W9-CAM-111

TYNDALE HANDBOOK OF
Bible Charts and Maps

Tyndale
HANDBOOK OF BIBLE CHARTS & MAPS

◆◆◆◆◆

Neil S. Wilson
AND
Linda K. Taylor

Tyndale House Publishers, Inc.
WHEATON, ILLINOIS

Visit Tyndale's exciting Web site at www.tyndale.com

Tyndale Handbook of Bible Charts and Maps copyright © 2001 by Tyndale House Publishers. All rights reserved.

Far left cover image copyright © 2000 by Jean Holmes. All rights reserved.
Far right cover image copyright © 2000 by Reed Holmes. All rights reserved.
Flower cover photograph copyright © 2000 by Richard Nowitz. All rights reserved.
Rock formation and tree photographs copyright © by Tyndale House Publishers, Inc. All rights reserved.

Charts and Jerusalem maps taken from the *Life Application Study Bible* copyright © 1996 by Tyndale House Publishers. All rights reserved.

Interior maps copyright © 2001 by Tyndale House Publishers, Inc. All rights reserved.

Charts taken from the *Life Application Bible Commentary* copyright © 1992, 1993, 1994, 1995, 1996, 1997, 1998, 1999, 2000 by the Livingstone Corporation. All rights reserved.

Permission is granted to make up to 300 copies of individual pages from the handbook or CD for nonprofit non-commercial use, such as handouts for teaching a class. The pages of maps and charts may not be modified in any manner. Permission is not granted to modify pages, to reprint maps or charts apart from the page setting, to reprint groups of pages in bound form, either electronically or physically, or to offer copies for sale or donation, either at cost or profit. All commercial use of these maps is reserved by Tyndale House Publishers, Inc. These maps may not be placed nor used on Web sites. Any other use of these maps and charts must be approved in writing by Tyndale House Publishers, Inc.

Tyndale House Publishers gratefully acknowledges the role of Youth for Christ/USA in preparing the Life Application Notes and Bible Helps.

Scripture quotations are taken from the *Holy Bible,* New Living Translation, copyright © 1996. Used by permission of Tyndale House Publishers, Inc., Wheaton, Illinois 60189. All rights reserved.

Edited by Shawn A. Harrison

Designed by Timothy R. Botts

Product management by Lisa M. Johnsrud
Typesetting by Gwendolyn R. Elliott

Library of Congress Cataloging-in-Publication Data

Wilson, Neil S., date
 Tyndale handbook of Bible charts and maps / by Neil S. Wilson and Linda K. Taylor.
   p. cm.— (The Tyndale reference library)
 Includes index.
 ISBN 0-8423-3552-8 (sc : alk. paper)
  1. Bible—Handbooks, manuals, etc. 2. Bible—Geography—Maps. I. Title: Handbook of Bible charts and maps.
 II. Taylor, Linda Chaffee, date. III. Title. IV. Series.

BS417.W53 2001
220′.022′3—dc21   2001027970

Printed in the United States of America

07 06 05 04 03
 8   7   6   5   4

CONTENTS

INTRODUCTION

We are pleased to present to you the *Tyndale Handbook of Bible Charts and Maps*, the most comprehensive and up-to-date collection of its kind. The over 530 Bible charts and over 200 high-resolution Bible maps will add a new dimension and depth to your personal or group study of Scripture. As an added benefit, the enclosed CD contains the entire handbook text, with full-color maps, powerful search and navigation features, and the entire text of the New Living Translation. The licensing arrangement for both the handbook and the CD allows you to print and photocopy charts and maps for personal study or to create handouts and overheads for group use. All in all, the *Tyndale Handbook of Bible Charts and Maps* is a powerful and flexible study and teaching tool!

How to Use the Handbook

The charts and maps in the *Tyndale Handbook of Bible Charts and Maps* are grouped by Bible book and arranged in the same order as the Bible text. So, as you are studying a passage of Scripture, you can easily open the handbook and see what charts and maps are available for that portion of Scripture.

Or, if you are doing a topical study of Scripture, you can look in the comprehensive index at the back of the handbook (p. 591) and see what charts and maps cover that topic. The index includes general topics as well as references to people and places covered by the charts and maps.

If you want to photocopy individual pages for personal study or group use, go ahead! The licensing agreement allows you to make up to 300 copies of individual pages for these purposes. (Of course, you shouldn't republish the maps or charts without written permission from Tyndale House Publishers.)

To get the greatest benefit from the *Tyndale Handbook of Bible Charts and Maps,* you should consider the other volumes of the Tyndale Reference Library. These include the *Tyndale Bible Dictionary,* which contains in-depth information about the people, places, and topics covered by the handbook; and the *Tyndale Concise Bible Commentary,* a succinct single-volume overview of Scripture that will help orient you as you study any Bible book or Scripture passage.

How to Use the CD

The enclosed CD contains the entire handbook, so the CD can be used in the same ways as the physical book. Charts and maps are organized by Bible book, and they appear in the order of the Bible text. Navigation features make it easy for you to click to find the map or chart covering the passage or topic you are studying. The table of contents allows you to "drill down" hierarchically to the map or chart you want, and the topical index contains active links to every chart or map that you can easily click from the index. And as with the handbook, you can print and copy the electronic charts and maps for personal study or group use. Each page of the CD contains self-explanatory navigational features that make it easy to use in these ways.

But the CD enables you to do more than you can do with the handbook. For instance, you can search the full text of the handbook electronically. You can view and print maps in color or black and white. You can click any Bible reference in the handbook text and view the corresponding text of the New Living Translation. In fact, the entire text of the New Living Translation is included for free, so you can do full-text searches of the NLT or just sit back and enjoy on-screen reading.

The CD uses the popular Adobe Acrobat® PDF format, and the Acrobat® Reader is included on the CD. To install the Reader software, simply go to the "reader" directory on the CD and choose the folder corresponding to your operating system. If you are unfamiliar with using the Acrobat® Reader, a tutorial is available through the "Help" menu in the Reader. The "README" file on the CD contains more information about how to install the handbook itself on your computer.

WE HOPE that you enjoy using the *Tyndale Handbook of Bible Charts and Maps,* that your study of Scripture is enriched and deepened, and that your relationship with God is strengthened by using this tool. May God bless your study of his word.

The Editors

GENESIS

MEGATHEMES IN GENESIS

Theme	Explanation	Importance
Beginnings	Genesis explains the beginning of many important realities: the universe, the earth, people, sin, and God's plan of salvation.	Genesis teaches us that the earth is well made and good. People are special to God and unique. God creates and sustains all life.
Disobedience	People are always facing great choices. Disobedience occurs when people choose not to follow God's plan of living.	Genesis explains why people are evil: They choose to do wrong. Even great Bible heroes failed God and disobeyed.
Sin	Sin ruins people's lives. It happens when we disobey God.	Living God's way makes life productive and fulfilling.
Promises	God makes promises to help and protect people. This kind of promise is called a "covenant."	God kept his promises then, and he keeps them now. He promises to love us, accept us, forgive us.
Obedience	The opposite of sin is obedience. Obeying God restores our relationship to him.	The only way to enjoy the benefits of God's promises is to obey him.
Prosperity	Prosperity is deeper than mere material wealth. True prosperity and fulfillment come as a result of obeying God.	When people obey God, they find peace with him, with others, and with themselves.
Israel	God started the nation of Israel in order to have a dedicated people who would (1) keep his ways alive in the world, (2) proclaim to the world what he is really like, and (3) prepare the world for the birth of Christ.	God is looking for people today to follow him. We are to proclaim God's truth and love to all nations, not just our own. We must be faithful to carry out the mission God has given us.

KEY PLACES IN GENESIS

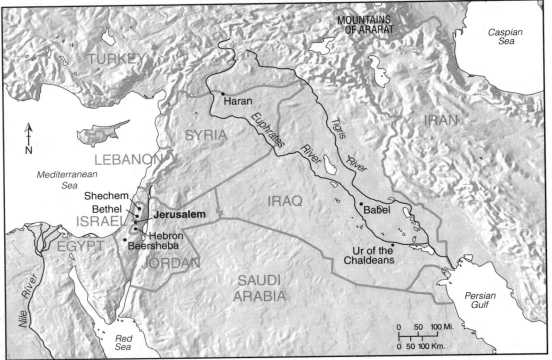

Modern names and boundaries are shown in gray.

God created the universe and the earth. Then he made man and woman, giving them a home in a beautiful garden. Unfortunately, Adam and Eve disobeyed God and were banished from the garden (3:23).

1. **Mountains of Ararat** Adam and Eve's sin brought sin into the human race. Years later, sin had run rampant and God decided to destroy the earth with a great flood. But Noah, his family, and two of each animal were safe in the boat. When the floods receded, the boat rested on the mountains of Ararat (8:4).

2. **Babel** People never learn. Again sin abounded, and the pride of the people led them to build a huge tower as a monument to their own greatness—obviously they had no thought of God. As punishment, God scattered the people by giving them different languages (11:8-9).

3. **Ur of the Chaldeans** Abram, a descendant of Shem and father of the Hebrew nation, was born in this region (11:27-28).

4. **Haran** Terah, Abram, Lot, and Sarai left Ur and, following the fertile crescent of the Euphrates River, headed toward the land of Canaan. Along the way, they settled in the city of Haran for a while (11:31).

5. **Shechem** God urged Abram to leave Haran and go to a place where he would become the father of a great nation (12:1-2). So Abram, Lot, and Sarai

traveled to the land of Canaan and settled near a city called Shechem (12:6).

6. **Hebron** Abraham moved on to Hebron where he put down his deepest roots (13:18). Abraham, Isaac, and Jacob all lived and were buried here.

7. **Beersheba** The well at Beersheba was a source of conflict between Abraham and King Abimelech and later became a sign of the oath that they swore there (21:31). Years later, as Isaac was moving from place to place, God appeared to him here and passed on to Isaac the covenant he had made with his father, Abraham (26:23-25).

8. **Bethel** After deceiving his brother, Jacob left Beersheba and fled to Haran. Along the way, God revealed himself to Jacob in a dream and passed on the covenant he had made with Abraham and Isaac (28:10-22). Jacob lived in Haran, worked for Laban, and married Leah and Rachel (29:15-30). After a tense meeting with his brother, Esau, Jacob returned to Bethel (35:1).

9. **Egypt** Jacob had 12 sons, including Joseph, Jacob's favorite. Joseph's 10 older brothers grew jealous, until one day the brothers sold him to Ishmaelite traders going to Egypt. Eventually, Joseph rose from Egyptian slave to Pharaoh's "right-hand man," saving Egypt from famine. His entire family moved from Canaan to Egypt and settled there (46:3-7).

DAYS OF CREATION / *Genesis 1:1–2:3*

First Day . . . . Light (so there was light and darkness)

Second Day . . . . . Sky and water (waters separated)

Third Day . . . . . . Land and seas (waters gathered); vegetation

Fourth Day . . . . . . Sun, moon, and stars (to govern the day and the night, and to mark seasons, days, and years)

Fifth Day . . . . Fish and birds (to fill the waters and the sky)

Sixth Day . . . . Animals (to fill the earth)
Man and woman (to care for the earth and to commune with God)

Seventh Day . . . . . God rested and declared all he had made to be very good

WHAT THE BIBLE SAYS ABOUT MARRIAGE / *Genesis 2:18-24*

Genesis 2:18-24	Marriage is God's idea
Genesis 24:58-60	Commitment is essential to a successful marriage
Genesis 29:10-11	Romance is important
Jeremiah 7:34	Marriage holds times of great joy
Malachi 2:14-15	Marriage creates the best environment for raising children
Matthew 5:32	Unfaithfulness breaks the bond of trust, the foundation of all relationships
Matthew 19:6	Marriage is permanent
Romans 7:2-3	Ideally, only death should dissolve marriage
Ephesians 5:21-33	Marriage is based on the principled practice of love, not on feelings
Ephesians 5:23-32	Marriage is a living symbol of Christ and the church
Hebrews 13:4	Marriage is good and honorable

SATAN'S PLAN / *Genesis 3:1-13*

Doubt . . . . Makes you question God's Word and his goodness

Discouragement . . . Makes you look at your problems rather than at God

Diversion . . . . . . Makes the wrong things seem attractive so that you will want them more than the right things

Defeat . . . . Makes you feel like a failure so that you don't even try

Delay . . . . Makes you put off doing something so that it never gets done

Name of God	Meaning	Reference	Significance
Elohim	God	Genesis 1:1; Numbers 23:19; Psalm 19:1	Refers to God's power and might. He is the only supreme and true God.
Yahweh	The LORD	Genesis 2:4; Exodus 6:2-3	The proper name of the divine person.
El Elyon	God Most High	Genesis 14:17-20; Numbers 24:16; Psalm 7:17; Isaiah 14:13-14	He is above all gods; nothing in life is more sacred.
El Roi	God Who Sees	Genesis 16:13	God oversees all of creation and the affairs of people.
El Shaddai	God Almighty	Genesis 17:1; Psalm 91:1	God is all-powerful.
Yahweh Yireh	The LORD Will Provide	Genesis 22:14	God will provide our real needs.
Yahweh Nissi	The LORD Is My Banner	Exodus 17:15	We should remember God for helping us.
Adonai	Lord	Deuteronomy 6:4	God alone is the head over all.
Yahweh Elohe Yisrael	LORD God of Israel	Judges 5:3; Psalm 59:5; Isaiah 17:6; Zephaniah 2:9	He is the God of the nation.
Yahweh Shalom	The LORD Is Peace.	Judges 6:24	God gives us peace so we need not fear.
Qedosh Yisrael	Holy One of Israel	Isaiah 1:4	God is morally perfect.
Yahweh Sabaoth	LORD of Hosts	1 Samuel 1:3; Isaiah 6:1-3	God is our savior and protector. (Host refers to armies but also to all the heavenly powers.)
El Olam	The Everlasting God	Isaiah 40:28-31	God is eternal. He will never die.
Yahweh Tsidkenu	The LORD Is Our Righteousness	Jeremiah 23:6; 33:16	God is our standard for right behavior. He alone can make us righteous.
Yahweh Shammah	The LORD Is There	Ezekiel 48:35	God is always present with us.
Attiq Yomin	Ancient of Days	Daniel 7:9, 13	God is the ultimate authority. He will one day judge all the nations.

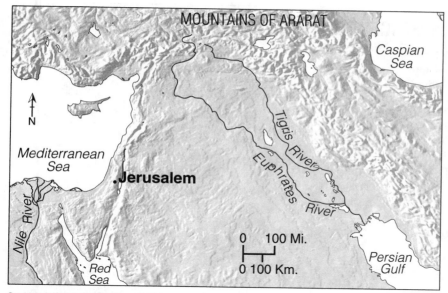

MOUN- TAINS OF ARARAT
Genesis 8:1-4

The boat touched land in the mountains of Ararat, located in present-day Turkey. There it rested for almost eight months before Noah, his family, and the animals stepped onto dry land.

Copyright © 2001 by Tyndale House Publishers

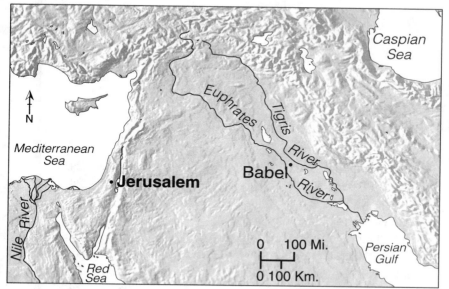

THE TOWER OF BABEL
Genesis 11:1-9

The plain between the Tigris and Euphrates Rivers offered a perfect location for the city and tower "that reaches to the skies."

Copyright © 2001 by Tyndale House Publishers

BIBLE NATIONS DESCENDED FROM NOAH'S SONS / *Genesis 10:1*

Shem's descendants were called Semites. Abraham, David, and Jesus descended from Shem. Ham's descendants settled in Canaan, Egypt, and the rest of Africa. Japheth's descendants settled mostly in Europe and Asia Minor.

Shem	Ham	Japheth
Hebrews	Canaanites	Greeks
Chaldeans	Egyptians	Thracians
Assyrians	Philistines	Scythians
Persians	Hittites	
Syrians	Amorites	

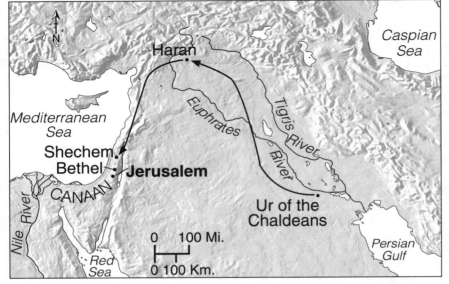

Copyright © 2001 by Tyndale House Publishers

ABRAM'S JOURNEY TO CANAAN

Genesis 11:31–12:9

Abram, Sarai, and Lot traveled from Ur of the Chaldeans to Canaan by way of Haran. Though indirect, this route followed the rivers rather than attempting to cross the vast desert.

ELIEZER: PROFILE OF A TRUE SERVANT / *Genesis 24*

Have you ever approached a responsibility with this kind of single-mindedness and careful planning, while ultimately depending on God?

Accepted the challenge	24:3, 9
Examined alternatives	24:5
Promised to follow instructions.	24:9
Made a plan	24:12-14
Submitted the plan to God	24:12-14
Prayed for guidance	24:12-14
Devised a strategy with room for God to operate	4:12-14
Waited	24:21
Watched closely	24:21
Accepted the answer thankfully	24:26
Explained the situation to concerned parties	24:34-49
Refused unnecessary delay	24:56
Followed through with entire plan	24:66

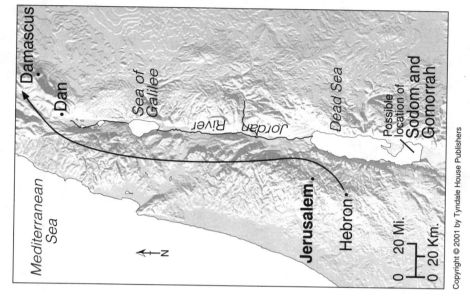

LOT'S RESCUE
Genesis 14:14-16

After conquering Sodom, Kedorlaomer left for his home country, taking many captives with him. Abram learned what had happened and chased Kedorlaomer past Dan and beyond Damascus. There he defeated the king and rescued the captives, among them Lot.

Damascus

Dan

Sea of Galilee

Jordan River

Mediterranean Sea

N

Dead Sea

Jerusalem.

Hebron.

Possible location of Sodom and Gomorrah

0   20 Mi.

0   20 Km.

Copyright © 2001 by Tyndale House Publishers

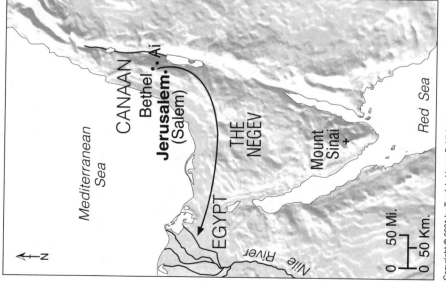

ABRAM'S JOURNEY TO EGYPT
Genesis 12:10

A famine could cause the loss of a shepherd's wealth. So Abram traveled through the Negev to Egypt, where there was plenty of food and good land for his flocks.

Mediterranean Sea

N

CANAAN

Bethel. • Ai

Jerusalem.
(Salem)

THE NEGEV

EGYPT

Mount Sinai +

Red Sea

Nile River

0   50 Mi.

0   50 Km.

Copyright © 2001 by Tyndale House Publishers

CAVE OF MACH-PELAH
Genesis 23:1-3, 16-17

Sarah died in Hebron. Abraham bought the cave of Machpelah, near Hebron, as her burial place. Abraham was also buried there, as were his son and grandson, Isaac and Jacob.

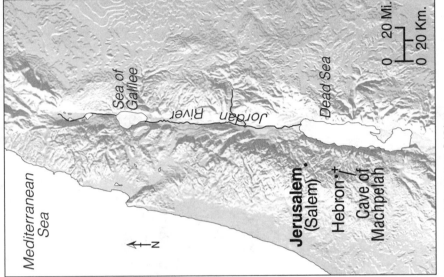

Mediterranean Sea

N

Sea of Galilee

Jordan River

Dead Sea

Jerusalem (Salem)

Hebron

Cave of Machpelah

0   20 Mi.
0   20 Km.

Copyright © 2001 by Tyndale House Publishers

ABRA-HAM'S TRIP TO MOUNT MORIAH
Genesis 22:1-19

Abraham and Isaac traveled the 50 or 60 miles from Beersheba to Mount Moriah in about three days. This was a very difficult time for Abraham, who was on his way to sacrifice his beloved son, Isaac.

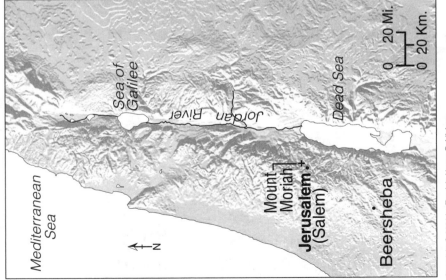

Mediterranean Sea

N

Sea of Galilee

Jordan River

Dead Sea

Mount Moriah

Jerusalem (Salem)

Beersheba

0   20 Mi.
0   20 Km.

Copyright © 2001 by Tyndale House Publishers

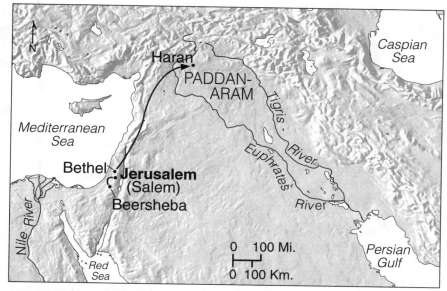

JACOB'S TRIP TO HARAN
Genesis 27:42-44; 28:5

After deceiving Esau, Jacob ran for his life, traveling more than 400 miles to Haran, where an uncle, Laban, lived. In Haran, Jacob married and started a family.

Copyright © 2001 by Tyndale House Publishers

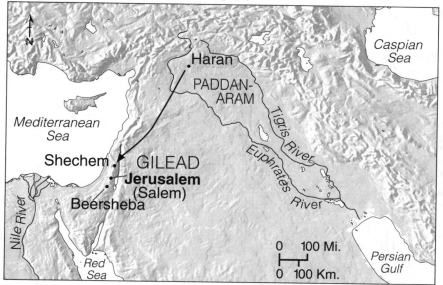

JACOB'S RETURN TO CANAAN
Genesis 31:3, 17-18

God told Jacob to leave Haran and return to his homeland. Jacob took his family, crossed the Euphrates River, and headed first for the hill country of Gilead. Laban caught up with him there.

Copyright © 2001 by Tyndale House Publishers

JACOB'S CHILDREN / *Genesis 30*

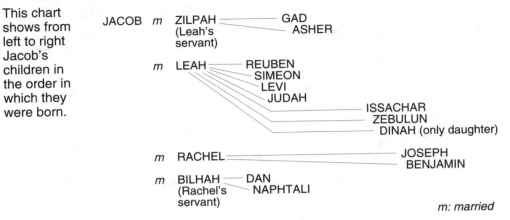

This chart shows from left to right Jacob's children in the order in which they were born.

JACOB *m* ZILPAH ———————— GAD
              (Leah's ———————— ASHER
              servant)

        m LEAH ——— REUBEN
                    ——— SIMEON
                    ——— LEVI
                    ——— JUDAH
                         ——————— ISSACHAR
                         ——————— ZEBULUN
                         ——————— DINAH (only daughter)

        m RACHEL ——————————— JOSEPH
                        ——————— BENJAMIN

        m BILHAH ——— DAN
              (Rachel's ——— NAPHTALI
              servant)

m: married

Jacob's many wives (two wives and two "substitute" wives) led to sad and bitter consequences among the children. Anger, resentment, and jealousy were common among Jacob's sons. It is interesting to note that the worst fighting and rivalry occurred between Leah's children and Rachel's children, and among the tribes that descended from them.

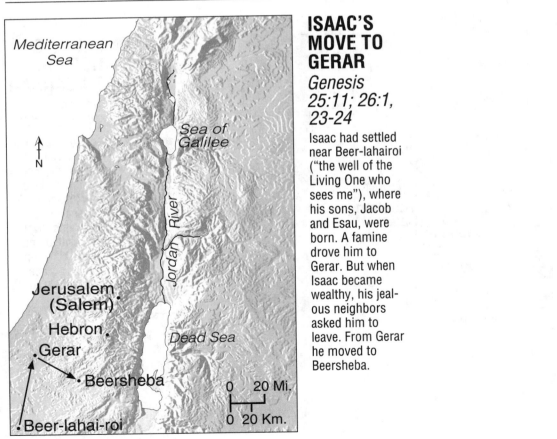

ISAAC'S MOVE TO GERAR
Genesis 25:11; 26:1, 23-24

Isaac had settled near Beer-lahairoi ("the well of the Living One who sees me"), where his sons, Jacob and Esau, were born. A famine drove him to Gerar. But when Isaac became wealthy, his jealous neighbors asked him to leave. From Gerar he moved to Beersheba.

Copyright © 2001 by Tyndale House Publishers

JACOB'S JOURNEY BACK TO HEBRON

Genesis 35:1-21

After Jacob's sons Simeon and Levi destroyed Shechem, God told Jacob to move to Bethel. There God reminded him that his name, Jacob, had been changed to Israel. He then traveled to Hebron, but along the way, his dear wife Rachel died near Ephrath (Bethlehem).

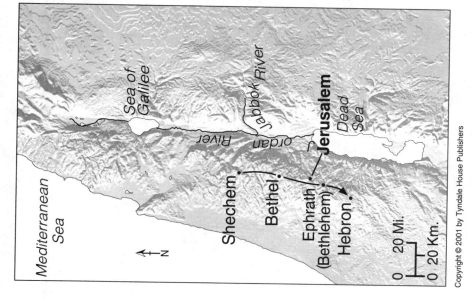

Mediterranean Sea

Sea of Galilee

Jabbok River

Jordan River

Dead Sea

Shechem

Bethel

Ephrath (Bethlehem)

Jerusalem

Hebron

N

0 20 Mi.
0 20 Km.

Copyright © 2001 by Tyndale House Publishers

JACOB'S JOURNEY TO SHECHEM

Genesis 33:1–34:31

After a joyful reunion with his brother, Esau (who journeyed from Edom), Jacob set up camp in Succoth. Later he moved on to Shechem where his daughter, Dinah, was raped and two of his sons took revenge on the city.

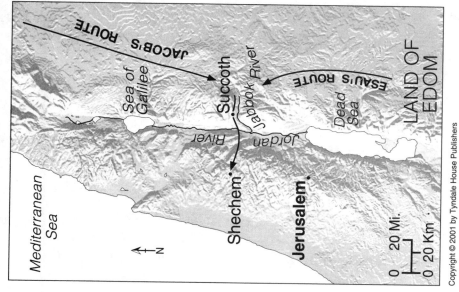

Mediterranean Sea

Sea of Galilee

JACOB'S ROUTE

Succoth

Jabbok River

Jordan River

ESAU'S ROUTE

Dead Sea

Shechem

Jerusalem

LAND OF EDOM

N

0 20 Mi.
0 20 Km.

Copyright © 2001 by Tyndale House Publishers

GENESIS

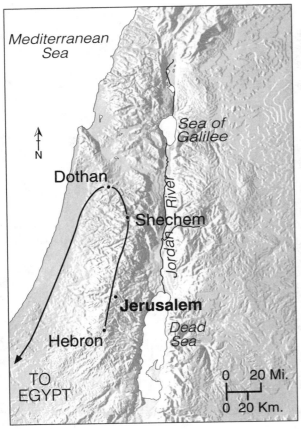

Mediterranean
Sea

Sea of
Galilee

↑
N

Dothan

Shechem

Jordan River

Jerusalem

Dead
Sea

Hebron

TO
EGYPT

0   20 Mi.

0   20 Km.

Copyright © 2001 by Tyndale House Publishers

JOSEPH GOES TO MEET HIS BROTHERS
Genesis 37:12-28

Jacob asked Joseph to go find his brothers, who were grazing their flocks near Shechem. When Joseph arrived, he learned that his brothers had gone on to Dothan, which lay along a major trade route to Egypt. There the jealous brothers sold Joseph as a slave to a group of Ishmaelite traders on their way to Egypt.

WOMEN IN JESUS' FAMILY TREE / *Genesis 38*

Tamar	Canaanite	Genesis 38:1-30
Rahab	Canaanite	Joshua 6:22-25
Ruth	Moabite	Ruth 4:13-22
Bathsheba	Israelite	2 Samuel 12:24-25

PARALLELS BETWEEN JOSEPH AND JESUS / *Genesis 37–50*

Joseph	Parallels	Jesus
37:3	Their fathers loved them dearly	Matthew 3:17
37:2	Shepherds of their fathers' sheep	John 10:11, 27
37:13-14	Sent by father to brothers	Hebrews 2:11
37:4	Hated by brothers	John 7:5
37:20	Others plotted to harm them	John 11:53
39:7	Tempted	Matthew 4:1
37:25, 28	Taken to Egypt	Matthew 2:14-15
37:23	Robes taken from them	John 19:23
37:28	Sold for the price of a slave	Matthew 26:15
39:20	Bound in chains	Matthew 27:2
39:16-18	Falsely accused	Matthew 26:59-60
40:2-3	Placed with two other prisoners, one who was saved and the other lost.	Luke 23:32
41:46	Both 30 years old at the beginning of public recognition.	Luke 3:23
41:41	Exalted after suffering	Philippians 2:9-11
45:1-15	Forgave those who wronged them	Luke 23:34
45:7	Saved their nation	Matthew 1:21
50:20	What people did to hurt them God turned to good	1 Corinthians 2:7-8

JACOB'S SONS AND THEIR NOTABLE DESCENDANTS / *Genesis 49*

Jacob's 12 sons were the ancestors of the 12 tribes of Israel. The entire nation of Israel came from these men.

Reuben	none
Simeon	none
Levi	Aaron, Moses, Eli, John the Baptist
Judah	David, Jesus
Dan	Samson
Naphtali	Barak, Elijah (?)
Gad	Jephthah(?)
Asher	none
Issachar	none
Zebulun	none
Joseph	Joshua, Gideon, Samuel
Benjamin	Saul, Esther, Paul

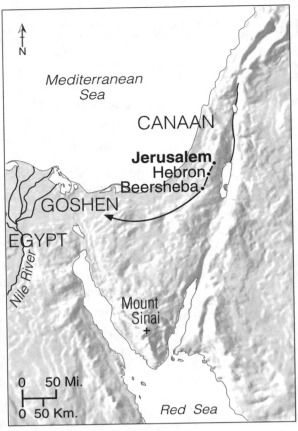

JACOB MOVES TO EGYPT

Genesis 46:1-5

After hearing the joyful news that Joseph was alive, Jacob packed up and moved his family to Egypt. Stopping first in Beersheba, Jacob offered sacrifices and received assurance from God that Egypt was where he should go. Jacob and his family settled in the region of Goshen, in the northeastern part of Egypt.

Copyright © 2001 by Tyndale House Publishers

EXODUS

MEGATHEMES IN EXODUS

Theme	Explanation	Importance
Slavery	During the Israelites 400-year stay in the land of Egypt, they became enslaved to the Egyptians. Pharaoh, the king of Egypt, oppressed them cruelly. They prayed to God for deliverance from this situation.	Like the Israelites, we need both human and divine leadership to escape from the slavery of sin. After their escape, the memory of slavery helped the Israelites learn to treat others generously. We need to stand against those who oppress others.
Rescue/ Redemption	God rescued Israel through the leader Moses and through mighty miracles. The Passover celebration was an annual reminder of their escape from slavery.	God delivers us from the slavery of sin. Jesus Christ celebrated the Passover with his disciples at the Last Supper and then went on to rescue us from sin by dying in our place.
Guidance	God guided Israel out of Egypt by using the plagues, Moses' heroic courage, the miracle of the Red Sea, and the Ten Commandments. God is a trustworthy guide.	Although God is all-powerful and can do miracles, he normally leads us by wise leadership and team effort. His Word gives us the wisdom to make daily decisions and govern our lives.
Ten Commandments	God's law system had three parts. The Ten Commandments were the first part, containing the absolutes of spiritual and moral life. The civil law was the second part, giving the people rules to manage their lives. The ceremonial law was the third part, showing them patterns for building the Tabernacle and for regular worship.	God was teaching Israel the importance of choice and responsibility. When they obeyed the conditions of the law, he blessed them; if they forgot or disobeyed, he punished them or allowed calamities to come. Many great countries of the world base their laws on the moral system set up in the book of Exodus. God's moral law is valid today.
The Nation	God founded the nation of Israel to be the source of truth and salvation to all the world. His relationship to his people was loving yet firm. The Israelites had no army, schools, governors, mayors, or police when they left Egypt. God had to instruct them in their constitutional laws and daily practices. He showed them how to worship and how to have national holidays.	Israel's newly formed nation had all the behavioral characteristics of Christians today. We are often disorganized, sometimes rebellious, and sometimes victorious. God's Person and Word are still our only guides. If our churches reflect his leadership, they will be effective in serving him.

KEY PLACES IN EXODUS

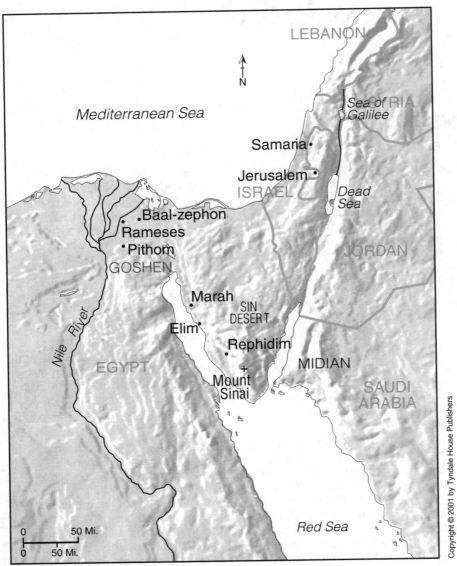

Modern names and boundaries are shown in gray.

KEY PLACES IN EXODUS *continued*

1. **Goshen** This area was given to Jacob and his family when they moved to Egypt (Genesis 47:5-6). It became the Hebrews' homeland for 400 years and remained separate from the main Egyptian centers, for Egyptian culture looked down upon shepherds and nomads. As the years passed, Jacob's family grew into a large nation (Exodus 1:7).

2. **Pithom and Rameses** During the Israelites' stay in the land of Egypt, a pharaoh came to the throne who had no respect for these descendants of Joseph and feared their large numbers. He forced them into slavery in order to oppress and subdue them. Out of their slave labor, the supply cities of Pithom and Rameses were built (1:11).

3. **Midian** Moses, an Egyptian prince who was born a Hebrew, killed an Egyptian and fled for his life to Midian. Here he became a shepherd and married a woman named Zipporah. It was while he was here that God commissioned him for the job of leading the Hebrew people out of Egypt (2:15–4:31).

4. **Baal-zephon** Slavery was not to last because God planned to deliver his people. After choosing Moses and Aaron to be his spokesmen to Pharaoh, God worked a series of dramatic miracles in the land of Egypt to convince Pharaoh to let the Hebrews go (5:1–12:33). When finally freed, the entire nation set out with the riches of Egypt (12:34-36). One of their first stops was at Baal-zephon (14:2), where Pharaoh, who had changed his mind, chased the Hebrews and trapped them against the sea. But God parted the waters and led the people through the sea on dry land. When Pharaoh's army tried to pursue, the waters collapsed around them, and they were drowned (14:5-31).

5. **Marah** Moses now led the people southward. The long trek across the desert brought hot tempers and parched throats for this mass of people. At Marah, the water they found was bitter, but God sweetened it (15:22-25).

6. **Elim** As they continued their journey, the Hebrews (now called Israelites) came to Elim, an oasis with 12 springs (15:27).

7. **Sin Desert** Leaving Elim, the people headed into the Sin Desert. Here the people became hungry, so God provided them with manna that came from heaven and covered the ground each morning (16:1, 13-15). The people ate this manna until they entered the Promised Land.

8. **Rephidim** Moses led the people to Rephidim where they found no water. But God miraculously provided water from a rock (17:1, 5-6). Here the Israelites encountered their first test in battle: the Amalekites attacked and were defeated (17:9-13). Moses' father-in-law, Jethro, then arrived on the scene with some sound advice on delegating responsibilities (18).

9. **Mount Sinai** God had previously appeared to Moses on this mountain and commissioned him to lead Israel (3:1-10). Now Moses returned with the people God had asked him to lead. For almost a year the people camped at the foot of Mount Sinai. During this time God gave them his Ten Commandments as well as other laws for right living. He also provided the blueprint for building the Tabernacle (19-40). God was forging a holy nation, prepared to live for and serve him alone.

MOSES RETURNS TO EGYPT
Exodus 3:1-3

God appeared to Moses in a mysterious burning bush on Mount Sinai. Later Aaron met Moses at the mountain, and together they returned to Egypt, a 200-mile trip.

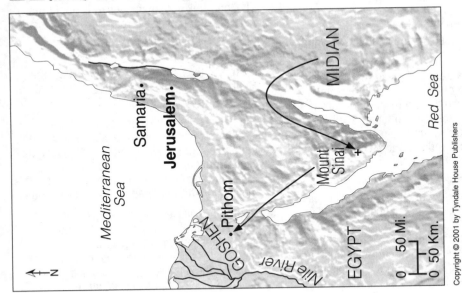

Mediterranean Sea

Samaria.

Jerusalem.

MIDIAN

Mount Sinai

Red Sea

GOSHEN • Pithom

Nile River

EGYPT

N

0   50 Mi.

0   50 Km.

Copyright © 2001 by Tyndale House Publishers

MOSES FLEES TO MIDIAN
Exodus 2:14-21

After murdering an Egyptian, Moses escaped into Midian. There he married Zipporah and became a shepherd.

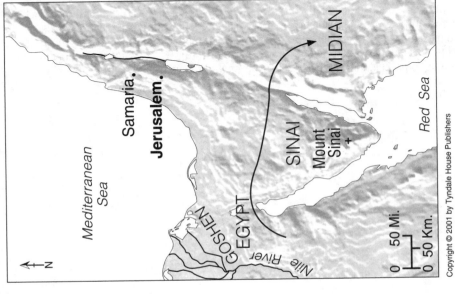

Mediterranean Sea

Samaria.

Jerusalem.

MIDIAN

SINAI

Mount Sinai

Red Sea

GOSHEN

EGYPT

Nile River

N

0   50 Mi.

0   50 Km.

Copyright © 2001 by Tyndale House Publishers

EXODUS

THE PLAGUES / *Exodus 7–12*

Reference	Plague	What Happened	Result
7:14-24	Blood	Fish die, the river smells, the people are without water	Pharaoh's magicians duplicate the miracle by "secret arts," and Pharaoh is unmoved
8:1-15	Frogs	Frogs come up from the water and completely cover the land	Again Pharaoh's magicians duplicate the miracle by sorcery, and Pharaoh is unmoved
8:16-19	Gnats	All the dust of Egypt becomes a massive swarm of gnats	Magicians are unable to duplicate this; they say it is the "finger of God," but Pharaoh's heart remains hard
8:20-32	Flies	Swarms of flies cover the land	Pharaoh promises to let the Hebrews go but then hardens his heart and refuses
9:1-7	Livestock	All the Egyptian livestock die—but none of Israel's is even sick	Pharaoh still refuses to let the people go
9:8-12	Boils	Horrible boils break out on everyone in Egypt	Magicians cannot respond because they are struck down with boils as well—Pharaoh refuses to listen
9:13-35	Hail	Hailstorms kill all the slaves and animals left out or unprotected and strip or destroy almost every plant	Pharaoh admits his sin but then changes his mind and refuses to let Israel go
10:1-20	Locusts	Locusts cover Egypt and eat everything left after the hail	Everyone advises Pharaoh to let the Hebrews go, but God hardens Pharaoh's heart and he refuses
10:21-29	Darkness	Total darkness covers Egypt for three days so no one can even move— except the Hebrews, who have light as usual	Pharaoh again promises to let Israel go but again changes his mind
11:1–12:33	Death of Firstborn	The firstborn of all the people and cattle of Egypt die—but Israel is spared	Pharaoh and the Egyptians urge Israel to leave quickly; after they are gone, Pharaoh again changes his mind and chases after them

THE HEBREW CALENDAR / *Exodus 13:4*

A Hebrew month began in the middle of a month on our calendar today. Crops are planted in November and December and harvested in March and April.

Month	Today's Calendar	Bible Reference	Israel's Holidays
1 Nisan (Abib)	March–April	Exodus 13:4; 23:15; 34:18; Deuteronomy 16:1	Passover (Leviticus 23:5); Unleavened Bread (Leviticus 23:6); Firstfruits (Leviticus 23:10)
2 Iyyar (Ziv)	April–May	1 Kings 6:1, 37	Second Passover (Numbers 9:10-11)
3 Sivan	May–June	Esther 8:9	Pentecost (Harvest) (Leviticus 23:16)
4 Tammuz	June–July		
5 Ab	July–August		
6 Elul	August–September	Nehemiah 6:15	
7 Tishri (Ethanim)	September–October	1 Kings 8:2	Trumpets (Leviticus 23:24; Numbers 29:1); Day of Atonement (Leviticus 23:27); Shelters (Leviticus 23:34)
8 Marcheshvan (Bul)	October–November	1 Kings 6:38	
9 Kislev	November–December	Nehemiah 1:1	Dedication (John 10:22)
10 Tebeth	December–January	Esther 2:16	
11 Shebat	January–February	Zechariah 1:7	Purim (Esther 9:24-32)
12 Adar	February–March	Esther 3:7	

JOURNEY TO MOUNT SINAI

Exodus 17:1; 19:1

God miraculously supplied food and water in the wilderness for the Israelites. In the Sin Desert, he provided manna (16). At Rephidim, he provided water from a rock (17:1-7). Finally God brought them to the foot of Mount Sinai, where he gave them his holy laws.

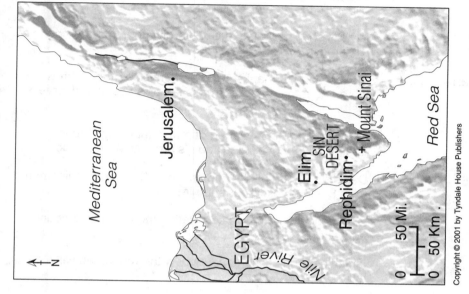

N

Mediterranean Sea

Jerusalem.

Elim
. SIN
  DESERT
Rephidim.
          + Mount Sinai

EGYPT

Nile River

Red Sea

0   50 Mi.
0   50 Km.

Copyright © 2001 by Tyndale House Publishers

THE EXODUS

Exodus 13:17–14:2; 14:22; 15:22–16:1

The Israelites left Succoth and camped first at Etham before going toward Baal-zephon to camp by the sea (14:2). God miraculously brought them across the sea, into the Shur Desert (15:22). After stopping at the oasis of Elim, the people moved into the Sin Desert (16:1).

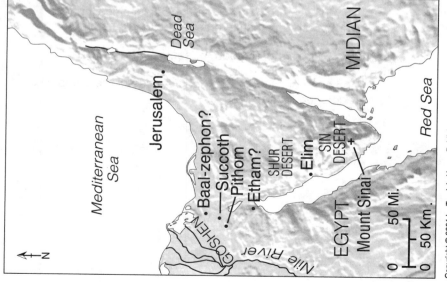

N

Mediterranean Sea

Dead Sea

Jerusalem.

Baal-zephon?
. Succoth
  Pithom
. Etham?

SHUR
DESERT

. Elim
   SIN
   DESERT
          +

MIDIAN

GOSHEN

Nile River

EGYPT
Mount Sinai

Red Sea

0   50 Mi.
0   50 Km.

Copyright © 2001 by Tyndale House Publishers

FAMOUS SONGS IN THE BIBLE / *Exodus 15*

Where	Purpose of Song
Exodus 15:1-21	Moses' song of deliverance and praise after God led Israel out of Egypt and saved them by parting the Red Sea; Miriam joined in the singing, too
Numbers 21:17.	Israel's song of praise to God for giving them water in the wilderness
Deuteronomy 32:1-43	Moses' song of thanksgiving and praise as the Hebrews were about to enter the Promised Land; recounted Israel's history
Judges 5:2-31	Deborah and Barak's song of praise thanking God for Israel's victory over King Jabin's army at Mount Tabor
2 Samuel 22:2-51	David's song of thanks and praise to God for rescuing him from Saul and his other enemies
Song of Songs	Solomon's song of love celebrating the union of husband and wife
Isaiah 26:1	Isaiah's prophetic song about how the redeemed will sing in the new Jerusalem
Ezra 3:11.	Israel's song of praise at the completion of the Temple's foundation
Luke 1:46-55	Mary's song of praise to God for the conception of Jesus
Luke 1:68-79	Zechariah's song of praise for the birth of his son
Acts 16:25	Paul and Silas sang hymns in prison
Revelation 5:9-10	The "new song" of the 24 elders acclaiming Christ as worthy to break the seven seals of God's scroll
Revelation 14:3	The song of the 144,000 redeemed from the earth
Revelation 15:3-4	The song of all the redeemed in praise of the Lamb who redeemed them

JESUS AND THE TEN COMMANDMENTS / *Exodus 20:1-17*

The Ten Commandments said . . .	Jesus said . . .
Exodus 20:3 "Do not worship any other gods besides me."	Matthew 4:10 "You must worship the Lord your God; serve only him."
Exodus 20:4 "Do not make idols of any kind."	Luke 16:13 "No one can serve two masters."
Exodus 20:7 "Do not misuse the name of the LORD your God."	Matthew 5:34 "But I say, don't make any vows! If you say, 'By heaven!' it is a sacred vow because heaven is God's throne."
Exodus 20:8 "Remember to observe the Sabbath day by keeping it holy."	Mark 2:27-28 "The Sabbath was made to benefit people and not people to benefit the Sabbath. And I, the Son of Man, am master even of the Sabbath!"
Exodus 20:12 "Honor your father and mother."	Matthew 10:37 "If you love your father or mother more than you love me, you are not worthy of being mine."
Exodus 20:13 "Do not murder."	Matthew 5:22 "If you are angry with someone, you are subject to judgment!"
Exodus 20:14 "Do not commit adultery."	Matthew 5:28 "Anyone who even looks at a woman with lust in his eye has already committed adultery with her in his heart."
Exodus 20:15 "Do not steal."	Matthew 5:40 "If you are ordered to court and your shirt is taken from you, give your coat, too."
Exodus 20:16 "Do not testify falsely against your neighbor."	Matthew 12:36 "You must give an account on judgment day of every idle word you speak."
Exodus 20:17 "Do not covet."	Luke 12:15 "Don't be greedy for what you don't have."

THEOPHANIES IN THE SCRIPTURE / *Exodus 20:18*

At the foot of Mount Sinai, God appeared to the people of Israel in a physical form. This is called a *theophany*. Here are some of the other times God appeared to Bible people.

Verse	Theophany
Genesis 16:7	The angel of the Lord appeared to Sarah's servant, Hagar, announcing the birth of Abraham's son Ishmael
Genesis 18:1-11 . . .	The Lord appeared to Abraham, foretelling Isaac's birth
Genesis 22:11-12 . .	The angel of the Lord stopped Abraham from sacrificing Isaac
Exodus 3:2	The angel of the Lord appeared to Moses as flames in a bush
Exodus 14:19	God appeared to Israel in pillars of cloud and fire to guide them through the wilderness
Exodus 33:11	The Lord spoke to Moses face-to-face
Daniel 3:25	One "like a divine being" appeared as the fourth man with Shadrach, Meshach, and Abednego in the fiery furnace

("Angel of the Lord" is a reverential way to refer to God in these passages.)

EIGHT WORDS FOR LAW / *Exodus 24:12*

Hebrew law served as the personal and national guide for living under God's authority. It directed the moral, spiritual, and social life. Its purpose was to produce better understanding of God and greater commitment to him.

Word	Meaning	Examples	Significance
Torah	Direction, Guidance, Instruction	Exodus 24:12	Need for law in general; a command from a higher person to a lower
Mitswah	Commandment, Command	Genesis 26:5; Exodus 15:26; 20:2-17	God's specific instruction to be obeyed rather than a general law; used of the Ten Commandments
Mishpat	Regulations, Judgment, Ordinance	Genesis 18:19; Deuteronomy 16:18; 17:9	Refers to the civil, social, and sanitation laws
Eduth	Testimony, Truth	Exodus 25:22	Refers to God's law as he deals with his people
Huqqim	Statutes, Laws	Leviticus 18:4; Deuteronomy 4:1	Dealt with the royal pronouncements; mainly connected to worship and feasts
Piqqudim	Orders, Commandments	Psalms 19:8; 103:18	Used often in the Psalms to describe God's orders and assignments
Dabar	Word, Terms	Exodus 34:28; Deuteronomy 4:13	Used to indicate divine oracles or revelations of God
Dath	Royal Edict, Public Law	Ezekiel 7:26; Daniel 6:8, 12	Refers to a public law or Jewish religious tradition

KEY TABERNACLE PIECES / *Exodus 35*

Name	Function and Significance
Ark of the Covenant	• A golden rectangular box that contained the Ten Commandments • Symbolized God's covenant with Israel's people • Located in the Most Holy Place
Atonement Cover	• The lid to the Ark of the Covenant • Symbolized the presence of God among his people
Curtain	• The curtain that divided the two sacred rooms of the Tabernacle—the Holy Place and the Most Holy Place • Symbolized how the people were separated from God because of sin
Table	• A wooden table located in the Holy Place of the Tabernacle. The Bread of the Presence and various utensils were kept on this table
Bread of the Presence	• Twelve loaves of baked bread, one for each tribe of Israel • Symbolized the spiritual nourishment God offers his people
Lampstands and Lamps	• A golden lampstand located in the Holy Place, which held seven burning oil lamps • The lampstand lit the Holy Place for the priests
Altar of Incense	• An altar in the Holy Place in front of the curtain • Used for burning God's special incense and symbolic of acceptable prayer
Anointing Oil	• A special oil used to anoint the priests and all the pieces in the Tabernacle • A sign of being set apart for God
Altar of Burnt Offering	• The bronze altar outside the Tabernacle used for the sacrifices • Symbolized how sacrifice restored one's relationship with God
Basin	• A large washbasin outside the Tabernacle used by the priests to cleanse themselves before performing their duties • Symbolized the need for spiritual cleansing

LEVITICUS

MEGATHEMES IN LEVITICUS

Theme	Explanation	Importance
Sacrifice/ Offering	There are five kinds of offerings that fulfill two main purposes: one to show praise, thankfulness, and devotion; the other for atonement, the covering and removal of guilt and sin. Animal offerings demonstrated that the person was giving his or her life to God by means of the life of the animal.	The sacrifices (offerings) were for worship and forgiveness of sin. Through them we learn about the cost of sin, for we see that we cannot forgive ourselves. God's system says that a life must be given for a life. In the Old Testament, an animal's life was given to save the life of a person. But this was only a temporary measure until Jesus' death paid the penalty of sin for all people forever.
Worship	Seven festivals were designated as religious and national holidays. They were often celebrated in family settings. These events teach us much about worshiping God in both celebration and quiet dedication.	God's rules about worship set up an orderly, regular pattern of fellowship with him. They allowed times for celebration and thanksgiving as well as for reverence and rededication. Our worship should demonstrate our deep devotion.
Health	Civil rules for handling food, disease, and sex were taught. In these physical principles, many spiritual principles were suggested. Israel was to be different from the surrounding nations. God was preserving Israel from disease and community health problems.	We are to be different morally and spiritually from the unbelievers around us. Principles for healthy living are as important today as in Moses' time. A healthy environment and a healthy body make our service to God more effective.
Holiness	Holy means "separated" or "devoted." God removed his people from Egypt; now he was removing Egypt from the people. He was showing them how to exchange Egyptian ways of living and thinking for his ways.	We must devote every area of life to God. God desires absolute obedience in motives as well as practices. Though we do not observe all the worship practices of Israel, we are to have the same spirit of preparation and devotion.
Levites	The Levites and priests instructed the people in their worship. They were the ministers of their day. They also regulated the moral, civil, and ceremonial laws and supervised the health, justice, and welfare of the nation.	The Levites were servants who showed Israel the way to God. They provide the historical backdrop for Christ, who is our High Priest and yet our Servant. God's true servants care for all the needs of their people.

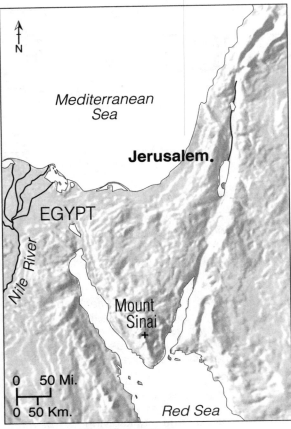

THE ISRAELITES AT MOUNT SINAI

Throughout the book of Leviticus, the Israelites were camped at the foot of Mount Sinai. It was time to be revitalized as a nation and learn the importance of following God as they prepared to march toward the Promised Land.

Mediterranean Sea

Jerusalem.

EGYPT

Nile River

Mount Sinai

0   50 Mi.

0   50 Km.

Red Sea

Copyright © 2001 by Tyndale House Publishers

THE OFFERINGS / *Leviticus 1–5*

Listed here are the five key offerings the Israelites made to God. They made these offerings in order to have their sins forgiven and to restore their fellowship with God. The death of Jesus Christ made these sacrifices unnecessary. Because of his death, our sins were completely forgiven, and fellowship with God has been restored.

Offering	Purpose	Significance	Christ, the Perfect Offering
Burnt Offering (Lev. 1— voluntary)	To make payment for sins in general	Showed a person's devotion to God	Christ's death was the perfect offering
Grain Offering (Lev. 2— voluntary)	To show honor and respect to God in worship	Acknowledged that all we have belongs to God	Christ was the perfect man, who gave all of himself to God and others
Peace Offering (Lev. 3— voluntary)	To express gratitude to God	Symbolized peace and fellowship with God	Christ is the only way to fellowship with God
Sin Offering (Lev. 4— required)	To make payment for unintentional sins of uncleanness, neglect, or thoughtlessness	Restored the sinner to fellowship with God; showed seriousness of sin	Christ's death restores our fellowship with God
Guilt Offering (Lev. 5— required)	To make payment for sins against God and others. A sacrifice was made to God, and the injured person was repaid or compensated	Provided compensation for injured parties	Christ's death takes away the deadly consequences of sin

OLD/NEW SYSTEMS OF SACRIFICE / *Leviticus 16:32*

Old System of Sacrifice	New System of Sacrifice
Was temporary (Hebrews 8:13)	Is permanent (Hebrews 7:21)
Aaron first high priest (Leviticus 16:32)	Jesus only High Priest (Hebrews 4:14)
From tribe of Levi (Hebrews 7:5)	From tribe of Judah (Hebrews 7:14)
Ministered on earth (Hebrews 8:4)	Ministers in heaven (Hebrews 8:1-2)
Used blood of animals (Leviticus 16:15)	Uses blood of Christ (Hebrews 10:4-12)
Required many sacrifices (Leviticus 22:19)	Requires one sacrifice (Hebrews 9:28)
Needed perfect animals (Leviticus 22:19)	Needs a perfect life (Hebrews 5:9)
Required careful approach to Tabernacle (Leviticus 16:2)	Encourages confident approach to throne (Hebrews 4:16)
Looked forward to new system (Hebrews 10:1)	Sets aside old system (Hebrews 10:9)

THE FESTIVALS / *Leviticus 23*

	Festival	What It Celebrated	Its Importance
Besides enjoying one Sabbath day of rest each week, the Israelites also enjoyed 19 days when national holidays were celebrated.	Passover One day (Leviticus 23:5)	When God spared the lives of Israel's firstborn children in Egypt and freed the Hebrews from slavery	Reminded the people of God's deliverance
	Unleavened Bread Seven days (Leviticus 23:6-8)	The exodus from Egypt	Reminded the people they were leaving the old life behind and entering a new way of living
	Firstfruits One day (Leviticus 23:9-14)	The first crops of the barley harvest	Reminded the people how God provided for them
	Pentecost (Harvest) One day (Leviticus 23:15-22)	The end of the barley harvest and beginning of the wheat harvest	Showed joy and thanksgiving over the bountiful harvest
	Trumpets One day (Leviticus 23:23-25)	The beginning of the seventh month (civil new year)	Expressed joy and thanksgiving to God
	Day of Atonement One day (Leviticus 23:26-32)	The removal of sin from the people and the nation	Restored fellowship with God
	Shelters Seven days (Leviticus 23:33-43)	God's protection and guidance in the wilderness	Renewed Israel's commitment to God and trust in his guidance and protection

NUMBERS

MEGATHEMES IN NUMBERS

Theme	Explanation	Importance
Census	Moses counted the Israelites twice. The first census organized the people into marching units to better defend themselves. The second prepared them to conquer the country east of the Jordan River.	People have to be organized, trained, and led to be effective in great movements. It is always wise to count the cost before setting out on some great undertaking. When we are aware of the obstacles before us, we can more easily avoid them. In God's work, we must remove barriers in our relationships with others so that our effectiveness is not diminished.
Rebellion	At Kadesh, 12 scouts were sent out into the land of Canaan to report on the fortifications of the enemies. When the scouts returned, 10 said that they should give up and go back to Egypt. As a result, the people refused to enter the land. Faced with a choice, Israel rebelled against God. Rebellion did not start with an uprising, but with griping and murmuring against Moses and God.	Rebellion against God is always a serious matter. It is not something to take lightly, for God's punishment for sin is often very severe. Our rebellion does not usually begin with all-out warfare, but in subtle ways—with griping and criticizing. Make sure your negative comments are not the product of a rebellious spirit.
Wandering	Because they rebelled, the Israelites wandered 40 years in the wilderness. This shows how severely God can punish sin. Forty years was enough time for all those who held on to Egypt's customs and values to die off. It gave time to train up a new generation in the ways of God.	God judges sin harshly because he is holy. The wanderings in the wilderness demonstrate how serious God considers flagrant disobedience of his commands. Purging our lives of sin is vital to God's purpose.
Canaan	Canaan is the Promised Land. It was the land God had promised to Abraham, Isaac, and Jacob—the land of the covenant. Canaan was to be the dwelling place of God's people, those set apart for true spiritual worship.	Although God's punishment for sin is often severe, he offers reconciliation and hope— his love is truly amazing. Just as God's love and law led Israel to the Promised Land, God desires to give purpose and destiny to our lives.

KEY PLACES IN NUMBERS

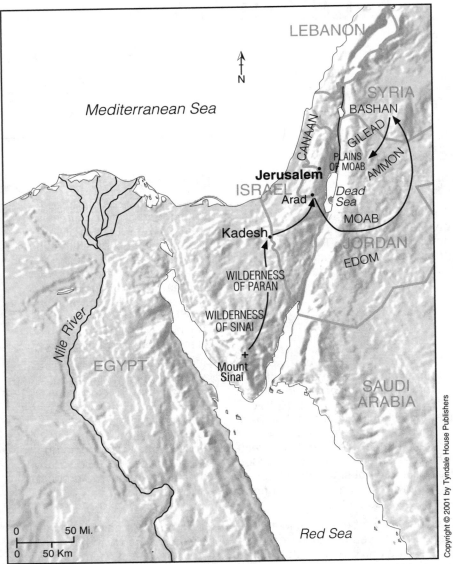

Modern names and boundaries are shown in gray.

1. **Mount Sinai**   Numbers begins at Mount Sinai in the wilderness of Sinai with Moses taking a census of the men eligible for battle. As the battle preparations began, the people also prepared for the spiritual warfare they would face. The Promised Land was full of wicked people who would try to entice the Israelites to sin. God, therefore, taught Moses and the Israelites how to live right (1:1–12:15).

2. **Wilderness of Paran**   After a full year at Mount Sinai, the Israelites broke camp and began their march toward the Promised Land by moving into the wilderness of Paran. From there, one leader from each tribe was sent to spy out the new land. After 40 days they returned, and all but Joshua and Caleb were too afraid to enter. Because of their lack of faith, the Israelites were made to wander in the wilderness for 40 years (12:16–19:22).

3. **Kadesh**   With the years of wandering nearing an end, the Israelites set their sights once again on the Promised Land. Kadesh was the oasis where they spent most of their wilderness years. Miriam died here. And it was here that Moses angrily struck the rock, which kept him from entering the Promised Land (20:1-13).

4. **Arad**   When the king there heard that Israel was on the move, he attacked, but he was soundly defeated. Moses then led the people southward and eastward around the Dead Sea (21:1-3).

5. **Edom**   The Israelites wanted to travel through Edom, but the king of Edom refused them passage (20:14-22). So they traveled around Edom and became very discouraged. The people complained, and God sent poisonous snakes to punish them. Only by looking at a bronze snake on a pole could those bitten be healed (21:4-9).

6. **Ammon**   Next, King Sihon of the Amorites refused Israel passage. When he attacked, Israel defeated his army and conquered the territory as far as the border of Ammon (21:21-32).

7. **Bashan**   Moses sent spies to Bashan. King Og attacked, but he was also defeated (21:33-35).

8. **Plains of Moab**   The people camped on the plains of Moab, east of the Jordan River across from Jericho. They were on the verge of entering the Promised Land (22:1).

9. **Moab**   King Balak of Moab, terrified of the Israelites, called upon Balaam, a famous sorcerer, to curse Israel from the mountains above where the Israelites camped. But the Lord caused Balaam to bless them instead (22:2–24:25).

10. **Gilead**   The tribes of Reuben and Gad decided to settle in the fertile country of Gilead east of the Jordan River because it was a good land for their sheep. But first they promised to help the other tribes conquer the land west of the Jordan River (32:1-42).

ARRANGEMENT OF TRIBES AROUND THE TABERNACLE
WHILE IN THE WILDERNESS / Numbers 2

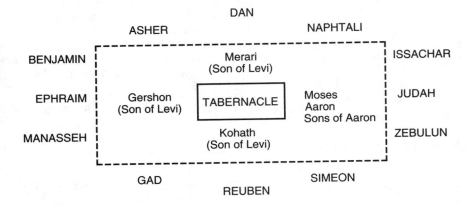

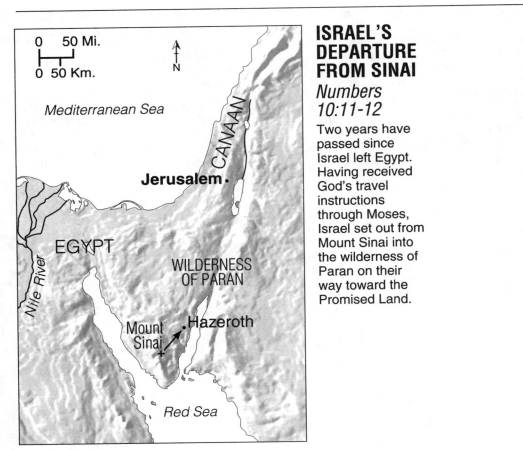

ISRAEL'S DEPARTURE FROM SINAI
Numbers 10:11-12

Two years have passed since Israel left Egypt. Having received God's travel instructions through Moses, Israel set out from Mount Sinai into the wilderness of Paran on their way toward the Promised Land.

Copyright © 2001 by Tyndale House Publishers

ISRAEL'S COMPLAINING / *Numbers 11*

	Complaint	Sin	Result
11:1	About their hardships	Complained about their problems instead of praying to God about them	Thousands of people were destroyed when God sent a plague of fire to punish them
11:4	About the lack of meat	Coveted things they didn't have	God sent quail; but as the people began to eat, God struck them with a plague that killed many
14:1-4	About being stuck in the wilderness, facing the giants of the Promised Land, and wishing to return to Egypt	Openly rebelled against God's leaders and failed to trust in his promises	All who complained were not allowed to enter the Promised Land, being doomed to wander in the wilderness until they died
16:3	About Moses' and Aaron's authority and leadership	Were greedy for more power and authority	The families, friends, and possessions of Korah, Dathan, and Abiram were swallowed up by the earth. Fire then burned up the 250 other men who rebelled
16:41	That Moses and Aaron caused the deaths of Korah and his conspirators	Blamed others for their own troubles	God began to destroy Israel with a plague. Moses and Aaron made atonement for the people, but 14,700 of them were killed
20:2-3	About the lack of water	Refused to believe that God would provide as he had promised	Moses sinned along with the people. For this he was barred from entering the Promised Land
21:5	That God and Moses brought them into the wilderness	Failed to recognize that their problems were brought on by their own disobedience	God sent poisonous snakes that killed many people and seriously injured many others

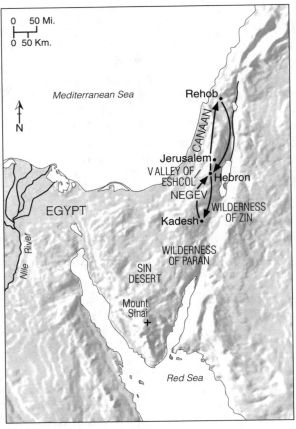

0 50 Mi.
0 50 Km.

Mediterranean Sea

Rehob

CANAAN

Jerusalem
VALLEY OF
ESHCOL
NEGEV

Hebron

EGYPT

Kadesh

WILDERNESS
OF ZIN

Nile River

WILDERNESS
OF PARAN

SIN
DESERT

Mount
Sinai

Red Sea

N

Copyright © 2001 by Tyndale House Publishers

ROUTE OF THE SCOUTS
Numbers 13:1-26

The scouts traveled from Kadesh at the southernmost edge of the wilderness of Zin to Rehob at the northern-most edge and back, a round trip of about 500 miles.

EVENTS AT KADESH
Numbers 20:1-22

After wandering in the wilderness for 40 years, Israel arrived at Kadesh, where Miriam died. There was not enough water and the people complained bitterly. Moses struck a rock, and it gave enough water for everyone. The king of Edom refused Israel passage through his land, forcing them to travel around his country.

Copyright © 2001 by Tyndale House Publishers

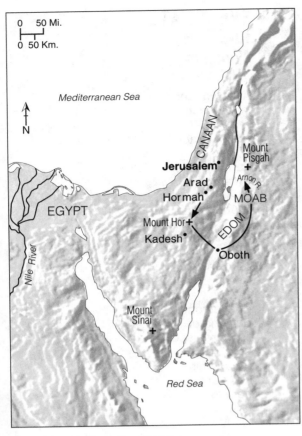

EVENTS IN THE WILDERNESS

Numbers 21:1-20

Israel next met resistance from the king of Arad but soundly defeated him. The next stop was Mount Hor (where Aaron died); then they traveled south and east around Edom. After camping at Oboth, they moved toward the Arnon River and onto the plains of Moab near Mount Pisgah.

Copyright © 2001 by Tyndale House Publishers

THE SNAKE IN THE WILDERNESS / *Numbers 21:7-9*

Compare the texts for yourself: Numbers 21:7-9 and John 3:14-15.

Israelites	Christians
Bitten by snakes	Bitten by sin
Little initial pain, then intense suffering	Little initial pain, then intense suffering
Physical death from snakes' poison	Spiritual death from sin's poison
Bronze snake lifted up in the wilderness	Christ lifted up on the cross
Looking to the snake spared one's life	Looking to Christ saves from eternal death

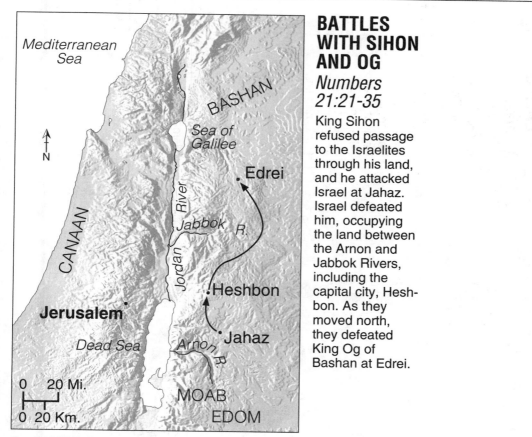

BATTLES WITH SIHON AND OG
Numbers 21:21-35

King Sihon refused passage to the Israelites through his land, and he attacked Israel at Jahaz. Israel defeated him, occupying the land between the Arnon and Jabbok Rivers, including the capital city, Heshbon. As they moved north, they defeated King Og of Bashan at Edrei.

Copyright © 2001 by Tyndale House Publishers

PREPARING TO ENTER THE PROMISED LAND

Numbers 33:50-54

The Israelites had been camped in the plains of Moab, across from Jericho. From this position, they were ready to enter the Promised Land.

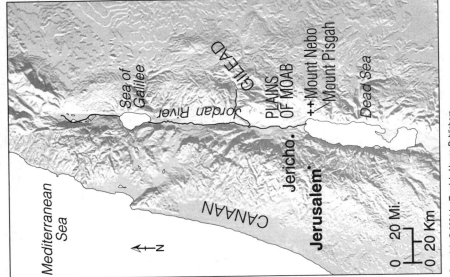

Copyright © 2001 by Tyndale House Publishers

THE STORY OF BALAAM

Numbers 22:1-41

At King Balak's request, Balaam traveled nearly 400 miles to curse Israel. Balak took Balaam to Bamoth-baal ("the high places of Baal"), then to Pisgah Peak, and finally to Mount Peor. Each place looked over the plains of Moab, where the Israelites were camped. But to the king's dismay, Balaam blessed, not cursed, Israel.

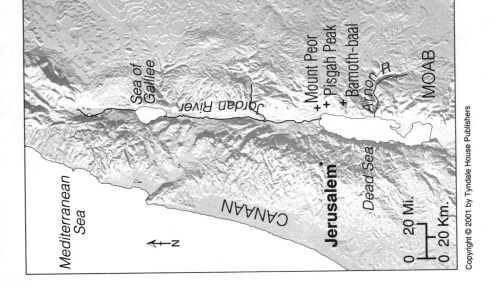

Copyright © 2001 by Tyndale House Publishers

CITIES OF REFUGE

Numbers 35:1-8

Six of the Levites' cities were designated as cities of refuge. They were spaced throughout the land and protected those who had accidentally committed a crime or who were awaiting trial.

Kedesh

Sea of Galilee

Golan

Ramoth

Bezer

Dead Sea

Jordan River

Shechem

CANAAN

Jerusalem

Hebron

Mediterranean Sea

N

0   20 Mi.

0   20 Km.

Copyright © 2001 by Tyndale House Publishers

THE BORDERS OF THE PROMISED LAND

Numbers 34:1-12

The borders of the Promised Land stretched from the wilderness of Zin and Kadesh-barnea in the south to Lebo-hamath and Riblah in the north, and from the Mediterranean seacoast on the west to the Jordan River on the east. The land of Gilead was also included.

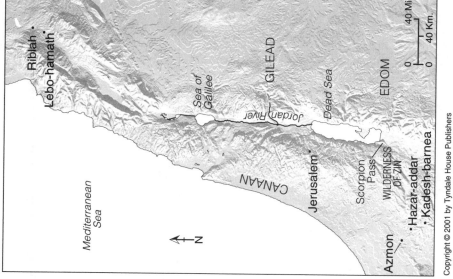

Riblah

Lebo-hamath

Sea of Galilee

GILEAD

Jordan River

Dead Sea

EDOM

Mediterranean Sea

N

CANAAN

Jerusalem

Scorpion Pass

WILDERNESS OF ZIN

Azmon

Hazar-addar

Kadesh-barnea

0   40 Mi.

0   40 Km.

Copyright © 2001 by Tyndale House Publishers

41

NUMBERS

PRIESTS IN ISRAEL'S HISTORY / *Numbers 35:25-28*

	Priest	Importance	Reference
Numbers 35:25-28 mentions the death of a high priest. Each new high priest had to come from the lineage of Aaron. Listed here are the ones whose stories are told elsewhere in the Bible.	Aaron	Moses' brother and first priest	Exodus 28:1-3
	Eleazar	Watched two of his brothers die in a fire from God because they did not follow God's instructions. He obeyed God and became chief leader of the Tabernacle.	Leviticus 10 Numbers 3:32
	Phinehas	Executed a young Israelite idol worshiper and his Midianite mistress to end a plague. He was then promised that his priestly line would never end.	Numbers 25:1-15
	Ahitub	A priest during King Saul's reign	1 Samuel 14:3
	Zadok	A faithful high priest under King David. He and Nathan anointed Solomon as the next king.	2 Samuel 8:17 1 Kings 1:38-39
	Ahimaaz	Carried the message of Absalom's death to King David but was apparently afraid to tell about it.	2 Samuel 18:19-29
	Azariah	High priest under King Solomon	1 Kings 4:2
	Azariah	High priest under Uzziah. He rebuked the king for burning incense himself.	2 Chronicles 26:17-21
		When Hezekiah became king, he reopened the Temple. Azariah again served as high priest.	2 Chronicles 26:17-21
	Amariah	King Jehoshaphat appointed him to judge religious disputes.	2 Chronicles 19:11
	Hilkiah	Found the Book of the Law during Josiah's reign	2 Kings 22:3-13 2 Chronicles 34:14-21
	Azariah	Probably one of the first to return to Israel from Babylon	1 Chronicles 9:10-11
	Seraiah	The father of Ezra	Ezra 7:1-5

DEUTERONOMY

MEGATHEMES IN DEUTERONOMY

Theme	Explanation	Importance
History	Moses reviewed the mighty acts of God whereby he liberated Israel from slavery in Egypt. He recounted how God had helped them and how the people had disobeyed.	By reviewing God's promises and mighty acts in history, we can learn about his character. We come to know God more intimately through understanding how he has acted in the past. We can also avoid mistakes in our own lives through learning from Israel's past failures.
Laws	God reviewed his laws for the people. The legal contract between God and his people had to be renewed by the new generation about to enter the Promised Land.	Commitment to God and his truth cannot be taken for granted. Each generation and each person must respond afresh to God's call for obedience.
Love	God's faithful and patient love is portrayed more often than his punishment. God shows his love by being faithful to his people and his promises. In response, God desires love from the heart, not merely a legalistic keeping of his law.	God's love forms the foundation for our trust in him. We trust him because he loves us. Because God loves us, we should maintain justice and respect.
Choices	God reminded his people that in order to ratify his agreement, they must choose the path of obedience. A personal decision to obey would bring benefits to their lives; rebellion would bring severe calamity.	Our choices make a difference. Choosing to follow God benefits us and improves our relationships with others. Choosing to abandon God's ways brings harm to ourselves and others.
Teaching	God commanded the Israelites to teach their children his ways. They were to use ritual, instruction, and memorization to make sure their children understood God's principles and passed them on to the next generation.	Quality teaching for our children must be a priority. It is important to pass on God's truth to future generations in our traditions. But God desires that his truth be in our hearts and minds and not merely in our traditions.

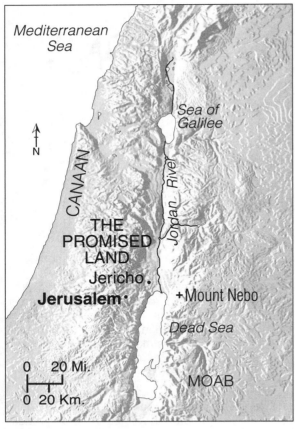

Mediterranean Sea

Sea of Galilee

N

CANAAN

Jordan River

THE PROMISED LAND

Jericho.

Jerusalem·

+Mount Nebo

Dead Sea

0   20 Mi.

0   20 Km.

MOAB

Copyright © 2001 by Tyndale House Publishers

EVENTS IN DEUTERONOMY
Deuteronomy 1:1-5

The book of Deuteronomy opens with Israel camped east of the Jordan River in the land of Moab. Just before the people crossed the river into the Promised Land, Moses delivered an inspirational speech indicating how they were to live.

BROKEN COMMANDMENTS / *Deuteronomy 5*

The Ten Commandments were God's standards for right living. To obey them was to obey God. Yet throughout the Old Testament, we can see how each commandment was broken. As you read the stories, notice the tragic consequences that occurred as a result of violating God's law.

Ten Commandments	Notable Violations
"Do not worship any other gods besides me."	Solomon (1 Kings 11)
"Do not make idols of any kind. . . . You must never worship or bow down to them."	The gold calf-idol incident (Exodus 32); generations after Joshua (Judges 2:10-14; 2 Kings 21:1-15; Jeremiah 1:16)
"Do not misuse the name of the LORD your God."	Zedekiah (Ezekiel 17:15-21)
"Observe the Sabbath day by keeping it holy."	Judah (2 Chronicles 36:21)
"Honor your father and mother."	Eli's sons—Hophni and Phinehas (1 Samuel 2:12, 23-25)
"Do not murder."	Hazael (2 Kings 8:15)
"Do not commit adultery."	David (2 Samuel 11:2-5)
"Do not steal."	Ahab (1 Kings 21:1-19)
"Do not testify falsely against your neighbor."	Saul (1 Samuel 15:13-25)
"Do not covet your neighbor's wife. Do not covet your neighbor's house or land, . . . or anything else your neighbor owns."	Achan (Joshua 7:19-26)

DANGER IN PLENTY / *Deuteronomy 6:11-12*

"When you have eaten your fill in this land, be careful not to forget the LORD" (Deuteronomy 6:11-12). It is often most difficult to follow God when life is easy—we can fall prey to temptation and fall away from God. Here are some notable examples of this truth.

Person	Reference	Comment
Adam	Genesis 3	Adam lived in a perfect world and had a perfect relationship with God. His needs were met; he had everything. But he fell to Satan's deception.
Noah	Genesis 9	Noah and his family had survived the Flood, and the whole world was theirs. They were prosperous, and life was easy. Noah shamed himself by becoming drunk and cursed his son Ham.
The nation of Israel	Judges 2	God had given Israel the Promised Land—rest at last with no more wandering. But as soon as brave and faithful Joshua died, they fell into the idolatrous practices of the Canaanites.
David	2 Samuel 11	David ruled well, and Israel was a dominant nation politically, economically, and militarily. In the midst of prosperity and success, he committed adultery with Bathsheba and had her husband, Uriah, murdered.
Solomon	1 Kings 11	Solomon truly had it all: power, wealth, fame, and wisdom. But his very abundance was the source of his downfall. He loved his pagan, idolatrous wives so much that he allowed himself and Israel to copy their detestable religious rites.

OBEDIENCE / *Deuteronomy 8:1*

Deuteronomy 8:1 tells us to obey God's commandments. We do this by obeying God with . . .

Our heart . . .	By loving him more than any relationship, activity, achievement, or possession
Our will	By committing ourselves completely to him
Our mind. . . .	By seeking to know him and his Word, so his principles and values form the foundation of all we think and do
Our body. . . .	By recognizing that our strengths, talents, and sexuality are given to us by God to be used for pleasure and fulfillment according to his rules, not ours
Our finances . .	By deciding that all of the resources we have ultimately come from God, and that we are to be managers of them and not owners
Our future . . .	By deciding to make service to God and man the main purpose of our life's work

VARIETY IN WORSHIP / *Deuteronomy 23*

Israel's worship used all of the senses. They reinforced the meaning of the ceremony. Every sense can be used to worship God.

Sight	The beauty and symbolism of the Tabernacle; every color and hue had a meaning
Hearing	The use of music; there were instructions for the use of a variety of instruments, and the Bible records many songs
Touch	The head of the animal to be sacrificed was touched, symbolizing the fact that it was taking their place
Smell	The sacrifices were burned, emitting a familiar aroma
Taste	The festivals were celebrations and memorials—much of the food was symbolic

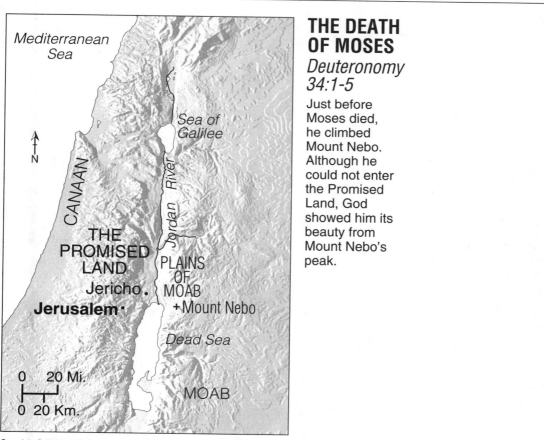

THE DEATH OF MOSES
Deuteronomy 34:1-5

Just before Moses died, he climbed Mount Nebo. Although he could not enter the Promised Land, God showed him its beauty from Mount Nebo's peak.

Copyright © 2001 by Tyndale House Publishers

JOSHUA

MEGATHEMES IN JOSHUA

Theme	Explanation	Importance
Success	God gave success to the Israelites when they obeyed his master plan, not when they followed their own desires. Victory came when they trusted in him rather than in their military power, money, muscle, or mental capacity.	God's work done in God's way will bring his success. The standard for success, however, is not to be set by the society around us but by God's Word. We must adjust our minds to God's way of thinking in order to see his standard for success.
Faith	The Israelites demonstrated their faith by trusting God daily to save and guide them. By noticing how God fulfilled his promises in the past, they developed strong confidence that he would be faithful in the future.	Our strength to do God's work comes from trusting him. His promises reassure us of his love and that he will be there to guide us in the decisions and struggles we face. Faith begins with believing he can be trusted.
Guidance	God gave instructions to Israel for every aspect of their lives. His law guided their daily living, and his specific marching orders gave them victory in battle.	Guidance from God for daily living can be found in his Word. By staying in touch with God, we will have the needed wisdom to meet the great challenges of life.
Leadership	Joshua was an example of an excellent leader. He was confident in God's strength, courageous in the face of opposition, and willing to seek God's advice.	To be a strong leader like Joshua, we must be ready to listen and to move quickly when God instructs us. Once we have his instructions, we must be diligent in carrying them out. Strong leaders are led by God.
Conquest	God commanded his people to conquer the Canaanites and take all their land. Completing this mission would have fulfilled God's promise to Abraham and brought judgment on the evil people living there. Unfortunately, Israel never finished the job.	The Israelites were faithful in accomplishing their mission at first, but their commitment faltered. To love God means more than being enthusiastic about him. We must complete all the work he gives us and apply his instructions to every corner of our lives.

KEY PLACES IN JOSHUA

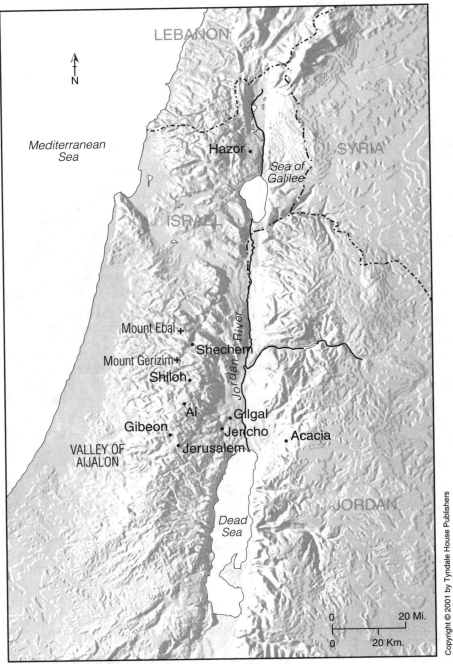

Modern names and boundaries are shown in gray.

KEY PLACES IN JOSHUA *continued*

1. **Acacia** The story of Joshua begins with the Israelites camping at Acacia. The Israelites under Joshua were ready to enter and conquer Canaan. But before the nation moved out, Joshua received instructions from God (1:1-18).

2. **Jordan River** The entire nation prepared to cross this river, which was swollen from spring rains. After the spies returned from Jericho with a positive report, Joshua prepared the priests and people for a miracle. As the priests carried the Ark into the Jordan River, the water stopped flowing, and the entire nation crossed on dry ground into the Promised Land (2:1–4:24).

3. **Gilgal** After crossing the Jordan River, the Israelites camped at Gilgal, where they renewed their commitment to God and celebrated the Passover, the festival commemorating their deliverance from Egypt (see Exodus). As Joshua made plans for the attack on Jericho, an angel appeared to him (5:1-15).

4. **Jericho** The walled city of Jericho seemed a formidable enemy. But when Joshua followed God's plans, the great walls were no obstacle. The city was conquered with only the obedient marching of the people (6:1-27).

5. **Ai** Victory could not continue without obedience to God. That is why the disobedience of one man, Achan, brought defeat to the entire nation in the first battle against Ai. But once the sin was recognized and punished, God told Joshua to take heart and try Ai once again. This time the city was taken (7:1–8:29).

6. **The Mountains of Ebal and Gerizim** After the defeat of Ai, Joshua built an altar at Mount Ebal. Then the people divided themselves, half at the foot of Mount Ebal, half at the foot of Mount Gerizim. The priests stood between the mountains holding the Ark of the Covenant as Joshua read God's law to all the people (8:30-35).

7. **Gibeon** It was just after the Israelites reaffirmed their covenant with God that their leaders made a major mistake in judgment: They were tricked into making a peace treaty with the city of Gibeon. The Gibeonites pretended that they had traveled a long distance and asked the Israelites for a treaty. The leaders made the agreement without consulting God. The trick was soon discovered, but because the treaty had been made, Israel could not go back on its word. As a result, the Gibeonites saved their own lives, but they were forced to become Israel's slaves (9:1-27).

8. **Valley of Aijalon** The king of Jerusalem was very angry at Gibeon for making a peace treaty with the Israelites. He gathered armies from four other cities to attack the city. Gibeon summoned Joshua for help. Joshua took immediate action. Leaving Gilgal, he attacked the coalition by surprise. As the battle waged on and moved into the valley of Aijalon, Joshua prayed for the sun to stand still until the enemy could be destroyed (10:1-43).

9. **Hazor** Up north in Hazor, King Jabin mobilized the kings of the surrounding cities to unite and crush Israel. But God gave Joshua and Israel victory (11:1-23).

10. **Shiloh** After the armies of Canaan were conquered, Israel gathered at Shiloh to set up the Tabernacle. This movable building had been the nation's center of worship during their years of wandering. The seven tribes who had not received their land were given their allotments (18:1–19:51).

11. **Shechem** Before Joshua died he called the entire nation together at Shechem to remind them that it was God who had given them their land and that only with God's help could they keep it. The people vowed to follow God. As long as Joshua was alive, the land was at rest from war and trouble (24:1-33).

TAKE THE LAND / *Joshua 1*

God told Joshua to lead the Israelites into the Promised Land (also called Canaan) and conquer it. This was not an act of imperialism or aggression but an act of judgment. Here are some of the earlier passages in the Bible where God promised to give this land to the Israelites and the reasons for doing so.

Genesis 12:1-3	God promised to bless Abraham and make his descendants into a great nation
Genesis 15:16	God would choose the right time for Israel to enter Canaan, because the nations living there then would be wicked and ripe for judgment (their sin would run its course)
Genesis 17:7-8	God promised to give all the land of Canaan to Abraham's descendants
Exodus 33:1-3	God promised to help the Israelites drive out all the evil nations from Canaan
Deuteronomy 4:5-8 . . .	The Israelites were to be an example of right living to the whole world; this would not work if they intermingled with the wicked Canaanites
Deuteronomy 7:1-5 . . .	The Israelites were to utterly wipe out the Canaanites because of their wickedness and because of Israel's call to purity
Deuteronomy 12:2 . . .	The Israelites were to completely destroy the Canaanite altars so nothing would tempt them away from worshiping God alone

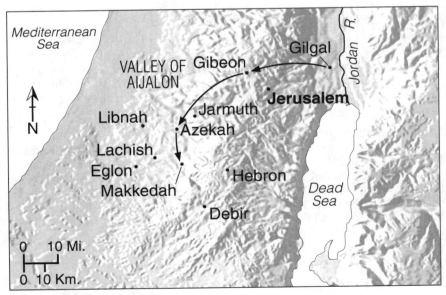

THE BATTLE FOR GIBEON
Joshua 10:1-43

Five Amorite kings conspired to destroy Gibeon. Israel came to the aid of the Gibeonites. The Israelites attacked the enemy armies outside of Gibeon and chased them through the valley of Aijalon as far as Makkedah and Azekah.

Copyright © 2001 by Tyndale House Publishers

THE BATTLE FOR AI

Joshua 8:1-29

During the night, Joshua sent one detachment of soldiers to the west of Ai to lie in wait. The next morning he led a second group north of Ai. When the army of Ai attacked, the Israelites to the north pretended to scatter, only to turn on the enemy as the men lying in ambush moved in and burned the city.

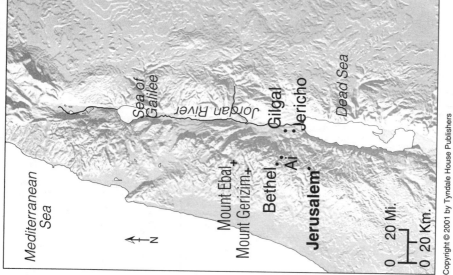

Copyright © 2001 by Tyndale House Publishers

SPY MISSION TO JERICHO

Joshua 2:1, 22-23

Two spies left the Israelite camp at Acacia, crossed the Jordan River, and slipped into Jericho. The city was built around an oasis in the midst of a hot and desolate valley 840 feet below sea level. Jericho was the first major city the Israelites set out to conquer.

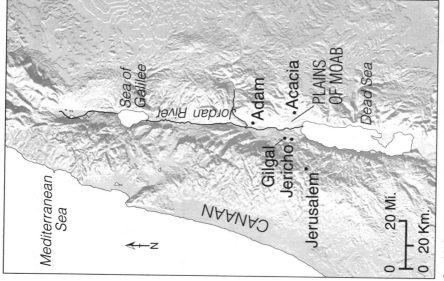

Copyright © 2001 by Tyndale House Publishers

53

THE LAND YET TO BE CONQUERED

Joshua 13:1-6

Canaan was now controlled by the Israelites, although much land and several cities still needed to be conquered. Joshua told the people to include both conquered and unconquered lands in the territorial allotments (13:7). He was certain the people would complete the conquest as God had commanded.

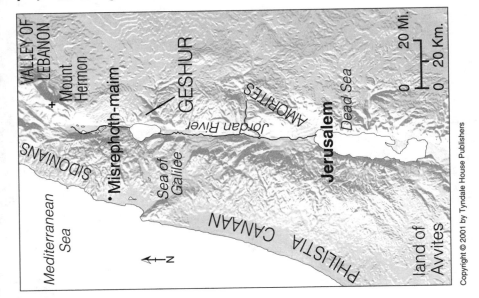

Copyright © 2001 by Tyndale House Publishers

THE BATTLE FOR HAZOR

Joshua 11:1-10

Kings from the north joined together to battle the Israelites who controlled the southern half of Canaan. They gathered by the water near Merom, but Joshua attacked them by surprise—the enemies' chariots were useless in the dense forests. Hazor, the largest Canaanite center in Galilee, was destroyed.

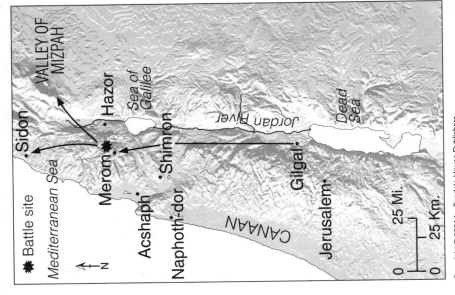

Copyright © 2001 by Tyndale House Publishers

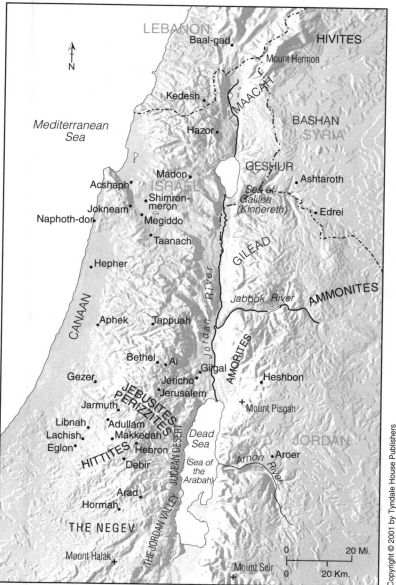

Modern names and boundaries are shown in gray.

THE CONQUERED LAND
Joshua 11:16–12:24

Joshua displayed brilliant military strategy in the way he went about conquering
the land of Canaan. He first captured the well-fortified Jericho to gain a foothold in
Canaan and to demonstrate the awesome might of the God of Israel. Then he gained
the hill country around Bethel and Gibeon. From there he subdued towns in the
lowlands. Then his army conquered important cities in the north, such as Hazor.
In all, Israel conquered land both east (12:1-6) and west (12:7-24) of the Jordan
River; from Mount Hermon in the north to beyond the Negev to Mount Halak in the
south. Thirty-one kings and their cities had been defeated. The Israelites had over-
powered the Hittites, the Amorites, the Canaanites, the Perizzites, the Hivites, and
the Jebusites. Other peoples living in Canaan were yet to be conquered.

THE TRIBES WEST OF THE JORDAN

Joshua 18:1-6

Judah, Ephraim, and the other half-tribe of Manasseh were the first tribes to receive land west of the Jordan because of their past acts of faith. The remaining seven tribes—Benjamin, Zebulun, Issachar, Asher, Naphtali, Simeon, and Dan—were slow to conquer and possess the land allotted to them.

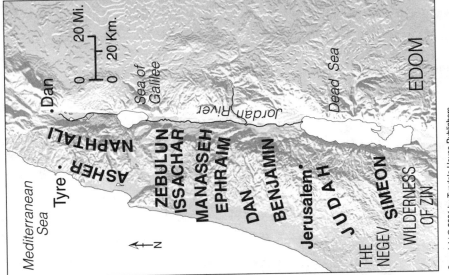

Mediterranean Sea

Tyre •

• Dan

Sea of Galilee

Jordan River

Dead Sea

ASHER

NAPHTALI

ZEBULUN

ISSACHAR

MANASSEH

EPHRAIM

DAN

BENJAMIN

Jerusalem •

J U D A H

THE NEGEV

SIMEON

WILDERNESS OF ZIN

EDOM

N

0   20 Mi.

0   20 Km.

Copyright © 2001 by Tyndale House Publishers

THE TRIBES EAST OF THE JORDAN

Joshua 13:8-12

Joshua assigned territory to the tribes of Reuben, Gad, and the half-tribe of Manasseh on the east side of the Jordan where they had chosen to remain because of the wonderful livestock country (Numbers 32:1-5).

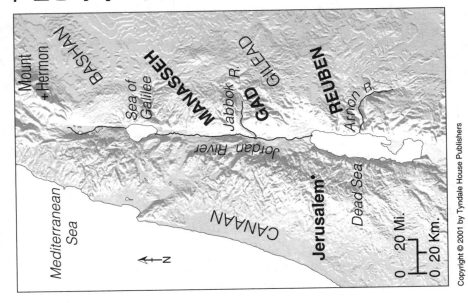

Mediterranean Sea

Mount + Hermon

BASHAN

Sea of Galilee

Jordan River

Jabbok R.

MANASSEH

GAD

GILEAD

REUBEN

Arnon R.

CANAAN

Jerusalem •

Dead Sea

N

0   20 Mi.

0   20 Km.

Copyright © 2001 by Tyndale House Publishers

JOSHUA'S FINAL SPEECH

Joshua 24:1, 29-30

Joshua called all the Israelites to Shechem to hear his final words. He challenged the people to make a conscious choice to always serve God. Soon afterward, Joshua died and was buried in his hometown of Timnath-serah.

Copyright © 2001 by Tyndale House Publishers

THE CITIES OF REFUGE

Joshua 20:1-8

A city of refuge was just that—refuge for someone who committed an unintentional murder that would evoke revenge from the victim's friends and relatives. The six cities of refuge were spaced throughout the land so that a person was never too far from one.

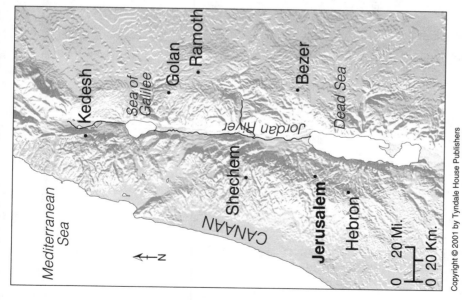

Copyright © 2001 by Tyndale House Publishers

JUDGES

MEGATHEMES IN JUDGES

Theme	Explanation	Importance
Decline/ Compromise	Whenever a judge died, the people faced decline and failure because they compromised their high spiritual purpose in many ways. They abandoned their mission to drive all the people out of the land, and they adopted the customs of the people living around them.	Society has many rewards to offer those who compromise their faith: wealth, acceptance, recognition, power, and influence. When God gives us a mission, it must not be polluted by a desire for approval from society. We must keep our eyes on Christ, who is our Judge and Deliverer.
Decay/ Apostasy	Israel's moral downfall had its roots in the fierce independence that each tribe cherished. It led to everyone doing whatever seemed good in his own eyes. There was no unity in government or in worship. Law and order broke down. Finally, idol worship and man-made religion led to the complete abandoning of faith in God.	We can expect decay when we value anything more highly than God. If we value our own independence more than dedication to God, we have placed an idol in our hearts. Soon our lives become temples to that god. We must constantly regard God's first claim on our lives and all our desires.
Defeat/ Oppression	God used evil oppressors to punish the Israelites for their sin, to bring them to the point of repentance, and to test their allegiance to him.	Rebellion against God leads to disaster. God may use defeat to bring wandering hearts back to him. When all else is stripped away, we recognize the importance of serving only him.
Repentance	Decline, decay, and defeat caused the people to cry out to God for help. They vowed to turn from idolatry and to turn to God for mercy and deliverance. When they repented, God delivered them.	Idolatry gains a foothold in our hearts when we make anything more important than God. We must identify modern idols in our hearts, renounce them, and turn to God for his love and mercy.
Deliverance/ Heroes	Because Israel repented, God raised up heroes to deliver his people from their path of sin and the oppression it brought. He used many kinds of people to accomplish this purpose by filling them with his Holy Spirit.	God's Holy Spirit is available to all people. Anyone who is dedicated to God can be used for his service. Real heroes recognize the futility of human effort without God's guidance and power.

KEY PLACES IN JUDGES

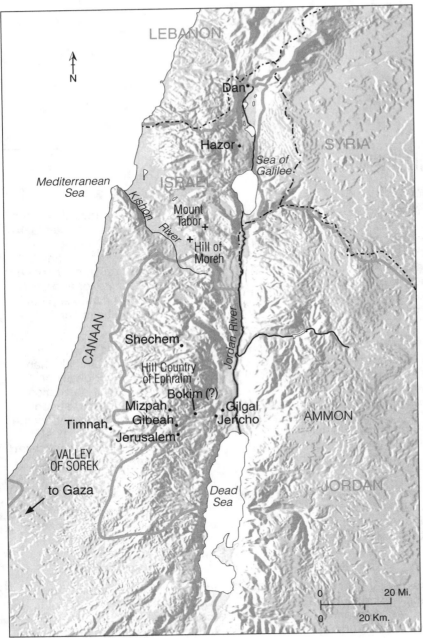

Modern names and boundaries are shown in gray.

ing the evil and idolatrous practices of the land's inhabitants. The angel of the Lord appeared at Bokim to inform the Israelites that their sin and disobedience had broken their agreement with God and would result in punishment through oppression (1:1–3:11).

2. Jericho The nation of Moab was one of the first to oppress Israel. Moab's king Eglon conquered much of Israel—including the city of Jericho—and forced the people to pay unreasonable taxes. The messenger chosen to deliver this tax money to King Eglon was named Ehud. But he had more than money to deliver, for he drew his hidden sword and killed the Moabite king. Ehud then escaped, only to return with an army that chased out the Moabites and freed Israel from its oppressors (3:12-31).

3. Hazor After Ehud's death, King Jabin of Hazor conquered Israel and oppressed the people for 20 years. Then Deborah became Israel's leader. She summoned Barak to fight Commander Sisera, the leader of King Jabin's army. Together Deborah and Barak led their army into battle against Jabin's forces in the land between Mount Tabor and the Kishon River and conquered them (4:1–5:31).

1. Bokim The book of Judges opens with the Israelites continuing their conquest of the Promised Land. Their failure to obey God and destroy all the evil inhabitants soon comes back to haunt them in two ways: (1) the enemies reorganized and counterattacked, and (2) Israel turned away from God, adopt-

4. Hill of Moreh After 40 years of peace, the Midianites began to harass the Israelites by destroying their flocks and crops. When the

Copyright © 2001 by Tyndale House Publishers

Israelites finally cried out to God, he chose Gideon, a poor and humble farmer, to be their deliverer. After struggling with doubt and feelings of inferiority, Gideon took courage and knocked down his town's altar to Baal, causing a great uproar among the citizens. Filled with the Spirit of God, he attacked the vast army of Midian, which was camped near the hill of Moreh. With just a handful of men, Gideon sent the enemy running away in confusion (6:1–7:25).

5. **Shechem**   Even great leaders make mistakes. Gideon's relations with a concubine in Shechem resulted in the birth of a son named Abimelech. Abimelech turned out to be treacherous and power hungry—stirring up the people to proclaim him king. To carry out his plan, he went so far as to kill 69 of his 70 half brothers. Eventually some men of Shechem rebelled against Abimelech, but he gathered together an army and defeated them. His lust for power led him to ransack two other cities, but he was killed by a woman who dropped a millstone onto his head (8:28–9:57).

6. **Land of Ammon**   Again Israel turned completely from God; so God turned from them. But when the Ammonites mobilized their army to attack, Israel threw away her idols and called upon God once again. Jephthah, a prostitute's son who had been run out of Israel, was asked to return and lead Israel's forces against the enemy. After defeating the Ammonites, Jephthah became involved in a war with the tribe of Ephraim over a misunderstanding (10:1–12:15).

7. **Timnah**   Israel's next judge, Samson, was a miracle child promised by God to a barren couple. He was the one who would begin to free Israel from their next and most powerful oppressor, the Philistines. According to God's command, Samson was to be a Nazirite—one who took a vow to be set apart for special service to God. One of the vow's stipulations was that Samson's hair could never be cut. But when Samson grew up, he did not always take his special responsibility to God seriously. He even fell in love with a Philistine girl in Timnah and asked to marry her. Before the wedding, Samson held a party for some men in the city, using a riddle to place a bet with them. The men, however, forced Samson's fiancée into giving the answer. Furious at being tricked, Samson paid his bet with the lives of 30 Philistines who lived in the nearby city of Ashkelon (13:1–14:20).

8. **Valley of Sorek**   Samson killed thousands of Philistines with his incredible strength. The nation's leaders looked for a way to stop him. They got their chance when another Philistine woman stole Samson's heart. Her name was Delilah, and she lived in the valley of Sorek. In exchange for a great sum of money, Delilah deceived Samson into entrusting her with the secret of his strength. One night while he slept, Delilah had his hair cut off. As a result, Samson fell helplessly into the hands of the enemy (15:1–16:20).

9. **Gaza**   Samson was blinded and led captive to a prison in Gaza. There his hair began to grow again. After a while, the Philistines held a great festival to celebrate Samson's imprisonment and to humiliate him before the crowds. When he was brought out as the entertainment, he literally brought down the house when he pushed on the main pillars of the banquet hall and killed the thousands trapped inside. The prophecy that he would begin to free Israel from the Philistines had come true (16:21-31).

10. **Hill Country of Ephraim**   In the hill country of Ephraim lived a man named Micah. Micah hired his own priest to perform priestly duties in the shrine that housed his collection of idols. He thought he was pleasing God with all his religiosity! Like many of the Israelites, Micah assumed that his own opinions of what was right would agree with God's (17:1-13).

11. **Dan**   The tribe of Dan migrated north in order to find new territory. They sent spies ahead of them to scout out the land. One night the spies stopped at Micah's home. Looking for some assurance of victory, the spies stole Micah's idols and priest. Rejoining the tribe, they came upon the city of Laish and slaughtered the unarmed and innocent citizens, renaming the conquered city Dan. Micah's idols were then set up in the city and became the focal point of the tribe's worship for many years (18:1-31).

12. **Gibeah**   The extent to which many people had fallen away from God became clear in Gibeah, a village in the territory of Benjamin. A man and his concubine were traveling north toward the hill country of Ephraim. They stopped for the night in Gibeah, thinking they would be safe. But some perverts in the city gathered around the home where they were staying and demanded that the man come out to have sexual relations with them. Instead, the man and his host pushed the concubine out the door. She was raped and abused all night. When the man found her lifeless body the next morning, he cut it into 12 pieces and sent the parts to each tribe of Israel. This tragic event demonstrated that the nation had sunk to its lowest spiritual level (19:1-30).

13. **Mizpah**   The leaders of Israel came to Mizpah to decide how to punish the wicked men from the city of Gibeah. When the city leaders refused to turn the criminals over, the whole nation of Israel took vengeance upon both Gibeah and the tribe of Benjamin where the city was located. When the battle ended, the entire tribe had been destroyed except for a handful of men who took refuge in the hills. Israel had become morally depraved. The stage was now set for the much-needed spiritual renewal that would come under the prophet Samuel (20:1–21:25).

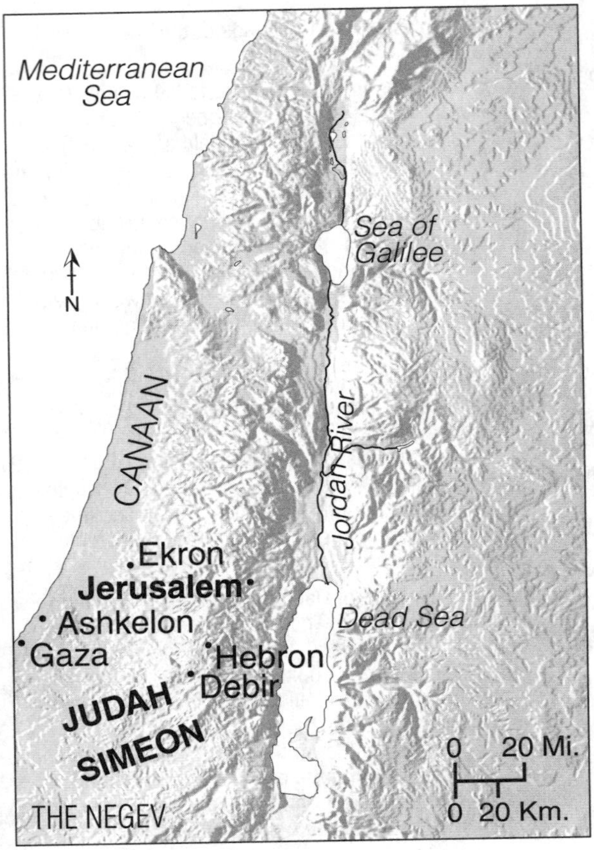
Mediterranean Sea
Sea of Galilee
N
CANAAN
Jordan River
Ekron
Jerusalem
Ashkelon
Gaza
Dead Sea
Hebron
Debir
JUDAH
SIMEON
0 20 Mi.
0 20 Km.
THE NEGEV

Copyright © 2001 by Tyndale House Publishers

JUDAH FIGHTS FOR ITS LAND

Judges 1:1-18

The tribe of Judah wasted no time beginning their conquest of the territory allotted to them. With help from the tribe of Simeon, Jerusalem was conquered, as were the Canaanites in the Negev and along the coast. Hebron and Debir fell to Judah, and later Gaza, Ashkelon, and Ekron.

WHY DID ISRAEL WANT TO WORSHIP IDOLS? / *Judges 2:10*

The temptation to follow false gods because of short-term benefits, good feelings, easy "rules," or convenience was always present. But the benefits were deceptive because the gods were false. We worship God because he is the one and only true God.

Worshiping God	Worshiping Idols
Long-range benefits	Short-range benefits
Gratification postponed	Self-gratification immediate
Morality required	Sensuality approved
High ethical standards demanded	Low ethical standards tolerated
Neighbors' sins disapproved	Neighbors' sins approved
Unseen God worshiped	Visible idols worshiped
Unselfishness expected	Selfishness condoned
Business relations hindered	Business relations improved
Strict religious practices maintained	Religious practices loosely regulated
Changed life demanded	Changed life not demanded
Ethical stand expected	Compromise and cooperation practiced
Concern for others taught	No concern for others expected

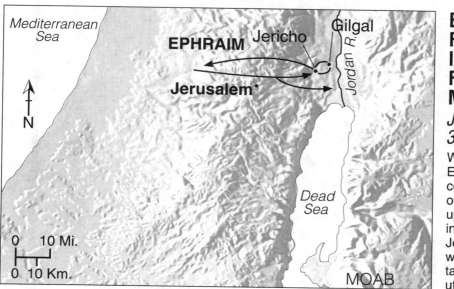

EHUD FREES ISRAEL FROM MOAB

Judges 3:12-30

When King Eglon of Moab conquered part of Israel, he set up his throne in the city of Jericho. Ehud was chosen to take Israel's tribute there. After delivering Israel's tribute, Ehud killed King Eglon and escaped into the hill country of Ephraim. From there he gathered together an army to cut off any Moabites trying to escape across the Jordan River.

Copyright © 2001 by Tyndale House Publishers

THE JUDGES OF ISRAEL / *Judges 3–16*

Judge	Years of Judging	Memorable Act(s)	Reference
Othniel	40	He captured a powerful Canaanite city	Judges 3:7-11
Ehud	80	He killed Eglon and defeated the Moabites	Judges 3:12-30
Shamgar	unrecorded	He killed 600 Philistines with an ox goad	Judges 3:31
Deborah (w/Barak)	40	She defeated Sisera and the Canaanites and later sang a victory song with Barak	Judges 4–5
Gideon	40	He destroyed his family idols, used a fleece to determine God's will, raised an army of 10,000, and defeated 135,000 Midianites with 300 soldiers	Judges 6–8
Tola	23	He judged Israel for 23 years	Judges 10:1-2
Jair	22	He had 30 sons	Judges 10:3-5
Jephthah	6	He made a rash vow, defeated the Ammonites, and later battled jealous Ephraim	Judges 10:6–12:7
Ibzan	7	He had 30 sons and 30 daughters	Judges 12:8-10
Elon	10	He judged Israel for 10 years	Judges 12:11-12
Abdon	8	He had 40 sons and 30 grandsons, each of whom had his own donkey	Judges 12:13-15
Samson	20	He was a Nazirite, killed a lion with his bare hands, burned the Philistine wheat fields, killed 1,000 Philistines with a donkey's jawbone, tore off an iron gate, was betrayed by Delilah, and destroyed thousands of Philistines in one last mighty act	Judges 13–16

THE JUDGES' FUNCTIONS / *Judges 3–16*

Regardless of an individual judge's leadership style, each one demonstrated that God's judgment follows apostasy, while repentance brings restoration.

Judges of Israel could be

saviors (deliverers) and redeemers . . *or* mediators and administrators
(Gideon) (Tola)

providers of rest and peace . . . . . . *or* rude, petty dictators
(Ehud and Jair) (Jephthah)

famous and powerful. . . . . *or* hardworking yet unsung
(Samson) (Elon and Abdon)

leaders of the nation . . . . *or* local heroes
(Othniel and Deborah) (Shamgar and Ibzan)

GIDEON'S BATTLE

Judges 6:1–7:22

In spite of Deborah and Barak's victory, the Canaanites still caused trouble in this fertile region. God appeared to Gideon at Ophrah and called him to defeat them. With only 300 fighting men, Gideon routed thousands of Midianites, chasing them to Zererah and Abel-meholah.

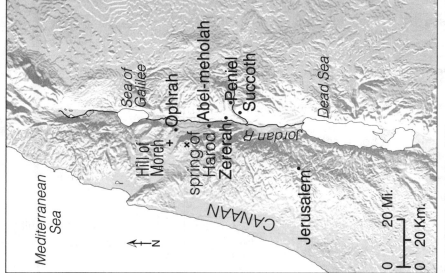

Copyright © 2001 by Tyndale House Publishers

KING JABIN IS DEFEATED

Judges 4:1–24

Deborah traveled from her home between Ramah and Bethel to march with Barak and the Israelite army against Hazor. Sisera, commander of Hazor's army, assembled his men at Harosheth-haggoyim. In spite of Sisera's 900 chariots and expertly trained army, Israel was victorious.

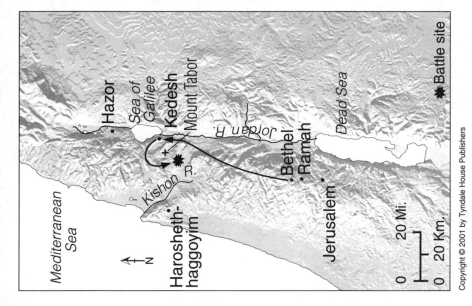

Copyright © 2001 by Tyndale House Publishers

GOD USES COMMON PEOPLE / *Judges 6:11*

God uses all sorts of people to do his work— like you and me!

Person	Known as	Task	Reference
Jacob	A deceiver	To "father" the Israelite nation	Genesis 27–28
Joseph	A slave	To save his family	Genesis 39ff
Moses	Shepherd in exile (and murderer)	To lead Israel out of bondage, to the Promised Land	Exodus 3
Gideon	A farmer	To deliver Israel from Midian	Judges 6:11-14
Jephthah	Son of a prostitute	To deliver Israel from the Ammonites	Judges 11
Hannah	A homemaker	To be the mother of Samuel	1 Samuel 1
David	A shepherd boy and last-born of the family	To be Israel's greatest king	1 Samuel 16
Ezra	A scribe	To lead the return to Judah and to write portions of the Bible	Ezra, Nehemiah
Esther	A slave girl	To save her people from massacre	Esther
Mary	A peasant girl	To be the mother of Christ	Luke 1:27-38
Matthew	A tax collector	To be an apostle and Gospel writer	Matthew 9:9
Luke	A Greek physician	To be a companion of Paul and a Gospel writer	Colossians 4:14
Peter	A fisherman	To be an apostle, a leader of the early church, and a writer of two New Testament letters	Matthew 4:18-20

JEPHTHAH'S VICTORY

Judges 12:1-7

The Ephraimites mobilized an army because they were angry at not being included in the battle against Ammon. They planned to attack Jephthah at his home in Gilead. Jephthah captured the shallows of the Jordan at the Jabbok River and killed the Ephraimites who tried to cross.

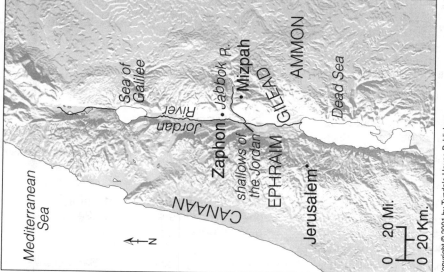

Mediterranean Sea

Sea of Galilee

Jordan River

Jabbok R.

Zaphon

shallows of the Jordan

Mizpah

GILEAD

AMMON

EPHRAIM

CANAAN

Jerusalem

Dead Sea

N

0   20 Mi.
0   20 Km.

Copyright © 2001 by Tyndale House Publishers

ABIMELECH'S FALL

Judges 9:1-57

Gideon's illegitimate son killed 69 of his half brothers in Ophrah and returned to Shechem to be acclaimed king. But three years later, Shechem rebelled. From Arumah, Abimelech attacked Shechem, Bethmillo ("the pillar at Shechem"), and Thebez, where he was killed.

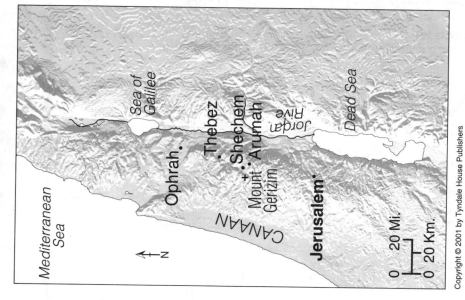

Mediterranean Sea

Sea of Galilee

Ophrah

Thebez

Shechem

Arumah

Mount Gerizim

Jordan River

CANAAN

Jerusalem

Dead Sea

N

0   20 Mi.
0   20 Km.

Copyright © 2001 by Tyndale House Publishers

RASH VOWS / *Judges 11:30-31*

Ecclesiastes 5:2 says: "And don't make rash promises to God, for he is in heaven, and you are only here on earth. So let your words be few." Scripture records the vows of many men and women. Some of these vows proved to be rash and unwise, and others, though extreme, were kept to the letter by those who made them. Let us learn from the examples in God's Word not to make rash vows.

Person	Vow	Result	Reference
Jacob	To "choose" the true God and to give back a tenth to him if he kept him safe	God protected Jacob, who kept his vow to follow God	Genesis 28:20
Jephthah	To offer to the Lord whoever came out to meet him after battle (it turned out to be his daughter)	He lost his daughter	Judges 11:30-31
Hannah	To give her child back to God if God would give her a son	When Samuel was born, she dedicated him to God	1 Samuel 1:9-11
Saul	To kill anyone who ate before evening (Jonathan, his son, had not heard the command and broke it)	Saul would have killed Jonathan if soldiers had not intervened	1 Samuel 14:24-45
David	To be kind to Jonathan's family	Mephibosheth, Jonathan's son, was treated royally by David	2 Samuel 9:7
Ittai	To remain loyal to David	He became one of the great men in David's army	2 Samuel 15:21
Micaiah	To say only what God told him to say	He was put in prison	1 Kings 22:14
Job	That he was not rebelling against God	His fortunes were restored	Job 42:10
Herod Antipas	To give Herodias's daughter anything she requested	Herod was forced to order John the Baptist's death	Mark 6:22-23
Paul	To offer a sacrifice of thanksgiving in Jerusalem	He made the sacrifice despite the danger	Acts 18:18

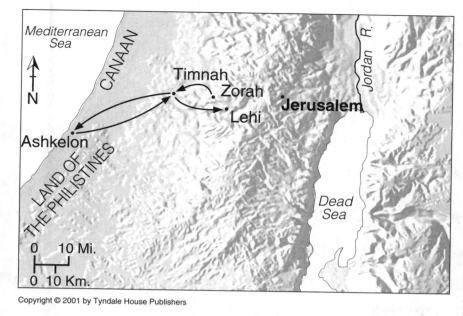

SAMSON'S VENTURES

Judges 13:1–15:20

Samson grew up in Zorah and wanted to marry a Philistine girl from Timnah. Tricked at his wedding feast, he went to Ashkelon and killed some Philistine men and stole their clothes to pay off a bet. Samson then let himself be captured and brought to Lehi, where he snapped his ropes and killed 1,000 people.

SAMSON AND DELILAH

Judges 16:1–31

Samson was seduced by a Philistine woman named Delilah who lived in the valley of Sorek. She betrayed the secret of his strength to the Philistines, who captured him and led him away in chains to Gaza. There he died. His relatives buried him between Zorah and Eshtaol.

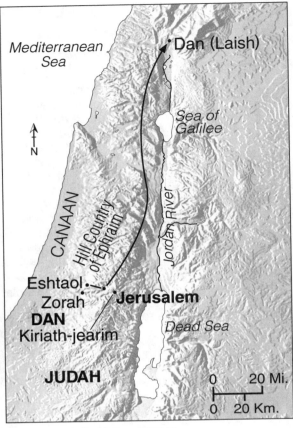

Mediterranean
Sea

Dan (Laish)

Sea of
Galilee

N

CANAAN

Hill Country
of Ephraim

Jordan River

Eshtaol

Zorah

Jerusalem

DAN

Kiriath-jearim

Dead Sea

JUDAH

0   20 Mi.

0   20 Km.

Copyright © 2001 by Tyndale House Publishers

THE TRIBE OF DAN MOVES NORTH

Judges 18:1-31

Troops from the tribe of Dan traveled from Zorah and Eshtaol into the hill country of Ephraim, where they persuaded Micah's priest to come with them. They continued north to Laish, where they ruthlessly butchered its citizens. The city was renamed Dan, and the priest's idols became the focus of their worship

RUTH

MEGATHEMES IN RUTH

Theme	Explanation	Importance
Faithfulness	Ruth's faithfulness to Naomi as a daughter-in-law and friend is a great example of love and loyalty. Ruth, Naomi, and Boaz are also faithful to God and his laws. Throughout the story we see God's faithfulness to his people.	Ruth's life was guided by faithfulness toward God, which showed itself in her loyalty toward the people she knew. To be loyal and loving in relationships, we must imitate God's faithfulness in our relationships with others.
Kindness	Ruth showed great kindness to Naomi. In turn, Boaz showed kindness to Ruth—a despised Moabite woman with no money. God showed his kindness to Ruth, Naomi, and Boaz by bringing them together for his purposes.	Just as Boaz showed his kindness by buying back land to guarantee Ruth and Naomi's inheritance, so Christ showed his kindness by dying for us to guarantee our eternal life. God's kindness should motivate us to love and honor him.
Integrity	Ruth showed high moral character by being loyal to Naomi, by her clean break from her former land and customs, and by her hard work in the fields. Boaz showed integrity in his moral standards, his honesty, and by following through on his commitments.	When we have experienced God's faithfulness and kindness, we should respond by showing integrity. Just as the values by which Ruth and Boaz lived were in sharp contrast to those of the culture portrayed in Judges, so our lives should stand out from the world around us.
Protection	We see God's care and protection over the lives of Naomi and Ruth. His supreme control over circumstances brings them safety and security. He guides the minds and activities of people to fulfill his purposes.	No matter how devastating our present situation may be, our hope is in God. His resources are infinite. We must believe that he can work in the life of any person— whether that person is a king or a stranger in a foreign land. Trust his protection.
Prosperity/ Blessing	Ruth and Naomi came to Bethlehem as poor widows, but they soon became prosperous through Ruth's marriage to Boaz. Ruth became the great-grandmother of King David. Yet the greatest blessing was not the money, the marriage, or the child; it was the quality of love and respect between Ruth, Boaz, and Naomi.	We tend to think of blessings in terms of prosperity rather than the high-quality relationships God makes possible for us. No matter what our economic situation, we can love and respect the people God has brought into our lives. In so doing, we give and receive blessings. Love is the greatest blessing.

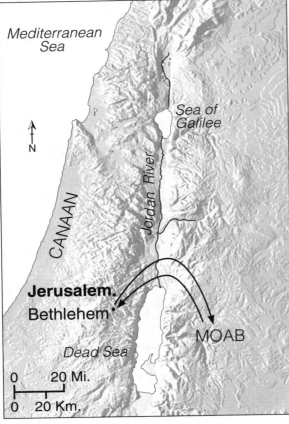

SETTING FOR THE STORY

Ruth 1

Elimelech, Naomi, and their sons traveled from Bethlehem to Moab because of a famine. After her husband and sons died, Naomi returned to Bethlehem with her daughter-in-law Ruth.

Copyright © 2001 by Tyndale House Publishers

1 SAMUEL

MEGATHEMES IN 1 SAMUEL

Theme	Explanation	Importance
King	Because Israel suffered from corrupt priests and judges, the people wanted a king. They wanted to be organized like the surrounding nations. Though it was against his original purpose, God chose a king for them.	Establishing a monarchy did not solve Israel's problems. What God desires is the genuine devotion of each person's mind and heart to him. No government or set of laws can substitute for the rule of God in your heart and life.
God's Control	Israel prospered as long as the people regarded God as their true king. When the leaders strayed from God's law, God intervened in their personal lives and overruled their actions. In this way, God maintained ultimate control over Israel's history.	God is always at work in this world, even when we can't see what he is doing. No matter what kinds of pressures we must endure or how many changes we must face, God is ultimately in control of our situation. Being confident of God's sovereignty, we can face the difficult situations in our lives with boldness.
Leadership	God guided his people using different forms of leadership: judges, priests, prophets, kings. Those whom he chose for these different offices, such as Eli, Samuel, Saul, and David, portrayed different styles of leadership. Yet the success of each leader depended on his devotion to God, not his position, leadership style, wisdom, age, or strength.	When Eli, Samuel, Saul, and David disobeyed God, they faced tragic consequences. Sin affected what they accomplished for God and how some of them raised their children. Being a real leader means letting God guide all aspects of your activities, values, and goals, including the way you raise your children.
Obedience	For God, "obedience is far better than sacrifice" (15:22). God wanted his people to obey, serve, and follow him with a whole heart rather than to maintain a superficial commitment based on tradition or ceremonial systems.	Although we are free from the sacrificial system of the Jewish law, we may still rely on outward observances to substitute for inward commitment. God desires that all our work and worship be motivated by genuine, heartfelt devotion to him.
God's Faithfulness	God faithfully kept the promises he made to Israel. He responded to his people with tender mercy and swift justice. In showing mercy, he faithfully acted in the best interest of his people. In showing justice, he was faithful to his word and perfect moral nature.	Because God is faithful, he can be counted on to be merciful toward us. Yet God is also just, and he will not tolerate rebellion against him. His faithfulness and unselfish love should inspire us to dedicate ourselves to him completely. We must never take his mercy for granted.

KEY PLACES IN 1 SAMUEL

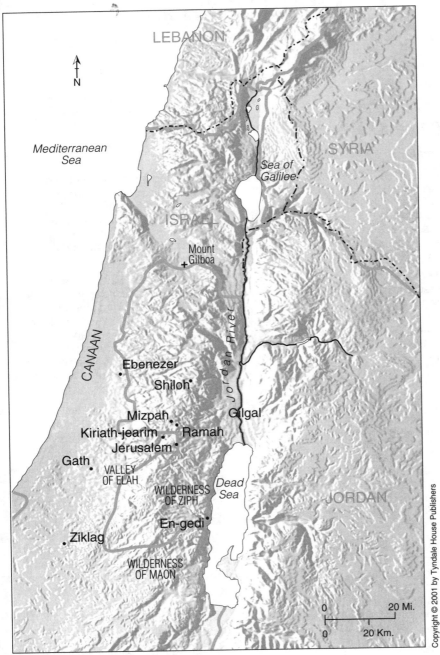

Modern names and boundaries are shown in gray.

Copyright © 2001 by Tyndale House Publishers

1. **Ramah** Samuel was born in Ramah. Before his birth, Samuel's mother, Hannah, made a promise to God that she would dedicate her son to serve God alongside the priests in the Tabernacle at Shiloh (1:1–2:11).

2. **Shiloh** The focal point of Israel's worship was at Shiloh, where the Tabernacle and the Ark of the Covenant resided. Eli was the high priest, but his sons, Hophni and Phinehas, were evil men who took advantage of the people. Samuel, however, served God faithfully, and God blessed him as he grew (2:12–3:21).

3. **Kiriath-jearim** Israel was constantly at odds with the Philistines, and another battle was brewing. Hophni and Phinehas brought the Ark of the Covenant from Shiloh to the battlefield, believing that its mere presence would bring the Israelites victory. The Israelites were defeated by the Philistines at Ebenezer, and the Ark was captured. However, the Philistines soon found out that the Ark was not quite the great battle trophy they expected. God sent plagues upon every Philistine city into which the Ark was brought. Finally, the Philistines sent it back to Kiriath-jearim in Israel (4:1–7:1).

4. **Mizpah** The Israelites' defeat made them realize that God was no longer blessing them. Samuel called the people together at Mizpah and asked them to fast and pray in sorrow for their sins. The assembly at Mizpah was a tempting target for the confident Philistines who advanced for an attack. But God intervened and routed their mighty army. Meanwhile, Samuel was judging cases throughout Israel. But as Samuel grew old, the people came to him at Ramah (his home base) demanding a king in order to be like the other nations. At Mizpah, Saul was chosen by sacred appointment to be Israel's first king with the blessing, but not the approval, of God and Samuel (7:2–10:27).

5. **Gilgal** A battle with the Ammonites proved Saul's leadership abilities to the people of Israel. He protected the people of Jabesh-gilead and scattered the Ammonite army. Samuel and the people crowned Saul as king of Israel at Gilgal (11:1-15).

6. **Valley of Elah** Saul won many other battles, but over time he proved to be arrogant, sinful, and rebellious, so God finally rejected him as king. Unknown to Saul, a young shepherd and musician named David was anointed to be Israel's next king. But it would be many years before David sat upon the throne. Ironically, Saul hired David to play the harp in his palace. Saul grew to like David so much that he made him his personal armor bearer. In one particular battle with the Philistines in the valley of Elah, David killed Goliath, the Philistines' mightiest soldier. But this victory was the beginning of the end of Saul's love for David. The Israelites praised David more than Saul, causing Saul to become so jealous that he plotted to kill David (12:1–22:23).

7. **The Wilderness** Even anointed kings are not exempt from troubles. David literally ran for his life from King Saul, hiding with his band of followers in the wilderness of Ziph (where the men of Ziph constantly betrayed him), the wilderness of Maon, and the wilderness of En-gedi. Though he had opportunities to kill Saul, David refused to do so because Saul was God's anointed king (23:1–26:25).

8. **Gath** David moved his men and family to Gath, the Philistine city where King Achish lived. Saul then stopped chasing him. The Philistines seemed to welcome this famous fugitive from Israel (27:1-4).

9. **Ziklag** Desiring privacy in return for his pretended loyalty to King Achish, David asked for a city in which to house his men and family. Achish gave him Ziklag. From there David conducted raids against the cities of the Geshurites, Girzites, and Amalekites, making sure no one escaped to tell the tale (27:5-12). David later conquered the Amalekites after they raided Ziklag (30:1-31).

10. **Mount Gilboa** War with the Philistines broke out again in the north, near Mount Gilboa. Saul, who no longer relied on God, consulted a medium in a desperate attempt to contact Samuel for help. In the meantime, David was sent back to Ziklag because the Philistine commanders did not trust his loyalty in battle against Israel. The Philistines slaughtered the Israelites on Mount Gilboa, killing King Saul and his three sons, including David's loyal friend Jonathan. Without God, Saul led a bitter and misguided life. The consequences of his sinful actions affected not only him but hurt his family and the entire nation as well (28:1–31:13).

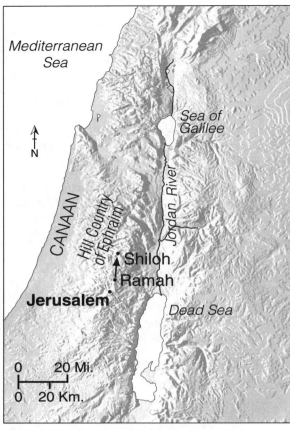

THE JOURNEY TO SHILOH

1 Samuel 1:1-18

Each year Elkanah and his family traveled from their home at Ramah to Shiloh, where they worshiped and sacrificed at God's Tabernacle.

Copyright © 2001 by Tyndale House Publishers

ISRAELITES VERSUS PHILISTINES / 1 Samuel 4:1

The Israelites and Philistines were archenemies and constantly fought. Here are some of their confrontations, found in 1 and 2 Samuel. When the Israelites trusted God for the victory, they always won.

Location	Winner of the Battle	Comments	Reference
Aphek to Ebenezer	Philistines	The Ark was captured and Eli's sons killed	1 Samuel 4:1-11
Mizpah	Israelites	After the Ark was returned, the Philistines planned to attack again, but God confused them. Israel chased the Philistines back to Beth-car	1 Samuel 7:7-14
Geba	Israelites under Jonathan	One detachment of Philistines destroyed	1 Samuel 13:3-4
Gilgal	A standoff	The Israelites lost their nerve and hid	1 Samuel 13:6-17
Micmash	Israelites	Jonathan and his armor bearer said it didn't matter how many enemies there were. If God was with them, they would win. They began the battle, and the army completed it	1 Samuel 13:23–14:23
Valley of Elah	Israelites	David and Goliath	1 Samuel 17:1-58
?	Israelites	David killed 200 Philistines to earn a wife	1 Samuel 18:17-30
Keilah	Israelites under David	David protected the threshing floors from Philistine looters	1 Samuel 23:1-5
Aphek, Jezreel, to Mount Gilboa	Philistines	Saul and Jonathan killed	1 Samuel 29:1; 31:1-13
Baal-perazim	Israelites	The Philistines tried to capture King David	2 Samuel 5:17-25
Gath	Israelites	There was very little trouble with the Philistines after this defeat	2 Samuel 8:1
?	Israelites	Abishai saved David from a Philistine giant	2 Samuel 21:15-17
Gob	Israelites	Other giants were killed, including Goliath's brother	2 Samuel 21:18-22

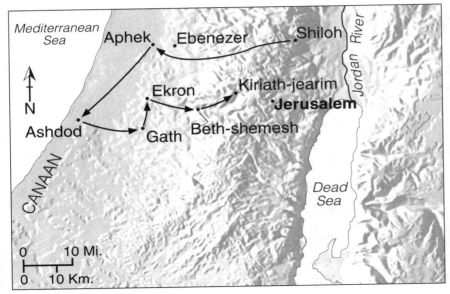

THE ARK'S TRAVELS

1 Samuel 4:1–7:2

Eli's sons took the Ark from Shiloh to the battlefield on the lower plains at Ebenezer and Aphek. The Philistines captured the Ark and took it to Ashdod, Gath, and Ekron. Plagues forced the people to send the Ark back to Israel, where it finally was taken by cattle-driven carts to Beth-shemesh and on to the home of Eleazar in Kiriath-jearim.

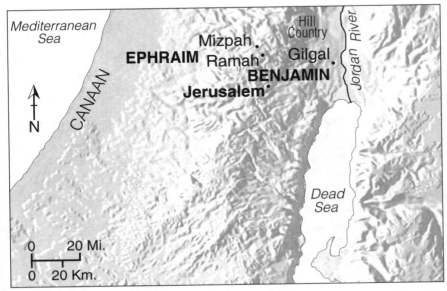

SAUL CHOSEN AS KING

1 Samuel 9:1–10:27

Saul and a servant searched for their lost donkeys in the hill country of Ephraim and the territory of Benjamin. They went to Ramah, looking for help from Samuel the prophet. While Saul was there, he found himself unexpectedly anointed by Samuel as Israel's first king. Samuel called Israel together at Mizpah to tell them God's choice for their king.

THE PROBLEMS WITH HAVING A KING / *1 Samuel 8:11-17*

Problems (warned by Samuel)	Reference	Fulfillment
Drafting young men into the army	8:11-12	14:52—"So whenever Saul saw a young man who was brave and strong, he drafted him into his army."
Having the young men "run before his chariots"	8:11	2 Samuel 15:1—"Absalom bought a chariot and horses, and he hired fifty footmen to run ahead of him."
Making slave laborers	8:12, 17	2 Chronicles 2:17-18—Solomon assigned laborers to build the Temple.
Taking the best fields and vineyards	8:14	1 Kings 21:5-16—Jezebel stole Naboth's vineyard.
Using property for his personal gain	8:14-16	1 Kings 9:10-14—Solomon gave away 20 cities to Hiram of Tyre.
Demanding a tenth of the harvest and flocks	8:15, 17	1 Kings 12:1-16—Rehoboam demanded heavier taxation than Solomon.

RELIGIOUS AND POLITICAL CENTERS OF ISRAEL
1 Samuel 10:3, 17, 26

During the period of the judges, Israel may have had more than one capital. This may explain why the Scriptures overlap with reference to some cities.

Gilgal	Joshua 4:19; Judges 2:1; Hosea 4:15; Micah 6:5
Shiloh	Joshua 18:1-10; 19:51; Judges 18:31; 1 Samuel 1:3; Jeremiah 7:12-14
Shechem	Joshua 24:1
Ramah	1 Samuel 7:17; 8:4
Mizpah	Judges 11:11; 20:1; 1 Samuel 10:17
Bethel	Judges 20:18, 26; 1 Samuel 10:3
Gibeah (political center only)	1 Samuel 10:26
Gibeon (religious center only)	1 Kings 3:4; 2 Chronicles 1:2-3
Jerusalem	1 Kings 8:1ff; Psalm 51:16-19

Samuel called the Israelites together at Mizpah, where he would anoint Saul as their first king. Up to this point, the political seat of the nation seems to have been the religious center of the nation as well. Above are the cities that probably served as both the religious and political centers of Israel since the days of Joshua. Saul may have been the first Israelite leader to separate the nation's religious center (probably Mizpah at this time) from its political center (Gibeah—1 Samuel 11:4; 26:1). Politically, the nation grew strong for a while. But when Saul and his officials stopped seeking God's will, internal jealousies and strife soon began to decay the nation from within. When David became king, he brought the Ark of the Covenant back to Jerusalem, his capital. King Solomon then completely united the religious and political centers at Jerusalem.

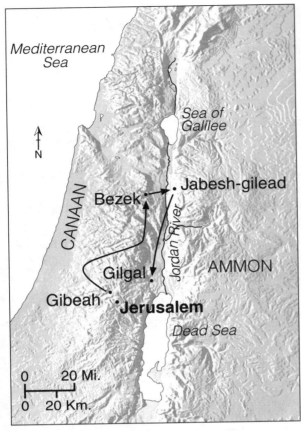

SAUL DEFEATS THE AMMONITES

1 Samuel 11:1-15

The Ammonites prepared to attack Jabesh-gilead. The people of Jabesh sent messengers to Saul in Gibeah asking for help. Saul mobilized an army at Bezek and then attacked the Ammonites. After the battle, the Israelites returned to Gilgal to crown Saul as king.

Copyright © 2001 by Tyndale House Publishers

GLOOM AND DOOM / *1 Samuel 13:13-14*

Reference	Message
3:11-14	Judgment will come to the house of Eli.
7:1-4	The nation must turn from idol worship.
8:10-22	Your kings will bring you nothing but trouble.
12:25	If you continue in sin, you will be destroyed by God.
13:13-14	Saul's kingdom will not continue.
15:17-31	Saul, you have sinned before God.

It wasn't easy being a prophet. Most of the messages they had to give were very unpleasant to hear. They preached of repentance, judgment, impending destruction, sin, and, in general, how displeased God was over the behavior of his people. Prophets were not the most popular people in town (unless they were *false* prophets and said what the people wanted to hear). But popularity was not the bottom line for true prophets of God—it was obedience to God and faithfully proclaiming his word. Samuel is a good example of a faithful prophet.

God has words for us to proclaim as well. And although his messages are loaded with "good news," there is also "bad news" to give. May we, like true prophets, faithfully deliver *all* God's words, regardless of their popularity or lack of it.

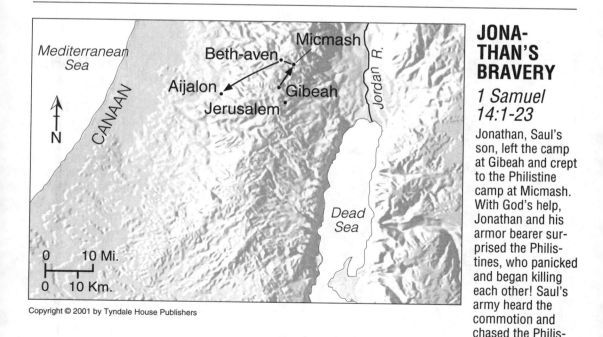

JONA-THAN'S BRAVERY

1 Samuel 14:1-23

Jonathan, Saul's son, left the camp at Gibeah and crept to the Philistine camp at Micmash. With God's help, Jonathan and his armor bearer surprised the Philistines, who panicked and began killing each other! Saul's army heard the commotion and chased the Philistines as far as Beth-aven and Aijalon.

Copyright © 2001 by Tyndale House Publishers

SIMPLE OBJECTS / 1 Samuel 17:40

God often uses simple, ordinary objects to accomplish his tasks in the world. It is important only that they be dedicated to him for his use. What do you have that God can use? Anything and everything is a possible "instrument" for him.

Object	Reference	Who Used It?	How Was It Used?
A staff	Exodus 4:2-4	Moses	To work miracles before Pharaoh
Horns	Joshua 6:3-5	Joshua	To flatten the walls of Jericho
A fleece	Judges 6:36-40	Gideon	To confirm God's will
Horns, jars, and torches	Judges 7:19-22	Gideon	To defeat the Midianites
Jawbone	Judges 15:15	Samson	To kill 1,000 Philistines
Smooth stone	1 Samuel 17:40	David	To kill Goliath
Olive oil	2 Kings 4:1-7	Elisha	To demonstrate God's power to provide
A river	2 Kings 5:9-14	Elisha	To heal a man of leprosy
Linen belt	Jeremiah 13:1-11	Jeremiah	As an object lesson of God's wrath
Clay jar	Jeremiah 19:1-13	Jeremiah	As an object lesson of God's wrath
Iron griddle, water, and food	Ezekiel 4:1-17	Ezekiel	As an object lesson of judgment
Five loaves and two fish	Mark 6:30-44	Jesus	To feed a crowd of more than 5,000 people

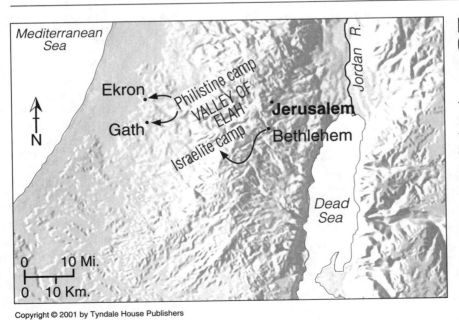

DAVID AND GOLIATH

1 Samuel 17:1-58

The armies of Israel and Philistia faced each other across the valley of Elah. David arrived from Bethlehem and offered to fight the giant Goliath. After David defeated Goliath, the Israelite army chased the Philistines to Ekron and Gath (Goliath's hometown).

Copyright © 2001 by Tyndale House Publishers

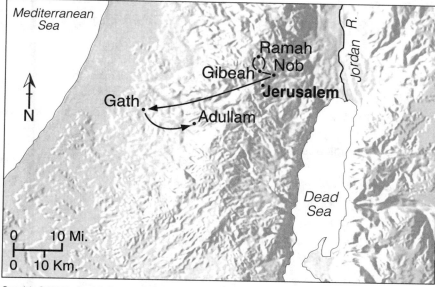

DAVID'S ESCAPE

1 Samuel 19:11–22:2

David learned of Saul's plans to kill him and fled to Samuel at Ramah. Returning to Gibeah to say good-bye to Jonathan, he then escaped to Nob, where he received food and a sword from the priest. He then fled to Gath in Philistine territory. When the Philistines became suspicious, he escaped to the cave of Adullam, where many men joined him.

DAVID FLEES FROM SAUL

1 Samuel 23:1-29

David and his men attacked the Philistines at Keilah from the forest of Hereth. Saul came from Gibeah to attack David, but David escaped into the wilderness of Ziph. At Horesh he met Jonathan, who encouraged him. Then he fled into the wilderness of Maon and into the strongholds of En-gedi.

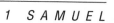

Copyright © 2001 by Tyndale House Publishers

LIFE OF DAVID VERSUS LIFE OF SAUL / *1 Samuel 18:6-8*

Life of David

David was God's kind of king
(2 Samuel 7:8-16)

David was a man after God's heart
(Acts 13:22)

David's kingship was eternal (through Jesus)
(2 Samuel 7:29)

David was kind and benevolent
(2 Samuel 9; 1 Chronicles 19:2)

David was forgiving
(1 Samuel 26)

David repented
(2 Samuel 12:13; 24:10)

David was courageous
(1 Samuel 17; 1 Chronicles 18)

David was at peace with God
(Psalms 4:8; 37:11)

Life of Saul

Saul was man's kind of king
(1 Samuel 10:23-24)

Saul was a man after people's praise
(1 Samuel 18:6-8)

Saul's kingship was rejected
(1 Samuel 15:23)

Saul was cruel
(1 Samuel 20:30-34; 22:11-19)

Saul was unforgiving
(1 Samuel 14:44; 18:9)

When confronted, Saul lied
(1 Samuel 15:10-31)

Saul was fearful
(1 Samuel 17:11; 18:12)

Saul was separated from God
(1 Samuel 16:14)

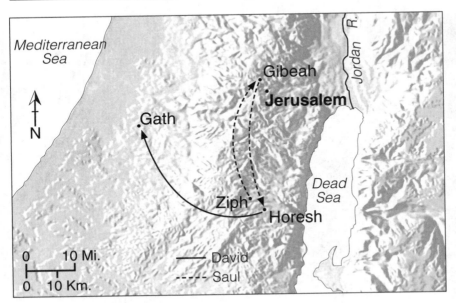

Copyright © 2001 by Tyndale House Publishers

SAUL CHASES DAVID

1 Samuel 26:1–27:12

The men of Ziph again betrayed David to Saul, who was in his palace in Gibeah. Saul took 3,000 troops to the area around Horesh in order to find David. David could have killed Saul, but he refused. Saul, feeling foolish at David's kindness, returned to Gibeah, and David went to Gath.

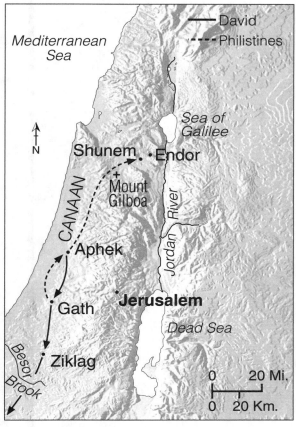

THE BATTLE AT GILBOA

1 Samuel 21:1–30:31

David pretended loyalty to Achish, but when war broke out with Israel, he was sent to Ziklag from Aphek. The Philistines defeated the Israelites at Mount Gilboa. David returned to Ziklag to find that the Amalekites had destroyed Ziklag. So David and his men pursued the Amalekite raiders and slaughtered them, recovering all that was taken.

Copyright © 2001 by Tyndale House Publishers

2 SAMUEL

MEGATHEMES IN 2 SAMUEL

Theme	Explanation	Importance
Kingdom Growth	Under David's leadership, Israel's kingdom grew rapidly. With the growth came many changes: from tribal independence to centralized government, from the leadership of judges to a monarchy, from decentralized worship to worship at Jerusalem.	No matter how much growth or how many changes we experience, God provides for us if we love him and highly regard his principles. God's work done in God's way never lacks God's supply of wisdom and energy.
Personal Greatness	David's popularity and influence increased greatly. He realized that the Lord was behind his success because he wanted to pour out his kindness on Israel. David regarded God's interests as more important than his own.	God graciously pours out his favor on us because of what Christ has done. God does not regard personal greatness as something to be used selfishly, but as an instrument to carry out his work among his people. The greatness we should desire is to love others as God loves us.
Justice	King David showed justice, mercy, and fairness to Saul's family, enemies, rebels, allies, and close friends alike. His just rule was grounded in his faith in and knowledge of God. God's perfect moral nature is the standard for justice.	Although David was the most just of all Israel's kings, he was still imperfect. His use of justice offered hope for a heavenly, ideal kingdom. This hope will never be satisfied in the heart of man until Christ, the Son of David, comes to rule in perfect justice forever.
Consequences of Sin	David abandoned his purpose as leader and king in time of war. His desire for prosperity and ease led him from triumph to trouble. Because David committed adultery with Bathsheba, he experienced consequences of his sin that destroyed both his family and the nation.	Temptation quite often comes when a person's life is aimless. We sometimes think that sinful pleasures and freedom from God's restraint will bring us a feeling of vitality; but sin creates a cycle of suffering that is not worth the fleeting pleasures it offers.
Feet of Clay	David not only sinned with Bathsheba, he murdered an innocent man. He neglected to discipline his sons when they got involved in rape and murder. This great hero showed a lack of character in some of his most important personal decisions. The man of iron had feet of clay.	Sin should never be considered as a mere weakness or flaw. Sin is fatal and must be eradicated from our lives. David's life teaches us to have compassion for all people, including those whose sinful nature leads them into sinful acts. It serves as a warning to us not to excuse sin in our own lives.

KEY PLACES IN 2 SAMUEL

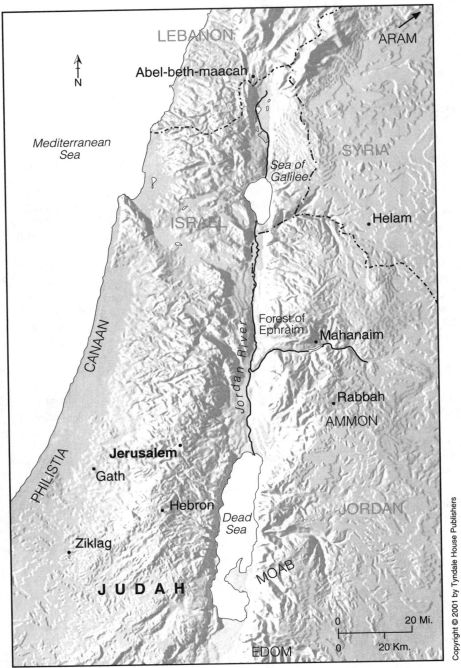

LEBANON

Abel-beth-maacah

Mediterranean
Sea

N

ARAM

Sea of
Galilee

SYRIA

ISRAEL

• Helam

CANAAN

Jordan River

Forest of
Ephraim

Mahanaim

• Rabbah

AMMON

Jerusalem •

• Gath

• Hebron

Dead
Sea

JORDAN

Ziklag •

MOAB

J U D A H

EDOM

0   20 Mi.

0   20 Km.

Copyright © 2001 by Tyndale House Publishers

Modern names and boundaries are shown in gray.

KEY PLACES IN 2 SAMUEL *continued*

1. **Hebron**   After Saul's death, David moved from the Philistine city of Ziklag to Hebron, where the tribe of Judah crowned him king. But the rest of Israel's tribes backed Saul's son Ishbosheth and crowned him king at Mahanaim. As a result, there was war between Judah and the rest of the tribes of Israel until Ishbosheth was assassinated. Then all of Israel pledged loyalty to David as their king (1:1–5:5).

2. **Jerusalem**   One of David's first battles as king occurred at the city of Zion (Jerusalem). David and his troops took the city by surprise, and it became his capital. It was here that David brought the Ark of the Covenant and made a special agreement with God (5:6–7:29).

3. **Gath**   The Philistines were Israel's constant enemy, though they did give David sanctuary when he was hiding from Saul (1 Samuel 27). But when Saul died and David became king, the Philistines planned to defeat him. In a battle near Jerusalem, David and his troops routed the Philistines (5:17-25), but they were not completely subdued until David conquered their largest city (8:1).

4. **Moab**   During the time of the judges, Moab controlled many cities in Israel and demanded heavy taxes (Judges 3:12-30). David conquered Moab and, in turn, levied tribute from them (8:2).

5. **Edom**   Though the Edomites and the Israelites traced their ancestry back to the same man, Isaac (Genesis 25:19-23), they were long-standing enemies. David defeated Edom and forced them to pay tribute also (8:14).

6. **Rabbah**   The Ammonites insulted David's delegation and turned a peacemaking mission into angry warfare. The Ammonites called troops from Aram, but David defeated this alliance first at Helam, then at Rabbah, the capital city (10:1–12:31).

7. **Mahanaim**   David had victory in the field, but problems at home. His son Absalom incited a rebellion and crowned himself king at Hebron. David and his men fled to Mahanaim. Acting on bad advice, Absalom mobilized his army to fight David (13:1–17:29).

8. **Forest of Ephraim**   The armies of Absalom and David fought in the forest of Ephraim. Absalom's hair got caught in a tree, and Joab, David's general, found and killed him. With Absalom's death the rebellion died, and David was welcomed back to Jerusalem (18:1–19:43).

9. **Abel-beth-maacah**   A man named Sheba also incited a rebellion against David. He fled to Abel-beth-maacah, but Joab and a small troop besieged the city. The citizens of Abel-beth-maacah killed Sheba themselves (20:1-26). David's victories laid the foundation for the peaceful reign of his son Solomon.

CHARACTERS IN THE DRAMA / 2 Samuel 1

It can be confusing to keep track of all the characters introduced in the first few chapters of 2 Samuel. Here is some help.

Character	Relation	Position	Whose Side?
Joab	Son of Zeruiah, David's half sister	One of David's military leaders and, later, commander in chief	David's
Abner	Saul's cousin	Saul's commander in chief	Saul and Ishbosheth's, but made overtures to David
Abishai	Joab's brother	High officer in David's army— Commander of "the Thirty"	Joab and David's
Asahel	Joab and Abishai's brother	High officer—one of David's 30 select warriors ("mighty men")	Joab and David's
Ishbosheth	Saul's son	Saul and Abner's selection as king	Saul's

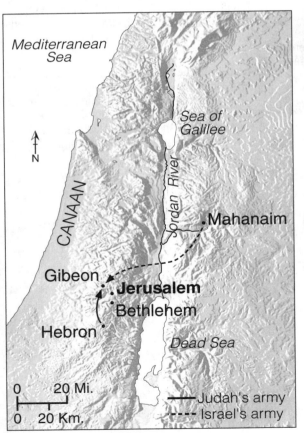

JOAB VERSUS ABNER

2 Samuel 2:1-32

David was crowned king of Judah in Hebron; Ishbosheth was crowned king of Israel in Mahanaim. The opposing armies of Judah and Israel met at Gibeon for battle—Judah under Joab, Israel under Abner.

Copyright © 2001 by Tyndale House Publishers

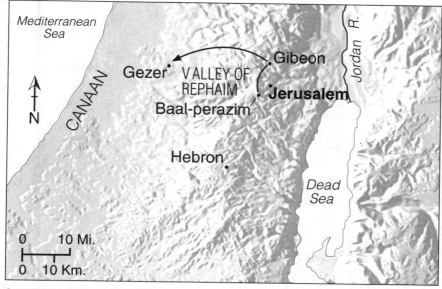

DAVID DEFEATS THE PHILISTINES

2 Samuel 5:17-25

The Philistines camped in the valley of Rephaim. David defeated them at Baal-perazim, but they remained in the valley. He attacked again and chased them from Gibeon to Gezer.

Copyright © 2001 by Tyndale House Publishers

CRITICIZING GOD'S LEADERS / *2 Samuel 6*

It is dangerous to criticize God's leaders. Consider the consequences for these men and women.

Person/Situation	Result	Reference
Miriam: Mocked Moses because he had a Cushite wife	Stricken with leprosy	Numbers 12
Korah and followers: Led the people of Israel to rebel against Moses' leadership	Swallowed by the earth	Numbers 16
Michal: Despised David because he danced before the Lord	Remained childless	2 Samuel 6
Shimei: Cursed and threw stones at David	Executed at Solomon's order	2 Samuel 16 1 Kings 2
Youths: Mocked Elisha and laughed at his baldness	Killed by bears	2 Kings 2
Sanballat and Tobiah: Spread rumors and lies to stop the building of Jerusalem's walls	Frightened and humiliated	Nehemiah 2; 4; 6
Hananiah: Contradicted Jeremiah's prophecies with false predictions	Died two months later	Jeremiah 28
Bar-Jesus, a sorcerer: Lied about Paul in an attempt to turn the governor against him	Stricken with blindness	Acts 13

COVENANTS / *2 Samuel 7:13*

A covenant is a legally binding obligation (promise). Throughout history God has made covenants with his people—he would keep his side if they would keep theirs. Here are seven covenants found in the Bible.

Name and Reference	God's Promise	Sign
In Eden Genesis 3:15	Satan and mankind will be enemies.	Pain of childbirth
Noah Genesis 9:8-17	God would never again destroy the earth with a flood.	Rainbow
Abraham Genesis 15:12-21; 17:1-14	Abraham's descendants would become a great nation if they obeyed God. God would be their God forever.	Smoking firepot and flaming torch
At Mount Sinai Exodus 19:5-6	Israel would be God's special people, a holy nation. But they would have to keep their part of the covenant—obedience.	The Exodus
The Priesthood Numbers 25:10-13	Aaron's descendants would be priests forever.	The Aaronic priesthood
David 2 Samuel 7:13; 23:5	Salvation would come through David's line through the birth of the Messiah.	David's line continued, and the Messiah was born a descendant of David
New Covenant Hebrews 8:6-13	Forgiveness and salvation are available through faith in Christ.	Christ's resurrection

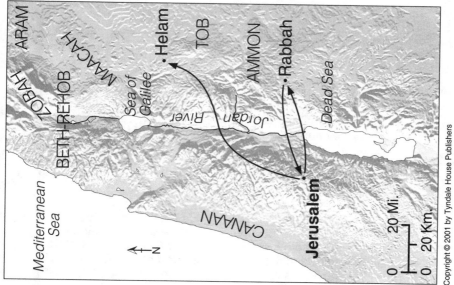

DAVID AND THE AMMON-ITES

2 Samuel 10:1-19

Ammon gathered together its troops from the north; Joab brought the Israelite army to attack them near Rabbah. Joab returned to Jerusalem victorious, but the enemy recruited additional forces and regrouped at Helam. David himself led the next victorious attack.

ARAM

ZOBAH

BETH-REHOB

MAACAH

• Helam

TOB

AMMON

• Rabbah

Sea of Galilee

Jordan River

Dead Sea

CANAAN

Jerusalem

Mediterranean Sea

N

0 ___ 20 Mi.
0 ___ 20 Km.

Copyright © 2001 by Tyndale House Publishers

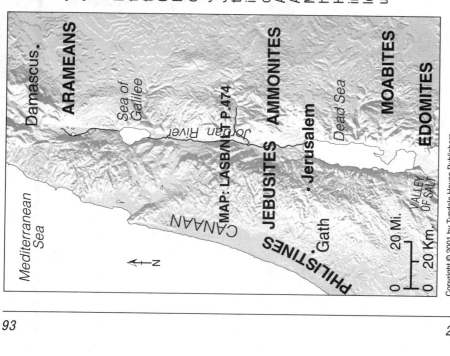

DAVID'S ENEMIES

2 Samuel 5:6-16; 8:1-18

David wanted to complete the conquest of Canaan begun by Joshua. He defeated the Jebusites at Jerusalem and the Philistines in the vicinity of Gath. The Ammonites, Arameans, and Moabites became his subjects. He put garrisons in Edom and levied a tax upon them.

Damascus •

ARAMEANS

Sea of Galilee

Jordan River

MAP: LASB/NLT, P. 474

AMMONITES

JEBUSITES • Jerusalem

PHILISTINES Gath

CANAAN

MOABITES

Dead Sea

VALLEY OF SALT

EDOMITES

Mediterranean Sea

N

0 ___ 20 Mi.
0 ___ 20 Km.

Copyright © 2001 by Tyndale House Publishers

DAVID'S FAMILY TROUBLES / 2 Samuel 11

David's many wives caused him much grief. And as a result of David's sin with Bathsheba, God said that murder would be a constant threat in his family, his family would rebel, and someone else would sleep with his wives. All this happened as the prophet Nathan had predicted. The consequences of sin affect not only us but those we know and love. Remember that the next time you are tempted to sin.

Wife	Children	What Happened?
Michal (Saul's daughter)	She was childless	David gave her five nephews to the Gibeonites to be killed because of Saul's sins.
Ahinoam (from Jezreel)	Amnon, David's firstborn	He raped Tamar, his half sister, and was later murdered by Absalom in revenge.
Maacah (daughter of King Talmai of Geshur)	Absalom, third son Tamar, the only daughter mentioned by name	Absalom killed Amnon for raping Tamar and then fled to Geshur. Later he returned, only to rebel against David. He set up a tent on the roof and slept with 10 of his father's concubines there. His pride led to his death.
Haggith	Adonijah, fourth son. He was very handsome, but it is recorded that he was never disciplined	He set himself up as king before David's death. His plot was exposed, and David spared his life, but his half brother Solomon later had him executed.
Bathsheba	Unnamed son	Died in fulfillment of God's punishment for David and Bathsheba's adultery.
Bathsheba	Solomon	Became the next king of Israel. Ironically, Solomon's many wives caused his downfall.

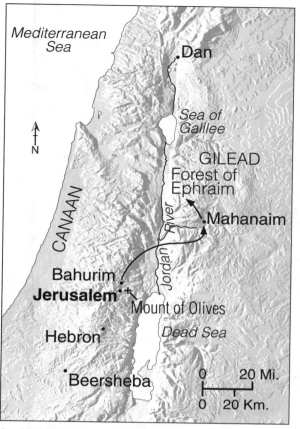

ABSALOM'S REBELLION

2 Samuel 15:1–18:33

Absalom crowned himself king in Hebron. David and his men fled from Jerusalem, crossed the Jordan, and went to Mahanaim. Absalom and his army followed, only to be defeated in the forest of Ephraim, where Absalom was killed.

Copyright © 2001 by Tyndale House Publishers

HIGHS AND LOWS OF DAVID'S LIFE / *2 Samuel 15*

The Bible calls David a man after God's own heart (1 Samuel 13:14; Acts 13:22), but that didn't mean his life was free of troubles. David's life was full of highs and lows. Some of David's troubles were a result of his sins; some were a result of the sins of others. We can't always control our ups and downs, but we can trust God every day. We can be certain that he will help us through our trials, just as he helped David. In the end, he will reward us for our consistent faith.

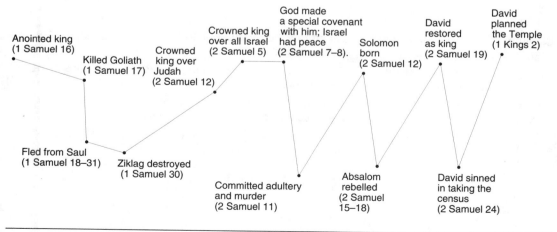

2 SAMUEL

REBELLION / 2 Samuel 15–18

The Bible records many rebellions. Many were against God's chosen leaders and were doomed for failure. Others were begun by wicked men against other wicked men. While these were sometimes successful, the rebel's life usually came to a violent end. Still other rebellions were made by good people against the wicked or unjust actions of others. This kind of rebellion sometimes freed the common people from oppression and gave them the freedom to turn back to God.

Who	Whom they rebelled against?	What happened?	Reference
Adam and Eve	God	Expelled from Eden	Genesis 3
Israelites	God, Moses	Forced to wander in wilderness for 40 years	Numbers 14
Korah	Moses	Swallowed by the earth	Numbers 16
Israelites	God	God took away his special promise of protection	Judges 2
Absalom (David's son)	David	Killed in battle	2 Samuel 15–18
Sheba	David	Killed in battle	2 Samuel 20
Adonijah (David's son)	David, Solomon	Killed for treason	1 Kings 1–2
Joab	David, Solomon	Supported Adonijah's kingship without seeking God's choice. Killed for treason	1 Kings 1–2
Ten tribes of Israel	Rehoboam	The kingdom was divided. The 10 tribes forgot about God, sinned, and were eventually taken into captivity.	1 Kings 12:16-20
Baasha, king of Israel	Nadab, king of Israel	Overthrew the throne and became king. God destroyed his descendants	1 Kings 15:27–16:7
Zimri, king of Israel	Elah, king of Israel	Overthrew the throne, but killed himself when his rule was not accepted	1 Kings 16:9-16
Jehu, king of Israel	Joram, king of Israel; Ahaziah, king of Judah	Killed both kings. Later turned from God and his dynasty was wiped out	2 Kings 9–10
Joash, king of Judah Jehoiada, a priest	Athaliah, queen of Judah	Athaliah, a wicked queen, was overthrown. This was a "good" rebellion.	2 Kings 11
Shallum, king of Israel	Zechariah, king of Israel	Overthrew the throne, but then was assassinated	2 Kings 15:8-15
Menahem, king of Israel	Shallum, king of Israel	Overthrew the throne, but then Israel was invaded by Assyrian army	2 Kings 15:16-22
Hoshea, king of Israel	Assyria	The city of Samaria was destroyed, the nation of Israel taken into captivity	2 Kings 17
Zedekiah, king of Judah	Nebuchadnezzar, king of Babylon	The city of Jerusalem was destroyed, the nation of Judah taken into captivity	2 Kings 24–25

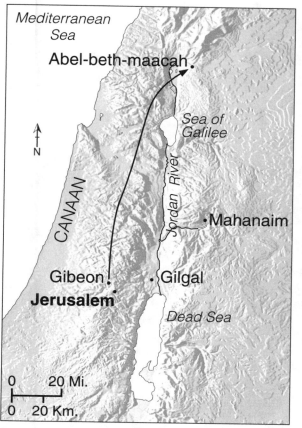

SHEBA'S REBELLION

2 Samuel 20:1-26

After defeating Absalom, David returned to Jerusalem from Mahanaim. But Sheba incited a rebellion against David, so David sent Joab, Abishai, and a small army after him. Joab and his troops besieged Abel-beth-maacah, Sheba's hideout, until the people of Abel-beth-maacah killed Sheba themselves.

Copyright © 2001 by Tyndale House Publishers

1 KINGS

MEGATHEMES IN 1 KINGS

Theme	Explanation	Importance
The King	Solomon's wisdom, power, and achievements brought honor to the Israelite nation and to God. All the kings of Israel and Judah were told to obey God and to govern according to his laws. But their tendency to abandon God's commands and to worship other gods led them to change the religion and government to meet their personal desires. This neglect of God's law led to their downfall.	Wisdom, power, and achievement do not ultimately come from any human source; they are from God. No matter what we lead or govern, we can't do well when we ignore God's guidelines. Whether or not we are leaders, effectiveness depends upon listening and obeying God's Word. Don't let your personal desires distort God's Word.
The Temple	Solomon's Temple was a beautiful place of worship and prayer. This sanctuary was the center of Jewish religion. It was the place of God's special presence and housed the Ark of the Covenant containing the Ten Commandments.	A beautiful house of worship doesn't always guarantee heartfelt worship of God. Providing opportunities for true worship doesn't ensure that it will happen. God wants to live in our hearts, not just meet us in a sanctuary.
Other Gods	Although the Israelites had God's law and experienced his presence among them, they became attracted to other gods. When this happened, their hearts became cold to God's law, resulting in the ruin of families and government, and eventually leading to the destruction of the nation.	Through the years, the people took on the false qualities of the false gods they worshiped. They became cruel, power hungry, and sexually perverse. We tend to become what we worship. Unless we serve the true God, we will become slaves to whatever takes his place.
The Prophet's Message	The prophet's responsibility was to confront and correct any deviation from God's law. Elijah was a bolt of judgment against Israel. His messages and miracles were a warning to the evil and rebellious kings and people.	The Bible, the truth in sermons, and the wise counsel of believers are warnings to us. Anyone who points out how we deviate from obeying God's Word is a blessing to us. Changing our lives in order to obey God and get back on track often takes painful discipline and hard work.
Sin and Repentance	Each king had God's commands, a priest or prophet, and the lessons of the past to draw him back to God. All the people had the same resources. Whenever they repented and returned to God, God heard their prayers and forgave them.	God hears and forgives us when we pray—if we are willing to trust him and turn from sin. Our desire to forsake our sin must be heartfelt and sincere. Then he will give us a fresh start and a desire to live for him.

KEY PLACES IN 1 KINGS

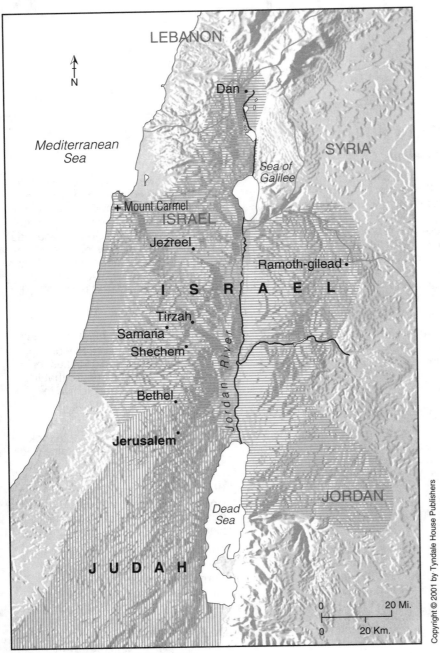

Modern names and boundaries are shown in gray.

Copyright © 2001 by Tyndale House Publishers

Solomon, David's son, brought Israel into its golden age. His wealth and wisdom were acclaimed worldwide. But he ignored God in his later years (1:1–11:43).

1. **Shechem**   After Solomon's death, Israel assembled at Shechem to inaugurate his son Rehoboam. However, Rehoboam foolishly angered the people by threatening even heavier burdens, causing a revolt (12:1-19).

2. **Israel**   Jeroboam, leader of the rebels, was made king of Israel, now called the northern kingdom. Jeroboam made Shechem his capital city (12:20, 25).

3. **Judah**   Only the tribes of Judah and part of Benjamin remained loyal to Rehoboam. These two tribes became the southern kingdom. Rehoboam returned to Judah from Shechem and prepared to force the rebels into submission, but a prophet's message halted these plans (12:21-24).

4. **Jerusalem**   Jerusalem was the capital city of Judah. Its Temple, built by Solomon, was the focal point of Jewish worship. This worried Jeroboam. How could he keep his people loyal if they were constantly going to Rehoboam's capital to worship (12:26-27)?

5. **Dan**   Jeroboam's solution was to set up his own worship centers. Two golden calves were made and proclaimed to be Israel's gods. One was placed in Dan, and the people were told they could go there instead of to Jerusalem to worship (12:28-29).

6. **Bethel**   The other golden calf was placed in Bethel. The people of the northern kingdom had two convenient locations for worship in

their own country, but their sin displeased God. In Jerusalem, meanwhile, Rehoboam was also allowing idolatry to creep in. The two nations were constantly at war (12:29–15:26).

7. **Tirzah**   Jeroboam had moved the capital city to Tirzah (1 Kings 14:17). Next, Baasha became king of Israel after assassinating Nadab (15:27–16:22).

8. **Samaria**   Israel continued to gain and lose kings through plots, assassinations, and warfare. When Omri became king, he bought a hill on which he built a new capital city, Samaria. Omri's son, Ahab, became the most wicked king of Israel. His wife, Jezebel, worshiped Baal. Ahab erected a temple to Baal in Samaria (16:23-34).

9. **Mount Carmel**   Great evil often brings great people who oppose it. Elijah challenged the prophets of Baal and Asherah at Mount Carmel, where he would prove that they were false prophets. There Elijah humiliated these prophets and then executed them (17:1–18:46).

10. **Jezreel**   Elijah returned to Jezreel. But Queen Jezebel, furious at the execution of her prophets, vowed to kill Elijah. He ran for his life, but God cared for and encouraged him. During his travels Elijah anointed the future kings of Aram and Israel, as well as Elisha, his own replacement (19:1-21).

11. **Ramoth-gilead**   The king of Aram declared war on Israel and was defeated in two battles. But the Arameans occupied Ramoth-gilead. Ahab and Jehoshaphat joined forces to recover the city. In this battle, Ahab was killed. Jehoshaphat later died (20:1–22:53).

WHO JOINED ADONIJAH'S CONSPIRACY AND WHO REMAINED LOYAL TO DAVID? / 1 Kings 1

Contrast the fate of those who rebelled and those who remained loyal to David, God's appointed leader. Adonijah, the leader of the conspiracy, met a violent death (2:25). Those who rebel against God's leaders rebel against God.

Joined Adonijah

JOAB (1:7)
Brilliant military general and commander of David's army. He continually demonstrated his belief that cold-blooded murder was as acceptable as a fairly fought battle. Solomon later had him executed.

ABIATHAR (1:7)
One of two high priests under David. He was a son of Ahimelech who had helped David, and David promised to protect him. Abiathar repaid David with his treachery. Solomon later had him banished, fulfilling the prophecy that Eli's priestly line would end (1 Samuel 2:31).

JONATHAN (1:42)
Abiathar's son. He helped David stop Absalom's rebellion (2 Samuel 17:17-22) but supported this rebellion by another of David's sons.

CHARIOTEERS (1:5)
Hired by Adonijah, apparently more loyal to money than to their king.

50 RUNNERS (1:5)
Recruited to give Adonijah a "royal" appearance.

Remained with David

BENAIAH (1:8)
Distinguished himself as a great warrior. Commanded a division of David's army—over 24,000 men. One of the Thirty, he was also placed in charge of David's bodyguard. Solomon later made him chief commander of the army.

ZADOK (1:8)
The other high priest under David. His loyalty gave him the privilege of crowning Solomon. He became the sole high priest under King Solomon.

NATHAN (1:8)
God's prominent prophet during David's reign. The Bible says he wrote a history of David and Solomon.

SHIMEI (1:8)
This man was probably the Shimei who was rewarded by Solomon and appointed district governor in Benjamin (4:18). (He was not the same person who cursed David at Bahurim and brought on his own death under Solomon.)

REI (1:8)
Only mentioned here. Possibly he was an army officer.

DAVID'S BODYGUARD (1:8, 10)
David's army was highly organized with several divisions of troops. It is enough to know that many of his leaders remained true to their king.

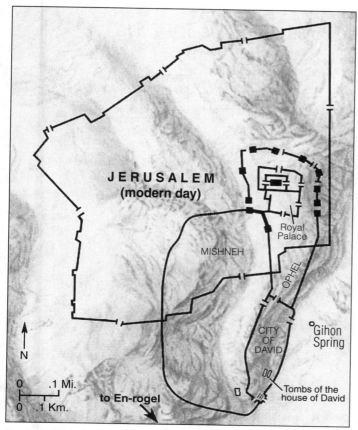

Copyright © 2001 by Tyndale House Publishers

TWO CORONA-TIONS

1 Kings 1:1-53

As David lay on his deathbed, his son Adonijah crowned himself king at En-rogel outside Jerusalem. When the news reached David, he declared that Solomon was to be the next ruler. Solomon was anointed at Gihon. It may have been more than coincidence that Gihon was not only within shouting distance of En-rogel but also closer to the royal palace.

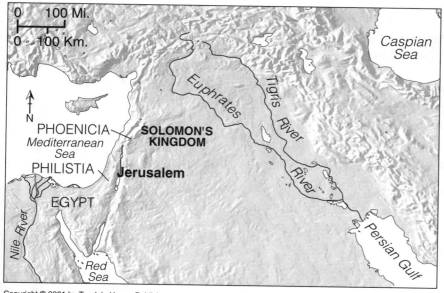

Copyright © 2001 by Tyndale House Publishers

SOLO-MON'S KINGDOM

1 Kings 4:1-34

Solomon's kingdom spread from the Euphrates River in the north to the borders of Egypt. The entire land was at peace under his rule.

SOLOMON'S TEMPLE 960-586 B.C. / *1 Kings 5:1–7:51*

Solomon's Temple was a beautiful sight. It took over seven years to complete and was a magnificent building containing gold, silver, bronze, and cedar. This house for God was without equal. The description is found in 2 Chronicles 2–4.

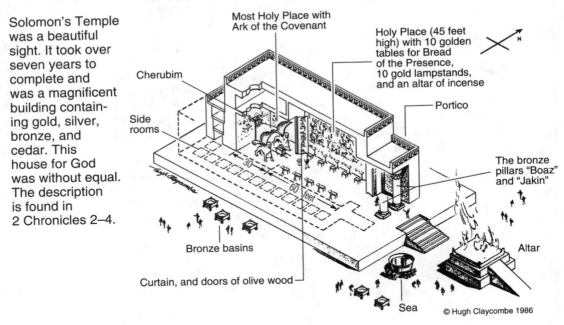

Most Holy Place with Ark of the Covenant

Holy Place (45 feet high) with 10 golden tables for Bread of the Presence, 10 gold lampstands, and an altar of incense

Cherubim

Side rooms

Portico

The bronze pillars "Boaz" and "Jakin"

Bronze basins

Altar

Curtain, and doors of olive wood

Sea

© Hugh Claycombe 1986

FURNISHINGS

Cherubim: represented heavenly beings, symbolized God's presence and holiness (gold-plated, 15 feet wide)

Ark of the Covenant: contained the law written on two tablets, symbolized God's presence with Israel (wood overlaid with gold)

Curtain: separated the Holy Place from the Most Holy Place (blue, purple, and crimson yarn and fine linen, with cherubim worked into it)

Doors: between Holy Place and Most Holy Place (wood overlaid with gold)

Golden tables (wood overlaid with gold), *gold lampstands* (with seven lamps on each stand), and *altar of incense* (wood overlaid with gold): instruments for priestly functions in the Holy Place

Bronze pillars: named Jakin (meaning "he establishes") and Boaz (meaning "in him is strength")—taken together they could mean "God provides the strength"

Altar: for burning of sacrifices (bronze)

Sea: for priests' washing (had 12,000-gallon capacity)

Bronze basins: for washing the sacrifices (water basins on wheeled bases)

This reconstruction uses known archaeological parallels to supplement the text, and assumes interior dimensions from 1 Kings 6:17-20. © Hugh Claycombe

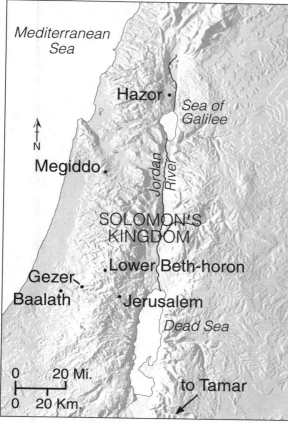

SOLOMON'S BUILDING PROJECTS

1 Kings 9:15-28

Solomon became known as one of the great builders in Israel's history. He built Hazor, Megiddo, and Gezer as fortress cities during his reign. He also rebuilt the cities of lower Beth-horon, Baalath, and Tadmor.

Copyright © 2001 by Tyndale House Publishers

TRIBAL ANIMOSITIES / 1 Kings 12

Although the kingdom of Israel was "united" under David and Solomon, the tensions between north and south were never resolved. The animosity behind this civil war didn't begin with Rehoboam and Jeroboam but had its roots in the days of the judges, when the people were more interested in tribal loyalty than in national unity. Note how easily tension arose between Ephraim, the most prominent tribe in the north, and Judah, the prominent tribe of the south.

- Ephraim claimed the promises in Genesis 48:17-22 and 49:22-26 for its leadership role.

- Joshua, who conquered the Promised Land, was an Ephraimite (Numbers 13:8).

- Samuel, Israel's greatest judge, was from Ephraim (1 Samuel 1:1ff).

- Ephraim allied with Ishbosheth in revolt against David, who was from the tribe of Judah (2 Samuel 2:8-11).

- David, a shepherd from the tribe of Judah, became king over all Israel, including Ephraim, which no longer had a claim to leadership.

- Although David helped to smooth over the bad feelings, the heavy yoke under Solomon and Rehoboam led the northern tribes to the breaking point.

Such tension developed because Ephraim was the key tribe in the north. They resented Judah's role in leadership under David and resented that the nation's capital and center of worship were located in Jerusalem.

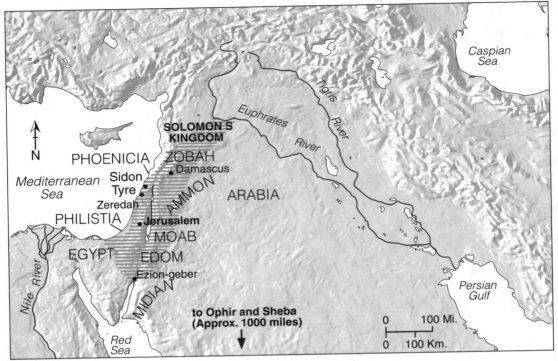

FRIENDS AND ENEMIES

1 Kings 11:14-43

Solomon's reputation brought acclaim and riches from many nations, but he disobeyed God, marrying pagan women and worshiping their gods. So God raised up enemies such as Hadad from Edom and Rezon from Zobah (modern-day Syria). Jeroboam from Zeredah was another enemy who would eventually divide this mighty kingdom.

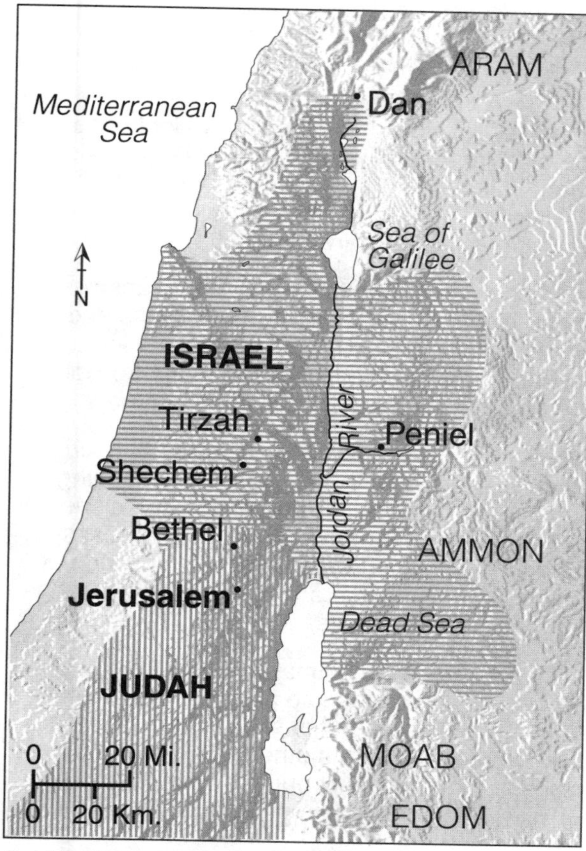
ARAM
Mediterranean Sea
Dan
Sea of Galilee
N
ISRAEL
Tirzah
Shechem
Bethel
Jerusalem
Jordan River
Peniel
AMMON
Dead Sea
JUDAH
0 20 Mi.
0 20 Km.
MOAB
EDOM

Copyright © 2001 by Tyndale House Publishers

THE KINGDOM DIVIDES

1 Kings 12:1-33

Rehoboam's threat of heavier burdens caused a rebellion and divided the nation. Rehoboam ruled the southern kingdom; Jeroboam ruled the northern kingdom. Jeroboam set up idols in Dan and Bethel to discourage worship in Jerusalem. At the same time Aram, Ammon, Moab, and Edom claimed independence from the divided nation.

THE APPEAL OF IDOLS / 1 Kings 15

On the surface, the lives of the kings don't make sense. How could they run to idolatry so fast when they had God's Word (at least some of it), prophets, and the example of David? Here are some of the reasons for the enticement of idols:

	The Appeal of Idols	Modern Parallel
POWER	The people wanted freedom from the authority of both God and the priests. They wanted their religion to fit their lifestyle, not their life-style to fit their religion.	People do not want to answer to a greater authority. Instead of having power *over* others, God wants us to have the Holy Spirit's power to *help* others.
PLEASURE	Idol worship exalted sensuality without responsibility or guilt. People acted out the vicious and sensuous personalities of the gods they worshiped, thus gaining approval for their degraded lives.	People deify pleasure, seeking it at the expense of everything else. Instead of seeking pleasure that leads to long-range disaster, God calls us to seek the kind of pleasure that leads to long-range rewards.
PASSION	Mankind was reduced to little more than animals. The people did not have to be viewed as unique individuals but could be exploited sexually, politically, and economically.	Like animals, people let physical drives and passion rule them. Instead of seeking passion that exploits others, God calls us to redirect our passions to areas that build others up.
PRAISE AND POPULARITY	The high and holy nature of God was replaced by gods who were more a reflection of human nature, thus more culturally suitable to the people. These gods no longer required sacrifice, just a token of appeasement.	Sacrifice is seen as self-inflicted punishment, making no sense. Success is to be sought at all costs. Instead of seeking praise for ourselves, God calls us to praise him and those who honor him.

As societies change, they often throw out norms and values no longer considered necessary or acceptable. Believers must be careful not to follow society's example if it discards God's Word. When society does that, only godlessness and evil remain.

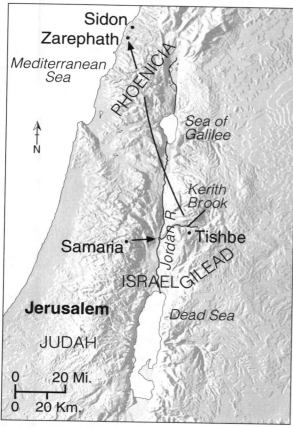

ELIJAH HIDES FROM AHAB

1 Kings 17:1-24

Elijah prophesied a drought and then hid from King Ahab by the Kerith Brook, where ravens fed him. When the brook dried up, God sent him to Zarephath in Phoenicia, where a widow and her son fed him and gave him lodging.

Copyright © 2001 by Tyndale House Publishers

PROPHETS—FALSE AND TRUE / 1 Kings 17

False Prophets	True Prophets
Worked for political purposes to benefit themselves	Worked for spiritual purposes to serve God and the people
Held positions of great wealth	Owned little or nothing
Gave false messages	Spoke only true messages
Spoke only what the people wanted to hear	Spoke only what God told them to say—no matter how unpopular

The false prophets were an obstacle to bringing God's word to the people. They would bring messages that contradicted the words of the true prophets. They gave "messages" that appealed to the people's sinful nature and comforted their fears. False prophets told people what they wanted to hear. True prophets told God's truth.

ELIJAH FLEES FROM JEZEBEL

1 Kings 19:1-18

After killing Baal's prophets, Elijah ran from the furious Queen Jezebel. He fled to Beersheba, then into the wilderness, and finally to Mount Horeb (Sinai). There, like Moses centuries earlier, he talked with God.

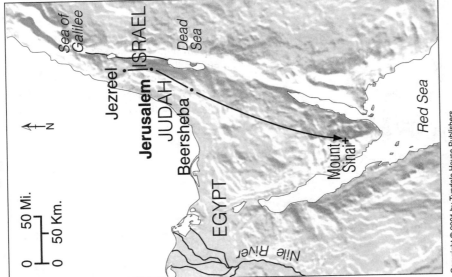

Copyright © 2001 by Tyndale House Publishers

THE SHOW-DOWN AT CARMEL

1 Kings 18:1-46

In a showdown with the false prophets of Baal at Mount Carmel, Elijah set out to prove to evil Ahab that only the Lord is God. Elijah then killed the false prophets by the Kishon River and fled back to Jezreel.

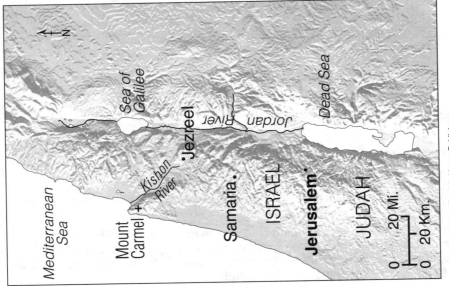

Copyright © 2001 by Tyndale House Publishers

GOD DELIVERS AHAB

1 Kings 20:1-43

Despite Ahab's wickedness, God approached him in love. When Samaria was surrounded by Aramean forces, God miraculously delivered the city. But Ahab refused to give God credit. A year later, the Arameans attacked near Aphek. Again God gave Ahab victory, but again the king refused to acknowledge God's help.

Copyright © 2001 by Tyndale House Publishers

DIVIDED KINGDOM OF ISRAEL / *Between 1 and 2 Kings*

AHIJAH 934–909

ELIJAH 875–848

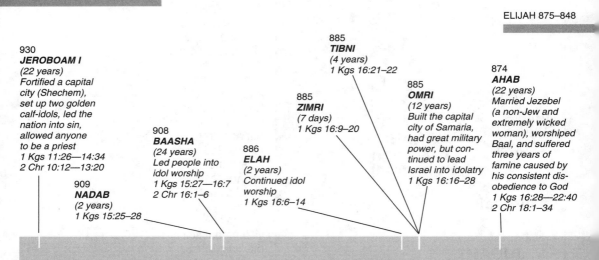

930
JEROBOAM I
(22 years)
Fortified a capital city (Shechem), set up two golden calf-idols, led the nation into sin, allowed anyone to be a priest
1 Kgs 11:26—14:34
2 Chr 10:12—13:20

909
NADAB
(2 years)
1 Kgs 15:25–28

908
BAASHA
(24 years)
Led people into idol worship
1 Kgs 15:27—16:7
2 Chr 16:1–6

886
ELAH
(2 years)
Continued idol worship
1 Kgs 16:6–14

885
ZIMRI
(7 days)
1 Kgs 16:9–20

885
TIBNI
(4 years)
1 Kgs 16:21–22

885
OMRI
(12 years)
Built the capital city of Samaria, had great military power, but continued to lead Israel into idolatry
1 Kgs 16:16–28

874
AHAB
(22 years)
Married Jezebel (a non-Jew and extremely wicked woman), worshiped Baal, and suffered three years of famine caused by his consistent disobedience to God
1 Kgs 16:28—22:40
2 Chr 18:1–34

CAPITAL: SHECHEM, THEN TIRZAH, THEN SAMARIA
THE NORTHERN KINGDOM OF ISRAEL (TEN TRIBES)

THE SOUTHERN KINGDOM OF JUDAH (TWO TRIBES)
CAPITAL: JERUSALEM

930
REHOBOAM
(17 years)
Built many fortified cities, strengthened the economy (despite the tribute paid to Egypt), followed God for three years, but then set up idols and shrines to foreign gods
1 Kgs 11:43—14:31
2 Chr 9:31—12:16

913
ABIJAH
(3 years)
Despite his wickedness, he called for God's help to win the battle against Israel
1 Kgs 14:31—15:8
2 Chr 13:1—14:1

910
ASA
(41 years)
Destroyed pagan altars and rebuilt altar of God, built fortified cities, gained much wealth from plunder of foreign conquest, removed the queen mother for worshiping Asherah, led the people to worship God with their hearts, provided peace on home soil, was greatly loved and given a beautiful funeral
1 Kgs 15:8–24
2 Chr 14:1—16:14

872
JEHOSHAPHAT
(25 years)
Arranged for the marriage of his son to a daughter of Ahab (who made trouble later on), had a strong military (kept troops in cities of Israel his father had conquered), collected tribute from the Philistines, worshiped the Lord and destroyed idols, established education, and appointed judges and courts
1 Kgs 15:24; 22:41–50
2 Chr 17:1—21:1

All dates are B.C. The total years of reign sometimes includes years of co-regency.

841
JEHU
(28 years)
Was responsible for
the deaths of Joram
(king of Israel),
Ahaziah (king of
Judah), and Jezebel
(wicked mother of
Joram); destroyed
the priests and
temples of Baal but
did not consistently
follow God
2 Kgs 9:1—10:36
2 Chr 22:7–12

798
JEHOASH
(16 years)
Even though he was
evil, he recognized
the authority of Elisha
as a prophet of God
2 Kgs 13:10—14:16
2 Chr 25:17–24

853
AHAZIAH
(2 years)
Proposed a
joint trade ven-
ture with Judah
1 Kgs 22:40—
2 Kgs 1:18
2 Chr 20:35–37

852
JORAM
(12 years)
Suffered famine
and war during
most of his
reign
2 Kgs 3:1—8:25
2 Chr 22:5–7

793
JEROBOAM II
(41 years)
Very evil but
politically
powerful; his
nation enjoyed
economic
prosperity and
military peace
2 Kgs
14:16–29

814
JEHOAHAZ
(17 years)
Evil reign included
worship of Asherah,
usually called
"detestable"
2 Kgs 13:1–9

853
JEHORAM
(8 years)
Married a
wicked daugh-
ter of Ahab,
compelled
the people to
worship idols,
and killed all
his brothers
2 Kgs 8:16–24
2 Chr 21:1–20

841
AHAZIAH
(1 year)
Friend of
Joram
of Israel
2 Kgs 8:24—
9:29
2 Chr 22:1–10

841
ATHALIAH
(QUEEN)
(6 years)
Killed all her
grandchildren
except Joash,
who was hidden
by her nurse for
six years, and
ravaged the
Temple to furnish
Baal's temple
2 Kgs 11:1–20
2 Chr 22:10—
23:21

835
JOASH
(40 years)
Was crowned
king at the age of
seven by Jehoiada
(the high priest),
promoted peace
and prosperity,
repaired the Temple,
and smashed the
altars to Baal;
but abandoned
God after Jehoiada
died, and even had
Jehoiada's son killed
2 Kgs 11:2—12:21
2 Chr 22:11—24:27

796
AMAZIAH
(29 years)
Was basically
good but did not
completely wipe
out idol worship;
organized and
mustered the
army
2 Kgs 14:1–20
2 Chr 25:1–28

792
AZARIAH
(UZZIAH)
(52 years)
Rebuilt a city
named Elath,
owned many farms
and vineyards,
constructed water
reservoirs and
fortified towers,
reorganized the
army (so powerful
that his fame
spread to Egypt),
but violated God's
laws for priestly
function—so God
struck him with
leprosy
2 Kgs 15:1–17
2 Chr 26:1–23

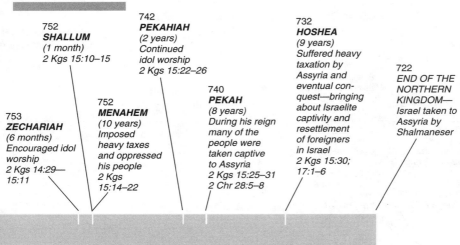

HOSEA 753–715

AMOS 760–750

752
SHALLUM
(1 month)
2 Kgs 15:10–15

742
PEKAHIAH
(2 years)
Continued
idol worship
2 Kgs 15:22–26

732
HOSHEA
(9 years)
Suffered heavy
taxation by
Assyria and
eventual con-
quest—bringing
about Israelite
captivity and
resettlement
of foreigners
in Israel
2 Kgs 15:30;
17:1–6

722
END OF THE
NORTHERN
KINGDOM—
Israel taken to
Assyria by
Shalmaneser

753
ZECHARIAH
(6 months)
Encouraged idol
worship
2 Kgs 14:29—
15:11

752
MENAHEM
(10 years)
Imposed
heavy taxes
and oppressed
his people
2 Kgs
15:14–22

740
PEKAH
(8 years)
During his reign
many of the
people were
taken captive
to Assyria
2 Kgs 15:25–31
2 Chr 28:5–8

ISRAEL

JUDAH

750
JOTHAM
(16 years)
Rebuilt the
Upper Gate of
the Temple,
rebuilt walls
and cities, but
still permitted
idol worship
2 Kgs 15:32–38
2 Chr 27:1–9

735
AHAZ
(16 years)
Sacrificed his
own son to
pagan gods,
nailed the
Temple doors
shut
2 Kgs 16:1–20
2 Chr 28:1–27

715
HEZEKIAH
(29 years)
Was a devoted follower of God,
reopened the Temple doors,
purified the Temple, reinstated
priests and their duties, organized
an orchestra to aid worship,
destroyed idols (including the
bronze snake of Moses because
people had begun to worship it),
celebrated the Passover and
even invited people who were
living in the north to participate,
constructed large public water-
works, was given 15 extra years
of life, foolishly showed messen-
gers the wealth in the Temple
2 Kgs 16:20; 18:1—20:21
2 Chr 29:1—32:33

697
MANASSEH
(55 years)
Rebuilt all the
pagan shrines,
sacrificed one
of his own sons,
practiced sor-
cery, set up an
idol right in the
Temple, mur-
dered many of
his own people,
but repented
during his
Assyrian
captivity
2 Kgs 21:1–18
2 Chr 33:1–20

MICAH 742–687

ISAIAH 740–681

586
END OF THE
SOUTHERN
KINGDOM—
carried off captive
to Babylon by
Nebuchadnezzar

642
AMON
(2 years)
2 Kgs
21:18–26
2 Chr
33:20–25

640
JOSIAH
(31 years)
Loved God with all his heart,
repaired the Temple, found
a lost scroll of the law (he
promised to obey it, thus God
delayed destruction for Judah
until after his death), person-
ally oversaw the major project
of destroying idol shrines,
reinstated the priests of God,
celebrated the Passover with
greater zeal than had been
since Samuel's day, was
greatly loved by his people
2 Kgs 21:26—23:30
2 Chr 33:25—35:27

609
JEHOAHAZ
(3 months)
Jailed and
taken to Egypt,
where he died
2 Kgs 23:30–34
2 Chr 36:1–4

609
JEHOIAKIM
(11 years)
Burned part of
God's Word given
to Jeremiah, was
a puppet king for
Egypt and then
Babylon, watched
gold and articles
taken from the
Temple to Bab-
ylon, saw first
exile (in which
Daniel was taken)
2 Kgs 23:34—
24:6 2 Chr 36:5–8

598
JEHOIACHIN
(3 months)
Saw next exile
to Babylon
2 Kgs
24:6–15;
25:27–30
2 Chr 36:8–10

597
ZEDEKIAH
(11 years)
Saw the Temple
burned and
Jerusalem
destroyed, was
tortured and
carried away
in the final exile
to Babylon
2 Kgs 24:17—
25:21
2 Chr 36:10–21

NAHUM
663–654

ZEPHANIAH 640–621

HABAKKUK 612–589

HULDAH 632

JEREMIAH 627–586

OBADIAH 598–580(?)

2 KINGS

MEGATHEMES IN 2 KINGS

Theme	Explanation	Importance
Elisha	The purpose of Elisha's ministry was to restore respect for God and his message, and he stood firmly against the evil kings of Israel. By faith, with courage and prayer, he revealed not only God's judgment on sin but also his mercy, love, and tenderness toward faithful people.	Elisha's mighty miracles showed that God controls not only great armies but also events in everyday life. When we listen to and obey God, he shows us his power to transform any situation. God's care is for all who are willing to follow him. He can perform miracles in our lives.
Idolatry	Every evil king in both Israel and Judah encouraged idolatry. These false gods represented war, cruelty, power, and sex. Although they had God's law, priests, and prophets to guide them, these kings sought priests and prophets whom they could manipulate to their own advantage.	An idol is any idea, ability, possession, or person that we regard more highly than God. We condemn Israel and Judah for foolishly worshiping idols, but we also worship other gods—power, money, physical attractiveness. Those who believe in God must resist the lure of these attractive idols.
Evil Kings/ Good Kings	Only 20 percent of Israel and Judah's kings followed God. The evil kings were shortsighted. They thought they could control their nations' destinies by importing other religions, forming alliances with pagan nations, and enriching themselves. The good kings had to spend most of their time undoing the evil done by their predecessors.	Although the evil kings led the people into sin, the priests, princes, heads of families, and military leaders all had to cooperate with the evil plans and practices in order for them to be carried out. We cannot discharge our responsibility to obey God by blaming our leaders. We are responsible to know God's Word and obey it.
God's Patience	God told his people that if they obeyed him, they would live successfully; if they disobeyed, they would be judged and destroyed. God had been patient with the people for hundreds of years. He sent many prophets to guide them. And he gave ample warning of coming destruction. But even God's patience has limits.	God is patient with us. He gives us many chances to hear his message, to turn from sin, and to believe him. His patience does not mean he is indifferent to how we live, nor does it mean we can ignore his warnings. His patience should make us want to come to him now.
Judgment	After King Solomon's reign, Israel lasted 209 years before the Assyrians destroyed it; Judah lasted 345 years before the Babylonians took Jerusalem. After repeated warnings to his people, God used these evil nations as instruments for his justice.	The consequences of rejecting God's commands and purpose for our lives are severe. He will not ignore unbelief or rebellion. We must believe in him and accept Christ's sacrificial death on our behalf, or we will be judged also.

KEY PLACES IN 2 KINGS

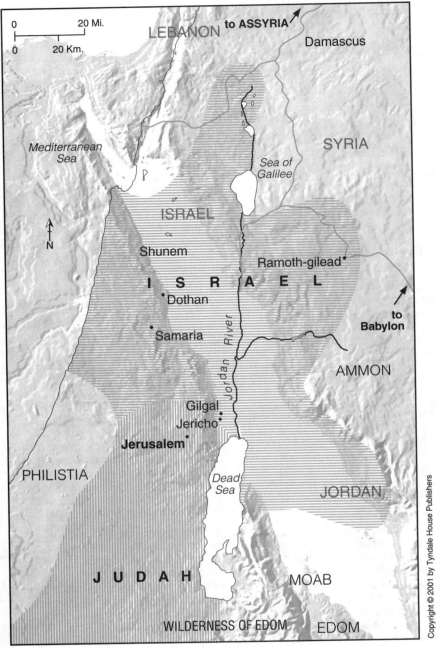

Modern names and boundaries are shown in gray.

KEY PLACES IN 2 KINGS *continued*

The history of both Israel and Judah was much affected by the prophet Elisha's ministry. He served Israel for 50 years, fighting the idolatry of its kings and calling its people back to God.

1. **Jericho** Elijah's ministry had come to an end. He touched his cloak to the Jordan River, and he and Elisha crossed on dry ground. Elijah was taken by God in a whirlwind, and Elisha returned alone with the cloak. The prophets in Jericho realized that Elisha was Elijah's replacement (1:1–2:25).

2. **Wilderness of Edom** The king of Moab rebelled against Israel, so the nations of Israel, Judah, and Edom decided to attack from the wilderness of Edom but ran out of water. The kings consulted Elisha, who said God would send both water and victory (3:1-27).

3. **Shunem** Elisha cared for individuals and their needs. He helped a woman clear a debt by giving her a supply of oil to sell. For another family in Shunem, he raised a son from the dead (4:1-37).

4. **Gilgal** Elisha cared for the young prophets in Gilgal—he removed poison from a stew, made a small amount of food feed everyone, and even caused an ax head to float so it could be retrieved. It was to Elisha that Naaman, a commander in the Aramean army, came to be healed of leprosy (4:38–6:7).

5. **Dothan** Although he cured an Aramean commander's leprosy, Elisha was loyal to Israel. He knew the Aramean army's battle plans and kept Israel's king informed. The Aramean king tracked Elisha down in Dothan and surrounded the city, hoping to kill him. But Elisha prayed that the Arameans would be blinded; then he led the blinded army into Samaria, Israel's capital city (6:8-23).

6. **Samaria** The Arameans didn't learn their lesson. They later besieged Samaria. Ironically, Israel's king thought it was Elisha's fault, but Elisha said food would be available in abundance the next day. True to Elisha's word, the Lord caused panic in the Aramean camp, and the enemy ran, leaving their supplies to Samaria's starving people (6:24–7:20).

7. **Damascus** Despite Elisha's loyalty to Israel, he obeyed God and traveled to Damascus, the capital of Aram. King Ben-hadad was sick, and he sent Hazael to ask Elisha if he would recover. Elisha knew the king would die and told this to Hazael. But Hazael then murdered Ben-hadad, making himself king. Later, Israel and Judah joined forces to fight this new Aramean threat (8:1-29).

8. **Ramoth-gilead** As Israel and Judah warred with Aram, Elisha sent a young prophet to Ramoth-gilead to anoint Jehu as Israel's next king. Jehu set out to destroy the wicked dynasties of Israel and Judah, killing kings Joram and Ahaziah, and wicked Queen Jezebel. He then destroyed King Ahab's family and all the Baal worshipers in Israel (9:1–11:1).

9. **Jerusalem** Power-hungry Athaliah became queen of Judah when her son Ahaziah was killed. She had all her grandsons killed except Joash, who was hidden by his aunt. Joash was crowned king at the age of seven and overthrew Athaliah. Meanwhile in Samaria, the Arameans continued to harass Israel. Israel's new king met with Elisha and was told that he would be victorious over Aram three times (11:2–13:19).

Following Elisha's death came a series of evil kings in Israel. Their idolatry and rejection of God caused their downfall. The Assyrian Empire captured Samaria and took most of the Israelites into captivity (13:20–17:41). Judah had a short reprieve because of a few good kings who destroyed idols and worshiped God. But many strayed from God. So Jerusalem fell to the next world power, Babylon (18:1–25:30).

MIRACLES OF ELIJAH AND ELISHA / 2 Kings 2

Baal, the false god worshiped by many Israelites, was the god of rain, fire, and farm crops. He also demanded child sacrifice. Elijah's and Elisha's miracles repeatedly show the power of the true God over the purported realm of Baal, as well as the value God places on the life of a child.

Miracle	Reference	Factors
ELIJAH		
1. Food brought by ravens	1 Kings 17:5-6	Food
2. Widow's food multiplied	1 Kings 17:12-16	Flour and oil
3. Widow's son raised to life	1 Kings 17:17-24	Life of a child
4. Altar and sacrifice consumed	1 Kings 18:16-46	Fire and water
5. Ahaziah's soldiers consumed	2 Kings 1:9-14	Fire
6. Jordan River parted	2 Kings 2:6-8	Water
7. Transported to heaven	2 Kings 2:11-12	Fire and wind
ELISHA		
1. Jordan River parted	2 Kings 2:13-14	Water
2. Spring purified at Jericho	2 Kings 2:19-22	Water
3. Widow's oil multiplied	2 Kings 4:1-7	Oil
4. Dead boy raised to life	2 Kings 4:18-37	Life of a child
5. Poison in stew purified	2 Kings 4:38-41	Flour
6. Prophets' food multiplied	2 Kings 4:42-44	Bread and grain
7. Naaman healed of leprosy	2 Kings 5:1-14	Water
8. Gehazi became leprous	2 Kings 5:15-27	Words alone
9. Ax head floated	2 Kings 6:1-7	Water
10. Aramean army blinded	2 Kings 6:8-23	Elisha's prayer

PEOPLE RAISED FROM THE DEAD / 2 Kings 4:34-35

God is all-powerful. Nothing in life is beyond his control, not even death.

Elijah raised a boy from the dead	1 Kings 17:22
Elisha raised a boy from the dead	2 Kings 4:34-35
Elisha's bones raised a man from the dead	2 Kings 13:20-21
Jesus raised a boy from the dead	Luke 7:14-15
Jesus raised a girl from the dead	Luke 8:52-56
Jesus raised Lazarus from the dead	John 11:38-44
Peter raised a woman from the dead	Acts 9:40-41
Paul raised a man from the dead	Acts 20:9-20

THE FAMILY IN SHUNEM

2 Kings 4:8-38

Elisha often stayed with a kind family in Shunem. When the son suddenly died, his mother traveled to Mount Carmel to find Elisha. He returned with her and raised the boy from the dead. Elisha then went to his home in Gilgal.

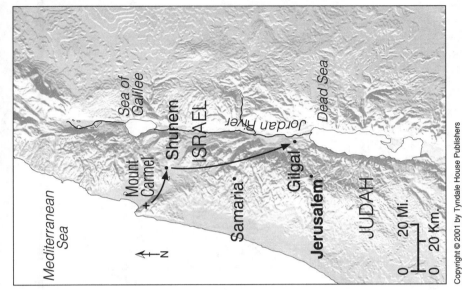

Copyright © 2001 by Tyndale House Publishers

WAR AGAINST MOAB

2 Kings 3:1-27

Moab's king rebelled against Israel. So Joram, Israel's king, and Jehoshaphat, Judah's king, attacked Moab. In the parched and rugged wilderness of Edom, the armies ran out of water, but Elisha promised that both water and victory would soon come.

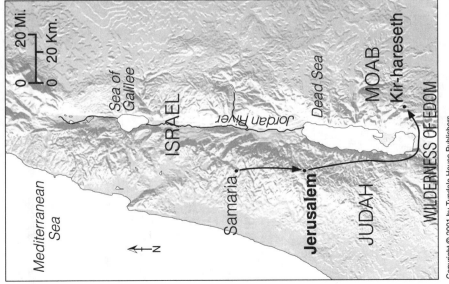

Copyright © 2001 by Tyndale House Publishers

JEHU TAKES OVER ISRAEL

2 Kings 9:1-37

Elisha sent a prophet to Ramoth-gilead to anoint Jehu as Israel's new king. Jehu immediately rode to Jezreel to find and kill King Joram of Israel and King Ahaziah of Judah. Jehu killed Joram; Ahaziah fled toward Beth-haggan, where he was wounded. He later died at Megiddo. Back in Jezreel, Jehu had Jezebel killed.

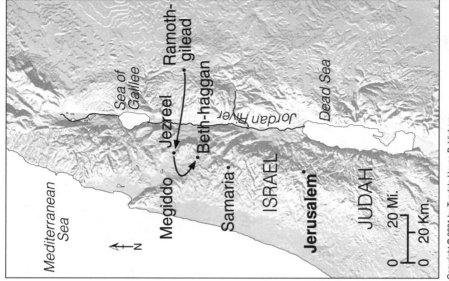

Copyright © 2001 by Tyndale House Publishers

ELISHA AND THE ARAMEANS

2 Kings 6:8-23

Elisha knew Aram's battle plans and kept Israel's king informed. The Aramean king tracked down Elisha at Dothan, but Elisha prayed that the Aramean army would be blinded. He then led the blind army into Samaria, Israel's capital city!

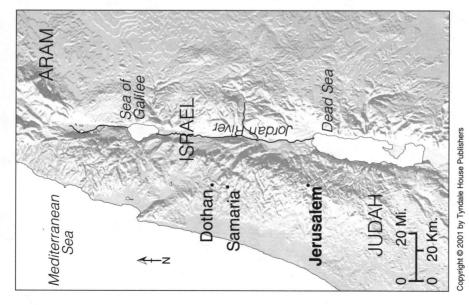

Copyright © 2001 by Tyndale House Publishers

GOD OR IDOLS / *2 Kings 12*

Why did people continually turn to idols instead of to God?

Idols were:

Tangible

Morally similar—had human characteristics

Comprehensible

Able to be manipulated

God is:

Intangible—no physical form

Morally dissimilar—had divine characteristics

Incomprehensible

Not able to be manipulated

Worshiping idols involved:

Materialism

Sexual immorality

Doing whatever a person wanted

Focusing on self

Worshiping God involves:

Sacrifice

Purity and commitment

Doing what God wants

Focusing on others

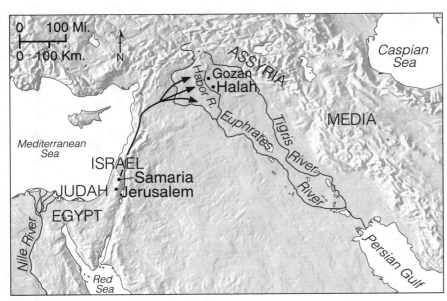

Copyright © 2001 by Tyndale House Publishers

ISRAEL TAKEN CAPTIVE

2 Kings 17:1-23

Finally the sins of Israel's people caught up with them. God allowed Assyria to defeat and disperse the people. They were led into captivity, swallowed up by the mighty, evil Assyrian Empire. Sin always brings discipline, and the consequences of that sin are sometimes irreversible.

WHO WERE THESE PROPHETS? / 2 Kings 17:13

Who?	When? (B.C.)	Ministered during the reign of these kings	Main message	Significance
AHIJAH	934-909	Jeroboam I of Israel (1 Kings 11:29-39)	Israel would split in two and God had chosen Jeroboam to lead the 10 tribes. Warned him to remain obedient to God.	We should not take lightly our God-given responsibilities. Jeroboam did and lost his kingdom.
ELIJAH	875-848	Ahab of Israel (1 Kings 17:1— 2 Kings 2:11)	In fiery style, urged wicked Ahab to turn back to God. Proved on Mount Carmel who the one true God is (1 Kings 18).	Even giants of faith can't force sinners to change. But those who remain faithful to God have a great impact for him.
MICAIAH	865-853	Ahab of Israel, Jehoshaphat of Judah (1 Kings 22:8; 2 Chronicles 18:28)	Ahab would be unsuccessful in fighting the Arameans.	It is foolish to move ahead with plans that are contrary to God's Word.
JEHU	853	Jehoshaphat of Judah (2 Chronicles 19:1-3)	Jehoshaphat should never have allied himself with wicked Ahab.	Partnerships with immoral people can lead us into trouble.
OBADIAH	855-840 (?)	Jehoram of Judah (The book of Obadiah)	God would judge the Edomites for taking advantage of God's people.	Pride is one of the most dangerous sins because it causes us to take advantage of others.
ELISHA	848-797	Joram, Jehu, Jehoahaz, and Jehoash, all of Israel (2 Kings 2:1—9:1; 13:10-21)	Expressed by his actions the importance of helping ordinary people in need.	God is concerned about the everyday needs of his people.
JOEL	835-796 (?)	Joash of Judah (The book of Joel)	Because a plague of locusts had come to punish the nation, called the people to turn back to God before an even greater judgment occurred.	While God judges all people for their sins, he gives eternal salvation only to those who have turned to him.
JONAH	793-753	Jeroboam II of Israel (2 Kings 14:25; the book of Jonah)	Warned Nineveh, the capital of Assyria, to repent of its sins.	God wants all nations to turn to him. His love reaches out to all peoples.
AMOS	760-750	Jeroboam II of Israel (The book of Amos)	Warned those who exploited or ignored the needy. (In Amos's day, Israel was an affluent and materialistic society.)	Believing in God is more than a personal matter. God calls all believers to work against injustices in society and to aid those less fortunate.
HOSEA	753-715	The last seven kings of Israel; Azariah (Uzziah), Jotham, Ahaz, and Hezekiah of Judah (The book of Hosea)	Condemned the people of Israel because they had sinned against God as an adulterous woman sins against her husband.	When we sin, we sever our relationship to God, breaking our commitment to him. While all must answer to God for their sins, those who seek God's forgiveness are spared from eternal judgment.

"Again and again the LORD had sent his prophets and seers to warn both Israel and Judah: 'Turn from all your evil ways. Obey my commands and laws . . . '" (2 Kings 17:13). Who were these prophets? Here are some of those who tried to turn their nations back to God. Predicting the future as revealed by God was just

Who?	When? (B.C.)	Ministered during the reign of these kings	Main message	Significance
MICAH	742-687	Jotham, Ahaz, and Hezekiah of Judah (The book of Micah)	Predicted the fall of both the northern and southern kingdoms. This was God's discipline on the people, actually showing how much he cared for them.	Choosing to live a life apart from God is making a commitment to sin. Sin leads to judgment and death. God alone shows us the way to eternal peace. His discipline often keeps us on the right path.
ISAIAH	740-681	Azariah (Uzziah), Jotham, Ahaz, Hezekiah, and Manasseh of Judah (The book of Isaiah)	Called the people back to a special relationship with God—although judgment through other nations was inevitable.	Sometimes we must suffer judgment and discipline before we are restored to God.
NAHUM	663-654	Manasseh of Judah (The book of Nahum)	The mighty empire of Assyria that oppressed God's people would soon tumble.	Those who do evil and oppress others will one day meet a bitter end.
ZEPHANIAH	640-621	Josiah of Judah (The book of Zephaniah)	A day would come when God, as Judge, would severely punish all nations; but afterward he would show mercy to his people.	We will all be judged for our disobedience to God, but if we remain faithful to him, he will show us mercy.
JEREMIAH	627-586	Josiah, Jehoahaz, Jehoiakim, Jehoiachin, Zedekiah of Judah (The book of Jeremiah)	Repentance would postpone Judah's coming judgment at the hands of Babylon.	Repentance is one of the greatest needs in our world of immorality. God's promises to the faithful shine brightly.
HABAKKUK	612-589	Josiah, Jehoahaz, Jehoiakim, Jehoiachin, Zedekiah of Judah (The book of Habakkuk)	Couldn't understand why God seemed to do nothing about the wickedness in society. Then realized that faith in God alone would one day supply the answer.	Instead of questioning the ways of God, we should realize that he is completely just, and we should have faith that he is in control and that one day evil will be utterly destroyed.
DANIEL	605-536	Prophesied as an exile in Babylon during the reigns of Nebuchadnezzar, Darius the Mede, and Cyrus of Persia (The book of Daniel)	Described both near and distant future events. Throughout it all, God is sovereign and triumphant.	We should spend less time wondering when future events will happen and more time learning how we should live *now* so we won't be victims when those events occur.
EZEKIEL	593-571	Prophesied as an exile in Babylon during the reign of Nebuchadnezzar (The book of Ezekiel)	Sent messages back to Jerusalem urging the people to turn back to God before they were all forced to join him in exile. After Jerusalem fell, he urged his fellow exiles to turn back to God so they could eventually return to their homeland.	God disciplines his people to draw them closer to him.

one part of a prophet's job; his main role was to preach God's word to the people—warning, instructing, and encouraging them to live as they ought. (The prophets Haggai, Zechariah, and Malachi were prophets to the people of Judah after they returned from exile. For more information, see the chart in Ezra 5.)

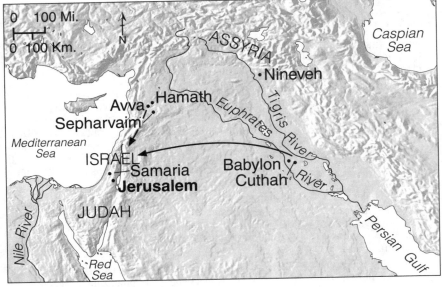

ISRAEL RESETTLED BY FOREIGNERS

2 Kings 17:24-41

After the Israelites were deported, foreigners from the Assyrian Empire were sent to resettle the land. This policy helped Assyria keep peace in conquered territories.

Copyright © 2001 by Tyndale House Publishers

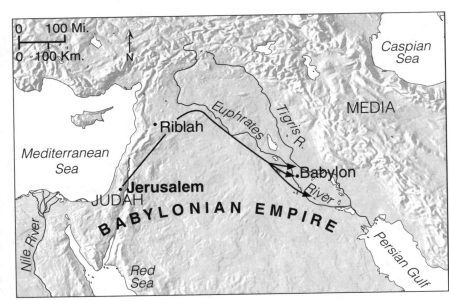

JUDAH EXILED

2 Kings 25:1-30

Evil permeated Judah, and God's anger flared against his rebellious people. Babylon conquered Assyria and became the new world power. The Babylonian army marched into Jerusalem, burned the Temple, tore down the city's massive walls, and carried off the people into captivity.

Copyright © 2001 by Tyndale House Publishers

1 CHRONICLES

MEGATHEMES IN 1 CHRONICLES

Theme	Explanation	Importance
Israel's History	By retelling Israel's history in the genealogies and the stories of the kings, the writer laid down the true spiritual foundation for the nation. God kept his promises, and we are reminded of them in the historical record of his people, leaders, prophets, priests, and kings.	Israel's past formed a reliable basis for reconstructing the nation after the Exile. Because God's promises are revealed in the Bible, we can know God and trust him to keep his word. Like Israel, we should have no higher goal in life than devoted service to God.
God's People	By listing the names of people in Israel's past, God established Israel's true heritage. They were all one family in Adam, one nation in Abraham, one priesthood under Levi, and one kingdom under David. The national and spiritual unity of the people was important to the rebuilding of the nation.	God is always faithful to his people. He protects them in every generation and provides leaders to guide them. Because God has been at work throughout the centuries, his people can trust him to work in the present. You can rely on his presence today.
David, the King	The story of David's life and his relationship with God showed that he was God's appointed leader. David's devotion to God, the law, the Temple, true worship, the people, and justice sets the standard for what God's chosen king should be like.	Jesus Christ came to earth as a descendant of David. One day he will rule as King over all the earth. His strength and justice will fulfill God's ideal for the king. He is our hope. We can experience God's Kingdom now by giving Christ complete control of our lives.
True Worship	David brought the Ark of the Covenant to the Tabernacle at Jerusalem to restore true worship to the people. God gave the plans for building the Temple, and David organized the priests to make worship central to all Israel.	The Temple stood as the throne of God on earth, the place of true worship. God's true throne is in the hearts of his people. When we acknowledge him as the true King over our lives, true worship takes place.
The Priests	God ordained the priests and Levites to guide the people in faithful worship according to his law. By leading the people in worship according to God's design, the priests and Levites were an important safeguard to Israel's faith.	For true worship to remain central in our lives, God's people need to take a firm stand for the ways of God recorded in the Bible. Today, all believers are priests for one another, and we should encourage each other to faithful worship.

KEY PLACES IN 1 CHRONICLES

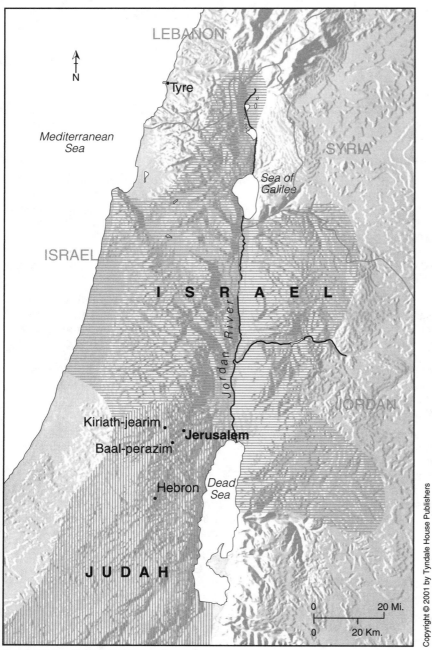

Modern names and boundaries are shown in gray.

The genealogies of 1 Chronicles present an overview of Israel's history. The first nine chapters are filled with genealogies tracing the lineages of people from the Creation to the exile in Babylon. Saul's death is recorded in chapter 10. Chapter 11 begins the history of David's reign over Israel.

1. **Hebron** Although David had been anointed king years earlier, his reign began when the leaders of Israel accepted him as king at Hebron (11:1-3).

2. **Jerusalem** David set out to complete the conquest of the land begun by Joshua. He attacked Jerusalem, captured it, and made it his capital (11:4–12:40).

3. **Kiriath-jearim** The Ark of the Covenant, which the Philistines had captured in battle and then returned (1 Samuel 4–6), was in safekeeping in Kiriath-jearim. David summoned all Israel to this city to join in bringing the Ark to Jerusalem. Unfortunately, it was not moved according to God's instructions, and as a result, one man died. David left the Ark in the home of Obed-edom until he could discover how to transport it correctly (13:1-14).

4. **Tyre** David did much building in Jerusalem. King Hiram of Tyre sent workers and supplies to help build David's palace. Cedar, abundant in the mountains north of Israel, was a valuable and hardy wood for the beautiful buildings in Jerusalem (14:1–17:27).

5. **Baal-perazim** David was not very popular with the Philistines because he had slain Goliath, one of their greatest warriors (1 Samuel 17). When David began to rule over a united Israel, the Philistines set out to capture him. But as David and his army approached Jerusalem, they attacked the Philistines at Baal-perazim. His army defeated the mighty Philistines twice, causing all the surrounding nations to fear David's power (14:11-17). After these battles, David moved the Ark to Jerusalem (this time in accordance with God's instructions for transporting the Ark). There was great celebration as the Ark was brought into Jerusalem (15:1–17:27). David spent the remainder of his life making preparations for the building of the Temple, a central place for the worship of God (18:1–29:30).

WHO'S WHO IN THE BIBLE / 1 Chronicles 1–8

Here are some of the people mentioned in this genealogy who are also mentioned elsewhere in the Bible. The writer of Chronicles reproduced a thorough history of Israel in one list of people. Many of the people in this list have exciting stories that can be traced through the Bible. Look up some of the names here that intrigue you. You may be surprised at what you discover!

Name	Key Life Lesson	Reference
Adam (1:1)	Our sins have far greater implications than we realize.	Genesis 2–3
Noah (1:4)	Great rewards come from obeying God.	Genesis 6–9
Abraham (1:27)	Faith alone makes one right in God's eyes.	Genesis 11:26–25:10
Isaac (1:28)	Seeking peace brings true respect.	Genesis 21–35
Esau (1:35)	It is never too late to put away bitterness and forgive.	Genesis 25:20–36:43
Amalek (1:36)	There are evil men and nations who seek to harm God's people.	Exodus 17:8-16
Israel (Jacob) (2:1)	While our sins may haunt us, God will honor our faith.	Genesis 25:20–50:13
Judah (2:3)	God can change the hearts of even the most wicked people.	Genesis 37–50
Tamar (2:4)	God works his purposes even through sinful events.	Genesis 38
Perez (2:5)	Your background does not matter to God.	Genesis 38:27-30
Boaz (2:12)	Those who are kind to others will receive kindness themselves.	The book of Ruth
Jesse (2:13)	Never take lightly the impact you may have on your children.	1 Samuel 16
David (2:15)	True greatness is having a heart for God.	The books of 1 and 2 Samuel
Joab (2:16)	Those who seek power die with nothing.	2 Samuel 2:13—1 Kings 2:34
Amnon (3:1)	Giving in to lust leads only to tragedy.	2 Samuel 13
Absalom (3:2)	Those seeking to oust a God-appointed leader will have a difficult battle.	2 Samuel 13–18
Adonijah (3:2)	God must determine what is rightfully ours.	1 Kings 1–2
Bathsheba (3:5)	One wrong act does not disqualify us from accomplishing things for God.	2 Samuel 11–12; 1 Kings 1–2
Solomon (3:5)	Man's wisdom is foolishness without God.	1 Kings 1–11
Reuben (5:1)	What is gained from a moment of passion is only perceived; what is lost is real and permanent.	Genesis 35:22; 37; 49:3-4
Aaron (6:3)	Don't expect God's leaders to be perfect, but don't let them get away with sin either.	Exodus 4—Numbers 20
Nadab (6:3)	Pretending to be God's representative is dangerous business.	Leviticus 10
Eleazar (6:3)	Those who are consistent in their faith are the best models to follow.	Numbers 20:25-29; 26–34; Joshua 24:33
Korah (6:22)	Rebelling against God's leaders is rebelling against God and will always be unsuccessful.	Numbers 16
Joshua (7:27)	Real courage comes from God.	The book of Joshua
Saul (8:33)	Those who say they follow God but don't live like it waste their God-given potential.	1 Samuel 8–31
Jonathan (8:33)	True friends always think of the other person, not just themselves.	1 Samuel 14–31

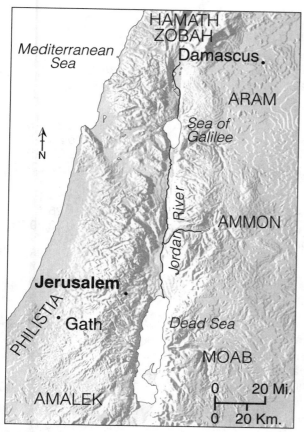

Copyright © 2001 by Tyndale House Publishers

DAVID SUBDUES HIS ENEMIES

1 Chronicles 18:1–20:8

David expanded his kingdom as the Lord continued to give him victory. He subdued the Philistines by taking Gath, conquered Moab, won battles as far north as Zobah and Hamath (conquering Aram when they came to help these enemy nations), and subdued the other surrounding nations of Ammon and Amalek.

DUTIES ASSIGNED IN THE TEMPLE / 1 Chronicles 23

King David charged all these people to do their jobs "to honor the LORD's name"
(1 Chronicles 22:17-19). God needs people of every talent—not just prophets and
priests—to obey him.

Administrative Duties	Supervisors	1 Chronicles 23:4-5
	Officials	1 Chronicles 23:4-5
	Judges	1 Chronicles 23:4-5
	Public administrators.	1 Chronicles 26:29-30
Ministerial Duties	Priests	1 Chronicles 24:1
	Prophets	1 Chronicles 25:1
	Assistants for sacrifices	1 Chronicles 23:29-31
	Assistants for purification ceremonies.	1 Chronicles 23:28
Service Duties.	Bakers of the sacred bread	1 Chronicles 23:29
	Those who checked the weights and measures.	1 Chronicles 23:29
	Caretakers	1 Chronicles 23:28
Financial Duties	Those who cared for the treasuries . .	1 Chronicles 26:20
	Those who cared for the dedicated things	1 Chronicles 26:26-28
Artistic Duties	Musicians	1 Chronicles 25:6
	Singers.	1 Chronicles 25:7
Protective Duties	Gatekeepers	1 Chronicles 26:12-18
Individual Assignments . . .	Chief of the gatekeepers.	1 Chronicles 9:19-21
	Secretary.	1 Chronicles 24:6
	Seer	1 Chronicles 25:5
	Prophet under the king.	1 Chronicles 25:2
	Chief officer of the treasuries	1 Chronicles 26:23-24

MUSIC IN BIBLE TIMES / 1 Chronicles 25

Paul clearly puts forth the Christian's view that things are not good or bad in and of themselves (see Romans 14 and 1 Corinthians 14:7-8, 26). The point should always be to worship the Lord or help others by means of the things of this world, including music. Music was created by God and can be returned to him in praise. Does the music you play or listen to have a negative or positive impact upon your relationship with God?

Highlights of Musical Use in Scripture	Reference
Jubal was father of all musicians	Genesis 4:21
Miriam and other women sang and danced to praise God	Exodus 15:1-21
The priest was to have bells on his robes	Exodus 28:34-35
Jericho fell to the sound of horns	Joshua 6:4-20
Saul experienced the soothing effect of music	1 Samuel 16:14-23
The king's coronation was accompanied by music	1 Kings 1:39-40
The Ark was accompanied by trumpeters	1 Chronicles 16:6
There were musicians for the king's court	Ecclesiastes 2:8
From David's time on, the use of music in worship was much more organized. Music for the Temple became refined	1 Chronicles 15:16-24 1 Chronicles 16:4-7 2 Chronicles 5:11-14
Everything was to be used by everyone to praise the Lord	Psalm 150

In the New Testament, worship continued in the synagogues until the Christians became unwelcome there, so there was a rich musical heritage already established. The fact that music is mentioned less often in the New Testament does not mean it was less important.

Jesus and the disciples sang a hymn	Matthew 26:30
Paul and Silas sang in jail	Acts 16:25
We are to sing to the Lord as a response to what he has done in our lives	Ephesians 5:19-20 Colossians 3:16 James 5:13

PRINCIPLES TO LIVE BY / 1 Chronicles 28:9-10

King David gave his son Solomon principles to guide him through life (see 1 Chronicles 28:9-10). These same ideas are ones that any Christian parent would want to present to a child:

1. Get to know God personally.

2. Learn God's commands and discover what he wants you to do.

3. Worship God with wholehearted devotion.

4. Serve God with a willing mind.

5. Be faithful.

6. Don't become discouraged.

2 CHRONICLES

MEGATHEMES IN 2 CHRONICLES

Theme	Explanation	Importance
Temple	The Temple was the symbol of God's presence and the place set aside for worship and prayer. Built by Solomon from the plans God gave to David, the Temple was the spiritual center of the nation.	As Christians meet together to worship God, they experience the presence of God in a way that no individual believer can, for the dwelling place of God is the people of God. The body of Christ is God's temple.
Peace	As Solomon and his descendants were faithful to God, they experienced victory in battle, success in government, and peace with other nations. Peace was the result of the people being unified and loyal to God and his law.	Only God can bring true peace. God is greater than any enemy, army, or nation. Just as Israel's faithful response was key to her peace and survival as a nation, so our obedience to God as individuals and nations is vital to peace today.
Prayer	After Solomon died, David's kingdom was divided. When a king led the Israelites into idolatry, the nation suffered. When the king and his people prayed to God for deliverance and they turned from their sinful ways, God delivered them.	God still answers prayer today. We have God's promise that if we humble ourselves, seek him, turn from our sin, and pray, God will hear, heal, and forgive us. If we are alert, we can pray for God's guidance before we get into trouble.
Reform	Although idolatry and injustice were common, some kings turned to God and led the people in spiritual revival—renewing their commitment to God and reforming their society. Revival included the destruction of idols, obedience to the law, and the restoration of the priesthood.	We must constantly commit ourselves to obeying God. We are never secure in what others have done before us. Believers in each generation must dedicate themselves to the task of carrying out God's will in their own lives as well as in society.
National Collapse	In 586 B.C. the Babylonians completely destroyed Solomon's beautiful Temple. The formal worship of God was ended. The Israelites had abandoned God. As a result, God brought judgment upon his people, and they were carried off into captivity.	Although our disobedience may not be as blatant as Israel's, quite often our commitment to God is insincere and casual. When we forget that all our power, wisdom, and wealth come from God and not ourselves, we are in danger of the same spiritual and moral collapse that Israel experienced.

KEY PLACES IN 2 CHRONICLES

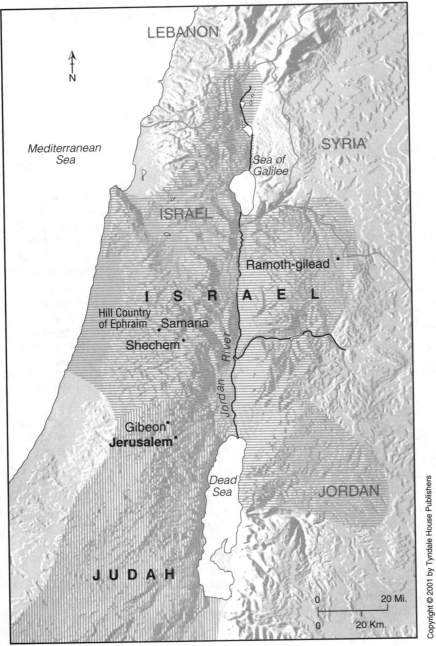

Modern names and boundaries are shown in gray.

Copyright © 2001 by Tyndale House Publishers

1. **Gibeon** David's son Solomon became king over Israel. He summoned the nation's leaders to a ceremony in Gibeon. Here God told Solomon to ask for whatever he desired. Solomon asked for wisdom and knowledge to rule Israel (1:1-12).

2. **Jerusalem** After the ceremony in Gibeon, Solomon returned to the capital city, Jerusalem. His reign began a golden age for Israel. Solomon implemented the plans for the Temple, which had been drawn up by his father, David. It was a magnificent construction. It symbolized Solomon's wealth and wisdom, which became known worldwide (1:13–9:31).

3. **Shechem** After Solomon's death, his son Rehoboam was ready to be crowned in Shechem. However, his promise of higher taxes and harder work for the people led to rebellion. Everyone but the tribes of Judah and Benjamin deserted Rehoboam and set up their own kingdom to the north called Israel. Rehoboam returned to Jerusalem as ruler over the southern kingdom called Judah (10:1–12:16). The remainder of 2 Chronicles records the history of Judah.

4. **Hill Country of Ephraim** Abijah became the next king of Judah, and soon war broke out between Israel and Judah. When the armies of the two nations arrived for battle in the hill country of Ephraim, Israel had twice as many troops as Judah. It looked as though Judah's defeat was certain. But they cried out to God, and God gave them victory over Israel. In their history as separate nations, Judah had a few godly kings, who instituted reforms and brought the people back to God. Israel, however, had a succession of only evil kings (13:1-22).

5. **Aram (Syria)** Asa, a godly king, removed every trace of pagan worship from Judah and renewed the people's covenant with God in Jerusalem. But King Baasha of Israel built a fortress to control traffic into Judah. Instead of looking to God for guidance, Asa took the silver and gold from the Temple and sent it to the king of Aram, requesting his help against King Baasha. As a result, God became angry with Judah (14:1–16:14).

6. **Samaria** Although Jehoshaphat was a godly king, he allied himself with Israel's most evil king, Ahab. Ahab's capital was Samaria. Ahab wanted help fighting against Ramoth-gilead. Jehoshaphat wanted advice, but rather than listening to God's prophet who had promised defeat, he joined Ahab in battle (17:1–18:27).

7. **Ramoth-gilead** The alliance with Israel against Ramoth-gilead ended in defeat and Ahab's death. Shaken by his defeat, Jehoshaphat returned to Jerusalem and to God. But his son Jehoram was a wicked king, as was his son Ahaziah, and history repeated itself. Ahaziah formed an alliance with Israel's king, Joram, to do battle with the Arameans at Ramoth-gilead. This led to the death of both kings (18:28–22:9).

8. **Jerusalem** The rest of Judah's history recorded in 2 Chronicles centers on Jerusalem. Some kings caused Judah to sin by bringing idol worship into their midst. Others cleaned up the idol worship, reopened and restored the Temple, and in the case of Josiah, tried to follow God's laws as they were written by Moses. In spite of the few good influences, a series of evil kings sent Judah into a downward spiral that ended with the Babylonian Empire overrunning the country. The Temple was burned, the walls of the city were broken down, and the people were deported to Babylon.

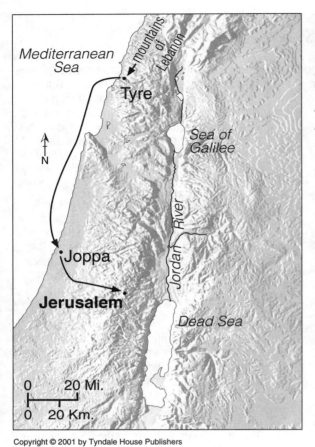

SHIPPING RESOURCES FOR THE TEMPLE

2 Chronicles 2:1-18

Solomon asked King Hiram of Tyre to provide supplies and skilled workmen to help build God's Temple in Jerusalem. The plan was to cut the cedar logs in the mountains of Lebanon, float them by sea to Joppa, then bring them inland to Jerusalem by the shortest and easiest route.

Copyright © 2001 by Tyndale House Publishers

CAREFUL OBEDIENCE / 2 Chronicles 4

Solomon and his workers carefully followed God's instructions. As a result, the Temple work was blessed by God and completed in every detail. Here are a few examples of people in the Bible who did not carefully follow one of God's instructions, and the resulting consequences. It is *not* enough to obey God halfheartedly.

Who?	God's Instruction	Disobedience	Result
Adam and Eve	Don't eat fruit from the tree of the knowledge of good and evil (Genesis 2:16-17)	Satan tempted them, and they ate (Genesis 3:1-6)	They were banished from the Garden of Eden, pain and death were inflicted on all people (Genesis 3:24; Romans 5:12)
Nadab and Abihu	Fire for the sacrifice must come from the proper source (Leviticus 6:12-13)	They used unauthorized fire for their sacrifice (Leviticus 10:1)	They were struck dead (Leviticus 10:2)
Moses	"Command the rock over there to pour out its water" (Numbers 20:8)	He spoke to the rock, but also struck it with his staff (Numbers 20:11)	He was not allowed to enter the Promised Land (Numbers 20:12)
Saul	Completely destroy the evil Amalekites (1 Samuel 15:3)	He spared the king and kept some of the plunder (1 Samuel 15:8-9)	God promised to end his reign (1 Samuel 15:16-26)
Uzzah	Only a priest can touch the sacred utensils and objects (Numbers 4:15)	He touched the Ark of the Covenant (2 Samuel 6:6)	He died instantly (2 Samuel 6:7)
Uzziah	Only the priests can offer incense in the Temple or Tabernacle sanctuary (Numbers 16:39-40; 18:7)	He entered the Holy Place in the Temple where only priests were allowed to go (2 Chronicles 26:16-18)	He became a leper (2 Chronicles 26:19)

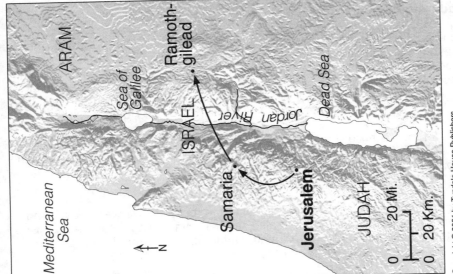

BATTLE WITH ARAM

2 Chronicles 18:1-34

King Jehoshaphat made an alliance with evil King Ahab of Israel. Together they decided to attack Ramoth-gilead and rout the Arameans who had occupied the city. But Jehoshaphat first wanted to seek the advice of a prophet. Ahab's prophets predicted victory, but Micaiah predicted defeat. The two kings were defeated, and Ahab was killed.

Copyright © 2001 by Tyndale House Publishers

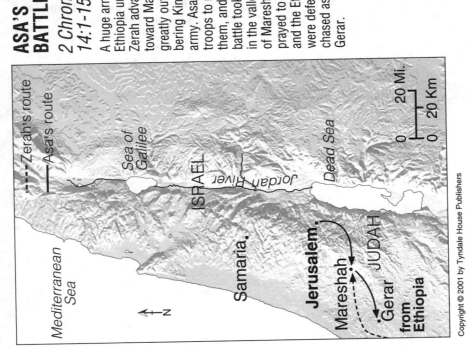

ASA'S BATTLES

2 Chronicles 14:1-15

A huge army from Ethiopia under Zerah advanced toward Mareshah, greatly outnumbering King Asa's army. Asa sent his troops to meet them, and the battle took place in the valley north of Mareshah. Asa prayed to God, and the Ethiopians were defeated and chased as far as Gerar.

Copyright © 2001 by Tyndale House Publishers

GREAT REVIVALS IN THE BIBLE / *2 Chronicles 29–31*

The Bible records several great revivals where people in substantial numbers turned to God and gave up their sinful ways of living. Each revival was characterized by a *leader* who recognized his nation's spiritual dryness. And in each case, the leader *took action* and was not afraid to make his desires known to the people.

Leader	Reference	How the People Responded
Moses	Exodus 32–33	Accepted God's laws and built the Tabernacle
Samuel	1 Samuel 7:2-13	Promised to make God first in their lives by destroying their idols
David	2 Samuel 6	Brought the Ark of the Covenant to Jerusalem; praised God with singing and musical instruments
Jehoshaphat	2 Chronicles 20	Decided to trust in God alone to help them, and their discouragement turned to joy
Hezekiah	2 Chronicles 29–31	Purified the Temple; got rid of idols; brought tithes to God's house
Josiah	2 Chronicles 34–35	Made a commitment to obey God's commands and remove sinful influences from their lives
Ezra	Ezra 9–10; Haggai 1	Stopped associating with those who caused them to compromise their faith; renewed their commitment to God's commands; began rebuilding the Temple
Nehemiah (with Ezra)	Nehemiah 8–10	Fasted, confessed their sins, read God's Word publicly, and promised in writing to again serve God wholeheartedly

BIBLE PERSECUTIONS / 2 Chronicles 18:12-26

The Persecuted	The Persecutors	Why the Persecution?	Result	Reference
Isaac	Philistines	God was blessing Isaac, and they envied him	The Philistines could not subdue Isaac, so they made peace with him	Genesis 26:12-33
Job	Satan	Satan wanted to prove that suffering would make a person abandon God	Job remained faithful to God and was restored	Job 1:8-12; 2:3-7
Moses	Israelites	The Israelites wanted water	God provided water in answer to Moses' prayer	Exodus 17:1-7
David	Saul and others	David was becoming a powerful leader, threatening Saul's position as king	David endured the persecution and became king	1 Samuel 20–27; Psalms 31:13; 59:1-4
Priests of Nob	Saul and Doeg	Saul and Doeg thought the priests helped David escape	85 priests were killed	1 Samuel 22
Prophets	Jezebel	Jezebel didn't like to have her evil ways pointed out	Many prophets were killed	1 Kings 18:3-4
Elijah	Ahab and Jezebel	Elijah confronted their sins	Elijah had to flee for his life	1 Kings 18:10–19:2
Micaiah	Ahab	Ahab thought Micaiah was stirring up trouble rather than prophesying from God	Micaiah was thrown into prison	2 Chronicles 18:12-26
Elisha	A king of Israel (Probably Joram)	The king thought Elisha had caused the famine	Elisha ignored the threatened persecution and prophesied the famine's end	2 Kings 6:31
Hanani	Asa	Hanani criticized Asa for trusting in Aram's help more than in God's help	Hanani was thrown in prison	2 Chronicles 16:7-10
Zechariah	Joash	Zechariah confronted the people of Judah for disregarding God's commands	Zechariah was executed	2 Chronicles 24:20-22
Uriah	Jehoiakim	Uriah confronted Jehoiakim about his evil ways	Uriah was killed with a sword	Jeremiah 26:20-23
Jeremiah	Zedekiah	Zedekiah thought Jeremiah was a traitor for prophesying Jerusalem's fall	Jeremiah was thrown in prison, then into a muddy cistern	Jeremiah 37:1–38:13

The Persecuted	The Persecutors	Why the Persecution?	Result	Reference
Shadrach, Meshach, Abednego	Nebuchad-nezzar	The three men refused to bow down to anyone but God	They were thrown into a fiery furnace, but God miraculously saved them	Daniel 3
Daniel	National leaders	Daniel was praying	Daniel was thrown into a den of lions, but God miraculously saved him	Daniel 6
John the Baptist	Herod and Herodias	John confronted King Herod's adultery	John was beheaded	Matthew 14:3-13
Jesus	Religious leaders	Jesus exposed their sinful motives	Jesus was crucified, but rose again from the dead to show his authority over all evil	Mark 7:1-16; Luke 22:63–24:7
Peter and John	Religious leaders	Peter and John preached that Jesus was God's Son and the only way to salvation	They were thrown into prison, but later released	Acts 4:1-31
Stephen	Religious leaders	Stephen exposed their guilt in crucifying Jesus	Stephen was stoned to death	Acts 6–7
The church	Paul and others	The Christians preached Jesus as the Messiah	Believers faced death, prison, torture, exile	Acts 8:1-3; 9:1-9
James	Herod Agrippa I	To appease the Jewish leaders	James was executed	Acts 12:1, 2
Peter	Herod Agrippa I	To appease the Jewish leaders	Peter was thrown into prison	Acts 12:3-17
Paul	Jews, city officials	Paul preached about Jesus and confronted those who made money by manipulating others	Paul was stoned; thrown into prison	Acts 14:19; 16:16-24
Timothy	Unknown	Unknown	Timothy was thrown into prison	Hebrews 13:23
John	Probably the Romans	John told others about Jesus	John was sent into exile on a remote island	Revelation 1:9

Micaiah, like thousands of believers before and after him, was persecuted for his faith. The chart shows that persecution comes from a variety of people and is given in a variety of ways. Sometimes God protects us from it; sometimes he doesn't. But as long as we remain faithful to God *alone,* we must expect persecution (see also Luke 6:22; 2 Corinthians 6:4-10; 2 Timothy 2:9-12; Revelation 2:10). God also seems to have a special reward for those who endure such persecution (Revelation 6:9-11; 20:4).

THE DAVIDIC DYNASTY / 2 Chronicles 33

David . . . 40 years, 1 Chr. 10–29

Solomon . . . 40 years, 2 Chr. 1–9

Rehoboam . . . 17 years, 2 Chr. 10–12

Abijah . . . 3 years, 2 Chr. 13

Asa . . . 41 years, 2 Chr. 14–16

Jehoshaphat . . . 25 years, 2 Chr. 17–20

Jehoram . . . 8 years, 2 Chr. 21

Ahaziah . . . 1 year, 2 Chr. 22:1-9

Athaliah . . . 6 years, 2 Chr. 22:10–23:21

Joash . . . 40 years, 2 Chr. 24

Amaziah . . . 29 years, 2 Chr. 25

Uzziah . . . Azariah . . . 52 years, 2 Chr. 26

Jotham . . . 16 years, 2 Chr. 27

Ahaz . . . 16 years, 2 Chr. 28

Hezekiah . . . 29 years, 2 Chr. 29–32

Manasseh . . . 55 years, 2 Chr. 33:1-20

Amon . . . 2 years, 2 Chr. 33:21-25

Josiah . . . 31 years, 2 Chr. 34–35

Jehoahaz . . . 3 months, 2 Chr. 36:1-4

Jehoiakim . . . 11 years, 2 Chr. 36:5-8

Jehoiachin . . . 3 months, 2 Chr. 36:9-10

Zedekiah . . . 11 years, 2 Chr. 36:11-16

The Lord promised David that his kingdom would endure and his throne would be established forever (2 Samuel 7:16). As a partial fulfillment of this promise, David and his descendants ruled Judah for over 400 years. Jesus Christ was a direct descendant of David and was the ultimate fulfillment of this promise (Acts 2:22-36).

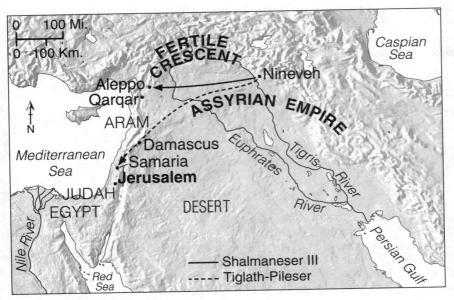

Copyright © 2001 by Tyndale House Publishers

THE ASSYRIAN EMPIRE

2 Chronicles 32:1-33

The mighty Assyrian Empire extended from the Persian Gulf, across the Fertile Crescent, and south to Egypt. Shalmaneser III extended the empire toward the Mediterranean Sea by conquering cities as far west as Qarqar. Tiglathpileser extended the empire south into Aram, Israel, Judah, and Philistia. It was Shalmaneser V who destroyed Samaria, Israel's capital.

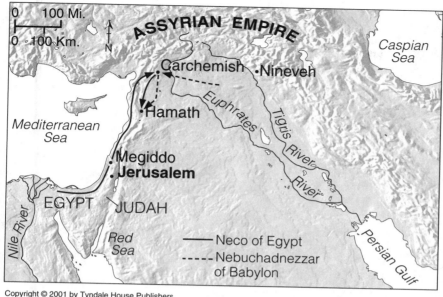

THE BATTLE AT CARCHEMISH

2 Chronicles 35:20-27

A world war was brewing in 609 B.C. when Pharaoh Neco of Egypt set out for the city of Carchemish to join the Assyrians in an attempt to defeat the Babylonians, who were rising to great power. Neco marched his armies through Judah, where King Josiah tried to stop him at Megiddo, but was killed. The battle began at Carchemish in 605 B.C., and the Egyptians and Assyrians were soundly defeated, chased to Hamath, and defeated again. Babylon was now the new world power.

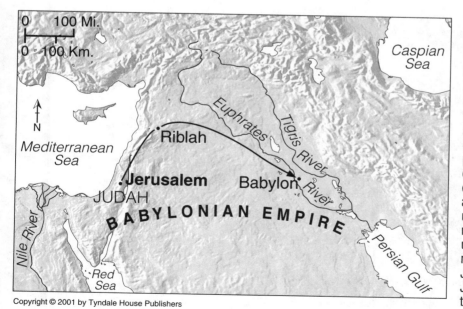

EXILE TO BABYLON

2 Chronicles 36:17-23

Despite Judah's few good kings and timely reforms, the people never truly changed. Their evil continued, and finally God used the Babylonian Empire, under Nebuchadnezzar, to conquer Judah, destroy Jerusalem, and take the people captive to Babylon.

EZRA

MEGATHEMES IN EZRA

Theme	Explanation	Importance
The Jews Return	By returning to the land of Israel from Babylon, the Jews showed their faith in God's promise to restore them as a people. They returned not only to their homeland but also to the place where their forefathers had promised to follow God.	God shows his mercy to every generation. He compassionately restores his people. No matter how difficult our present "captivity," we are never far from his love and mercy. He restores us when we return to him.
Rededication	In 536 B.C., Zerubbabel led the people in rebuilding the altar and laying the Temple foundation. They reinstated daily sacrifices and annual festivals, and rededicated themselves to a new spiritual worship of God.	In rededicating the altar, the people were recommitting themselves to God and his service. To grow spiritually, our commitment must be reviewed and renewed often. As we rededicate ourselves to God, our lives become altars to him.
Opposition	Opposition came soon after the altar was built and the Temple foundation laid. Enemies of the Jews used deceit to hinder the building for over six years. Finally, there was a decree to stop the building altogether. This opposition severely tested their wavering faith.	There will always be adversaries who oppose God's work. The life of faith is never easy. But God can overrule all opposition to his service. When we face opposition, we must not falter or withdraw, but keep active and patient.
God's Word	When the people returned to the land, they were also returning to the influence of God's Word. The prophets Haggai and Zechariah helped encourage them, while Ezra's preaching of Scripture built them up. God's Word gave them what they needed to do God's work.	We also need the encouragement and direction of God's Word. We must make it the basis for our faith and actions to finish God's work and fulfill our obligations. We must never waver in our commitment to hear and obey his Word.
Faith and Action	The urging of Israel's leaders motivated the people to complete the Temple. Over the years they had intermarried with idol worshipers and adopted their pagan practices. Their faith, tested and revived, also led them to remove these sins from their lives.	Faith led them to complete the Temple and to remove sin from their society. As we trust God with our hearts and minds, we must also act by completing our daily responsibilities. It is not enough to say we believe; we must make the changes God requires.

PROPHECIES FULFILLED BY THE RETURN OF ISRAEL FROM EXILE / *Ezra 1*

Reference	Prophecy	Approximate Date	Fulfillment Date	Significance
Isaiah 44:28	Cyrus would be used by God to guarantee the return of a remnant. Jerusalem would be rebuilt and the Temple restored.	688 B.C.	538 B.C.	As God named Cyrus even before he was born, God knows what will happen—he is in control.
Jeremiah 25:12	Babylon would be punished for destroying Jerusalem and exiling God's people.	605 B.C.	539 B.C.	Babylon was conquered by Cyrus the Great. God may seem to allow evil to go unpunished, but consequences for wrongdoing are inevitable. God will punish evil.
Jeremiah 29:10	The people would spend 70 years in Babylon; then God would bring them back to their homeland.	594 B.C.	538 B.C.	The 70 years of captivity passed, and God provided the opportunity for Zerubbabel to lead the first group of captives home. God's plans may allow for hardship, but his desire is for our good.
Daniel 5:17-30	God had judged the Babylonian Empire. It would be given to the Medes and the Persians, forming a new world power.	539 B.C.	539 B.C.	Belshazzar was killed and Babylon was conquered the same night. God's judgment is accurate and swift. God knows the point of no return in each of our lives. Until then, he allows the freedom for us to repent and seek his forgiveness.

God, through his faithful prophets, predicted that the people of Judah would be taken into captivity because of their sinfulness. But he also predicted that they would return to Jerusalem and rebuild the city, the Temple, and the nation.

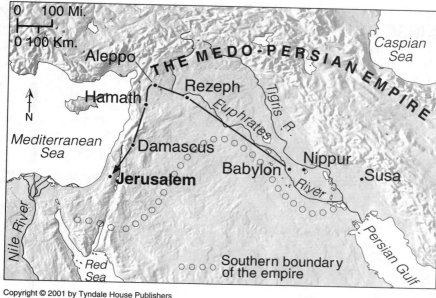

The vast Medo-Persian Empire included all the area on this map and more. A group of exiles began the long trip back to their homeland. Many exiles, however, preferred the comfort and security they had in Babylon to the dangerous trip back to Jerusalem, and so they decided to stay in Babylon.

Map labels: 0 100 Mi. / 0 100 Km. / Aleppo / THE MEDO-PERSIAN EMPIRE / Caspian Sea / Rezeph / Hamath / N / Euphrates / Tigris R. / Mediterranean Sea / Damascus / Nippur / Babylon / Susa / Jerusalem / Nile River / Red Sea / River / Persian Gulf / Southern boundary of the empire

Copyright © 2001 by Tyndale House Publishers

THE RETURN FROM EXILE / *Ezra 2*

Year	Number of People Returned	Persian King	Jewish Leader	Main Accomplishment
538 B.C.	50,000	Cyrus	Zerubbabel	They rebuilt the Temple, but only after a 20-year struggle. The work was halted for several years but was finally finished.
458 B.C.	2,000 men and their families	Artaxerxes	Ezra	Ezra confronted the spiritual disobedience of the people, and they repented and established worship at the Temple. But the wall of Jerusalem remained in ruins.
445 B.C.	Small group	Artaxerxes	Nehemiah	The city was rebuilt, and a spiritual awakening followed. But the people still struggled with ongoing disobedience.

Babylon, the once-mighty nation that had destroyed Jerusalem and carried the people of Judah into captivity, had itself become a defeated nation. Persia was the new world power, and under its new foreign policy, captured peoples were allowed to return to their homelands. The people of Judah and Israel returned to their land in three successive waves.

THE PERSIAN KINGS OF EZRA'S DAY / *Ezra 4*

Name	Date of Reign	Relationship to Israel
Cyrus	559–530 B.C.	Conquered Babylon. Established a policy of returning exiles to their homelands. Sent Zerubbabel to Jerusalem, financed his project, and returned the gold and silver articles that Nebuchadnezzar had taken from the Temple. He probably knew Daniel.
Darius	522–486 B.C.	Supported construction of the Temple in Jerusalem.
Xerxes (Ahasuerus)	486–465 B.C.	Was Esther's husband. Allowed the Jews to protect themselves against Haman's attempt to eliminate their people.
Artaxerxes I	465–424 B.C.	Had Nehemiah as his cupbearer. Allowed both Ezra and Nehemiah to return to Jerusalem.

THE POSTEXILIC PROPHETS / *Ezra 5*

God used these men to confront and comfort his people after their return to their homeland from exile in Babylon.

Who?	When?	Ministered to These Contemporary Leaders	Main Message	Significance
Haggai	520 B.C.	Zerubbabel Joshua	• Encouraged the leaders and the people to continue rebuilding the Temple, which God would bless • Challenged the people's careless worship, which God would not bless	Disobedience and careless obedience of God's commands lead to judgment.
Zechariah	520 B.C.	Zerubbabel Joshua	• Emphasized God's command to rebuild his Temple • Gave the people another look at God's plan to bless the world through Israel and its coming King—the Messiah (9:9-10)	Encouragement for today's effort sometimes requires that we remember God has a plan and purpose for tomorrow. Meanwhile the challenge is to live for him today.
Malachi	430 B.C.	The priests are the only leaders mentioned	• Confronted the people and priests with God's promises of judgment on those who reject him and God's blessing on those who live as he desires	God expects our obedience to him to affect our attitude toward him and our treatment of one another.

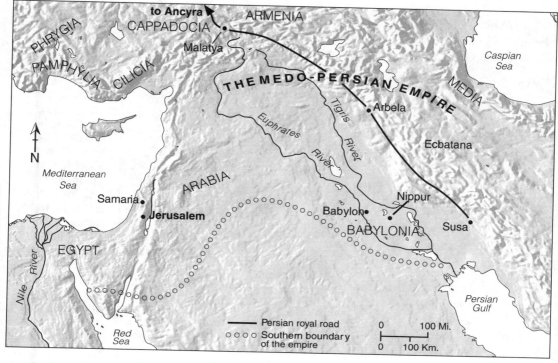

THE MEDO-PERSIAN EMPIRE

The Medo-Persian Empire included the lands of Media and Persia, much of the area shown on this map and more. The Jewish exiles were concentrated in the area around Nippur in the Babylonian province. The decree by King Cyrus that allowed the Israelites to return to their homeland and rebuild the Temple was discovered in the palace at Ecbatana.

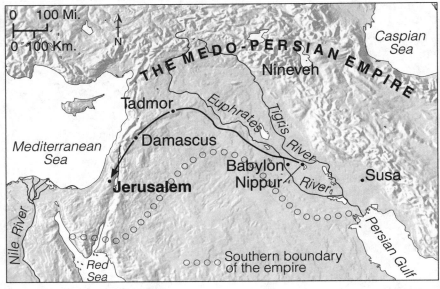

EZRA'S JOURNEY

Ezra 7:1–8:36

Ezra led a second group of exiles back to Judah and Jerusalem about 80 years after the first group. He traveled the dangerous route without military escort (8:22), but the people prayed and, under Ezra's godly leadership, arrived safely in Jerusalem after several months.

Copyright © 2001 by Tyndale House Publishers

NEHEMIAH

MEGATHEMES IN NEHEMIAH

Theme	Explanation	Importance
Vision	Although the Jews completed the Temple in 515 B.C., the city walls remained in shambles for the next 70 years. These walls represented power, protection, and beauty to the city of Jerusalem. They were also desperately needed to protect the Temple from attack and to ensure the continuity of worship. God put the desire to rebuild the walls in Nehemiah's heart, giving him a vision for the work.	Does God have a vision for us? Are there "walls" that need to be built today? God still wants his people to be united and trained to do his work. As we recognize deep needs in our world, God can give us the vision and desire to "build." With that vision, we can mobilize others to pray and put together a plan of action.
Prayer	Both Nehemiah and Ezra responded to problems with prayer. When Nehemiah began his work, he recognized the problem, immediately prayed, and then acted on the problem.	Prayer is still God's mighty force in solving problems today. Prayer and action go hand in hand. Through prayer, God guides our preparation, teamwork, and diligent efforts to carry out his will.
Leadership	Nehemiah demonstrated excellent leadership. He was spiritually ready to heed God's call. He used careful planning, teamwork, problem solving, and courage to get the work done. Although he had tremendous faith, he never avoided the extra work necessary for good leadership.	Being God's leader is not just gaining recognition, holding a position, or being the boss. It requires planning, hard work, courage, and perseverance. Positive expectations are never a substitute for doing the difficult work. And in order to lead others, you need to listen for God's direction in your own life.
Problems	After the work began, Nehemiah faced scorn, slander, and threats from enemies, as well as fear, conflict, and discouragement from his own workers. Although these problems were difficult, they did not stop Nehemiah from finishing the work.	When difficulties come, there is a tendency for conflict and discouragement to set in. We must recognize that there are no triumphs without troubles. When problems arise, we must face them squarely and press on to complete God's work.
Repentance/ Revival	Although God had enabled them to build the wall, the work wasn't complete until the people rebuilt their lives spiritually. Ezra instructed the people in God's Word. As they listened, they recognized the sin in their lives, admitted it, and took steps to remove it.	Recognizing and admitting sin are not enough; revival must result in reform, or it is merely the expression of enthusiasm. God does not want halfhearted measures. We must not only remove sin from our lives but also ask God to move into the center of all we do.

HOW NEHEMIAH USED PRAYER / *Nehemiah 1:4-11*

Reference	Occasion	Summary of His Prayer	What Prayer Accomplished	Our Prayers
1:4-11	After receiving the bad news about the state of Jerusalem's walls	Recognized God's holiness. Asked for a hearing. Confessed sin. Asked for specific help in approaching the king.	Included God in Nehemiah's plans and concerns. Prepared Nehemiah's heart and gave God room to work	How often do you pour out your heart to God? How often do you give him a specific request to answer?
2:4	During his conversation with the king	"Here's where you can help, God!"	Put the expected results in God's hands	Giving God credit for what happens before it happens keeps us from taking more credit than we should.
4:4-5	After being taunted and ridiculed by Tobiah and Sanballat	"They're mocking you, God. You decide what to do with them."	Expressed anger to God, but Nehemiah did not take matters into his own hands	We are prone to do exactly the opposite—take matters into our hands and not tell God how we feel.
4:9	After threats of attack by enemies	"We are in your hands, God. We'll keep our weapons handy in case you want us to use them."	Showed trust in God even while taking necessary precautions	Trusting God does not mean we do nothing. Action does not mean we do not trust.
6:9	Responding to threats	"O Lord God, please strengthen me!"	Showed Nehemiah's reliance on God for emotional and mental stability	How often do you ask God for help when under pressure?
13:29	Reflecting on the actions of his enemies	Asked God to deal with the enemies and their evil plans	Took away the compulsion to get revenge, and entrusted justice to God	When did you last settle a desire for revenge by turning the matter over to God?
5:19; 13:14, 22, 31	Reflecting on his own efforts to serve God	"Remember me, God."	Kept clear in Nehemiah's mind his own motives for action	How many of your actions today will be done with the purpose of pleasing God?

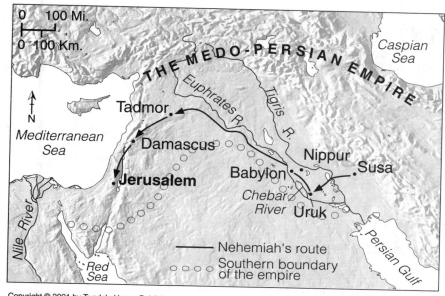

NEHEMIAH GOES TO JERUSALEM

Nehemiah 1:1–2:20

Nehemiah worked in Susa as a personal assistant for the king of the vast Medo-Persian Empire. When he heard that the rebuilding projects in Jerusalem were progressing slowly, he asked the king if he could go there to help his people complete the task of rebuilding their city's walls. The king agreed to let him go; so he left as soon as possible, traveling along much the same route Ezra had taken.

Copyright © 2001 by Tyndale House Publishers

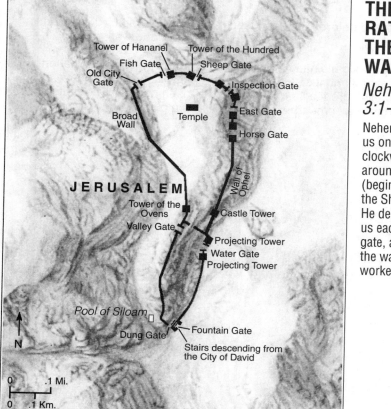

THE RESTORATION OF THE CITY WALLS

Nehemiah 3:1-32

Nehemiah takes us on a counter-clockwise tour around Jerusalem (beginning with the Sheep Gate). He describes for us each section, gate, and tower on the wall and who worked to rebuild it.

Copyright © 2001 by Tyndale House Publishers

NEHEMIAH

GOING HOME: TWO GREAT JOURNEYS OF ISRAEL / Nehemiah 2

What about the Journeys?	The Exodus	The Return from Exile
Where were they?	Egypt (430 years)	Babylon (70 years)
How many?	About 1 million	60,000
How long did the journey take them?	40 years and 2 attempts	100 years and 3 journeys
Who led them?	Moses/Aaron/Joshua	Zerubbabel/Ezra/Nehemiah
What was their purpose?	To reclaim the Promised Land	To rebuild the Temple and city of Jerusalem
What obstacles did they face?	Red Sea/Wilderness/Enemies	Ruins/Limited Resources/Enemies
What failures did they experience?	Complaining/Disobedience/Retreat—all of which turned a journey of a few weeks into a 40-year ordeal	Fear/Discouragement/Apathy—all of which turned a project of a few months into one that required a century to complete
What successes did they have?	Eventually entered the Promised Land	Eventually rebuilt Jerusalem's Temple and wall
What lessons did they learn?	God will build his nation. God is both faithful and just. God will accomplish great acts to make his promises come true.	God will preserve his nation. God will continue to have a chosen people, a home for them, and a plan to offer himself to them.

ESTHER

MEGATHEMES IN ESTHER

Theme	Explanation	Importance
God's Sovereignty	The book of Esther tells of the circumstances that were essential to the survival of God's people in Persia. These "circumstances" were not the result of chance but of God's grand design. God is sovereign over every area of life.	With God in charge, we can take courage. He can guide us through the circumstances we face in our lives. We should expect God to display his power in carrying out his will. As we unite our life's purposes to God's purpose, we benefit from his sovereign care.
Racial Hatred	The Jews in Persia had been a minority since their deportation from Judah 100 years earlier. Haman was a descendant of King Agag, an enemy of the Jews. Lust for power and pride drove Haman to hate Mordecai, Esther's cousin. Haman convinced the king to kill all the Jews.	Racial hatred is always sinful. We must never condone it in any form. Every person on earth has intrinsic worth because God created people in his own image. Therefore, God's people must stand against racism whenever and wherever it occurs.
Deliverance	In February or March, the Jews celebrate the Festival of Purim, which symbolizes God's deliverance. *Purim* means "lots," such as those used by Haman to set the date for the extermination of all Jews from Persia. But God overruled, using Queen Esther to intercede on behalf of the Jews.	Because God is in control of history, he is never frustrated by any turn of events or human action. He is able to save us from the evil of this world and deliver us from sin and death. Because we trust God, we are not to fear what people may do to us; instead, we are to be confident in God's control.
Action	Faced with death, Esther and Mordecai set aside their own fear and took action. Esther risked her life by asking King Xerxes to save the Jews. They were not paralyzed by fear.	When outnumbered and powerless, it is natural for us to feel helpless. Esther and Mordecai resisted this temptation and acted with courage. It is not enough to know that God is in control; we must act with self-sacrifice and courage to follow God's guidance.
Wisdom	The Jews were a minority in a world hostile to them. It took great wisdom for Mordecai to survive. Serving as a faithful official of the king, Mordecai took steps to understand and work with the Persian law. Yet he did not compromise his integrity.	It takes great wisdom to survive in a nonbelieving world. In a setting that is for the most part hostile to Christianity, we can demonstrate wisdom by giving respect to what is true and good and by humbly standing against what is wrong.

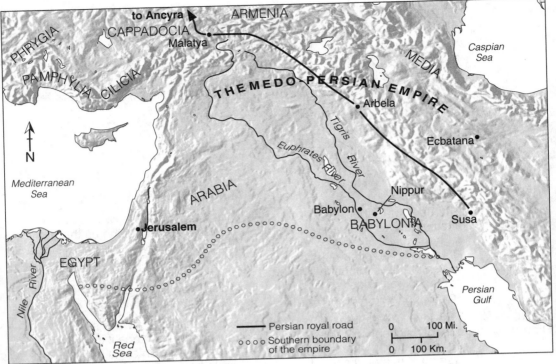

THE WORLD OF ESTHER'S DAY
Esther 1:1-4; 10:1-3

Esther lived in the capital of the vast Medo-Persian Empire, which incorporated the provinces of Media and Persia, as well as the previous empires of Assyria and Babylon. Esther, a Jewess, was chosen by King Xerxes to be his queen. The story of how she saved her people takes place in the palace in Susa.

GOD BEHIND THE SCENES IN ESTHER / *Esther 2:21, 23*

Although God's name is not mentioned in the Hebrew text of Esther, he makes himself known in these ways:

Indirect References . . 2:17 . . . . Esther, who worshiped God, became queen.

4:14 . . . . God's existence and his power over the affairs of people are assumed.

4:16 . . . . Fasting was a distinct spiritual activity usually connected with prayer.

Divine Incidents . . . . 2:21, 23 . . Mordecai overhears a death plot and saves the king's life.
The book of Esther is filled with divine interventions

6:1 . . . . Xerxes can't sleep and decides to read a history book.

6:2 . . . . Xerxes reads the exact page needed for the moment, reminding him of an unpaid reward to Mordecai.

7:9-10. . . Haman's plan is exactly reversed—the intended victims are the victors.

Why was God's name hidden in the book of Esther? There were many gods in the Middle East and Persian Empire. Usually, their names were mentioned in official documents in order to control the peoples who worshiped those particular gods. The Jews were unique in being the people of one God. A story about them was naturally a story about God, for even the name "Jew" carried with it the connotation of one who worshiped Yahweh.

HOW GOD WORKS IN THE WORLD / *Esther 8*

God's Will	**What God wants done—he works through . . .**		
	↞ *Natural Order*	↞ *Miracles*	↞ *Providence*
God's Action	↞ God set into action through Creation a normal working of his universe. He also revealed his expectations of people through his Word and people's consciences.	↞ God breaks into the natural order to respond to the expressed needs of people.	↞ God overrules the natural order to accomplish an act that people may or may not have requested.
Examples from Esther	↞ God gave Esther natural beauty.	↞ God allowed Esther to speak to the king.	↞ God allowed Mordecai to overhear a plot.
	↟ Esther planned a way to save her people.	↟ The people prayed and fasted.	↟ Mordecai trusted God to accomplish what was impossible in human terms.
People's Will	**What people want done—they either . . .**		
	↟ *Plan*	↟ *Pray*	↟ *Trust and Obey*
Action We Can Take	↟ Can make plans based on the order and dependability of God's creation. Know and obey his words.	↟ Can ask God to intervene in certain affairs while realizing that our knowledge and perspective are limited.	↟ Can trust that God is in control even when circumstances seem to indicate that he is not.
	or . . .		
Mistakes We Can Make	↞ *Disobey*	↞ *Demand*	↞ *Despair*
	↞ Can violate the natural order; disobey God's commands.	↞ Can assume that we understand what is needed and expect God to agree and answer our prayers that way.	↞ Can assume God doesn't answer prayer or respond to our needs and live as though there is nothing but the natural order.

JOB

MEGATHEMES IN JOB

Theme	Explanation	Importance
Suffering	Through no fault of his own, Job lost his wealth, children, and health. Even his friends were convinced that Job had brought this suffering upon himself. For Job, the greatest trial was not the pain or the loss; it was not being able to understand why God allowed him to suffer.	Suffering can be, but is not always, a penalty for sin. In the same way, prosperity is not always a reward for being good. Those who love God are not exempt from trouble. Although we may not be able to understand fully the pain we experience, it can lead us to rediscover God.
Satan's Attacks	Satan attempted to drive a wedge between Job and God by getting Job to believe that God's governing of the world was not just and good. Satan had to ask God for permission to take Job's wealth, children, and health away. Satan was limited to what God allowed.	We must learn to recognize but not fear Satan's attacks because Satan cannot exceed the limits that God sets. Don't let any experience drive a wedge between you and God. Although you can't control how Satan may attack, you can always choose how you will respond when it happens.
God's Goodness	God is all-wise and all-powerful. His will is perfect, yet he doesn't always act in ways that we understand. Job's suffering didn't make sense because everyone believed good people were supposed to prosper. When Job was at the point of despair, God spoke to him, showing him his great power and wisdom.	Although God is present everywhere, at times he may seem far away. This may cause us to feel alone and to doubt his care for us. We should serve God for who he is, not what we feel. He is never insensitive to our suffering. Because God is sufficient, we must hold on to him.
Pride	Job's friends were certain that they were correct in their judgment of him. God rebuked them for their pride and arrogance. Human wisdom is always partial and temporary, so undue pride in our own conclusions is sin.	We must be careful not to judge others who are suffering. We may be demonstrating the sin of pride. We must be cautious in maintaining the certainty of our own conclusions about how God treats us. When we congratulate ourselves for being right, we become proud.
Trusting	God alone knew the purpose behind Job's suffering, and yet he never explained it to Job. In spite of this, Job never gave up on God— even in the midst of suffering. He never placed his hope in his experience, his wisdom, his friends, or his wealth. Job focused on God.	Job showed the kind of trust we are to have. When everything is stripped away, we are to recognize that God is all we ever really had. We should not demand that God explain everything. God gives us himself, but not all the details of his plans. We must remember that this life, with all its pain, is not our final destiny.

THE SOURCES OF SUFFERING / *Job 2*

Sources	Who is Responsible	Who is Affected	Needed Response
My sin	I am	Myself and others	Repentance and confession to God
Others' sin	Person who sinned and others who allowed the sin	Probably many people, including those who sinned	Active resistance to the sinful behavior, while accepting the sinner
Avoidable physical (or natural) disaster	Persons who ignore the facts or refuse to take precautions	Most of those exposed to the cause	Prevent them if possible; be prepared if they can't be prevented
Unavoidable physical (or natural) disaster	God, Satan	Most of those present	Ongoing trust in God's faithfulness

When suffering or troubles happen, do they always come from Satan? In Job's story, his series of tragedies did come from Satan, but this is not always the case. The chart above demonstrates the four main causes of suffering. Any one of these or a combination of them may create suffering. If knowing why we are suffering will teach us to avoid the cause, then the causes are worth knowing. However, it is most important to know how to respond during suffering.

ADVICE FROM FRIENDS / *Job 4*

Overwhelmed by suffering, Job was not comforted but condemned by his friends. Each of their views represents a well-known way to understand suffering. God proves that each explanation given by Job's friends has less than the whole answer.

Who They Were	Reference	How They Helped	Their Reasoning	Their Advice	Job's Response	God's Response
Eliphaz the Temanite	Job 4–5; 15; 22		Job is suffering because he has sinned.	"Go to God and present your case to him." (5:8)	"Stop assuming my guilt." (6:29)	
Bildad the Shuhite	Job 8; 18; 25	They sat in silence with Job for seven days. (2:11-13)	Job won't admit he sinned, so he's still suffering.	"How long will you go on like this?" (8:2)	"I will say to God, . . . Tell me the charge you are bringing against me." (10:2)	God rebukes Job's friends. (42:7)
Zophar the Naamathite	Job 11; 20		Job's sin deserves even more suffering than he's experienced.	"Get rid of your sins." (11:13-14)	"I will be proved innocent." (13:18)	
Elihu the Buzite	Job 32–37		God is using suffering to mold and train Job.	"Keep silent and I will teach you wisdom." (33:33)	No response	God does not directly address Elihu.
God	Job 38–41	Confronted Job with the need to be content even though he didn't know why he was suffering	Did not explain the reason for the pain	"Do you still want to argue with the Almighty?" (40:2)	"I was talking about things I did not understand." (42:3-5)	

WHERE CAN WISDOM BE FOUND? / *Job 28:20-28*

Job and his friends differed in their ideas of how people become wise.

Person	His Source of Wisdom	Attitude toward God
Eliphaz	Wisdom is learned by observing and experiencing life. He based his advice to Job on his confident, firsthand knowledge (4:7-8; 5:3, 27).	"I have personally observed how God works and have figured him out."
Bildad	Wisdom is inherited from the past. Trustworthy knowledge is secondhand. He based his advice to Job on traditional proverbs and sayings that he frequently quoted (8:8-9; 18:5-21).	"Those who have gone before us figured God out, and all we have to do is use that knowledge."
Zophar	Wisdom belongs to the wise. He based his advice on his wisdom that had no other source than himself (11:6; 20:1-29).	"The wise know what God is like, but there aren't many of us around."
Job	God is the source of wisdom, and the first step toward wisdom is to fear God (28:20-28).	"God reveals his wisdom to those who humbly trust him."

HOW SUFFERING AFFECTS US / *Job 30*

Suffering is helpful when:

We turn to God for understanding, endurance, and deliverance

We ask important questions we might not take time to think about in our normal routine

We are prepared by it to identify with and comfort others who suffer

We are open to being helped by others who are obeying God

We are ready to learn from a trustworthy God

We realize we can identify with what Christ suffered on the cross for us

We are sensitized to the amount of suffering in the world

Suffering is harmful when:

We become hardened and reject God

We refuse to ask any questions and miss any lessons that might be good for us

We allow it to make us self-centered and selfish

We withdraw from the help others can give

We reject the fact that God can bring good out of calamity

We accuse God of being unjust and perhaps lead others to reject him

We refuse to be open to any changes in our lives

GOD SPEAKS / *Job 38*

On various occasions in the Old Testament, God chose to communicate audibly with individuals. God will always find a way to make contact with those who want to know him. Some of those occasions are listed here.

To Whom He Spoke	What He Said	Reference
Adam and Eve	Confronted them about sin	Genesis 3:8-13
Noah	Gave him directions about building the boat	Genesis 6:13-22; 7:1; 8:15-17
Abraham	Commanded him to follow God's leading and promised to bless him	Genesis 12:1-9
	Tested his obedience by commanding him to sacrifice his son	Genesis 22:1-14
Jacob	Permitted him to go to Egypt	Genesis 46:1-4
Moses	Sent him to lead the people out of Egypt	Exodus 3:1-10
	Gave him the Ten Commandments	Exodus 19:1–20:20
Moses, Aaron, Miriam	Pronounced judgment on a family conflict	Numbers 12:1-15
Joshua	Promised to be with him as he was with Moses	Joshua 1:1-9
Samuel	Chose him to be his spokesman	1 Samuel 3:1-18
Isaiah	Sent him to the people with his message	Isaiah 6:1-13
Jeremiah	Encouraged him to be his prophet	Jeremiah 1:4-10
Ezekiel	Sent him to Israel to warn them of coming judgment	Ezekiel 2:1-8

GOD'S JUSTICE / *Job 38*

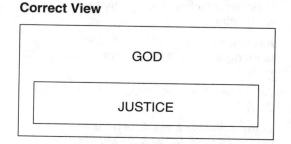

Wrong View

> LAW OF FAIRNESS

> GOD

Correct View

> GOD
>> JUSTICE

There is a law of fairness or justice that is higher and more absolute than God. It is binding even for God. God must act in response to that law in order to be fair. Our response is to appeal to that law.

God himself is the standard of justice. He uses his power according to his own moral perfection. Thus, whatever he does is fair, even if we don't understand it. Our response is to appeal directly to him.

FOUR VIEWS OF SUFFERING / Job 41

Satan's view . . . . People believe in God only when they are prospering and not suffering. This is wrong.

The view of Job's three friends . . . Suffering is God's judgment for sin. This is not always true.

Elihu's view . . . . Suffering is God's way to teach, discipline, and refine. This is true, but an incomplete explanation.

God's view . . . . Suffering causes us to trust God for who he is, not what he does.

JOB AND JESUS / Job 42

The book of Job is intimately tied to the New Testament because Job's questions and problems are answered perfectly in Jesus Christ.

Subject/Reference in Job	How Jesus is the Answer
Someone must help us approach God (9:32-33)	1 Timothy 2:5
Is there life after death? (14:14)	John 11:25
There is one in heaven working on our behalf (16:19)	Hebrews 9:24
There is one who can save us from judgment (19:25)	Hebrews 7:24-25
What is important in life? (21:7-15)	Matthew 16:26; John 3:16
Where do we find God? (23:3-5)	John 14:9

WHEN WE SUFFER / Job 42

Here are six questions to ask ourselves when we suffer, and what to do if the answer is yes.

Questions	Our Response
Am I being punished by God for sin?	Confess known sin.
Is Satan attacking me as I try to survive as a Christian?	Call on God for strength.
Am I being prepared for a special service, learning to be compassionate to those who suffer?	Resist self-pity. Ask God to open up doors of opportunity and help you discover others who suffer as you do.
Am I specifically selected for testing, like Job?	Accept help from the body of believers. Trust God to work his purpose through you.
Is my suffering a result of natural consequences for which I am not directly responsible?	Recognize that in a sinful world, both good and evil people will suffer. But the good person has a promise from God that his or her suffering will one day come to an end.
Is my suffering because of some unknown reason?	Don't draw inward from the pain. Proclaim your faith in God, know that he cares, and wait patiently for his aid.

PSALMS

MEGATHEMES IN PSALMS

Theme	Explanation	Importance
Praise	Psalms are songs of praise to God as our Creator, Sustainer, and Redeemer. Praise is recognizing, appreciating, and expressing God's greatness.	Focusing our thoughts on God moves us to praise him. The more we know him, the more we can appreciate what he has done for us.
God's power	God is all-powerful; and he always acts at the right time. He is sovereign over every situation. God's power is shown by the ways he reveals himself in creation, history, and his Word.	When we feel powerless, God can help us. His strength can overcome the despair of any pain or trial. We can always pray that he will deliver, protect, and sustain us.
Forgiveness	Many psalms are intense prayers asking God for forgiveness. God forgives us when we confess our sin and turn from it.	Because God forgives us, we can pray to him honestly and directly. When we receive his forgiveness, we move from alienation to intimacy, from guilt to love.
Thankfulness	We are grateful to God for his personal concern, help, and mercy. Not only does he protect, guide, and forgive us, but his creation provides everything we need.	When we realize how we benefit from knowing God, we can fully express our thanks to him. By thanking him often, we develop spontaneity in our prayer life.
Trust	God is faithful and just. When we put our trust in him, he quiets our hearts. Because he has been faithful throughout history, we can trust him in times of trouble.	People can be unfair and friends may desert us. But we can trust God. Knowing God intimately drives away doubt, fear, and loneliness.

REASONS TO READ PSALMS / *Psalm 1*

When you want . . .	Read . . .
to know how to come to God each day	Psalm 5
to understand yourself more clearly	Psalm 8
to please God	Psalm 15
to find comfort	Psalm 23
to learn more about God	Psalm 24
to be forgiven for your sins	Psalm 51
to learn a new song	Psalm 92
to meet God intimately	Psalm 103
to know why you should worship God	Psalm 104
to understand why you should read the Bible	Psalm 119
to give thanks to God	Psalm 136
to learn a new prayer	Psalm 136
to feel worthwhile	Psalm 139
to give praise to God	Psalm 145
to know that God is in control	Psalm 146

God's Word was written to be studied, understood, and applied, and the book of Psalms lends itself most directly to application. We understand the psalms best when we "stand under" them and allow them to flow over us like a rain shower. We may turn to Psalms looking for something, but sooner or later we will meet Someone. As we read and memorize the psalms, we will gradually discover how much they are already part of us. They put into words our deepest hurts, longings, thoughts, and prayers. They gently push us toward being what God designed us to be—people loving and living for him.

PSALMS FROM DAVID'S LIFE / *Psalm 3*

Of the more than 70 psalms attributed to David, at least 14 of them are connected with specific events in his life. From them we see an outline of a growing relationship with God. They are listed here, roughly in chronological order.

Event in David's Life	Reference	Psalm	What David Learned about God
When Saul sent men to David's home to kill him	1 Samuel 19	59	God is my refuge.
While running from Saul	1 Samuel 21	34	I will praise the Lord at all times.
While running from Saul	1 Samuel 21	56	When I am afraid, I put my trust in God.
While hiding in the cave of Adullam	1 Samuel 22	142	God is my refuge.
After learning that Doeg had murdered 85 priests and their families	1 Samuel 22	52	God will bring evil people down to everlasting ruin.
When the Ziphites tried to betray him	1 Samuel 23	54	God is my helper.
While hiding in a cave	1 Samuel 24	57	I will take refuge in the shadow of God's wings until the violent storm has passed.
While hiding in the wilderness of En-gedi	1 Samuel 24	63	My soul thirsts for God; his right hand holds me securely.
When Saul's pursuit was over	2 Samuel 22	18	To the faithful, God shows himself faithful.
After being confronted about his adultery with Bathsheba	2 Samuel 12	51	The sacrifices of God are a broken spirit; a broken and repentant heart he will not despise.
During Absalom's rebellion	2 Samuel 15	3	From the Lord comes victory.
During Absalom's rebellion	2 Samuel 15	7	He is a righteous God who searches minds and hearts and can bring to an end the violence of the wicked and make the righteous secure.

TROUBLES AND COMPLAINTS IN PSALMS / Psalm 13

We can relate to the psalms because they express our feelings. We all face troubles, as did the psalm writers hundreds of years ago, and we often respond as they did. In Psalm 3, David told God how he felt about the odds against him. But within three verses, the king realized that God's presence and care made the odds meaningless. This experience is repeated in many of the psalms. Usually, the hope and confidence in God outweigh the fear and suffering; sometimes they do not. Still, the psalm writers consistently poured out their thoughts and emotions to God. When they felt abandoned by God, they told him so. When they were impatient with how slowly God seemed to be answering their prayers, they also told him so. Because they recognized the difference between themselves and God, they were free to be men and to be honest with their Creator. That is why so many of the dark psalms end in the light. The psalmists started by expressing their feelings and ended up remembering to whom they were speaking!

Although we have much in common with the psalmists, we may differ in two ways: We might not tell God what we are really thinking and feeling; therefore, we also might not recognize, even faintly, who is listening to our prayers!

Notice this pattern as you read Psalms, and put the psalmists' insights to the test. You may well find that your awareness and appreciation of God will grow as you are honest with him. (See Psalms 3; 6; 13; 31; 37; 64; 77; 102; 121; 142.)

PSALMS TO LEARN AND LOVE / Psalm 24

Almost everyone, whether religious or not, has heard Psalm 23 because it is quoted so frequently. Many other psalms are also familiar because they are quoted in music, in literature, or in the words of the worship service.

The psalms we know and love are the ones that come into our minds when we need them. They inspire us, comfort us, correct us just when we need a word from the Lord. If you want to begin memorizing psalms, start with some of these favorites. Memorize the whole psalm or just the verses that speak most directly to you. Or read the psalm aloud several times a day until it is part of you.

Psalms to bring us into God's presence	29; 95:1-7; 96; 100
Psalms about goodness	1; 19; 24; 133; 136; 139
Psalms of praise	8; 97; 103; 107; 113; 145; 150
Psalms of repentance and forgiveness	32:1-5; 51; 103
Psalms for times of trouble	3; 14; 22; 37:1-11; 42; 46; 53; 116:1-7
Psalms of confidence and trust	23; 40:1-4; 91; 119:11; 121; 127

CHRIST IN THE PSALMS / *Psalm 22*

Both the Jewish and Christian faiths have long believed that many psalms referred as much to the promised Messiah as they did to events at the time. Because the Messiah was to be a descendant of David, it was expected that many of the royal psalms would apply to him. Christians noted how many of the passages seemed to describe in detail events from Christ's life and death. Jesus himself frequently quoted from Psalms. Almost everything that happened at the Crucifixion and most of Jesus' words during his final hours were prophesied in Psalms.

The following is a list of the main references in Psalms pertaining to Christ.

Reference in Psalms	Reference to Christ	Fulfillment in the New Testament
2:7	The Messiah will be God's Son	Hebrews 1:5-6
16:8-10	He will rise from the dead	Luke 24:5-7
22:1-21	He will experience agony on the cross	Matthew 26; 27
22:15	He thirsts while on the cross	John 19:28
22:18	Evil men throw dice for his clothing	Matthew 27:35; John 19:23-24
22:22	He will declare God's name	Hebrews 2:12
34:20	His bones would not be broken	John 19:36-37
40:6-8	He came to do God's will	Hebrews 10:5-7
41:9	His close friend would betray him	Luke 22:48
45:6-7	His throne will last forever	Hebrews 1:8-9
68:18	He ascended into heaven	Ephesians 4:8-10
69:9	He is zealous for God	John 2:17
69:21	He was offered vinegar for his thirst on the cross	Matthew 27:48
89:3-4, 35-36	He will be a descendant of David	Luke 1:31-33
96:13	He will return to judge the world	1 Thessalonians 1:10
110:1	He is David's son and David's Lord	Matthew 22:44
110:4	He is the eternal priest-king	Hebrews 6:20
118:22	He is rejected by many but accepted by God	1 Peter 2:7-8

CONFESSION, REPENTANCE, AND FORGIVENESS IN PSALMS
Psalm 32

Over the centuries, many believers, overcome by an awareness of their own sins, have found in the words of the penitential (repentance) psalms a ray of hope. The psalmists shared with God the depth of their sorrow and repentance, as well as the height of joy at being forgiven. They rejoiced in the knowledge that God would respond to confession and repentance with complete forgiveness. We who live on the other side of the cross of Christ can rejoice even more because we understand more. God has shown us that he is willing to forgive because his judgment on sin was satisfied by Christ's death on the cross.

As you read these psalms, note the pattern followed by the psalmists in responding to God: (1) They recognized their sinfulness and tendency to do wrong; (2) they realized that sin was rebellion against God himself; (3) they admitted their sins to God; (4) they trusted in God's willingness to forgive; and (5) they accepted his forgiveness. Use these psalms as a reminder of how easy it is to drift away from God and fall into sin, and what is needed to reestablish that fellowship.

Selected psalms that emphasize these themes are Psalms 6; 14; 31; 32; 38; 41; 51; 102; 130; 143.

PSALMS THAT HAVE INSPIRED HYMNS / Psalm 46

Psalm 23	The King of Love My Shepherd Is My Shepherd Shall Supply My Need The Lord Is My Shepherd
Psalm 46	A Mighty Fortress Is Our God
Psalm 61	Hiding in Thee (O safe to the Rock that is higher than I . . .)
Psalm 87	Glorious Things of Thee Are Spoken
Psalm 90	O God, Our Help in Ages Past
Psalm 100	All People That on Earth Do Dwell Before Jehovah's Awful Throne
Psalm 103	Praise to the Lord, the Almighty
Psalm 104	O Worship the King, All Glorious Above
Psalm 126	Bringing in the Sheaves

PRAYER IN THE BOOK OF PSALMS / *Psalm 79*

Prayer is human communication with God. Psalms could be described as a collection of song-prayers. Probably the most striking feature of these prayers is their unedited honesty. The words often express our own feelings—feelings that we would prefer no one, much less God, ever knew. Making these psalms our prayers can teach us a great deal about how God wants us to communicate with him. Too often we give God a watered-down version of our feelings, hoping we won't offend him or make him curious about our motives. As we use the psalms to express our feelings, we learn that honesty, openness, and sincerity are valuable to God.

Following are several types of prayers with examples from Psalms. Note that the psalm writers communicated with God in a variety of ways for a variety of reasons. Each of us is invited to communicate with God. Using the psalms will enrich your personal prayer life.

Prayers of:	Psalms:
Praise to God	100; 113; 117
Thanksgiving by a community	67; 75; 136
Thanksgiving by an individual	18; 30; 32
Request by the community	79; 80; 123
Request by an individual	3; 55; 86
Sorrow by the community	44; 74; 137
Sorrow by an individual	5; 6; 120
Anger	35; 109; 140
Confession	6; 32; 51
Faith	11; 16; 23

JUSTICE IN THE BOOK OF PSALMS / *Psalm 94*

Justice is a major theme in Psalms. The Psalmists praise God because he is just; they plead for him to intervene and bring justice where there is oppression and wickedness; they condemn the wicked who trust in their wealth; they extol the righteous who are just toward their neighbors.

Justice in Psalms is more than honesty. It is active intervention on behalf of the helpless, especially the poor. The psalmists do not merely wish the poor could be given what they need—they plead with God to destroy those nations that are subverting justice and oppressing God's people.

Here are some example of psalms that speak about justice. As you read them, ask yourself, Who is my neighbor? Does my lifestyle—my work, my play, my buying habits, my giving—help or hurt people who have less than I do? What one thing could I do this week to help a helpless person?

Selected psalms that emphasize this theme are Psalms 7; 9; 15; 37; 50; 72; 75; 82; 94; 145.

HOW GOD IS DESCRIBED IN PSALMS / Psalm 104

Most of the psalms speak to God or about God. Because they were composed in a variety of situations, various facets of God's character are mentioned. Here is a sample of God's characteristics as understood and experienced by the psalm writers. As you read these psalms, ask yourself if this is the God you know.

God is . . .	Reference
All-knowing and ever present	Psalm 139
Beautiful and desirable	Psalms 27; 36; 45
Creator	Psalms 8; 104; 148
Good and generous	Psalms 34; 81; 107
Great and sovereign	Psalms 33; 89; 96
Holy	Psalms 66; 99; 145
Loving and faithful	Psalms 23; 42; 51
Merciful and forgiving	Psalms 32; 111; 130
Powerful	Psalms 76; 89; 93
Willing to reveal his will, law, and direction	Psalms 1; 19; 119
Righteous and just	Psalms 71; 97; 113
Spirit	Psalms 104; 139; 143

HISTORY IN THE BOOK OF PSALMS / Psalm 105

For the original hearers, the historical psalms were vivid reminders of God's past acts on behalf of Israel. These history songs were written for passing on important lessons to succeeding generations. They celebrated the many promises God had made and faithfully kept; they also recounted the faithlessness of the people.

We cannot read this ancient history without reflecting on how consistently God's people failed to learn from the past. They repeatedly turned from fresh examples of God's faithfulness and forgiveness only to plunge back into sin. God can use these psalms to remind us how often we do exactly the same thing: Having every reason to live for God, we choose instead to live for everything but God. If we paid more attention to "his story," we wouldn't make so many mistakes in our own stories.

Selected historical psalms include Psalms 68; 78; 95; 105; 106; 111; 114; 135; 136; 149.

ANGER AND VENGEANCE IN THE BOOK OF PSALMS / *Psalm 140*

Several psalms shock those familiar with New Testament teachings. The psalmists didn't hesitate to demand God's justice and make vivid suggestions on how he might carry it out. Apparently, no subject was unsuitable for discussion with God, but our tendency is to avoid the subjects of anger and vengeance in the book of Psalms.

To understand the words of anger and vengeance, we need to understand several things:

(1) The judgments asked for are to be carried out by God and are written out of intense personal and national suffering. The people are unable or unwilling to take revenge themselves and are asking God to intervene. Because few of us have suffered intense cruelty on a personal or national level, we find it difficult to grasp these outbursts.

(2) These writers were intimately aware of God's justice. Some of their words are efforts to vividly imagine what God might allow to happen to those who had harmed his people.

(3) If we dared to write down our thoughts while being unjustly attacked or suffering cruelty, we might be shocked at our own bold desire for vengeance. We would be surprised at how much we have in common with these men of old. The psalmists did not have Jesus' command to pray for one's enemies, but they did point to the right place to start. We are challenged to pay back good for evil, but until we respond to this challenge, we will not know how much we need God's help in order to forgive others.

(4) There is a helpful parallel between the psalms of anger and the psalms of vengeance. The "angry" psalms are intense and graphic, but they are directed at God. He is boldly told how disappointing it is when he turns his back on his people or acts too slowly. But while these thoughts and feelings were sincerely expressed, we know from the psalms themselves that these passing feelings were followed by renewed confidence in God's faithfulness. It is reasonable to expect the same of the "vengeance" psalms. We read, for example, David's angry outburst against Saul's pursuit in Psalm 59, yet we know that David never took personal revenge on Saul. The psalmists freely spoke their minds to God, having confidence that he could sort out what was meant and what was felt. Pray with that same confidence—God can be trusted with your heart.

Selected psalms that emphasize these themes are Psalms 10; 23; 28; 35; 59; 69; 109; 137; 139; 140.

PRAISE IN THE BOOK OF PSALMS / *Psalm 145*

Most of the psalms are prayers, and most of the prayers include praise to God. Praise expresses admiration, appreciation, and thanks. Praise in the book of Psalms is often directed to God, and just as often the praise is shared with others. Considering all that God has done and does for us, what could be more natural than outbursts of heartfelt praise?

As you read Psalms, note the praise given to God, not only for what he does—his creation, his blessings, his forgiveness—but also for who he is—loving, just, faithful, forgiving, patient. Note also those times when the praise of God is shared with others and they, too, are encouraged to praise him. In what ways have you recently praised God or told others all that he has done for you?

Selected psalms that emphasize this theme are Psalms 8; 19; 30; 65; 84; 96; 100; 136; 145; 150.

WHERE TO GET HELP IN THE BOOK OF PSALMS / Psalm 150

When you feel . . .

Afraid: 3; 4; 27; 46; 49; 56; 91; 118

Alone: 9; 10; 12; 13; 27; 40; 43

"Burned out": 6; 63

Cheated: 41

Confused: 10; 12; 73

Depressed: 27; 34; 42; 43; 88; 143

Distressed: 13; 25; 31; 40; 107

Elated: 19; 96

Guilty: 19; 32; 38; 51

Hateful: 11

Impatient: 13; 27; 37; 40

Insecure: 3; 5; 12; 91

Insulted: 41; 70

Jealous: 37

Like quitting: 29; 43; 145

Lost: 23; 139

Overwhelmed: 25; 69; 142

Penitent/Sorry: 32; 51; 66

Proud: 14; 30; 49

Purposeless: 14; 25; 39; 49; 90

Sad: 13

Self-confident: 24

Tense: 4

Thankful: 118; 136; 138

Threatened: 3; 11; 17

Tired/Weak: 6; 13; 18; 28; 29; 40; 86

Trapped: 7; 17; 42; 88; 142

Unimportant: 8; 90; 139

Vengeful: 3; 7; 109

Worried: 37

Worshipful: 8; 19; 27; 29; 150

When you're facing . . .

Atheists: 10; 14; 19; 52; 53; 115

Competition: 133

Criticism: 35; 56; 120

Danger: 11

Death: 6; 71; 90

Decisions: 1; 119

Discrimination: 54

Doubts: 34; 37; 94

Enemies: 3; 25; 35; 41; 56; 59

Evil people: 10; 35; 36; 49; 52; 109; 140

Heresy: 14

Hypocrisy: 26; 28; 40; 50

Illness: 6; 139

Lies: 5; 12; 120

Old age: 71; 92

Persecution: 1; 3; 7; 56

Poverty: 9; 10; 12

Punishment: 6; 38; 39

Slander/Insults: 7; 15; 35; 43; 120

Slaughter: 6; 46; 83

Sorrow: 23; 34

Success: 18; 112; 127; 128

Temptation: 38; 141

Troubles: 34; 55; 86; 102; 142; 145

Verbal cruelty: 35; 120

When you want . . .

Acceptance: 139

Answers: 4; 17

Confidence: 46; 71

Courage: 11; 42

Fellowship with God: 5; 16; 25; 27; 37; 133

Forgiveness: 32; 38; 40; 51; 69; 86; 103; 130

Friendship: 16

Godliness: 15; 25

Guidance: 1; 5; 15; 19; 25; 32; 48

Healing: 6; 41

Hope: 16; 17; 18; 23; 27

Humility: 19; 147

Illumination: 19

Integrity: 24; 25

Joy: 9; 16; 28; 126

Justice: 2; 7; 14; 26; 37; 49; 58; 82

Knowledge: 2; 8; 18; 19; 25; 29; 97; 103

Leadership: 72

Miracles: 60; 111

Money: 15; 16; 17; 49

Peace: 3; 4

Perspective: 2; 11

Prayer: 5; 17; 27; 61

Protection: 3; 4; 7; 16; 17; 18; 23; 27; 31; 91; 121; 125

Provision: 23

Rest: 23; 27

Salvation: 26; 37; 49; 126

Stability: 11; 33; 46

Vindication: 9; 14; 28; 35; 109

Wisdom: 1; 16; 19; 64; 111

PROVERBS

MEGATHEMES IN PROVERBS

Theme	Explanation	Importance
Wisdom	God wants his people to be wise. Two kinds of people portray two contrasting paths of life. The fool is the wicked, stubborn person who hates or ignores God. The wise person seeks to know and love God.	When we choose God's way, he grants us wisdom. His Word, the Bible, leads us to live right, have right relationships, and make right decisions.
Relationships	Proverbs gives us advice for developing our personal relationships with friends, family members, and coworkers. In every relationship, we must show love, dedication, and high moral standards.	To relate to people, we need consistency, tact, and discipline to use the wisdom God gives us. If we don't treat others according to the wisdom God gives, our relationships will suffer.
Speech	What we say shows our real attitude toward others. How we talk reveals what we're really like. Our speech is a test of how wise we have become.	To be wise in our speech we need to use self-control. Our words should be honest and well chosen.
Work	God controls the final outcome of all we do. We are accountable to carry out our work with diligence and discipline, not laziness.	Because God evaluates how we live, we should work purposefully. We must never be lax or self-satisfied in using our skills.
Success	Although people work very hard for money and fame, God views success as having a good reputation, moral character, and the spiritual devotion to obey him.	A successful relationship with God counts for eternity. Everything else is perishable. All our resources, time, and talents come from God. We should strive to use them wisely.

UNDERSTANDING PROVERBS / *Proverbs 1*

Most often, proverbs are written in the form of couplets. These are constructed in three ways:

Type	Description	Key Word(s)	Examples
Contrasting	Meaning and application come from the differences or contrast between the two statements of the proverb.	"but"	10:3; 14:11, 18
Comparing	Meaning and application come from the similarities or comparison between the two statements of the proverb.	"as/so" "better/than" "like"	15:16-17; 22:7; 25:25
Complementing	Meaning and application come from the way the second statement complements the first.	"and"	11:16; 14:10, 17

WISDOM: APPLIED TRUTH / *Proverbs 4*

The book of Proverbs tells us about people who have wisdom and enjoy its benefits.

Reference	The Person Who Has Wisdom	Benefits of Wisdom
Proverbs 3–4 A father's instructions	Is kind Is loyal Trusts in the Lord Puts God first Turns away from evil Knows right from wrong Listens and learns Does what is right	Long, satisfying life Favor with God and people Reputation for good judgment Success Health, vitality Riches, honor, pleasure, peace Protection
Proverbs 8–9 Wisdom speaks	Discovers knowledge and discernment Hates pride, arrogance, and corruption Respects and fears God Gives good advice and has common sense Loves correction and is teachable Knows God	Riches, honor Justice Righteousness Life God's approval Constant learning Understanding

PEOPLE CALLED "WISE" IN THE BIBLE / *Proverbs 3*

The special description "wise" is used for 12 significant people in the Bible. They can be helpful models in our own pursuit of wisdom.

The Person	His or Her Role	Reference	How He or She Practiced Wisdom
Joseph	Wise leader	Acts 7:10	Prepared for a major famine; helped rule Egypt
Moses	Wise leader	Acts 7:20-22	Learned all the Egyptian wisdom, then graduated to God's lessons in wisdom to lead Israel out of Egypt
Bezalel	Wise artist	Exodus 31:1-5	Designed and supervised the construction of the Tabernacle and its utensils in the wilderness
Joshua	Wise leader	Deuteronomy 34:9	Learned by observing Moses, obeyed God, led the people into the Promised Land
David	Wise leader	2 Samuel 14:20	Never let his failures keep him from the source of wisdom—reverence for God
Abigail	Wise wife	1 Samuel 25:3	Managed her household well in spite of a mean and dishonest husband
Solomon	Wise leader	1 Kings 3:5-14; 4:29-34	Knew what to do even though he often failed to put his own wisdom into action
Daniel	Wise counselor	Daniel 5:11-12	Known as a man in touch with God; a solver of complex problems with God's help
Astrologers	Wise learners	Matthew 2:1-12	Not only received special knowledge of God's visit to earth but checked it out personally
Stephen	Wise leader	Acts 6:8-10	Organized the distribution of food to the Grecian widows; preached the gospel to the Jews
Paul	Wise messenger	2 Peter 3:15-16	Spent his life communicating God's love to all who would listen
Christ	Wise youth Wise Savior Wisdom of God	Luke 2:40, 52; 1 Corinthians 1:20-25	Not only lived a perfect life but died on the cross to save us and make God's wise plan of eternal life available to us

THINGS GOD HATES / *Proverbs 6:16-19*

The book of Proverbs notes 14 types of people and actions that God hates. Let these be guidelines of what we are *not* to be and do!

Violent people . . . . Proverbs 3:31

Haughtiness, lying, murdering, scheming, eagerness to do wrong,
a false witness, stirring up discord . . . . Proverbs 6:16-19

Those who are untruthful . . . . Proverbs 12:22

The sacrifice of the wicked . . . . Proverbs 15:8

The way of the wicked . . . . Proverbs 15:9

The thoughts of the wicked . . . . Proverbs 15:26

Those who are proud . . . . Proverbs 16:5

Those who judge unjustly . . . . Proverbs 17:15

STRATEGY FOR EFFECTIVE LIVING / *Proverbs 9*

Begins with	God's wisdom	Respecting and appreciating who God is; reverence and awe in recognizing the almighty God
Requires	Moral application	Trusting in God and his Word; allowing his Word to speak to us personally; willing to obey
Requires	Practical application	Acting on God's direction in daily devotions
Results in	Effective living	Experiencing what God does with our obedience

GOD'S ADVICE ABOUT MONEY / Proverbs 11:24-26

Proverbs gives some practical instruction on the use of money, although sometimes it is advice we would rather not hear. It's more comfortable to continue in our habits than to learn how to use money more wisely. The advice includes

Be generous in giving 11:24-25; 22:9

Place people's needs ahead of profit 11:26

Be cautious of co-signing for another 17:18; 22:26-27

Don't accept bribes. 17:23

Help the poor. 19:17; 21:13

Store up for the future 21:20

Be careful about borrowing. 22:7

Other verses to study include 11:15; 20:16; 25:14; 27:13.

TEACHING AND LEARNING / Proverbs 12:15

Good teaching comes from good learning—and Proverbs has more to say to students than to teachers. Proverbs is concerned with the learning of wisdom. The book makes it clear that there are no good alternatives to learning wisdom. We are either becoming wise learners or refusing to learn and becoming foolish failures. Proverbs encourages us to make the right choice.

Wise Learners	Proverb(s)	Foolish Failures
Quietly accept instruction	10:8; 15:23; 23:12	Ignore instruction
Love discipline	12:1	Hate correction
Listen to advice	12:15; 21:11; 24:6	Think they need no advice
Accept parents' discipline	13:1	Mock parents
Lead others to life	10:17	Lead others astray
Receive honor	13:18	End in poverty and disgrace
Profit from constructive criticism	15:31-32; 29:1	Self-destruct by refusing criticism

Advice to Teachers:
Help people avoid traps (13:14), use pleasant words (16:21), and speak at the right time (15:23; 18:20).

WISDOM AND FOOLISHNESS / *Proverbs 15:14*

The wise and the foolish are often contrasted in Proverbs. The characteristics, reputation, and results of each are worth knowing if wisdom is our goal.

	The Wise	The Foolish	Reference
Characteristics	Give good advice	Lack common sense	10:21
	Enjoy wisdom	Enjoy foolishness	10:23
	Consider their steps	Gullible	14:15
		Avoid the wise	15:12
	Hungry for truth	Feed on foolishness	15:14
	Value wisdom above riches		16:16
	Receive life	Receive punishment	16:22
	Respond to correction	Do not respond to punishment	17:10
	Pursue wisdom	Pursue illusive dreams	17:24
		Blame failure on God	19:3
	Profit from correction	An example to others	19:25
		Are proud and arrogant	21:24
		Despise wise advice	23:9
		Make truth useless	26:7
		Repeat their folly	26:11
	Trust in wisdom	Trust in themselves	28:26
	Control their anger	Unleash their anger	29:11
Reputation	Admired as counselors	Punished as servants	10:13
	Crowned with knowledge	Inherit folly	14:18
		Cause strife and quarrels	22:10
		Receive no honor	26:1
	Keep peace	Stir up anger	29:8
Results	Stay on the right path	Go the wrong way	15:21
		Lash out when discovered in folly	17:12
		Endangered by their words	18:6-7
	Their wisdom conquers others' strength		21:22
	Avoid wicked paths	Walk a troublesome path	22:5
	Have great advice		24:5
		Will never be chosen as counselors	24:7
		Must be guided by hardship	26:3
		Persist in foolishness	27:22

HOW GOD IS DESCRIBED IN PROVERBS / *Proverbs 16:2*

Proverbs is a book about wise living. It often focuses on a person's response and attitude toward God, who is the source of wisdom. And a number of proverbs point out aspects of God's character. Knowing God helps us on the way to wisdom.

God . . .

is aware of all that happens (15:3)

knows the heart of all people (15:11; 16:2; 21:2)

controls all things (16:33; 21:30)

is a place of safety (18:10)

rescues good people from danger (11:8, 21)

condemns the wicked (11:31)

delights in our prayers (15:8, 29)

loves those who obey him (15:9; 22:12)

cares for the poor and needy (15:25; 22:22-23)

purifies hearts (17:3)

hates evil (17:5; 21:27; 28:9)

Our response should be . . .

to fear and reverence God (10:27; 14:26-27; 15:16; 16:6; 19:23; 28:14)

to obey God's Word (13:13; 19:16)

to please God (21:3)

to trust in God (22:17-19; 29:25)

HUMILITY AND PRIDE / *Proverbs 18:12*

Results of . . .	Humility	Pride	
	Leads to wisdom	Leads to disgrace	11:2
	Takes advice	Produces arguments	13:10
	Leads to honor		15:33
		Leads to punishment	16:5
		Leads to destruction	16:18
	Ends in honor	Ends in downfall	18:12
	Brings one to honor	Brings one to humiliation	29:23

Proverbs is direct and forceful in rejecting pride. The proud attitude heads the list of seven things God hates (6:16-17). The harmful results of pride are constantly contrasted with humility and its benefits.

HOW TO SUCCEED IN GOD'S EYES / *Proverbs 17:27*

Proverbs notes two significant by-products of wise living: success and good reputation. Several verses also point out what causes failure and poor reputation.

Qualities that promote success and a good reputation

Godliness (righteousness) 10:7; 12:3; 28:12

Hating what is false 13:5

Committing all work to the Lord 16:3

Using words with restraint; being even-tempered. 17:27-28

Loving wisdom and understanding 19:8

Humility and fear of the Lord 22:4

Willingness to confess and forsake sin 28:13

Qualities that prevent success and cause a bad reputation

Wickedness 10:7; 12:3; 28:12

Seeking honors 25:27

Hatred 26:24-26

Praising oneself 27:2

Concealing sin 28:13

Other verses dealing with one's reputation are 11:10, 16; 14:3; 19:10; 22:1; 23:17-18; 24:13-14.

HONESTY AND DISHONESTY / *Proverbs 20:7*

Proverbs tells us plainly that God despises all forms of dishonesty. Not only does God hate dishonesty, but we are told that it works against us—others no longer trust us, and we cannot even enjoy our dishonest gains. It is wiser to be honest because "the godly escape such trouble" (12:13).

Others' Opinions

Leaders value those who speak honestly 16:13

In the end most people will appreciate truth more than flattery 28:23

Quality of Life

The godly person's plans are just 12:5

Truthful witnesses do not lie; false witnesses breathe lies. 14:5

Truthful witnesses save lives 14:25

The children of the righteous are blessed 20:7

Short-Term Results

Ill-gotten gain has no lasting value. 10:2

The righteous are rescued from trouble 11:8

The wicked are trapped by their own words 12:13

Fraudulent gain is sweet for a while 20:17

Long-Term Results

Good people are guided by their honesty 11:3

Truth endures 12:19

Riches gained quickly don't last 20:21

Riches gained dishonestly don't last. 21:6

The honest are rescued from harm 28:18

God's Opinion

God delights in honesty 11:1

God delights in those who are truthful 12:22

God despises double standards 20:10

God is pleased when we do what is right and just 21:3

RIGHTEOUSNESS AND WICKEDNESS / *Proverbs 21:29*

Proverbs often compares the lifestyles of the wicked and the righteous, and makes a strong case for living by God's pattern. The advantages of righteous living and the disadvantages of wicked living are pointed out. The kind of person we decide to be will affect every area of our lives.

	Righteous	Wicked	Reference
Outlook on life	Hopeful	Fearful	10:24
	Concerned about the welfare of God's creation	Even their kindness is cruel	12:10
	Understand justice	Don't understand justice	28:5
Response to life	Showered with blessings	Covered with violence	10:6
		Plot evil	16:30
	Proceed with care	Put up a bold front	21:29
	Persevere against evil	Brought down by calamity	24:15-16
		Hate the honest	29:10
How they are seen by others	Seek out the honest	Do not endure	13:15
	Are respected	Lead others into sin	16:29
	Conduct is upright	Conduct is devious	21:8
	Are not to desire the company of godless people	Plot violence	24:1-2
	Others are glad when they succeed	Others hide when they rise to power	28:12
	Care for the poor	Unconcerned about the poor	29:7
	Despise the wicked	Despise the godly	29:27
Quality of life	Stand firm	Swept away	10:25
	Rescued by godliness	Trapped by evil desires	11:6

	Righteous	Wicked	Reference
Quality of life (cont.)	No real harm befalls them	Constant trouble befalls them	12:21
	Income results in treasure	Income results in trouble	15:6
	Avoid evil		16:17
		Fall into constant trouble	17:20
	Are bold as lions	Are fearful constantly	28:1
	Will be safe	Will suddenly fall	28:18
Short-term results	Walk securely	Will be found out	10:9
	Chased by blessings	Chased by trouble	13:21
Long-term results	God protects them	God destroys them	10:29
	Evil people will bow to them	Will bow to the righteous	14:19
		Will be punished for rebellion	17:11
Eternal expectations	Never uprooted	Will not remain	10:30
	Earn a sure reward	Earn deceptive wages	11:18
	Attain life	Go to death	11:19
	End only in good	End only in wrath	11:23
	Will stand firm	Will perish	12:7
	Have a refuge when they die	Crushed by their sins	14:32
God's opinion of them	Delights in the good	Detests the perverse	11:20

THE FOUR TONGUES / *Proverbs 21:23*

What we say probably affects more people than any other action we take. It is not surprising, then, to find that Proverbs gives special attention to words and how they are used. Four common speech patterns are described in Proverbs. The first two should be copied, while the last two should be avoided.

The Controlled Tongue	Those with this speech pattern think before speaking, know when silence is best, and give wise advice.	10:19; 11:12-13; 12:16; 13:3; 15:1, 4, 28; 16:23; 17:14, 27-28; 21:23; 24:26
The Caring Tongue	Those with this speech pattern speak truthfully while seeking to encourage.	10:32; 12:18, 25; 15:23; 16:24; 25:15; 27:9
The Conniving Tongue	Those with this speech pattern are filled with wrong motives, gossip, slander, and a desire to twist truth.	6:12-14; 8:13; 16:28; 18:8; 25:18; 26:20-28
The Careless Tongue	Those with this speech pattern are filled with lies, curses, quick-tempered words—which can lead to rebellion and destruction.	10:18, 32; 11:9; 12:16, 18; 15:4; 17:9, 14, 19; 20:19; 25:23

Other verses about our speech include 10:11, 20, 31; 12:6, 17-19; 13:2; 14:3; 19:5, 28; 25:11; 27:2, 5, 14, 17; 29:9.

DILIGENCE AND LAZINESS / *Proverbs 22:13*

Proverbs makes it clear that diligence—being willing to work hard and do one's best at any job given to him or her—is a vital part of wise living. We work hard, not to become rich, famous, or admired (although those may be by-products), but to serve God with our very best during our lives.

The Diligent	The Lazy	Reference
Become rich.	Are soon poor	10:4
Gather their crops.	Sleep during harvest.	10:5
Are an annoyance.		10:26
Are prosperous	Are idle.	12:11
Gain many benefits		12:14
Will become leaders	Will become slaves	12:24
Make good use of resources	Waste good resources.	12:27
Are fully satisfied	Want much but get little	13:4
Bring profit	Experience poverty	14:23
Have an easy path	Have trouble all through life	15:19
	Are like those who destroy.	18:9
	Go hungry	19:15
	Won't feed themselves.	19:24
	Won't plow in season	20:4
Stay awake and have food to spare	Love sleep and grow poor	20:13
Make careful plans	Make hasty shortcuts	21:5
	Love leisure and become poor.	21:17
Love to give.	Desire things but refuse to work for them	21:25-26
	Are full of excuses for not working.	22:13
Will serve before kings		22:29
	Sleep too much, which leads to poverty	24:30-34
Reap abundance through hard work	Experience poverty because of laziness.	28:19

LEADERSHIP / *Proverbs 29:2*

Since many of the proverbs came from King Solomon, it is natural to expect some of his interest to be directed toward leadership. Other verses to study: 24:27; 25:13; 27:18.

Qualities of a good leader	Reference
Works hard.	12:24
Doesn't penalize people for honesty.	17:26
Listens before answering	18:13
Open to new ideas.	18:15
Listens to both sides of the story.	18:17
Stands up under pressure	24:10
Stands up under praise	27:21

What happens without good leadership	
Fools are honored	26:8
A wicked ruler is dangerous	28:15
People despair.	29:2
A wicked ruler has wicked advisers	29:12

ECCLESIASTES

MEGATHEMES IN ECCLESIASTES

Theme	Explanation	Importance
Searching	Solomon searched for satisfaction almost as though he was conducting a scientific experiment. Through this process, he discovered that life without God is a long and fruitless search for enjoyment, meaning, and fulfillment. True happiness is not in our power to attain because we always want more than we can have. In addition, there are circumstances beyond our control that can snatch away our possessions or attainments.	People are still searching. Yet the more they try to get, the more they realize how little they really have. No pleasure or happiness is possible without God. Without him, satisfaction is a lost search. Above everything we should strive to know and love God. He gives wisdom, knowledge, and joy.
Emptiness	Solomon shows how empty it is to pursue the pleasures that this life has to offer rather than seek to have a relationship with the eternal God. The search for pleasure, wealth, and success is ultimately disappointing. Nothing in the world can fill the emptiness and satisfy the deep longings in our restless hearts.	The cure for emptiness is to center on God. His love also can fill the emptiness of human experience. Fear God throughout your life, and fill your life with serving God and others rather than with selfish pleasures.
Work	Solomon tried to shake people's confidence in their own efforts, abilities, and wisdom and to direct them to faith in God as the only sound basis for living. Without God, there is no lasting reward or benefit in hard work.	Work done with the wrong attitude will leave us empty, but work accepted as an assignment from God can be seen as a gift. Examine what you expect from your efforts. God gives you abilities and opportunities to work so that you can use your time well.
Death	The certainty of death makes all human achievements futile. God has a plan for each one of us that goes beyond life and death. The reality of aging and dying reminds each individual of the end to come when God will judge each person's life.	Because life is short, we need wisdom that is greater than this world can offer. We need the words of God so we can live right. If we listen to him, his wisdom spares us the bitterness of futile human experience and gives us a hope that goes beyond death.
Wisdom	Human wisdom doesn't contain all the answers. Knowledge and education have their limits. To understand life and make right choices, we need the wisdom that can be found only in God's Word—the Bible.	When we realize that God will evaluate all that we do, we should learn to live wisely, remembering that he is present each day, and learn to obey his guidelines for living. But in order to have God's wisdom, we must first get to know and honor him.

SONG OF SONGS

MEGATHEMES IN SONG OF SONGS

Theme	Explanation	Importance
Sex	Sex is God's gift to his creatures. He endorses sex but restricts its expression to those committed to each other in marriage.	God wants sex to be motivated by love and commitment, not lust. It is for mutual pleasure, not selfish enjoyment.
Love	As the relationship developed, the beauty and wonder of a romance unfolded between Solomon and his bride. The intense power of love affected the hearts, minds, and bodies of the two lovers.	Because love is such a powerful expression of feeling and commitment between two people, it is not to be regarded casually. We are not to manipulate others into loving us, and love should not be prematurely encouraged in a relationship.
Commitment	The power of love requires more than the language of feeling to protect it. Sexual expression is such an integral part of our selfhood that we need the boundary of marriage to safeguard our love. Marriage is the celebration of daily commitment to each other.	While romance keeps a marriage interesting, commitment keeps romance from dwindling away. The decision to commit yourself to your spouse alone *begins* at the marriage altar. It must be maintained day by day.
Beauty	The two lovers praise the beauty they see in each other. The language they use shows the spontaneity and mystery of love. Praise should not be limited to physical beauty; beautiful personality and moral purity should also be praised.	Our love for someone makes him or her appear beautiful to us. As you consider marriage, don't just look for physical attractiveness in a person. Look for the inner qualities that don't fade with time— spiritual commitment, sensitivity, and sincerity.
Problems	Over time, feelings of loneliness, indifference, and isolation came between Solomon and his bride. During those times, love grew cold, and barriers were raised.	Through careful communication, lovers can be reconciled, commitment can be renewed, and romance can be refreshed. Don't let walls come between you and your partner. Take care of problems while they are still small.

ISAIAH

MEGATHEMES IN ISAIAH

Theme	Explanation	Importance
Holiness	God is highly exalted above all his creatures. His moral perfection stands in contrast to evil people and nations. God is perfect and sinless in all his motives and actions, so he is in perfect control of his power, judgment, love, and mercy. His holy nature is our yardstick for morality.	Because God is without sin, he alone can help us with our sin. It is only right that we regard him as supreme in power and moral perfection. We must never treat God as common or ordinary. He alone deserves our devotion and praise. He is always truthful, fair, and just.
Punishment	Because God is holy, he requires his people to treat others justly. He promised to punish Israel, Judah, and other nations for faithless immorality and idolatry. True faith had degenerated into national pride and empty religious rituals.	We must trust in God alone and fulfill his commands. We cannot forsake justice nor give in to selfishness. If we harden our heart against his message, punishment will surely come to us.
Salvation	Because God's judgment is coming, we need a Savior. No man or nation can be saved without God's help. Christ's perfect sacrifice for our sins is foretold and portrayed in Isaiah. All who trust God can be freed from their sin and restored to him.	Christ died to save us from our sin. We cannot save ourselves. He is willing to save all those who turn from their sin and come to him. Salvation is from God alone. No amount of good works can earn it.
Messiah	God will send the Messiah to save his people. He will set up his own Kingdom as the faithful Prince of Peace, who rules with righteousness. He will come as sovereign Lord, but he will do so as a servant who will die to take away sins.	Our trust must be in the Messiah, not in ourselves or in any nation or power. There is no hope unless we believe in him. Trust Christ fully and let him rule in your life as your sovereign Lord.
Hope	God promises comfort, deliverance, and restoration in his future Kingdom. The Messiah will rule over his faithful followers in the age to come. Hope is possible because Christ is coming.	We can be refreshed because there is compassion for those who repent. No matter how bleak our situation or how evil the world is, we must continue to be God's faithful people who hope for his return.

THE PROPHET ISAIAH / *Isaiah 1*

Served as a prophet to Judah from 740–681 B.C.

Climate of the times . . . . . . Society was in a great upheaval. Under King Ahaz and King Manasseh, the people reverted to idolatry, and there was even child sacrifice.

Main message . . . . Although judgment from other nations was inevitable, the people could still have a special relationship with God.

Importance of message . . . . Sometimes we must suffer judgment and discipline before we are restored to God.

Contemporary prophets . . . . Hosea (753–715 B.C.), Micah (742–687 B.C.)

NAMES FOR MESSIAH / *Isaiah 9:6*

Isaiah uses four names in 9:6 to describe the Messiah. These names have special meaning to us.

Wonderful Counselor . . . . . He is exceptional, distinguished, and without peer, the one who gives the right advice.

Mighty God . . . . He is God himself.

Everlasting Father . . . . He is timeless; he is God our Father.

Prince of Peace . . . . His government is one of justice and peace.

ALLIANCES TODAY / *Isaiah 21*

Government. . . . . We rely on government legislation to protect the moral decisions we want made, but legislation cannot change people's hearts.

Science . . . . We enjoy the benefits of science and technology. We look to scientific predictions and analysis before we look to the Bible.

Education . . . . We act as though education and degrees can guarantee our future and success without considering God's plans for our future.

Medical care . . . . . . We regard medicine as the way to prolong life and preserve the quality—quite apart from faith and moral living.

Financial systems. . . . We place our faith in financial "security"—making as much money as we can for ourselves—forgetting that, while being wise with our money, we must trust God for our needs.

Isaiah warned Judah not to ally with Egypt (20:5; 30:1-2; 31:1). He knew that trust in any nation or any military might was futile. Judah's only hope was to trust in God. Although we don't consciously put our hope for deliverance in political alliances in quite the same way, we often put our hope in other forces.

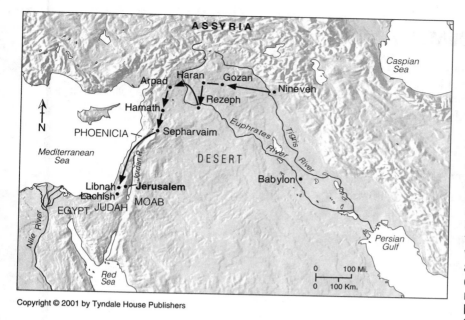

ASSYRIA ADVANCES
Isaiah 36:1–37:38

As Sennacherib beautified his capital city, Nineveh, Hezekiah withheld tribute and prepared for battle. The Assyrians advanced toward their rebellious western border, attacking swiftly down the Mediterranean coast. From Lachish, Sennacherib threatened to take Jerusalem, but Isaiah knew his threats would die with him on his return to Nineveh.

Copyright © 2001 by Tyndale House Publishers

THE SERVANT IN ISAIAH / Isaiah 42:19

The nation Israel is called the servant: 41:8; 42:19; 43:10; 44:1-2, 21; 45:4; 48:20

The Messiah is called the Servant: 42:1-17; 49:3, 5-7; 50:10; 52:13; 53:11

The nation was given a mission to serve God, to be custodian of his word, and to be a light to the Gentile nations. Because of sin and rebellion, they failed. God sent his Son, Christ, as Messiah to fulfill his mission on earth.

TODAY'S IDOLATRY / *Isaiah 44*

Isaiah tells us, "Who but a fool would make his own god—an idol that cannot help him one bit!" We think of idols as statues of wood or stone, but in reality an idol is anything natural that is given sacred value and power. If your answer to any of the following questions is anything or anyone other than God, you may need to check out who or what you are worshiping.

- Who created me?
- Whom do I ultimately trust?
- Whom do I look to for ultimate truth?
- Whom do I look to for security and happiness?
- Who is in charge of my future?

MAJOR IDOLS MENTIONED IN THE BIBLE / *Isaiah 46*

Name	Where they were worshiped	What they stood for	What the worship included
Bel (Marduk)	Babylon	Weather, war, sun god	Prostitution, child sacrifice
Nebo (son of Marduk)	Babylon	Learning, astronomy, science	
Ashtoreth (Asherah)	Canaan	Goddess of love, childbirth, and fertility	Prostitution
Chemosh	Moab		Child sacrifice
Molech	Ammon	National god	Child sacrifice
Baal	Canaan	Rain, harvest, symbolized strength and fertility	Prostitution
Dagon	Philistia	Harvest, grain, success in farming	Child sacrifice

THE SPIRIT IN ISAIAH / *Isaiah 63:10-11*

Reference	Main Teaching
11:2	The Spirit of the Lord brings wisdom, understanding, knowledge, and the fear of the Lord.
32:15	The Spirit of the Lord brings abundance.
34:16	The Spirit of the Lord carries out God's word.
40:13	The Spirit of the Lord is the Master Counselor.
42:1	The Messiah, God's Servant, will be given the Spirit.
44:3-5	Through the Spirit, God's true children will thrive.
48:16	The Spirit of the Lord sent Isaiah to prophesy.
61:1	God's servants (Isaiah and then Jesus) were appointed by the Spirit to proclaim the Good News.
63:10-11	The Spirit of the Lord was grieved because of God's people.
63:14	The Spirit of the Lord gives rest.

JEREMIAH

MEGATHEMES IN JEREMIAH

Theme	Explanation	Importance
Sin	King Josiah's reformation failed because the people's repentance was shallow. They continued in their selfishness and worship of idols. All the leaders rejected God's law and will for the people. Jeremiah lists all their sins, predicts God's judgment, and begs for repentance.	Judah's deterioration and disaster came from a callous disregard and disobedience of God. When we ignore sin and refuse to listen to God's warning, we invite disaster. Don't settle for half measures in removing sin.
Punishment	Because of sin, Jerusalem was destroyed, the Temple was ruined, and the people were captured and carried off to Babylon. The people were responsible for their destruction and captivity because they refused to listen to God's message.	Unconfessed sin brings God's full punishment. It is useless to blame anyone else for our sin; we are accountable to God before anyone else. We must answer to him for how we live.
God Is Lord of All	God is the righteous Creator. He is accountable to no one but himself. He wisely and lovingly directs all creation to fulfill his plans, and he brings events to pass according to his timetable. He is Lord over all the world.	Because of God's majestic power and love, our only duty is to submit to his authority. By following his plans, not our own, we can have a loving relationship with him and serve him with our whole heart.
New Hearts	Jeremiah predicted that after the destruction of the nation, God would send a new shepherd, the Messiah. He would lead them into a new future, a new covenant, and a new day of hope. He would accomplish this by changing their sinful hearts into hearts of love for God.	God still transforms people by changing their hearts. His love can eliminate the problems created by sin. We can have assurance of a new heart by loving God, trusting Christ to save us, and repenting of our sin.
Faithful Service	Jeremiah served God faithfully for 40 years. During that time the people ignored, rejected, and persecuted him. Jeremiah's preaching was unsuccessful by human standards, yet he did not fail in his task. He remained faithful to God.	People's acceptance or rejection of us is not the measure of our success. God's approval alone should be our standard for service. We must bring God's message to others even when we are rejected. We must do God's work even if it means suffering for it.

THE PROPHET JEREMIAH / *Jeremiah 2*

Served as a prophet to Judah from 627 B.C. until the Exile in 586 B.C.

Climate of the times	Society was deteriorating economically, politically, spiritually. Wars and captivity dominated the world scene. God's word was deemed offensive.
Main message	Repentance from sin would postpone Judah's coming judgment at the hands of Babylon.
Importance of message	Repentance is one of the greatest needs in our immoral world. God's promises to the faithful shine brightly by bringing hope for tomorrow and strength for today.
Contemporary prophets	Habakkuk (612–589 B.C.), Zephaniah (640–621 B.C.)

THE KINGS OF JEREMIAH'S LIFETIME / *Jeremiah 3*

King	Story of of his reign	Dates of his reign	Character of reign	Jeremiah's message to the king
Josiah	2 Kings 22:1–23:30	640–609 B.C.	Mostly good	3:6-25
Jehoahaz	2 Kings 23:31-33	609 B.C.	Evil	22:11-17
Jehoiakim	2 Kings 23:34–24:7	609–598 B.C.	Evil	22:18-23; 25:1-38; 26:1-24; 27:1-11; 35:1-19; 36:1-32
Jehoiachin	2 Kings 24:8-17	598–597 B.C.	Evil	13:18-27; 22:24-30
Zedekiah	2 Kings 24:18–25:26	597–586 B.C.	Evil	21:1-14; 24:8-10; 27:12-22; 32:1-5; 34:1-22; 37:1-21; 38:1-28; 51:59-64

GOD'S OBJECT LESSONS IN JEREMIAH / *Jeremiah 19*

Reference	Object Lesson	Significance
1:11-12	Branch of an almond tree	God will carry out his threats of punishment.
1:13	Boiling pot, tipping southward	God will punish Judah.
13:1-11	A useless linen belt	Because the people refused to listen to God, they had become useless, good for nothing, like a useless linen belt.
18:1-17	Potter's clay	God could destroy his sinful people if he so desired. This is a warning to them to repent before he is forced to bring judgment.
19:1-12	Broken clay jars	God would smash Judah just as Jeremiah smashed the clay jars.
24:1-10	Two baskets of figs	Good figs represent God's remnant. Bad figs are the people left behind.
27:2-11	Yoke	Any nation who refused to submit to Babylon's yoke of control would be punished.
43:8-13	Large rocks	The rocks marked the place where Nebuchadnezzar would set his throne when God allowed him to conquer Egypt.
51:59-64	Scroll sunk in the river	Babylon would sink to rise no more.

ESCAPE TO EGYPT

Jeremiah 40:1–43:13

With Judah in turmoil after the murder of Gedaliah, the people turned to Jeremiah for guidance. Jeremiah had God's answer, "Stay in this land." But the leaders disobeyed and went to Egypt, taking Jeremiah with them. In Egypt, Jeremiah told them they were in grave danger.

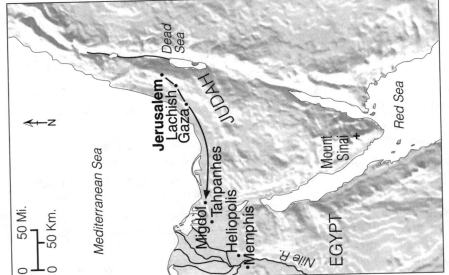

Copyright © 2001 by Tyndale House Publishers

BABYLON ATTACKS JUDAH

Jeremiah 34:1-7; 37:1–39:10

Zedekiah incurred Babylon's wrath in allying with Egypt (37:5) and not surrendering as God told him through Jeremiah (38:17). Nebuchadnezzar attacked Judah for the third and final time, moving systematically until all its cities fell. Jerusalem withstood siege for several months but was burned, as Jeremiah predicted (chapter 39).

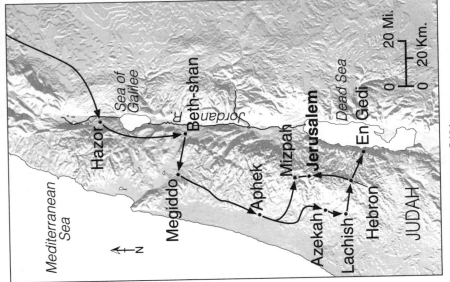

Copyright © 2001 by Tyndale House Publishers

LAMENTATIONS

MEGATHEMES IN LAMENTATIONS

Theme	Explanation	Importance
Destruction of Jerusalem	Lamentations is a sad funeral song for the great capital city of the Jews. The Temple has been destroyed, the king is gone, and the people are in exile. God had warned that he would destroy them if they abandoned him. Now, afterward, the people realize their condition and confess their sin.	God's warnings are justified. He does what he says he will do. His punishment for sin is certain. Only by confessing and renouncing our sin can we turn to him for deliverance. How much better to do so before his warnings are fulfilled.
God's Mercy	God's compassion was at work even when the Israelites were experiencing the affliction of their Babylonian conquerors. Although the people had been unfaithful, God's faithfulness was great. He used this affliction to bring his people back to him.	God will always be faithful to his people. His merciful, refining work is evident even in affliction. At those times, we must pray for forgiveness and then turn to him for deliverance.
Sin's Consequences	God was angry at the prolonged rebellion by his people. Sin was the cause of their misery, and destruction was the result of their sin. The destruction of the nation shows the vanity of human glory and pride.	To continue in rebellion against God is to invite disaster. We must never trust our own leadership, resources, intelligence, or power more than God. If we do, we will experience consequences similar to Jerusalem's.
Hope	God's mercy in sparing some of the people offers hope for better days. One day, the people will be restored to a true and fervent relationship with God.	Only God can deliver us from sin. Without him there is no comfort or hope for the future. Because of Christ's death for us and his promise to return, we have a bright hope for tomorrow.

EZEKIEL

MEGATHEMES IN EZEKIEL

Theme	Explanation	Importance
God's Holiness	Ezekiel saw a vision that revealed God's absolute moral perfection. God was spiritually and morally superior to members of Israel's corrupt and compromising society. Ezekiel wrote to let the people know that God in his holiness was also present in Babylon, not just in Jerusalem.	Because God is morally perfect, he can help us live above our tendency to compromise with this world. When we focus on his greatness, he gives us the power to overcome sin and to reflect his holiness.
Sin	Israel had sinned, and God's punishment came. The fall of Jerusalem and the Babylonian exile were used by God to correct the rebels and draw them back from their sinful way of life. Ezekiel warned them that not only was the nation responsible for sin but each individual was also accountable to God.	We cannot excuse ourselves from our responsibilities before God. We are accountable to God for our choices. Rather than neglect him, we must recognize sin for what it is—rebellion against God—and choose to follow him instead.
Restoration	Ezekiel consoles the people by telling them that the day will come when God will restore those who turn from sin. God will be their King and shepherd. He will give his people a new heart to worship him, and he will establish a new government and a new Temple.	The certainty of future restoration encourages believers in times of trial. But we must be faithful to God because we love him, not merely for what he can do for us. Is our faith in *him* or merely in our future benefits?
Leaders	Ezekiel condemned the shepherds (unfaithful priests and leaders), who led the people astray. By contrast, he served as a caring shepherd and a faithful watchman to warn the people about their sin. One day God's perfect shepherd, the Messiah, will lead his people.	Jesus is our perfect leader. If we truly want him to lead us, our devotion must be more than talk. If we are given the responsibility of leading others, we must take care of them even if it means sacrificing personal pleasure, happiness, time, or money. We are responsible for those we lead.
Worship	An angel gave Ezekiel a vision of the Temple in great detail. God's holy presence had departed from Israel and the Temple because of sin. The building of a future Temple portrays the return of God's glory and presence. God will cleanse his people and restore true worship.	All of God's promises will be fulfilled under the rule of the Messiah. The faithful followers will be restored to perfect fellowship with God and with one another. To be prepared for this time, we must focus on God. We do this through regular worship. Through worship we learn about God's holiness and the changes we must make in how we live.

THE PROPHET EZEKIEL / *Ezekiel 1*

Served as a prophet to the exiles in Babylon from 593– 571 B.C.

Climate of the times . . . . . . Ezekiel and his people are taken to Babylon as captives. The Jews become foreigners in a strange land ruled by an authoritarian government.

Main message . . . . Because of the people's sins, God allowed the nation of Judah to be destroyed. But there was still hope—God promised to restore the land to those who remained faithful to him.

Importance of message . . . . God never forgets those who faithfully seek to obey him. They have a glorious future ahead.

Contemporary prophets . . . . Daniel (605–536 B.C.), Habakkuk (612–589 B.C.), Jeremiah (627–586 B.C.)

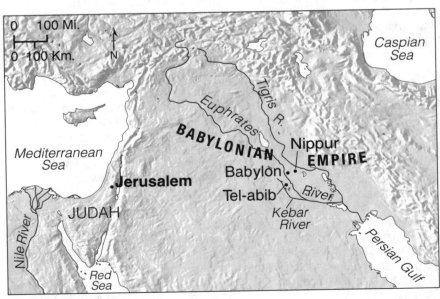

EXILE IN BABYLON
Ezekiel 1:1-3
Ezekiel worked for God right where he was—among the exiles in various colonies near the Kebar River in Babylonia. Jerusalem and its Temple lay over 500 miles away, but Ezekiel helped the people understand that, although they were far from home, they did not need to be far from God.

Copyright © 2001 by Tyndale House Publishers

EZEKIEL'S ACTS OF OBEDIENCE / *Ezekiel 4:1*

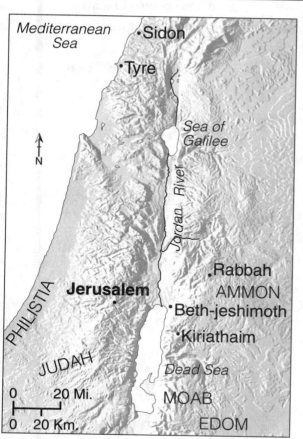

JUDAH'S ENEMIES

Ezekiel 25:1-17

Ammon, Moab, Edom, and Philistia, although once united with Judah against Babylon, had abandoned Judah and rejoiced to see its ruin. But these nations were as sinful as Judah and would also feel the sting of God's judgment.

Copyright © 2001 by Tyndale House Publishers

BAD SHEPHERDS VERSUS GOOD SHEPHERDS / Ezekiel 34

Bad Shepherds	Good Shepherds
Take care of themselves	Take care of their flock
Worry about their own health	Strengthen the weak and sick; search for the lost
Rule harshly and brutally	Rule lovingly and gently
Abandon and scatter the sheep	Gather and protect the sheep
Keep the best for themselves	Give their best to the sheep

OLD AND NEW COVENANTS / Ezekiel 36

Old Covenant	New Covenant
Placed upon stone	Placed upon people's hearts
Based on the law	Based on desire to love and serve God
Must be taught	Known by all
Legal relationship with God	Personal relationship with God

DANIEL

MEGATHEMES IN DANIEL

Theme	Explanation	Importance
God Is in Control	God is all-knowing, and he is in charge of world events. God overrules and removes rebellious leaders who defy him. God will overcome evil; no one is exempt. But he will deliver the faithful who follow him.	Although nations vie for world control now, one day Christ's Kingdom will replace and surpass the kingdoms of this world. Our faith is sure because our future is secure in Christ. We must have courage and put our faith in God, who controls everything.
Purpose in Life	Daniel and his three friends are examples of dedication and commitment. They determined to serve God regardless of the consequences. They did not give in to pressures from an ungodly society because they had a clear purpose in life.	It is wise to make trusting and obeying God alone our true purpose in life. This will give us direction and peace in spite of the circumstances or consequences. We should disobey anyone who asks us to disobey God. Our first allegiance must be to God.
Perseverance	Daniel served for 70 years in a foreign land that was hostile to God, yet he did not compromise his faith in God. He was truthful, persistent in prayer, and disinterested in power for personal glory.	In order to fulfill your life's purpose, you need staying power. Don't let your Christian distinctness become blurred. Be relentless in your prayers, maintain your integrity, and be content to serve God wherever he puts you.
God's Faithfulness	God was faithful in Daniel's life. He delivered him from a den of lions and from enemies who hated him. God cares for his people and deals patiently with them.	We can trust God to be with us through any trial. Because he has been faithful to us, we should remain faithful to him.

THE PROPHET DANIEL / *Daniel 1*

Served as a prophet to the exiles in Babylon from 605–536 B.C.

Climate of the times . . . . The people of Judah were captives in a strange land, feeling hopeless.

Main message. . . . . God is sovereign over all human history, past, present, and future.

Importance of message . . . . We should spend less time wondering when future events will happen and more time learning how we should live now.

Contemporary prophets . . . . Jeremiah (627–586 B.C.), Habakkuk (612–589 B.C.), Ezekiel (593–571 B.C.)

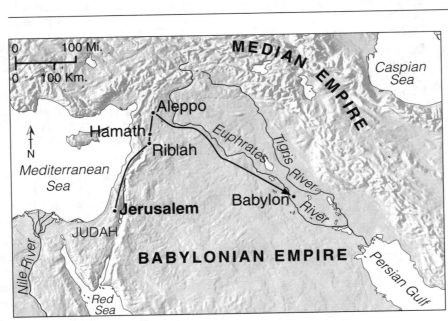

TAKEN TO BABYLON

Daniel 1:1-7

Daniel, as a captive of Babylonian soldiers, faced a long and difficult march to a new land. The 500-mile trek, under harsh conditions, certainly tested his faith in God.

Copyright © 2001 by Tyndale House Publishers

THE FULFILLMENT OF DANIEL'S INTERPRETATION / Daniel 2

The large statue in Nebuchadnezzar's dream (2:24-45) represented the four kingdoms that would dominate as world powers. We recognize these as the Babylonian Empire, the Medo-Persian Empire, the Grecian Empire, and the Roman Empire. All of these will be crushed and brought to an end by the Kingdom of God, which will continue forever.

Part	Material	Empire	Period of Domination
Head	Gold	Babylonian	606 B.C.–539 B.C.
Chest and Arms	Silver	Medo-Persian	539 B.C.–331 B.C.
Belly and Thighs	Bronze	Grecian	331 B.C.–146 B.C.
Legs and Feet	Iron and Clay	Roman	146 B.C.–A.D. 476

KINGS DANIEL SERVED / Daniel 6

Name	Empire	Story told in	Memorable event
Nebuchad-nezzar	Babylonia	chapters 1–4	Shadrach, Meshach, and Abednego thrown into blazing furnace; Nebuchad-nezzar became insane for 7 years
Belshazzar	Babylonia	chapters 5, 7–8	The writing on the wall—which signaled the end of the Babylonian Empire
Darius	Medo-Persia	chapters 6, 9	Daniel thrown into a lions' den
Cyrus	Medo-Persia	chapters 10–12	The exiles return to their homeland in Judah and their capital city, Jerusalem

HOSEA

MEGATHEMES IN HOSEA

Theme	Explanation	Importance
The Nation's Sin	Just as Hosea's wife, Gomer, was unfaithful to him, so the nation of Israel had been unfaithful to God. Israel's idolatry was like adultery. They sought illicit relationships with Assyria and Egypt in pursuit of military might, and they mixed Baal worship with the worship of God.	Like Gomer, we can chase after other loves—love of power, pleasure, money, or recognition. The temptations in this world can be very seductive. Are we loyal to God, remaining completely faithful, or have other loves taken his rightful place?
God's Judgment	Hosea solemnly warned Judah against following Israel's example. Because Judah broke the covenant, turned away from God, and forgot her Maker, she experienced a devastating invasion and exile. Sin has terrible consequences.	Disaster surely follows ingratitude toward God and rebellion. The Lord is our only true refuge. If we harden our heart against him, there is no safety or security anywhere else. We cannot escape God's judgment.
God's Love	Just as Hosea went after his unfaithful wife to bring her back, so the Lord pursues us with his love. His love is tender, loyal, unchanging, and undying. No matter what, God still loves us.	Have you forgotten God and become disloyal to him? Don't let prosperity diminish your love for him or let success blind you to your need for his love.
Restoration	Although God will discipline his people for sin, he encourages and restores those who have repented. True repentance opens the way to a new beginning. God forgives and restores.	There is still hope for those who turn back to God. No loyalty, achievement, or honor can be compared to loving him. Turn to the Lord while the offer is still good. No matter how far you have strayed, God is willing to forgive you.

THE PROPHET HOSEA / *Hosea 1*

Served as a prophet to Israel (the northern kingdom) from 753–715 B.C.

Climate of the times	Israel's last six kings were especially wicked; they promoted heavy taxes, oppression of the poor, idol worship, and total disregard for God. Israel was subjected to Assyria and was forced to pay tribute, which depleted its few remaining resources.
Main message	The people of Israel had sinned against God, as an adulterous woman sins against her husband. Judgment was sure to come for living in total disregard for God and fellow humans. Israel fell to Assyria in 722 B.C.
Importance of message . . .	When we sin, we sever our relationship with God, breaking our commitment to him. While all must answer to God for their sins, those who seek God's forgiveness are spared eternal judgment.
Contemporary prophets . . .	Jonah (793–753 B.C.), Amos (760–750 B.C.), Micah (742–687 B.C.), Isaiah (740–681 B.C.)

SPIRITUAL UNFAITHFULNESS / *Hosea 2*

Spiritual adultery and physical adultery are alike in many ways, and both are dangerous. God was disappointed with his people, because they had committed spiritual adultery against him, as Gomer had committed physical adultery against Hosea.

Parallels	The Danger
Both spiritual and physical adultery are against God's law.	When we break God's law in full awareness of what we're doing, our hearts become hardened to the sin, and our relationship with God is broken.
Both spiritual and physical adultery begin with disappointment and dissatisfaction—either real or imagined—with an already existing relationship.	The feeling that God disappoints can lead you away from him. Feelings of disappointment and dissatisfaction are normal and, when endured, will pass.
Both spiritual and physical adultery begin with diverting affection from one object of devotion to another.	The diverting of our affection is the first step in the blinding process that leads into sin.
Both spiritual and physical adultery involve a process of deterioration; it is not usually an impulsive decision.	The process is dangerous because you don't always realize it is happening until it is too late.
Both spiritual and physical adultery involve the creation of a fantasy about what a new object of love can do for you.	Such fantasy creates unrealistic expectations of what a new relationship can do and only leads to disappointment in all existing and future relationships.

OBEDIENCE VERSUS SACRIFICES / *Hosea 6:6*

God says many times that he doesn't want our gifts and sacrifices when we give them out of ritual or hypocrisy. God wants us first to love and obey him.

1 Samuel 15:22-23 . . . . Obedience is far better than sacrifice.

Psalm 40:6-8 . . . . God doesn't want burnt offerings; he wants our lifelong service.

Psalm 51:16-19 . . . . God isn't interested in penance; he wants a broken and repentant heart.

Jeremiah 7:21-23 . . . . It isn't sacrifices God wants; he desires our obedience and promises he will be our God and we will be his people.

Hosea 6:6 . . . . God doesn't want sacrifices; he wants our loving loyalty. He doesn't want offerings; he wants us to acknowledge him.

Amos 5:21-24 . . . . God hates pretense and hypocrisy; he wants to see justice roll on like a river.

Micah 6:6-8 . . . . God is not satisfied with offerings; he wants us to do what is right, love mercy, and walk humbly with him.

Matthew 9:13 . . . . God doesn't want sacrifices; he wants us to be merciful.

CYCLES OF JUDGMENT/SALVATION IN HOSEA / *Hosea 13:16*

Judgment 1:2-9; 2:2-13; 4:1–5:14; 6:4–11:7; 11:12–13:16

Salvation 1:10–2:1; 2:14–3:5; 5:15–6:3; 11:8-11; 14:1-9

God promises to judge, but he also promises mercy. Here you can see the cycles of judgment and salvation in Hosea. Prophecies of judgment are consistently followed by prophecies of forgiveness.

JOEL

MEGATHEMES IN JOEL

Theme	Explanation	Importance
Punishment	Like a destroying army of locusts, God's punishment for sin is overwhelming, dreadful, and unavoidable. When it comes, there will be no food, no water, no protection, and no escape. The day for settling accounts with God for how we have lived is fast approaching.	God is the one with whom we all must reckon— not nature, the economy, or a foreign invader. We can't ignore or offend God forever. We must pay attention to his message now, or we will face his anger later.
Forgiveness	God stood ready to forgive and restore all those who would come to him and turn away from sin. God wanted to shower his people with his love and restore them to a proper relationship with him.	Forgiveness comes by turning from sin and turning toward God. It is not too late to receive God's forgiveness. God's greatest desire is for you to come to him.
Promise of the Holy Spirit	Joel predicts the time when God will pour out his Holy Spirit on all people. It will be the beginning of new and fresh worship of God by those who believe in him, as well as the beginning of judgment on all who reject him.	God is in control. Justice and restoration are in his hands. The Holy Spirit confirms God's love for us just as he did for the first Christians (Acts 2). We must be faithful to God and place our life under the guidance and power of his Holy Spirit.

THE PROPHET JOEL / *Joel 1*

Served as a prophet to Judah, possibly from 835–796 B.C.

Climate of the times . . . . . . Wicked Queen Athaliah seized power in a bloody coup but was overthrown after a few years. Joash was crowned king, but he was only seven years old and in great need of spiritual guidance. Joash followed God in his early years but then turned away from him.

Main message . . . . A plague of locusts had come to discipline the nation. Joel called the people to turn back to God before an even greater judgment occurred.

Importance of message . . . . God judges all people for their sins, but he is merciful to those who turn to him and offers them eternal salvation.

Contemporary prophets . . . . Elisha (848–797 B.C.), Jonah (793–753 B.C.)

AMOS

MEGATHEMES IN AMOS

Theme	Explanation	Importance
Everyone Answers to God	Amos pronounced judgment from God on all the surrounding nations. Then he included Judah and Israel. God is in supreme control of all the nations. Everyone is accountable to him.	All people will have to account for their sin. When those who reject God seem to get ahead, don't envy their prosperity or feel sorry for yourself. Remember that we all must answer to God for how we live.
Complacency	Everyone was optimistic, business was booming, and people were happy (except for the poor and oppressed). With all the comfort and luxury came self-sufficiency and a false sense of security. But prosperity brought corruption and destruction.	A complacent present leads to a disastrous future. Don't congratulate yourself for the blessings and benefits you now enjoy. They are from God. If you are more satisfied with yourself than with God, remember that everything is meaningless without him. A self-sufficient attitude may be your downfall.
Oppressing the Poor	The wealthy and powerful people of Samaria, the capital of Israel, had become prosperous, greedy, and unjust. Illegal and immoral slavery came as the result of over-taxation and landgrabbing. There was also cruelty and indifference towards the poor. God is weary of greed and will not tolerate injustice.	God made all people; therefore, to ignore the poor is to ignore those whom God loves and whom Christ came to save. We must go beyond feeling bad for the poor and oppressed. We must act compassionately to stop injustice and to help care for those in need.
Superficial Religion	Although many people had abandoned real faith in God, they still pretended to be religious. They were carrying on superficial religious exercises instead of having spiritual integrity and practicing heartfelt obedience toward God.	Merely participating in ceremony or ritual falls short of true religion. God wants simple trust in him, not showy external actions. Don't settle for impressing others with external rituals when God wants heartfelt obedience and commitment.

THE PROPHET AMOS / Amos 1

Served as a prophet to Israel (the northern kingdom) from 760–750 B.C.

Climate of the times . . . . Israel was enjoying peace and economic prosperity. But this blessing had caused her to become a selfish, materialistic society. Those who were well-off ignored the needs of those less fortunate. The people were self-centered and indifferent toward God.

Main message . . . . Amos spoke against those who exploited or ignored the needy.

Importance of message . . . . . . Believing in God is more than a matter of individual faith. God calls all believers to work against injustices in society and to aid those less fortunate.

Contemporary prophets . . . . . . Jonah (793–753 B.C.), Hosea (753–715 B.C.)

AMOS'S VISIONS / Amos 8

Vision/Reference	Significance
Swarm of locusts 7:1-3	God was preparing punishment, which he delayed only because of Amos's intervention.
Fire 7:4-6	God was preparing to devour the land, but Amos intervened on behalf of the people.
Wall and plumb line 7:7-9	God would see if the people were crooked, and if they were, he would punish them.
Basket of ripe fruit 8:1ff	The people were ripe for punishment; though once beautiful, they were now rotten.
God standing by the altar 9:1ff	Punishment was executed.

Amos had a series of visions concerning God's judgment on Israel. God was planning to judge Israel by sending a swarm of locusts or by sending fire. In spite of Amos' intercession on Israel's behalf, God would still carry out his judgment because Israel persisted in her disobedience.

OBADIAH

MEGATHEMES IN OBADIAH

Theme	Explanation	Importance
Justice	Obadiah predicted that God would destroy Edom as punishment for standing by when Babylon invaded Judah. Because of their treachery, Edom's land would be given to Judah in the day when God rights the wrongs against his people.	God will judge and fiercely punish all who harm his people. We can be confident in God's final victory. He is our champion, and we can trust him to bring about true justice.
Pride	Because of their seemingly invincible rock fortress, the Edomites were proud and self-confident. But God humbled them and their nation disappeared from the face of the earth.	All those who defy God will meet their doom as Edom did. Any nation who trusts in its power, wealth, technology, or wisdom more than in God will be brought low. All who are proud will one day be shocked to discover that no one is exempt from God's justice.

THE PROPHET OBADIAH / *Obadiah 1*

Served as a prophet to Judah possibly around 853 B.C.

Climate of the times . . . . . Edom was a constant thorn in Judah's side. The Edomites often participated in attacks initiated by other enemies.

Main message. . . . . God will judge Edom for its evil actions toward God's people.

Importance of message . . . Just as Edom was destroyed and disappeared as a nation, so God will destroy proud and wicked people.

Contemporary prophets . . . Elijah (875–848 B.C.), Micaiah (865–853 B.C.), Jehu (853 B.C.)

HISTORY OF THE CONFLICT BETWEEN ISRAEL AND EDOM
Obadiah 1

The nation of Israel descended from Jacob; the nation of Edom descended from Esau . . . . Genesis 25:23

Jacob and Esau struggled in their mother's womb. . . . . Genesis 25:19-26

Esau sold his birthright and blessing to Jacob . . . . Genesis 25:29-34

Edom refused to let the Israelites pass through its land . . . . Numbers 20:14-22

Israel's kings had constant conflict with Edom.

- Saul. . . . . 1 Samuel 14:47
- David . . . . 2 Samuel 8:13-14
- Solomon . . . . 1 Kings 11:14-22
- Jehoram . . . . 2 Kings 8:20-22;
2 Chronicles 21:8ff
- Ahaz . . . . 2 Chronicles 28:16

Edom urged Babylon to destroy Jerusalem . . . . Psalm 137:7

JONAH

MEGATHEMES IN JONAH

Theme	Explanation	Importance
God's Sovereignty	Although the prophet Jonah tried to run away from God, God was in control. By controlling the stormy seas and a great fish, God displayed his absolute, yet loving guidance.	Rather than running from God, trust him with your past, present, and future. Saying no to God quickly leads to disaster. Saying yes brings new understanding of God and his purpose in the world.
God's Message to All the World	God had given Jonah a purpose—to preach to the great Assyrian city of Nineveh. Jonah hated Nineveh, and so he responded with anger and indifference. Jonah had yet to learn that God loves all people. Through Jonah, God reminded Israel of its missionary purpose.	We must not limit our focus to our own people. God wants his people to proclaim his love in words and actions to the whole world. He wants us to be his missionaries wherever we are, wherever he sends us.
Repentance	When the reluctant preacher went to Nineveh, there was a great response. The people repented and turned to God. This was a powerful rebuke to the people of Israel, who thought they were better but refused to respond to God's message. God will forgive all those who turn from their sin.	God doesn't honor sham or pretense. He wants the sincere devotion of each person. It is not enough to share the privileges of Christianity; we must ask God to forgive us and to remove our sin. Refusing to repent shows that we still love our sin.
God's Compassion	God's message of love and forgiveness was not for the Jews alone. God loves all the people of the world. The Assyrians didn't deserve it, but God spared them when they repented. In his mercy, God did not reject Jonah for aborting his mission. God has great love, patience, and forgiveness.	God loves each of us, even when we fail him. But he also loves other people, including those not of our group, background, race, or denomination. When we accept his love, we must also learn to accept all those whom he loves. We will find it much easier to love others when we truly love God.

Copyright © 2001 by Tyndale House Publishers

JONAH'S ROUND-ABOUT JOURNEY

Jonah 1:1-3; 3:1-5

God told Jonah to go to Nineveh, the capital of the Assyrian Empire. Many of Jonah's countrymen had experienced the atrocities of these fierce people. The last place Jonah wanted to go was on a missionary trip to Nineveh!

So he went in the opposite direction. He boarded a ship in Joppa that was headed for Tarshish. But Jonah could not run from God.

THE PROPHET JONAH / *Jonah 1*

Served as a prophet to Israel and Assyria from 793–753 B.C.

Climate of the times	Nineveh was the most important city in Assyria and would soon become the capital of the huge Assyrian Empire. But Nineveh was also a very wicked city.
Main message	Jonah, who hated the powerful and wicked Assyrians, was called by God to warn the Assyrians that they would receive judgment if they did not repent.
Importance of message . . .	Jonah didn't want to go to Nineveh, so he tried to run from God. But God has ways of teaching us to obey and follow him. When Jonah preached, the city repented and God withheld his judgment. Even the most wicked will be saved if they truly repent of their sins and turn to God.
Contemporary prophets . . .	Joel (835–796? B.C.), Amos (760–750 B.C.)

MIRACLES IN THE BOOK OF JONAH / *Jonah 4:6*

God sent a violent storm	1:4
God provided a great fish to swallow Jonah	1:17
God ordered the fish to spit up Jonah	2:10
God made a leafy plant to shade Jonah	4:6
God provided a worm to eat the plant	4:7
God provided a scorching wind to blow on Jonah	4:8

MICAH

MEGATHEMES IN MICAH

Theme	Explanation	Importance
Perverting Faith	God will judge the false prophets, dishonest leaders, and selfish priests in Israel and Judah. While they publicly carried out religious ceremonies, they were privately seeking to gain money and influence. To mix selfish motives with an empty display of religion is to pervert faith.	Don't try to mix your own selfish desires with true faith in God. One day God will reveal how foolish it is to substitute anything for loyalty to him. Coming up with your own private blend of religion will pervert your faith.
Oppression	Micah predicted ruin for all nations and leaders who were oppressive toward others. The upper classes oppressed and exploited the poor. Yet no one was speaking against them or doing anything to stop them. God will not put up with such injustice.	We dare not ask God to help us while we ignore those who are needy and oppressed, or while we silently condone the actions of those who oppress them.
The Messiah—King of Peace	God promised to provide a new king to bring strength and peace to his people. Hundreds of years before Christ's birth, God promised that the eternal King would be born in Bethlehem. It was God's great plan to restore his people through the Messiah.	Christ our king leads us just as God promised. But until his final judgment, his leadership is only visible among those who welcome his authority. We can have God's peace now by giving up our sins and welcoming him as king.
Pleasing God	Micah preached that God's greatest desire was not the offering of sacrifices at the Temple. God delights in faith that produces justice, love for others, and obedience to him.	True faith in God generates kindness, compassion, justice, and humility. We can please God by seeking these attributes in our work, our family, our church, and our neighborhood.

THE PROPHET MICAH / *Micah 1*

Served as a prophet to Judah from 742–687 B.C.

Climate of the times	King Ahaz set up pagan idols in the Temple and finally nailed the Temple doors shut. Four different nations harassed Judah. When Hezekiah became king, the nation began a slow road to recovery and economic strength. Hezekiah probably heeded much of Micah's advice.
Main message	Prediction of the fall of both the northern kingdom of Israel and the southern kingdom of Judah. This was God's discipline upon the people, actually showing how much he cared for them. Hezekiah's good reign helped postpone Judah's punishment.
Importance of message	Choosing to live a life apart from God is making a commitment to sin. Sin leads to judgment and death. God alone shows us the way to eternal peace. His discipline often keeps us on the right path.
Contemporary prophets	Hosea (753–715 B.C.), Isaiah (740–681 B.C.)

MICAH'S CHARGES OF INJUSTICE / *Micah 3:9*

Micah charged the people with injustice of many kinds.

Plotting evil	2:1
Fraud, coveting, violence	2:2
Stealing, dishonesty	2:8
Evicting women from their homes	2:9
Hating good, loving evil	3:1-2
Despising justice, distorting what is right	3:9
Murder	3:10
Taking bribes	3:11

NAHUM

MEGATHEMES IN NAHUM

Theme	Explanation	Importance
God Judges	God would judge the city of Nineveh for its idolatry, arrogance, and oppression. Although Assyria was the leading military power in the world, God would completely destroy this "invincible" nation. God allows no person or power to usurp or scoff at his authority.	Anyone who remains arrogant and resists God's authority will face his anger. No ruler or nation will get away with rejecting him. No individual will be able to hide from his judgment. Yet those who keep trusting God will be kept safe forever.
God Rules	God rules over all the earth, even over those who don't acknowledge him. God is all-powerful, and no one can thwart his plans. God will overcome any who attempt to defy him. Human power is futile against God.	If you are impressed by or afraid of any weapons, armies, or powerful people, remember that God alone can truly rescue you from fear or oppression. We must place our confidence in God because he alone rules all of history, all the earth, and our life.

NAHUM / *Nahum 1*

Served as a prophet to Judah from 663–612 B.C.

Climate of the times . . . . . . Manasseh, one of Judah's most wicked kings, ruled the land. He openly defied God and persecuted God's people. Assyria, the world power at that time, made Judah one of its vassal states. The people of Judah wanted to be like the Assyrians, who seemed to have all the power and possessions they wanted.

Main message . . . . The mighty empire of Assyria that oppressed God's people would soon tumble.

Importance of message . . . . Those who do evil and oppress others will one day meet a bitter end.

Contemporary prophets . . . . Zephaniah (640–621 B.C.)

HABAKKUK

MEGATHEMES IN HABAKKUK

Theme	Explanation	Importance
Struggle and Doubt	Habakkuk asked God why the wicked in Judah were not being punished for their sin. He couldn't understand why a just God would allow such evil to exist. God promised to use the Babylonians to punish Judah. When Habakkuk cried out for answers in his time of struggle, God answered him with words of hope.	God wants us to come to him with our struggles and doubts. But his answers may not be what we expect. God sustains us by revealing himself to us. Trusting him leads to quiet hope, not bitter resignation.
God's Sovereignty	Habakkuk asked God why he would use the wicked Babylonians to punish his people. God said that he would also punish the Babylonians after they had fulfilled his purpose.	God is still in control of this world in spite of the apparent triumph of evil. God doesn't overlook sin. One day he will rule the whole earth with perfect justice.
Hope	God is the Creator; he is all-powerful. He has a plan, and he will carry it out. He will punish sin. He is our strength and our place of safety. We can have confidence that he will love us and guard our relationship with him forever.	Hope means going beyond our unpleasant daily experiences to the joy of knowing God. We live by trusting in him, not by the benefits, happiness, or success we may experience in this life. Our hope comes from God.

THE PROPHET HABAKKUK / *Habakkuk 1*

Served as a prophet to Judah from 612–589 B.C.

Climate of the times	Judah's last four kings were wicked men who rejected God and oppressed their own people. Babylon invaded Judah twice before finally destroying it in 586 B.C. It was a time of fear, oppression, persecution, lawlessness, and immorality.
Main message	Habakkuk couldn't understand why God seemed to do nothing about the wickedness in society. Then he realized that faith in God alone would supply the answers to his questions.
Importance of message	Instead of questioning the ways of God, we should realize that he is totally just, and we should have faith that he is in control and that one day evil will be utterly destroyed.
Contemporary prophets	Jeremiah (627–586 B.C.), Daniel (605–536 B.C.), Ezekiel (593–571 B.C.)

ZEPHANIAH

MEGATHEMES IN ZEPHANIAH

Theme	Explanation	Importance
Day of Judgment	Destruction was coming because Judah had forsaken the Lord. The people worshiped Baal, Molech, and the starry hosts. Even the priests mixed pagan practices with faith in God. God's punishment for sin was on the way.	To escape God's judgment we must listen to him, accept his correction, trust him, and seek his guidance. If we accept him as our Lord, we can escape his condemnation.
Indifference to God	Although there had been occasional attempts at renewal, Judah had no sorrow for its sins. The people were prosperous, and they no longer cared about God. God's demands for righteous living seemed irrelevant to the people, whose security and wealth made them complacent.	Don't let material comfort be a barrier to your commitment to God. Prosperity can lead to an attitude of proud self-sufficiency. We need to admit that money won't save us and that we cannot save ourselves. Only God can save us.
Day of Cheer	The day of judgment will also be a day of cheer. God will judge all those who mistreat his people. He will purify his people, purging away all sin and evil. God will restore his people and give them hope.	When people are purged of sin, there is great relief and hope. No matter how difficult our experience now, we can look forward to the day of celebration when God will completely restore us. It will truly be a day to rejoice!

THE PROPHET ZEPHANIAH / *Zephaniah 1*

Served as a prophet to Judah from 640–621 B.C.

Climate of the times . . . . . . Josiah was the last good king in Judah. His bold attempts to reform the nation and turn it back to God were probably influenced by Zephaniah.

Main message . . . . A day will come when God, as judge, will severely punish all nations. But after judgment, he will show mercy to all who have been faithful to him.

Importance of message . . . . We will all be judged for our disobedience to God; but if we remain faithful to him, he will show us mercy.

Contemporary prophet . . . . . Jeremiah (627–586 B.C.)

HAGGAI

MEGATHEMES IN HAGGAI

Theme	Explanation	Importance
Right Priorities	God had given the Jews the assignment to finish the Temple in Jerusalem when they returned from captivity. After 15 years, they still had not completed it. They were more concerned about building their own homes than finishing God's work. Haggai told them to get their priorities straight.	It is easy to make other priorities more important than doing God's work. But God wants us to follow through and build up his Kingdom. Don't stop and don't make excuses. Set your heart on what is right and do it. Get your priorities straight.
God's Encouragement	Haggai encouraged the people as they worked. He assured them of the divine presence of the Holy Spirit and of final victory, and instilled in them the hope that the Messiah would reign.	If God gives you a task, don't be afraid to get started. His resources are infinite. God will help you complete it by giving you encouragement from others along the way.

THE PROPHET HAGGAI / *Haggai 1*

Served as a prophet to Judah about 520 B.C., after the return from exile.

Climate of the times . . . . . The people of Judah had been exiled to Babylon in 586 B.C., and Jerusalem and the Temple had been destroyed. Under Cyrus, king of Persia, the Jews were allowed to return to Judah and rebuild their Temple.

Main message . . . . The people returned to Jerusalem to begin rebuilding the Temple, but they hadn't finished. Haggai's message encouraged the people to finish rebuilding God's Temple.

Importance of message . . . The Temple lay half-finished while the people lived in beautiful homes. Haggai warned them against putting their possessions and jobs ahead of God. We must put God first in our lives.

Contemporary prophet . . . . Zechariah (520–480 B.C.)

ZECHARIAH

MEGATHEMES IN ZECHARIAH

Theme	Explanation	Importance
God's Jealousy	God was angry at his people for ignoring his prophets through the years, and he was concerned that they not follow the careless and false leaders who exploited them. Disobedience was the root of their problems and the cause of their misery. God was jealous for their devotion to him.	God is jealous for our devotion. To avoid Israel's ruin, don't walk in their steps. Don't reject God, follow false teachers, or lead others astray. Turn to God, faithfully obey his commands, and make sure you are leading others correctly.
Rebuild the Temple	The Jews were discouraged. They were free from exile, yet the Temple was not completed. Zechariah encouraged them to rebuild it. God would both protect his workmen and empower them by his Holy Spirit to carry out his work.	More than the rebuilding of the Temple was at stake—the people were staging the first act in God's wonderful drama of the end times. Those of us who love God must complete his work. To do so we must have the Holy Spirit's help. God will empower us with his Spirit.
The King Is Coming	The Messiah will come both to rescue people from sin and to reign as king. He will establish his Kingdom, conquer all his enemies, and rule over all the earth. Everything will one day be under his loving and powerful control.	The Messiah came as a servant to die for us. He will return as a victorious king. At that time, he will usher in peace throughout the world. Submit to his leadership now to be ready for the King's triumphant return.
God's Protection	There was opposition to God's plan in Zechariah's day, and he prophesied future times of trouble. But God's Word endures. God remembers the agreements he makes with his people. He cares for his people and will deliver them from all the world powers that oppress them.	Although evil is still present, God's infinite love and personal care have been demonstrated through the centuries. God keeps his promises. Although our bodies may be destroyed, we need never fear our ultimate destiny if we love and obey him.

THE PROPHET ZECHARIAH / *Zechariah 1*

Served as a prophet to Judah about 520 B.C., after the return from exile.

Climate of the times . . . . . . The exiles had returned from captivity to rebuild their Temple. But work on the Temple had stalled, and the people were ignoring their service to God.

Main message . . . . Zechariah, like Haggai, encouraged the people to finish rebuilding the Temple. His visions gave the people hope. He told the people of a future king who would one day establish an eternal kingdom.

Importance of message . . . . Even in times of discouragement and despair, God is working out his plan. God protects and guides us; we must trust and follow him.

Contemporary prophet. . . . . Haggai (approximately 520 B.C.)

ZECHARIAH'S VISIONS / *Zechariah 3*

Vision	Reference	Significance
Zechariah sees messengers reporting to God that the surrounding nations that have oppressed Judah are living in careless and sinful ease.	1:7-17	The people were asking, "Why isn't God punishing the wicked?" Wicked nations may prosper, but not forever. God will bring upon them the judgment they deserve.
Zechariah sees four horns, representing the four world powers that oppressed and scattered the people of Judah and Israel. Then he sees four blacksmiths who will throw down the horns.	1:18-21	God will do what he promised. After the evil nations have carried out his will in punishing his people, God will destroy these nations for their sin.
Zechariah sees a man measuring the city of Jerusalem. The city will one day be full of people, and God himself will be a wall around the city.	2:1-13	The city will be restored in God's future Kingdom. God will keep his promise to protect his people.
Zechariah sees Jeshua the high priest standing before God. Jeshua's filthy clothes are exchanged for fine new clothes; Satan's accusations against him are rejected by God.	3:1-10	The story of Jeshua the high priest pictures how the filthy clothes of sin are replaced with the pure linen of God's righteousness. Christ has taken our clothes of sin and replaced them with God's righteousness. (See Ephesians 4:24; 1 John 1:9.)
Zechariah sees a lampstand that is continually kept burning by an unlimited reservoir of oil. This picture reminds the people that it is only through God's Spirit that they will succeed, not by their own might and resources.	4:1-14	The Spirit of God is given without measure. Human effort does not make a difference. The work of God is not accomplished in human strength.
Zechariah sees a flying scroll, which represents God's curse.	5:1-4	By God's word and Spirit, every person will be judged. The individual's sin is the focus here, not the sins of the nation. God's curse is a symbol of destruction; all sin will be judged and removed.
Zechariah sees a vision of a woman in a basket. She represents the wickedness of the nations. The angel packed the woman back into the basket and sent her back to Babylon.	5:5-11	Sins of the individual were judged in the last vision (5:1-4); now sin is being removed from society. Sin has to be eradicated in order to clean up the nation and the individual.
Zechariah sees a vision of four horses and chariots. The horses represent God's judgment on the world—one is sent north; the direction from which most of Judah's enemies came. The other horses are patrolling the world, ready to execute judgment at God's command.	6:1-8	Judgment will come upon those who oppress God's people—it will come in God's time and at his command.

MALACHI

MEGATHEMES IN MALACHI

Theme	Explanation	Importance
God's Love	God loves his people even when they ignore or disobey him. He has great blessings to bestow on those who are faithful to him. His love never ends.	Because God loves us so much, he hates hypocrisy and careless living. This kind of living denies him the relationship he wants to have with us. What we give and how we live reflects the sincerity of our love for God.
The Sin of the Priests	Malachi singled out the priests for condemnation. They knew what God required, yet their sacrifices were unworthy and their service was insincere; they were lazy, arrogant, and insensitive. They had a casual attitude toward the worship of God and observance of God's standards.	If religious leaders go wrong, how will the people be led? We are all leaders in some capacity. Don't neglect your responsibilities or be ruled by what is convenient. Neglect and insensitivity are acts of disobedience. God wants leaders who are faithful and sincere.
The Sin of the People	The people had not learned the lesson of the Exile, nor had they listened to the prophets. Men were callously divorcing their faithful wives to marry younger pagan women. This was against God's law because it disobeyed his commands about marriage and threatened the religious training of the children. But pride had hardened the hearts of the people.	God deserves our very best honor, respect, and faithfulness. But sin hardens our heart to our true condition. Pride is unwarranted self-esteem; it is setting your own judgment above God's and looking down on others. Don't let pride keep you from giving God your devotion, money, marriage, and family.
The Lord's Coming	God's love for his faithful people is demonstrated by the Messiah's coming. The Messiah will lead the people to the realization of all their fondest hopes. The day of the Lord's coming will be a day of comfort and healing for a faithful few, and a day of judgment for those who reject him.	At Christ's first coming, he refined and purified all those who believed in him. Upon his return, he will expose and condemn those who are proud, insensitive, or unprepared. Yet God is able to heal and forgive. Forgiveness is available to all who come to him.

THE PROPHET MALACHI / *Malachi 1*

Served as a prophet to Judah about 430 B.C. He was the last of the Old Testament prophets.

Climate of the times	The city of Jerusalem and the Temple had been rebuilt for almost a century, but the people had become complacent in their worship of God.
Main message	The people's relationship with God was broken because of their sin, and they would soon be punished. But the few who repented would receive God's blessing, highlighted in his promise to send a Messiah.
Importance of message	Hypocrisy, neglecting God, and careless living have devastating consequences. Serving and worshiping God must be the primary focus of our life, both now and in eternity.
Contemporary prophets	None

MATTHEW

MEGATHEMES IN MATTHEW

Theme	Explanation	Importance
Jesus Christ, the King	Jesus is revealed as the King of kings. His miraculous birth, his life and teaching, his miracles, and his triumph over death show his true identity.	Jesus cannot be equated with any person or power. He is the supreme ruler of time and eternity, heaven and earth, humans and angels. We should give him his rightful place as King of our life.
The Messiah	Jesus was the Messiah, the one for whom the Jews had waited to deliver them from Roman oppression. Yet, tragically, they didn't recognize him when he came because his kingship was not what they expected. The true purpose of God's anointed deliverer was to die for all people to free them from sin's oppression.	Because Jesus was sent by God, we can trust him with our life. It is worth everything we have to acknowledge him and give ourselves to him, because he came to be our Messiah, our Savior.
Kingdom of God	Jesus came to earth to begin his Kingdom. His full Kingdom will be realized at his return and will be made up of anyone who has faithfully followed him.	The way to enter God's Kingdom is by faith— believing in Christ to save us from sin and change our life. We must do the work of his Kingdom now to be prepared for his return.
Teachings	Jesus taught the people through sermons, illustrations, and parables. Through his teachings, he showed the true ingredients of faith and how to guard against a fruitless and hypocritical life.	Jesus' teachings show us how to prepare for life in his eternal Kingdom by living properly right now. He lived what he taught, and we, too, must practice what we preach.
Resurrection	When Jesus rose from the dead, he rose in power as the true King. In his victory over death, he established his credentials as King and his power and authority over evil.	The Resurrection shows Jesus' all-powerful life for us—not even death could stop his plan of offering eternal life. Those who believe in Jesus can hope for a resurrection like his. Our role is to tell his story to all the earth so that everyone may share in his victory.

KEY PLACES IN MATTHEW

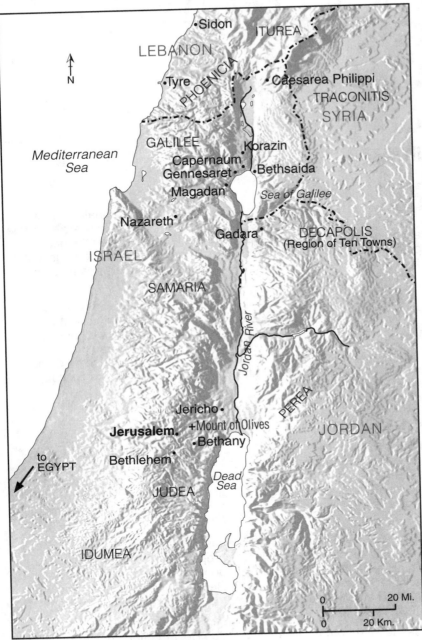

Jesus' earthly story begins in the town of Bethlehem in the Roman province of Judea (2:1). A threat to kill the infant king led Joseph to take his family to Egypt (2:14). When they returned, God led them to settle in Nazareth in Galilee (2:22-23). At about age 30, Jesus was baptized in the Jordan River and was tempted by Satan in the Judean wilderness (3:13; 4:1). Jesus set up his base of operations in Capernaum (4:12-13) and from there ministered throughout Israel, telling parables, teaching about the Kingdom, and healing the sick. He traveled to Gadara and healed two demon-possessed men (8:28ff); fed over 5,000 people with five loaves and two fish on the shores of Galilee near Bethsaida (14:15ff); healed the sick in Gennesaret (14:34ff); ministered to the Gentiles in Tyre and Sidon (15:21ff); visited Caesarea Philippi, where

The broken lines (·–·–·) indicate modern boundaries.

Copyright © 2001 by Tyndale House Publishers

Peter declared him to be the Messiah (16:13ff); and taught in Perea, across the Jordan (19:1). As he set out on his last visit to Jerusalem, he told the disciples what would happen to him there (20:17ff). He spent some time in Jericho (20:29) and then stayed in Bethany at night as he went back and forth to Jerusalem during his last week (21:17ff). In Jerusalem he was crucified, but then he rose again.

GOSPEL ACCOUNTS FOUND ONLY IN MATTHEW

Matthew records nine special events that are not mentioned in any of the other Gospels. In each case, the most apparent reason for Matthew's choice has to do with his purpose in communicating the gospel to Jewish people. Five cases are fulfillments of Old Testament prophecies (marked with asterisks below). The other four would have been of particular interest to the Jews of Matthew's day.

Passage	Subject
1:20-24	Joseph's dream*
2:1-12	The visit of the astrologers
2:13-15	Escape to Egypt*
2:16-18	Slaughter of the male children*
27:3-10	The death of Judas*
27:19	The dream of Pilate's wife
27:52	The other resurrections
28:11-15	The bribery of the guards
28:19-20	The baptism emphasis in the great commission*

JESUS BEGINS HIS MINISTRY

Matthew 3:13–4:17 See also *Mark 1:9-15; Luke 3:21–4:15; John 4:43-45*

From his childhood home, Nazareth, Jesus set out to begin his earthly ministry. He was baptized by John the Baptist in the Jordan River, tempted by Satan in the wilderness, and then returned to Galilee.

Between the temptation and his move to Capernaum (4:12-13), he ministered in Judea, Samaria, and Galilee (see John 1–4).

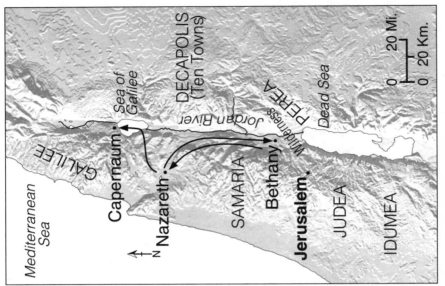

Copyright © 2001 by Tyndale House Publishers

THE FLIGHT TO EGYPT

Matthew 2:13-18

Herod planned to kill the baby Jesus, whom he perceived to be a future threat to his position. Warned of this treachery in a dream, Joseph took his family to Egypt until Herod's death, which occurred a year or two later. They then planned to return to Judea, but God led them instead to Nazareth in Galilee.

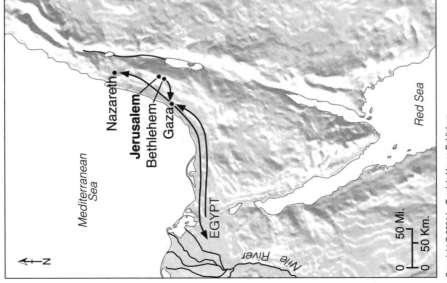

Copyright © 2001 by Tyndale House Publishers

THE PHARISEES AND SADDUCEES / Matthew 3

The Pharisees and Sadducees were the two major religious groups in Israel at the time of Christ. The Pharisees were more religiously minded, while the Sadducees were more politically minded. Although the groups disliked and distrusted each other, they became allies in their common hatred for Jesus.

Name	Positive Characteristics	Negative Characteristics
Pharisees	Were committed to obeying all of God's commands	Behaved as though their own religious rules were just as important as God's rules for living
	Were admired by the common people for their apparent piety	Their piety was often hypocritical, and their efforts often forced others to try to live up to standards they themselves could not live up to
	Believed in a bodily resurrection and eternal life	Believed that salvation came from perfect obedience to the law and was not based on forgiveness of sins
	Believed in angels and demons	Became so obsessed with obeying their legal interpretations in every detail that they completely ignored God's message of mercy and grace
		Were more concerned with appearing to be good than obeying God
Sadducees	Believed strongly in the Mosaic law and in Levitical purity	Relied on logic while placing little importance on faith
	Were more practically minded than the Pharisees	Did not believe all the Old Testament was God's Word
	Did not believe in a bodily resurrection or eternal life	Did not believe in angels or demons
		Were often willing to compromise their values with the Romans and others in order to maintain their status and influential positions

KNOW THE ENEMY, KNOW THE METHOD / *Matthew 4:2*

Satan, the archenemy of all believers, has been tempting people to turn from God since the first woman on earth listened to his lies. Interestingly enough, his methods have never really changed. He tempted Eve in the Garden of Eden, Jesus in the wilderness, and tempts us in our daily lives. When we know how he attacks, we can be prepared.

How Satan tempted . . .

Jesus	**Eve**	**Us**
Turned stones to bread to eat	Fruit would be good to eat	Lust of the flesh
Prove his divine sonship	Gain wisdom so as to be like God	Pride of life
Obtain all he could see	Look at the fruit and see that it looks tasty	Lust of the eyes

THE TEMPTATIONS / *Matthew 4*

As if going through a final test of preparation, Jesus was tempted by Satan in the wilderness. Three specific parts of the Temptation are listed by Matthew. They are familiar because we face the same kinds of temptations. As the chart shows, temptation is often the combination of a real need and a possible doubt that creates an inappropriate desire. Jesus demonstrates both the importance and effectiveness of knowing and applying Scripture to combat temptation.

Temptation	Real needs used as basis for temptation	Possible doubts that made the temptations real	Potential weaknesses Satan sought to exploit	Jesus' answer
Make bread	Physical need: Hunger	Would God provide food?	Hunger, impatience, need to "prove his sonship"	Deuteronomy 8:3 "Depend on God" Focus: God's purpose
Dare God to rescue you (based on misapplied Scripture, Psalm 91:11-12)	Emotional need: Security	Would God protect?	Pride, insecurity, need to test God	Deuteronomy 6:16 "Don't test God" Focus: God's plan
Worship me! (Satan)	Psychological need: significance, power, achievement	Would God rule?	Desire for quick power, easy solutions, need to prove equality with God	Deuteronomy 6:13 "No compromise with evil" Focus: God's person

KEY LESSONS FROM THE SERMON ON THE MOUNT / *Matthew 5:3*

In his longest recorded sermon, Jesus began by describing the traits he was looking for in his followers. He called those who lived out those traits blessed because God had something special in store for them. Each beatitude is an almost direct contradiction of society's typical way of life. In the last beatitude, Jesus even points out that a serious effort to develop these traits is bound to create opposition. The best example of each trait is found in Jesus himself. If our goal is to become like him, the Beatitudes will challenge the way we live each day.

Beatitude	Old Testament anticipation	Clashing worldly values	God's reward	How to develop this attitude
Realize need for God (5:3)	Isaiah 57:15	Pride and personal independence	Kingdom of Heaven	James 4:7-10
Mourn (5:4)	Isaiah 61:1-2	Happiness at any cost	Comfort (2 Corinthians 1:4)	Psalm 51; James 4:7-10
Gentle and lowly (5:5)	Psalm 37:5-11	Power	Receive the earth	Matthew 11:27-30
Hunger and thirst for justice (5:6)	Isaiah 11:4-5; 42:1-4	Pursuing personal needs	See it happen	John 16:5-11; Philippians 3:7-11
Merciful (5:7)	Psalm 41:1	Strength without feeling	Be shown mercy	Ephesians 5:1-2
Pure in heart (5:8)	Psalm 24:3-4; 51:10	Deception is acceptable	See God	1 John 3:1-3
Work for peace (5:9)	Isaiah 57:18-19; 60:17	Personal peace is pursued without concern for the world's chaos	Be called children of God	Romans 12:9-21; Hebrews 12:10-11
Persecuted (5:10)	Isaiah 52:13; 53:12	Weak commitments	Inherit the Kingdom of Heaven	2 Timothy 3:12

THE UNBEATITUDES / *Matthew 5:3*

We can understand the Beatitudes by looking at them from their opposites. Some, Jesus implied, will not be blessed. Their condition could be described this way:

Wretched are the spiritually self-sufficient, for theirs is the kingdom of hell.

Wretched are those who deny the tragedy of their sinfulness, for they will be troubled.

Wretched are the self-centered, for they will be empty.

Wretched are those who ceaselessly justify themselves, for their efforts will be in vain.

Wretched are the merciless, for no mercy will be shown to them.

Wretched are those with impure hearts, for they will not see God.

Wretched are those who reject peace, for they will earn the title "sons of Satan."

Wretched are the uncommitted for convenience's sake, for their destination is hell.

SIX WAYS TO THINK LIKE CHRIST / *Matthew 5:21*

We, more often than not, avoid the extreme sins but regularly commit the types of sins with which Jesus was most concerned. In these six examples, our real struggle with sin is exposed. Jesus pointed out what kind of lives would be required of his followers. Are you living as Jesus taught?

Reference	Example	It's not enough to	We must also
5:21-22	Murder	Avoid killing	Avoid anger and hatred
5:23-26	Offerings	Offer regular gifts	Have right relationships with God and others
5:27-30	Adultery	Avoid adultery	Keep our hearts from lusting and be faithful
5:31-32	Divorce	Be legally married	Live out marriage commitments
5:33-37	Vows	Keep a vow	Avoid casual and irresponsible commitments to God
5:38-47	Revenge	Seek justice for ourselves	Show mercy and love to others

JESUS AND THE OLD TESTAMENT LAW / *Matthew 5:38*

What seems to be a case of Jesus contradicting the laws of the Old Testament deserves a careful look. It is too easy to overlook how much mercy was written into the Old Testament laws. Below are several examples. What God designed as a system of justice with mercy had been distorted over the years into a license for revenge. It was this misapplication of the law that Jesus attacked.

Reference	Examples of Old Testament mercy in justice:
Leviticus 19:18	"Never seek revenge or bear a grudge against anyone, but love your neighbor as yourself. I am the LORD."
Proverbs 24:28-29	"Do not testify spitefully against innocent neighbors; don't lie about them. And don't say, 'Now I can pay them back for all their meanness to me! I'll get even!' "
Proverbs 25:21-22	"If your enemies are hungry, give them food to eat. If they are thirsty, give them water to drink. You will heap burning coals on their heads, and the LORD will reward you."
Lamentations 3:30-31	"Let them turn the other cheek to those who strike them. Let them accept the insults of their enemies. For the Lord does not abandon anyone forever."

SEVEN REASONS NOT TO WORRY / *Matthew 6:25*

6:25 . . . . The same God who created life in you can be trusted with the details of your life.

6:26 . . . . Worrying about the future hampers your efforts for today.

6:27 . . . . Worrying is more harmful than helpful.

6:28-30 . . . . . . God does not ignore those who depend on him.

6:31-32 . . . . . . Worrying shows a lack of faith in and understanding of God.

6:33 . . . . Worrying keeps us from real challenges God wants us to pursue.

6:34 . . . . Living one day at a time keeps us from being consumed with worry.

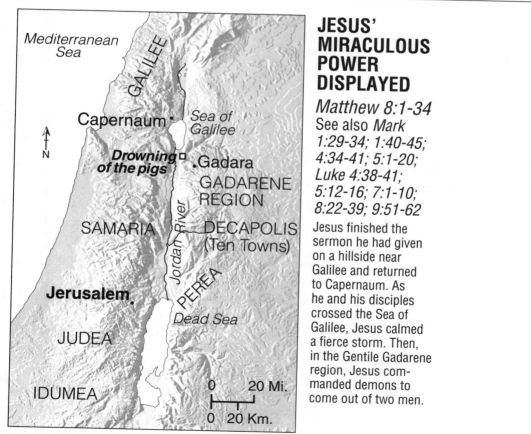

JESUS' MIRACULOUS POWER DISPLAYED

Matthew 8:1-34
See also *Mark 1:29-34; 1:40-45; 4:34-41; 5:1-20; Luke 4:38-41; 5:12-16; 7:1-10; 8:22-39; 9:51-62*

Jesus finished the sermon he had given on a hillside near Galilee and returned to Capernaum. As he and his disciples crossed the Sea of Galilee, Jesus calmed a fierce storm. Then, in the Gentile Gadarene region, Jesus commanded demons to come out of two men.

Copyright © 2001 by Tyndale House Publishers

COUNTING THE COST OF FOLLOWING CHRIST / *Matthew 10:17*

Jesus helped his disciples prepare for the rejection many of them would experience by being Christians. Being God's person will usually create reactions from others who are resisting him.

Who may oppose us?	Natural response	Possible pressures	Needed truth
Government 10:18-19		Threats 10:26	The truth will be revealed (10:26)
	Fear and worry	Physical harm 10:28	Our soul cannot be harmed (10:28)
Religious People 10:17		Public ridicule 10:22	God himself will acknowledge us if we acknowledge him (10:32)
Family 10:21		Rejection by loved ones 10:34-37	God's love can sustain us (10:31)

THE HOLY SPIRIT IN MATTHEW / *Matthew 12:17-21*

For further study on the Holy Spirit in Matthew, see the following passages:

Matthew 1:18, 20.	The Spirit was involved in Jesus' conception.
Matthew 3:11.	John promised judgment and referred to the work of the Spirit.
Matthew 3:16.	Jesus received the Spirit, heralding his ministry and empowering him.
Matthew 4:1	Jesus was led into the wilderness by the Spirit to defeat Satan's temptations.
Matthew 12:18	The Spirit anointing Jesus was an indication that he was the Messiah.
Matthew 12:28	Exorcism and healing were accomplished by the Spirit.
Matthew 12:31-32	Blasphemy against the Holy Spirit is an unforgivable sin.
Matthew 28:19	The Holy Spirit is promised as a gift to those who believe (see also 10:20).

JESUS WALKS ON THE SEA

Matthew 14:13-36

See also *Mark 6:30-56; Luke 9:10-17; John 6:1-21*

The miraculous feeding of the 5,000 occurred on the shores of the Sea of Galilee near Bethsaida. Jesus then sent his disciples across the lake. Several hours later they encountered a storm, and Jesus came to them—walking on the water. The boat then landed at Gennesaret.

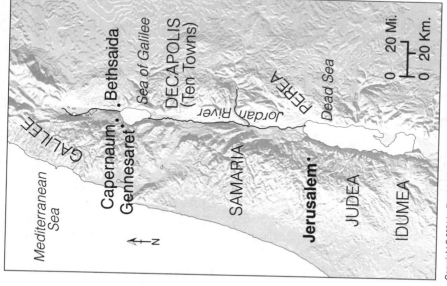

Copyright © 2001 by Tyndale House Publishers

NAZARETH REJECTS JESUS

Matthew 13:53-58

See also *Mark 6:1-6*

Chronologically, this return to Nazareth occurred after Jesus was in the Gadarene region and healed the demon-possessed men (8:28-34), then recrossed the sea to Capernaum. From there he traveled to Nazareth, where he had grown up, only to discover that the people refused to believe he was the Christ.

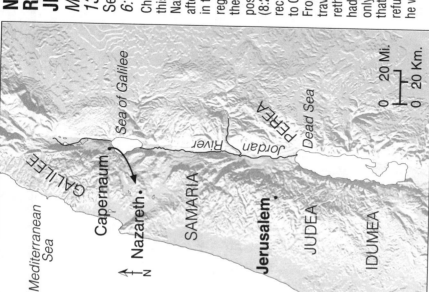

Copyright © 2001 by Tyndale House Publishers

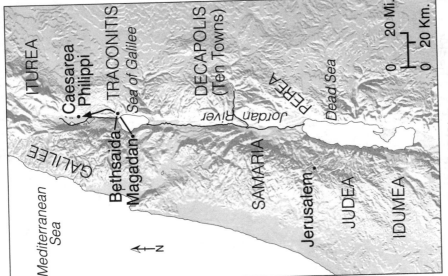

MINISTRY IN PHOENICIA

Matthew 15:1-39
See also *Mark 7:1–8:10*

After preaching again in Capernaum, Jesus left Galilee for Phoenicia, where he preached in Tyre and Sidon. On his return, he traveled through the region of the Decapolis (Ten Towns), fed the 4,000 beside the sea, then crossed to Magadan.

Copyright © 2001 by Tyndale House Publishers

JOURNEY TO CAESAREA PHILIPPI

Matthew 16:1-20; Matthew 19
See also *Mark 8:11-30; Luke 9:18-20*

Jesus left Magadan, crossed the lake, and landed in Bethsaida. There he healed a man who had been born blind. From there, he and his disciples went to Caesarea Philippi, where Peter confessed Jesus as the Messiah and Son of God.

Copyright © 2001 by Tyndale House Publishers

MATTHEW

254

JESUS' REWARDS / *Matthew 16:27*

Jesus had much to say about rewards.

5:12	A great reward awaits you in heaven.	When we are persecuted and remain faithful, our reward in heaven is being with God himself.
6:2,4	They have received all the reward they will ever get. . . . Give your gifts in secret, and your Father, who knows all secrets, will reward you.	Empty acts done for worldy recognition receive human praise, but that is the only reward they get. The acts that God rewards are those done with goodness and kindness as the only motives.
10:41	If you welcome a prophet as one who speaks for God, you will receive the same reward a prophet gets. And if you welcome good and godly people because of their godliness, you will be given a reward like theirs.	Anyone who helps or even shows hospitality to a Christian brother or sister (particularly a Christian worker) will reap the benefit of eternal life.
16:27	For I, the Son of Man, will come in the glory of my Father with his angels and will judge all people according to their deeds.	Jesus Christ will judge each person's life. As we are reviewed and evaluated for how we utilized the resources God has given us, we will be rewarded. This is not something we can earn, but a by-product of faithful obedience.
19:29	And everyone who has given up houses or brothers or sisters or father or mother or children or property, for my sake, will receive a hundred times as much in return and will have eternal life.	God rewards according to his justice. We who believe will receive eternal life, and it will mean more to us than any sacrifice for the gospel that we made on earth.
20:15	Is it against the law for me to do what I want with my money? Should you be angry because I am kind?	In this parable, Jesus taught that God himself decides the reward he will give.
25:34	Then the King will say to those on the right, "Come, you who are blessed by my Father, inherit the Kingdom prepared for you from the foundation of the world."	We should love and serve everyone we can, especially the needy people in Christ's church. Our reward is God himself and eternal life with him.

JESUS AND FORGIVENESS / Matthew 18

Jesus not only taught frequently about forgiveness, he also demonstrated his own willingness to forgive. Here are several examples that should be an encouragement to recognize his willingness to forgive us also.

Jesus forgave . . .	Reference
the paralyzed man lowered on a mat through the roof	Matthew 9:2-8
the woman caught in adultery	John 8:3-11
the woman who anointed his feet with perfume	Luke 7:44-50
Peter, for denying he knew Jesus	John 18:15-18, 25-27; 21:15-19
the criminal on the cross	Luke 23:39-43
the people who crucified him	Luke 23:34

THE SEVEN WOES / Matthew 23:14

Jesus mentioned seven ways to guarantee God's anger, often called the "seven woes." These seven statements about the religious leaders must have been spoken with a mixed tone of judgment and sorrow. They were strong and unforgettable. They are still applicable anytime we become so involved in perfecting the practice of religion that we forget that God is also concerned with mercy, real love, and forgiveness.

23:14	Not letting others enter the Kingdom of Heaven and not entering yourselves
23:15	Converting people away from God to be like yourselves
23:16-22	Blindly leading God's people to follow man-made traditions instead of God's Word
23:23-24	Involving yourself in every last detail and ignoring what is really important: justice, mercy, and faith
23:25-26	Keeping up appearances while your private world is corrupt
23:27-28	Acting spiritual to cover up sin
23:29-36	Pretending to have learned from history, but your present behavior shows you have learned nothing

PREPARATION FOR THE TRIUMPHAL ENTRY

Matthew 21:1-11; Matthew 26 See also Mark 11:1-11; Luke 19:28-44; John 12:12-19

On their way from Jericho, Jesus and the disciples neared Bethphage, on the slope of the Mount of Olives, just outside Jerusalem. Two disciples went into the village, as Jesus told them, to bring back a donkey and its colt. Jesus rode into Jerusalem on the colt, an unmistakable sign of his kingship.

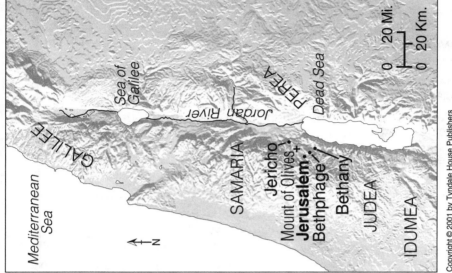

Copyright © 2001 by Tyndale House Publishers

JESUS TRAVELS TOWARD JERUSALEM

Matthew 19:1–20:34; Matthew 21 See also Mark 10:1-52; Luke 18:15-43

Jesus left Galilee for the last time—heading toward Jerusalem and death. He again crossed the Jordan, spending some time in Perea before going on to Jericho.

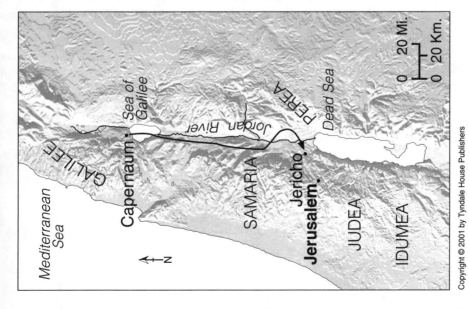

Copyright © 2001 by Tyndale House Publishers

257

MATTHEW

CONCERN FOR THE POOR / *Matthew 25:40*

Concern and care for the poor are essential to truly biblical Christianity.	We are not to take advantage of the needy.	Exodus 22:25-27
	We are not to charge interest or make a profit on food sold to them.	Leviticus 25:35-37
	Every third year the tithe was to be given to the poor people.	Deuteronomy 14:28-29
	We are instructed to give generously to the poor.	Deuteronomy 15:11; Matthew 6:2-4
	Jesus had special concern for the place of the poor.	Luke 4:18-19; 6:20-21
	Paul was eager to remember the poor.	Galatians 2:10
The Bible teaches that Christians should care for the poor, so what can you do?	Feed the poor.	Contribute to a food relief organization.
		Volunteer to help in a community program.
		Work through your church to develop a project to help the needy.
		Consider giving extra tithe to help ministries that assist the poor.
	Secure justice for the poor.	Help widows, orphans, aliens, and the oppressed.
		Help agencies that work for housing, education, and job opportunities for needy people.
	Uphold the cause of the poor.	Stand against oppression.
		Intercede for even one person.
		Write to Christian missions and encourage them to support the cause of the poor.
		Tell your deacons that you will help a poor person under their supervision.

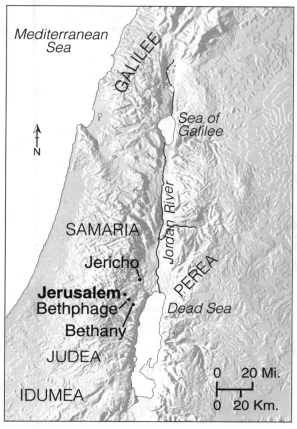

VISIT IN BETHANY

Matthew 26:6-13
See also *Mark 14:3-9; John 12:1-11*

Chronologically, the events of Matthew 26:6-13 precede the events of 21:1ff. In 20:29, Jesus left Jericho, heading toward Jerusalem. Then he arrived in Bethany, where a woman anointed him. From there he went toward Bethphage, where two of his disciples got the colt that he would ride into Jerusalem.

Copyright © 2001 by Tyndale House Publishers

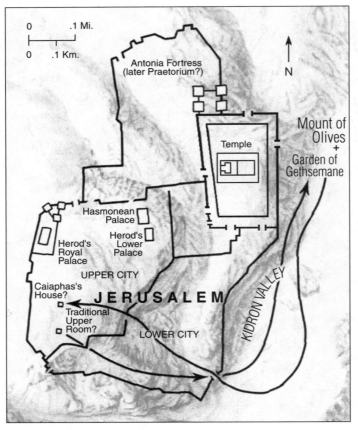

0   .1 Mi.
0   .1 Km.

Antonia Fortress
(later Praetorium?)

N

Temple

Mount of
Olives
+
Garden of
Gethsemane

Hasmonean
Palace

Herod's
Lower
Palace

Herod's
Royal
Palace

UPPER CITY

Caiaphas's
House?

JERUSALEM

KIDRON VALLEY

Traditional
Upper
Room?

LOWER CITY

Copyright © 2001 by Tyndale House Publishers

THE PASSOVER MEAL AND GETHSEMANE

Matthew 26:17-46
See also *Mark 14:12-42; Luke 22:7-46; John 13:21-38*

Jesus, who would soon be the final Passover Lamb, ate the traditional Passover meal with his disciples in the upper room of a house in Jerusalem. During the meal they partook of the bread and wine, which would be the elements of future Communion celebrations, and then went out to the Garden of Gethsemane on the Mount of Olives.

BETRAYED! / *Matthew 26:46*

Delilah betrayed Samson to the Philistines.	Judges 16:16-21
Absalom betrayed David, his father	2 Samuel 15:10-16
Jehu betrayed Joram and killed him	2 Kings 9:14-27
Officials betrayed Joash and killed him.	2 Kings 12:20-21
Judas betrayed Jesus	Matthew 26:46-56

Scripture records a number of occasions on which a person or group was betrayed. The tragedies caused by these violations of trust are a strong lesson about the importance of keeping our commitments.

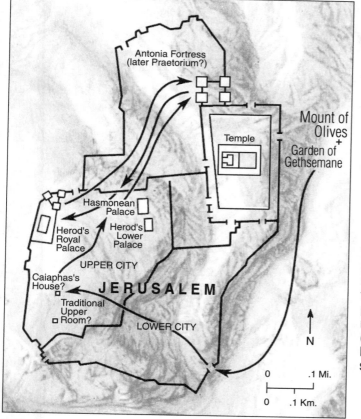

Copyright © 2001 by Tyndale House Publishers

JESUS' TRIAL

Matthew 26:47–27:26

See also *Mark 14:43–15:15; Luke 22:47–23:25; John 18:1–19:16*

After Judas singled Jesus out for arrest, the mob took Jesus first to Caiaphas, the high priest. This trial, a mockery of justice, ended at daybreak with their decision to kill him; but the Jews needed Rome's permission for the death sentence. Jesus was taken to Pilate (who was probably in the Praetorium), then to Herod (Luke 23:5-12), and back to Pilate, who sentenced him to die.

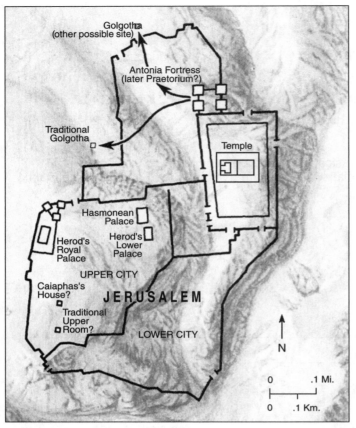

THE WAY OF THE CROSS

Matthew 27:27-44
See also *Mark 15:16-32; Luke 23:26-43; John 19:17-27*

The Roman soldiers took Jesus into the Praetorium and mocked him, dressing him in a scarlet robe and a crown of thorns. They then led him to the crucifixion site outside the city. He was so weakened by his beatings that he could not carry his cross, and a man from Cyrene was forced to carry it to Golgotha.

Golgotha (other possible site)

Antonia Fortress (later Praetorium?)

Traditional Golgotha

Temple

Hasmonean Palace

Herod's Royal Palace

Herod's Lower Palace

UPPER CITY

Caiaphas's House?

JERUSALEM

Traditional Upper Room?

LOWER CITY

N

0   .1 Mi.

0   .1 Km.

Copyright © 2001 by Tyndale House Publishers

THE SEVEN LAST STATEMENTS OF JESUS ON THE CROSS
Matthew 27:46; Luke 23:46

"Father, forgive these people because they don't know what they are doing." . . . . Luke 23:34

"I assure you, today you will be with me in paradise." . . . . Luke 23:43

Speaking to Mary and John, "Woman, he is your son. . . . She is your mother.". . . . . John 19:26-27

"My God, my God, why have you forsaken me?" . . . . Matthew 27:46; Mark 15:34

"I am thirsty." . . . . John 19:28

"It is finished!" . . . . John 19:30

"Father, I entrust my spirit into your hands!" . . . . Luke 23:46

The statements that Jesus made from the cross have been treasured by all who have followed him as Lord. They demonstrate both his humanity and his divinity. They also capture the last moments of all that Jesus went through to gain our forgiveness.

HOW JESUS' TRIAL WAS ILLEGAL / Matthew 26:59

1. Even before the trial began, it had been determined that Jesus must die (Mark 14:1; John 11:50). There was no "innocent until proven guilty" approach.

2. False witnesses were sought to testify against Jesus (Matthew 26:59). Usually the religious leaders went through an elaborate system of screening witnesses to ensure justice.

3. No defense for Jesus was sought or allowed (Luke 22:67-71).

4. The trial was conducted at night (Mark 14:53-65; 15:1), which was illegal according to the religious leaders' own laws.

5. The high priest put Jesus under oath, but then incriminated him for what he said (Matthew 26:63-66).

6. Cases involving such serious charges were to be tried only in the high council's regular meeting place, not in the high priest's home (Mark 14:53-65).

The religious leaders were not interested in giving Jesus a fair trial. In their minds, Jesus had to die. This blind obsession led them to pervert the justice they were appointed to protect. Above are many examples of the actions taken by the religious leaders that were illegal according to their own laws.

JESUS' APPEARANCES AFTER HIS RESURRECTION

Matthew 28:19-20 See also *Mark 16:7; Luke 23:46; John 20:10; 1 Corinthians 15:5*

The truth of Christianity rests heavily on the Resurrection. If Jesus rose from the grave, who saw him? How trustworthy were the witnesses? Those who claimed to have seen the risen Jesus went on to turn the world upside down. Most of them also died for being followers of Christ. People rarely die for halfhearted belief. These are the people who saw Jesus risen from the grave.

1. Mary Magdalene . . . . Mark 16:9-11; John 20:10-18

2. The other women at the tomb . . . . Matthew 28:8-10

3. Peter in Jerusalem . . . . Luke 24:34; 1 Corinthians 15:5

4. The two travelers on the road . . . . Mark 16:12-13; Luke 24:13-35

5. Ten disciples behind closed doors . . . . . Mark 16:14; Luke 24:36-43; John 20:19-25

6. All eleven disciples (including Thomas) . . . John 20:26-31; 1 Corinthians 15:5

7. Seven disciples while fishing on the Sea of Galilee . . . . John 21:1-14

8. Eleven disciples on a mountain in Galilee . . Matthew 28:16-20; Mark 16:15-18

9. A crowd of 500 . . . . 1 Corinthians 15:6

10. Jesus' brother James . . . . 1 Corinthians 15:7

11. Those who watched Jesus ascend into heaven . . . . Mark 16:19-20; Luke 24:44-49; Acts 1:3-8

MARK

MEGATHEMES IN MARK

Theme	Explanation	Importance
Jesus Christ	Jesus Christ alone is the Son of God. In Mark, Jesus demonstrates his divinity by overcoming disease, demons, and death. Although he had the power to be king of the earth, Jesus chose to obey the Father and die for us.	When Jesus rose from the dead, he proved that he was God, that he could forgive sin, and that he has the power to change our lives. By trusting in him for forgiveness, we can begin a new life with him as our guide.
Servant	As the Messiah, Jesus fulfilled the prophecies of the Old Testament by coming to earth. He did not come as a conquering king; he came as a servant. He helped people by telling them about God and healing them. Even more, by giving his life as a sacrifice for sin, he performed the ultimate act of service.	Because of Jesus' example, we should be willing to serve God and others. Real greatness in Christ's kingdom is shown by service and sacrifice. Ambition or love of power or position should not be our motive; instead, we should do God's work because we love him.
Miracles	Mark records more of Jesus' miracles than sermons. Jesus is clearly a man of power and action, not just words. Jesus did miracles to convince the people who he was and to confirm to the disciples his true identity—God.	The more convinced we become that Jesus is God, the more we will see his power and his love. His mighty works show us he is able to save anyone regardless of his or her past. His miracles of forgiveness bring healing, wholeness, and changed lives to those who trust him.
Spreading the Gospel	Jesus directed his public ministry to the Jews first. When the Jewish leaders opposed him, Jesus also went to the non-Jewish world, healing and preaching. Roman soldiers, Syrians, and other Gentiles heard the Good News. Many believed and followed him. Jesus' final message to his disciples challenged them to go into all the world and preach the gospel of salvation.	Jesus crossed national, racial, and economic barriers to spread his Good News. Jesus' message of faith and forgiveness is for the whole world—not just our church, neighborhood, or nation. We must reach out beyond our own people and needs to fulfill the worldwide vision of Jesus Christ so that people everywhere may hear this great message and be saved from sin and death.

KEY PLACES IN MARK

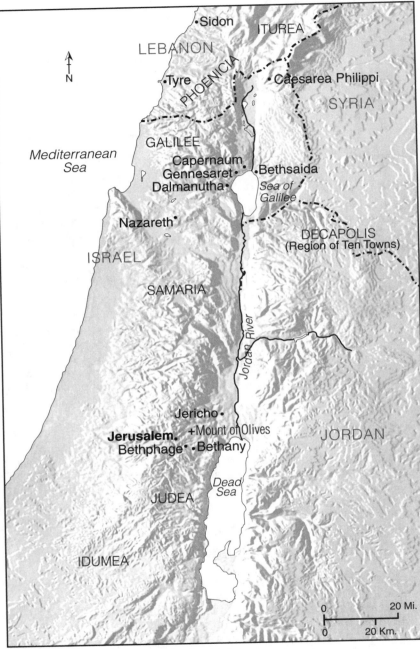

The broken lines (·–·–·) indicate modern boundaries.

Of the four Gospels, Mark's narrative is the most chronological—that is, most of the stories are positioned in the order they actually occurred. Though the shortest of the four, the Gospel of Mark contains the most events; it is action-packed. Most of this action centers in **Galilee**, where Jesus began his ministry. **Capernaum** served as his base of operation (1:21; 2:1; 9:33), from which he would go out to cities like **Bethsaida**, where he healed a blind man (8:22ff); **Gennesaret**, where he performed many healings (6:53ff); **Tyre and Sidon** (to the far north), where he healed many, drove out demons, and met the woman from Syrian Phoenicia (3:8; 7:24ff); and **Caesarea Philippi**, where

Peter declared him to be the Messiah (8:27ff). After his ministry in **Galilee** and the surrounding regions, Jesus headed for **Jerusalem** (10:1). Before going there, Jesus told his disciples three times that he would be crucified there and then come back to life (8:31; 9:31; 10:33-34).

Copyright © 2001 by Tyndale House Publishers

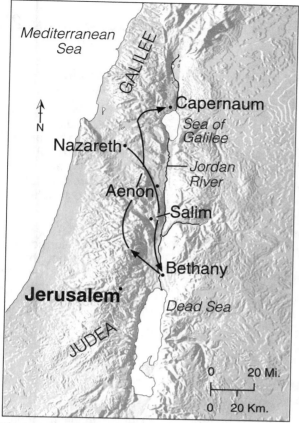

JESUS BEGINS HIS MINISTRY

Mark 1:9-15
See also
Matthew 3:13–4:17; Luke 3:21–4:15; John 4:43-45

When Jesus came from his home in Nazareth to begin his ministry, he first took two steps in preparation—baptism by John in the Jordan River and temptation by Satan in the rough Judean wilderness. After the temptations, Jesus returned to Galilee and later set up his home base in Capernaum.

Copyright © 2001 by Tyndale House Publishers

COMPARISON OF JOHN'S BAPTISM TO JESUS' BAPTISM / *Mark 1:8*

John	Jesus
Baptized with water	Would baptize with the Holy Spirit
Signified preparation for Christ's work	Would convey fulfillment of Christ's work
Person entered the water	The Holy Spirit enters the person to make him or her part of the body of Christ
A ceremonial cleansing that could not save	The presence of the Holy Spirit is evidence of having received salvation

---

See also *John 3:1-2*

Name and Selected References	Description	Agreement with Jesus	Disagreement with Jesus
PHARISEES Matthew 5:20; Matthew 23:1-36; Luke 6:2; Luke 7:36-47	Strict group of religious Jews who advocated obedience to the most minute portions of the Jewish law and traditions. Very influential in the synagogues.	Respect for the law, belief in the resurrection of the dead, commitment to obeying God's will.	Rejected Jesus' claim to be Messiah because he did not follow all their traditions and associated with notoriously wicked people.
SADDUCEES Matthew 3:7; Matthew 16:11-12; Mark 12:18	Wealthy, upper class, Jewish priestly party. Rejected the authority of the Bible beyond the five books of Moses. Profited from business in the Temple. They, along with the Pharisees, were one of the two major parties of the Jewish high council.	Showed great respect for the five books of Moses, as well as the sanctity of the Temple.	Denied the resurrection of the dead. Thought the Temple could also be used as a place to transact business.
TEACHERS OF RELIGIOUS LAW Matthew 7:29; Mark 2:6; Mark 2:16	Professional interpreters of the law—who especially emphasized the traditions. Many teachers of religious law were Pharisees.	Respect for the law. Committed to obeying God.	Denied Jesus' authority to reinterpret the law. Rejected Jesus as Messiah because he did not obey all of their traditions.
SUPPORTERS OF HEROD Matthew 22:16 Mark 3:6; Mark 12:13	A Jewish political party of King Herod's supporters.	Unknown. In the Gospels they tried to trap Jesus with questions and plotted to kill him.	Afraid of Jesus causing political instability. They saw Jesus as a threat to their political future at a time when they were trying to regain from Rome some of their lost political power.
ZEALOTS Luke 6:15; Acts 1:14	A fiercely dedicated group of Jewish patriots determined to end Roman rule in Israel.	Concerned about the future of Israel. Believed in the Messiah but did not recognize Jesus as the one sent by God.	Believed that the Messiah must be a political leader who would deliver Israel from Roman occupation.
ESSENES none	Jewish monastic group practicing ritual purity and personal holiness.	Emphasized justice, honesty, commitment.	Believed ceremonial rituals made them righteous.

KEY CHARACTERISTICS OF CHRIST IN THE GOSPELS / *Mark 2:12*

Characteristic	References
Jesus is the Son of God	Matthew 16:15-16 Mark 1:1 Luke 22:70-71 John 8:24
Jesus is God who became human	John 1:1-2, 14; 20:28
Jesus is the Christ, the Messiah	Matthew 26:63-64 Mark 14:61-62 Luke 9:20 John 4:25-26
Jesus came to help sinners.	Luke 5:32 Matthew 9:13
Jesus has power to forgive sins	Mark 2:9-12 Luke 24:47
Jesus has authority over death	Mark 5:22-24, 35-42 John 11:1-44 Luke 24:5-6 Matthew 28:5-6
Jesus has power to give eternal life	John 10:28; 17:2
Jesus healed the sick.	Matthew 8:5-13 Mark 1:32-34 Luke 5:12-15 John 9:1-7
Jesus taught with authority	Mark 1:21-22 Matthew 7:29
Jesus was compassionate	Mark 1:41; 8:2 Matthew 9:36
Jesus experienced sorrow	Matthew 26:38 John 11:35
Jesus never disobeyed God	Matthew 3:15 John 8:46

THE TWELVE DISCIPLES / Mark 3

Jesus' faithful disciples were ordinary men who became extraordinary because of Jesus Christ. Despite their confusion and lack of understanding during his lifetime, they became powerful witnesses to his resurrection. Their lives were transformed by God's power. The story of Jesus' disciples does not end with the Gospels. It continues in the book of Acts and many of the letters.

Name	Occupation	Outstanding Characteristics	Major Events in His Life
SIMON PETER (son of John)	Fisherman	Impulsive; later—bold in preaching about Jesus	One of three in core group of disciples; recognized Jesus as the Messiah; denied Christ and repented; preached Pentecost sermon; a leader of the Jerusalem church; baptized Gentiles; wrote 1 and 2 Peter.
JAMES (son of Zebedee), he and his brother, John, were called the "Sons of Thunder"	Fisherman	Ambitious, short-tempered, judgmental, deeply committed to Jesus	Also in core group; he and his brother, John, asked Jesus for places of honor in his Kingdom; wanted to call fire down to destroy a Samaritan village; first disciple to be martyred.
JOHN (son of Zebedee), James's brother, and "the disciple whom Jesus loved"	Fisherman	Ambitious, judgmental, later—very loving	Third disciple in core group; asked Jesus for a place of honor in his Kingdom; wanted to call down fire on a Samaritan village; a leader of the Jerusalem church; wrote the Gospel of John and 1, 2, 3 John and Revelation.
ANDREW (Peter's brother)	Fisherman	Eager to bring others to Jesus	Accepted John the Baptist's testimony about Jesus; told Peter about Jesus; he and Philip told Jesus that Greeks wanted to see him.
PHILIP	Fisherman	Questioning attitude	Told Nathanael about Jesus; wondered how Jesus could feed the 5,000; asked Jesus to show his followers God the Father; he and Andrew told Jesus that Greeks wanted to see him.
BARTHOLOMEW (Nathanael)	Unknown	Honest and straightforward	Initially rejected Jesus because Jesus was from Nazareth but acknowledged him as the "Son of God" and "King of Israel" when they met.
MATTHEW (Levi)	Tax collector	Despised outcast because of his dishonest career	Abandoned his corrupt (and financially profitable) way of life to follow Jesus; invited Jesus to a party with his notorious friends; wrote the Gospel of Matthew.
THOMAS (the Twin)	Unknown	Courage and doubt	Suggested the disciples go with Jesus to Bethany—even if it meant death; asked Jesus about where he was going; refused to believe Jesus was risen until he could see Jesus alive and touch his wounds.
JAMES (son of Alphaeus)	Unknown	Unknown	Became one of Jesus' disciples.
THADDAEUS (Judas son of James)	Unknown	Unknown	Asked Jesus why he would reveal himself to his followers and not to the world.
SIMON THE ZEALOT	Unknown	Fierce patriotism	Became a disciple of Jesus.
JUDAS ISCARIOT	Unknown	Treacherous and greedy	Became one of Jesus' disciples; betrayed Jesus; killed himself.

What Jesus Said about Him	A Key Lesson from His Life	Selected References
Named him Peter, "rock"; called him "Satan" when he urged Jesus to reject the cross; said he would fish for people; he received revelation from God; he would deny Jesus; he would later be crucified for his faith.	Christians falter at times, but when they return to Jesus, he forgives them and strengthens their faith.	Matthew 4:18-20 Mark 8:29-33 Luke 22:31-34 John 21:15-19 Acts 2:14-41 Acts 10:1–11:18
Called James and John "Sons of Thunder"; said he would fish for people; would drink the cup Jesus drank.	Christians must be willing to die for Jesus.	Mark 3:17 Mark 10:35-40 Luke 9:52-56 Acts 12:1-2
Called John and James "Sons of Thunder"; said he would fish for people; he would drink the cup Jesus drank; and he would take care of Jesus' mother after Jesus' death.	The transforming power of the love of Christ is available to all.	Mark 1:19 Mark 10:35-40 Luke 9:52-56 John 19:26-27 John 21:20-24
Said he would fish for people.	Christians are to tell other people about Jesus.	Matthew 4:18-20 John 1:35-42; 6:8-9 John 12:20-24
Asked if Philip realized that to know and see him was to know and see the Father.	God uses our questions to teach us.	Matthew 10:3 John 1:43-46; 6:2-7 John 12:20-22 John 14:8-11
Called him "a true son of Israel" and "an honest man."	Jesus respects honesty in people—even if they challenge him because of it.	Mark 3:18 John 1:45-51 John 21:1-13
Called him to be a disciple.	Christianity is not for people who think they're already good; it is for people who know they've failed and want help.	Matthew 9:9-13 Mark 2:15-17 Luke 5:27-32
Said Thomas believed because he actually saw Jesus after the Resurrection.	Even when Christians experience serious doubts, Jesus reaches out to them to restore their faith.	Matthew 10:3 John 14:5; 20:24-29 John 21:1-13
Unknown	Unknown	Matthew 10:3 Mark 3:18 Luke 6:15
Unknown	Christians follow Jesus because they believe in him; they do not always understand the details of God's plan.	Matthew 10:3 Mark 3:18 John 14:22
Unknown	If we are willing to give up our plans for the future, we can participate in Jesus' plans.	Matthew 10:4 Mark 3:18 Luke 6:15
Called him "a devil"; said Judas would betray Jesus.	It is not enough to be familiar with Jesus' teachings. Jesus' true followers love and obey him.	Matthew 26:20-25 Luke 22:47-48 John 12:4-8

TODAY'S THORNS / *Mark 4:18-19*

We must welcome God's Word exclusively so nothing stifles or distracts us. We must weed out or avoid the thorn patches. As James wrote, "It is a message to obey, not just to listen to" (James 1:22).

The Thorn	The Problem	The Solution
Worries of this life. Society says, "Take care of yourself; no one else will."	Fear of persecution for being identified with Christ can neutralize people who are worried that they will be ridiculed. Daily concerns, schedules, and pressures can snuff out our time and energy to grow. Worry consumes our thoughts, disrupts our productivity, and reduces our trust in God.	James 1:12 "God blesses the people who patiently endure testing. Afterward they will receive the crown of life that God has promised to those who love him." Philippians 4:6 "Don't worry about anything; instead, pray about everything. Tell God what you need, and thank him for all he has done." Matthew 6:31 "So don't worry about having enough food or drink or clothing."
Deceitfulness of wealth. Society says, "Wealth brings security, power, and happiness."	Wealth can take God's place in our lives. It can become an idol—the focus of our activities and devotion. It tempts us to deny our dependence on God, keeping our eyes off of eternal values. Wealth leads to pride.	Jeremiah 9:23 "This is what the LORD says: 'Let not the wise man gloat in his wisdom, or the mighty man in his might, or the rich man in his riches.'" Luke 12:34 "Wherever your treasure is, there your heart and thoughts will also be." 1 Timothy 6:6 "Yet true religion with contentment is great wealth." 1 Timothy 6:10 "For the love of money is at the root of all kinds of evil. And some people, craving money, have wandered from the faith and pierced themselves with many sorrows."
Desires for other things. Society says, "Indulge yourself; try it all; get all you can."	Indulging our desires leads to all kinds of problems. It weakens our will power, stifles and distracts us from growing, and leads to companions who will pull us down.	Romans 13:14 "But let the Lord Jesus Christ take control of you, and don't think of ways to indulge your evil desires." 1 Corinthians 15:33 "Don't be fooled by those who say such things, for "bad company corrupts good character." 1 Peter 1:13-14 "So think clearly and exercise self-control. Look forward to the special blessings that will come to you at the return of Jesus Christ. Obey God because you are his children. Don't slip back into your old ways of doing evil; you didn't know any better then."

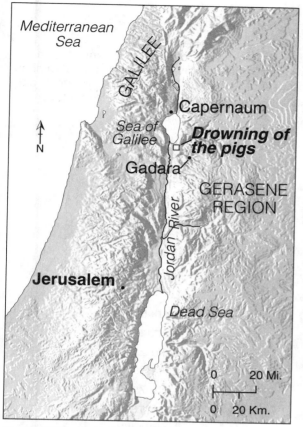

Mediterranean Sea

GALILEE

Capernaum

Sea of Galilee

Drowning of the pigs

Gadara

GERASENE REGION

Jordan River

Jerusalem

Dead Sea

N

0   20 Mi.

0   20 Km.

Copyright © 2001 by Tyndale House Publishers

HEALING A DEMON-POSSESSED MAN

Mark 4:35–5:20

See also *Matthew 8:23-34; Luke 8:22-39*

From Capernaum, Jesus and his disciples crossed the Sea of Galilee. A storm blew up unexpectedly, but Jesus calmed it. Landing in the region of the Gerasenes, Jesus sent demons out of a man and into a herd of pigs that plunged over the steep bank into the lake.

THE TOUCH OF JESUS / *Mark 5:41*

What kind of people did Jesus associate with? Whom did he consider important enough to touch? Here we see many of the people Jesus came to know. Some reached out to him; he reached out to them all. Regardless of how great or unknown, rich or poor, young or old, sinner or saint—Jesus cares equally for each one. No person is beyond the loving touch of Jesus.

Jesus talked with . . .	Reference
A despised tax collector	Matthew 9:9
An insane hermit	Mark 5:1-15
The Roman governor	Mark 15:1-15
A young boy	Mark 9:17-27
A prominent religious leader	John 3:1-21
A homemaker	Luke 10:38-42
An expert in the law	Matthew 22:35
A criminal	Luke 23:40-43
A synagogue ruler	Mark 5:22
Fishermen	Matthew 4:18-20
A king	Luke 23:7-11
A poor widow	Luke 7:11-17; 21:1-4
A Roman centurion	Luke 7:1-10
A group of children	Mark 10:13-16
A prophet	Matthew 3
An adulterous woman	John 8:1-11
The Jewish council	Luke 22:66-71
A sick woman	Mark 5:25-34
A rich man	Mark 10:17-23
A blind beggar	Mark 10:46
Jewish political leaders	Mark 12:13
A group of women	Luke 8:2-3
The high priest	Matthew 26:62-68
An outcast with leprosy	Luke 17:11-19
A royal official	John 4:46-53
A young girl	Mark 5:41-42
A traitor	John 13:1-3, 27
A helpless and paralyzed man	Mark 2:1-12
An angry mob of soldiers and police	John 18:3-9
A woman from a foreign land	Mark 7:25-30
A doubting follower	John 20:24-29
An enemy who hated him	Acts 9:1-9
A Samaritan woman	John 4:1-26

REAL LEADERSHIP / *Mark 6:29*

Mark gives us some of the best insights into Jesus' character.

Herod as a leader	Jesus as a leader
Selfish	Compassionate
Murderer	Healer
Immoral	Just and good
Political opportunist	Servant
Ruler over small territory	King over all creation

CONTRASTING FEASTS / *Mark 6:42-43*

Who's in charge	Herod, the official ruler (6:14)	The people, who were "without a leader" (6:34)	Jesus, the Shepherd supreme (6:39-40)
Occasion	All-male birthday party and sumptuous feast for rich and influential people (6:21)	Following Jesus into the wilderness (6:35-36)	Provides a simple "poor man's" meal of bread and fish (6:41)
Result	Ends in murder, grief, and guilt (6:26-28)	Wondering where to get food (6:37)	This meal points to the heavenly banquet and rest promised to all believers (6:42)

JESUS WALKS ON THE WATER

Mark 6:30-56 See also *Matthew 14:13-36; Luke 9:10-17; John 6:1-21*

After feeding the people who had followed to hear him at Bethsaida, Jesus sent the people home, sent his disciples by boat toward Bethsaida, and went to pray. The disciples encountered a storm, and Jesus walked to them on the water. They landed at Gennesaret.

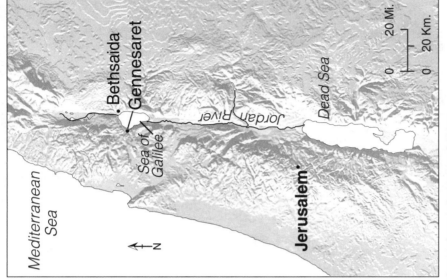

Mediterranean Sea

Bethsaida

Gennesaret

Sea of Galilee

Jordan River

Dead Sea

Jerusalem

N

20 Mi.

20 Km.

0

0

Copyright © 2001 by Tyndale House Publishers

PREACHING IN GALILEE

Mark 6:1-34 See also *Matthew 10:1-15; 13:53-58; 14:1-21; Luke 9:1-17*

After returning to his hometown, Nazareth, from Capernaum, Jesus preached in the villages of Galilee and sent his disciples out to preach as well. After meeting back in Capernaum, they left by boat to rest, only to be met by the crowds who followed the boat along the shore.

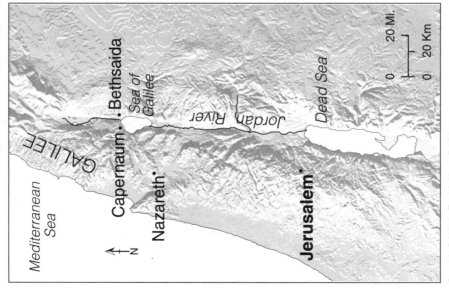

Mediterranean Sea

GALILEE

Capernaum

Bethsaida

Sea of Galilee

Nazareth

Jordan River

Dead Sea

Jerusalem

N

20 Mi.

20 Km

0

0

Copyright © 2001 by Tyndale House Publishers

CONTINUED MINISTRY

Mark 7:31–8:38

See also
*Matthew 15:29–16:28;
Luke 9:18–27*

After taking a roundabout way back to Galilee through Decapolis (the Ten Towns), Jesus returned to Dalmanutha where Jewish leaders questioned his authority. From there he went to Bethsaida and on to Caesarea Philippi. Here he talked with his disciples about his authority and coming events.

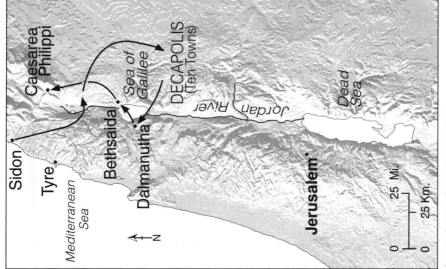

Caesarea Philippi

Sidon

Tyre

Mediterranean Sea

Bethsaida

Dalmanutha

Sea of Galilee

DECAPOLIS (Ten Towns)

Jordan River

Dead Sea

Jerusalem

N

0 ____ 25 Mi.

0 ____ 25 Km.

Copyright © 2001 by Tyndale House Publishers

MINISTRY IN PHOENICIA

Mark 7:1–30

See also
Matthew 15:1–28

Jesus' ministry was to all people—first to Jews but also to Gentiles. Jesus took his disciples from Galilee to Tyre and Sidon, large cities in Phoenicia, where he healed a Gentile woman's daughter.

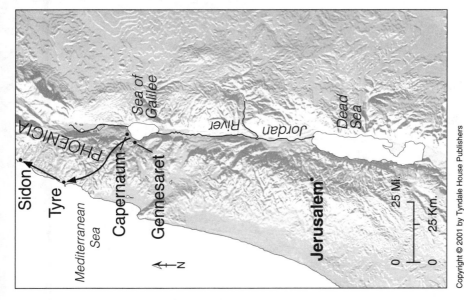

Sidon

Tyre

Mediterranean Sea

PHOENICIA

Capernaum

Gennesaret

Sea of Galilee

Jordan River

Dead Sea

Jerusalem

N

0 ____ 25 Mi.

0 ____ 25 Km.

Copyright © 2001 by Tyndale House Publishers

GOSPEL ACCOUNTS FOUND ONLY IN MARK / *Mark 7:31*

Section	Topic	Significance
4:26-29	Story of the growing seed	We must share the Good News of Jesus with other people, but only God makes it grow in their lives
7:31-37	Jesus healed a deaf man who could hardly talk	Jesus cares about our physical as well as spiritual needs
8:22-26	Jesus healed the blind man at Bethsaida	Jesus is considerate because he made sure this man's sight was fully restored

WHAT THE BIBLE SAYS ABOUT MARRIAGE / *Mark 10:9*

See also *1 Corinthians 7:12-13*

Reference	Characteristic
Genesis 2:18-24	Marriage is God's idea.
Genesis 24:58-60	Commitment is essential to a successful marriage.
Genesis 29:10-11	Romance is important.
Jeremiah 7:34	Marriage holds times of great joy.
Malachi 2:14-15	Marriage creates the best environment for raising children.
Matthew 5:32	Unfaithfulness breaks the bond of trust, the foundation of all relationships.
Matthew 19:6	Marriage is permanent.
Romans 7:2-3	Ideally, only death should dissolve marriage.
Ephesians 5:21-33	Marriage is based on the principled practice of love, not on feelings.
Ephesians 5:23-32	Marriage is a living symbol of Christ and the church.
Hebrews 13:4	Marriage is good and honorable.

FINAL TRIP TO JUDEA

Mark 10:1-52
See also *Matthew 19:1–20:34; Luke 18:15-43*

Jesus quietly left Capernaum, heading toward the borders of Judea before crossing the Jordan River. He preached there before going to Jericho. This trip from Galilee was his last; he would not return before his death.

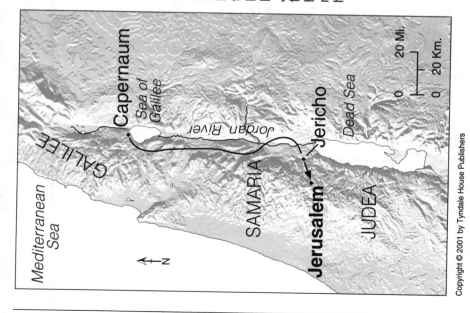

Copyright © 2001 by Tyndale House Publishers

JESUS NEARS JERUSALEM

Mark 11:1-11
See also *Matthew 21:1-11; Luke 19:28-44; John 12:12-19*

Leaving Jericho, Jesus headed toward acclaim, then crucifixion, in Jerusalem. During his last week, he stayed outside the city in Bethany, a village on the eastern slope of the Mount of Olives, entering Jerusalem to teach, eat the Passover, and finally be crucified.

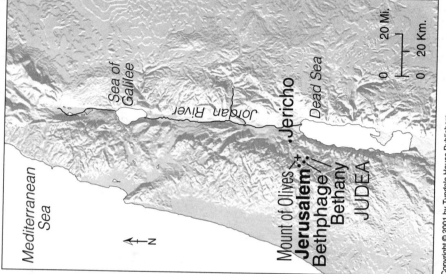

Copyright © 2001 by Tyndale House Publishers

KEY CHARACTERISTICS OF CHRIST IN THE GOSPELS / *Mark 11*

Characteristic	Reference
Jesus is the Son of God	Matthew 16:15-16; Mark 1:1; Luke 22:70-71; John 8:24
Jesus is God who became human	John 1:1-2, 14; 20:28
Jesus is the Christ, the Messiah	Matthew 26:63-64; Mark 14:61-62; Luke 9:20; John 4:25-26
Jesus came to help sinners	Matthew 9:13; Luke 5:32
Jesus has power to forgive sins	Mark 2:9-12; Luke 24:47
Jesus has authority over death	Matthew 28:5-6; Mark 5:22-24, 35-42; Luke 24:5-6; John 11:1-44
Jesus has power to give eternal life	John 10:28; 17:2
Jesus healed the sick	Matthew 8:5-13; Mark 1:32-34; Luke 5:12-15; John 9:1-7
Jesus taught with authority	Matthew 7:29; Mark 1:21-22
Jesus was compassionate	Matthew 9:36; Mark 1:41; 8:2
Jesus experienced sorrow	Matthew 26:38; John 11:35
Jesus never disobeyed God	Matthew 3:15; John 8:46

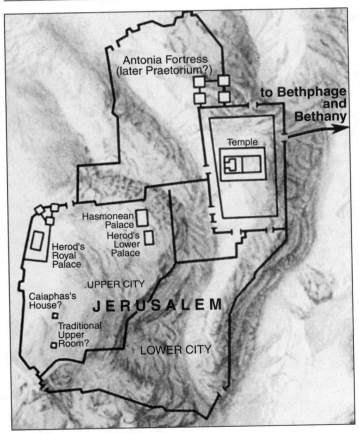

CLEARING THE TEMPLE

Mark 11:12-19
See also *Matthew 21:12-17; Luke 19:45-48*

On Monday morning of his last week, Jesus left Bethany, entered Jerusalem, and cleared the Temple of money changers and merchants.

Copyright © 2001 by Tyndale House Publishers

PERSECUTED PROPHETS / *Mark 12:1-8* See also *James 5:10*

The Persecuted	The Persecutors	Reason	Result	Reference
Prophets	Jezebel	Jezebel didn't like to have her evil ways pointed out.	Many prophets were killed.	1 Kings 18:3-4
Elijah	Ahab and Jezebel	Elijah confronted their sins.	Elijah had to flee for his life.	1 Kings 18:10–19:2
Micaiah	Ahab	Ahab thought Micaiah was stirring up trouble rather than prophesying from God.	Micaiah was thrown into prison.	2 Chronicles 18:12-26
Elisha	A king of Israel	The king thought Elisha had caused the famine.	Elisha ignored the threatened persecution and prophesied the famine's end.	2 Kings 6:31
Hanani	Asa	Hanani criticized Asa for trusting in Syria's help more than in God's help.	Hanani was thrown in jail.	2 Chronicles 16:7-10
Zechariah	Joash	Zechariah confronted the people of Judah for disregarding God's Word.	Zechariah was executed.	2 Chronicles 24:20-22
Uriah (Urijah)	Jehoiakim	Uriah confronted Jehoiakim about his evil ways.	Uriah was butchered.	Jeremiah 26:20-23
Jeremiah	Zedekiah	Zedekiah thought Jeremiah was a traitor for prophesying Jerusalem's fall.	Jeremiah was thrown in prison, then into a muddy cistern.	Jeremiah 37:1–38:13
John the Baptist	Herod and Herodias	John confronted their adultery.	John was beheaded.	Mark 6:14-29

WHAT WE KNOW ABOUT HEAVEN / *Mark 12:18*

Heaven is being prepared by Christ himself . . . . John 14:3

Heaven is only for those who have been born again . . John 3:3

Heaven is described as a glorious city . . . . Revelation 21:11, 18

Heaven will shine with and be lighted by God's glory . . Revelation 21:11, 23; 22:5

Heaven's gates will never be shut . . . . Revelation 21:25

Heaven has the River of Life to insure everlasting life . . Revelation 22:1

Heaven has the Tree of Life to insure abundant life . . . Revelation 2:7; 22:19

Heaven has the throne of God at its center . . . . Revelation 4:2; 22:1

Heaven is a place of holiness . . . . Revelation 21:27

Heaven is beautiful . . . . Psalm 50:2

Heaven is a place of unity . . . . Ephesians 1:10

Heaven is a place of perfection . . . . 1 Corinthians 13:10

Heaven is joyful . . . . Psalm 16:11

Heaven is a place for all eternity . . . . John 3:15; Psalm 23:6

Heaven has no night . . . . Revelation 21:25; 22:5

Heaven has singing . . . . Isaiah 44:23; Revelation 14:3; 15:3

Heaven has serving . . . . Revelation 7:15; 22:3

Heaven has learning . . . . 1 Corinthians 13:9-10

WHAT WE KNOW ABOUT OUR BODIES IN HEAVEN / *Mark 12:25*

Our bodies will . . .	Reference
be recognizable	1 Corinthians 13:2
be like Christ's body	1 John 3:2
be bodies in which the spirit predominates	1 Corinthians 15:44, 49
be unlimited by time, gravity, or space	Luke 24:31; John 20:19, 26
be eternal	2 Corinthians 5:1
be glorious	Romans 8:18; 1 Corinthians 15:43
shed no tears	Revelation 7:17; 21:4
not get sick	Revelation 22:2
not have pain	Revelation 21:4
not die	1 Corinthians 15:26; Revelation 21:4
not hunger or thirst	Revelation 7:16
not sin	Revelation 21:27

WHAT JESUS SAID ABOUT LOVE / *Mark 12:31*

In Mark 12:28 a teacher of the law asked Jesus which of all the commandments was the most important to follow. Jesus mentioned two commandments, one from Deuteronomy 6:5, the other from Leviticus 19:18. Both had to do with love. Why is love so important? Jesus said that all of the commandments were given for two simple reasons—to help us love God and love others as we should.

What else did Jesus say about love?	**Reference**
God loves us.	John 3:16
We are to love God.	Matthew 22:37
Because God loves us, he cares for us.	Matthew 6:25-34
God wants everyone to know how much he loves them.	John 17:23
God loves even those who hate him; we are to do the same.	Matthew 5:43-47; Luke 6:35
God seeks out even those most alienated from him.	Luke 15
God must be your first love.	Matthew 6:24; 10:37
You love God when you obey him.	John 14:21; 15:10
God loves Jesus, his Son.	John 5:20; 10:17
Jesus loves God.	John 14:31
Those who refuse Jesus don't have God's love.	John 5:41-44
Jesus loves us just as God loves Jesus.	John 15:9
Jesus proved his love for us by dying on the cross so that we could live eternally with him.	John 3:14-15; 15:13-14
The love between God and Jesus is the perfect example of how we are to love others.	John 17:21-26
We are to love one another (John 13:34-35) and demonstrate that love.	Matthew 5:40-42; 10:42
We are not to love the praise of people (John 12:43), selfish recognition (Matthew 23:6), earthly belongings (Luke 16:19-31), or anything more than God.	Luke 16:13
Jesus' love extends to each individual.	John 10:11-15; Mark 10:21
Jesus wants us to love him through the good and the bad times.	Matthew 26:31-35
Jesus wants our love to be genuine.	John 21:15-17

SACRIFICES OF THE HEART / *Mark 12:33*

God says many times that he doesn't want our gifts and sacrifices when we give them out of ritual or hypocrisy. God wants us first to love and obey him.

1 Samuel 15:22-23 . . . . Obedience is far better than sacrifice.

Psalm 40:6-8 . . . . God doesn't want burnt animals; he wants our lifelong service.

Psalm 51:16-19 . . . . God isn't interested in penance; he wants a broken and contrite heart.

Jeremiah 7:21-23 . . . . It isn't offerings God wants; he desires our obedience and promises that he will be our God and we shall be his people.

Hosea 6:6 . . . . God doesn't want sacrifices, he wants love; he doesn't want offerings, he wants us to know him.

Amos 5:21-24 . . . . God hates pretense and hypocrisy; he wants to see a flood of justice.

Micah 6:6-8 . . . . God is not satisfied with sacrifices; he wants us to be fair and just and merciful, and to walk humbly with him.

Matthew 9:13 . . . . God doesn't want gifts; he wants us to be merciful.

KING DAVID'S FAMOUS DESCENDANT / *Mark 12:37*

David's descendant will be on the throne forever . . . . 2 Samuel 7:8-16

David was promised that his line would last forever . . . . Psalm 89:3-4

David's descendant shall be born who will be called Wonderful Counselor, Mighty God, Everlasting Father, Prince of Peace. His reign on David's throne will last forever. . . . . Isaiah 9:2-7

David's descendant will have the Spirit of the Lord upon him and his rule will bring lasting peace . . . . Isaiah 11:1-9

David's descendant will reign wisely, do what is just and right, and be called the Lord Our Righteousness . . . . Jeremiah 23:5-6

David's descendant will be raised up by the Lord and will restore Israel . . . . Jeremiah 30:9

David's descendant will be a righteous "Branch" who will restore Judah and Jerusalem . . . . Jeremiah 33:15-17, 22

David's descendant will rule over God's people and be a prince among them . . . . Ezekiel 34:23-24

David's descendant will be the people's king and shepherd . . . . . Ezekiel 37:24

The Israelites will turn back to God and to David's great descendant . . . . Hosea 3:5

JESUS' PROPHECIES IN THE OLIVET DISCOURSE / *Mark 13:8*

In Mark 13, often called the Olivet Discourse, Jesus talked a lot about two future events: the end times and his second coming. Jesus was not trying to encourage his disciples to speculate about exactly when he would return by sharing these prophecies with them. Instead, he was urging all his followers to be watchful and prepared for his second coming. Serve Jesus faithfully now and you will be ready for his return.

Type of Prophecy	Old Testament References	Other New Testament References
THE LAST DAYS		
Mark 13:1-23	Daniel 9:26-27	John 15:21
Matthew 24:1-28	Daniel 11:31	Revelation 11:2
Luke 21:5-24	Joel 2:2	1 Timothy 4:1-2
THE SECOND COMING		
Mark 13:24-27	Isaiah 13:6-10	Revelation 6:12
Luke 21:25-28	Ezekiel 32:7	Mark 14:62
Matthew 24:29-31	Daniel 7:13-14	1 Thessalonians 4:16

ENDURE TO THE END / *Mark 13:13*

"And everyone will hate you because of your allegiance to me. But those who endure to the end will be saved."

Matthew 10:22

"They give us hope and encouragement as we wait patiently for God's promises."

Romans 15:4

"We have worked wearily with our own hands to earn our living. We bless those who curse us. We are patient with those who abuse us."

1 Corinthians 4:12

"So when we are weighed down with troubles, it is for your benefit and salvation! For when God comforts us, it is so that we, in turn, can be an encouragement to you. Then you can patiently endure the same things we suffer."

2 Corinthians 1:6

"In everything we do we try to show that we are true ministers of God. We patiently endure troubles and hardships and calamities of every kind."

2 Corinthians 6:4

"We also pray that you will be strengthened with his glorious power so that you will have all the patience and endurance you need. May you be filled with joy."

Colossians 1:11

"As we talk to our God and Father about you, we think of your faithful work, your loving deeds, and your continual anticipation of the return of our Lord Jesus Christ."

1 Thessalonians 1:3

"But you, Timothy, belong to God; so run from all these evil things, and follow what is right and good. Pursue a godly life, along with faith, love, perseverance, and gentleness."

1 Timothy 6:11

"Endure suffering along with me, as a good soldier of Christ Jesus."

2 Timothy 2:3

"I am willing to endure anything if it will bring salvation and eternal glory in Christ Jesus to those God has chosen."

2 Timothy 2:10

"If we endure hardship, we will reign with him. If we deny him, he will deny us."

2 Timothy 2:12

"But you know what I teach, Timothy, and how I live, and what my purpose in life is. You know my faith and how long I have suffered. You know my love and my patient endurance."

2 Timothy 3:10

"But you should keep a clear mind in every situation. Don't be afraid of suffering for the Lord. Work at bringing others to Christ. Complete the ministry God has given you."

2 Timothy 4:5

"Teach the older men to exercise self-control, to be worthy of respect, and to live wisely. They must have strong faith and be filled with love and patience."

Titus 2:2

"As you endure this divine discipline, remember that God is treating you as his own children. Whoever heard of a child who was never disciplined?"

Hebrews 12:7

"This suffering is all part of what God has called you to. Christ, who suffered for you, is your example. Follow in his steps.

He did not retaliate when he was insulted. When he suffered, he did not threaten to get even. He left his case in the hands of God, who always judges fairly."

1 Peter 2:21, 23

"I am John, your brother. In Jesus we are partners in suffering and in the Kingdom and in patient endurance. I was exiled to the island of Patmos for preaching the word of God and speaking about Jesus."

Revelation 1:9

"You have patiently suffered for me without quitting."

Revelation 2:3

"The people who are destined for prison will be arrested and taken away. Those who are destined for death will be killed. But do not be dismayed, for here is your opportunity to have endurance and faith.

Let this encourage God's holy people to endure persecution patiently and remain firm to the end, obeying his commands and trusting in Jesus."

Revelation 13:10; 14:12

JESUS AND THE FATHER ARE ONE / *Mark 13:32*

During his earthly life, Jesus subordinated himself to the will of his Father. He perfectly obeyed what his Father willed (see John 4:34; 5:30; 6:38; 7:28; 8:29). The cult called Jehovah's Witnesses have used these verses to attack Jesus' divinity. Others have used similar arguments to undermine faith in Jesus.

Incorrect Conclusions

Jesus is a creature. Those who believe this use Acts 2:36, "So let it be clearly known by everyone in Israel that God has made this Jesus whom you crucified to be both Lord and Messiah!" and Colossians 1:15, "Christ is the visible image of the invisible God. He existed before God made anything at all and is supreme over all creation."

Jesus is not God. Those who believe this use John 17:3, "And this is the way to have eternal life—to know you, the only true God, and Jesus Christ, the one you sent to earth."

Jesus is inferior to the Father. Those who believe this use John 14:28 where Jesus said, "Remember what I told you: I am going away, but I will come back to you again. If you really love me, you will be very happy for me, because now I can go to the Father, who is greater than I am."

Jesus didn't have divine knowledge, so couldn't be divine. Those who believe this use Mark 13:32 where Jesus said, "However, no one knows the day or hour when these things will happen, not even the angels in heaven or the Son himself. Only the Father knows."

The Complete Truth

BUT in context, these verses apply to Jesus' office and function, not his origin. In Colossians, "supreme" means first in rank.

BUT in context, Jesus' prayer was contrasting the Father with false gods and spiritual rivals—not with himself, the Son.

BUT in context, in his earthly ministry, Jesus took upon himself a functional subordination of his will and divine powers. During the incarnation, he was dependent upon God for his divine attributes.

BUT in context, Jesus voluntarily took on limitations to accommodate his humanity. These are not limitations of his essential divinity, but only of his physical humanity.

Jesus and the Bible affirm the Trinity, and Jesus' essential oneness, equality, and interchangeability with God, the Father. See Matthew 28:19; John 10:30; 17:21-22; 2 Corinthians 13:14.

MAJOR EVENTS OF PASSION WEEK / *Mark 14:10*

Sunday through Wednesday Jesus spent each night in Bethany, just two miles east of Jerusalem on the opposite slope of the Mount of Olives. He probably stayed at the home of Mary, Martha, and Lazarus. Jesus spent Thursday night praying in the Garden of Gethsemane. During Friday and Saturday nights, Jesus' body lay in the garden tomb.

Day	Event	References
Sunday	Triumphal Entry into Jerusalem	Matthew 21:1-11; Mark 11:1-10; Luke 19:29-40; John 12:12-19
Monday	Jesus clears the temple	Matthew 21:12-13; Mark 11:15-17; Luke 19:45-46
Tuesday	Jesus' authority is challenged in the temple Jesus teaches in stories and confronts the Jewish leaders Greeks ask to see Jesus Jesus gives the Olivet Discourse Judas agrees to betray Jesus	Matthew 21:23-27; Mark 11:27-33; Luke 20:1-8; Matthew 21:28–23:36; Mark 12:1-40; Luke 20:9-47; John 12:20-26; Matthew 24; Mark 13; Luke 21:5-38; Matthew 26:14-16; Mark 14:10-11; Luke 22:3-6
Wednesday	The Bible does not say what Jesus did on this day. He probably remained in Bethany with his disciples	
Thursday	Jesus and the disciples celebrate the Last Supper Jesus speaks to the disciples in the upper room Jesus struggles in Gethsemane Jesus is betrayed and arrested	Matthew 26:26-29; Mark 14:22-25; Luke 22:14-20; John 13–17; Matthew 26:36-46; Mark 14:32-42; Luke 22:39-46; John 18:1; Matthew 26:47-56; Mark 14:43-52; Luke 22:47-53; John 18:2-12
Friday	Jesus is tried by Jewish and Roman authorities and denied by Peter Jesus is crucified	Matthew 26:57–27:2, 11-31; Mark 14:53–15:20; Luke 22:54–23:25; John 18:13–19:16; Matthew 27:31-56; Mark 15:20-41; Luke 23:26-49; John 19:17-30
Sunday	Jesus rises from the dead	Matthew 28:1-10; Mark 16:1-11; Luke 24:1-12; John 20:1-18

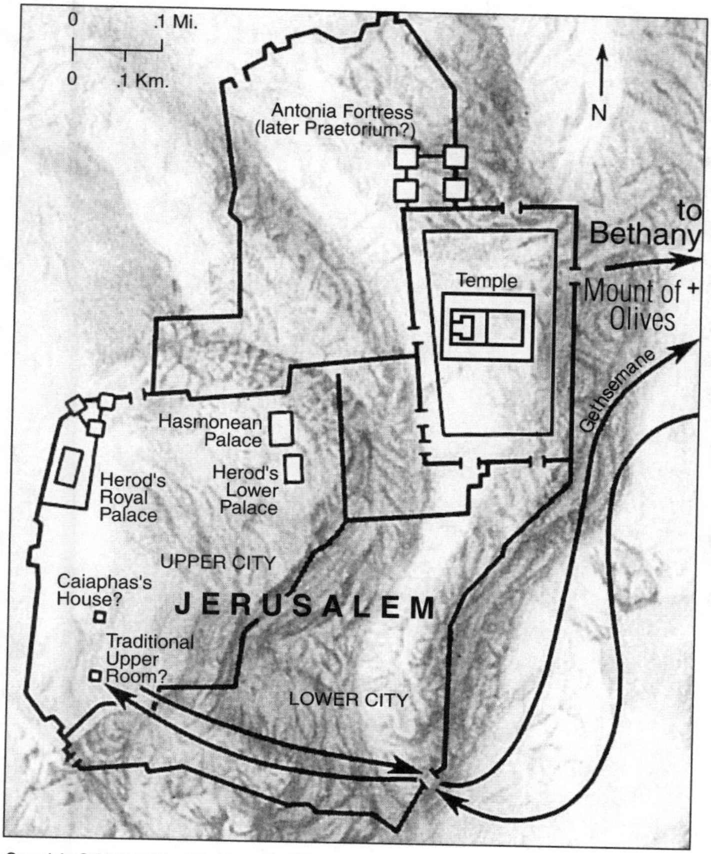
0 .1 Mi.
0 .1 Km.
N
Antonia Fortress
(later Praetorium?)
to
Bethany
Temple
Mount of
Olives
Gethsemane
Hasmonean
Palace
Herod's
Lower
Palace
Herod's
Royal
Palace
UPPER CITY
Caiaphas's
House?
JERUSALEM
Traditional
Upper
Room?
LOWER CITY

Copyright © 2001 by Tyndale House Publishers

UPPER ROOM AND GETHSEMANE

Mark 14:12-42
See also *Matthew 26:17-46; Luke 22:7-46; John 13:21-38*

Jesus and the disciples ate the traditional Passover meal in an upper room in the city and then went to the Mount of Olives into a garden called Gethsemane. In the cool of the evening, Jesus prayed for strength to face the trial and suffering ahead.

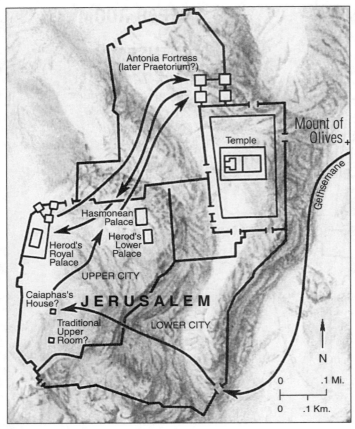

JESUS' TRIAL

Mark 14:43–15:15
See also *Matthew 26:47–27:26; Luke 22:47–23:25; John 18:1–19:16*

From Gethsemane, Jesus' trial began at the home of Caiaphas, the high priest. Jesus was then taken to Pilate, the Roman governor. Luke records that Pilate sent him to Herod, who was in Jerusalem—presumably in one of his two palaces (Luke 23:5-12). Herod sent him back to Pilate, who handed Jesus over to be crucified.

Map labels: Antonia Fortress (later Praetorium?); Mount of Olives; Temple; Gethsemane; Hasmonean Palace; Herod's Lower Palace; Herod's Royal Palace; UPPER CITY; Caiaphas's House?; JERUSALEM; Traditional Upper Room?; LOWER CITY; N; 0 .1 Mi.; 0 .1 Km.

Copyright © 2001 by Tyndale House Publishers

MARK CONTRASTS MARY AND JUDAS / *Mark 14:10*

When Mark placed the response of Mary prior to the response of Judas in his Gospel account, he was deliberately telling us to be like Mary, not like Judas. We need Mary's heart.

Mary	Judas
Had a loving heart.	Had a loveless heart
Gave generously	Bartered greedily
Praised Jesus by her actions	Plotted against Jesus
Attributed worth to Christ	Doubted and despaired
Pursued heavenly values	Sought earthly solutions
Remembered for her unselfishness.	Remembered as a traitor

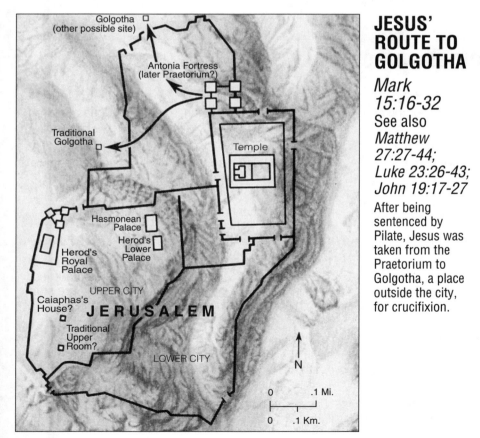

JESUS' ROUTE TO GOLGOTHA

Mark 15:16-32
See also *Matthew 27:27-44; Luke 23:26-43; John 19:17-27*

After being sentenced by Pilate, Jesus was taken from the Praetorium to Golgotha, a place outside the city, for crucifixion.

Copyright © 2001 by Tyndale House Publishers

WHY DID JESUS HAVE TO DIE? / Mark 15:39

The Problem	We have all done things that are wrong, and we have failed to obey God's laws. Because of this, we have been separated from God our Creator. Separation from God is death; but, by ourselves, we can do nothing to become united with God.
Why Jesus Could Help	Jesus was not only a man; he was God's unique Son. Because Jesus never disobeyed God and never sinned, only he can bridge the gap between the sinless God and sinful mankind.
The Solution	Jesus freely offered his life for us, dying on the cross in our place, taking all our wrongdoing upon himself, and saving us from the consequences of sin—including God's judgment and death.
The Results	Jesus took our past, present, and future sins upon himself so that we could have new life. Because all our wrongdoing is forgiven, we are reconciled to God. Furthermore, Jesus' resurrection from the dead is the proof that his substitutionary sacrifice on the cross was acceptable to God, and his resurrection has become the source of new life for whoever believes that Jesus is the Son of God. All who believe in him may have this new life and live it in union with him.

OUR CONDITION WITHOUT SALVATION / Mark 15:33

In Scripture, darkness is a key concept.

Darkness represents the power of God's presence.	"As the people stood in the distance, Moses entered into the deep darkness where God was" (Exodus 20:21).
Darkness stands for God's judgment.	"So Moses lifted his hand toward heaven, and there was deep darkness over the entire land for three days" (Exodus 10:22).
Darkness is controlled by God.	"I am the one who creates the light and makes the darkness. I am the one who sends good times and bad times. I, the LORD, am the one who does these things" (Isaiah 45:7).
Darkness represents people's sinful rebellion against God.	"But the way of the wicked is like complete darkness. Those who follow it have no idea what they are stumbling over" (Proverbs 4:19; see also John 3:19; Romans 1:21; Ephesians 4:18).
Darkness represents people's ignorance of God.	". . . the people who sat in darkness have seen a great light. And for those who lived in the land where death casts its shadow, a light has shined" (Matthew 4:16; see also John 1:5; Ephesians 4:18).
Darkness represents people's condition without hope in God.	"LORD, you have brought light to my life; my God, you light up my darkness" (Psalm 18:28; see also 1 Peter 2:9).

EVIDENCE THAT JESUS ACTUALLY DIED AND AROSE / *Mark 16:22*

This evidence demonstrates Jesus' uniqueness in history and proves that he is God's Son. No one else was able to predict his own resurrection and then accomplish it.

Proposed Explanations for the Empty Tomb	Evidence Against These Explanations	References
Jesus was only unconscious and later revived.	A Roman soldier told Pilate that Jesus was dead.	Mark 15:44-45
	The Roman soldiers did not break Jesus' legs because he had already died, and one of them pierced Jesus' side with a spear.	John 19:32-34
	Joseph of Arimathea and Nicodemus wrapped Jesus' body and placed it in the tomb.	John 19:38-40
The women made a mistake and went to the wrong tomb.	Mary Magdalene and Mary the mother of Joseph saw Jesus placed in the tomb.	Matthew 27:59-61 Mark 15:47 Luke 23:55
Unknown thieves stole Jesus' body.	On Sunday morning, Peter and John also went to the same tomb.	John 20:3-9
The disciples stole Jesus' body.	The tomb was sealed and guarded by Roman soldiers.	Matthew 27:65-66
	The disciples were ready to die for their faith. Stealing Jesus' body would have been admitting that their faith was meaningless.	Acts 12:2
The religious leaders stole Jesus' body to produce it later.	If the religious leaders had taken Jesus' body, they would have produced it to stop the rumors of his resurrection.	none

LUKE

MEGATHEMES IN LUKE

Theme	Explanation	Importance
Jesus Christ, the Savior	Luke describes how God's Son entered human history. Jesus lived as the perfect example of a human. After a perfect ministry, he provided a perfect sacrifice for our sin so we could be saved.	Jesus is our perfect leader and Savior. He offers forgiveness to all who will accept him as Lord of their lives and believe that what he says is true.
History	Luke was a medical doctor and historian. He put great emphasis on dates and details, connecting Jesus to events and people in history.	Luke gives details so we can believe in the reliability of the history of Jesus' life. Even more important, we can believe with certainty that Jesus is God.
People	Jesus was deeply interested in people and relationships. He showed warm concern for his followers and friends—men, women, and children.	Jesus' love for people is good news for everyone. His message is for all people in every nation. Each one of us has an opportunity to respond to him in faith.
Compassion	As a perfect human, Jesus showed tender sympathy to the poor, the despised, the hurt, and the sinful. No one was rejected or ignored by him.	Jesus is more than a good teacher— he cares for you. Because of his deep love for you, he can satisfy your needs.
Holy Spirit	The Holy Spirit was present at Jesus' birth, baptism, ministry, and resurrection. As a perfect example for us, Jesus lived in dependence on the Holy Spirit.	The Holy Spirit was sent by God as confirmation of Jesus' authority. The Holy Spirit is given to enable people to live for Christ. By faith we can have the indwelling Holy Spirit's presence and power to witness and to serve.

KEY PLACES IN LUKE

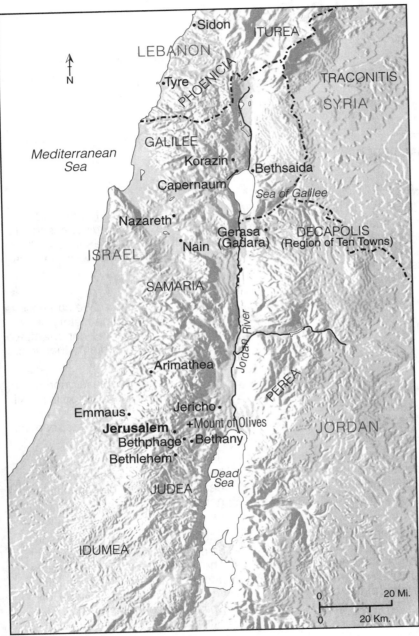

The broken lines (·–·–·) indicate modern boundaries.

Luke begins his account in the Temple in Jerusalem, giving us the background for the birth of John the Baptist, then moves on to the town of Nazareth and the story of Mary, chosen to be Jesus' mother (1:26ff). As a result of Caesar's call for a census, Mary and Joseph had to travel to Bethlehem, where Jesus was born in fulfillment of prophecy (2:1ff). Jesus grew up in Nazareth and began his earthly ministry by being baptized by John (3:21-22) and tempted by Satan (4:1ff). Much of his ministry focused on Galilee: He set up his "home" in Capernaum (4:31ff), and from there he taught throughout the region (8:1ff). Later he visited Gerasa (also called Gadara), where he healed a demon-possessed man (8:36ff). He fed more than 5,000 people with one lunch on the shores of the Sea of Galilee near Bethsaida (9:10ff). Jesus always traveled to Jerusalem for the major festivals, and he enjoyed visiting friends in nearby Bethany (10:38ff). He healed 10 men with leprosy on the border between Galilee and Samaria (17:11) and helped a dishonest tax collector in Jericho turn his life around (19:1ff). The little villages of Bethphage and Bethany on the Mount of Olives were Jesus' resting places during his last days on earth. He was crucified outside Jerusalem's walls, but then he rose again. Two of Jesus' followers walking on the road leading to Emmaus were among the first to see the resurrected Christ (24:13ff).

Copyright © 2001 by Tyndale House Publishers

COUPLES AND CHILDREN / Luke 1:6-7

Zechariah and Elizabeth were by no means alone in their strong desire to have children, as well as in their inability to do so. The Bible records the stories of other couples who desperately wanted to be parents. Some remained faithful to God through the pain (as did Elizabeth), others used other methods to obtain children—methods that led only to sorrow (as did Sarah).

Abraham and Sarah	Genesis 11:30; 15:1–17:27; 21:1-7
Isaac and Rebekah	Genesis 25:21-24
Jacob and Rachel	Genesis 29:31–30:20; 35:1-20
Manoah and his wife	Judges 13:1-25
Elkanah and Hannah	1 Samuel 1:1-20

GABRIEL'S MISSIONS / Luke 1:19

Gabriel appeared in the Old Testament to Daniel and brought announcements regarding the end times. Compare Daniel's experience with that of Zechariah in the chart below:

Daniel	Zechariah
I went on praying and confessing my sin and the sins of my people, pleading with the LORD my God for Jerusalem, his holy mountain. As I was praying, Gabriel, whom I had seen in the earlier vision, came swiftly to me at the time of the evening sacrifice. *Daniel 9:20-21*	While the incense was being burned, a great crowd stood outside, praying. *Luke 1:10*
	But the angel said, "Don't be afraid, Zechariah! For God has heard your prayer, and your wife, Elizabeth, will bear you a son! And you are to name him John." *Luke 1:13*
As Gabriel approached the place where I was standing, I became so terrified that I fell to the ground. "Son of man," he said, "you must understand that the events you have seen in your vision relate to the time of the end." *Daniel 8:17*	Zechariah was overwhelmed with fear. *Luke 1:12*
I, Daniel, am the only one who saw this vision. The men with me saw nothing, but they were suddenly terrified and ran away to hide. *Daniel 10:7*	
In the third year of the reign of King Cyrus of Persia, Daniel (also known as Belteshazzar) had another vision. It concerned events certain to happen in the future—times of war and great hardship—and Daniel understood what the vision meant. *Daniel 10:1*	When he finally did come out, he couldn't speak to them. Then they realized from his gestures that he must have seen a vision in the Temple sanctuary. *Luke 1:22*
While he was speaking to me, I looked down at the ground, unable to say a word. *Daniel 10:15*	"And now, since you didn't believe what I said, you won't be able to speak until the child is born. For my words will certainly come true at the proper time." *Luke 1:20*

GOD'S UNUSUAL METHODS / *Luke 1:13*

One of the best ways to understand God's willingness to communicate to people is to note the various methods, some of them quite unexpected, that he has used to give his message. Following is a sample of his methods and the people he contacted.

Person/Group	Method	Reference
Jacob, Zechariah, Mary, Shepherds	Angels	Genesis 32:22-32; Luke 1:13, 30; 2:10
Jacob, Joseph, a baker, a cup-bearer, Pharaoh, Isaiah, Joseph, the Magi	Dreams	Genesis 28:10-22; 37:5-10; 40:5; 41:7-8; Isaiah 1:1; Matthew 1:20; 2:12-13
Belshazzar	Writing on the wall	Daniel 5:5-9
Balaam	Talking donkey	Numbers 22:21-35
People of Israel	Pillar of cloud and fire	Exodus 13:21-22
Jonah	Being swallowed by a fish	Jonah 2
Abraham, Moses, Jesus at his baptism, Paul	Verbal	Genesis 12:1-4; Exodus 7:8; Matthew 3:13-17; Acts 18:9
Moses	Fire	Exodus 3:2
Us	God's Son	Hebrews 1:1-2

DOUBTERS IN THE BIBLE / *Luke 1:18*

Many of the people God used to accomplish great things started out as real doubters. With all of them, God showed great patience. Honest doubt was not a bad starting point as long as they didn't stay there. How great a part does doubt have in your willingness to trust God?

Doubter	Doubtful Moment	Reference
Abraham	When told he would be a father in old age	Genesis 17:17
Sarah	When she heard she would be a mother in old age	Genesis 18:12
Moses	When told to return to Egypt to lead the people	Exodus 3:10-15
Israelites	Whenever they faced difficulties in the wilderness	Exodus 16:1-3
Gideon	When told he would be a judge and leader	Judges 6:14-23
Zechariah	When told he would be a father in old age	Luke 1:18
Thomas	When told Jesus had risen from the dead	John 20:24-25

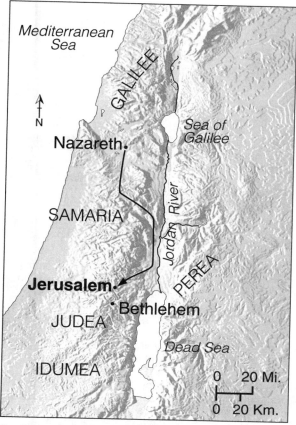

THE JOURNEY TO BETHLEHEM

Luke 2:1-7

Caesar's decree for a census of the entire Roman Empire made it necessary for Joseph and Mary to leave their hometown, Nazareth, and journey the 70 miles to the Judean village of Bethlehem.

Copyright © 2001 by Tyndale House Publishers

TO FEAR OR NOT TO FEAR / *Luke 2:10*

People in the Bible who were confronted by God or his angels all had one consistent response—fear. To each of them, God's response was always the same—don't be afraid. As soon as they sensed that God accepted them and wanted to communicate with them, their fear subsided. He had given them freedom to be his friends. Has he given you the same freedom?

Person	Reference
Abraham	Genesis 15:1
Moses	Numbers 21:34 Deuteronomy 3:2
Joshua	Joshua 8:1
Jeremiah	Lamentations 3:57
Daniel	Daniel 10:12, 19
Mary	Luke 1:30
Shepherds	Luke 2:10
Peter	Luke 5:10
Paul	Acts 27:23-24
John	Revelation 1:17-18

PRAISING GOD / Luke 2:38

The Bible speaks often of people praising God and encourages continual praise. What does it mean to praise God? Why should we do it? How should we do it? The Bible gives us answers to those questions.

Verse

Explanation

Verse

I will thank you, Lord, with all
my heart;
I will tell of all the marvelous
things you have done.
I will be filled with joy because
of you.
I will sing praises to your name,
O Most High. *Psalm 9:1-2*

Explanation

Praise is giving thanks to God for who he is. Praise is saying thank you for each aspect of his divine nature and for all the marvelous works that God has done. One's inward attitude becomes outward expression. When people praise God, they expand their awareness of who he is.

Praise the LORD!
Praise the LORD, I tell myself.
I will praise the LORD as long
as I live.
I will sing praises to my God
even with my dying breath.
Psalm 146:1-2

Praise is focusing one's heart on God. The last five psalms (146–150) are filled with praise. Each begins and ends with "Praise the Lord!" What does praise do? (1) Praise takes people's minds off their problems and shortcomings and focuses them on God. (2) Praise leads from individual meditation to corporate worship. (3) Praise causes believers to consider and appreciate God's character. (4) Praise lifts one's perspective from the earthly to the heavenly.

Praise the LORD, I tell myself,
and never forget the good
things he does for me.
Psalm 103:2

Praise is thanking God for his many gracious gifts. It is easy to complain about life, but there is much for which to praise God—he forgives sins, heals diseases, redeems from death, crowns with love and compassion, satisfies desires, and gives righteousness and justice. Believers receive all of these without deserving any of them. No matter how difficult your life's journey, you can always count your blessings—past, present, and future.

God saved you by his special
favor when you believed. And
you can't take credit for this;
it is a gift from God.
    Salvation is not a reward for
the good things we have done,
so none of us can boast about it.
Ephesians 2:8-9

Praise is thanking God for salvation. When someone gives you a gift, do you say, "That's very nice—now how much do I owe you?" No, the appropriate response to a gift is "Thank you." Yet, often Christians, even after they have been given the gift of salvation, feel obligated to try to work their way to God. Because salvation and even faith are gifts, believers should respond with gratitude, praise, and joy.

With Jesus' help, let us continually offer our sacrifice of praise
to God by proclaiming the glory
of his name.   *Hebrews 13:15*

Praise is a spiritual offering. Jewish Christians, because of their witness to the Messiah, no longer worshiped with other Jews. So praise and acts of service became their sacrifices—ones they could offer anywhere, anytime. The prophet Hosea wrote, "Forgive all our sins and receive us graciously, that we may offer the fruit of our lips" (Hosea 14:2). A "sacrifice of praise" today would include thanking Christ for his sacrifice on the cross and telling others about it. Acts of kindness and sharing are particularly pleasing to God, even when they go unnoticed.

JESUS' TEMPTATION AND RETURN TO GALILEE

Luke 4:1-30
See also *Matthew 3:13–4:17;*
Mark 1:9-15;
John 4:43-45

Jesus was tempted by Satan in the rough Judean wilderness before returning to his boyhood home, Nazareth. John's Gospel tells of Jesus' journeys in Galilee, Samaria, and Judea (see John 1–4) before he moved to Capernaum to set up his base of operations (see Matthew 4:12-13).

Copyright © 2001 by Tyndale House Publishers

AS GOD IS MERCIFUL / *Luke 6:36*

The Old Testament records over 130 references to God the Father's mercy on people. Many references also say that his people are to follow his example. Below is a sampling of some of these verses:

Reference:	How God shows mercy:
Genesis 19:16	When Lot still hesitated, the angels seized his hand and the hands of his wife and two daughters and rushed them to safety outside the city, for the LORD was merciful.
Deuteronomy 4:31	For the LORD your God is merciful—he will not abandon you or destroy you or forget the solemn covenant he made with your ancestors.
2 Samuel 24:14	"This is a desperate situation!" David replied to Gad. "But let us fall into the hands of the LORD, for his mercy is great. Do not let me fall into human hands."
Nehemiah 9:31	But in your great mercy, you did not destroy them completely or abandon them forever. What a gracious and merciful God you are!
Isaiah 55:7	Let the people turn from their wicked deeds. Let them banish from their minds the very thought of doing wrong! Let them turn to the LORD that he may have mercy on them. Yes, turn to our God, for he will abundantly pardon.
Daniel 9:9	But the Lord our God is merciful and forgiving, even though we have rebelled against him.
Titus 3:5	He saved us, not because of the good things we did, but because of his mercy. He washed away our sins and gave us a new life through the Holy Spirit.
Hebrews 4:16	So let us come boldly to the throne of our gracious God. There we will receive his mercy, and we will find grace to help us when we need it.

Reference:	How believers are to show mercy:
Hosea 6:6	I want you to be merciful; I don't want your sacrifices. I want you to know God; that's more important than burnt offerings.
Micah 6:8	No, O people, the LORD has already told you what is good, and this is what he requires: to do what is right, to love mercy, and to walk humbly with your God.
Zechariah 7:9	"This is what the LORD Almighty says: Judge fairly and honestly, and show mercy and kindness to one another.
James 3:17	But the wisdom that comes from heaven is first of all pure. It is also peace loving, gentle at all times, and willing to yield to others. It is full of mercy and good deeds. It shows no partiality and is always sincere.
Jude 22-23	Show mercy to those whose faith is wavering. Rescue others by snatching them from the flames of judgment. There are still others to whom you need to show mercy, but be careful that you aren't contaminated by their sins.

RAISED FROM THE DEAD / *Luke 7:16*

There are many similarities between this story and the one recorded in 1 Kings 17:8-24. The location and the nature of the miracle caused the townspeople to recognize that a "great prophet" was among them.

Elijah/Elisha

Elisha raised a boy from the dead, the only child of a woman in Shunem (2 Kings 4:8, 32-37).

Elijah also raised the son of a widow in Zarephath. He first met the widow at the village gate (1 Kings 17:10).

The boy who died was the son of a widow (1 Kings 17:9, 17).

The expression is that Elijah "gave" the boy back to his mother (1 Kings 17:23).

The recognition that a man of God had done the miracle (1 Kings 17:24).

However:

Elijah had to cry out to the Lord and stretch himself on the boy three times (1 Kings 17:20-21).

Elisha prayed and stretched himself out on the boy (2 Kings 4:32-35).

Jesus

Jesus raised a boy from the dead, the only son of a widow in Nain (Luke 7:11). Scholars place Nain on the other side of the hill of Moreh from Shunem, thus placing this miracle in the same general location as Elisha's. The people would have remembered this from Scripture and the life of the great prophet Elisha.

Jesus met the woman as he approached the village gate (Luke 7:12).

The boy who died was the son of a widow (Luke 7:12).

The expression is repeated that Jesus "gave him back to his mother" (Luke 7:15).

The recognition that "a mighty prophet has risen among us" (Luke 7:16).

However:

Jesus merely had to speak a word of command. Jesus spoke and the boy came back to life. Jesus' power was clearly superior to that of the greatest OT prophets.

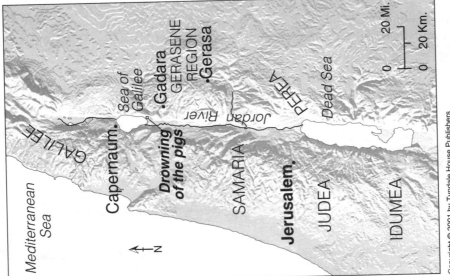

HEALING A DEMON-POSSESSED MAN

Luke 8:22-39

See also *Matthew 8:23-34; Mark 4:35–5:20*

As he traveled through Galilee, Jesus told many parables and met many people, as recorded in Matthew and Mark. Later, from Capernaum, Jesus and the disciples set out in a boat, only to encounter a fierce storm. Jesus calmed the storm and, when they landed, exorcised a "legion" of demons.

Copyright © 2001 by Tyndale House Publishers

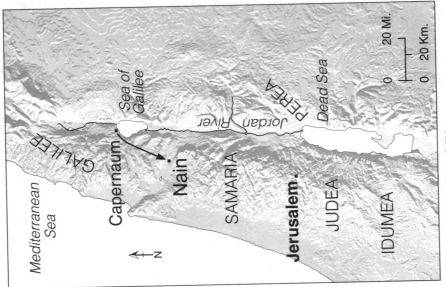

JESUS RAISES A WIDOW'S SON

Luke 7:11-17

Jesus traveled to Nain and met a funeral procession leaving the village. A widow's only son had died, leaving her virtually helpless, but Jesus brought the young man back to life. This miracle, recorded only in Luke, reveals Jesus' compassion for people's needs.

Copyright © 2001 by Tyndale House Publishers

JESUS AND WOMEN / Luke 8:3

As a non-Jew recording the words and works of Jesus' life, Luke demonstrates a special sensitivity to other "outsiders" with whom Jesus came into contact. For instance, Luke records five events involving women that are not mentioned in the other Gospels. In first-century Jewish culture, women were usually treated as second-class citizens with few of the rights men had. But Jesus crossed those barriers, and Luke showed the special care Jesus had for women. Jesus treated all people with equal respect. The following passages tell of his encounters with women.

Jesus talks to a Samaritan woman at the well	John 4:1-26
Jesus raises a widow's son from the dead	Luke 7:11-17
A sinful woman anoints Jesus' feet	Luke 7:36-50
The adulterous woman	John 8:1-11
The group of women travels with Jesus	Luke 8:1-3
Jesus visits Mary and Martha	Luke 10:38-42
Jesus heals a crippled woman	Luke 13:10-17
Jesus heals the daughter of a Gentile woman	Mark 7:24-30
Weeping women follow Jesus on his way to the cross	Luke 23:27-31
Jesus' mother and other women gather at the cross	John 19:25-27
Jesus appears to Mary Magdalene	Mark 16:9-11
Jesus appears to other women after his resurrection	Matthew 28:8-10

A COLLECTION OF ATTITUDES / Luke 10

To the expert in religious law	the wounded man was a subject to discuss.
To the bandits	the wounded man was someone to use and exploit.
To the religious men	the wounded man was a problem to be avoided.
To the innkeeper	the wounded man was a customer to serve for a fee.
To the Samaritan	the wounded man was a human being worth being cared for and loved.
To Jesus	all of them and all of us were worth dying for.

Confronting the needs of others brings out various attitudes in us. Jesus used the story of the good but despised Samaritan to make clear what attitude was acceptable to him. If we are honest, we often will find ourselves in the place of the expert in religious law, needing to learn again who our neighbor is. Note these different attitudes toward the wounded man.

WHO IS MY NEIGHBOR? / *Luke 10:29*

Reference	Faith in God	Love for Neighbor
John 13:34-35	So now I am giving you a new commandment: Love each other. Just as I have loved you, you should love each other.	Your love for one another will prove to the world that you are my disciples.
John 15:10, 12	When you obey me, you remain in my love, just as I obey my Father and remain in his love.	I command you to love each other in the same way that I love you.
Colossians 1:4-5	For we have heard that you trust in Christ Jesus and that you love all of God's people.	You do this because you are looking forward to the joys of heaven—as you have been ever since you first heard the truth of the Good News.
1 Thessalonians 1:3	As we talk to our God and Father about you, we think of your faithful work, . . .	. . . your loving deeds, and your continual anticipation of the return of our Lord Jesus Christ.
Philemon 5	"I keep hearing of your trust in the Lord Jesus . . ."	". . . and your love for all of God's people."
1 Peter 2:17	"Fear God."	"Show respect for everyone. Love your Christian brothers and sisters."
1 John 4:11	"Dear friends, since God loved us that much . . ."	". . . we surely ought to love each other."

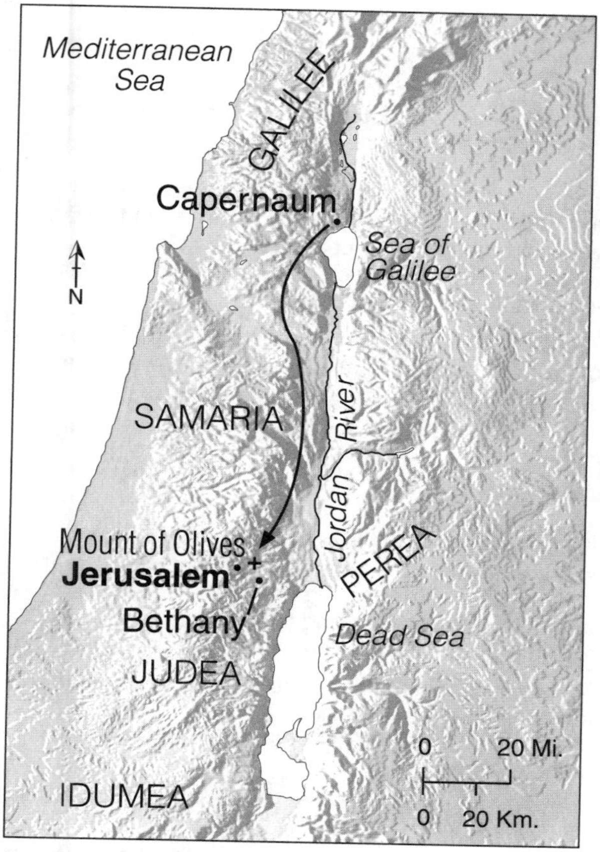

Mediterranean Sea
GALILEE
Capernaum
Sea of Galilee
N
SAMARIA
Jordan River
Mount of Olives
Jerusalem
Bethany
PEREA
Dead Sea
JUDEA
IDUMEA
0 20 Mi.
0 20 Km.

Copyright © 2001 by Tyndale House Publishers

JESUS VISITS MARY AND MARTHA

Luke 10:38-42

After teaching throughout Galilee, Jesus returned to Jerusalem for the Festival of Shelters (John 7:2ff). He spoke in Jerusalem and then visited his friends Mary and Martha in Bethany, a tiny village on the eastern slope of the Mount of Olives.

THE POOR / Luke 12:33-34

Jesus' example and attitude toward the poor gives believers a picture of how they ought to hold lightly to their worldly possessions, willingly sharing with those in need.

Luke 4:18, "The Spirit of the Lord is upon me, for he has appointed me to preach Good News to the poor."

We must not spiritualize away Jesus' concern for the poor. Jesus' ministry, as the promised Messiah, would focus on calling people back to God—those who saw their need, such as the poor, the outcasts, the disabled, and the Gentiles.

Luke 7:22, Then he told John's disciples, "Go back to John and tell him what you have seen and heard—the blind see, the lame walk, the lepers are cured, the deaf hear, the dead are raised to life, and the Good News is being preached to the poor."

The prophet Isaiah had prophesied that the "one to come" would do such miracles. See also Matthew 4:23; 9:35; Mark 1:14-15; Luke 4:43; 8:1.

Luke 11:41, "So give to the needy what you greedily possess, and you will be clean all over."

It is a "cleansing" act to give generously. Jesus wanted to stress the importance of the inward over the outward, here focusing on the importance of a right attitude when giving to the poor. The inner attitude must match the outward act.

Luke 12:33, "Sell what you have and give to those in need. This will store up treasure for you in heaven! And the purses of heaven have no holes in them. Your treasure will be safe—no thief can steal it and no moth can destroy it."

Treasure in heaven far surpasses any accumulated treasure on earth. Why have abundance when others are starving? Why hoard when others could be helped?

Luke 14:13, 21, Instead, invite the poor, the crippled, the lame, and the blind.

"The servant returned and told his master what they had said. His master was angry and said, 'Go quickly into the streets and alleys of the city and invite the poor, the crippled, the lame, and the blind.'"

When God's people can do good, without expectation of reward or repayment, they have truly served him unselfishly.

Luke 18:22, "There is still one thing you lack," Jesus said. "Sell all you have and give the money to the poor, and you will have treasure in heaven. Then come, follow me."

The task of selling possessions will not give anyone eternal life. But such obedience shows the desire to follow Jesus in complete commitment. Only when money is no longer lord of one's life can Jesus become Lord.

Luke 19:8, Meanwhile, Zacchaeus stood there and said to the Lord, "I will give half my wealth to the poor, Lord, and if I have overcharged people on their taxes, I will give them back four times as much!"

Jesus took the initiative with Zacchaeus, and Zacchaeus took the initiative to follow wherever the path of obedience to Jesus might lead. Zacchaeus was able to give away his wealth in order to follow Jesus. This was the heart attitude Jesus was always looking for. When he perceived it in Zacchaeus, he lost no time in bringing this man the Good News.

Luke 21:2-3, Then a poor widow came by and dropped in two pennies. "I assure you," he said, "this poor widow has given more than all the rest of them."

Jesus judged this woman's gift not by how much she gave, but by how much she had left after giving. She gave everything. She could have kept back one coin, but she willingly gave both coins and trusted God to care for her. Jesus wanted the disciples to see this lesson in total surrender of self, commitment to God, and willingness to trust in his provision.

SEVEN SABBATH MIRACLES / *Luke 13:10* See also *John 5:10*

Over the centuries, the Jewish religious leaders had added rule after rule to God's law. For example, God's law said the Sabbath is a day of rest (Exodus 20:10-11). But the religious leaders added to that law, creating one that said, "You cannot heal on the Sabbath" because that is "work." Seven times Jesus healed people on the Sabbath. In doing this, he was challenging these religious leaders to look beyond their rules to their true purpose—to honor God by helping those in need. Would God have been pleased if Jesus had ignored these people?

Jesus sends a demon out of a man	Mark 1:21-28
Jesus heals Peter's mother-in-law	Mark 1:29-31
Jesus heals a lame man by the pool of Bethesda	John 5:1-18
Jesus heals a man with a deformed hand	Mark 3:1-6
Jesus restores a crippled woman	Luke 13:10-17
Jesus heals a man with dropsy	Luke 14:1-6
Jesus heals a man born blind	John 9:1-16

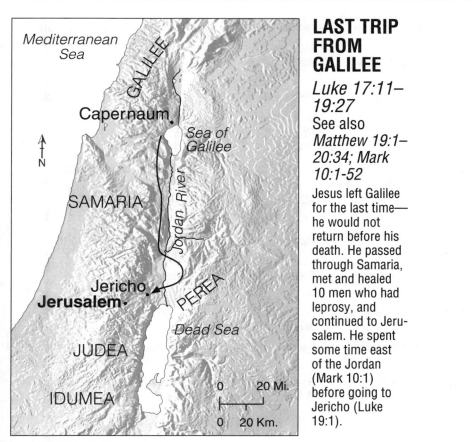

LAST TRIP FROM GALILEE

Luke 17:11– 19:27
See also *Matthew 19:1– 20:34; Mark 10:1-52*

Jesus left Galilee for the last time— he would not return before his death. He passed through Samaria, met and healed 10 men who had leprosy, and continued to Jerusalem. He spent some time east of the Jordan (Mark 10:1) before going to Jericho (Luke 19:1).

Copyright © 2001 by Tyndale House Publishers

MESSIANIC PROPHECIES AND FULFILLMENTS / *Luke 18:31*

For the Gospel writers, one of the main reasons for believing in Jesus was the way his life fulfilled the Old Testament prophecies about the Messiah. Following is a list of some of the main prophecies.

Old Testament Prophecies		New Testament Fulfillment
1. Messiah was to be born in Bethlehem	Micah 5:2	Matthew 2:1-6; Luke 2:1-20
2. Messiah was to be born of a virgin	Isaiah 7:14	Matthew 1:18-25; Luke 1:26-38
3. Messiah was to be a prophet like Moses	Deuteronomy 18:15, 18-19	John 7:40
4. Messiah was to enter Jerusalem in triumph	Zechariah 9:9	Matthew 21:1-9; John 12:12-16
5. Messiah was to be rejected by his own people	Isaiah 53:1, 3; Psalm 118:22	Matthew 26:3-4; John 12:37-43; Acts 4:1-12
6. Messiah was to be betrayed by one of his followers	Psalm 41:9	Matthew 26:14-16, 47-50; Luke 22:19-23
7. Messiah was to be tried and condemned	Isaiah 53:8	Luke 23:1-25; Matthew 27:1-2
8. Messiah was to be silent before his accusers	Isaiah 53:7	Matthew 27:12-14; Mark 15:3-4; Luke 23:8-10
9. Messiah was to be struck and spat on by his enemies	Isaiah 50:6	Matthew 26:67; 27:30; Mark 14:65
10. Messiah was to be mocked and insulted	Psalm 22:7-8	Matthew 27:39-44; Luke 23:11, 35
11. Messiah was to die by crucifixion	Psalm 22:14, 16-17	Matthew 27:31; Mark 15:20, 25
12. Messiah was to suffer with criminals and pray for his enemies	Isaiah 53:12	Matthew 27:38; Mark 15:27-28; Luke 23:32-34
13. Messiah was to be given vinegar and gall	Psalm 69:21	Matthew 27:34; John 19:28-30
14. Others were to cast lots for Messiah's garments	Psalm 22:18	Matthew 27:35; John 19:23-24
15. Messiah's bones were not to be broken	Exodus 12:46	John 19:31-36
16. Messiah was to die as a sacrifice for sin	Isaiah 53:5-6, 8, 10-12	John 1:29; 11:49-52; Acts 10:43; 13:38-39
17. Messiah was to be raised from the dead	Psalm 16:10	Acts 2:22-32; Matthew 28:1-10
18. Messiah is now at God's right hand	Psalm 110:1	Mark 16:19; Luke 24:50-51

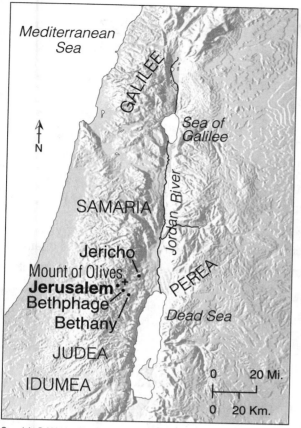

Copyright © 2001 by Tyndale House Publishers

LAST WEEK IN JERUSALEM

Luke 19:1-44
See also *Matthew 21:1-11; Mark 11:1-11; John 12:12-19*

As they approached Jerusalem from Jericho (19:1), Jesus and the disciples came to the villages of Bethany and Bethphage, nestled on the eastern slope of the Mount of Olives, only a few miles outside Jerusalem. Jesus stayed in Bethany during the nights of that last week, entering Jerusalem during the day.

GOSPEL ACCOUNTS FOUND ONLY IN LUKE / *Luke 19:27*

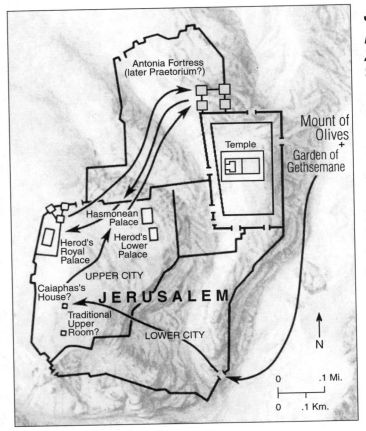

JESUS' TRIAL

Luke 22:47–23:25
See also *Matthew 26:47–27:26; Mark 14:43–15:15; John 18:1–19:16*

Taken from Gethsemane, Jesus first appeared before the Jewish high council, which had convened at daybreak at Caiaphas's house. From there he went to Pilate, the Roman governor; then to Herod, tetrarch of Galilee, who was visiting in Jerusalem; and back to Pilate, who, in desperation, sentenced Jesus to die.

Copyright © 2001 by Tyndale House Publishers

PERSEVERE TO THE END / *Luke 21:19*

Luke 21:19, "By standing firm, you will win your souls."

Perseverance grows out of commitment to Jesus Christ. Standing firm is not the way to be saved but the evidence that a person is really committed to Jesus. Endurance is not a means to earn salvation; it is the by-product of a truly devoted life.

2 Timothy 4:5, "But you should keep a clear mind in every situation. Don't be afraid of suffering for the Lord. Work at bringing others to Christ. Complete the ministry God has given you."

God will make believers' perseverance worthwhile. He will help his people complete whatever work he has called them to do; he will help them draw others into the kingdom.

Hebrews 3:6, "But Christ, the faithful Son, was in charge of the entire household. And we are God's household, if we keep up our courage and remain confident in our hope in Christ."

Perseverance keeps believers courageous and hopeful because they can trust Christ. Because Christ lives in Christians and because he is completely trustworthy to fulfill all his promises, believers can remain courageous and hopeful.

Revelation 14:12, "Let this encourage God's holy people to endure persecution patiently and remain firm to the end, obeying his commands and trusting in Jesus."

Believers' ability to persevere is related to the quality of our relationship with God. The secret to perseverance is trust and obedience. Trust God to give you the patience to endure even the small trials you face daily. The fact of God's ultimate triumph can encourage believers to remain steadfast in their faith through every trial and persecution.

TO NOT BE OVERCOME BY TEMPTATION / *Luke 22:40*

Scripture explains what to do to not be overcome by temptation.

Reference	Lesson about temptation
Genesis 3	Satan wants to see all believers stumble and will actively work to make it happen.
Genesis 39	When you are tempted, focus on your relationship with God and obey him.
2 Samuel 11:2-4	Temptation will come at weak spots and unexpected times.
Psalm 51:4	Temptation can lead to sin and its consequences.
Proverbs 7:1-5	Avoid temptation by storing up God's commands in your heart.
Matthew 4:1-11	Combat temptation by using the Word of God.
Matthew 6:13	God doesn't lead us into temptation, but sometimes he allows believers to be tested by it.
Matthew 8:7-9	Being tempted is not a sin, but you must not let temptation lead you into sin.
Matthew 26:40	Watch and pray to avoid falling into sin.
1 Corinthians 10:13	God will not allow temptations you cannot handle.
1 Timothy 6:11-12	To avoid temptation, you must fight as in a battle.
2 Timothy 2:22	At times you may need to turn and run from temptation.
Hebrews 2:16-18	Because Jesus Christ was tempted, he understands how you feel and knows how to help you resist.
James 1:12-16	You sometimes cause your own temptations.
James 4:7-8	Submit to God; resist the devil.

JESUS' TRIAL / Luke 22:71

Jesus' trial was actually a series of hearings, carefully controlled to accomplish the death of Jesus. The verdict was predecided, but certain "legal" procedures were necessary. A lot of effort went into condemning and crucifying an innocent man. Jesus went through an unfair trial in our place so that we would not have to face a fair trial and receive the well-deserved punishment for our sins.

Event	Probable Reasons	References
Trial before Annas (powerful ex-high priest)	Although no longer the high priest, he may still have wielded much power	John 18:13-23
Trial before Caiaphas (the ruling high priest)	To gather evidence for the full high council hearing to follow	Matthew 26:57-68 Mark 14:53-65 Luke 22:54, 63-65 John 18:24
Trial before the high council (Sanhedrin)	Formal religious trial and condemnation to death	Matthew 27:1 Mark 15:1 Luke 22:66-71
Trial before Pilate (highest Roman authority)	All death sentences needed Roman approval	Matthew 27:2, 11-14 Mark 15:1-5 Luke 23:1-6 John 18:28-38
Trial before Herod (ruler of Galilee)	A courteous and guilt-sharing act by Pilate because Jesus was from Galilee, Herod's district	Luke 23:7-12
Trial before Pilate	Pilate's last effort to avoid condemning an obviously innocent man	Matthew 27:15-26 Mark 15:6-15 Luke 23:13-25 John 18:39–19:16

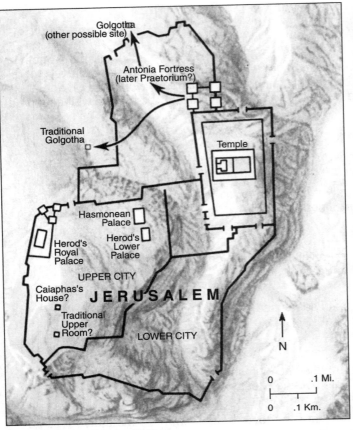

JESUS LED AWAY TO DIE

Luke 23:26-43
See also *Matthew 27:27-44; Mark 15:16-32; John 19:17-27*

As Jesus was led away through the streets of Jerusalem, he could no longer carry his cross, and Simon of Cyrene was given the burden. Jesus was crucified, along with common criminals, on a hill outside Jerusalem.

Map labels:
Golgotha (other possible site)
Antonia Fortress (later Praetorium?)
Traditional Golgotha
Temple
Hasmonean Palace
Herod's Lower Palace
Herod's Royal Palace
UPPER CITY
Caiaphas's House?
JERUSALEM
Traditional Upper Room?
LOWER CITY
N
0 .1 Mi.
0 .1 Km.

Copyright © 2001 by Tyndale House Publishers

WHAT DOES THE CROSS MEAN? / *Luke 23:26*

The cross is . . .

Reference

a place of ransom—Jesus made the payment for believers' debt of sin.

Mark 10:45
1 Timothy 2:6
Hebrews 9:15

a place of substitution—Jesus took the punishment that everyone deserves.

John 6:51
Romans 8:3
2 Corinthians 5:21

a place of propitiation—Jesus' perfect sacrifice removed God's punishment from those who believe.

Romans 3:25

a place of victory—Jesus' sacrifice defeated Satan's hold on humanity.

John 3:14-15; 8:28; 12:31-32; 18:32

a place of beginning—Jesus' shed blood began the church.

Acts 20:28

a place of ending—Jesus' sacrifice ended all other sacrifices for sin.

Hebrews 8–10

a place of separation—Jesus' death is the basis on which God sets apart a people to be a holy community.

1 Peter 1:2, 18-25; 2:1-11

a place of mediation—Jesus became mediator between sinful humanity and holy God.

Galatians 3:13, 19-20

a place of reconciliation—Jesus reconciled God and sinners, and reconciled Jews and Gentiles.

Romans 5:8-11
2 Corinthians 5:20-21
Ephesians 2:11-22
Colossians 1:21-22; 2:11-15

a place of justification—Jesus' death makes it possible for God to declare believers righteous before him.

Romans 3:21-31

OLD TESTAMENT PASSAGES QUOTED BY CHRIST / *Luke 24*

New Testament	Old Testament	Occasion
Matthew 4:4	Deuteronomy 8:3	Temptation
Matthew 4:7	Deuteronomy 6:16	
Matthew 4:10	Deuteronomy 6:13	
Matthew 5:21	Exodus 20:13	Sermon on the Mount
Matthew 5:27	Exodus 20:14	
Luke 4:18-19	Isaiah 61:1-2	Hometown Sermon
Matthew 9:13	Hosea 6:6	Confrontations with the Jewish Rulers
Mark 10:7-8	Genesis 2:24	
Mark 12:29-30	Deuteronomy 6:4-5	
Matthew 15:7-9	Isaiah 29:13	
John 8:17	Deuteronomy 17:6	
Luke 7:27	Malachi 3:1	Tribute to John
Matthew 21:16	Psalm 8:2	Triumphal Entry
Luke 19:46	Isaiah 56:7	Temple Cleansing
Matthew 21:42, 44	Psalm 118:22-23	Parable about Israel
Mark 12:36	Psalm 110:1	Temple Question Session
John 15:25	Psalm 35:19; 69:4	Last Passover
Matthew 27:46	Psalm 22:1	On the Cross
Luke 23:46	Psalm 31:5	

WHY IS THE RESURRECTION SO IMPORTANT? / *Luke 24:5-7*

The resurrection of Jesus from the dead is the central fact of Christian history. On it, the church is built; without it, there would be no Christian church today. Jesus' resurrection is unique. Other religions have strong ethical systems, concepts about paradise and afterlife, and various holy scriptures. Only Christianity has a God who became human, literally died for his people, and was raised again in power and glory to rule his church forever.

1. Because Christ was raised from the dead, Christians know that the kingdom of heaven has broken into earth's history. The world is now headed for redemption, not disaster. God's mighty power is at work destroying sin, creating new lives, and preparing believers for Jesus' second coming.

2. Because of the resurrection, Christians know that death has been conquered and that they, too, will be raised from the dead to live forever with Christ.

3. The resurrection gives authority to the church's witness in the world. Look at the early evangelistic sermons in the book of Acts: the apostles' most important message was the proclamation that Jesus Christ had been raised from the dead!

4. The resurrection gives meaning to the church's regular feast, the Lord's Supper. Like the disciples on the Emmaus Road, believers break bread with their risen Lord, who comes in power to save them.

5. The resurrection helps Christians find meaning even in great tragedy. No matter what happens in their walk with the Lord, the resurrection gives them hope for the future.

6. The resurrection assures Christians that Christ is alive and ruling his kingdom. He is not legend; he is alive and real.

7. God's power that brought Jesus back from the dead is available to believers so that they can live for him in an evil world.

Christians can look very different from one another, and they can hold widely varying beliefs about politics, lifestyle, and even theology. But one central belief unites and inspires all true Christians—Jesus Christ rose from the dead! (For more on the importance of the resurrection, see 1 Corinthians 15:12-58.)

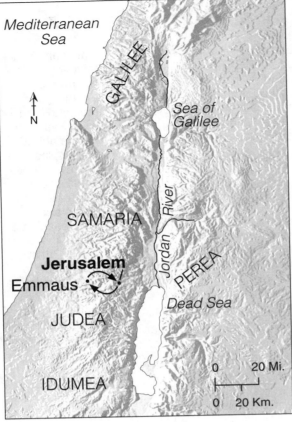

ON THE ROAD TO EMMAUS

Luke 24:13-34
See also *Mark 16:12-13*

After Jesus' death, two of his followers were walking from Jerusalem back toward Emmaus when a stranger joined them. During dinner in Emmaus, Jesus revealed himself to them and then disappeared. They immediately returned to Jerusalem to tell the disciples the good news that Jesus was alive!

Copyright © 2001 by Tyndale House Publishers

JOHN

MEGATHEMES IN JOHN

Theme	Explanation	Importance
Jesus Christ, Son of God	John shows us that Jesus is unique as God's special Son, yet he is fully God. Because he is fully God, Jesus is able to reveal God to us clearly and accurately.	Because Jesus is God's Son, we can perfectly trust what he says. By trusting him, we can gain an open mind to understand God's message and fulfill his purpose in our lives.
Eternal Life	Because Jesus is God, he lives forever. Before the world began, he lived with God, and he will reign forever with him. In John we see Jesus revealed in power and magnificence even before his resurrection.	Jesus offers eternal life to us. We are invited to begin living in a personal, eternal relationship with him now. Although we must grow old and die, by trusting him we can have a new life that lasts forever.
Belief	John records eight specific signs, or miracles, that show the nature of Jesus' power and love. We see his power over everything created, and we see his love of all people. These signs encourage us to believe in him.	Believing is active, living, and continuous trust in Jesus as God. When we believe in his life, his words, his death, and his resurrection, we are cleansed from sin and receive power to follow him. But we must respond to him by believing.
Holy Spirit	Jesus taught his disciples that the Holy Spirit would come after he ascended from earth. The Holy Spirit would then indwell, guide, counsel, and comfort those who follow Jesus. Through the Holy Spirit, Christ's presence and power are multiplied in all who believe.	Through God's Holy Spirit, we are drawn to him in faith. We must know the Holy Spirit to understand all Jesus taught. We can experience Jesus' love and guidance as we allow the Holy Spirit to do his work in us.
Resurrection	On the third day after he died, Jesus rose from the dead. This was verified by his disciples and many eyewitnesses. This reality changed the disciples from frightened deserters to dynamic leaders in the new church. This fact is the foundation of the Christian faith.	We can be changed as the disciples were and have confidence that our bodies will one day be raised to live with Christ forever. The same power that raised Christ to life can give us the ability to follow Christ each day.

KEY PLACES IN JOHN

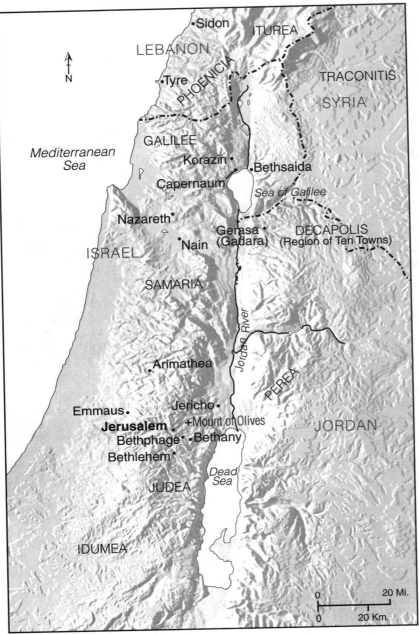

The broken lines (·—··—·) indicate modern boundaries.

John's story begins as John the Baptist ministers near Bethany east of the Jordan (1:28ff). Jesus also begins his ministry, talking to some of the men who would later become his 12 disciples. Jesus' ministry in Galilee began with a visit to a wedding in Cana (2:1ff). Then he went to Capernaum, which became his new home (2:12). He journeyed to Jerusalem for the special festivals (2:13) and there met with Nicodemus, a religious leader (3:1ff). When Jesus left Judea, he traveled through Samaria and ministered to the Samaritans (4:1ff). Jesus did miracles in Galilee (4:46ff) and in Judea and Jerusalem (5:1ff). We follow him as he fed 5,000 near Bethsaida beside the Sea of Galilee (Sea of Tiberias) (6:1ff), walked on the water to his frightened disciples (6:16ff), preached through Galilee (7:1), returned to Jerusalem (7:2ff), preached beyond the Jordan in Perea (10:40), raised Lazarus from the dead in Bethany (11:1ff), and finally entered Jerusalem for the last time to celebrate the Passover with his disciples and give them key teachings about what was to come and how they should act. His last hours before his crucifixion were spent in the city (13:1ff), in a grove of olive trees (the Garden of Gethsemane) (18:1ff), and finally in various buildings in Jerusalem during his trial (18:12ff). There he was crucified, but then he rose again as he had promised.

Copyright © 2001 by Tyndale House Publishers

PARALLELS BETWEEN JOHN'S PROLOGUE AND HIS GOSPEL
John 1:14

Theme from Prologue	Parallel in John's Gospel	Significance
Preexisting Word (1:1-2)	17:5	Christ has equal status with God.
Life itself was in him (1:4)	5:26	Christ is the source of life; we must come to him for eternal life.
This life gives light (1:4)	8:12	Only Christ can light our path. We must follow him.
Darkness rejects the light (1:5)	3:19	Those bound by sin reject Christ's life and truth.
Darkness can never extinguish the light (1:5)	12:35	The hostility of unbelievers can never destroy Christ's light.
Real light comes into the world (1:9)	3:19; 12:46	Christ shows us the way to have a personal relationship with God, but we must believe and follow.
Jesus' own people did not receive him (1:11)	4:44	We must not be like those who refused to believe.
Being born of God (1:13)	3:6; 8:41-42	To experience God's love we must be born again.
We have seen Christ's glory (1:14)	12:41	We know his real identity and his true nature as the Son of God.
Jesus is the one and only (1:14, 18)	3:16	Christ is the unique, unparalleled, and unrivaled Son of God.
Truth comes through Jesus (1:17)	14:6	Christ's life and teaching demonstrate God's revealed will. Those who listen to and follow his truth will be saved.
Only Jesus has seen God (1:18)	6:44-46	Christ is the ultimate authority on what God is like. We should not trust anyone else.

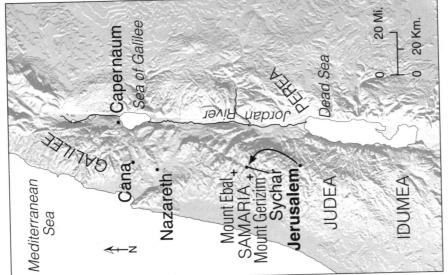

THE VISIT IN SAMARIA

John 2:13–4:42

Jesus went to Jerusalem for the Passover, cleared the Temple, and talked with Nicodemus, a religious leader, about eternal life. He then left Jerusalem and traveled in Judea. On his way to Galilee, he visited Sychar and other villages in Samaria. Unlike most Jews of the day, he did not try to avoid the region of Samaria.

Copyright © 2001 by Tyndale House Publishers

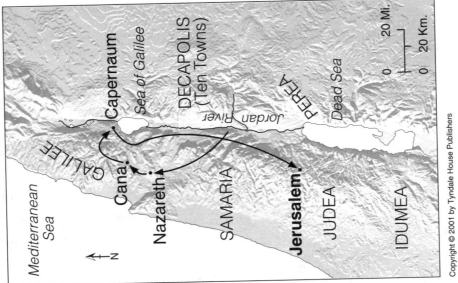

JESUS' FIRST TRAVELS

John 1:29–2:25

After his baptism by John in the Jordan River and the temptation by Satan in the wilderness (see the map in Mark 1), Jesus returned to Galilee. He visited Nazareth, Cana, and Capernaum, and then returned to Jerusalem for the Passover.

Copyright © 2001 by Tyndale House Publishers

THE TEMPLE IN JESUS' DAY

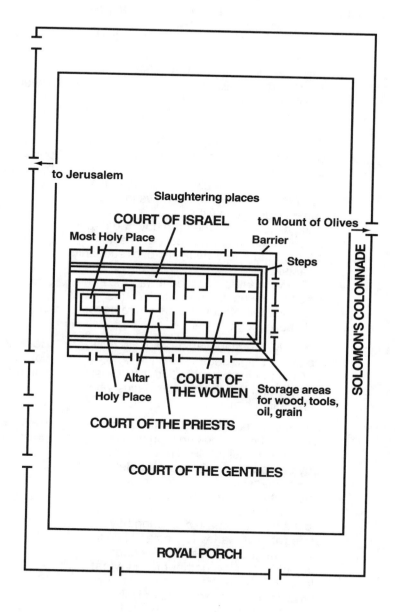

to Jerusalem

Slaughtering places

COURT OF ISRAEL

to Mount of Olives

Most Holy Place

Barrier

Steps

Altar

COURT OF THE WOMEN

Holy Place

Storage areas for wood, tools, oil, grain

COURT OF THE PRIESTS

SOLOMON'S COLONNADE

COURT OF THE GENTILES

ROYAL PORCH

MIRACLES RECORDED IN JOHN'S GOSPEL AND THEIR SIGNIFICANCE / *John 2:11*

Jesus' miracles were always performed to show his nature—his compassion and love for people. But more than that, they revealed his glory. They were his "credentials," but they weren't done for show. The miracles were performed to help people believe that Jesus was the promised Messiah. The miracles also reveal Jesus' great power over the temporal world.

Passage	Key Verses	Significance
Jesus turns water into wine (2:1-11)	This miraculous sign at Cana in Galilee was Jesus' first display of his glory. And his disciples believed in him.	Reveals Jesus' power over creation.
Jesus heals an official's son (4:46-54)	Then Jesus told him, "Go back home. Your son will live!" And the man believed Jesus' word and started home. While he was on his way, some of his servants met him with the news that his son was alive and well. He asked them when the boy had begun to feel better, and they replied, "Yesterday afternoon at one o'clock his fever suddenly disappeared!" Then the father realized it was the same time that Jesus had told him, "Your son will live." And the officer and his entire household believed in Jesus.	Reveals that Jesus' power is not limited by time or space.
Jesus heals a lame man (5:1-16)	Instantly, the man was healed! He rolled up the mat and began walking! . . . Then the man went to find the Jewish leaders and told them it was Jesus who had healed him.	Reveals Jesus' power over disease and disability.
Jesus feeds over five thousand people (6:5-14)	Jesus soon saw a great crowd of people climbing the hill, looking for him. Turning to Philip, he asked, "Philip, where can we buy bread to feed all these people?" He was testing Philip, for he already knew what he was going to do. Then Andrew, Simon Peter's brother, spoke up. . . . "There's a young boy here with five barley loaves and two fish. But what good is that with this huge crowd?" . . . "Now gather the leftovers," Jesus told his disciples, "so that nothing is wasted." . . . There were only five barley loaves to start with, but twelve baskets were filled with the pieces of bread the people did not eat!	Reveals Jesus' power to supply humanity.

Passage	Key Verses	Significance
Jesus walks on the water (6:17-21)	Soon a gale swept down upon them as they rowed, and the sea grew very rough. They were three or four miles out when suddenly they saw Jesus walking on the water toward the boat. They were terrified, but he called out to them, "I am here! Don't be afraid." Then they were eager to let him in, and immediately the boat arrived at their destination!	Reveals Jesus' power over the forces of nature.
Jesus heals a man born blind (9:1-7)	As Jesus was walking along, he saw a man who had been blind from birth. "Teacher," his disciples asked him, "why was this man born blind? Was it a result of his own sins or those of his parents?" "It was not because of his sins or his parents' sins," Jesus answered. "He was born blind so the power of God could be seen in him. But while I am still here in the world, I am the light of the world."	Reveals Jesus' power over birth defects.
Jesus raises Lazarus from the dead (11:1-44)	Jesus responded, "Didn't I tell you that you will see God's glory if you believe?" So they rolled the stone aside. Then Jesus looked up to heaven and said, "Father, thank you for hearing me. You always hear me, but I said it out loud for the sake of all these people standing here, so they will believe you sent me." Many of the people who were with Mary believed in Jesus when they saw this happen.	Reveals Jesus' power over death.
Jesus gives the disciples a miraculous catch of fish (21:1-14)	At dawn the disciples saw Jesus standing on the beach, but they couldn't see who he was. He called out, "Friends, have you caught any fish?" "No," they replied. Then the disciple whom Jesus loved said to Peter, "It is the Lord!" . . . This was the third time Jesus had appeared to his disciples since he had been raised from the dead.	Reveals Jesus' power over circumstances.

Those who read the life of Christ are faced with one unavoidable question—was Jesus God? Part of any reasonable conclusion has to include the fact that he did claim to be God. We have no other choice but to agree or disagree with his claim. Eternal life is at stake in the choice.

Jesus claimed to be:	Matthew	Mark	Luke	John
the fulfillment of Old Testament prophecies	5:17 14:33 16:16, 17 26:31, 53-56 27:43	14:21, 61-62	4:16-21 7:18-23 18:31 22:37 24:44	2:22 5:45-47 6:45 7:40 10:34-36 13:18 15:25 20:9
the Son of Man	8:20 12:8 16:27 19:28 20:18-19 24:27, 44 25:31 26:2, 45, 64	8:31, 38 9:9 10:45 14:41	6:22 7:33-34 12:8 17:22 18:8, 31 19:10 21:36	1:51 3:13-14 6:27, 53 12:23, 34
the Son of God	11:27 14:33 16:16-17 27:43	3:11-12 14:61-62	8:28 10:22	1:18 3:35-36 5:18-26 6:40 10:36 11:4 17:1 19:7
the Messiah/ the Christ	23:9-10 26:63-64	8:29-30	4:41 23:1-2 24:25-27	4:25-26 10:24-25 11:27
Teacher/Master	26:18			13:13-14
one with authority to forgive		2:1-12	7:48-49	
Lord		5:19		13:13-14 20:28-29
Savior			19:10	3:17 10:9

THE KINGDOM OF GOD / John 3:3

Statement	Scripture
To enter you must confess and repent of sin	Matthew 4:17
Those persecuted for their faith will receive rewards there	Matthew 5:10-12
Not all who talk about it belong there	Matthew 7:21
Small beginning but great results	Matthew 13:31-32
Worldwide impact	Matthew 13:33
Priceless value	Matthew 13:44-46
Cannot judge who will be in it	Matthew 13:47-49
Good news to all.	Luke 4:43
Equally available to all.	Luke 10:21
Must be the believer's top priority	Luke 12:31
The door is now open to all, but one day it will close	Luke 13:22-30
To enter you must be born again	John 3:3

ALL THE GREATEST / John 3:16

God . . . *the greatest Lover*

So loved . . . *the greatest degree*

The world . . . *the greatest number*

That he gave . . . *the greatest act*

His only Son . . . *the greatest gift*

So that everyone . . . *the greatest invitation*

Who believes . . . *the greatest simplicity*

In him . . . *the greatest person*

Will not perish . . . *the greatest escape*

But . . . *the greatest difference*

Have . . . *the greatest certainty*

Eternal life . . . *the greatest destiny*

—J. Edwin Hortell

JESUS TEACHES IN JERU-SALEM

John 5:1-47

Between chapters 4 and 5 of John, Jesus ministered throughout Galilee, especially in Capernaum. He had been calling certain men to follow him, but it wasn't until after this trip to Jerusalem (5:1) that he chose his 12 disciples from among them.

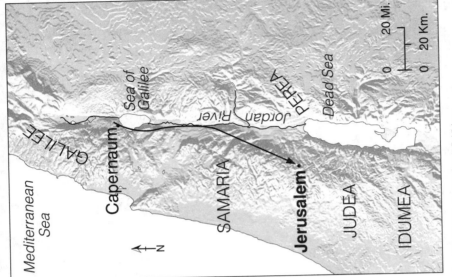

Copyright © 2001 by Tyndale House Publishers

JESUS RETURNS TO GALILEE

John 4:43-54
See also *Matthew 4:12-17; Mark 1:14-15; Luke 4:14-15*

Jesus stayed in Sychar for two days, then went on to Galilee. He visited Nazareth and various towns in Galilee before arriving in Cana. From there he spoke the word of healing, and a government official's son in Capernaum was healed. The Gospel of Matthew tells us Jesus then settled in Capernaum (Matthew 4:12-13).

Copyright © 2001 by Tyndale House Publishers

LIVING WATER / *John 4:10*

What did Jesus mean by "living water"? In the Old Testament many verses speak of thirsting after God. In promising to bring living water that could forever quench a person's thirst for God, Jesus was claiming to be the Messiah. Only the Messiah could give this gift that satisfies the soul's desire.

Psalm 36:8-9	"You feed them from the abundance of your own house, letting them drink from your rivers of delight."
Psalm 42:1-2	"As the deer pants for streams of water, so I long for you, O God."
Isaiah 55:1	"Is anyone thirsty? Come and drink—even if you have no money! Come, take your choice of wine or milk—it's all free!"
Jeremiah 2:13	"For my people have done two evil things: They have forsaken me—the fountain of living water. And they have dug for themselves cracked cisterns that can hold no water at all!"
Jeremiah 17:13	"O LORD, the hope of Israel, all who turn away from you will be disgraced and shamed. They will be buried in a dry and dusty grave, for they have forsaken the LORD, the fountain of living water."

JESUS, THE MESSIAH / *John 5:19-30*

What God does	**What Messiah does**	**What Jesus did**
1. God alone judges (Psalm 7:6-17; 9:7-8; Joel 3:12)	Messiah has authority to judge (Daniel 7:13-14; Jeremiah 23:5-6)	Jesus claimed and demonstrated his authority to judge (5:27)

Because Jesus demonstrated his authority, we have no reason to fear judgment, or what people may do to us.

2. God alone heals (Isaiah 35:5-7)	Messiah has the power to heal (Isaiah 53:4-5; 61:1-3)	Jesus demonstrated the power to heal (5:8, 20, 26)

Because Jesus demonstrated his power to heal, we can claim that power in our own lives for now and eternity.

3. God alone gives life (Genesis 1:20-27; Deuteronomy 32:39; 1 Samuel 2:6; 2 Kings 5:7)	Messiah has the power to give life (Daniel 7:13-14)	Jesus claimed and demonstrated the power to give life (5:21, 28-29, 40)

Because Jesus demonstrated his power over death, we do not have to fear dying.

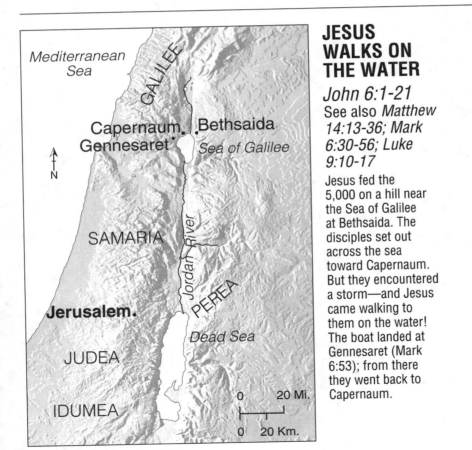

Mediterranean Sea

GALILEE

Capernaum. .Bethsaida
Gennesaret. *Sea of Galilee*

N

SAMARIA

Jordan River

PEREA

Jerusalem.

Dead Sea

JUDEA

0   20 Mi.

0   20 Km.

IDUMEA

JESUS WALKS ON THE WATER

John 6:1-21
See also *Matthew 14:13-36; Mark 6:30-56; Luke 9:10-17*

Jesus fed the 5,000 on a hill near the Sea of Galilee at Bethsaida. The disciples set out across the sea toward Capernaum. But they encountered a storm—and Jesus came walking to them on the water! The boat landed at Gennesaret (Mark 6:53); from there they went back to Capernaum.

Copyright © 2001 by Tyndale House Publishers

A SAMPLING OF HARD SAYINGS / *John 6:60*

At least seventy hard sayings of Jesus have been identified in the Gospels. The following allow us to sense their impact on Jesus' followers, for they still challenge us.

Reference	Saying
Matthew 5:22	But I say, if you are angry with someone, you are subject to judgment! If you call someone an idiot, you are in danger of being brought before the high council. And if you curse someone, you are in danger of the fires of hell.
Matthew 5:29	So if your eye—even if it is your good eye—causes you to lust, gouge it out and throw it away. It is better for you to lose one part of your body than for your whole body to be thrown into hell.
Mark 8:12	When he heard this, he sighed deeply and said, "Why do you people keep demanding a miraculous sign? I assure you, I will not give this generation any such sign."
Mark 9:1	Jesus went on to say, "I assure you that some of you standing here right now will not die before you see the Kingdom of God arrive in great power!"
Luke 12:10	Yet those who speak against the Son of Man may be forgiven, but anyone who speaks blasphemies against the Holy Spirit will never be forgiven.
Luke 14:26	"If you want to be my follower you must love me more than your own father and mother, wife and children, brothers and sisters—yes, more than your own life. Otherwise, you cannot be my disciple."
John 6:53	So Jesus said again, "I assure you, unless you eat the flesh of the Son of Man and drink his blood, you cannot have eternal life within you."

EVENTS FROM JESUS' GALILEAN MINISTRY / *John 7:1*

Event	Reference
Jesus sent a demon out of a girl	Matthew 15:21-28; Mark 7:24-30
Jesus fed 4,000	Matthew 15:32-39; Mark 8:1-9
Religious leaders asked for a sign in the sky	Matthew 16:1-4; Mark 8:10-12
Jesus restored sight to a blind man	Mark 8:22-26
Jesus took Peter, James, and John to see his transfiguration	Matthew 17:1-13; Mark 9:2-13; Luke 9:28-36
Jesus healed a demon-possessed boy	Matthew 17:14-21; Mark 9:14-29; Luke 9:37-43
Jesus twice predicted his death	Matthew 16:21-28; 17:22-23; Mark 8:31–9:1; 9:30-32; Luke 9:21-27; 9:44-45
The disciples argued about who would be the greatest	Matthew 18:1-6; Mark 9:33-37; Luke 9:46-48

VIEWS OF JESUS / *John 7:9*

John 7 could be titled "A Catalogue of Opinions about Jesus." Among the clearest opinions are that Jesus was:

View	Reference in John 7
a good man	7:12
a deceiver	7:12
a great teacher	7:15
demon-possessed	7:20
a doer of miraculous signs	7:31
the Prophet	7:40
the Messiah	7:41

But the key question is, What do *you* believe about Jesus? It makes a difference, both now and for eternity.

IF YOU KNEW ME / *John 8:19*

For John, "knowing God" was a key theme of Jesus' ministry. To be enlightened by God in order to understand clearly the nature of God and Jesus was both a gift and a prerequisite for salvation. Each individual must be given the ability to recognize Jesus and God. Once given, we must grow in our knowledge of God by knowing Christ better and better.

Knowledge of Christ is not innate

1:5   The light shines through the darkness, and the darkness can never extinguish it.

1:10   But although the world was made through him, the world didn't recognize him when he came.

Knowledge of God comes to us through Christ

7:28-29   While Jesus was teaching in the Temple, he called out, "Yes, you know me, and you know where I come from. But I represent one you don't know, and he is true. I know him because I have come from him, and he sent me to you."

8:19   "Where is your father?" they asked. Jesus answered, "Since you don't know who I am, you don't know who my Father is. If you knew me, then you would know my Father, too."

8:55   But you do not even know him. I know him. If I said otherwise, I would be as great a liar as you! But it is true—I know him and obey him.

Knowing God is every believer's opportunity

14:7   If you had known who I am, then you would have known who my Father is. From now on you know him and have seen him!

14:9   Jesus replied, "Philip, don't you even yet know who I am, even after all the time I have been with you? Anyone who has seen me has seen the Father! So why are you asking to see him?"

14:17   He is the Holy Spirit, who leads into all truth. The world at large cannot receive him, because it isn't looking for him and doesn't recognize him. But you do, because he lives with you now and later will be in you.

Knowing the Father through the Son was the end result of Jesus' mission on earth

17:3   And this is the way to have eternal life—to know you, the only true God, and Jesus Christ, the one you sent to earth.

17:6   "I have told these men about you. They were in the world, but then you gave them to me. Actually, they were always yours, and you gave them to me; and they have kept your word."

THE NAMES OF JESUS / *John 10:7*

In different settings, Jesus gave himself names that pointed to special roles he was ready to fulfill for people. Some of these refer back to the Old Testament promises of the Messiah. Others were ways to help people understand him.

Reference	Name	Significance
6:27	Son of Man	Jesus' favorite reference to himself. It emphasized his humanity—but the way he used it, it was a claim to divinity.
6:35	Bread of life	Refers to his life-giving role—that he is the only source of eternal life.
8:12	Light of the world	Light is a symbol of spiritual truth. Jesus is the universal answer for people's need of spiritual truth.
10:7	Gate for the sheep	Jesus is the only way into God's Kingdom.
10:11	Good shepherd	Jesus appropriated the prophetic images of the Messiah pictured in the Old Testament. This is a claim to divinity, focusing on Jesus' love and guidance.
11:25	The resurrection and the life	Not only is Jesus the source of life; he is the power over death.
14:6	The way, the truth, and the life	Jesus is the method, the message, and the meaning for all people. With this title, he summarized his purpose in coming to earth.
15:1	The true vine	This title has an important second part, "you are the branches." As in so many of his other names, Jesus reminds us that just as branches gain life from the vine and cannot live apart from it, so we are completely dependent on Christ for spiritual life.

RESPONSES TO JESUS / John 11:51-54

Throughout chapter 11 we are given a variety of responses to Jesus. None of them are neutral. People who met Jesus formed a variety of opinions about him. Among them are the following:

Response:	Do you know someone who:
Some, like Mary and Martha, displayed faith that needed to deepen.	. . . needs to deepen his/her faith?
Some saw the miracle of Lazarus's resurrection and concluded that Jesus must be telling the truth about his identity. So they put their faith in him.	. . . needs to put his/her faith in Christ?
Some saw the miracle and concluded that it was merely another reason to get rid of Jesus the troublemaker.	. . . considers Jesus merely a source of trouble?
Some heard about the miracle and could only see Jesus as a threat to their power and position.	. . . finds Jesus threatening?
Some decided that Jesus must be killed and planned accordingly.	. . . would remove Jesus if that were possible?
Some arrived in Jerusalem for the Passover curious about Jesus, moving toward acceptance or rejection.	. . . is curious and might be open to the Good News?

Tell Them the Good News, that New Life Is Available in Christ!

WE ARE HIS SHEEP / John 10:1-2

Jesus' love for his people is contrasted with the treatment given the people by the Jewish religious leaders of the day. That contrast would hold for any leader who attempts to use the flock of God for his or her own selfish purposes.

Religious Leaders	Jesus
Self-centered (thieves and/or hired hands)	From God, true
Strangers	Knows his sheep and they recognize him
Lead sheep away from God	Leads sheep to God
Flee when danger threatens	Provides real saftey and assurance (Psalm 23)
Have no heart of compassion for the sheep	Lays down his life for the sheep (Psalm 22)
Will abandon the sheep in time of trouble	Will return for his sheep (Psalm 24)

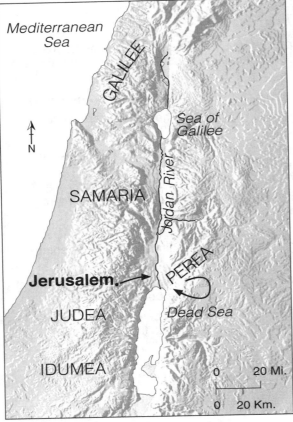

MINISTRY EAST OF THE JORDAN
John 10:22-42

Jesus had been in Jerusalem for the Festival of Shelters (7:2); then he preached in various towns, probably in Judea, before returning to Jerusalem for Hanukkah. He again angered the religious leaders, who tried to arrest him, but he left the city and went to the region east of the Jordan to preach.

Copyright © 2001 by Tyndale House Publishers

LIFE! / John 10:12-13

John emphasized the theme of "life" in his Gospel. The word was constantly on Jesus' lips. It was John who recorded Jesus saying: "I am the resurrection and the life. Those who believe in me, even though they die like everyone else, will live again" (11:25). The following are several other aspects of life found in the Gospel of John:

Aspects of Life	Reference in John's Gospel
Life is God's gift	1:4; 10:28
Jesus is the Life	11:25; 14:6
Eternal life is living fellowship with God now and forever	3:15-16
Life is found only in trusting Christ, not just knowing about him	5:40
Life begins by believing in Jesus	20:31

J O H N

338

LIVING TO DIE / *John 10:14-16*

Everything about Jesus' life pointed toward a purpose. His passing through the world illustrated many spiritual truths about God and his plan, but Jesus' main reason for coming was to die in our behalf. Without Christ's death for us there would be no hope for us!

Reference	Passage
Romans 5:8	But God showed his great love for us by sending Christ to die for us while we were still sinners.
Ephesians 5:2	Live a life filled with love for others, following the example of Christ, who loved you and gave himself as a sacrifice to take away your sins. And God was pleased, because that sacrifice was like sweet perfume to him.
Hebrews 9:14	Just think how much more the blood of Christ will purify our hearts from deeds that lead to death so that we can worship the living God. For by the power of the eternal Spirit, Christ offered himself to God as a perfect sacrifice for our sins.
1 Peter 2:24	He personally carried away our sins in his own body on the cross so we can be dead to sin and live for what is right. You have been healed by his wounds!
1 Peter 3:18	Christ also suffered when he died for our sins once for all time. He never sinned, but he died for sinners that he might bring us safely home to God. He suffered physical death, but he was raised to life in the Spirit.

GOD IS GREATER / *John 10:31-33*

The invincibility of God in protecting those who trust in him is attested throughout the Bible. And nowhere else is that power more clear than toward those whom God has promised to save. The following are a sample of biblical affirmations on God's protection.

God's Greatness	Reference
Then Asa cried out to the LORD his God, "O LORD, no one but you can help the powerless against the mighty! Help us, O LORD our God, for we trust in you alone. It is in your name that we have come against this vast horde. O LORD, you are our God; do not let mere men prevail against you!"	2 Chronicles 14:11
But God is my helper. The Lord is the one who keeps me alive!	Psalm 54:4
With God's help we will do mighty things, for he will trample down our foes.	Psalm 60:12
It is better to trust the LORD than to put confidence in people.	Psalm 118:8
Sin is no longer your master, for you are no longer subject to the law, which enslaves you to sin. Instead, you are free by God's grace.	Romans 6:14
And I am convinced that nothing can ever separate us from his love. Death can't, and life can't. The angels can't, and the demons can't. Our fears for today, our worries about tomorrow, and even the powers of hell can't keep God's love away. Whether we are high above the sky or in the deepest ocean, nothing in all creation will ever be able to separate us from the love of God that is revealed in Christ Jesus our Lord.	Romans 8:38-39
And that is why I am suffering here in prison. But I am not ashamed of it, for I know the one in whom I trust, and I am sure that he is able to guard what I have entrusted to him until the day of his return.	2 Timothy 1:12
And now, all glory to God, who is able to keep you from stumbling, and who will bring you into his glorious presence innocent of sin and with great joy. All glory to him, who alone is God our Savior, through Jesus Christ our Lord. Yes, glory, majesty, power, and authority belong to him, in the beginning, now, and forevermore. Amen.	Jude 24-25

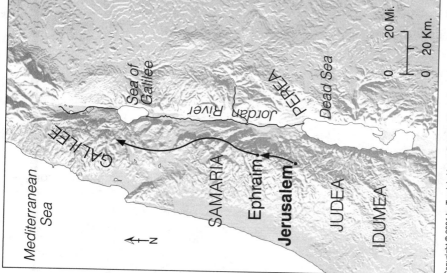

JESUS RAISES LAZARUS

John 11:1-44

Jesus had been preaching in the villages beyond the Jordan, probably in Perea, when he received the news of Lazarus's sickness. Jesus did not leave immediately, but waited two days before returning to Judea. He knew Lazarus would be dead when he arrived in Bethany, but he was going to do a great miracle.

Copyright © 2001 by Tyndale House Publishers

TIME WITH THE DISCIPLES

John 11:45-54

Lazarus's return to life became the last straw for the religious leaders, who were bent on killing Jesus. So Jesus stopped his public ministry and took his disciples away from Jerusalem to Ephraim. From there they returned to Galilee for a while (see the map in Luke 17).

Copyright © 2001 by Tyndale House Publishers

GREAT EXPECTATIONS / *John 11:53*

Wherever he went, Jesus exceeded people's expectations.

What was expected	What Jesus did	Reference
A man looked for healing.	Jesus also forgave his sins.	Mark 2:1-12
The disciples were expecting an ordinary day of fishing.	They found the Savior.	Luke 5:1-11
A widow was resigned to bury her dead son.	Jesus restored her son to life.	Luke 7:11-17
The religious leaders wanted a miracle.	Jesus offered them the Creator of miracles.	Matthew 12:38-45
A woman who wanted to be healed touched Jesus.	Jesus helped her see it was her faith that had healed her.	Mark 5:25-34
The disciples thought the crowd should be sent home because there was no food.	Jesus used a small meal to feed thousands, and there were leftovers!	John 6:1-15
The crowds looked for a political leader to set up a new kingdom to overthrow Rome's control.	Jesus offered them an eternal, spiritual kingdom to overthrow sin's control.	A theme throughout the Gospels
The disciples wanted to eat the Passover meal with Jesus, their Master.	Jesus washed their feet, showing that he was also their servant.	John 13:1-20
The religious leaders wanted Jesus killed and got their wish.	But Jesus rose from the dead!	John 11:53; 19:30; 20:1-29

BARRIERS TO FRUITFULNESS / *John 15:1-2*

Barrier	Explanation	Implication
Lack of proper nourishment	Poor supply of water or nutrients will destroy the vine.	If Christ's life and love do not flow in us, we will be spiritually unproductive.
Disease	Insects and disease move from dead wood into healthy plants.	Ongoing sin and unresolved past issues will lead to spiritual ineffectiveness.
Immature branches	New branches require several years of pruning before they can produce.	We need time to grow. Growth may involve suffering.
Improper pruning	A wise gardener knows what to remove in order to bring about fruitfulness.	Our priorities and the focus of our energies must be guided by Christ and his Word, not our own wisdom and desires.
No Gardener	Vines need constant attention.	Resistance to God's guidance and pruning leads to unfruitfulness.
Separated from the Vine	Branches must be attached to a healthy root stock.	We must not think for a moment that we are capable of surviving apart from Jesus Christ. He is the giver and sustainer of life!

THE JUDGMENT OF SATAN / *John 16:9*

Satan has been judged so that his darkness cannot overcome believers' light.

Reference	Quotation	Explanation
Luke 10:18	"Yes," he told them, "I saw Satan falling from heaven as a flash of lightning!"	Pride was Satan's downfall. Jesus spoke of his fall from glory and pointed to his total destruction.
John 12:31	The time of judgment for the world has come, when the prince of this world will be cast out.	Jesus' crucifixion gave him the victory over Satan.
John 16:11	Judgment will come because the prince of this world has already been judged.	Jesus announced that Satan's judgment was complete.
Hebrews 2:14	Because God's children are human beings—made of flesh and blood—Jesus also became flesh and blood by being born in human form. For only as a human being could he die, and only by dying could he break the power of the Devil, who had the power of death.	Jesus' crucifixion shattered Satan's deadly power.
1 John 3:8	But when people keep on sinning, it shows they belong to the Devil, who has been sinning since the beginning. But the Son of God came to destroy these works of the Devil.	Jesus' purpose was fulfilled in overcoming Satan.
Revelation 20:10	Then the Devil, who betrayed them, was thrown into the lake of fire that burns with sulfur, joining the beast and the false prophet. There they will be tormented day and night forever and ever.	Jesus will have the complete and final victory over Satan.

CHRIST IS IN US; WE ARE IN CHRIST / *John 17:22-23*

Christ is in us

He takes up residence in our lives by his Spirit.

He goes everywhere with us.

We represent Jesus everywhere we go.

Jesus helps us obey him.

His presence guarantees our hope.

We are in Christ

Our salvation is guaranteed by him.

We live in His protection.

Our purpose for living is focused in Christ.

We seek to obey Jesus.

He accomplished what we now look forward to with hope.

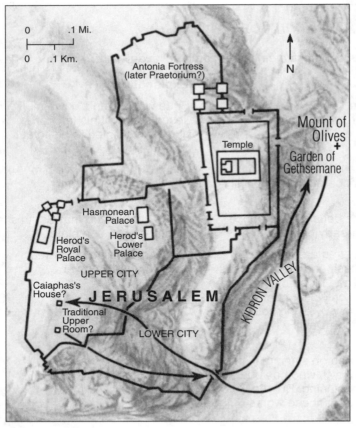

BETRAYAL IN THE GARDEN

John 18:1-24
See also *Matthew 26:47-56; Mark 14:43-52; Luke 22:47-53*

After eating the Passover meal in the upper room, Jesus and his disciples went to Gethsemane, where Judas led the Temple guard to arrest Jesus. Jesus was then taken to Caiaphas's house for his first of many trials.

Map labels:

- 0 — .1 Mi.
- 0 — .1 Km.
- Antonia Fortress (later Praetorium?)
- N
- Temple
- Mount of Olives
- Garden of Gethsemane
- Hasmonean Palace
- Herod's Royal Palace
- Herod's Lower Palace
- UPPER CITY
- Caiaphas's House?
- JERUSALEM
- KIDRON VALLEY
- Traditional Upper Room?
- LOWER CITY

Copyright © 2001 by Tyndale House Publishers

THE SIX STAGES OF JESUS' TRIAL / *John 18:12*

Although Jesus' trial lasted less than 18 hours, he was taken to six different hearings.

Before Jewish Authorities	Preliminary Hearing before Annas (John 18:12-24)	Because the office of high priest was for life, Annas was still the "official" high priest in the eyes of the Jews, even though the Romans had appointed another. Thus, Annas still carried much weight in the high council.
	Hearing before Caiaphas (Matthew 26:57-68)	Like the hearing before Annas, this hearing was conducted at night in secrecy. It was full of illegalities that made a mockery of justice.
	Trial before the High Council (Matthew 27:1-2)	Just after daybreak, 70 members of the high council met to rubber-stamp their approval of the previous hearings to make them appear legal. The purpose of this trial was not to determine justice, but to justify their own preconceptions of Jesus' guilt.
Before Roman Authorities	First Hearing before Pilate (Luke 23:1-5)	The religious leaders had condemned Jesus to death on religious grounds, but only the Roman government could grant the death penalty. Thus, they took Jesus to Pilate, the Roman governor, and accused him of treason and rebellion, crimes for which the Roman government gave the death penalty. Pilate saw at once that Jesus was innocent, but he was afraid of the uproar being caused by the religious leaders.
	Hearing before Herod (Luke 23:6-12)	Because Jesus' home was in the region of Galilee, Pilate sent Jesus to Herod Antipas, the ruler of Galilee, who was in Jerusalem for the Passover celebration. Herod was eager to see Jesus do a miracle, but when Jesus remained silent, Herod wanted nothing to do with him and sent him back to Pilate.
	Last Hearing before Pilate (Luke 23:13-25)	Pilate didn't like the religious leaders. He wasn't interested in condemning Jesus because he knew Jesus was innocent. However, he knew that another uprising in his district might cost him his job. First he tried to compromise with the religious leaders by having Jesus beaten, an illegal action in itself. But finally he gave in and handed Jesus over to be executed. Pilate's self-interest was stronger than his sense of justice.

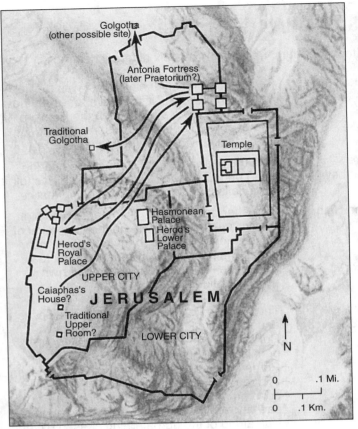

JESUS' TRIAL AND CRUCIFIXION

John 18:28–19:16 See also *Matthew 27:11-26; Mark 15:2-15; Luke 23:1-25*

Jesus was taken from trial before the Jewish high council to trial before the Roman governor, Pilate, in Pilate's palace. Pilate sent him to Herod (Luke 23:5-12), but Herod just returned Jesus to Pilate. Responding to threats from the mob, Pilate finally turned Jesus over to be crucified.

Copyright © 2001 by Tyndale House Publishers

OLD TESTAMENT PASSAGES QUOTED BY CHRIST / *John 21:25*

New Testament	Old Testament	Occasion
Matthew 4:4	Deuteronomy 8:3	Temptation
Matthew 4:7	Deuteronomy 6:16	Temptation
Matthew 4:10	Deuteronomy 6:13	Temptation
Matthew 5:21	Exodus 20:13	Sermon on the Mount
Matthew 5:27	Exodus 20:14	Sermon on the Mount
Luke 4:18-19	Isaiah 61:1-2	Hometown Sermon
Matthew 9:13	Hosea 6:6	Supper at Matthew's
Mark 10:7-8	Genesis 2:24	Confrontations with the Jewish Rulers
Mark 12:29-30	Deuteronomy 6:4-5	Temple Question Session
Matthew 15:7-9	Isaiah 29:13	Confrontations with the Jewish Rulers
John 8:17	Deuteronomy 17:6	Confrontations with the Jewish Rulers
Luke 7:27	Malachi 3:1	Tribute to John
Matthew 21:16	Psalm 8:2	Temple Cleansing
Luke 19:46	Isaiah 56:7	Temple Cleansing
Matthew 21:42, 44	Psalm 118:22-23	Confrontations with the Jewish Rulers
Mark 12:36	Psalm 110:1	Temple Question Session
John 15:25	Psalms 35:19; 69:4	Parable about Israel
Matthew 27:46	Psalm 22:1	On the Cross
Luke 23:46	Psalm 31:5	On the Cross

COMPARISON OF THE FOUR GOSPELS / *John 21:25*

All four Gospels present the life and teachings of Jesus. Each book, however, focuses on a unique facet of Jesus and his character. To understand more about the specific characteristics of Jesus, read any one of the four Gospels.

	Matthew	Mark	Luke	John
Jesus is	The promised King	The Servant of God	The Son of Man	The Son of God
The original readers were	Jews	Gentiles, Romans	Greeks	Christians throughout the world
Significant themes	Jesus is the Messiah because he fulfilled Old Testament prophecy	Jesus backed up his words with action	Jesus was God but also fully human	Belief in Jesus is required for salvation
Character of the writer	Teacher	Storyteller	Historian	Theologian
Greatest emphasis is on	Jesus' sermons and words	Jesus' miracles and actions	Jesus' humanity	The principles of Jesus' teaching

250 EVENTS IN THE LIFE OF CHRIST / *A Harmony of the Gospels*

All four books in the Bible that tell the story of Jesus Christ—Matthew, Mark, Luke, and John—stand alone, emphasizing a unique aspect of Jesus' life. But when these are blended into one complete account, or harmonized, we gain new insights about the life of Christ.

This harmony combines the four Gospels into a single chronological account of Christ's life on earth. It includes every chapter and verse of each Gospel, leaving nothing out.

The harmony is divided into 250 events. The title of each event is identical to the title found in the corresponding Gospel. Parallel passages found in more than one Gospel have identical titles, helping you to identify them quickly.

Each of the 250 events in the harmony is numbered. The number of the event corresponds to the number next to the title in the Bible text. When reading one of the Gospel accounts, you will notice, at times, that some numbers are missing or out of sequence. The easiest way to locate these events is to refer to the harmony.

In addition, if you are looking for a particular event in the life of Christ, the harmony can help you locate it more rapidly than paging through all four Gospels. Each of the 250 events has a distinctive title keyed to the main emphasis of the passage to help you locate and remember the events.

This harmony will help you to better visualize the travels of Jesus, study the four Gospels comparatively, and appreciate the unity of their message.

I. BIRTH AND PREPARATION OF JESUS CHRIST

	Matthew	Mark	Luke	John
1. Luke's purpose in writing			1:1-4	
2. God became a human				1:1-18
3. The record of Jesus' ancestors	1:1-17		3:23-38	
4. An angel promises the birth of John to Zechariah			1:5-25	
5. An angel promises the birth of Jesus to Mary			1:26-38	
6. Mary visits Elizabeth			1:39-56	
7. John the Baptist is born			1:57-80	
8. An angel appears to Joseph	1:18-25			
9. Jesus is born in Bethlehem			2:1-7	
10. Shepherds visit Jesus			2:8-20	
11. Mary a77nd Joseph bring Jesus to the Temple			2:21-40	
12. Visitors arrive from eastern lands	2:1-12			
13. The escape to Egypt	2:13-18			
14. The return to Nazareth	2:19-23			
15. Jesus speaks with the religious teachers			2:41-52	
16. John the Baptist prepares the way for Jesus	3:1-12	1:1-8	3:1-18	
17. The baptism of Jesus	3:13-17	1:9-11	3:21-22	
18. Satan tempts Jesus in the wilderness	4:1-11	1:12-13	4:1-13	
19. John the Baptist declares his mission				1:19-28
20. John the Baptist proclaims Jesus as the Messiah			1:29-34	
21. The first disciples follow Jesus				1:35-51
22. Jesus turns water into wine				2:1-12

II. MESSAGE AND MINISTRY OF JESUS CHRIST

	Matthew	Mark	Luke	John
23. Jesus clears the Temple	2:13-25			
24. Nicodemus visits Jesus at night				3:1-21
25. John the Baptist tells more about Jesus				3:22-36
26. Herod puts John in prison			3:19-20	
27. Jesus talks to a woman at the well				4:1-26
28. Jesus tells about the spiritual harvest				4:27-38
29. Many Samaritans believe in Jesus				4:39-42
30. Jesus preaches in Galilee	14:12-17	1:14-15	4:14-15	4:43-45
31. Jesus heals a government official's son				4:46-54
32. Jesus is rejected at Nazareth			4:16-30	
33. Four fishermen follow Jesus	4:18-22	1:16-20		
34. Jesus teaches with great authority		1:21-28	4:31-37	
35. Jesus heals Peter's mother-in-law and many others	8:14-17	1:29-34	4:38-41	
36. Jesus preaches throughout Galilee	4:23-25	1:35-39	4:42-44	
37. Jesus provides a miraculous catch of fish			5:1-11	
38. Jesus heals a man with leprosy	8:1-4	1:40-45	5:12-16	
39. Jesus heals a paralyzed man	9:1-8	2:1-12	5:17-26	
40. Jesus eats with sinners at Matthew's house	9:9-13	2:13-17	5:27-32	
41. Religious leaders ask Jesus about fasting	9:14-17	2:18-22	5:33-39	
42. Jesus heals a lame man by a pool				5:1-15
43. Jesus claims to be the Son of God				5:16-30
44. Jesus supports his claim				5:31-47
45. The disciples pick wheat on the Sabbath	12:1-8	2:23-28	6:1-5	
46. Jesus heals a man's hand on the Sabbath	12:9-14	3:1-6	6:6-11	
47. Large crowds follow Jesus	12:15-21	3:7-12		
48. Jesus chooses the twelve disciples		3:13-19	6:12-16	
49. Jesus gives the Beatitudes	5:1-12		6:17-26	
50. Jesus teaches about salt and light	5:13-16			
51. Jesus teaches about the law	5:17-20			
52. Jesus teaches about anger	5:21-26			
53. Jesus teaches about lust	5:27-30			
54. Jesus teaches about divorce	5:31-32			
55. Jesus teaches about vows	5:33-37			
56. Jesus teaches about revenge	5:38-42			
57. Jesus teaches about loving enemies	5:43-48		6:27-36	
58. Jesus teaches about giving to the needy	6:1-4			
59. Jesus teaches about prayer	6:5-15			
60. Jesus teaches about fasting	6:16-18			
61. Jesus teaches about money	6:19-24			
62. Jesus teaches about worry	6:25-34			
63. Jesus teaches about judging others	7:1-6	6:37-42		
64. Jesus teaches about asking, looking, knocking	7:7-12			
65. Jesus teaches about the way to heaven	7:13-14			
66. Jesus teaches about fruit in people's lives	7:15-20		6:43-45	
67. Jesus teaches about building on a solid foundation	7:21-29		6:46-49	
68. A Roman officer demonstrates faith	8:5-13		7:1-10	

	Matthew	Mark	Luke	John
69. Jesus raises a widow's son from the dead			7:11-17	
70. Jesus eases John's doubt	11:1-19		7:18-35	
71. Jesus promises rest for the soul	11:20-30			
72. A sinful woman anoints Jesus' feet			7:36-50	
73. Women accompany Jesus and the disciples			8:1-3	
74. Religious leaders accuse Jesus of getting his power from Satan	12:22-37	3:20-30		
75. Religious leaders ask Jesus for a miracle	12:38-45			
76. Jesus describes his true family	12:46-50	3:31-35	8:19-21	
77. Jesus tells the parable of the four soils	13:1-9	4:1-9	8:4-8	
78. Jesus explains the parable of the four soils	13:10-23	4:10-25	8:9-18	
79. Jesus tells the parable of the growing seed		4:26-29		
80. Jesus tells the parable of the weeds	13:24-30			
81. Jesus tells the parable of the mustard seed	13:31-32	4:30-34		
82. Jesus tells the parable of the yeast	13:33-35			
83. Jesus explains the parable of the weeds	13:36-43			
84. Jesus tells the parable of hidden treasure	13:44			
85. Jesus tells the parable of the pearl merchant	13:45-46			
86. Jesus tells the parable of the fishing net	13:47-52			
87. Jesus calms the storm	8:23-27	4:35-41	8:22-25	
88. Jesus sends demons into a herd of pigs	8:28-34	5:1-20	8:26-39	
89. Jesus heals a bleeding woman and restores a girl to life	9:18-26	5:21-43	8:40-56	
90. Jesus heals the blind and mute	9:27-34			
91. The people of Nazareth refuse to believe		6:1-6	13:53-58	
92. Jesus urges the disciples to pray for workers			9:35-38	
93. Jesus sends out the twelve disciples	10:1-15	6:7-13	9:1-6	
94. Jesus prepares the disciples for persecution	10:16-42			
95. Herod kills John the Baptist	14:1-12	6:14-29	9:7-9	
96. Jesus feeds 5,000	14:13-21	6:30-44	9:10-17	6:1-15
97. Jesus walks on water	14:22-33	6:45-52		6:16-21
98. Jesus heals all who touch him	14:34-36	6:53-56		
99. Jesus is the true bread from heaven				6:22-40
100. The people disagree that Jesus is from heaven				6:41-59
101. Many disciples desert Jesus				6:60-71
102. Jesus teaches about inner purity	15:1-20	7:1-23		
103. Jesus sends a demon out of a girl	15:21-28	7:24-30		
104. Jesus heals many people	15:29-31	7:31-37		
105. Jesus feeds 4,000	15:32-39	8:1-10		
106. Leaders demand a miraculous sign	16:1-4	8:11-13		
107. Jesus warns against wrong teaching	16:5-12	8:14-21		
108. Jesus restores sight to a blind man		8:22-26		
109. Peter says Jesus is the Messiah	16:13-20	8:27-30	9:18-20	
110. Jesus predicts his death the first time	16:21-28	8:31–9:1	9:21-27	
111. Jesus is transfigured on the mountain	17:1-13	9:2-13	9:28-36	
112. Jesus heals a demon-possessed boy	17:14-21	9:14-29	9:37-43	
113. Jesus predicts his death the second time	17:22-23	9:30-32	9:44-45	

II. MESSAGE AND MINISTRY OF JESUS CHRIST *Continued*

	Matthew	Mark	Luke	John
114. Peter finds the coin in the fish's mouth	17:24-27			
115. The disciples argue about who would be the greatest	18:1-6	9:33-37	9:46-48	
116. The disciples forbid another to use Jesus' name		9:38-41	9:49-50	
117. Jesus warns against temptation	18:7-9	9:42-50		
118. Jesus warns against looking down on others	18:10-14			
119. Jesus teaches how to treat a believer who sins	18:15-20			
120. Jesus tells the parable of the unforgiving debtor	18:21-35			
121. Jesus' brothers ridicule him				7:1-9
122. Jesus teaches about the cost of following him	8:18-22		9:51-62	
123. Jesus teaches openly at the Temple				7:10-31
124. Religious leaders attempt to arrest Jesus				7:32-52
125. Jesus forgives an adulterous woman				7:53– 8:11
126. Jesus is the light of the world				8:12-20
127. Jesus warns of coming judgment				8:21-30
128. Jesus speaks about God's true children				8:32-47
129. Jesus states he is eternal				8:48-59
130. Jesus sends out 72 messengers			10:1-16	
131. The 72 messengers return			10:17-24	
132. Jesus tells the parable of the Good Samaritan			10:25-37	
133. Jesus visits Mary and Martha			10:38-42	
134. Jesus teaches his disciples about prayer			11:1-13	
135. Jesus answers hostile accusations			11:14-28	
136. Jesus warns against unbelief			11:29-32	
137. Jesus teaches about the light within			11:33-36	
138. Jesus criticizes the religious leaders			11:37-54	
139. Jesus speaks against hypocrisy			12:1-12	
140. Jesus tells the parable of the rich fool			12:13-21	
141. Jesus warns about worry			12:22-34	
142. Jesus warns about preparing for his coming			12:35-48	
143. Jesus warns about coming division			12:49-53	
144. Jesus warns about the future crisis			12:54-59	
145. Jesus calls the people to repent			13:1-9	
146. Jesus heals the crippled woman			13:10-17	
147. Jesus teaches about the Kingdom of God			13:18-21	
148. Jesus heals the man who was born blind				9:1-12
149. Religious leaders question the blind man				9:13-34
150. Jesus teaches about spiritual blindness				9:35-41
151. Jesus is the good shepherd				10:1-21
152. Religious leaders surround Jesus at the Temple				10:22-42
153. Jesus teaches about entering the Kingdom			13:22-30	
154. Jesus grieves over Jerusalem			13:31-35	
155. Jesus heals a man with swollen limbs			14:1-6	

	Matthew	Mark	Luke	John
156. Jesus teaches about seeking honor			14:7-14	
157. Jesus tells the parable of the great festival			14:15-24	
158. Jesus teaches about the cost of being a disciple			14:25-35	
159. Jesus tells the parable of the lost sheep			15:1-7	
160. Jesus tells the parable of the lost coin			15:8-10	
161. Jesus tells the parable of the lost son			15:11-32	
162. Jesus tells the parable of the shrewd manager			16:1-18	
163. Jesus tells about the rich man and the beggar			16:19-31	
164. Jesus tells about forgiveness and faith			17:1-10	
165. Lazarus becomes ill and dies				11:1-16
166. Jesus comforts Mary and Martha				11:17-37
167. Jesus raises Lazarus from the dead				11:38-44
168. Religious leaders plot to kill Jesus				11:45-57
169. Jesus heals ten men with leprosy			17:11-19	
170. Jesus teaches about the coming of the Kingdom of God			17:20-37	
171. Jesus tells the parable of the persistent widow			18:1-8	
172. Jesus tells the parable of two men who prayed			18:9-14	
173. Jesus teaches about marriage and divorce	19:1-12	10:1-12		
174. Jesus blesses the children	19:13-15	10:13-16	18:15-17	
175. Jesus speaks to the rich young man	19:16-30	10:17-31	18:18-30	
176. Jesus tells the parable of the vineyard workers	20:1-16			
177. Jesus predicts his death the third time	20:17-19	10:32-34	18:31-34	
178. Jesus teaches about serving others	20:20-28	10:35-45		
179. Jesus heals a blind beggar	20:29-34	10:46-52	18:35-43	
180. Jesus brings salvation to Zacchaeus's home			19:1-10	
181. Jesus tells the parable of the king's ten servants			19:11-27	
182. A woman anoints Jesus with perfume	26:6-13	14:3-9		12:1-11
183. Jesus rides into Jerusalem on a young donkey	21:1-11	11:1-11	19:28-44	12:12-19
184. Jesus clears the Temple again	21:12-17	11:12-19	19:45-48	
185. Jesus explains why he must die				12:20-36
186. Most of the people do not believe in Jesus				12:37-43
187. Jesus summarizes his message				12:44-50
188. Jesus says the disciples can pray for anything	21:18-22	11:20-26		
189. Religious leaders challenge Jesus' authority	21:23-27	11:27-33	20:1-8	
190. Jesus tells the parable of the two sons	21:28-32			
191. Jesus tells the parable of the evil farmers	21:33-46	12:1-12	20:9-19	

II. MESSAGE AND MINISTRY OF JESUS CHRIST Continued

	Matthew	Mark	Luke	John
192. Jesus tells the parable of the wedding dinner	22:1-14			
193. Religious leaders question Jesus about paying taxes	22:15-22	12:13-17	20:20-26	
194. Religious leaders question Jesus about the Resurrection	22:23-33	12:18-27	20:27-40	
195. Religious leaders question Jesus about the greatest commandment	22:34-40	12:28-34		
196. Religious leaders cannot answer Jesus' question	22:41-46	12:35-37	20:41-44	
197. Jesus warns against the religious leaders	23:1-12	12:38-40	20:45-57	
198. Jesus condemns the religious leaders	23:13-36			
199. Jesus grieves over Jerusalem again	23:37-39			
200. A poor widow gives all she has		12:41-44	21:1-4	
201. Jesus tells about the future	24:1-25	13:1-23	21:5-24	
202. Jesus tells about his return	24:26-35	13:24-31	21:25-33	
203. Jesus tells about remaining watchful	24:36-51	13:32-37	21:34-38	
204. Jesus tells the parable of the ten bridesmaids	25:1-13			
205. Jesus tells the parable of the loaned money	25:14-30			
206. Jesus tells about the final judgment	25:31-46			

III. DEATH AND RESURRECTION OF JESUS CHRIST

	Matthew	Mark	Luke	John
207. Religious leaders plot to kill Jesus	26:1-5	14:1-2	22:1-2	
208. Judas agrees to betray Jesus	26:14-16	14:10-11	22:3-6	
209. Disciples prepare for the Passover	26:17-19	14:12-16	22:7-13	
210. Jesus washes the disciples' feet				13:1-20
211. Jesus and the disciples share the Last Supper	26:20-30	14:17-26	22:14-30	13:21-30
212. Jesus predicts Peter's denial			22:31-38	13:31-38
213. Jesus is the way to the Father				14:1-14
214. Jesus promises the Holy Spirit				14:15-31
215. Jesus teaches about the vine and the branches				15:1-17
216. Jesus warns about the world's hatred				15:18–16:4
217. Jesus teaches about the Holy Spirit				16:5-15
218. Jesus teaches about using his name in prayer				16:16-33
219. Jesus prays for himself				17:1-5
220. Jesus prays for his disciples				17:6-19
221. Jesus prays for future believers				17:20-26
222. Jesus again predicts Peter's denial	26:31-35	14:27-31		
223. Jesus agonizes in the garden	26:36-46	14:32-42	22:39-46	
224. Jesus is betrayed and arrested	26:47-56	14:43-52	22:47-53	18:1-11
225. Annas questions Jesus				18:12-24

III. DEATH AND RESURRECTION OF JESUS CHRIST *Continued*

	Matthew	Mark	Luke	John
226. Caiaphas questions Jesus	26:57-68	14:53-65		
227. Peter denies knowing Jesus	26:69-75	14:66-72	22:54-65	18:25-27
228. The council of religious leaders condemns Jesus	27:1-2	15:1	22:66-71	
229. Judas hangs himself	27:3-10			
230. Jesus' trial before Pilate	27:11-14	15:2-5	23:1-5	18:28-37
231. Jesus stands trial before Herod			23:6-12	
232. Pilate hands Jesus over to be crucified	27:15-26	15:6-15	23:13-25	18:38–19:16
233. Roman soldiers mock Jesus	27:27-31	15:16-20		
234. Jesus is led away to be crucified	27:32-34	15:21-24	23:26-31	19:17
235. Jesus is placed on the cross	27:35-44	15:25-32	23:32-43	19:18-27
236. Jesus dies on the cross	27:45-56	15:33-41	23:44-49	19:28-37
237. Jesus is laid in the tomb	27:57-61	15:42-47	23:50-56	19:38-42
238. Guards are posted at the tomb	27:62-66			
239. Jesus rises from the dead	28:1-7	16:1-8	24:1-12	20:1-10
240. Jesus appears to Mary Magdalene		16:9-11		20:11-18
241. Jesus appears to the women	28:8-10			
242. Religious leaders bribe the guards	28:11-15			
243. Jesus appears to two believers traveling on the road		16:12-13	24:13-34	
244. Jesus appears to his disciples			24:35-43	20:19-23
245. Jesus appears to Thomas		16:14		20:24-31
246. Jesus appears to seven disciples				21:15-25
247. Jesus challenges Peter				21:15-25
248. Jesus gives the great commission	28:16-20	16:15-18		
249. Jesus appears to the disciples in Jerusalem			24:44-49	
250. Jesus ascends into heaven		16:19-20	24:50-53	

THE PARABLES OF JESUS

I. Teaching Parables
  A. About the Kingdom of God
    1. The Soils (Matthew 13:3-8; Mark 4:4-8; Luke 8:5-8)
    2. The Weeds (Matthew 13:24-30)
    3. The Mustard Seed (Matthew 13:31-32; Mark 4:30-32; Luke 13:18-19)
    4. The Yeast (Matthew 13:33; Luke 13:20-21)
    5. The Treasure (Matthew 13:44)
    6. The Pearl (Matthew 13:45-46)
    7. The Fishing Net (Matthew 13:47-50)
    8. The Growing Wheat (Mark 4:26-29)
  B. About Service and Obedience
    1. The Workers in the Harvest (Matthew 20:1-16)
    2. The Loaned Money (Matthew 25:14-30)
    3. The Nobleman's Servants (Luke 19:11-27)
    4. The Servant's Role (Luke 17:7-10)
  C. About Prayer
    1. The Friend at Midnight (Luke 11:5-8)
    2. The Unjust Judge (Luke 18:1-8)
  D. About Neighbors
    1. The Good Samaritan (Luke 10:30-37)
  E. About Humility
    1. The Wedding Feast (Luke 14:7-11)
    2. The Proud Pharisee and the Corrupt Tax Collector (Luke 18:9-14)
  F. About Wealth
    1. The Rich Fool (Luke 12:16-21)
    2. The Great Festival (Luke 14:16-24)
    3. The Shrewd Manager (Luke 16:1-9)

II. Gospel Parables
  A. About God's Love
    1. The Lost Sheep (Matthew 18:12-14; Luke 15:3-7)
    2. The Lost Coin (Luke 15:8-10)
    3. The Lost Son (Luke 15:11-32)
  B. About Thankfulness
    1. The Forgiven Debts (Luke 7:41-43)

III. Parables of Judgment and the Future
  A. About Christ's Return
    1. The Ten Bridesmaids (Matthew 25:1-13)
    2. The Wise and Faithful Servants (Matthew 24:45-51; Luke 12:42-48)
    3. The Traveling Owner of the House (Mark 13:34-37)
  B. About God's Values
    1. The Two Sons (Matthew 21:28-32)
    2. The Evil Farmers (Matthew 21:33-34; Mark 12:1-9; Luke 20:9-16)
    3. The Unproductive Fig Tree (Luke 13:6-9)
    4. The Wedding Feast (Matthew 22:1-14)
    5. The Unforgiving Servant (Matthew 18:23-35)

JESUS' MIRACLES

John and the other Gospel writers were able to record only a fraction of the people who were touched and healed by Jesus. But enough of Jesus' words and works have been saved so that we also might be able to know him and be his disciples in this day. There follows a listing of the miracles that are included in the Gospels. They were supernatural events that pointed people to God, and they were acts of love by one who is love.

	Matthew	Mark	Luke	John
5,000 people are fed	14:15-21	6:35-44	9:12-17	6:5-14
Calming the storm	8:23-27	4:35-41	8:22-25	
Demons sent into the pigs	8:28-34	5:1-20	8:26-39	
Jairus's daughter raised	9:18-26	5:22-24, 35-43	8:41-42, 49-56	
A sick woman is healed	9:20-22	5:25-34	8:43-48	
Jesus heals a paralytic	9:1-8	2:1-12	5:17-26	
A leper is healed at Gennesaret	8:1-4	1:40-45	5:12-15	
Peter's mother-in-law healed	8:14-17	1:29-31	4:38-39	
A deformed hand is restored	12:9-13	3:1-5	6:6-11	
A boy with an evil spirit is healed	17:14-21	9:14-29	9:37-42	
Jesus walks on the water	14:22-33	6:45-52		6:17-21
Blind Bartimaeus receives sight	20:29-34	10:46-52	18:35-43	
A girl is freed from a demon	15:21-28	7:24-30		
4,000 are fed	15:32-38	8:1-9		
Cursing the fig tree	21:18-22	11:12-14, 20-24		
A centurion's servant is healed	8:5-13		7:1-10	
An evil spirit is sent out of a man		1:23-27	4:33-36	
A mute demoniac is healed	12:22		11:14	
Two blind men find sight	9:27-31			
Jesus heals the mute man	9:32-33			
A coin in a fish's mouth	17:24-27			
A deaf and mute man is healed		7:31-37		
A blind man sees at Bethsaida		8:22-26		
The first miraculous catch of fish			5:1-11	
A widow's son is raised			7:11-16	
A crippled woman is healed			13:10-17	
Jesus heals a sick man			14:1-6	
Ten lepers are healed			17:11-19	
Jesus restores a man's ear			22:49-51	
Jesus turns water into wine				2:1-11
An official's son is healed at Cana				4:46-54
A lame man is healed				5:1-16
Jesus heals a man born blind				9:1-7
Lazarus is raised from the dead				11:1-45
The second miraculous catch of fish				21:1-14

For the Gospel writers, one of the main reasons for believing in Jesus was the way his life fulfilled the Old Testament prophecies about the Messiah. Following is a list of some of the main prophecies.

	Old Testament Prophecies	New Testament Fulfillment
1. Messiah was to be born in Bethlehem	Micah 5:2	Matthew 2:1-6 Luke 2:1-20
2. Messiah was to be born of a virgin	Isaiah 7:14	Matthew 1:18-25 Luke 1:26-38
3. Messiah was to be a prophet like Moses	Deuteronomy 18:15, 18-19	John 7:40
4. Messiah was to enter Jerusalem in triumph	Zechariah 9:9	Matthew 21:1-9 John 12:12-16
5. Messiah was to be rejected by his own people	Isaiah 53:1, 3 Psalm 118:22	Matthew 26:3-4 John 12:37-43 Acts 4:1-12
6. Messiah was to be betrayed by one of his followers	Psalm 41:9	Matthew 26:14-16, 47-50 Luke 22:19-23
7. Messiah was to be tried and condemned	Isaiah 53:8	Luke 23:1-25 Matthew 27:1-2
8. Messiah was to be silent before his accusers	Isaiah 53:7	Matthew 27:12-14 Mark 15:3-4 Luke 23:8-10
9. Messiah was to be struck and spat on by his enemies	Isaiah 50:6	Matthew 26:67; 27:30 Mark 14:65
10. Messiah was to be mocked and insulted	Psalm 22:7-8	Matthew 27:39-44 Luke 23:11, 35
11. Messiah was to die by crucifixion	Psalm 22:14, 16-17	Matthew 27:31 Mark 15:20, 25
12. Messiah was to suffer with criminals and pray for his enemies	Isaiah 53:12	Matthew 27:38 Mark 15:27, 28 Luke 23:32-34
13. Messiah was to be given vinegar	Psalm 69:21	Matthew 27:34 John 19:28-30
14. Others were to cast lots for Messiah's garments	Psalm 22:18	Matthew 27:35 John 19:23-24
15. Messiah's bones were not to be broken	Exodus 12:46	John 19:31-36
16. Messiah was to die as a sacrifice for sin	Isaiah 53:5-6, 8, 10-12	John 1:29; 11:49-52 Acts 10:43; 13:38, 39
17. Messiah was to be raised from the dead	Psalm 16:10	Matthew 28:1-10 Acts 2:22-32
18. Messiah is now at God's right hand	Psalm 110:1	Mark 16:19 Luke 24:50-51

ACTS

MEGATHEMES IN ACTS

Theme	Explanation	Importance
Church Beginnings	Acts is the history of how Christianity was founded and organized and solved its problems. The community of believers began by faith in the risen Christ and in the power of the Holy Spirit, who enabled them to witness, to love, and to serve.	New churches are continually being founded. By faith in Jesus Christ and through the power of the Holy Spirit, the church can be a vibrant agent for change. As we face new problems, Acts gives important remedies for solving them.
Holy Spirit	The church did not start or grow by its own power or enthusiasm. The disciples were empowered by God's Holy Spirit. He was the promised Counselor and Guide sent when Jesus went to heaven.	The Holy Spirit's work demonstrated that Christianity was supernatural. Thus, the church became more Holy Spirit conscious than problem conscious. By faith, any believer can claim the Holy Spirit's power to do Christ's work.
Church Growth	Acts presents the history of a dynamic, growing community of believers from Jerusalem to Syria, Africa, Asia, and Europe. In the first century, Christianity spread from believing Jews to non-Jews in 39 cities and 30 countries, islands, or provinces.	When the Holy Spirit works, there is movement, excitement, and growth. He gives us the motivation, energy, and ability to get the gospel to the whole world. How are you fitting into God's plan for spreading Christianity? What is your place in this movement?
Witnessing	Peter, John, Philip, Paul, Barnabas, and thousands more witnessed to their new faith in Christ. By personal testimony, preaching, or defense before authorities, they told the story with boldness and courage to groups of all sizes.	We are God's people, chosen to be part of his plan to reach the world. In love and by faith, we can have the Holy Spirit's help as we witness or preach. Witnessing is also beneficial to us because it strengthens our faith as we confront those who challenge it.
Opposition	Through imprisonment, beatings, plots, and riots, Christians were persecuted by both Jews and Gentiles. But the opposition became a catalyst for the spread of Christianity. Growth during times of oppression showed that Christianity was not the work of humans, but of God.	God can work through any opposition. When persecution from hostile unbelievers comes, realize that it has come because you have been a faithful witness and you have looked for the opportunity to present the Good News about Christ. Seize the opportunities that opposition brings.

KEY PLACES IN ACTS

Modern names and boundaries are shown in gray.

Copyright © 2001 by Tyndale House Publishers

KEY PLACES IN ACTS *Continued*

The apostle Paul, whose missionary journeys fill much of this book, traveled tremendous distances as he tirelessly spread the gospel across much of the Roman Empire. His combined trips, by land and sea, equal more than 13,000 air miles.

1. **Judea** Jesus ascended to heaven from the Mount of Olives, outside Jerusalem, and his followers returned to the city to await the infilling of the Holy Spirit, which occurred at Pentecost. Peter gave a powerful sermon that was heard by Jews from across the empire. The Jerusalem church grew, but Stephen was martyred for his faith by Jewish leaders who did not believe in Jesus (1:1–7:60).

2. **Samaria** After Stephen's death, persecution of Christians intensified, but it caused the believers to leave Jerusalem and spread the gospel to other cities in the empire. Philip took the gospel into Samaria, and even to a man from Ethiopia (8:1-40).

3. **Syria** Paul (Saul) began his story as a persecutor of Christians, only to be met by Jesus himself on the road to Damascus. He became a believer, but his new faith caused opposition, so he returned to Tarsus, his home, for safety. Barnabas sought out Paul in Tarsus and brought him to the church in Antioch of Syria, where they worked together. Meanwhile, Peter had received a vision that led him to Caesarea, where he presented the gospel to a Gentile family, who became believers (9:1–12:25).

4. **Cyprus and Galatia** Paul and Barnabas were dedicated by the church in Antioch of Syria for God's work of spreading the gospel to other cities. They set off on their first missionary journey through Cyprus and Galatia (13:1–14:28).

5. **Jerusalem** Controversy between Jewish Christians and Gentile Christians over the matter of keeping the law led to a special council, with delegates from the churches in Antioch and Jerusalem meeting in Jerusalem. Together, they resolved the conflict and the news was taken back to Antioch (15:1-35).

6. **Macedonia** Barnabas traveled to Cyprus while Paul took a second missionary journey. He revisited the churches in Galatia and headed toward Ephesus, but the Holy Spirit said no. So he turned north toward Bithynia and Pontus but again was told not to go. He then received the "Macedonian call," and followed the Spirit's direction into the cities of Macedonia (15:36–17:14).

7. **Achaia** Paul traveled from Macedonia to Athens and Corinth in Achaia, then traveled by ship to Ephesus before returning to Caesarea, Jerusalem, and finally back to Antioch (17:15–18:22).

8. **Ephesus** Paul's third missionary journey took him back through Cilicia and Galatia, this time straight to Ephesus in Asia. He visited other cities in Asia before going back to Macedonia and Achaia. He returned to Jerusalem by ship, despite his knowledge that arrest awaited him there (18:23–23:30).

9. **Caesarea** Paul was arrested in Jerusalem and taken to Antipatris, then on to Caesarea under Roman guard. Paul always took advantage of any opportunity to share the gospel, and he did so before many Gentile leaders. Because Paul appealed to Caesar, he began the long journey to Rome (23:31–26:32).

10. **Rome** After storms, layovers in Crete, and shipwreck on the island of Malta, Paul arrived in Sicily and finally in Italy, where he traveled by land, under guard, to his long-awaited destination: Rome, the capital of the Empire (27:1–28:31).

A JOURNEY THROUGH THE BOOK OF ACTS

Beginning with a brief summary of **Jesus' last days on earth** with his disciples, his ascension, and the selection of a replacement for Judas Iscariot, Luke moves quickly to his subject—the spread of the gospel and the growth of the church. **Pentecost**, highlighted by the filling of the Holy Spirit (2:1-13) and Peter's powerful sermon (2:14-42), was the beginning. Then **the Jerusalem church** grew daily through the bold witness of Peter and John and the love of the believers (2:43–4:37). The infant church was not without problems, however, with external opposition (resulting in imprisonment, beatings, and death) and internal deceit and complaining. Greek-speaking Jewish believers were appointed to help with the administration of the church to free the apostles to preach. **Stephen and Philip** were among the first deacons, and Stephen became the church's first martyr (5:1–8:3).

Instead of stopping Christianity, opposition and persecution served as catalysts for its spread because the believers took the message with them wherever they fled (8:4). Soon there were converts throughout **Samaria** and even in **Ethiopia** (8:5-40).

At this point, Luke introduces us to a bright young Jew, zealous for the law and intent on ridding Judaism of the Jesus heresy. But on the way to Damascus to capture believers, **Saul** was converted when he was confronted in person by the risen Christ (9:1-9). Through the ministry of Ananias and the sponsorship of Barnabas, Saul (Paul) was welcomed into the fellowship and then sent to Tarsus for safety (9:10-30).

Meanwhile, the church continued to thrive throughout Judea, Galilee, and Samaria. Luke recounts **Peter's preaching** and how Peter healed **Aeneas** in Lydda and **Dorcas** in Joppa (9:31-43). While in Joppa, Peter learned through a vision that he could take the gospel to the "unclean" Gentiles. Peter understood, and he faithfully shared the truth with **Cornelius**, whose entire household became believers (chapter 10). This was startling news to the Jerusalem church; but when Peter told his story, they praised God for his plan for *all* people to hear the Good News (11:1-18). This pushed the church into even wider circles as the message was preached to Greeks in Antioch, where **Barnabas** went to encourage the believers. Then he went on to Tarsus to find Saul (11:20-26).

To please the Jewish leaders, Herod joined in the **persecution of the Jerusalem church**, killing James (John's brother) and imprisoning Peter. But God freed Peter, and Peter walked from prison to a prayer meeting on his behalf at **John Mark's house** (chapter 12).

Here Luke shifts the focus to Paul's ministry. Commissioned by **the Antioch church** for a missionary tour (13:1-3), **Paul and Barnabas** took the gospel to **Cyprus** and **south Galatia** with great success (13:4–14:28). But **the Jewish-Gentile controversy** still smoldered, and with so many Gentiles responding to Christ, the controversy threatened to divide the church. So a **council** met in Jerusalem to rule on the relationship of Gentile Christians to the Old Testament laws. After hearing both sides, **James** (Jesus' brother and the leader of the Jerusalem church) resolved the issue and sent messengers to the churches with the decision (15:1-31).

After the council, **Paul and Silas** preached in Antioch. Then they left for **Syria and Cilicia** as **Barnabas and Mark** sailed for **Cyprus** (15:35-41). On this second missionary journey, Paul and Silas traveled throughout **Macedonia and Achaia**, establishing churches in **Philippi, Thessalonica, Berea, Corinth, and Ephesus** before returning to Antioch (16:1–18:22). Luke also tells of the ministry of **Apollos** (18:24-28).

On Paul's third missionary trip, he traveled through **Galatia, Phrygia, Macedonia, and Achaia**, encouraging and teaching the believers (19:1–21:9). During this time, he felt compelled to go to **Jerusalem**; and although he was warned by **Agabus** and others of impending imprisonment (21:10-12), he continued his journey in that direction.

While in Jerusalem, Paul was accosted in the Temple by an angry mob and taken into protective custody by the Roman commander (21:17–22:29). Now we see Paul as a prisoner and on trial before the Jewish high council (23:1-9), **Governor Felix** (23:23–24:27), and **Festus and Agrippa** (25:1–26:32). In each case, Paul gave a strong and clear witness for his Lord.

Because Paul appealed to **Caesar**, however, he was sent to **Rome** for the final hearing of his case. But on the way, the ship was destroyed in a storm, and the sailors and prisoners had to swim ashore. Even in this circumstance Paul shared his faith (27:1–28:10). Eventually the journey continued and Paul arrived in Rome, where he was held under **house arrest** while awaiting trial (28:11-31).

Luke ends Acts abruptly with the encouraging word that Paul had freedom in his captivity as he talked to visitors and guards, "proclaiming the Kingdom of God with all boldness and teaching about the Lord Jesus Christ. And no one tried to stop him" (28:31).

THE TWELVE DISCIPLES / Acts 1:12-13

Name	Major Events in His Life	Selected References
Simon Peter (son of John)	One of three in core group of disciples; recognized Jesus as the Messiah; denied Christ and repented; preached Pentecost sermon; a leader of the Jerusalem church; baptized Gentiles; wrote 1 and 2 Peter.	Matthew 4:18-20 Mark 8:29-33 Luke 22:31-34 John 21:15-19 Acts 2:14-41; 10:1–11:18
James (son of Zebedee)	Also in core group; he and his brother, John, asked Jesus for places of honor in his kingdom; wanted to call fire down to destroy a Samaritan village; first disciple to be martyred.	Mark 3:17; 10:35-40 Luke 9:52-56 Acts 12:1-2
John (son of Zebedee)	Third disciple in core group; asked Jesus for a place of honor in his kingdom; wanted to call down fire on a Samaritan village; a leader of the Jerusalem church; wrote the Gospel of John, 1, 2, 3 John, and Revelation.	Mark 1:19; 10:35-40 Luke 9:52-56 John 19:26-27; 21:20-24
Andrew (Peter's brother)	Accepted John the Baptist's testimony about Jesus; told Peter about Jesus; he and Philip told Jesus that Greeks wanted to see him.	Matthew 4:18-20 John 1:35-42; 6:8-9; 12:20-22
Philip	Told Nathanael about Jesus; wondered how Jesus could feed the 5,000; he and Andrew told Jesus that Greeks wanted to see him; asked Jesus to show his followers God the Father.	Matthew 10:3 John 1:43-46; 6:2-7; 12:20-22; 14:8-11
Bartholomew (Nathanael)	Initially rejected Jesus because Jesus was from Nazareth but acknowledged him as the "Son of God" and "King of Israel" when they met.	Mark 3:18 John 1:45-51; 21:1-13
Matthew (Levi)	Abandoned his corrupt (and financially profitable) way of life to follow Jesus; invited Jesus to a party with his notorious friends; wrote the Gospel of Matthew.	Matthew 9:9-13 Mark 2:15-17 Luke 5:27-32
Thomas (the Twin)	Suggested the disciples go with Jesus to Bethany—even if it meant death; asked Jesus about where he was going; refused to believe Jesus was risen until he could see Jesus alive and touch his wounds.	Matthew 10:3 John 14:5; 20:24-29; 21:1-13
James (son of Alphaeus)	Became one of Jesus' disciples.	Matthew 10:3 Mark 3:18 Luke 6:15
Judas son of James (Thaddeus)	Asked Jesus why he would reveal himself to his followers and not to the world.	Matthew 10:3 Mark 3:18 John 14:22
Simon the Zealot	Became a disciple of Jesus.	Matthew 10:4 Mark 3:18 Luke 6:15
Matthias	Chosen to replace Judas Iscariot (who had betrayed Jesus and then killed himself).	Acts 1:15-26

A RECIPE FOR THE SUCCESS OF THE CHURCH / *Acts 1:26*

In Acts 1, Luke was setting the stage *for* and previewing the material *of* the balance of the book of Acts. He included many of the ingredients for the successful spread of the gospel message:

People	People have always been God's plan for the delivery of his message (Acts 1:2, 8, 11, 13-14, 21-26).
Prayer	Prayer was the first, best step in every decision of the early church (Acts 1:14, 24-26).
Preparation	The apostles demonstrated their knowledge of and belief in the importance of the Scriptures. God's Word should be learned, trusted, obeyed, and applied to life situations (Acts 1:1-4, 7-8, 16, 20).
Power	Christ's promised Holy Spirit power forms the basis of the church's ability to accomplish great things for him (Acts 1:8).
Promise	The church must always live in the conscious reality of a returning Savior who will come back in the same way he departed (Acts 1:9-11).
Pattern	Our task is not so much to be preachers as it is to be witnesses. A witness tells what he or she has seen and heard. We speak the news and spread the news (Acts 1:8, 11).

"BAPTISM IN THE SPIRIT" IN THE NEW TESTAMENT / *Acts 2:4*

The term (or concept) occurs only a few times in the New Testament. It is used in basically three different ways:

Prophetic	Historical	Doctrinal
Matthew 3:11	Acts 2:1-4	1 Corinthians 12:12-13
Mark 1:8	Acts 11:15-17	Romans 6:1-4
Luke 3:16		
John 1:33		
Acts 1:5		

- In the Gospels, John the Baptist used the term in describing Jesus' ministry.
- In Acts 1:5, Jesus quotes John's prophecy looking forward to Pentecost.
- In Acts 2, *the process was initiated* on the day of Pentecost: the Holy Spirit came to make the church his residence, indwelling every believer.
- In Acts 11:16 the term is used by Peter, who referred to Jesus' quote of John's prophecy.
- In Romans 6:1-4 and 1 Corinthians 12:13 Paul taught its significance.

JOY IN ACTS / Acts 2:46-47

Wherever the gospel message went, it brought joy to those who believed. Follow this theme through the book of Acts:

2:46 . . . . "They worshiped together at the Temple each day, met in homes for the Lord's Supper, and shared their meals with great joy and generosity."

5:41 . . . . "The apostles left the high council rejoicing that God had counted them worthy to suffer dishonor for the name of Jesus."

8:8 . . . . [Philip in Samaria] "So there was great joy in that city."

8:39 . . . . "When they came up out of the water, the Spirit of the Lord caught Philip away. The eunuch never saw him again but went on his way rejoicing."

11:23 . . . . "When he [Barnabas] arrived and saw this proof of God's favor, he was filled with joy, and he encouraged the believers to stay true to the Lord."

12:14 . . . . "When she recognized Peter's voice, she was so overjoyed that, instead of opening the door, she ran back inside and told everyone, 'Peter is standing at the door!'"

13:48 . . . . [In Iconium] "When the Gentiles heard this, they were very glad and thanked the Lord for his message; and all who were appointed to eternal life became believers."

13:52 . . . . "And the believers were filled with joy and with the Holy Spirit."

14:17 . . . . [Paul speaking in Lystra] "But he never left himself without a witness. There were always his reminders, such as sending you rain and good crops and giving you food and joyful hearts."

15:3 . . . . "The church sent the delegates [Paul and Barnabas] to Jerusalem, and they stopped along the way in Phoenicia and Samaria to visit the believers. They told them—much to everyone's joy—that the Gentiles, too, were being converted."

15:31 . . . . "And there was great joy throughout the church that day as they read this encouraging message." [the letter from Jerusalem]

16:34 . . . . "Then he [the Philippian jailer] brought them into his house and set a meal before them. He and his entire household rejoiced because they all believed in God."

TIME TO PRAY / Acts 3:1

The Jews had set times of prayer, but the clear teaching (and example) of the New Testament is that believers are to be in a spirit of prayerfulness at all times. Our lives should be one long running conversation with the Father.

Scripture	Command
Romans 1:9-10	"Day and night I bring you and your needs in prayer to God."
Ephesians 6:18	"Pray at all times and on every occasion. . . . be persistent in your prayers for all Christians everywhere."
Colossians 1:3	"We always pray for you."
1 Thessalonians 1:2.	"We . . . pray for you constantly."
1 Thessalonians 2:13	"We will never stop thanking God."
1 Thessalonians 5:17	"Keep on praying."
2 Timothy 1:3	"Night and day I constantly remember you in my prayers."

A LESSON FROM ANANIAS AND SAPPHIRA / Acts 5:11

How to destroy yourself . . . a church . . . a life:

Desire the esteem of people more than God (Acts 4:36; 5:1-4, 9).

Envy the success of others (Acts 4:37; 5:2).

Attempt to cheat God (Acts 5:2-4, 8-9).

Destroy everything you are trying to achieve/obtain (Acts 4:36; 5:1-4, 9).

How to be the person or the church that God wants you to be:

Work for God's approval, not people's (Acts 5:3-4; Luke 16:15; Galatians 1:10).

Improve yourself from the example of others, rather than envying them.

Serve God wholeheartedly, rather than hypocritically.

Enjoy the rewards of righteousness.

MAJOR THEMES OF STEPHEN'S SPEECH / Acts 7:39-52

1. The Jews always reject God's leaders.	Acts 7:39
2. God doesn't dwell in temples made with hands.	Acts 7:48
3. God transcends the laws.	Acts 7:50
4. Israel tends toward apostasy.	Acts 7:51
5. Israel rejects God's redeemers.	Acts 7:52

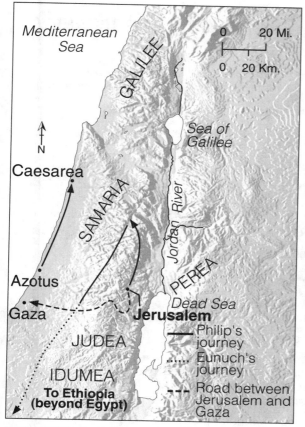

Copyright © 2001 by Tyndale House Publishers

PHILIP'S MINISTRY

Acts 8:4-40

To escape persecution in Jerusalem, Philip fled to Samaria, where he continued preaching the gospel. While he was there, an angel commanded him to meet an Ethiopian official on the road between Jerusalem and Gaza. The man became a believer before continuing on to Ethiopia. Philip then went from Azotus to Caesarea.

THE EFFECTS OF STEPHEN'S DEATH / *Acts 8:4*

Stephen's death was not in vain. Below are some of the events that were by-products (either directly or indirectly) of the persecution that began with Stephen's martyrdom.

1. Philip's evangelistic tour	Acts 8:4-40
2. Paul's (Saul's) conversion	Acts 9:1-30
3. Peter's missionary tour	Acts 9:32–11:18
4. The church in Antioch of Syria founded	Acts 11:19ff

MISSIONARIES OF THE NEW TESTAMENT AND THEIR JOURNEYS

Acts 9:1

Name	Journey's Purpose	Scripture Reference in Acts
Philip	One of the first to preach the gospel outside Jerusalem	8:4-40
Peter and John	Visited new Samaritan believers to encourage them	8:14-25
Paul (journey to Damascus)	Set out to capture Christians but was captured by Christ	9:1-25
Peter	Led by God to one of the first Gentile families to become Christians—Cornelius's family	9:32–10:48
Barnabas	Went to Antioch as an encourager; traveled on to Tarsus to bring Paul back to Antioch; took famine relief to Jerusalem	11:25-30
Barnabas, Paul, John Mark	Left Antioch for Cyprus, Pamphylia, and Galatia on the first missionary journey	13:1–14:28
Barnabas and John Mark	Left Antioch for Cyprus after a break with Paul	15:36-41
Paul, Silas, Timothy, Luke	Left Antioch to revisit churches in Galatia; then traveled on to Asia, Macedonia, and Achaia on the second missionary journey	15:36–18:22
Apollos	Left Alexandria for Ephesus; learned the complete gospel story from Priscilla and Aquila; preached in Athens and Corinth	18:24-28
Paul, Timothy, Erastus	Revisited churches in Galatia, Asia, Macedonia, and Achaia on the third major missionary journey	18:23; 19:1–21:14

SAUL'S RETURN TO TARSUS

Acts 9:19-30

At least three years elapsed between Acts 9:22 and 9:26. After time alone in Arabia (see Galatians 1:16-18), Saul (Paul) returned to Damascus and then to Jerusalem. The apostles were reluctant to believe that this former persecutor could have become one of them. He escaped to Caesarea, where he caught a ship and returned to Tarsus.

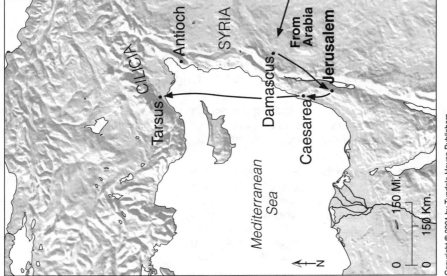

Copyright © 2001 by Tyndale House Publishers

SAUL TRAVELS TO DAMASCUS

Acts 9:1-19

Many Christians fled Jerusalem when persecution began after Stephen's death, seeking refuge in other cities and countries. Saul tracked them down, even traveling 150 miles to Damascus in Syria to bring Christians back in chains to Jerusalem. But as he neared the ancient city, he discovered that God had other plans for him (9:15).

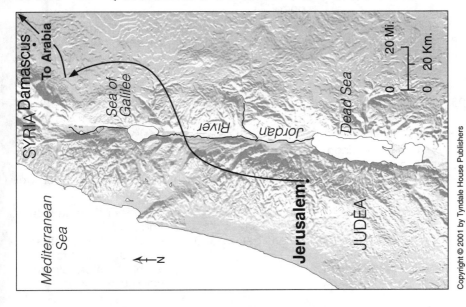

Copyright © 2001 by Tyndale House Publishers

GREAT ESCAPES IN THE BIBLE / Acts 9:23

Who escaped	Reference	What happened	What the escape accomplished	Application
Jacob	Genesis 31:1-55	Fled from his father-in-law, Laban, after almost 20 years of service	Allowed Jacob to return home for Isaac's death and for reconciliation with Esau, his brother	A time away from home often puts the really important things into perspective
Moses	Exodus 2:11-15	Fled Egypt after killing an Egyptian in defense of a fellow Israelite	Saved his own life and began another part of God's training	God fits even our mistakes into his plan
Israelites	Exodus 12:28-42	Escaped Egypt after 430 years, most of that time in slavery	God confirmed his choice of Abraham's descendants	God will not forget his promises
Spies	Joshua 2:1-24	Escaped searchers in Jericho by hiding in Rahab's house	Prepared the destruction of Jericho and preserved Rehab, who would become one of David's ancestors—as well as an ancestor of Jesus	God's plan weaves lives together in a pattern beyond our understanding
Ehud	Judges 3:15-30	Escaped undetected after assassinating the Moabite king Eglon	Broke the control of Moab over Israel and began 80 years of peace	Punishments by God are often swift and deadly
Samson	Judges 16:1-3	Escaped a locked city by ripping the gates from their hinges	Merely postponed Samson's self-destruction because of his lack of self-control	Without dependence on God and his guidance, even great ability is wasted
Elijah	1 Kings 19:1-18	Fled into the wilderness out of fear of Queen Jezebel	Preserved Elijah's life but also displayed his human weakness	Even at moments of real success, our per- sonal weaknesses are our greatest challenges
Saul (Paul)	Acts 9:23-25	Lowered over the wall in a basket to get out of Damascus	Saved this new Christian for great service to God	God has a purpose for every life, which leads to a real adventure for those willing to cooperate
Peter	Acts 12:1-11	Freed from prison by an angel	Saved Peter for God's further plans for his life	God can use extraordinary means to carry out his plan—often when we least expect it
Paul and Silas	Acts 16:22-40	Chains loosened and doors opened by an earthquake, but they chose not to leave the prison	Pointed out the powerlessness of humans before God	When our dependence and attention are focused on God rather than our problems, he is able to offer help in unexpected ways

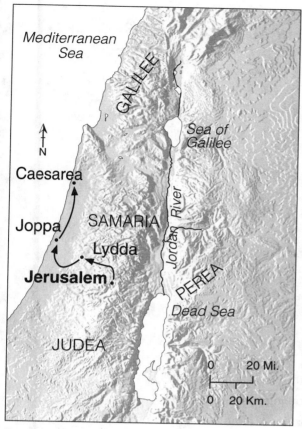

Mediterranean
Sea

GALILEE

Sea of
Galilee

↑
N

Caesarea

Joppa

SAMARIA

Jordan River

Lydda

Jerusalem

PEREA

Dead Sea

JUDEA

0   20 Mi.

0   20 Km.

Copyright © 2001 by Tyndale House Publishers

PETER'S MINISTRY

Acts 9:32–10:48

Peter traveled to the ancient cross-roads town of Lydda, where he healed crippled Aeneas. The believers in Joppa, an old port city, sent for him after a wonderful woman died. Peter went and brought her back to life. While in Joppa, Peter had a vision that led him to take the gospel to Cornelius, a Gentile, in Caesarea.

NAMES AND TITLES FOR JESUS IN ACTS / *Acts 10:36*

Reference	Name/Title
1:6	Lord
1:21	Lord Jesus
2:22	Jesus of Nazareth
2:27	Holy One
2:30-31, 36	Messiah
2:38	Jesus Christ
3:13	his [God's] servant Jesus
3:15	"the author of life"
3:20	"Jesus your Messiah"
5:31	"Prince and Savior"
7:52	"the Righteous One"
7:56	the Son of Man
9:20	Son of God
10:36	"Lord of all"
10:42	"the judge of all—the living and the dead"
10:43	"the one all the prophets testified about"
13:23	God's promised Savior of Israel
16:7	the Spirit of Jesus
17:7	king
24:24	Christ Jesus
28:20	the hope of Israel

FIVE KEYS TO MAKING A DIFFERENCE / Acts 10:48

Peter and Cornelius provide a great lesson for believers who want to make a real difference in the world. See the following acronym for **world:**

1. *W* alk closely with God. (Acts 10:1-4, 9)

The text carefully reports on the quality of the spiritual life of Cornelius and the explicit time of prayer of both Cornelius and Peter. Both were devout men, apparently with a regular, consistent habit of walking with God, praying to God, and expecting God to work in their lives. The reason they both were involved in the work of God—Cornelius as the first genuine Gentile convert; Peter as the human instrument in opening the door to the Gentiles—was that they were both in the habit of walking with, talking to, and hearing from God on a regular basis.

2. *O* bey God. (Acts 9:39, 43; 10:8, 23-25, 28-29)

A predisposition to obedience that comes from a deep relationship with God marked both these men. Cornelius got "found," and Peter had the privilege of finding him because they responded positively to God's command. We will not be involved in real world change if we have a predisposition to disobey. To be habitually disobedient is to be habitually useless for the real work of God.

3. *R* each out to people outside your comfort zone. (Acts 9:32-43; 10:5-6, 20, 25, 48)

It is hard to feel what Peter would have felt about moving into the Gentile world. He was going against that with his move to Lydda, then Joppa, then to the leatherworker's house, and certainly with Cornelius. The Jewish part of him would balk at every turn, every doorstep, every meal. But Peter understood the great commission and was committed to spreading the Word to whomever God was calling. How readily do you move outside the confines of your safe relationships? That's where the lost are and where God wants us to be.

4. *L* ook for those God is reaching or softening. (Acts 9:32-43; 10:19, 22-23)

This constant theme of Acts shows that God is working, and we must find out where and with whom, and get in on it.

5. *D* isregard the criticism. (Acts 10:13-14, 20, 28; 11:1-3, 18)

Jewish culture was resistant; Peter himself was resistant; the church was resistant, critical, skeptical. But Peter, Cornelius, Peter's traveling companions, and ultimately the church itself overcame the resistance to be a part of what God wanted to do. God was moving, spreading his message by softening and wooing hearts, by awakening souls.

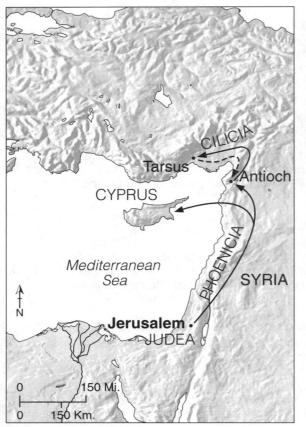

BARNABAS AND SAUL IN ANTIOCH
Acts 11:19-26

Persecution scattered the believers into Phoenicia, Cyprus, and Antioch, and the gospel went with them. Most spoke only to Jews, but in Antioch, some Gentiles were converted. The church sent Barnabas to investigate, and he was pleased with what he found. Barnabas went to Tarsus to bring Saul (Paul) back to Antioch.

Copyright © 2001 by Tyndale House Publishers

TITLES FOR THE REDEEMED PEOPLE OF GOD IN ACTS
Acts 11:25-26

Title	Reference in Acts
Believers	1:15; 2:44; 4:32; 5:12; 9:41; 10:45; 15:2, 23; 16:1, 15; 21:25
The church	5:11; 8:1, 3; 9:31; 11:22; 12:1, 5; 13:1; 14:23; 15:3-4, 41; 16:5; 18:22; 20:17
Disciples	6:1-2, 7; 9:1, 10, 19, 26, 36; 11:29; 13:52; 14:20-22; 18:23; 19:9; 21:4-5, 16
Brother/brothers	6:3; 9:17, 30; 10:23; 11:1, 29; 12:17; 14:2; 15:3, 22, 32-33, 36; 16:2, 40; 17:6, 10; 18:18, 27; 21:7, 17; 28:14-15
The Way	9:2; 19:9, 23; 24:22
The Lord's people	9:32
Christians	11:26; 26:28
Follower/followers	17:34; 22:4; 24:14
The flock	20:28-29

SIX CHARACTERISTICS OF A *USABLE* CHRISTIAN / *Acts 11:29-30*

1. *U* nstained by our Culture. (11:19-20, 22, 26)

At Antioch the believers were first called Christians, the Christ-ones. There are some distinctions of a church that must be kept intact. We bear the name of our Savior.

2. *S* tretched to our Limits. (11:19; 12:1-3)

From a close look at the early church, we see clearly that struggle, rejection, criticism, and even death for believers was the norm.

3. *A* dhering to the Savior. (11:21, 23, 26)

Barnabas encouraged the believers to make a serious, solid attachment to Christ and Christ alone.

4. *B* old in our Witness. (11:19-21, 24)

This church spoke, told, and preached the Good News. People believed and turned to the Lord.

5. *L* iberal in our Giving. (11:22, 24, 27-30)

The Antioch church gave. They were unselfish, other-centered, and giving oriented, even to a culturally and racially different congregation.

6. *E* quipped in the Scriptures. (11:23, 26)

This church was taught. The picture here is of classrooms, courses, study, memorization . . . work. Before Antioch became a *sending* place it was a *studying* place. We have the picture of an equipping church and an equipped people. No wonder they changed the world.

THE FATE OF THE APOSTLES / *Acts 12:2*

Name	Fate
Simon Peter	Crucified upside down (reported by Origen)
James, son of Zebedee	Martyred by Herod Agrippa (Acts 12:1-2)
John, son of Zebedee	Exiled to Patmos; later died of old age (one legend is that Domitian had John thrown into a pot of boiling oil, but he was unharmed)
Andrew	According to tradition, was crucified (in the form of an X) at Patrae, a city of Achaia, because he rebuked Aegeas, the proconsul, for idolatry
Philip	According to tradition, died as a martyr at Hierapolis
Bartholomew/ Nathanael	Said to have preached the gospel in India or perhaps Armenia where conflicting reports have him flayed alive or crucified upside down
Matthew/Levi	According to legend, preached in unspecified foreign nations
Thomas	According to tradition, preached in Parthia and Persia and died as a martyr by being speared with a lance
James, son of Alphaeus	Not known
Thaddaeus/Judas, son of James	Not known
Simon the Zealot	Not known
Judas Iscariot	Committed suicide by hanging himself (Matthew 27:5; Acts 1:18)
Matthias	According to tradition, went to Ethiopia to minister, where he was eventually martyred
Saul/Paul	According to tradition, was beheaded at Nero's command along the Appian Way

PAUL'S FIRST MISSIONARY JOURNEY / *Acts 13:1–14:28*

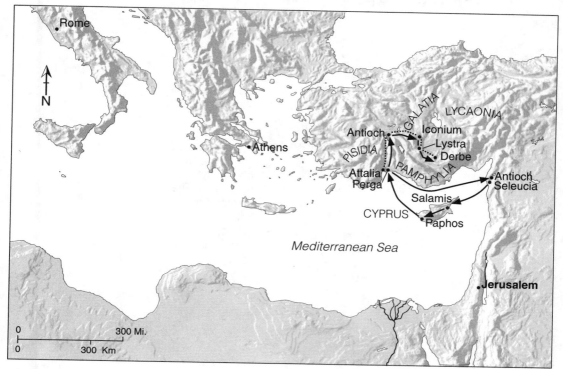

Copyright © 2001 by Tyndale House Publishers

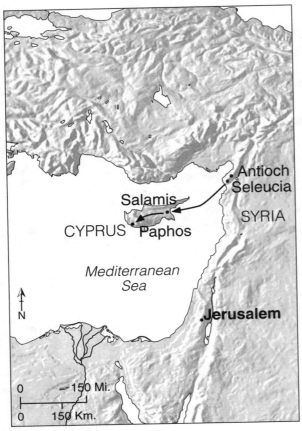

MINISTRY IN CYPRUS

Acts 13:4-12

The leaders of the church in Antioch chose Paul and Barnabas to take the gospel westward. Along with John Mark, they boarded ship at Seleucia and set out across the Mediterranean for Cyprus. They preached in Salamis, the largest city, and went across the island to Paphos.

Copyright © 2001 by Tyndale House Publishers

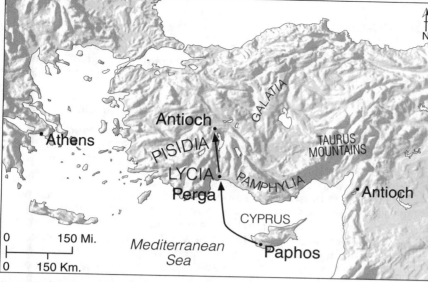

MINISTRY IN PAMPHYLIA AND GALATIA

Acts 13:13-52

Paul, Barnabas, and John Mark left Paphos and landed at Perga in the humid region of Pamphylia, a narrow strip of land between the sea and the Taurus Mountains. John Mark left them in Perga, but Paul and Barnabas traveled up the steep road into the higher elevation of Pisidia in Galatia. When the Jews rejected his message, Paul preached to Gentiles, and the Jews drove Paul and Barnabas out of the Pisidian city of Antioch.

Copyright © 2001 by Tyndale House Publishers

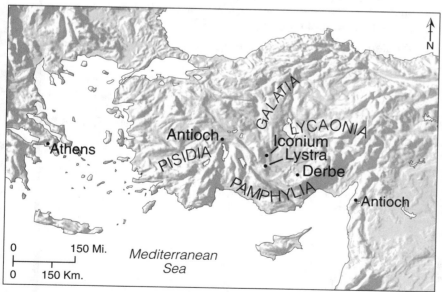

CONTINUED MINISTRY IN GALATIA

Acts 14:1-20

Paul and Barnabas, thrown out of Antioch in Pisidia, descended the mountains, going east into Lycaonia. They went first to Iconium, a commercial center on the road between Asia and Syria. After preaching there, they had to flee to Lystra, 25 miles south. Paul was stoned in Lystra, but he and Barnabas traveled the 50 miles to Derbe, a border town. The pair then boldly retraced their steps.

Copyright © 2001 by Tyndale House Publishers

ELDERS / *Acts 14:23*

Near the end of their first missionary journey, Paul and Barnabas went back through the cities where they had ministered and "appointed elders in every church . . . turning them over to the care of the Lord" (14:23). What does the New Testament teach about the office of elder?

Meaning of term	The Greek term is *presbyteros,* meaning, literally, "an older person."
Function/role	To rule the church (Titus 1:7; 1 Peter 5:2-3); to watch over/shepherd God's flock (Acts 20:28; 1 Peter 5:2; Hebrews 13:17); to teach the truths of God (1 Timothy 3:2; Titus 1:9) to the people of God.
Qualifications	To be one "whose life cannot be spoken against. He must be faithful to his wife. He must exhibit self-control, live wisely, and have a good reputation. He must enjoy having guests in his home and must be able to teach. He must not be a heavy drinker or be violent. He must be gentle, peace loving, and not one who loves money. He must manage his own family well, with children who respect and obey him. For if a man cannot manage his own household, how can he take care of God's church? . . . not be a new Christian, because he might be proud of being chosen so soon, and the Devil will use that pride to make him fall. Also, people outside the church must speak well of him so that he will not fall into the Devil's trap and be disgraced (1 Timothy 3:2-7; see similar list in Titus 1:6-9).
Number of elders	A plurality of elders is described, if not prescribed, in the New Testament (Acts 14:23; Philippians 1:1; Titus 1:5). Nowhere is a certain number mandated, however.
Length of term	The New Testament does not specify a precise term of eldership.
How elected?	Those meeting the qualifications seem to be appointed or chosen by those already functioning as elders (Acts 14:23; Titus 1:5). Ordination to the office involved a ceremony that included laying on of hands, prayer, and fasting (Acts 14:23).
Proper response to	Obedience and submission (Hebrews 13:17); respect (1 Corinthians 16:16; 1 Thessalonians 5:12).
Discipline of elders	Accusations or criticisms against an elder should be received according to 1 Timothy 5:19-21. If the elder is guilty of an offense, he is to be counseled by fellow elders with a view toward restoration (Galatians 6:1-2). If the sinning elder refuses to repent, he is to be removed from office and disciplined according to Matthew 18:15-17.

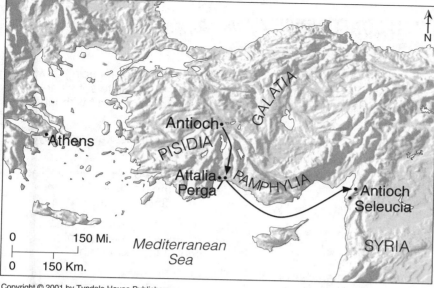

THE END OF THE FIRST JOURNEY

Acts 14:21-28

From Antioch in Pisidia, Paul and Barnabas went down the mountains back to Pamphylia on the coast. Stopping first in Perga, where they had landed, they went west to Attalia, the main port that sent goods from Asia to Syria and Egypt. There they found a ship bound for Seleucia, the port of Antioch in Syria. This ended their first missionary journey.

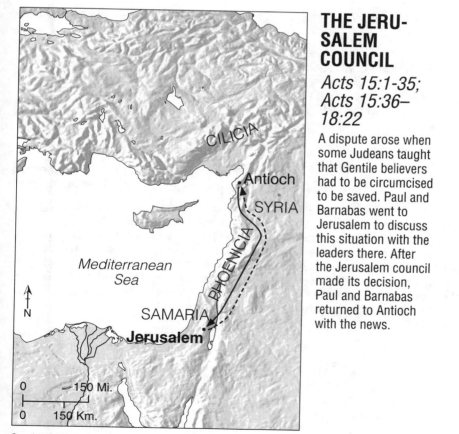

THE JERU-SALEM COUNCIL

Acts 15:1-35;
Acts 15:36–
18:22

A dispute arose when some Judeans taught that Gentile believers had to be circumcised to be saved. Paul and Barnabas went to Jerusalem to discuss this situation with the leaders there. After the Jerusalem council made its decision, Paul and Barnabas returned to Antioch with the news.

Copyright © 2001 by Tyndale House Publishers

THE FIRST CHURCH CONFERENCE / Acts 15

Group	Position	Reasons
Judaizers (some Jewish Christians)	Gentiles must become Jewish first to be eligible for salvation	1. They were devout, practicing Jews who found it difficult to set aside a tradition of gaining merit with God by keeping the law. 2. They thought grace was too easy for the Gentiles. 3. They were afraid of seeming too non-Jewish in the practice of their new faith—which could lead to death. 4. The demands on the Gentiles were a way of maintaining control and authority in the movement.
Gentile Christians	Faith in Christ as Savior is the only requirement for salvation	1. To submit to Jewish demands would be to doubt what God had already done for them by grace alone. 2. They resisted exchanging their pagan rituals for a system of Jewish rituals—neither of which had power to save. 3. They sought to obey Christ by baptism (rather than by circumcision) as a sign of their new faith.
Peter and James	Faith is the only requirement, but there must be evidence of change by rejecting the old lifestyle	1. They tried to distinguish between what was true from God's Word versus what was just human tradition. 2. They had Christ's command to preach to all the world. 3. They wanted to preserve unity. 4. They saw that Christianity could never survive as just a sect within Judaism.

As long as most of the first Christians were Jewish, there was little difficulty in welcoming new believers; however, Gentiles (non-Jews) began to accept Jesus' offer of salvation. The evidence in their lives and the presence of God's Spirit in them showed that God was accepting them. Some of the early Christians believed that non-Jewish Christians needed to meet certain conditions before they could be worthy to accept Christ. The issue could have destroyed the church, so a conference was called in Jerusalem, and the issue was formally settled there, although it continued to be a problem for many years following. Above is an outline of the three points of view at the conference.

JUDAIZERS VERSUS PAUL / Acts 15:2

As the debate raged between the Gentile Christians and the Judaizers, Paul found it necessary to write to the churches in Galatia. The Judaizers were trying to undermine Paul's authority. The debate over Jewish laws and Gentile Christians was officially resolved at the Jerusalem council.

What the Judaizers said about Paul	Paul's defense
They said he was perverting the truth.	He had received his message from Christ himself (Acts 9:15; Galatians 1:11-12).
They said he was a traitor to the Jewish faith.	He was one of the most dedicated Jews of his time. Yet, in the midst of one of his most zealous acts, God had transformed him through a revelation of the good news about Jesus (Acts 9:1-30; Galatians 1:13-16).
They said he compromised and diluted his message for the Gentiles.	The other apostles declared that the message Paul was preaching was the true gospel (Acts 9:28; Galatians 2:1-10).
They said he was disregarding the law of Moses.	Far from degrading the law, Paul put the law in its proper place. He wrote that it shows people where they have sinned and points them to Christ (Galatians 3:19-29).

CHURCH CRISES: DANGEROUS OPPORTUNITIES! / *Acts 15:31*

The Chinese word for "crisis" consists of two letters: one means "danger" and the other means "opportunity." Indeed, every church crisis involves a dangerous opportunity to bring either great glory or great shame to the name of Christ. Acts 15 is a good example of this truth.

Dangerous Opportunity?	How Seen in Acts 15?	The Root of the Danger?	How to Avoid the Danger and Seize the Opportunity	How the Situation Can Glorify God if Properly Handled
Disputes over doctrine	Judaizers wanted Gentile converts to be circumcised and to keep Mosaic law.	Presuppositions	Submit to the Word of God (rather than our own opinions).	Purity
Diversity in membership	Those from Jewish backgrounds (tending toward legalism) were in the same body with those from pagan back-grounds (tending toward license).	Prejudice	Submit to one another in love (rather than segregate from one another in suspicion).	Unity
Decisions by authority	Some Judaizers did not submit to decision by Jerusalem council; they defiantly continued their divisive campaign of deception and distortion (as seen in later epistles, such as Titus 1:10).	Pride	Submit to God-appointed lead-ership (rather than demanding and advancing our own agenda).	Humility

PAUL'S SECOND MISSIONARY JOURNEY / *Acts 15:36–18:22*

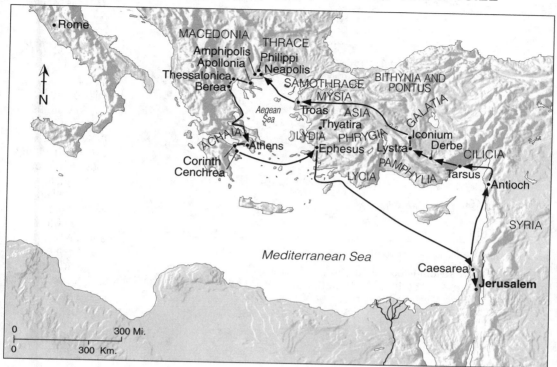

Rome

MACEDONIA
THRACE
Amphipolis
Philippi
Apollonia
Neapolis
Thessalonica
Berea
SAMOTHRACE
BITHYNIA AND
PONTUS

*Aegean
Sea*
Troas
MYSIA
Thyatira
ASIA
GALATIA
ACHAIA
LYDIA
PHRYGIA
Iconium
Athens
Ephesus
Lystra
Derbe
Corinth
Cenchrea
PAMPHYLIA
CILICIA
LYCIA
Tarsus
Antioch

Mediterranean Sea
SYRIA

Caesarea
Jerusalem

0   300 Mi.
0   300 Km.

Copyright © 2001 by Tyndale House Publishers

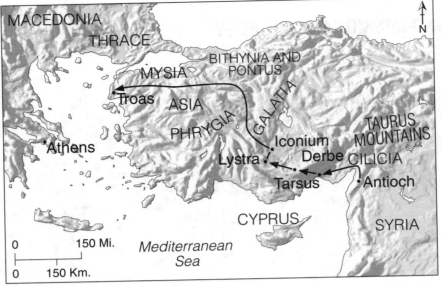

THE SECOND JOURNEY BEGINS

Acts 16:1-8

Paul and Silas set out on a second missionary journey to visit the cities Paul had preached in earlier. This time they set out by land rather than sea, traveling the Roman road through Cilicia and the Cilician Gates—a gorge through the Taurus Mountains—then northwest toward Derbe, Lystra, and Iconium. The Spirit told them not to go into Asia, so they turned northward toward Bithynia. Again the Spirit said no, so they turned west through Mysia to the harbor city of Troas.

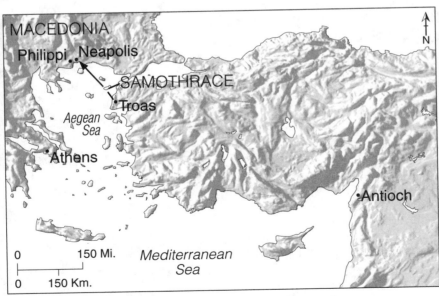

PAUL TRAVELS TO MACEDONIA

Acts 16:9-40

At Troas, Paul received the Macedonian call (16:9), and he, Silas, Timothy, and Luke boarded a ship. They sailed to the island of Samothrace, then on to Neapolis, the port for the city of Philippi. Philippi sat on the Egnatian Way, a main transportation artery connecting the eastern provinces with Italy.

HOW GOD SOVEREIGNLY GUIDED HIS PEOPLE IN ACTS / Acts 16:6

Means	Reference in Acts
Through direct revelation	1:4-5, 11; 8:29; 10:19; 13:2; 16:6-7; 20:23
Through Scripture	1:20
Through the casting of lots	1:23-26
Through unexpected, supernatural acts	2:1-41
Through the apostles' teaching	2:42
Through judgment	5:1-11
Through church "growing pains"	6:1-7
Through persecution and evil opposition	7:54–8:1; 14:5-7; 20:3
Through angelic messengers	8:26; 10:3-8; 27:22-26
Through miraculous relocation	8:39
Through direct, life-altering encounters with the risen Lord	9:3-9
Through visions	9:10; 10:3-8, 9-16; 11:5; 16:9-10; 18:9-11; 23:11
Through human instruments/messengers	9:17-19, 27-28
Through times of intense prayer	10:9; 13:2-3
Through bringing to their minds the words of the Lord	11:16
Through prophetic utterances	11:28; 21:4, 10-12
Through God-honoring, Spirit-led discussions among church leaders	15:1-31
Through promptings by the Spirit	15:28; 19:21; 20:22
Through closed doors	16:6-7
Through favorable circumstances	19:8-11
Through having them take advantage of civil/legal/political rights	25:10-12

MINISTRY IN MACE-DONIA
Acts 17:1-34

Luke stayed in Philippi while Paul, Silas, and Timothy continued on the Egnatian Way to Amphipolis, Apollonia, and Thessalonica. But trouble arose in Thessalonica, and they fled to Berea. When their enemies from Thessalonica pursued them, Paul set out by sea to Athens, leaving Silas and Timothy to encourage the believers.

Copyright © 2001 by Tyndale House Publishers

THE BOOKS OF THE NEW TESTAMENT: WHEN WERE THEY WRITTEN? / *Acts 17*

(Dates are approximate A.D.)

Galatians	49	Philemon	60	Acts	66/68
James	49	Philippians	61	2 Peter	66/68
1, 2 Thessalonians	51/52	Matthew	61/64	2 Timothy	66/67
1, 2 Corinthians	55	Luke	61/64	Hebrews	68/70
Romans	57	1 Timothy	64	John	85
Mark	58/60	Titus	64	1, 2, 3 John	85/90
Ephesians	60	1 Peter	64/65	Revelation	95
Colossians	60	Jude	65		

ATTACKING THE WORK OF GOD / Acts 17:13

The Bible is full of examples of people who, operating under the seemingly purest of motives, undermine the very work of God. Look at just a few:

People	Reference	Actions
Miriam and Aaron	Numbers 12	asked, "Has the Lord spoken only through Moses?"
The men of Korah	Numbers 16	rose up against Moses, accusing him of setting himself above them. It was a rebellion—refusal to follow God's ordained leadership.
Abimelech	Judges 9	manipulated his kinsmen to overthrow Gideon's legacy after murdering all but one of Gideon's sons.
Absalom	2 Samuel 15	met people at the city gate, bad-mouthed his father, King David, and "stole the hearts of the men of Israel."
Troublemakers	Ezra 4	shut down construction on the temple for fifteen years with their false accusations.
Sanballat and Tobiah	Nehemiah 4 and 6	kept trying to get Nehemiah off the wall and on a retreat in order to stop the building of the Jerusalem wall.

While the motives vary in all these examples, and some are not known at all, envy seems to be the common one, envy and a desire to control. Such people have been and will always be around. The keepers of the Light must not allow them to stop the work. Paul certainly didn't.

SECULAR WRITERS / Acts 17:28

On four occasions at least, the apostle Paul quoted popular literary/dramatic works. While these references do not prove that Paul attended plays or read many secular writers, they do indicate that he was familiar enough with certain works to include their sayings as illustrations in his sermons and letters.

Name	When lived	Quote	From what source?	Quoted where in Scripture
Epimenides (a Cretan poet)	c. 600 B.C.	"For in him we live and move and exist."	Cretica	Acts 17:28
Aratus (a Cilician poet)	c. 315-240 B.C.	"We are his offspring."	Phaenomena 5	Acts 17:28
Menander (a Greek poet)	c. 342-292 B.C.	"Bad company corrupts good character."	Thais	1 Corinthians 15:33
Epimenides	c. 600 B.C.	"The people of Crete are all liars; they are cruel animals and lazy gluttons."	De Oraculis	Titus 1:12

SEVEN EFFECTIVE WAYS TO APPROACH A KNOW-IT-ALL WORLD
Acts 17:33-34

From Paul's approach to the Athenians, we find some great pointers on how to approach a culture that takes itself far too seriously. The way to win some is to be **winsome:**

1. *W*atch for ways to find common ground (Acts 17:22-23).
Paul went where people were physically and began where they were intellectually.

2. *I*lluminate poor views of God (Acts 17:24-26).
Paul gently but firmly exposed the errant views of the Athenians. There *is* a knowable God. On that front they were wrong and needed correction.

3. *N*urture that part of each person that wants to know God (Acts 17:27).
Paul knew that there is a God-built part of every person that wants to know God. When we talk to those who don't know God, we need to assume this and nurture it.

4. *S*tudy the world and its ways (Acts 17:28-30).
Paul was a student of the culture. Christians tend to isolate, insulate, run and hide, gather up in our holy huddle and avoid the world—their way of thinking, writing, singing, reasoning, influencing. We must learn to speak in a language that the world understands.

5. *O*ffer the proof of Christianity—the Resurrection (Acts 17:31).
Paul spoke of the Resurrection. Christ's resurrection is the focal point of the faith, proving the central theme of Christianity. Without that fact we have no religion (1 Corinthians 15:13-14).

6. *M*ake clear every person's accountability for his or her life (Acts 17:30-31).
Paul didn't mince words. There comes a time when folks need to be told of a life audit.

7. *E*xpect a variety of responses (Acts 17:5-9, 13, 18-20, 32-34).
Paul received varied responses. Some will be jealous. Others will misrepresent what we are doing, accusing *us* of being troublemakers, agitating those we're trying to reach. But some will believe. And they are worth it!

MINISTRY IN CORINTH AND EPHESUS / *Acts 18:1-23*

Paul left Athens and traveled on to Corinth, one of the greatest commercial centers of the empire, located on a narrow neck of land offering direct passage between the Aegean and Adriatic seas. When Paul left from the port of Corinth at Cenchrea, he visited Ephesus. He then traveled to Caesarea, from where he went on to Jerusalem to report on his trip before returning to Antioch.

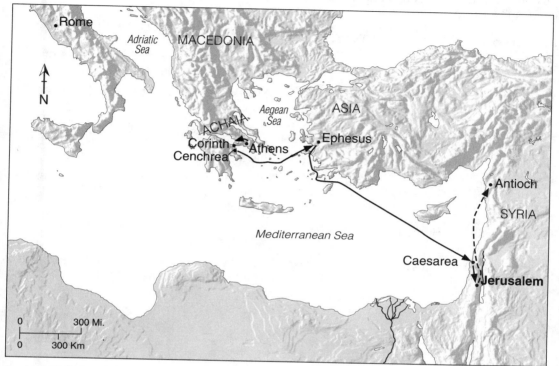

Copyright © 2001 by Tyndale House Publishers

MARRIAGE WITH A MISSION / *Acts 18:19-21*

One of the more interesting couples in the New Testament is Priscilla and Aquila. Colleagues of the apostle Paul, this husband-and-wife team left a legacy of tireless labor for the work of Christ. Always willing to serve wherever needed, they are a wonderful role model for modern-day couples who want to use their marriages to make an eternal difference in this world.

Reference	Location	Date	Event
Acts 18:2	Rome	A.D. 49	Ordered to leave Rome (with all the other Jews) by Claudius
Acts 18:2-3	Corinth	A.D. 50–51	Made tents and ministered with the apostle Paul
Acts 18:18-19	Ephesus	A.D. 52	Left in Ephesus by Paul, where, among other things, they helped Apollos sharpen his message
1 Corinthians 16:19	Ephesus	A.D. 55–56	Hosted a church in their home in Ephesus and sent greetings via Paul to Christian friends in Corinth
Romans 16:3-5	Rome	A.D. 56–57	Ministered back in Rome and hosted a house church
2 Timothy 4:19	Ephesus	A.D. 67	In Ephesus once again, probably assisted young Timothy as he pastored there

PARALLELS BETWEEN THE MINISTRIES OF PETER AND PAUL IN ACTS / *Acts 19:6-7*

Similarity	Peter	Paul
Healing crippled men	3:2-8	14:8-10
Healing via extraordinary means	5:15 (his shadow!)	19:12 (handkerchiefs!)
Casting out demons	5:16	16:18
Being flogged or beaten	5:40	16:23
Defeating sorcerers	8:18-24	13:6-11
Raising the dead	9:36-41	20:9-12
Escaping from prison	12:6-11	16:25-26

PAUL'S THIRD MISSIONARY JOURNEY / Acts 18:23–21:16

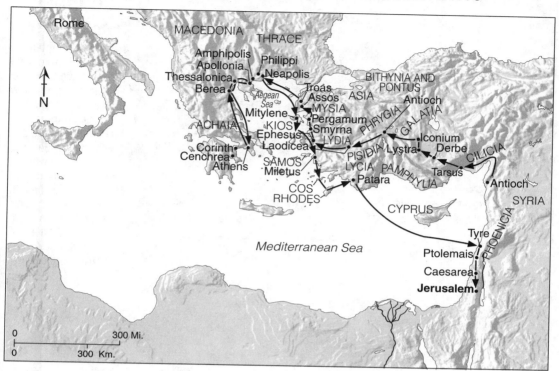

Copyright © 2001 by Tyndale House Publishers

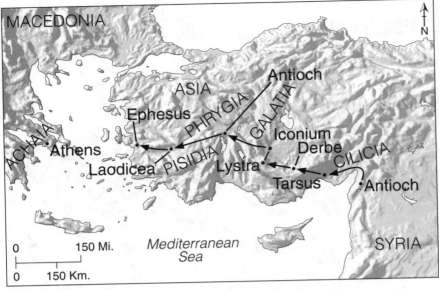

Copyright © 2001 by Tyndale House Publishers

PAUL TAKES A THIRD JOURNEY

Acts 19:1-41

What prompted Paul's third journey may have been the need to correct any misunderstandings in the churches Paul had planted. So he hurried north, then west, returning to many of the cities he had previously visited. This time, however, he stayed on a more direct west-ward route toward Ephesus.

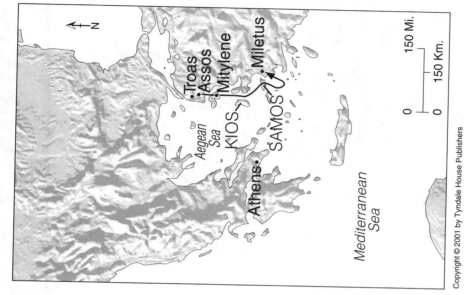

PAUL TRAVELS FROM TROAS TO MILETUS

Acts 20:6-38

From Troas, Paul traveled overland to Assos, then boarded a ship to Mitylene and Samos on its way to Miletus. He summoned the elders of the Ephesian church to say farewell to them, because he knew he would probably not see them again.

Copyright © 2001 by Tyndale House Publishers

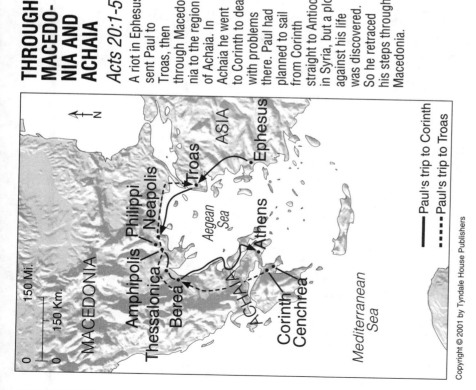

THROUGH MACEDONIA AND ACHAIA

Acts 20:1-5

A riot in Ephesus sent Paul to Troas, then through Macedonia to the region of Achaia. In Achaia he went to Corinth to deal with problems there. Paul had planned to sail from Corinth straight to Antioch in Syria, but a plot against his life was discovered. So he retraced his steps through Macedonia.

—— Paul's trip to Corinth
----- Paul's trip to Troas

Copyright © 2001 by Tyndale House Publishers

PAUL RETURNS TO JERUSALEM / *Acts 21:1-17*

The ship sailed from Miletus to Cos, Rhodes, and Patara. Paul and his companions then boarded a cargo ship bound for Phoenicia. They passed Cyprus and landed at Tyre, then Ptolemais, and finally Caesarea, where Paul disembarked and returned by land to Jerusalem.

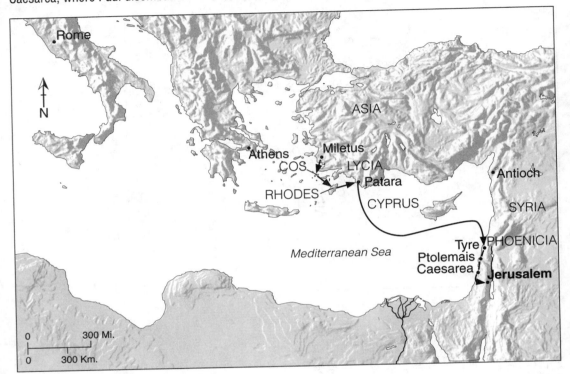

Copyright © 2001 by Tyndale House Publishers

PAUL'S JOURNEY TO ROME / *Acts 21:17–28:31*

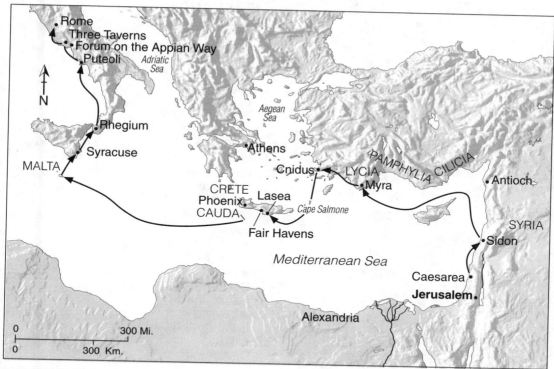

Copyright © 2001 by Tyndale House Publishers

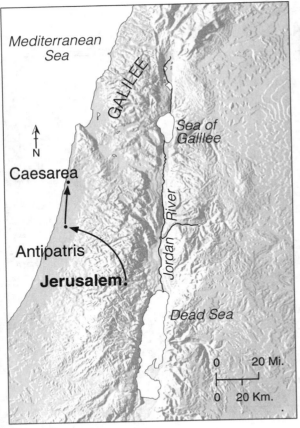

IMPRISON-MENT IN CAESAREA

Acts 21:18–23:35

Paul brought news of his third journey to the elders of the Jerusalem church, who rejoiced at his ministry. But Paul's presence soon stirred up the Jews, who persuaded the Romans to arrest him. A plot to kill Paul was uncovered, so Paul was taken by night to Antipatris and then transferred to the provincial prison in Caesarea.

Mediterranean Sea

GALILEE

Sea of Galilee

Caesarea

Jordan River

Antipatris

Jerusalem

Dead Sea

0   20 Mi.

0   20 Km.

Copyright © 2001 by Tyndale House Publishers

"ENCOURAGEMENT" VISITS OF GOD TO PAUL / Acts 23:11

Passage	Purpose	Result
Acts 16:9	To send him on to Macedonia to preach	Many converts and churches planted.
Acts 18:9-10	To get him to stay and preach boldly in Corinth	Many converts, some new close friends/coworkers, and a solid ministry begun.
Acts 22:17	To send him from Jerusalem for his safety	Protection by the Roman military given.
Acts 23:11	To send him to preach the gospel in Rome	Effective ministry in Rome and beyond continued.
Acts 27:24	To promise him protection and guidance through the shipwreck	Safety for him and his companions provided.
2 Timothy 4:16-17	To encourage him in his trial in Rome	Deliverance from the "lions" provided.

A C T S

UNSUNG HEROES IN ACTS / *Acts 23:16*

When we think of the success of the early church, we often think of the work of the apostles. But the church could have died if it hadn't been for the unsung heroes, the men and women who through some small but committed act moved the church forward.

Hero	Reference	Heroic Action
Crippled man	3:9-12	After his healing, he praised God. As the crowds gathered to see what happened, Peter used the opportunity to tell many about Jesus.
Five deacons	6:2-5	Everyone has heard of Stephen, and many know of Philip, but there were five other men chosen to be deacons. They not only laid the foundation for service in the church, but their hard work also gave the apostles the time they needed to preach the gospel.
Ananias	9:10-19	He had the responsibility of being the first to demonstrate Christ's love to Saul (Paul) after his conversion.
Cornelius	10:30-35	His example showed Peter that the gospel was for all people, Jews and Gentiles.
Rhoda	12:13-15	Her persistence brought Peter inside Mary's home, where he would be safe.
James	15:13-21	He took command of the Jerusalem council and had the courage and discernment to help form a decision that would affect literally millions of Christians over many generations.
Lydia	16:13-15	She opened her home to Paul, from which he led many to Christ and founded a church in Philippi.
Jason	17:5-9	He risked his life for the gospel by allowing Paul to stay in his home. He stood up for what was true and right, even though he faced persecution for it.
Paul's nephew	23:16-24	He saved Paul's life by telling officials of a murder plot.
Julius	27:1, 43	He spared Paul when the other soldiers wanted to kill him.

GOD'S SOVEREIGNTY / *Acts 25:1-2*

God's sovereignty over all things is a theme throughout Scripture, especially in the book of Acts as the gospel message is spread across the world. God is always completely in charge, and what may appear as hindrances are in his control.

Reference

Exodus 15:18	"The LORD will reign forever and ever!"
Deuteronomy 4:39	"So remember this and keep it firmly in mind: The LORD is God both in heaven and on earth, and there is no other god!"
1 Chronicles 29:11	"Yours, O LORD, is the greatness, the power, the glory, the victory, and the majesty. Everything in the heavens and on earth is yours, O LORD, and this is your kingdom. We adore you as the one who is over all things."
Job 25:2	"God is powerful and dreadful. He enforces peace in the heavens."
Job 41:11	"Who will confront me and remain safe? Everything under heaven is mine."
Psalm 22:27	"The whole earth will acknowledge the LORD and return to him. People from every nation will bow down before him."
Psalm 24:1	"The earth is the LORD'S, and everything in it. The world and all its people belong to him."
Psalm 67:4	"How glad the nations will be, singing for joy, because you govern them with justice and direct the actions of the whole world."
Psalm 93:1	"The LORD is king! He is robed in majesty. Indeed, the LORD is robed in majesty and armed with strength. The world is firmly established; it cannot be shaken."
Isaiah 33:22	"For the LORD is our judge, our lawgiver, and our king. He will care for us and save us."
Ezekiel 18:4	"For all people are mine to judge—both parents and children alike. And this is my rule: The person who sins will be the one who dies."
Daniel 4:34	"After this time had passed, I, Nebuchadnezzar, looked up to heaven. My sanity returned, and I praised and worshiped the Most High and honored the one who lives forever. His rule is everlasting, and his kingdom is eternal."
Romans 11:36	"For everything comes from him; everything exists by his power and is intended for his glory. To him be glory evermore. Amen."
1 Timothy 1:17	"Glory and honor to God forever and ever. He is the eternal King, the unseen one who never dies; he alone is God. Amen."
1 Timothy 6:15	"For at the right time Christ will be revealed from heaven by the blessed and only almighty God, the King of kings and Lord of lords."
Revelation 19:6	"Then I heard again what sounded like the shout of a huge crowd, or the roar of mighty ocean waves, or the crash of loud thunder: 'Hallelujah! For the Lord our God, the Almighty, reigns.'"

THE HEROD FAMILY / *Acts 25:21-22*

Name	Reference	Date of Rule	Description
Herod the Great	Matthew 2:1-18; Luke 1:5	37–4 B.C.	Half Jewish; eager to please the Roman authorities who decreed him king of the Jews; slaughtered the innocent baby boys of Bethlehem
Herod Philip I	Matthew 14:3b; Mark 6:17	4 B.C.–A.D. 34	Son of Herod the Great; married Herodias, his niece
Herod Antipas	Mark 6:14-29; Luke 3:1; 13:31-33; 23:7-12	4 B.C.–A.D. 39	Son of Herod the Great; Tetrarch of Galilee and Perea; called a "fox" by Jesus; ordered the execution of John the Baptist; presided over the trial of Jesus
Herod Archelaus	Matthew 2:22	4 B.C.–A.D. 6	Son of Herod the Great; Ethnarch of Judea, Samaria, and Idumea
Herod Philip II	Luke 3:1	4 B.C.–A.D. 34	Son of Herod the Great; Tetrarch of Iturea and Trachonitis; married Salome, the daughter of Herodias
Herod Agrippa I	Acts 12:1-11	A.D. 37–44	Grandson of Herod the Great; king over Palestine; had James the apostle killed and Peter imprisoned
Herodias	Matthew 14:3; Mark 6:17		Granddaughter of Herod the Great; sister of Agrippa I; married her Uncle Herod Philip I, and later her uncle Herod Antipas
Herod Agrippa II	Acts 25:13–26:32	A.D. 50–70	Son of Herod Agrippa I; Tetrarch of Chalcis; presided over Paul's trial
Drusilla	Acts 23:25–24:27		Daughter of Herod Agrippa I; wife of Felix (procurator of Judea, A.D. 52–59)
Bernice	Acts 25:13; 26:30		Daughter of Herod Agrippa I; sister and mistress of Herod Agrippa II

THE TRIP TOWARD ROME / *Acts 27:1–28:1*

Paul began his 2,000-mile trip to Rome at Caesarea. To avoid the open seas, the ship followed the coastline. At Myra, Paul was put on a vessel bound for Italy. It arrived with difficulty at Cnidus, then went to Crete, landing at the port of Fair Havens. The next stop was Phoenix, but the ship was blown south around the island of Cauda, then drifted for two weeks until it was shipwrecked on the island of Malta.

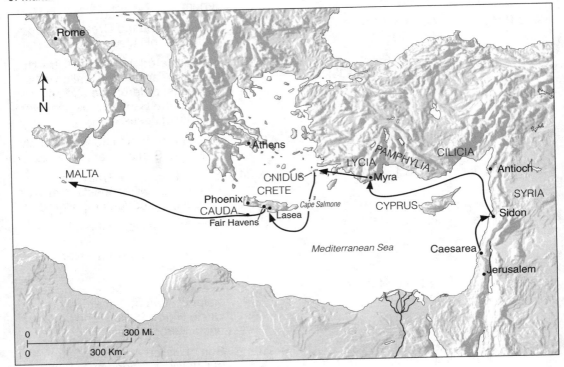

Copyright © 2001 by Tyndale House Publishers

PAUL'S JOURNEY TO ROME / Acts 27:1–28:1

One of Paul's most important journeys was to Rome, but he didn't get there the way he expected. It turned out to be more of a legal journey than a missionary journey. Through a series of legal trials and transactions, Paul was delivered to Rome, where his presentation of the gospel would even penetrate the walls of the emperor's palace. Sometimes when our plans don't work out as we want them to, they work out even better than we expected.

Reference	What Happened
21:30-34	When Paul arrived in Jerusalem, a riot broke out. Seeing the riot, Roman soldiers put Paul into protective custody. Paul asked for a chance to defend himself to the people. His speech was interrupted by the crowd when he told about what God was doing in the lives of Gentiles.
22:24-25	A Roman commander ordered a beating to get a confession from Paul. Paul claimed Roman citizenship and escaped the whip.
22:30	Paul was brought before the Jewish high council. Because of his Roman citizenship, he was rescued from the religious leaders who wanted to kill him.
23:10	The Roman commander put Paul back under protective custody.
23:21-24	Due to a plot to kill Paul, the commander transferred him to Caesarea, which was under Governor Felix's control.
23:35	Paul was in prison until the Jews arrived to accuse him. Paul defended himself before Felix.
24:25-26	Paul was in prison for two years, speaking occasionally to Felix and Drusilla.
24:27	Felix was replaced by Festus.
25:1, 10	New accusations were brought against Paul—Jews wanted him back in Jerusalem for a trial. Paul claimed his right to a hearing before Caesar.
25:12	Festus promised to send him to Rome.
25:13-14	Festus discussed Paul's case with Herod Agrippa II.
26:1	Agrippa and Festus heard Paul speak. Paul again told his story.
26:24-28	Agrippa interrupted with a sarcastic rejection of the gospel.
26:30-32	Group consensus was that Paul was guilty of nothing and could have been released if he had not appealed to Rome.
27:1-2	Paul left for Rome, courtesy of the Roman Empire.

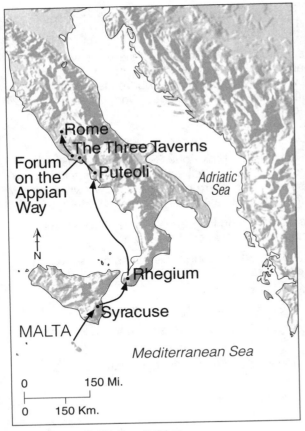

PAUL ARRIVES IN ROME

Acts 28:1-16

The shipwreck occurred on Malta, where the ship's company spent three months. Finally, another ship gave them passage for the 100 miles to Syracuse, capital of Sicily, then sailed on to Rhegium, finally dropping anchor at Puteoli. Paul was taken to the Forum on the Appian Way and to The Three Taverns before arriving in Rome.

Copyright © 2001 by Tyndale House Publishers

ROMANS

MEGATHEMES IN ROMANS

Theme	Explanation	Importance
Sin	Sin means refusing to do God's will and failing to do all that God wants. Since Adam's rebellion against God, our nature is to disobey him. Our sin cuts us off from God. Sin causes us to want to live our own way rather than God's way. Because God is morally perfect, just, and fair, he is right to condemn sin.	Each person has sinned, either by rebelling against God or by ignoring his will. No matter what our background or how hard we try to live good and moral lives, we cannot earn salvation or remove our sin. Only Christ can save us.
Salvation	Our sin points out our need to be forgiven and cleansed. Although we don't deserve it, God, in his kindness, reached out to love and forgive us. He provides the way for us to be saved. Christ's death paid the penalty for our sin.	It is good news that God saves us from our sin. But in order to enter into a wonderful new relationship with God, we must believe that Jesus died for us and that he forgives all our sin.
Growth	By God's power, believers are sanctified— made holy. This means we are set apart from sin, enabled to obey and to become more like Christ. When we are growing in our relationship with Christ, the Holy Spirit frees us from the demands of the law and from fear of judgment.	Because we are free from sin's control, the law's demands, and fear of God's punishment, we can grow in our relationship with Christ. By trusting in the Holy Spirit and allowing him to help us, we can overcome sin and temptation.
Sovereignty	God oversees and cares about his people—past, present, and future. God's ways of dealing with people are always fair. Because God is in charge of all creation, he can save whomever he wills.	Because of God's mercy, both Jews and Gentiles can be saved. We all must respond to his mercy and accept his gracious offer of forgiveness. Because he is sovereign, let him reign in your heart.
Service	When our purpose is to give credit to God for his love, power, and perfection in all we do, we can serve him properly. Serving him unifies all believers and enables them to show love and sensitivity to others.	None of us can be fully Christlike by ourselves—it takes the entire body of Christ to fully express Christ. By actively and vigorously building up other believers, Christians can be a symphony of service to God.

THE GOSPEL GOES TO ROME / *Romans 1:6-15*

When Paul wrote his letter to the church in Rome, he had not yet been there, but he had taken the gospel "from Jerusalem clear over into Illyricum" (15:19). He planned to visit and preach in Rome one day and hoped to continue to take the gospel farther west—even to Spain.

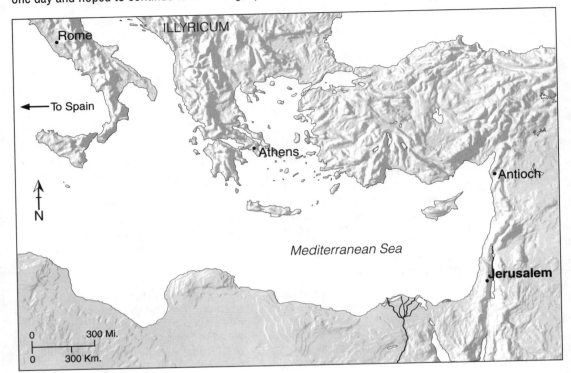

Copyright © 2001 by Tyndale House Publishers

FAITH / *Romans 1*

Faith is a word with many meanings. It can mean **faithfulness** (Matthew 24:45). It can mean **absolute trust**, as shown by some of the people who came to Jesus for healing (Luke 7:2-10). It can mean **confident hope** (Hebrews 11:1). Or, as James points out, it can even mean a **barren belief** that does not result in good deeds (James 2:14-26). What does Paul mean when, in Romans, he speaks of "saving faith"?

We must be very careful to understand faith as Paul uses the word because he ties faith so closely to salvation. It is *not* something we must do in order to earn salvation—if that were true, then faith would be just one more deed, and Paul clearly states that human deeds can never save us (Galatians 2:16). Instead, faith is a gift God gives us *because* he is saving us (Ephesians 2:8). It is God's grace, not our faith, that saves us. In his mercy, however, when he saves us, he gives us faith—a relationship with his Son that helps us become like him. Through the faith he gives us, he carries us from death into life (John 5:24).

Even in Old Testament times, grace, not deeds, was the basis of salvation. As Hebrews points out, "it is not possible for the blood of bulls and goats to take away sins" (10:4). God intended for his people to look beyond the animal sacrifices to him, but all too often they instead put their confidence in fulfilling the requirements of the law—that is, performing the required sacrifices. When Jesus triumphed over death, he cancelled the charges against us and opened the way to the Father (Colossians 2:12-15). Because he is merciful, he offers us faith. How tragic if we turn faith into a deed and try to develop it on our own! We can never come to God through our own faith any more than his Old Testament people could come through their own sacrifices. Instead, we must accept his gracious offer with thanksgiving and allow him to plant the seed of faith within us.

THE PROPHETS WROTE OF GOD'S PLAN / Romans 1:2

Paul did not specify the passages from the prophets he had in mind when he wrote of "the gospel [God] promised . . . through his prophets in the Holy Scriptures," probably because of his reader's familiarity with those Scriptures. For these early Christians, the Old Testament continued to be their authority, and they knew of many references to God's plan and the Messiah. Here are several references Paul might have pointed to:

Genesis 12:3	The Messiah would come from Abraham's line, and through the Messiah "all the families of the earth will be blessed through you."
Psalm 16:10	The promise of the resurrection given to David: the Messiah, "your godly one" would be resurrected.
Psalm 40:6-10	The Messiah would "take joy in doing your will, my God," and would accomplish that will so completely as to die on the cross.
Psalm 118:22	The Messiah would be rejected by his own people, but would become the "cornerstone," the most important part of the church.
Isaiah 11:1ff	The Messiah will be the "Branch" that will be "bearing fruit" in the form of believers. "The Spirit of the Lord will rest on him."
Isaiah 49:5-6	The Messiah will gather Israel and be a light for the Gentiles.
Zechariah 9:9-11	The Messiah would come to his people "riding on a donkey," which he did in his Triumphal Entry into Jerusalem.
Zechariah 12:10	The Messiah would be "pierced" on the cross, and many would mourn his death.
Malachi 4:1-5	The Messiah's arrival will be heralded by one like the "prophet Elijah," who was to be John the Baptist.

RIGHTEOUSNESS AND WICKEDNESS / Romans 2:3

See also *Proverbs 21:29*

	Righteous	Wicked	Reference
Outlook on life	Hopeful	Fearful	10:24
Response to life	Showered with blessings	Covered with violence	10:6
How they are seen by others	Conduct is upright	Conduct is devious	21:8
Quality of life	Stand firm	Swept away	10:25
Short-term results	Walk securely	Will be found out	10:9
Long-term results	God protects them	God destroys them	10:29
Eternal expectations	Attain life	Go to death	11:19
God's opinion of them	Delights in the good	Detests the perverse	11:20

HOW CAN GOD ACCEPT US? / *Romans 2:1*

The Problem:

We resist God.
We ignore God.
We attempt to deceive God.
We work against God's interests.
We acknowledge God only when we are in trouble.
We consider our plans and desires before God's.
We do not love God with all our heart, soul, and mind.

How can we even hope to have an intimate relationship with God, or to go to heaven after this life?

False solutions:

Deny there is a God, but create our own god out of something or someone else.

Live in guilt, punishing ourselves or masking the guilt behind alcohol and drugs.

Use religion (works, church attendance, service) as a substitute for faith, loving God, and obeying him.

Assume or vaguely hope God will save us anyway.

Conclude God is too demanding and live in despair or apathy.

True solution:

Recognize the answer to our problem is faith and trust in Christ.

Accept God's gracious gift of forgiveness, believing in his love.

Realize that God is willing to declare us not guilty, and that he alone can do that.

Live in the freedom provided by God, enjoying the opportunity to express our thanks by obedience rather than trying to earn his acceptance.

Humbly accept the fact that Christ's substitution for us accomplished what we could not have done for ourselves.

SALVATION'S FREEWAY / *Romans 3:23*

Romans 3:23	Everyone has sinned.
Romans 6:23	The penalty for our sin is death.
Romans 5:8	Jesus Christ died for sin.
Romans 10:8-10	To be forgiven for our sin, we must believe and confess that Jesus is Lord. Salvation comes through Jesus Christ.

CRUCIAL CONCEPTS IN ROMANS / *Romans 3:25*

Election *Romans 9:10-13*	God's choice of an individual or group for a specific purpose or destiny.
Justification *Romans 4:25; 5:18*	God's act of declaring us "not guilty" for our sins, making us "right" with him.
Propitiation *Romans 3:25*	The removal of God's punishment for sin through the perfect sacrifice of Jesus Christ.
Redemption *Romans 3:24; 8:23*	Jesus Christ has paid the price so we can go free. The price of sin is death; Jesus paid the price.
Sanctification *Romans 5:2; 15:16*	Becoming more and more like Jesus Christ through the work of the Holy Spirit.
Glorification *Romans 8:18-19, 30*	The ultimate state of the believer after death when he or she becomes like Christ (1 John 3:2).

STEPS OF ABRAHAM'S FAITH / *Romans 4:12*

Abraham's faith was tested a number of times. Each response was a step of faith. Some of these steps were not what we would call big tests, but together they establish a picture of Abraham as a man of genuine faith. After the last test, the angel of the LORD said, "Lay down the knife, . . . Do not hurt the boy in any way, for now I know that you truly fear God. You have not withheld even your beloved son from me" (Genesis 22:12). Note that these "steps" are not "works" in that they earn God's approval; rather, they are the natural outflowing of the inward faith that God counts as righteousness.

Abraham's faith-steps can have applications for us:

Reference	Step	Application
Genesis 12:1-7	At God's direction, Abraham left Ur and Haran for a destination unknown.	Do I trust God with my future? Is his will part of my decision making?
Genesis 14:17-24	Abraham gave a tithe of loot to the godly king of Salem, Melchizedek, but he refused the gift from the king of Sodom.	In my dealings with people, am I careful to give proper honor to God and refuse to receive honor that belongs to him?
Genesis 15:1-6	Abraham trusted God's promise that he would have a son.	How often do I consciously reaffirm my trust in God's promise?
Genesis 15:7-11	Abraham received the Promised Land by faith, though God warned him the fulfillment would not come for many generations.	How have I demonstrated my continued trust in God during those times when I have been required to wait?
Genesis 17:9-27	At God's command, Abraham circumcised every male in his family.	On what occasions in my life have I acted simply in obedience to God?
Genesis 18:22-33	Abraham prayed for Sodom.	Am I a person who cares for people in spite of their sinfulness?
Genesis 20:1-17	Abraham admitted to wrongdoing and took the actions necessary to set things right.	When I sin, do I tend to cover up or admit my fault? When needed, do I accompany my apology with restitution?
Genesis 22:1-12	Abraham prepared to sacrifice his son Isaac.	How have I demonstrated that I will not allow anything in my life to come before God?

SUFFERING WITH CHRIST / *Romans 5:3*

If we serve the Lord, suffering is unavoidable. As we bring Christ's message to the world, we will suffer opposition. Christ participates with us when we suffer.

Colossians 1:24
I am glad when I suffer for you in my body, for I am completing what remains of Christ's sufferings for his body, the church.

Philippians 1:29
For you have been given not only the privilege of trusting in Christ but also the privilege of suffering for him.

Philippians 3:10
As a result, I can really know Christ and experience the mighty power that raised him from the dead. I can learn what it means to suffer with him, sharing in his death.

1 Peter 2:21
This suffering is all part of what God has called you to. Christ, who suffered for you, is your example. Follow in his steps.

1 Peter 4:13
Instead, be very glad—because these trials will make you partners with Christ in his suffering, and afterward you will have the wonderful joy of sharing his glory when it is displayed to all the world.

Until the world knows him, there is always more work to do. As we work for him, we can face suffering joyfully because we know people are being saved as a result of our work.

Our suffering and how we handle it are signs to others that we belong to Christ.

Sharing in Christ's mission for the world implies that we must share in his sacrifice. We must be ready to give up plans, pleasure, and even our life in order to serve him.

Christ never sinned, yet he suffered so we could be set free. We should face suffering as he did—with patience, calmness, and confidence that God is in control of the future.

God strengthens us by his Holy Spirit when we face persecution for him. We know that one day he will overcome all suffering when we are with him in glory.

WHAT WE HAVE AS CHILDREN / *Romans 5:8*

What we have as Adam's children	What we have as God's children
Ruin . . . 5:9	Rescue . . . 5:8
Sin . . . 5:12, 15, 21	Righteousness . . . 5:18
Death . . . 5:12, 16, 21	Eternal life . . . 5:17, 21
Separation from God . . . 5:18	Relationship with God . . . 5:11, 19
Disobedience . . . 5:12, 19	Obedience . . . 5:19
Judgment . . . 5:18	Deliverance . . . 5:10-11
Law . . . 5:20	Grace . . . 5:20

WHAT HAS GOD DONE ABOUT SIN? / *Romans 6:2*

He has given us	Reference	Principle	Importance
New life	6:2-3 6:4 6:6	Sin's power is broken. Sin-loving nature is buried. You are no longer under sin's control.	We can be certain that sin's power is broken.
New nature	6:5 6:11	Now you share his new life. Look upon your old self as dead; instead, be alive to God.	We can see ourselves as unresponsive to the old power and alive to the new.
New Freedom	6:12 6:13 6:14 6:16	Do not let sin control you. Give yourselves completely to God. You are free. You can choose your own master.	We can commit ourselves to obey Christ in perfect freedom.

UNITED IN CHRIST / *Romans 6:6*

Crucified Together	**Old Identity**
	Sin dies; the old slave master died; the power and lordship of sin have been destroyed; we are free from the obligation, addition, and necessity to sin. If sin is dead, it can no longer rule.
Resurrected Together	**New Identity**
	We have new life, a new master, new fellowship with God, and new union with Christ. We have been set free to serve.
Workers Together	**New Service**
	We have new direction, new purpose, new gifts, and new power to accomplish Christ's work (see 1 Corinthians 3:9).

MAKE HEAVENLY TRUTH AN EARTHLY REALITY / *Romans 6:15*

Truth
We must . . .

Count ourselves dead to sin but alive to God (6:11)

Not let sin reign, but allow Christ to reign as Lord (6:12)

Not offer our bodies to sin, but offer ourselves to God (6:13)

Remember we are not under law, but under grace (6:14)

Reality

When sin presents itself to tempt us, we must show our new I.D. stamped "In Christ." Sin's power is no longer valid.

We must forget our past master and fight Satan's designs for our lives.

We must place our whole self at Christ's disposal for service, and then serve him in love.

We should not obey God out of obligation or fear, but out of love, remembering all that he has done for us.

SLAVERY VS. SPIRITUAL FREEDOM / *Romans 7:6*

We have been released front the penalty of the law.

We are cleansed from sin and counted as righteous.

We are free from the external regulations that must be filled in order to be right with God.

We are free from the ceremonial regulations that pointed to Christ (sacrifices and symbols—Hebrews 10:1-18) because Christ has fulfilled them.

Slavery under the law	New Way of the Soirit
Guilt	Love
Restraint	Joy
Sacrifices	Peace
Ceremonies	Patience
Emphasis on sin	Kindness
Rule keeping	Goodness
Extreme pressures	Faithfulness
Failure	Gentleness
Hopelessness	Self-control

WHY DO GOD'S LAWS AROUSE OUR SINFUL DESIRES?
Romans 7:7-25

Because sin in us seizes the opportunity and becomes:

A sharpshooter, picking the best time and place for a kill

A magnet, creating an attraction as the object comes near

A temptress, working seduction at the point of need

A lawyer, trapping a victim in his own arguments

An engineer, building elaborate traps

An army, occupying undefended areas in our morality

A guerrilla, instigating rebellion behind the scenes

DIFFERENT WAYS TO HAVE YOUR MIND SET / Romans 8:6

When a person is determined to do something or to hold a certain belief or idea, we say that person has a certain mind-set. A mind-set:

Determines how a person acts

Motivates a person

Influences who or what a person chooses as sources of knowledge and authority

Affects a person's view of every experience

Shapes a person's value system

Dominates a person's private and public life

Paul indicates that all mind-sets can be reduced to two categories: sinful and spiritual. The two mind-sets are not parts of a person or even forces within a person. They signify powers and dominant features of two realms, the spirit and the flesh (former sinful nature).

The sinful mind-set	**The spiritual mind-set**
Consciously and unconsciously will be oriented toward:	Consciously and unconsciously will be oriented toward:
Death	Life and peace
Hostility toward God	Friendship with God
Resistance to any form of submission	Obedience to the Spirit's influence
Actions and attitudes that will not please God	Guidance by the Holy Spirit
	Love for God and neighbor
	Knowing and following the words of Jesus

THE TRINITY IN THE NEW TESTAMENT / *Romans 8:9-11*

In addition to Romans 8:9, where all three persons of the Trinity are working together in our salvation, there are some other key passages that portray the Trinity.

Baptism of Jesus—Matthew 3:17

The Father spoke.

The Son was in the water.

The Holy Spirit appeared as a dove.

Baptism of all believers—Matthew 28:19

All believers are baptized in name of

The Father,
The Son,
And the Holy Spirit.

The angel Gabriel's words to Mary—Luke 1:35

"The Holy Spirit will come upon you."

"The power of the Most High will overshadow you."

"The holy one to be born will be called the Son of God."

Paul's benediction—2 Corinthians 13:14

"May the grace of our Lord Jesus Christ"

"The love of God"

"The fellowship of the Holy Spirit"

INAPPROPRIATE RESPONSES TO THE MISDEEDS OF THE BODY
Romans 8:13

We should terminate the practices that the Holy Spirit points out as wrong. But instead, we often try to make excuses.

Response	Example
Denying that these habits or actions are part of our life	"I haven't done or couldn't do something like that."
Disclaiming our knowing participation	"I wasn't sure if it was right or wrong."
Continuing to give in to those patterns	"I'm weak, but at least I'm being honest about it."
Creating elaborate excuses	"I was deprived as a child. It's not really a habit. I tried to resist."
Minimizing or covering up the misdeeds	"At least I'm not as bad as she is."
Hiding behind a façade of legalism	"I'm doing so many things right; those wrong things don't count!"

BENEFITS OF BEING A JEW / *Romans 9:4-5*

- They are sons of God by adoption.
  - ➤ "Israel is my first born son" (Exodus 4:22).
  - ➤ "Yet the time will come when Israel will prosper and become a great nation. In that day its people will be like the sands of the seashore—too many to count! Then, at the place where they were told, 'You are not my people,' it will be said, 'You are children of the living God'" (Hosea 1:10).
  - ➤ "When Israel was a child, I loved him as a son, and I called my son out of Egypt" (Hosea 11:1).
- They had divine glory, or visible presence of God, dwelling among them.
  - ➤ "The LORD guided them by a pillar of cloud during the day and a pillar of fire at night. That way they could travel whether it was day or night. And the LORD did not remove the pillar of cloud or pillar of fire from their sight" (Exodus 13:21-22).
  - ➤ "Then the cloud covered the Tabernacle, and the glorious presence of the LORD filled it. Moses was no longer able to enter the Tabernacle because the cloud had settled down over it, and the Tabernacle was filled with the awesome glory of the LORD" (Exodus 40:34-35).
  - ➤ ". . . the glorious presence of the LORD filled the Temple" (1 Kings 8:11).
- They were given the covenants. God made covenants with his people. God's promises never go unfilled. The Old Testament records five covenants:
  - ➤ The Abrahamic Covenant—So the LORD made a covenant with Abram that day and said, "I have given this land to your descendants" (Genesis 15:18, see also 17:4-21).
  - ➤ The Mosiac Covenant—The Ten Commandments (Exodus 20: 1-17).
  - ➤ The Reestablished Covenant—"But you are not the only ones with whom the LORD is making this covenant with its obligations. The LORD your God is making this covenant with you who stand in his presence today and also with all future generations of Israel" (Deuteronomy 29:14-15).
  - ➤ The Davidic Covenant—"Your dynasty and your kingdom will continue for all time before me, and your throne will be secure forever" (2 Samuel 7:16).
  - ➤ The New Covenant through Jeremiah—"But this is the new covenant I will make with the people of Israel on that day," says the LORD. "I will put my laws in their minds, and I will write them on their hearts. I will be their God, and they will be my people" (Jeremiah 31:33).
- They received the law. God gave his law to Israel (see Exodus 20:1ff.; Deuteronomy 5:1-22).
- They worshiped in the Temple. Israel also was given the worship ceremony prescribed for the Tabernacle and the Temple (see especially the book of Leviticus).
- They were given God's promises. This refers especially to the promised Messiah—promises of his arrival are found throughout the Old Testament (see Luke 24:27).
- Last in this list of blessings are the patriarchs—Abraham, Isaac, Jacob, and Jacob's twelve sons. From the patriarchs is traced the human ancestry of Jesus Christ (Matthew 1:1-16; Romans 1:3), thus all Israel is in line to receive God's promises. And it is in Christ that all of God's promises to Israel are fulfilled.
- They have Christ, who is God over all and will be forever praised! For some, Christ is not really a separate benefit but the reason behind all the other benefits. Everything that God had given the Jews prepared the way for Christ.

STAGES IN THE HARDENING PROCESS / *Romans 9:20*

Stage	**Example**
Stage 1	
Abandoning God's guidance from his Word or believers	"I don't read the Bible or attend church."
	"Who are they to tell me what to do?"
Stage 2	
Willfully disobeying God, based on desire for sin or unresolved conflict with God	"I know it's wrong, but I want it."
	"Where was God when I needed him?"
	"How could he do this to me?"
Stage 3	
Justifying sin as not really being sin, but as being essential for the person's welfare	"I'm not sure this is really wrong."
	"I'm not as bad as the others."
	"I'll feel better."
Stage 4	
Rejecting the Holy Spirit's conviction	"I know I'll feel guilty, but I don't care."
	"I'll just ignore it."
Stage 5	
Becoming entrenched in the sinful behavior	"I'm in too deep to get out."
	"I might as well finish what I started."

HEBREW WORDS FOR LAW / *Romans 10:5*

Hebrew law served as the personal and national guide for living under God's authority. It directed their moral, spiritual, and social life. Its purpose was to produce better understanding of God and commitment to him.

Word	Meaning	Examples	Significance
Torah	Direction, Guidance, Instruction	Exodus 24:12; Isaiah 30:20	Need for law in general; a command from a higher person to a lower
Mitsvah	Commandment, Command	Genesis 25:5; Exodus 15:26; 20:2-17; Deuteronomy 5:6-21	God's specific instruction to be obeyed rather than a general law; used in reference to the Ten Commandments
Mishpat	Judgment, Ordinance	Genesis 18:19; Deuteronomy 16:18; 17:19	This refers to the civil, social, and sanitation laws
Huqqim	Statutes, Ordinances	Leviticus 18:4; Deuteronomy 4:1	Dealt with the royal pronouncements—mainly connected to worship and festivals

YOU ARE NOT ALONE / *Romans 11:4*

The prophets of Israel, for all their severity, consistently revealed God's ongoing commitment to a remnant. The messages God used to remind the people of his faithfulness were varied and persistent. You are not the only faithful follower of Christ; God has others. Together you are the remnant that he wants to use to impact the world.

Isaiah	Named his son Shear-Jashub, which means "a remnant will return" (Isaiah 7:3).
Jeremiah	Wrote of God as one who "will gather together the remnant of my flock from wherever I have driven them" Jeremiah 23:3).
Micah	Recorded God as saying, "Someday, O Israel, I will gather the few of you who are left. I will bring you together again like sheep in a fold, like a flock in its pasture. Yes, your land will again be filled with noisy crowds!" (Micah 2:12).
Zephaniah	Told Israel that "those who are left will be the lowly and the humble, for it is they who trust in the name of the LORD. The people of Israel who survive will do no wrong to each other, never telling lies or deceiving one another. They will live peaceful lives, lying down to sleep in safety; there will be no one to make them afraid" (Zephaniah 3:12-13).

WARNING SIGNS OF DEVELOPING HARDNESS / *Romans 11:9-10*

Hardening is like a callus or like the tough bone that bridges a fracture. Spiritual hardening begins with self-sufficiency, security in one's self, and self-satisfaction. The real danger is that at some point, repeated resistance to God will yield an actual inability to respond, which the Bible describes as a hardened heart. Insensitivity indicates advanced hardening. Here are some of the warning signs:

Warning Sign	Reference
Disobeying—Pharaoh's willful disobedience led to his hardened heart.	Exodus 4:21
Having wealth and prosperity—Taking God's blessings for granted can cause us to feel as if they were owed to us.	Deuteronomy 8:6-14
Rebelling and being discontented—Suffering or discomfort can create an attitude that blames God.	Psalm 95:8
Rejecting a deserved rebuke—Rejecting God's gift makes our necks stiff and heart hard.	Proverbs 29:1
Refusing to listen—Refusing to listen leads to a loss of spiritual hearing.	Zechariah 7:11-13
Failing to respond—Listening to God with no intention of obeying produces an inability to obey.	Matthew 13:11-15

DISGUISED ELITISM / *Romans 11:22*

To remember that God bases our salvation on faith and not on any merit in ourselves provides an effective antidote for elitism. But knowing some of the subtle ways that elitism can take root will keep us on guard.

When we say this . . .	We're actually doing this . . .
"They're not welcome in our church!"	Rejecting people because of race
"Everybody knows that at our church."	Excluding people on the basis of knowledge
"You're not part of that denomination?"	Rejecting people on the basis of denominational affiliation, with no reference to their personal relationship with Christ
"This is our family's church."	Excluding people because they are not in the "family"
"We need to dress up for church and use only the best for God."	Excluding people on the basis of wealth.
"Our church is growing so fast that soon we'll be the biggest and the best."	Rejecting people on the basis of success
"We have the best people."	Excluding people because of their reputation
"We know the truth."	Rejecting people because of doctrinal pride.

SACRIFICES COMPARED / *Romans 12:1*

In the old sacrifices . . .	But for the new sacrifices . . .
An altar was required	There is no altar
Animals were slain	The sacrifice lives
Sacrifices were cut up	The sacrifice is whole
Sacrifices were burned up	The sacrifice serves
It was based on legal obligation	It is based on mercy and gratitude
Death was not defeated	Eternal life is celebrated

DO NOT CONFORM / *Romans 12:3*

What causes us to conform to the world's pattern?

- We believe that the world is more likely to allow us pleasure than God is.
- We find certain exhilaration in rushing along with the world.
- We are afraid of what might happen if we really think about life and change.
- We are crippled by pride or a negative self-image and believe there really isn't an alternative.
- We reject the life of service and humility necessary to conform ourselves to God's pattern.

Conforming to the world's pattern will involve the following way of thinking:

- We have a right to have all our desires fulfilled (see Romans 8:5; 1 Peter 4:3-4).
- We have a right to pursue and use power (see Mark 10:42-45).
- We have a right to abuse people (see Luke 11:43, 46-52).
- We have a right to accumulate wealth for purely selfish reasons (see Matthew 16:26).
- We have a right to use personal abilities and wisdom for self-advancement rather than for serving others (see 1 Corinthians 3:19).
- We have a right to ignore or even hate God (see James 4:4).

GIFT DISCOVERY / *Romans 12:7-8*

Believers will respond differently in the same circumstances. Recognizing what our initial response might be will help us identify the general nature of our gifts. For example, imagine that a destitute family attends your worship service next Sunday. How will different believers respond? The responses that are most similar to what you would do will give you clues to your gifts.

The prophets will ask the congregation . . .	"What went wrong here that needs to be corrected? What caused this family to experience these problems?"
The servers will ask . . .	"What can we do for you?"
The teachers will ask . . .	"How can we help you avoid this situation in the future? What skills, wisdom, and spiritual insights will give you better direction?"
The encouragers will ask . . .	"You must be feeling bad. Please know that we will care for you any way we can. Before you know it, you will be helping someone else."
The givers will ask . . .	"How much will you need to meet your needs? How can we respond to this need in the most effective way?"
The leaders will ask the church . . .	"Are there any others we need to help?"
The merciful . . .	Will probably not ask any questions, but welcome the person with smiles, hugs, warm acceptance, and understanding.

CONSCIENTIOUS OBJECTORS / *Romans 13:3*

In the Bible, God's faithful resisted or disobeyed corrupt political or religious structures:

Daniel	Declined food for a king (Daniel 1:8-21)
Daniel's friends	Refused to bow down to the king's image (Daniel 3:1-30)
Jesus	Healed on the Sabbath (Luke 6:6-11; 14:1-6)
Jesus' disciples	Picked grain on the Sabbath (Luke 6:1-5) and refused to be silenced (Acts 1-22; 5:17-31)

PROFILE OF A STRONG CHURCH / *Romans 15:4*

A place of refuge, where people can find help 15:1

A place of instruction, where people's faith and lives are built up 15:2

A place centered on Christ, where Jesus is held up as a model 15:3

A place filled with the Word, where the Scriptures are known and applied. 15:4

A place of prayer, where endurance and encouragement are sought from God . . . 15:4-5

A place of acceptance, where there is an atmosphere and understanding of hope . 15:4

A place of togetherness, where unity is recognized as a product of God's work . . . 15:5

A place of witness, where acceptance of others is Christlike. 15:8

1 CORINTHIANS

MEGATHEMES IN 1 CORINTHIANS

Theme	Explanation	Importance
Loyalties	The Corinthians were rallying around various church leaders and teachers—Peter, Paul, and Apollos. These loyalties led to intellectual pride and created a spirit of division in the church.	Our loyalty to human leaders or human wisdom must never divide Christians into camps. We must care for our fellow believers, not fight with them. Your allegiance must be to Christ. Let him lead you.
Immorality	Paul received a report of uncorrected sexual sin in the church at Corinth. The people had grown indifferent to immorality. Others had misconceptions about marriage. We are to live morally, keeping our bodies for God's service at all times.	Christians must never compromise with sinful ideas and practices. We should not blend in with people around us. You must live up to God's standard of morality and not condone immoral behavior, even if society accepts it.
Freedom	Paul taught freedom of choice on practices not expressly forbidden in Scripture. Some believers felt certain actions—like eating the meat of animals used in pagan rituals—were corrupt by association. Others felt free to participate in such actions without feeling that they had sinned.	We are free in Christ, yet we must not abuse our Christian freedom by being inconsiderate and insensitive to others. We must never encourage others to do something they feel is wrong just because we have done it. Let love guide your behavior.
Worship	Paul addressed disorder in worship. People were taking the Lord's Supper without first confessing sin. There was misuse of spiritual gifts and confusion over women's roles in the church.	Worship must be carried out properly and in an orderly manner. Everything we do to worship God should be done in a manner worthy of his high honor. Make sure that worship is harmonious, useful, and edifying to all believers.
Resurrection	Some people denied that Christ rose from the dead. Others felt that people would not physically be resurrected. Christ's resurrection assures us that we will have new, living bodies after we die. The hope of the resurrection forms the secret of Christian confidence.	Since we will be raised again to life after we die, our life is not in vain. We must stay faithful to God in our morality and our service. We are to live today knowing we will spend eternity with Christ.

CORINTH AND EPHESUS / *1 Corinthians 1:1-3; 16:5-9*

Paul wrote this letter to Corinth during his three-year visit in Ephesus on his third missionary journey. The two cities sat across from each other on the Aegean Sea—both were busy and important ports. Titus may have carried this letter from Ephesus to Corinth (2 Corinthians 12:18).

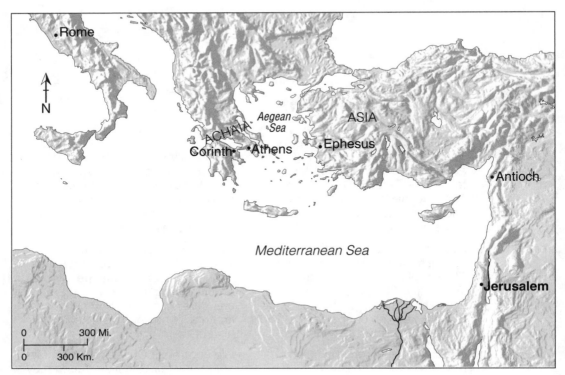

Copyright © 2001 by Tyndale House Publishers

EIGHT ISSUES IN THE FIRST LETTER TO THE CORINTHIANS
1 Corinthians 1:2

1. Paul's authority as an apostle had been challenged, so Paul defended his authority against the false teachers (chapters 2–4).

2. Paul rebuked the church for not disciplining the blatant sin of one of its members. Their laxness in dealing with sin could become a severe problem (chapter 5).

3. Paul explained that the believers should not take one another to the civil courts but should handle their disputes among themselves (6:1-8).

4. Paul's teaching about freedom in Christ had been changed to the point that some thought that even fornication was allowable among believers. Paul corrected that error by explaining that freedom in Christ did not mean freedom to sin (6:9-20).

5. Paul answered the questions about marriage that the Corinthians had sent to him. Many new Christians were already married to unbelievers and did not know what to do. Other new Christians did not know whether or not they should marry. Paul gave forthright advice on the matter (chapter 7).

6. Paul answered questions about dealing with a world filled with idolatry. Surrounded by the pagan religious cults and immorality of Corinth, the new believers wondered about how to deal with the issue of eating food sacrificed to idols. Paul explained freedom in Christ yet also held them responsible to deal carefully with those among them with weak consciences in these matters (chapters 8–10).

7. Paul delineated matters of respect and order in worship services. Male and female roles needed to be understood in the context of this time period and culture (chapters 11–14).

8. Paul reminded the Corinthian believers of their wonderful faith in the resurrection of Jesus Christ because false teachers had come along denying it as truth. Paul defended the resurrection and explained that without it, their faith was worthless (chapter 15).

HIGHLIGHTS OF 1 CORINTHIANS / Corinthians 1:18

The Meaning of the Cross (1:18–2:16)	Be considerate of one another because of what Christ has done for us. There is no place for pride or a know-it-all attitude. We are to have the mind of Christ.
The Story of the Last Supper (11:23-29)	The Last Supper is a time of reflection on Christ's final words to his disciples before he died on the cross; believers must celebrate this in an orderly and correct manner.
The Poem of Love (13:1-13)	Love is to guide all that believers do. Christians have different gifts, abilities, likes, dislikes—but they are called, without exception, to love.
The Christian's Destiny (15:42-58)	Christ, who died for sins, promised that just as he had come back to life after death, so believers' perishable bodies will be exchanged for heavenly bodies. They will live and reign with Christ.

PLEASING GOD / *1 Corinthians 4:3-4*

The New Testament illustrates the importance of pleasing God, not people. The secret to pleasing God is faith, obedience, and service.

Reference	Key Phrase	Significance
John 8:29	"Jesus said, 'When you have lifted up the Son of Man on the cross, then you will realize that . . . I do nothing on my own, but I speak what the Father taught me.' "	Believers are to follow God totally, just as Christ did.
2 Corinthians 5:9	"So our aim is to please him always, whether we are here in this body or away from this body."	Believers should aim always to please God in their words and actions.
Galatians 6:8	"Those who live to please the Spirit will harvest everlasting life from the Spirit."	Believers are assured of great reward when they live to please and honor God.
Colossians 1:9-10	"We ask [God] to make you wise with spiritual wisdom. Then the way you live will always honor and please the Lord, and you will continually do good, kind things for others."	Believers can ask God for wisdom to help them live to honor and please him.
1 Thessalonians 2:4	"Our purpose is to please God, not people. He is the one who examines the motives of our hearts."	Believers must always focus on pleasing God, then even if they don't please people, they know that their consciences are clear.
1 Thessalonians 4:1	"Finally . . . we urge you in the name of the Lord Jesus to live in a way that pleases God."	Believers are urged to please God because of what Jesus has done for them.
Hebrews 11:6	"It is impossible to please God without faith."	The first ingredient to pleasing God is faith that trusts him for salvation.
1 John 3:22	"And we will receive whatever we request because we obey him and do the things that please him."	Believers have access to God because of their faith and obedience.

SET AN EXAMPLE / 1 Corinthians 4:17

Throughout Scripture, setting an example is an important element of discipleship.

- Matthew 11:29—"Take my yoke upon you."
  Jesus told his followers to learn from his example of gentleness and humility.
- Philippians 3:17—"Pattern your lives after mine."
  Paul urged believers to follow his example of enthusiasm, perseverance, and maturity.
- 1 Thessalonians 1:6-7—"You imitated both us and the Lord . . . You yourselves became an example."
  The new Christians at Thessalonica received training in discipleship from Paul, and even in suffering they modeled before others what they had learned.
- 1 Timothy 1:16—"But that is why God had mercy on me, so that Christ Jesus could use me as a prime example of his patience with even the worse sinners."
  Paul used his unworthiness to receive Christ as an example of grace so that no one would hold back from coming to Christ.
- 1 Peter 5:3—"Don't lord it over the people assigned to your care, but lead them by your good example."
  Peter taught Christian leaders to lead by example, not by commands.

Paul told the Corinthian believers to follow his example. As the body of Christ, believers must show Christ to the world by being examples. Nonbelievers should be able to see Christ in believers and be so drawn to what they see that they seek Christ and his salvation. What kind of example are you?

CHURCH DISCIPLINE / 1 Corinthians 5:13

The church, at times, must exercise discipline toward members who have sinned. But church discipline must be handled carefully, straightforwardly, and lovingly.

Situations	Steps (Matthew 18:15-17)
Unintentional error or private sin	1. Go to the brother or sister, show the fault to him or her in private.
Public sin or those done flagrantly and arrogantly	2. If he or she does not listen, go with one or two witnesses.
	3. If he or she refuses to listen, take the matter before the church.

After these steps have been carried out, the next steps are:

1. Remove the one in error from the fellowship (1 Corinthians 5:2-13).
2. The church gives united disapproval, but forgiveness and comfort are in order if he or she chooses to repent (2 Corinthians 2:5-8).
3. Do not associate with the disobedient person; and if you must, speak to him or her as to one who needs a warning (2 Thessalonians 3:14-15).
4. After two warnings, reject the person from the fellowship (Titus 3:10).

STRONGER, WEAKER BELIEVERS / *1 Corinthians 8:9*

Paul advises those who are more mature in the faith about how they must care about their brothers and sisters in Christ who have more tender consciences; those "weaker" brothers and sisters are advised concerning their growth; and pastors and leaders are instructed on how to deal with the conflicts that easily could arise between these groups.

Advice to:

Stronger believer	Don't be proud of your maturity; don't flaunt your freedom. Act in love so you do not cause a weaker believer to stumble.
Weaker believer	Although you may not feel the same freedom in some areas as in others, take your time and pray to God, but do not force others to adhere to your stipulations. You would hinder other believers by making up rules and standards for how everyone ought to behave. Make sure your convictions are based on God's Word and are not simply an expression of your opinions.
Pastors and leaders	Teach correctly from God's Word, helping Christians understand what is right and wrong in God's eyes and helping them see that they can have varied opinions on other issues and still be unified. Don't allow potential problems to get out of hand, causing conflicts and divisions.

WHY WE DON'T GIVE UP / *1 Corinthians 9:27*

Perseverance, persistence, the prize! Christ never promised us an easy way to live; instead, these verses (9:26-27) remind us that we must have a purpose and a plan because times will be difficult and Satan will attack. We must be diligent, all the while remembering that we never run alone. God keeps his promises.

Reference	The Purpose	The Plan	The Prize
1 Corinthians 9:24-27	Run to get the prize Run straight to the goal	Deny yourself whatever is potentially harmful Discipline your body, training it	A crown that will last forever
Galatians 6:7-10	Don't become weary in doing good Don't get discouraged and give up Do good to everyone	Sow to please the Spirit	Reap eternal life
Ephesians 6:10-20	Put on the full armor of God Pray on all occasions	Use all the pieces of God's armor provided for you	Taking your stand against the devil's schemes
Philippians 3:12-14	Press on toward the day when you will be all God wants you to be	Forget the past, strain toward what is ahead	The prize for which God calls you heavenward
2 Timothy 2:1-13	Entrust these great truths to people who will teach them to others Be strong in Christ's grace, even when your faith is faltering	Endure hardship like a soldier and don't get involved in worldly affairs Follow the Lord's rules, as an athlete must do in order to win Work hard, like a farmer who tends his crops for the harvest	You will live with Christ; you will reign with him He always remains faithful to you and always carries out his promises

GOD OR IDOLS / 1 Corinthians 10:7

Why did people continually turn to idols instead of to God?

Idols were:

Tangible

Morally similar—had human characteristics

Comprehensible

Able to be manipulated

Worshiping idols involved:

Materialism

Sexual immorality

Doing whatever a person wanted

Focusing on self

God is:

Intangible—no physical form

Morally dissimilar—has divine characteristics

Incomprehensible

Not able to be manipulated

Worshiping God involved:

Sacrifice

Purity and commitment

Doing what God wants

Focusing on others

MAKING CHOICES IN SENSITIVE ISSUES / 1 Corinthians 10:32

Every person makes hundreds of choices every day. Most choices have no right or wrong attached to them—like what a person wears or eats. But many decisions carry a little more weight. You don't want to do wrong, and you don't want to cause others to do wrong, so how can you make such decisions? Ask yourself the following questions.

If I choose one course of action:

- Does it help my witness for Christ? (9:19-22)
- Am I motivated by a desire to help others to know Christ? (9:23; 10:33)
- Does it help me do my best? (9:25)
- Is it against a specific command in Scripture and would thus cause me to sin? (10:12)
- Is it the best and most beneficial course of action? (10:23, 33)
- Am I thinking only of myself, or do I truly care about the other person? (10:24)
- Am I acting lovingly or selfishly? (10:28-31)
- Does it glorify God? (10:31)
- Will it cause someone else to sin? (10:32)

PROPHETS IN NEW TESTAMENT TIMES / *1 Corinthians 14:1*

The word "prophets" refers to those who speak for God. The New Testament gives us many of the characteristics and activities of those called prophets.

The early believers saw the Spirit come at Pentecost, fulfilling the prophet Joel's prediction that all God's people would prophesy.	Acts 2:17
Prophets ranked second in importance only to the apostles.	1 Corinthians 12:28-31 Ephesians 4:11
Some people are given a special gift of prophecy.	1 Corinthians 12:29; 13:2
Prophets are called "pneumatics" (spiritual ones).	1 Corinthians 14:37
Prophets played a foundational role in the early church.	1 Corinthians 12:28-31 Ephesians 2:20; 4:11
Prophets function primarily in the worship of the church	Acts 13:1-2
Prophets may sometimes predict the future.	Acts 11:28; 20:23; 27:22-26
Prophets may announce judgments.	Acts 13:11; 28:25-28
Prophets may act symbolically.	Acts 21:10-11
Prophets may receive visions.	Acts 9:10-11 2 Corinthians 12:1
Prophets may identify specific persons for specific Christian tasks, even at times equipping them with the spiritual gifts necessary to carry out the tasks.	Acts 11:27-28; 13:1-2 1 Timothy 4:14
Prophets may preach long messages or give exposition of the Bible.	Luke 1:67-79 Acts 15:32 Romans 11:25-36 Ephesians 3:5
Prophets are saturated in the Old Testament Scriptures and their words are influenced by the language of the Bible.	Romans 11:27 with Isaiah 27:9 1 Corinthians 15:51, 54-55 with Isaiah 25:8 and Hosea 13:14
While teaching and prophecy are different, they can be related.	Acts 13:1-2; Revelation 2:20
Prophets use phrases such as "the Lord says" or "the Holy Spirit says" as introductory formulas for prophetic insight.	Acts 21:11; Hebrews 3:7
Prophecy in the New Testament included prophetic words given for the benefit of the body of believers.	1 Corinthians 14:3-4
Prophecy in the New Testament also included the work of the Spirit on the prophet whereby the Spirit revealed to the prophet a word from Christ.	John 16:12-14 Revelation 1:10; 4:1-2

WHAT THE BIBLE TEACHES ABOUT WORSHIP / *1 Corinthians 14:26*

Worship is first and foremost an encounter with the living and holy God.	" 'Do not come any closer,' God told him. 'Take off your sandals, for you are standing on holy ground' " (Exodus 3:5).	God is our friend, but he is also our sovereign Lord. To approach him frivolously shows a lack of respect and sincerity. When you come to God in worship, do you approach him casually, or do you come as though you were an invited guest before a king?
Worship is only as real as the involvement of those participating.	"The Lord gave these instructions to Moses on Mount Sinai when he commanded the Israelites to bring their offerings to the Lord in the wilderness of Sinai" (Leviticus 7:38).	All the rituals in Leviticus were meant to teach the people valuable lessons. But over time, the people became indifferent. When your church appears to be conducting dry, meaningless rituals, try rediscovering the meaning and purpose behind them. Your worship will be revitalized.
A true worship experience is often a direct result of preparation for worship.	"The Lord said to Moses, 'Give these instructions to the people of Israel: The offerings you present to me by fire on the altar are my food, and they are very pleasing to me. See to it that they are brought at the appointed times and offered according to my instructions' " (Numbers 28:1-2).	Following these rituals took time, and this gave the people the opportunity to prepare their heart for worship. Unless your heart is ready, worship is meaningless. God is delighted when you are prepared to come before him in a spirit of thankfulness.
Believers should take advantage of every opportunity to worship and praise God.	"Sing praises to God, our strength. Sing to the God of Israel. Sing! Beat the tambourine. Play the sweet lyre and the harp. Sound the trumpet for a sacred feast when the moon is new, when the moon is full" (Psalm 81:1-3).	Israel's holidays reminded the nation of God's great miracles. Remember the spiritual origin of the holidays you celebrate and use them as opportunities to worship God for his goodness to you, your family, and your nation.
Worship and music go hand in hand.	"David and the army commanders then appointed men from the families of Asaph, Heman, and Jeduthun to proclaim God's message to the accompaniment of harps, lyres, and cymbals" (1 Chronicles 25:1).	David instituted music for the temple worship services. Worship should involve the whole person, and music helps lift a person's thoughts and emotions to God. Through music you can celebrate God's greatness.

WHAT THE BIBLE TEACHES ABOUT WORSHIP / *1 Corinthians 14:26*
Continued

Worship is bringing the best believers have to Christ.

"They entered the house where the child and his mother, Mary, were, and they fell down before him and worshiped him. Then they opened their treasure chests and gave him gifts of gold, frankincense, and myrrh" (Matthew 2:11).

The wise men brought gifts and worshiped Jesus for who he was. This is the essence of true worship—honoring Christ for who he is and being willing to give him what is valuable to you. Worship God because he is worthy of the best you have to give.

Genuine worship results in submission and obedience to Jesus.

"But even as he said it, a bright cloud came over them, and a voice from the cloud said, 'This is my beloved Son, and I am fully pleased with him. Listen to him'" (Matthew 17:5).

Jesus is more than just a great leader. He is the Son of God. When you understand this profound truth, the only adequate response is worship. When you have a correct understanding of Christ, you will obey him.

Everything done in corporate worship must be beneficial to the worshipers.

"Since you are so eager to have spiritual gifts, ask God for those that will be of real help to the whole church" (1 Corinthians 14:12).

This principle touches every aspect of worship. Those contributing to a worship service must have love as their chief motivation, speaking useful words or participating in a way that will strengthen the faith of other believers.

In worship, everything must be done in harmony and with order.

"Be sure that everything is done properly and in order" (1 Corinthians 14:40).

Even when the gifts of the Holy Spirit are being exercised, there is no excuse for disorder. When there is chaos, the church is not allowing God to work among believers as he would like. Make sure that what you bring to worship is appropriate, but also make sure that you participate.

WHY BELIEVE THE RESURRECTION? / *1 Corinthians 15:1-2*

The Resurrection is the central theme of the gospel message.	15:2-4
The Resurrection is a fulfillment of the promises of the Old Testament Scriptures.	15:3-4
The Resurrection was attested to by many eyewitnesses.	15:5-8
If there is no such thing as resurrection, then Christ could not have been raised.	15:13, 16
If Christians will not one day be resurrected, then their faith is useless.	15:14, 17
If there is no Resurrection, then the apostles were all liars.	15:15
If there is no Resurrection, then the Christian faith is only for this life. Why then should believers face persecution for their faith? Why believe something that is only good for this life but only brings trouble in this life?	15:19, 30-32
The resurrection of Christ is a factual, historical event.	15:20
The resurrection of believers is a factual event to occur when Christ returns.	15:23
Resurrection includes a resurrection of physical bodies, not just spirits.	15:35-49
Resurrected bodies will live for eternity, never to die again.	15:50, 53-56
Because of the promised resurrection, nothing done for Christ is done in vain.	15:58

PHYSICAL AND RESURRECTION BODIES / *1 Corinthians 15:45-55*

All people have bodies—each looks different, each has different strengths and weaknesses. But as physical, earthly bodies, they are all alike. All believers are promised life after death and bodies like Christ's (15:49)—resurrection bodies.

Physical Bodies	Resurrection Bodies
Perishable.	Imperishable
Sown in dishonor	Raised in glory
Sown in weakness	Raised in power
Natural	Spiritual
From the dust	From heaven

2 CORINTHIANS

MEGATHEMES IN 2 CORINTHIANS

Theme	Explanation	Importance
Trials	Paul experienced great suffering, persecution, and opposition in his ministry. He even struggled with a personal weakness—a "thorn" in the flesh. Through it all, Paul affirmed God's faithfulness.	God is faithful. His strength is sufficient for any trial. When trials come, they keep us from pride and teach us dependence on God. He comforts us so we can comfort others.
Church Discipline	Paul defends his role in church discipline. Neither immorality nor false teaching could be ignored. The church was to be neither too lax nor too severe in administering discipline. The church was to restore the corrected person when he or she repented.	The goal of all discipline in the church should be correction, not vengeance. For churches to be effective, they must confront and solve problems, not ignore them. In everything, we must act in love.
Hope	To encourage the Corinthians as they faced trials, Paul reminded them that they would receive new bodies in heaven. This would be a great victory in contrast to their present suffering.	To know we will receive new bodies offers us hope. No matter what adversity we face, we can keep going. Our faithful service will result in triumph.
Giving	Paul organized a collection of funds for the poor in the Jerusalem church. Many of the Asian churches gave money. Paul explains and defends his beliefs about giving, and he urges the Corinthians to follow through on their previous commitment.	Like the Corinthians, we should follow through on our financial commitments. Our giving must be generous, sacrificial, well planned, and based on need. Our generosity not only helps those in need but enables them to thank God.
Sound Doctrine	False teachers were challenging Paul's ministry and authority as an apostle. Paul asserts his authority in order to preserve correct Christian doctrine. His sincerity, his love for Christ, and his concern for the people were his defense.	We should share Paul's concern for correct teaching in our churches. But in so doing, we must share his motivation—love for Christ and people—and his sincerity.

PAUL SEARCHES FOR TITUS / *2 Corinthians 2:12-13*

Paul had searched for Titus, hoping to meet him in Troas and receive news about the Corinthian church. When he did not find Titus in Troas, he went on to Macedonia (2:13), most likely to Philippi, where he found Titus.

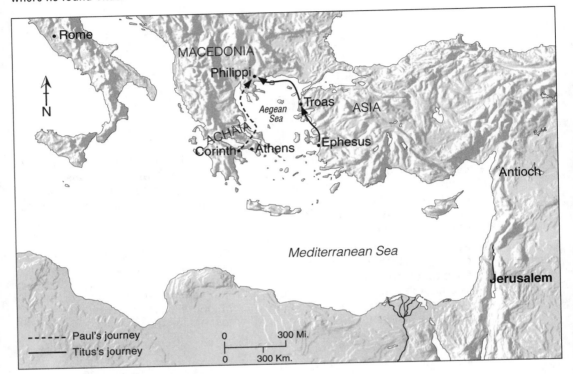

Copyright © 2001 by Tyndale House Publishers

DIFFERENCES BETWEEN 1 AND 2 CORINTHIANS / *2 Corinthians 1*

The two letters to the Corinthian church that we find in the Bible are very different, with different tones and focuses.

1 Corinthians/Practical	2 Corinthians/Personal
Focuses on the character of the Corinthian church	Focuses on Paul as he bares his soul and tells of his love for the Corinthian church
Deals with questions on marriage, freedom, spiritual gifts, and order in the church	Deals with the problem of false teachers, whereby Paul defends his authority and the truth of his message
Paul instructs in matters concerning the church's well-being	Paul gives his testimony because he knows that acceptance of his advice is vital to the church's well-being
Contains advice to help the church combat the pagan influences in the wicked city of Corinth	Contains testimony to help the church combat the havoc caused by false teachers

PRINCIPLES OF CONFRONTATION IN 2 CORINTHIANS
2 Corinthians 7:9

Sometimes rebuke is necessary, but it must be used with caution. The purpose of any rebuke, confrontation, or discipline is to help people, not hurt them.

Method	Reference
Be firm and bold.	7:9; 10:2
Affirm all you see that is good.	7:4
Be accurate and honest.	7:14; 8:21
Know the facts	11:22-27
Follow up after the confrontation	7:13; 12:14
Be gentle after being firm	7:15; 13:11-13
Speak words that reflect Christ's message, not your own ideas	10:3; 10:12-13; 12:19
Use discipline only when all else fails.	13:2

NEEDS FOR A FUND-RAISING PROJECT / *2 Corinthians 8:4*

The topic of fund-raising is not one to be avoided or one that should embarrass us, but all fund-raising efforts should be planned and conducted responsibly.

Information 8:4
Enthusiasm 8:7-8, 11
Definite purpose. 8:4
Persistence 8:2ff
Readiness and willingness 9:7
Honesty and integrity 8:21
Dedication. 8:5
Accountability 9:3
Leadership 8:7
Someone to keep it moving 8:18-22

PAUL'S CREDENTIALS / 2 Corinthians 11:23

Paul was concerned because the church in Corinth viewed him as no more than a blustering preacher; thus, they were not taking seriously his advice in his letters and on his visits. Paul addressed this attitude in the letter of 2 Corinthians, pointing out his credentials as an apostle of Christ and why the Corinthians should take his advice.

Reference	Credential
1:1, 21; 4:1	Commissioned by God
1:12	Acted in holiness, sincerity, and dependence on God alone in his dealings with them
1:13-14	Was straightforward and sincere in his letters
1:18; 4:2	Spoke truthfully
1:22	Had God's Holy Spirit
2:4; 6:11; 11:11	Loved the Corinthian believers
2:17	Spoke with sincerity and Christ's power
3:2-3	Worked among them and changed their lives
3:4; 12:6	Lived as an example to the believers
4:1, 16	Did not give up
4:2	Taught the Bible with integrity
4:5	Had Christ as the center of his message
4:8-12; 6:4-5, 9, 10	Endured persecution as he taught the Good News
5:18-20	Was Christ's ambassador, called to tell the Good News
6:3-4	Tried to live an exemplary life so others would not be kept from God
6:6	Led a pure life, understood the gospel, and displayed patience with the Corinthians
6:7	Was truthful and filled with God's power
6:8	Stood true to God first and always
7:2; 11:7-9	Never corrupted or exploited anyone
8:20-21	Handled their offering for the Jerusalem believers in a responsible, blameless manner
10:1-6	Used God's weapons, not his own, for God's work
10:7-8	Was confident that he belonged to Christ
10:12-13	Would boast not in himself but in the Lord
10:14-15	Had authority because he taught them the Good News
11:23-33	Endured pain and danger as he fulfilled his calling
12:2-4	Was blessed with an astounding vision
12:7-10	Was constantly humbled by a "thorn" in the flesh that God refused to take away
12:12	Did miracles among them
12:19	Was always motivated to strengthen others spiritually
13:4	Was filled with God's power
13:5-6	Passed the test
13:9	Was always concerned that his spiritual children become mature believers

GALATIANS

MEGATHEMES IN GALATIANS

Theme	Explanation	Importance
Law	A group of Jewish teachers insisted that non-Jewish believers must obey Jewish law and traditional rules. They believed a person was saved by following the law of Moses (with emphasis on circumcision, the sign of the covenant), in addition to faith in Christ. Paul opposed them by showing that the law can't save anyone.	We can't be saved by keeping the Old Testament law, even the Ten Commandments. The law served as a guide to point out our need to be forgiven. Christ fulfilled the obligations of the law for us. We must turn to him to be saved. He alone can make us right with God.
Faith	We are saved from God's judgment and penalty for sin by God's gracious gift to us. We receive salvation by faith—trusting in him—not in anything else. Becoming a Christian is in no way based on our initiative, wise choice, or good character. We can be right with God only by believing in him.	Your acceptance with God comes by believing in Christ alone. You must never add to or twist this truth. We are saved by faith, not by the good that we do. Have you placed your whole trust and confidence in Christ? He alone can forgive you and bring you into a relationship with God.
Freedom	Galatians is our charter of Christian freedom. We are not under the jurisdiction of Jewish laws and traditions nor under the authority of Jerusalem. Faith in Christ brings true freedom from sin and from the futile attempt to be right with God by keeping the law.	We are free in Christ, and yet freedom is a privilege. We are not free to disobey Christ or practice immorality, but we are free to serve the risen Christ. Let us use our freedom to love and to serve, not to do wrong.
Holy Spirit	We become Christians through the work of the Holy Spirit. He brings new life; even our faith to believe is a gift from him. The Holy Spirit instructs, guides, leads, and gives us power. He ends our bondage to evil desires, and he creates in us love, joy, peace, and many other wonderful changes.	When the Holy Spirit leads us, he produces his fruit in us. Just as we are saved by faith, not deeds, we also grow by faith. By believing, we can have the Holy Spirit within us, helping us live for Christ. Obey Christ by following the Holy Spirit's leading.

CITIES IN GALATIA / *Galatians 1:1-5, 13-24*

Paul visited several cities in Galatia on each of his three missionary journeys. On his first journey he went through Antioch in Pisidia, Iconium, Lystra, and Derbe, and then retraced his steps; on his second journey he went by land from Antioch of Syria through the four cities in Galatia; on his third journey he also went through those cities on the main route to Ephesus.

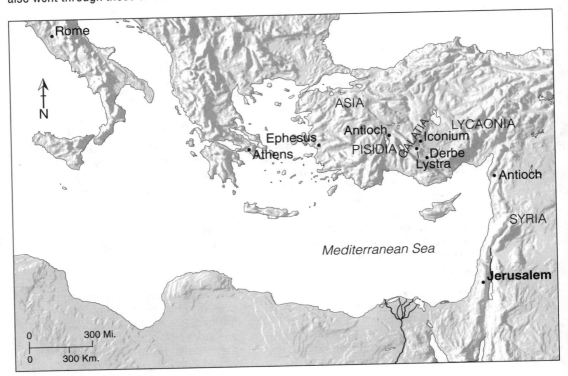

Copyright © 2001 by Tyndale House Publishers

LEGALISM AND LABELISM / *Galatians 1*

Paul encountered two forms of Jewish attitudes toward the law. Modern forms of these same attitudes can be found in Christianity today.

Legalism

"Legalism" is attempting to win God's favor by our own determined efforts of dedication and obedience.

Then

In Paul's time, Jews and many Jewish Christians believed that by faithful adherence to the law, they could win God's approval. By strict adherence to the Mosaic code, they could earn righteous standing with God.

Now

Often without realizing it, we try to live up to God's and other people's expectations of how Christians should be—all this as a means of winning God's approval. We do this by our efforts at obedience, dedication, full-time Christian service, academic study, and volunteer work. Some people try to be saved by working their way into heaven—they try to win God's love or approval through perfectionistic duty.

Lesson

We must obey and serve freely out of love and gratitude to Christ. The Holy Spirit must empower us. Our dedicated service cannot remove sin or obtain saving grace.

Labelism

"Labelism" is pride of ownership for having the "right" religion.

Then

Jews saw their commitment to the law (primarily the Jewish food laws and circumcision) as a badge of ownership, a symbol of their performance of the historic covenant between them and God. They felt superior for their religious correctness and for upholding the "right" religion. Too often this adherence to the law was in name only.

Now

Some Christians display this same love for having the "right" label, identifying with the right church, pastor, denomination, or religious viewpoint. Often their only identity as believers is a stance taken quite proudly on a single issue. By comparing themselves spiritually, they demean others who don't hold their view.

Lesson

Only Christ's faithful work on the cross, which enables us to respond in faith, can save us.

THE MARKS OF THE TRUE GOSPEL AND OF FALSE GOSPELS
Galatians 1:9

Marks of a false gospel

2:21 . . . . . . Treats Christ's death as meaningless

3:12 . . . . . . Says people must obey the law in order to be saved

4:10 . . . . . . Tries to find favor with God by observing certain rituals

5:4 . . . . Counts on keeping laws to erase sin

3:26-28 . . . Says that all believers are one in Christ, so there is no basis for discrimination of any kind

Marks of the true gospel

1:11-12 . . . Teaches that the source of the gospel is God

2:20 . . . . . . Knows that life is obtained through death; we trust in the God who loves us and died for us so that we might die to sin and live for him

3:14 . . . . . . Eplains that all believers have the Holy Spirit through faith

3:21-22 . . . Declares that we cannot be saved by keeping laws; the only way of salvation is through faith in Christ, which is available to all

5:24-25 . . . Proclaims that we are free from the grip of sin and that the Holy Spirit's power fills and guides us

---

A WHOLE PART, AND PART OF THE WHOLE / *Galatians 2:1-10*

In the early chapters of Galatians, Paul conveyed both his *independence* as an apostle, called and commissioned by God, as well as his *solidarity* as he ministered with the other apostles. Paul's problems were not with the other apostles, but with those false teachers who sought to drive a wedge between Paul and the apostles.

Evidence of Independence:

Paul was not sent by human authority (1:1).

Paul claimed that his account-ability was to God (1:10).

Paul's aim was to please God (1:10).

Paul's message was not derived from human sources, or reason, but by divine revelation (1:11).

Paul's conversion and subse-quent ministry did not come as a result of consultations with anyone (1:16).

Paul took the initiative in contacting Peter (1:18).

Evidence of Solidarity:

By traveling with Barnabas and Titus, Paul demon-strated that he was unified with the Christian com-munity. The fact that Barnabas was a Jew and Titus was a Greek showed that Paul could work with others and had support from key leaders in Asia (2:1).

Paul "placed his message on the table" for the other apostles to examine (2:2).

The rest of the apostles affirmed Paul's message to be the true gospel and his ministry to be directed to the Gentiles (2:7).

Jesus was clearly working through both Peter and Paul (2:8).

The apostolic band demonstrated their unity with Paul and Barnabas by publicly accepting them as co-workers. They were adding their endorsement to Christ's commission (2:9).

Later Paul lovingly confronted Peter as an equal about an inconsistency in Peter's behavior (2:14).

JUDAIZERS VERSUS PAUL / *Galatians 2:1*

As the debate raged between the Gentile Christians and the Judaizers, Paul found it necessary to write to the churches in Galatia. The Judaizers were trying to undermine Paul's authority, and they taught a false gospel. In reply, Paul defended his authority as an apostle and the truth of his message. The debate over Jewish laws and Gentile Christians was officially resolved at the Jerusalem council (Acts 15), yet it continued to be a point of contention after that time.

What the Judaizers said about Paul	Paul's defense
They said he was perverting the truth.	He received his message from Christ himself (1:11-12).
They said he was a traitor to the Jewish faith.	Paul was one of the most dedicated Jews of his time. Yet, in the midst of one of his most zealous acts, God transformed him through a revelation of the Good News about Jesus (1:13-16; Acts 9:1-30).
They said he compromised and watered down his message for the Gentiles.	The other apostles declared that the message Paul preached was the true gospel (2:1-10).
They said he was disregarding the law of Moses.	Far from degrading the law, Paul puts the law in its proper place. He says it shows people where they have sinned, and it points them to Christ (3:19-29).

COMPARISON OF HUMAN EFFORT VS. LIFE IN THE SPIRIT
Galatians 3:3

It's easy to try to attain maturity in Christ the wrong way. Much of devoted and dedicated service is in reality human effort. All of our service and good work must flow out of a life of faith and the enabling power of the Holy Spirit.

	Religion by Human Effort	Life in the Spirit
Goal	Please God by our own good works	Trust in Christ and then live to please God
Means	Practice, diligent service, discipline, and obedience in hope of reward	Confess, submit, and commit yourself to Christ's control
Power	Good, honest effort through self-determination	The Holy Spirit in us helps us do good work for Christ's kingdom
Control	Self-motivation; self-control	Christ in me; I in Christ
Results	Chronic guilt, apathy, depression, failure, constant desire for approval	Joy, thankfulness, love, guidance, service, forgiveness

PROMISES MADE TO ABRAHAM / *Galatians 3:16*

Genesis 12:1-3, 7	The promises of inhabiting a new land, becoming a great nation, being blessed, having a great name. Through Abraham all families of the earth would be blessed.
Genesis 15:1-5, 18	The promise of an heir and descendants too numerous to count, and the promise of inheriting the land.
Genesis 17:1-8	The promise that Abraham would be the ancestor of many nations, kings would be among his descendants, the covenant would be eternal, and the land would belong to his descendants forever.
Genesis 22:16-18	The promise of descendants as numerous as the stars of heaven and the sand on the seashore. The promise that through him all nations of the earth would be blessed.

WHAT IS THE LAW? / *Galatians 3:25*

Part of the Jewish law included those laws found in the Old Testament. When Paul says that non-Jews (Gentiles) are no longer bound by these laws, he is not saying that the Old Testament laws do not apply to us today. He is saying that certain types of laws may not apply to us. In the Old Testament there were three categories of laws.

Ceremonial law	This kind of law relates specifically to Israel's worship (see, for example, Leviticus 1:1-13). Its primary purpose was to point forward to Jesus Christ. Therefore, these laws were no longer necessary after Jesus' death and resurrection. While we are no longer bound by ceremonial laws, the principles behind them—to worship and love a holy God—still apply. The Jewish Christians often accused the Gentile Christians of violating the ceremonial law.
Civil law	This type of law dictated Israel's daily living (see Deuteronomy 24:10-11, for example). Because modern society and culture are so radically different, some of these guidelines cannot be followed specifically. But the principles behind the commands should guide our conduct. At times, Paul asked Gentile Christians to follow some of these laws, not because they had to, but in order to promote unity.
Moral law	This sort of law is the direct command of God—for example, the Ten Commandments (Exodus 20:1-17). It requires strict obedience. It reveals the nature and will of God, and it still applies to us today. We are to obey this moral law not to obtain salvation, but to live in ways pleasing to God.

THREE DISTORTIONS OF CHRISTIANITY / Galatians 4

Almost from the beginning there were forces at work within Christianity that would have destroyed or sidetracked the movement. Of these, three created many problems then and have continued to reappear in other forms even today. The three aberrations are contrasted to true Christianity.

Group	Their definition of a Christian	Their genuine concern	The danger	Application question
Judaized Christianity	Christians are Jews who have recognized Jesus as the promised Savior. Therefore, any Gentile desiring to become a Christian must first become a Jew.	Having a high regard for the Scriptures and God's choice of Jews as his people, they did not want to see God's commands overlooked or broken.	Tends to add human traditions and standards to God's law. Also subtracts from the Scriptures God's clear concern for all nations.	Do you appreciate God's choice of a unique people through whom he offered forgiveness and eternal life to all peoples?
Legalized Christianity	Christians are those who live by a long list of "don'ts." God's favor is earned by good behavior.	Recognized that real change brought about by God should lead to changes in behavior.	Tends to make God's love something to earn rather than to accept freely. Would reduce Christianity to a set of impossible rules and transform the Good News into bad news.	As important as change in action is, can you see that God may be desiring different changes in you than in others?
Lawless Christianity	Christians live above the law. They need no guidelines. God's Word is not as important as our personal sense of God's guidance.	Recognized that forgiveness from God cannot be based on our ability to live up to his perfect standards. It must be received by faith as a gift made possible by Christ's death on the cross.	Forgets that Christians are still human and fail consistently when trying to live only by what they "feel" God wants.	Do you recognize the ongoing need for God's expressed commands as you live out your gratitude for his great salvation?
True Christianity	Christians are those who believe inwardly and outwardly that Jesus' death has allowed God to offer them forgiveness and eternal life as a gift. They have accepted that gift through faith and are seeking to live a life of obedient gratitude for what God has done for them.	Christianity is both private and public, with heart-belief and mouth-confession. Our relationship to God and the power he provides result in obedience. Having received the gift of forgiveness and eternal life, we are now daily challenged to live that life with his help.	Avoids the above dangers.	How would those closest to you describe your Christianity? Do they think you live so that God will accept you, or do they know that you live because God has accepted you in Christ?

CONTRAST OF SARAH AND HAGAR / *Galatians 4:21*

Paul contrasted those who were enslaved to the law (represented by Hagar) with those who are free from the law (represented by Sarah).

	Sarah	Hagar	Significance
Name of child	Isaac	Ishmael	Isaac represented God's intervention. Ishmael was born by the ordinary process.
What the child represented	Covenant of Promise (grace)	Covenant of Mt. Sinai (law)	God's promise to Abraham was prior to the covenant with Moses at Mt. Sinai.
Source	Based on Jerusalem above (Spirit)	Based on present Jerusalem (flesh)	The present Jerusalem represents legalism. The Jerusalem above represents life in the Spirit.
Results in life	Leads to freedom	Leads to slavery	Paul wanted the Galatians to experience Christian freedom, not a return to the law.

BELIEVERS' TRUE IDENTITY IN CHRIST / *Galatians 5:6*

See also *Ephesians 1:3*

Romans 3:24	We are justified (declared "not guilty" of sin).
Romans 8:1	We await no condemnation.
Romans 8:2	We are set free from the law of sin and death.
1 Corinthians 1:2	We are sanctified and made acceptable in Jesus Christ.
1 Corinthians 1:30	We are righteous and holy in Christ.
1 Corinthians 15:22	We will be made alive at the resurrection.
2 Corinthians 5:17	We are new creations.
2 Corinthians 5:21	We receive God's righteousness.
Galatians 3:28	We are one in Christ with all other believers.
Ephesians 1:3	We are blessed with every spiritual blessing in Christ.
Ephesians 1:4	We are holy, blameless, and covered with God's love.
Ephesians 1:5-6	We are adopted as God's children.
Ephesians 1:7	We are forgiven—our sins are taken away.
Ephesians 1:10-11	We will be brought under Christ's headship.
Ephesians 1:13	We are marked as belonging to God by the Holy Spirit.
Ephesians 2:6	We have been raised up to sit with Christ in glory.
Ephesians 2:10	We are God's work of art.
Ephesians 2:13	We have been brought near to God.
Ephesians 3:6	We share in the promise in Christ.
Ephesians 3:12	We can come with freedom and confidence into God's presence.
Ephesians 3:29-30	We are members of Christ's body, the church.
Colossians 2:10	We have been given fullness in Christ.
Colossians 2:11	We are set free from our sinful nature.
2 Timothy 2:10	We will have eternal glory.

VICES AND VIRTUES / 5:21

The Bible mentions many specific actions and attitudes that are either right or wrong. Look at the list included here. Are there a number of characteristics from the wrong column that are influencing you?

Vices
(Neglecting God and others)

Sexual immorality (Galatians 5:19)

Impure thoughts (Galatians 5:19)

Lust (Colossians 3:5)

Hostility (Galatians 5:20)

Quarreling (Galatians 5:20)

Jealousy (Galatians 5:20)

Anger (Galatians 5:20)

Selfish ambition (Galatians 5:20)

Divisions (Galatians 5:20)

Conceit (2 Corinthians 12:20; Galatians 5:20)

Envy (Galatians 5:21)

Murder (Revelation 22:12-16)

Idolatry (Galatians 5:20; Ephesians 5:5)

Demonic activities (Galatians 5:20)

Drunkenness (Galatians 5:21)

Wild living (Luke 15:13; Galatians 5:21)

Cheating (1 Corinthians 6:8)

Adultery (1 Corinthians 6:9-10)

Homosexuality (1 Corinthians 6:9-10)

Greed (1 Corinthians 6:9, 10; Ephesians 5:5)

Stealing (1 Corinthians 6:9-10)

Lying (Revelation 22:12-16)

Virtues
(The by-products of living for God)

Love (Galatians 5:22)

Joy (Galatians 5:22)

Peace (Galatians 5:22)

Patience (Galatians 5:22)

Kindness (Galatians 5:22)

Goodness (Galatians 5:22)

Faithfulness (Galatians 5:22)

Gentleness (Galatians 5:23)

Self-control (Galatians 5:23)

THE OLD SELF IS DEAD BUT SINFUL HUMAN DESIRES LIVE ON
Galatians 5:24

In Scripture, the *old self* (old man) represents the corrupt sinful state we inherited from Adam. The *sinful human desires* (flesh) represent our tendency to sin. In Christ, our old self was crucified but our sinful human desires live on.

The Old Self → Dead when we became believers

Romans 6:6	"Our old sinful selves were crucified with Christ so that sin might lose its power in our lives. We are no longer slaves to sin."
Romans 6:11	"So you should consider yourselves dead to sin and able to live for the glory of God through Christ Jesus."
Romans 6:22	"But now you are free from the power of sin and have become slaves of God. Now you do those things that lead to holiness and result in eternal life."
2 Corinthians 5:17	"What this means is that those who become Christians become new persons. They are not the same anymore, for the old life is gone. A new life has begun!"
Galatians 2:20	"I myself no longer live, but Christ lives in me. So I live my life in this earthly body by trusting in the Son of God, who loved me and gave himself for me."
Ephesians 4:22-24	"Throw off your old evil nature and your former way of life, which is rotten through and through, full of lust and deception.
	Instead, there must be a spiritual renewal of your thoughts and attitudes.
	You must display a new nature because you are a new person, created in God's likeness—righteous, holy, and true."
Colossians 3:3	"For you died when Christ died, and your real life is hidden with Christ in God."
Colossians 3:9-10	"Don't lie to each other, for you have stripped off your old evil nature and all its wicked deeds.
	In its place you have clothed yourselves with a brand-new nature that is continually being renewed as you learn more and more about Christ, who created this new nature within you."

Sinful Human Desires → Active as long as believers live

Romans 8:5	"Those who are dominated by the sinful nature think about sinful things, but those who are controlled by the Holy Spirit think about things that please the Spirit."
Romans 8:7	"For the sinful nature is always hostile to God. It never did obey God's laws, and it never will."
Galatians 5:16	"So I advise you to live according to your new life in the Holy Spirit. Then you won't be doing what your sinful nature craves."
Galatians 5:24	"Those who belong to Christ Jesus have nailed the passions and desires of their sinful nature to his cross and crucified them there."
Colossians 3:5	"So put to death the sinful, earthly things lurking within you. Have nothing to do with sexual sin, impurity, lust, and shameful desires. Don't be greedy for the good things of this life, for that is idolatry."

OUR WRONG DESIRES VERSUS THE FRUIT OF THE SPIRIT
Galatians 5:26

The will of the Holy Spirit is in constant opposition to our sinful desires. The two are on opposite sides of the spiritual battle.

Our wrong desires are	The fruit of the Spirit is
Evil	Good
Destructive	Productive
Easy to ignite	Difficult to ignite
Difficult to stifle	Easy to stifle
Self-centered	Self-giving
Oppressive and possessive	Liberating and nurturing
Decadent	Uplifting
Sinful	Holy
Deadly	Abundant life

WHAT GOD WANTS US TO DO FOR OTHERS / *Galatians 6:2*

Besides the command to "carry each other's burdens" (Galatians 6:2), the New Testament tells us many attitudes we should have toward others and actions we should do for others. Below is a sampling:

Love one another	John 13:34-35; 15:12, 17 Romans 12:10; 13:8 1 Thessalonians 3:12; 4:9 1 Peter 1:22; 4:8 1 John 3:11, 23; 4:7, 11-12 2 John 5
Encourage one another	Ephesians 5:19 1 Thessalonians 4:18; 5:11 Hebrews 3:13; 10:24-25
Be at peace with one another	Mark 9:50 Romans 12:16 1 Peter 3:8
Humbly serve and submit to one another	John 13:14 Galatians 5:13 Ephesians 5:21 Philippians 2:3 1 Peter 4:9-10; 5:5
Show kindness and honor to one another	Romans 12:10; 15:7 1 Corinthians 11:33; 12:25 Ephesians 4:2, 32 Colossians 3:13 James 4:11; 5:9
Instruct one another	Romans 15:14 Colossians 3:16
Forgive one another	Colossians 3:13
Stop judging one another	Romans 14:13
Pray for one another	James 5:16

EPHESIANS

MEGATHEMES IN EPHESIANS

Theme	Explanation	Importance
God's Purpose	According to God's eternal, loving plan, he directs, carries out, and sustains our salvation.	When we respond to Christ's love by trusting in him, his purpose becomes our mission. Have you committed yourself to fulfilling God's purpose?
Christ the Center	Christ is exalted as the center of the universe and the focus of history. He is the head of the body, the church. He is the Creator and sustainer of all creation.	Because Christ is central to everything, his power must be central in us. Begin by placing all your priorities under his control.
Living Church	Paul describes the nature of the church. The church, under Christ's control, is a living body, a family, a dwelling. God gives believers special abilities by his Holy Spirit to build the church.	We are part of Christ's body, and we must live in vital union with him. Our conduct must be consistent with this living relationship. Use your God-given abilities to equip believers for service. Fulfill your role in the living church.
New Family	Because God through Christ paid our penalty for sin and forgave us, we have been reconciled—brought near—to him. We are a new society, a new family. Being united with Christ means we are to treat one another as family members.	We are one family in Christ, so there should be no barriers, no divisions, no basis for discrimination. We all belong to him, so we should live in harmony with one another.
Christian Conduct	Paul encourages all Christians to wise, dynamic Christian living, for with privileges goes family responsibility. As a new community, we are to live by Christ's new standards.	God provides his Holy Spirit to enable us to live his way. To utilize the Spirit's power, we must lay aside our evil desires and draw on the power of his new life. Submit your will to Christ, and seek to love others.

LOCATION OF EPHESUS / *Ephesians 1:1-2*

Ephesus was a strategic city, ranking in importance with Alexandria in Egypt and Antioch of Syria as a port. It lay on the most western edge of Asia Minor (modern-day Turkey), the most important port on the Aegean Sea on the main route from Rome to the east.

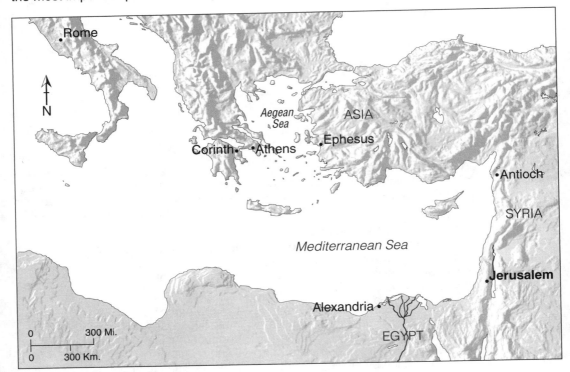

Copyright © 2001 by Tyndale House Publishers

SIMILARITIES BETWEEN EPHESIANS AND COLOSSIANS
Ephesians 1

Ephesians	Colossians	Theme
1:7	1:14	freedom and forgiveness
1:10	1:20	reconciliation under Christ
1:19; 2:5	2:12-13	new life
3:2	1:25	Paul's ministry to Gentiles
4:2-4	3:12-15	harmony
4:16	2:19	Christ's body
4:22-24	3:9-10	a new nature
4:32	3:13	forgiving others
5:6-8	3:6-8	God's anger toward sin
5:15-16	4:5	using opportunities
5:19	3:16	singing
5:20-33	3:17-18	submission and love
6:19-20	4:3-4	praying for preachers
6:22	4:8	the encourager, Tychicus

BLAMELESS / *Ephesians 1:4*

Christ is blameless . . . . Hebrews 9:14; 1 Peter 1:19

The ideal church is blameless . . . . Ephesians 5:27

Christians are blameless now . . . . Philippians 2:15

Christians will be blameless at the end
of the age . . . . Colossians 1:22; 2 Peter 3:14; Jude 24

GOD'S RICHES GIVEN TO US / *Ephesians 1:7*

God is rich in kindness, tolerance, and patience. . . . . Romans 2:4

God makes known the riches of his glory. . . . . Romans 9:23

God is rich in wisdom and knowledge. Romans 11:33

Though Christ was rich, he became poor for the sake of sinners,
so that through his poverty, we might be made rich. . . . . 2 Corinthians 8:9

Believers' redemption and forgiveness are in accordance with the
riches of God's grace. . . . . Ephesians 1:7

Paul prayed that the believers would know the riches of their
inheritance. . . . . Ephesians 1:18

God is rich in mercy. . . . . Ephesians 2:4

The riches of God's grace are incomparable. . . . . Ephesians 2:7

Paul was called to preach to the Gentiles the unsearchable
riches of Christ. . . . . Ephesians 3:8

Paul prayed that God would strengthen the believers out of his
glorious riches. . . . . Ephesians 3:16

Paul prayed that God would grant the believers' needs according
to his glorious riches. . . . . Philippians 4:19

God is making known the riches of this mystery—Christ in human
beings. . . . . Colossians 1:27

Paul wanted the believers to have the full riches of complete
understanding in order to understand the mystery of Christ's
work in people. . . . . Colossians 2:2

THE SEAL OF THE SPIRIT / *Ephesians 1:13*

The Spirit marks the beginning of the Christian experience.

We cannot belong to Christ without his Spirit. . . . . Romans 8:9

We cannot be united to Christ without his Spirit. . . . . 1 Corinthians 6:17

We cannot be adopted as his children without his Spirit. . . . . Romans 8:14-17
Galatians 4:6-7

We cannot be in the body of Christ except by baptism in the Spirit. . . . 1 Corinthians
12:13

The Spirit is the power of our new lives.

The Spirit lives within us. . . . . 1 Corinthians 6:19

The Spirit changes us from within, helping us produce "fruit." . . . . . . Galatians 5:22-23

The Spirit helps us become more like Christ. . . . . 2 Corinthians 3:18;
Ephesians 3:16-20

The Spirit unites the Christian community.

The Spirit is building us into a holy dwelling. . . . . Ephesians 2:22

The Spirit can be experienced by all and works through all. . . . . 1 Corinthians
12:4-11

NOT OF WORKS, BUT OF GRACE / Ephesians 2:9

Acts 15:11   We believe that we are all saved the same way, by the special favor of the Lord Jesus.

Acts 18:27   Apollos had been thinking about going to Achaia, and the brothers and sisters in Ephesus encouraged him in this. They wrote to the believers in Achaia, asking them to welcome him. When he arrived there, he proved to be of great benefit to those who, by God's grace, had believed.

Romans 3:24   Yet now God in his gracious kindness declares us not guilty. He has done this through Christ Jesus, who has freed us by taking away our sins.

Romans 4:16   So that's why faith is the key! God's promise is given to us as a free gift. And we are certain to receive it, whether or not we follow Jewish customs, if we have faith like Abraham's. For Abraham is the father of all who believe.

Romans 11:6   And if they are saved by God's kindness, then it is not by their good works. For in that case, God's wonderful kindness would not be what it really is—free and undeserved.

Galatians 3:18   For if the inheritance could be received only by keeping the law, then it would not be the result of accepting God's promise. But God gave it to Abraham as a promise.

Ephesians 2:5   That even while we were dead because of our sins, he gave us life when he raised Christ from the dead. (It is only by God's special favor that you have been saved!)

Ephesians 2:8   God saved you by his special favor when you believed. And you can't take credit for this; it is a gift from God.

2 Timothy 1:9   It is God who saved us and chose us to live a holy life. He did this not because we deserved it, but because that was his plan long before the world began—to show his love and kindness to us through Christ Jesus.

Titus 3:4-7   But then God our Savior showed us his kindness and love.

He saved us, not because of the good things we did, but because of his mercy. He washed away our sins and gave us a new life through the Holy Spirit.

He generously poured out the Spirit upon us because of what Jesus Christ our Savior did.

He declared us not guilty because of his great kindness. And now we know that we will inherit eternal life.

OUR LIVES BEFORE AND AFTER CHRIST / *Ephesians 3:6*

Before	After
Dead because of sin	Made alive with Christ
Under God's anger	Shown God's mercy and given salvation
Followed the ways of the world	Stand for Christ and truth
God's enemies	God's children
Enslaved to Satan	Free in Christ to love, serve, and sit with him
Followed our evil thoughts and desires	Raised up with Christ to glory

THE ONENESS OF ALL BELIEVERS / *Ephesians 4:4-6*

Too often believers are separated because of minor differences in doctrine. But Paul here shows those areas where Christians must agree to attain true unity. When believers have this unity of spirit, petty differences should never be allowed to dissolve that unity.

Believers are one in	Our unity is experienced in
Body	The fellowship of believers—the church
Spirit	The Holy Spirit, who activates the fellowship
Hope	That glorious future to which we are all called
Lord	Christ, to whom we all belong
Faith	Our singular commitment to Christ
Baptism	Baptism—the sign of entry into the church
God	God, who is our Father who keeps us for eternity

SPIRITUAL GIFTS / *Ephesians 4:16*

What does the Bible say about the nature and use of spiritual gifts?

Read Romans 12; Ephesians 4.	God gives us spiritual gifts so we can work together to serve him and each other.
	God gives us gifts so we can build up his church.
	Our gifts, though different, are all useful.
	Christians using their gifts to serve God and each other create an exciting fellowship.
Read 1 Corinthians 12; 1 Peter 4:10-11.	Spiritual gifts have a single source and a special purpose.
	Spiritual gifts have at times been divisive because of pride and jealousy.
	Spiritual gifts ought to be humbly used in service of others.
Read 1 Thessalonians 5:12-28.	Spiritual maturity neither denies nor overemphasizes spiritual gifts.

CHRISTIAN RELATIONSHIPS / *Ephesians 5:30-33*

A Christian Husband and Father

Remains faithful to his wife in a lifelong commitment to her (1 Corinthians 7:10-11)

Meets his wife's sexual needs (1 Corinthians 7:3-5)

Loves his wife as much as he loves himself (Ephesians 5:25-30)

Joins with his wife in total and complete unity (Ephesians 5:31)

Brings up his children in the training and instruction of the Lord (Ephesians 6:4)

Treats his wife kindly (Colossians 3:19)

Provides for the material needs of his family (1 Timothy 5:8)

Treats his wife with consideration and respect (1 Peter 3:7)

A Christian Wife and Mother

Remains faithful to her husband in a lifelong commitment to him (1 Corinthians 7:10-11)

Meets her husband's sexual needs (1 Corinthians 7:3-5)

Submits to her husband's leadership role in the home (Ephesians 5:22, 24; Colossians 3:18; 1 Peter 3:1)

Shows respect for her husband (Ephesians 5:33)

Develops inward charm and beauty (1 Peter 3:3-5)

CHILDREN AND THEIR PARENTS / *Ephesians 6:2-3*

The Scriptures have much to say about how children should treat their parents.

Who said it	Where it's said	Do	Don't
Moses in the Law	Exodus 20:12; Deuteronomy 5:16 Exodus 21:15 Exodus 21:17; Leviticus 20:9 Deuteronomy 21:18-21	Honor and respect them Obey them	Strike them Curse them Rebel against them
Solomon in the Proverbs	Proverbs 23:22 Proverbs 28:24 Proverbs 30:11 Proverbs 30:17	Listen to them	Rob them Curse them Mock them
Jesus in the Gospels	Matthew 15:4-6; Mark 7:10-13 Matthew 19:19 Mark 10:19 Luke 14:26	Honor and provide for them Honor them Respect them	Curse and neglect them Honor them above God
Paul in the Epistles	Ephesians 6:1 Ephesians 6:2	Obey them Honor them	

GOD'S ARMOR FOR US / *Ephesians 6:17*

We are engaged in a spiritual battle—all believers find themselves subject to Satan's attacks because they are no longer on Satan's side. Thus, Paul tells us to use *every piece* of God's armor to resist Satan's attacks and to stand true to God in the midst of those attacks.

Piece of Armor	Use	Application
Belt	Truth	Satan fights with lies, and sometimes his lies sound like truth; but only believers have God's truth, which can defeat Satan's lies.
Body armor	Righteousness	Satan often attacks our heart—the seat of our emotions, self-worth, and trust. God's righteousness is the body armor that protects our heart and ensures his approval. He approves of us because he loves us and sent his Son to die for us.
Shoes	Readiness to spread the Good News	Satan wants us to think that telling others the Good News is a worthless and hopeless task—the size of the task is too big and the negative responses are too much to handle. But the shoes God gives us are the motivation to continue to proclaim the true peace that is available in God—news everyone needs to hear.
Shield	Faith	What we see are Satan's attacks in the form of insults, setbacks, and temptations. But the shield of faith protects us from Satan's fiery arrows. With God's perspective, we can see beyond our circumstances and know that ultimate victory is ours.
Helmet	Salvation	Satan wants to make us doubt God, Jesus, and our salvation. The helmet protects our mind from doubting God's saving work for us.
Sword	Word of God	The sword is the only weapon of offense in this list of armor. There are times when we need to take the offensive against Satan. When we are tempted, we need to trust in the truth of God's Word.

PHILIPPIANS

MEGATHEMES IN PHILIPPIANS

Theme	Explanation	Importance
Humility	Christ showed true humility when he laid aside his rights and privileges as God to become human. He poured out his life to pay the penalty we deserve. Laying aside self-interest is essential to all our relationships.	We are to take Christ's attitude in serving others. We must renounce personal recognition and merit. When we give up our self-interest, we can serve with joy, love, and kindness.
Self-Sacrifice	Christ suffered and died so we might have eternal life. With courage and faithfulness, Paul sacrificed himself for the ministry. He preached the gospel even while he was in prison.	Christ gives us power to lay aside our personal needs and concerns. To utilize his power, we must imitate those leaders who show self-denying concern for others. We dare not be self-centered.
Unity	In every church, in every generation, there are divisive influences (issues, loyalties, and conflicts). In the midst of hardships, it is easy to turn on one another. Paul encouraged the Philippians to agree with one another, stop complaining, and work together.	As believers, we should not contend with one another but unite against a mutual enemy. When we are unified in love, Christ's strength is most abundant. Keep before you the ideals of teamwork, consideration of others, and unselfishness.
Christian Living	Paul shows us how to live successful Christian lives. We can become mature by being so identified with Christ that his attitude of humility and self-sacrifice becomes ours. Christ is both our source of power and our guide.	Developing our character begins with God's work in us. But growth also requires self-discipline, obedience to God's Word, and concentration on our part.
Joy	Believers can have profound contentment, serenity, and peace no matter what happens. This joy comes from knowing Christ personally and from depending on his strength rather than our own.	We can have joy, even in hardship. Joy does not come from outward circumstances but from inward strength. As Christians, we must not rely on what we have or what we experience to give us joy but on Christ within us.

LOCATION OF PHILIPPI / *Philippians 1:27-30*

Philippi sat on the Egnatian Way, the main transportation route in Macedonia, an extension of the Appian Way, which joined the eastern empire with Italy.

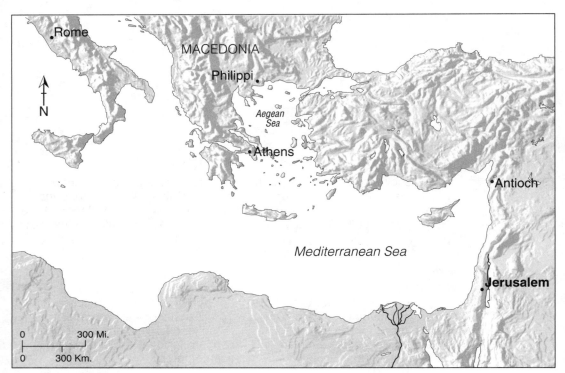

Copyright © 2001 by Tyndale House Publishers

THE GLORIOUS INCARNATION / *Philippians 2:7*

When Christ was born, God became a man. He was not part man and part God; he was completely human and completely divine. After Christ came, people could know God fully because he became visible and tangible in Christ.

John 1:1-14

The Good News is that Jesus Christ came as a human, was part of the Jewish royal line through David, died and was raised from the dead, and opened the door for God's grace and kindness to be poured out on us.

Romans 1:2-5

As a man, Jesus was subject to human limitations. He did not give up his eternal power when he became human, but he did set aside his glory and rights of his pre-incarnate state as equal with God. He became "poor" so that we could become "rich" in salvation and eternal life.

2 Corinthians 8:9

As a man, Jesus lived a perfect life, and so he is a perfect example of how to live. As God, Jesus gives us the power to do what is right. It is possible to live a godly life—through following Christ.

1 Timothy 3:16

Jesus had to become human so that he could die and rise again, in order to destroy the devil's power over death. Only then could Christ deliver those who had lived in fear of death.

Hebrews 2:14

Christ is eternal, God came into the world as a human, and the apostles were eyewitnesses to Jesus' life. We have not seen Christ, but we can trust the writings of those who did see him.

1 John 1:1-3

PRAYER IN PAUL'S LIFE AND LETTERS / *Philippians 1:4*

For Opportunities to Minister

Romans 1:10	One of the things I always pray for is the opportunity, God willing, to come at last to see you.
Philippians 1:19	For I know that as you pray for me and as the Spirit of Jesus Christ helps me, this will all turn out for my deliverance.
Colossians 4:3	Don't forget to pray for us, too, that God will give us many opportunities to preach about his secret plan—that Christ is also for you Gentiles. That is why I am here in chains.
1 Thessalonians 3:10	Night and day we pray earnestly for you, asking God to let us see you again to fill up anything that may still be missing in your faith.

For Knowledge and Insight for Believers

Ephesians 1:18-19	I pray that your hearts will be flooded with light so that you can understand the wonderful future he has promised to those he called. I want you to realize what a rich and glorious inheritance he has given to his people. I pray that you will begin to understand the incredible greatness of his power for us who believe him.
Philippians 1:9	I pray that your love for each other will overflow more and more, and that you will keep on growing in your knowledge and understanding.
Colossians 1:9	So we have continued praying for you ever since we first heard about you. We ask God to give you a complete understanding of what he wants to do in your lives, and we ask him to make you wise with spiritual wisdom.

For Progress and Growth for Believers

2 Corinthians 13:9	We are glad to be weak, if you are really strong. What we pray for is your restoration to maturity.
1 Thessalonians 3:13	As a result, Christ will make your hearts strong, blameless, and holy when you stand before God our Father on that day when our Lord Jesus comes with all those who belong to him.

For the Believers to Live Holy Lives

2 Corinthians 13:7	We pray to God that you will not do anything wrong. We pray this, not to show that our ministry to you has been successful, but because we want you to do right even if we ourselves seem to have failed.
Colossians 1:10	Then the way you live will always honor and please the Lord, and you will continually do good, kind things for others. All the while, you will learn to know God better and better.
2 Thessalonians 1:11	And so we keep on praying for you, that our God will make you worthy of the life to which he called you. And we pray that God, by his power, will fulfill all your good intentions and faithful deeds.

For the Believers to Persevere

Romans 12:12	Be glad for all God is planning for you. Be patient in trouble, and always be prayerful.
Colossians 4:2	Devote yourselves to prayer with an alert mind and a thankful heart.
Colossians 4:12	Epaphras, from your city, a servant of Christ Jesus, sends you his greetings. He always prays earnestly for you, asking God to make you strong and perfect, fully confident of the whole will of God.

To Encourage the Believers

Ephesians 1:16	I have never stopped thanking God for you. I pray for you constantly.
Ephesians 3:16, 19	I pray that from his glorious, unlimited resources he will give you mighty inner strength through his Holy Spirit.
	May you experience the love of Christ, though it is so great you will never fully understand it. Then you will be filled with the fullness of life and power that comes from God.
Colossians 1:3	We always pray for you, and we give thanks to God the Father of our Lord Jesus Christ.
1 Thessalonians 1:2	We always thank God for all of you and pray for you constantly.

For the Spread of the Gospel

Romans 10:1	Dear brothers and sisters, the longing of my heart and my prayer to God is that the Jewish people might be saved.
Ephesians 6:19	And pray for me, too. Ask God to give me the right words as I boldly explain God's secret plan that the Good News is for the Gentiles, too.
2 Thessalonians 3:1	Finally, dear brothers and sisters, I ask you to pray for us. Pray first that the Lord's message will spread rapidly and be honored wherever it goes, just as when it came to you.
Philemon 6	You are generous because of your faith. And I am praying that you will really put your generosity to work, for in so doing you will come to an understanding of all the good things we can do for Christ.

For Others

Philippians 1:4-5	I always pray for you, and I make my requests with a heart full of joy because you have been my partners in spreading the Good News about Christ from the time you first heard it until now.
1 Timothy 2:1	I urge you, first of all, to pray for all people. As you make your requests, plead for God's mercy upon them, and give thanks.
2 Timothy 1:3	Timothy, I thank God for you. He is the God I serve with a clear conscience, just as my ancestors did. Night and day I constantly remember you in my prayers.
Philemon 4	I always thank God when I pray for you, Philemon.

I SAY IT AGAIN, "REJOICE" / *Philippians 3:1*

Paul used forms of the words "joy" and "rejoice" several times in his letter:

1. He referred to believers and their progress in the faith as a cause for joy, particularly those he had led to Christ.

Philippians 2:2	Then make me truly happy by agreeing wholeheartedly with each other, loving one another, and working together with one heart and purpose.
Colossians 2:5	For though I am far away from you, my heart is with you. And I am very happy because you are living as you should and because of your strong faith in Christ.
1 Thessalonians 2:19-20	After all, what gives us hope and joy, and what is our proud reward and crown? It is you! Yes, you will bring us much joy as we stand together before our Lord Jesus when he comes back again. For you are our pride and joy.

   (*See also* Romans 15:32; 16:19; 2 Corinthians 1:24; 7:9, 16; 13:9; Philippians 1:3-5, 25; 4:1; Philemon 7)

2. Many times, Christian joy comes as a result of suffering for Christ. Although it is difficult to grasp this concept, knowing that God is working in salvation produces this joy.

Philippians 2:17-18	But even if my life is to be poured out like a drink offering to complete the sacrifice of your faithful service (that is, if I am to die for you), I will rejoice, and I want to share my joy with all of you. And you should be happy about this and rejoice with me.
Colossians 1:11-12	We also pray that you will be strengthened with his glorious power so that you will have all the patience and endurance you need. May you be filled with joy, always thanking the Father, who has enabled you to share the inheritance that belongs to God's holy people, who live in the light.
Colossians 1:24	I am glad when I suffer for you in my body, for I am completing what remains of Christ's sufferings for his body, the church.

   (*See also* Romans 12:12-15; 1 Corinthians 8:2; 2 Corinthians 6:4-10)

3. Joy is ultimately a gift of the Holy Spirit, not something we can produce in ourselves. It comes as a result of God's love for us.

Romans 14:17	For the Kingdom of God is not a matter of what we eat or drink, but of living a life of goodness and peace and joy in the Holy Spirit.
Romans 15:13	So I pray that God, who gives you hope, will keep you happy and full of peace as you believe in him. May you overflow with hope through the power of the Holy Spirit.
Galatians 5:22	But when the Holy Spirit controls our lives, he will produce this kind of fruit in us: love, joy, peace, patience, kindness, goodness, faithfulness.
1 Thessalonians 1:6	So you received the message with joy from the Holy Spirit in spite of the severe suffering it brought you. In this way, you imitated both us and the Lord.

THREE STAGES OF PERFECTION / *Philippians 3:1*

Perfect Relationship	We are perfect because of our eternal union with the infinitely perfect Christ. When we become his children, we are declared "not guilty" and thus righteous because of what Christ, God's beloved Son, has done for us. This perfection is absolute and unchangeable, and it is this perfect relationship that guarantees that we will one day be "completely perfect" (below). See Colossians 2:8-10; Hebrews 10:8-14.
Perfect Progress	We can grow and mature spiritually as we continue to trust Christ, learn more about him, draw closer to him, and obey him. Our progress is changeable (in contrast to our relationship, above) because it depends on our daily walk—at times in life we mature more than at other times. But we are growing toward perfection if we "keep working" (Philippians 3:12). These good deeds do not perfect us; rather, as God perfects us, we do good deeds for him. See Philippians 3:1-15.
Completely Perfect	When Christ returns to take us into his eternal Kingdom, we will be glorified and made completely perfect. See Philippians 3:20-21. All phases of perfection are grounded in faith in Christ and what he has done, not what we can do for him. We cannot perfect ourselves; only God can work in and through us to "continue his work until it is finally finished on that day Christ Jesus comes back again" (1:6).

TRAINING FOR THE CHRISTIAN LIFE / *Philippians 3:14*

As a great amount of training is needed for athletic activities, so we must train diligently for the Christian life. Such training takes time, dedication, energy, continued practice, and vision. We must commit ourselves to the Christian life, but we must first know the rules as prescribed in God's Word (2 Timothy 2:5).

Reference	Metaphors	Training	Our Goal as Believers
1 Corinthians 9:24-27	Race	Go into strict training in order to get the prize.	We train ourselves to run the race of life. So we keep our eyes on Christ—the goal—and don't get sidetracked or slowed down. When we do this, we will win a reward in Christ's Kingdom.
Philippians 3:13-14	Race	Focus all your energies toward winning the race.	Living the Christian life demands all of our energies. We can forget the past and strain to reach the goal because we know Christ promises eternity with him at the race's end.
1 Timothy 4:7-10	Exercise	Spiritual exercise will help you grow in faith and character.	Just as we exercise to keep physically fit, we must also train ourselves to be spiritually fit. As our faith develops, we become better Christians, living in accordance with God's will. Such a life will attract others to Christ and pay dividends in both this life and the next.
2 Timothy 4:7-8	Fight Race	Fighting the good fight and persevering to the end.	The Christian life is a fight against evil forces from without and temptation from within. If we stay true to God through it all, he promises an end, a rest, and a crown.

COLOSSIANS

MEGATHEMES IN COLOSSIANS

Theme	Explanation	Importance
Christ Is God	Jesus Christ is God in the flesh, Lord of all creation, and Lord of the new creation. He is the expressed reflection of the invisible God. He is eternal, preexistent, omnipotent, and equal with the Father. He is supreme and complete.	Because Christ is supreme, our life must be Christ-centered. To recognize him as God means to regard our relationship with him as most vital and to make his interests our top priority.
Christ Is Head of the Church	Because Christ is God, he is the head of the church, his true believers. Christ is the founder, the leader, and the highest authority on earth. He requires first place in all our thoughts and activities.	To acknowledge Christ as our head, we must welcome his leadership in all we do or think. No person, group, or church can regard any loyalty as more critical than that of loyalty to Christ.
Union with Christ	Because our sin has been forgiven and we have been reconciled to God, we have a union with Christ that can never be broken. In our faith connection with him, we identify with his death, burial, and resurrection.	We should live in constant contact and communication with God. When we do, we all will be unified with Christ and with one another.
Man-Made Religion	False teachers were promoting a heresy that stressed self-made rules (legalism). They also sought spiritual growth by discipline of the body (asceticism) and visions (mysticism). This search created pride in their self-centered efforts.	We must not cling to our own ideas and try to blend them into Christianity. Nor should we let our hunger for a more fulfilling Christian experience cause us to trust in a teacher, a group, or a system of thought more than in Christ himself. Christ is our hope and our true source of wisdom.

LOCATION OF COLOSSE / *Colossians 1:1-2; 2:1-5*

Paul had no doubt been through Laodicea on his third missionary journey, as it lay on the main route to Ephesus, but he had never been to Colosse. Though a large city with a significant population, Colosse was smaller and less important than the nearby cities of Laodicea and Hierapolis.

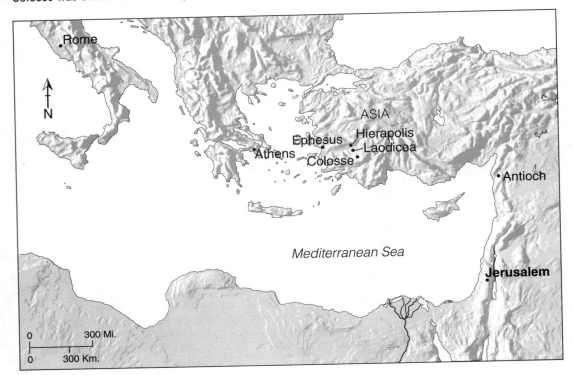

Copyright © 2001 by Tyndale House Publishers

THE COLOSSIAN HERESY / *Colossians 1:15*

Paul answered the various tenets of the Colossian heresy that threatened the church. This heresy was a "mixed bag," containing elements from several different heresies, some of which contradicted each other (as the chart shows).

The Heresy	Reference	Paul's Answer
Spirit is good; matter is evil.	1:15-20	God created heaven and earth for his glory.
One must follow ceremonies, rituals, and restrictions in order to be saved or perfected.	2:11, 16-23; 3:11	These were only shadows that ended when Christ came. He is all you need to be saved.
One must deny the body and live in strict asceticism.	2:20-23	Asceticism is no help in conquering evil thoughts and desires; instead, it leads to pride.
Angels must be worshiped.	2:18	Angels are not to be worshiped; Christ alone is worthy of worship.
Christ could not be both human and divine.	1:15-20; 2:2-3	Christ is God in the flesh; he is the eternal one, head of the body, first in everything, supreme.
One must obtain "secret knowledge" in order to be saved or perfected—and this was not available to everyone.	2:2, 18	God's secret is Christ, and he has been revealed to all.
One must adhere to human wisdom, tradition, and philosophies.	2:4, 8-10; 3:15-17	By themselves, these can be misleading and shallow because they have human origin; instead, we should remember what Christ taught and follow his words as our ultimate authority.
It is even better to combine aspects of several religions.	2:10	You have everything when you have Christ; he is all-sufficient.
There is nothing wrong with immorality.	3:1-11	Get rid of sin and evil because you have been chosen by God to live a new life as a representative of the Lord Jesus.

HOW TO PRAY FOR OTHER CHRISTIANS / *Colossians 1*

1. Be thankful for their faith and changed lives (1:3).
2. Ask God to help them know what he wants them to do (1:9).
3. Ask God to give them deep spiritual understanding (1:9).
4. Ask God to help them live for him (1:10).
5. Ask God to give them more knowledge of himself (1:10).
6. Ask God to give them strength for endurance (1:11).
7. Ask God to fill them with joy, strength, and thankfulness (1:11).

How many people in your life could be touched if you prayed in this way?

WHO IS CHRIST? / *Colossians 1:20*

Colossians 1:15-20 lists seven characteristics of Christ:

1. The visible image of the invisible God 1:15
2. Existed before God made anything. 1:15
3. He is the one through whom God created everything 1:16
4. He is the head of the body, the church 1:18
5. He is the first of all who will rise from the dead 1:18
6. All God's fullness lives in him. 1:19
7. Through Christ, God was pleased to reconcile to himself all things . . . 1:20

Because of who Christ is:
- we ought to worship him with praise and thanks
- we ought to learn about him for he is God
- we ought to obey him for he is the ultimate authority
- we ought to love him for what he has done for us

CALLED TO SUFFER / *Colossians 1:24*

Paul never feared suffering for he knew that God was in control, that his suffering helped others to be more courageous in spreading the gospel, and that one day all suffering would end and he (along with all believers) would be with the Father. The New Testament abounds with warnings about and words of comfort in suffering.

Speaker	Reference	Words about Suffering
Jesus	Matthew 5:10-12	Those who are persecuted are called "blessed."
Jesus	Matthew 20:23	The Son of Man will return and end all suffering.
Jesus	John 15:20	Jesus was persecuted; we will be persecuted.
The apostles	Acts 5:41	We can rejoice at being worthy to suffer for Christ.
Jesus	Acts 9:16	Paul was called to suffer for Jesus' name.
Paul	Romans 8:17	As children and heirs, we will share in Jesus' suffering.
Paul	2 Corinthians 1:3-7	God gives comfort in suffering.
Paul	2 Corinthians 4:7-12	Paul suffered so that others might be saved.
Paul	2 Corinthians 6:4-5, 9-10	Paul suffered, yet rejoiced.
Paul	Ephesians 3:13	Our sufferings can glorify God.
Paul	Philippians 1:29	Suffering for Christ's name is a privilege.
Paul	2 Timothy 1:12	We must not be ashamed of suffering; trust Christ.
Paul	2 Timothy 2:10	Paul suffered for the sake of other believers.
Paul	2 Timothy 3:11	God will rescue us from suffering—now or in eternity.
Paul	2 Timothy 4:5	We are called to endure hardship.
Author of Hebrews	Hebrews 10:32-34	We can face suffering knowing we have God's inheritance.
James	James 1:2	We can consider it pure joy to face trials.
Peter	1 Peter 1:6	Our suffering is refining our faith.
Peter	1 Peter 2:21	We suffer because Christ suffered.
Peter	1 Peter 3:13-14	We are blessed for suffering for what is right.
Peter	1 Peter 4:1, 13, 16	We suffer yet rejoice because we suffer for Christ.
Peter	1 Peter 5:9-10	Resist Satan, stand firm, God is with you.
Jesus	Revelation 2:10	We must be faithful, even to death; the crown of life awaits us.

TRUST: YESTERDAY, TODAY, AND TOMORROW! / *Colossians 2:7*

Living under the lordship of Christ means realizing that each day brings new opportunities to trust Christ and experience his powerful work in us. Have you trusted this day to Christ?

Trusting Christ	= Living in vital union with Christ day by day (2:2-7)
Accepting Christ as Head or Lord	= He is in control (1:15-18; 2:19; 3:10-17)
Experiencing the power of the Holy Spirit	= God's mighty energy at work in us (1:11, 28-29)
Inward and outward results	= Assurance of forgiveness (2:15) Freedom from evil desires (2:11) Joy (2:7) Personal growth (1:28) Opportunities to tell others the gospel (1:4, 28) Thankfulness to God (2:7)
Direction	= God becoming involved in our decisions (3:1, 16)

SALVATION THROUGH FAITH / *Colossians 2:16-23*

Salvation through faith in Christ sounds too easy for many people. They would rather think that they have done something to save themselves. Their religion becomes one of self-effort that leads either to disappointment or pride, but finally to eternal death. Christ's simple way is the only way, and it alone leads to eternal life.

	Religion by Self-effort	Salvation through Faith
Goal	Please God by our own good deeds	Trust in Christ and then live to please God
Means	Practice, diligent service, discipline, and obedience in hope of reward	Confess, submit, and commit yourself to Christ's control
Power	Good, honest effort through self-determination	The Holy Spirit in us helps us do good work for Christ's kingdom
Control	Self-motivation, self-control	Christ in me; I in Christ
Results	Chronic guilt, apathy, depression, failure, constant desire for approval	Joy, thankfulness, love, guidance, service, forgiveness

FROM DEATH TO LIFE / *Colossians 3:3*

The Bible uses many illustrations to teach what happens when we choose to let Jesus be Lord of our life. Following are some of the most vivid pictures:

Because Christ died for us, we have been crucified with him.	Romans 6:2-13; 7:4-6 2 Corinthians 5:14 Galatians 2:20; 5:24; 6:14 Colossians 2:20; 3:3-5 1 Peter 2:24
Our old, rebellious nature died with Christ.	Romans 6:6; 7:4-6 Colossians 3:9-10
Christ's resurrection guarantees our new life now and eternal life with him later.	Romans 6:4, 11 Colossians 2:12-13; 3:1, 3

This process is acted out in baptism (Colossians 2:12), based on our faith in Christ:

1. The old sinful nature dies (crucified).
2. We are ready to receive a new life (buried).
3. Christ gives us new life (resurrected).

SINS VS. SIGNS OF LOVE / *Colossians 3:5-13*

In Colossians 3:5 Paul tells us to put to death the things found in list 1. In 3:8-9 he tells us to rid ourselves of the things found in list 2. In 3:12-13 we're told to practice the things found in list 3. List 1 deals with sins of sexual attitudes and behavior—they are particularly destructive because of what they do to destroy any group or church. List 2 deals with sins of speech—these are the relationship breakers. List 3 contains the relationship builders, which we are to express as members of Christ's body.

Sins of Sexual Attitude and Behavior	Sins of Speech	Signs of Love
Shameful desires	Anger	Mercy
Sexual sin	Malicious behavior	Kindness
Impurity	Slander	Humility
Lust	Dirty language	Gentleness
Greed	Lying	Patience
		Forgiveness

RULES OF SUBMISSION / *Colossians 3:18–4:1*

The New Testament includes many instructions concerning relationships. Most people read these instructions for the other person and ignore the ones that apply to themselves. But you can't control another person's behavior, only your own. Start by following your own instructions and not insisting on the obedience of others first.

Wives, submit to your husbands (3:18).	Husbands, love your wives and don't be harsh with them (3:19).
Children, obey your parents (3:20).	Parents, don't aggravate your children so that they become discouraged (3:21).
Slaves, obey your masters (3:22).	Masters, be just and fair to your slaves (4:1).
(Employees, work hard for your employers.)	(Employers, be just and fair with your employees.)

1 THESSALONIANS

MEGATHEMES IN 1 THESSALONIANS

Theme	Explanation	Importance
Persecution	Paul and the new Christians at Thessalonica experienced persecution because of their faith in Christ. We can expect trials and troubles as well. We need to stand firm in our faith in the midst of trials, being strengthened by the Holy Spirit.	The Holy Spirit helps us to remain strong in faith, able to show genuine love to others and maintain our moral character even when we are being persecuted, slandered, or oppressed.
Paul's Ministry	Paul expressed his concern for this church even while he was being slandered. Paul's commitment to share the gospel in spite of difficult circumstances is a model we should follow.	Paul not only delivered his message, but gave of himself. In our ministries, we must become like Paul—faithful and bold, yet sensitive and self-sacrificing.
Hope	One day all believers, both those who are alive and those who have died, will be united with Christ. To those Christians who die before Christ's return, there is hope—the hope of the resurrection of the body.	If we believe in Christ, we will live with him forever. All those who belong to Jesus Christ—from throughout history—will be present with him at his second coming. We can be confident that we will be with loved ones who have trusted in Christ.
Being Prepared	No one knows the time of Christ's return. We are to live moral and holy lives, ever watchful for his coming. Believers must not neglect daily responsibilities, but always work and live to please the Lord.	The gospel is not only what we believe but also what we must live. The Holy Spirit leads us in faithfulness, so we can avoid lust and fraud. Live as though you expect Christ's return at any time. Don't be caught unprepared.

LOCATION OF THESSALONICA / *1 Thessalonians 1:1-10*

Paul visited Thessalonica on his second and third missionary journeys. It was a seaport and trade center located on the Egnatian Way, a busy international highway. After Paul visited Thessalonica on his second missionary journey, he went on to Berea, Athens, and Corinth (Acts 17–18). From Corinth, Paul wrote his two letters to the Thessalonian church.

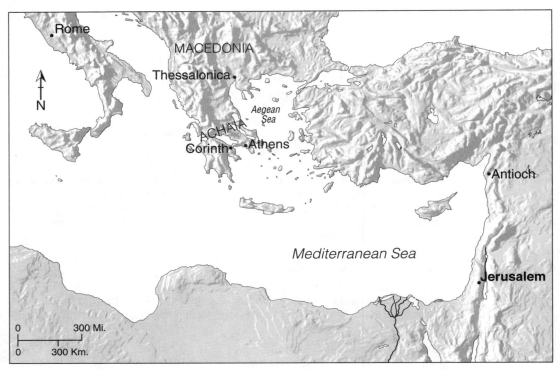

Copyright © 2001 by Tyndale House Publishers

FAITH, HOPE, AND LOVE / *1 Thessalonians 1:3*

In our days of complex formulas, this simple program for Christian living still holds true.

Romans 5:1-5	"Therefore, since we have been made right in God's sight by faith . . . Because of our faith, Christ has brought us into this place of highest privilege where we now stand, . . . God loves us, because he has given us the Holy Spirit to fill our hearts with his love."
1 Corinthians 13:13	"There are three things that will endure—faith, hope, and love— and the greatest of these is love."
Galatians 5:5-6	"But we who live by the Spirit eagerly wait to receive everything promised to us who are right with God through faith. . . . What is important is faith expressing itself in love."
Ephesians 1:15-18	"Ever since I first heard of your strong faith . . . and your love . . . I have never stopped thanking God for you."
Ephesians 4:2-5	"Making allowance for each other's faults because of your love. . . . Always keep yourselves united in the Holy Spirit, and bind yourselves together with peace. . . . There is only one Lord, one faith, one baptism."
Colossians 1:4	"Love all of God's people."
1 Thessalonians 5:8	"But let us who live in the light think clearly, protected by the body armor of faith and love, and wearing as our helmet the confidence of our salvation."
Hebrews 6:10-12	"And how you have shown your love to him by caring for other Christians. Our great desire is that you will keep right on loving others as long as life lasts, in order to make certain that what you hope for will come true. Instead, you will follow the example of those who are going to inherit God's promises because of their faith and patience."
Hebrews 10:23-24	"Without wavering, let us hold tightly to the hope we say we have, for God can be trusted to keep his promise. Think of ways to encourage one another to outbursts of love and good deeds."
1 Peter 1:5,7-8	"And God, in his mighty power, will protect you until you receive this salvation, because you are trusting him. . . . These trials are only to test your faith, to show that it is strong and pure. It is being tested as fire tests and purifies gold—and your faith is far more precious to God than mere gold. So if your faith remains strong after being tried by fiery trials, it will bring you much praise and glory and honor on the day when Jesus Christ is revealed to the whole world. . . . You love him even though you have never seen him."
1 Peter 1:21-22	"Your faith and hope can be placed confidently in God. Now you can have sincere love for each other as brothers and sisters because you were cleansed from your sins when you accepted the truth of the Good News. So see to it that you really do love each other intensely with all your hearts."

CHARACTERISTICS OF A CHRISTIAN MINISTER
1 Thessalonians 2:3-12

First Thessalonians 2 gives a rich description of how a true Christian minister (missionary, pastor, teacher) should look. Too often the bad examples are paraded in the media, while the many solid, Spirit-filled servants of God get little notice. Believers ought to be able to distinguish godly ministers from frauds, and Paul gave several ways to know.

Verse	A Godly Minister . . .
2:3. . . .	speaks the truth and has pure motives in doing so
2:4. . . .	seeks to please God, not people
2:5. . . .	does not flatter; is not greedy
2:6. . . .	does not seek people's praise
2:7. . . .	is gentle, like a mother caring for her children
2:8. . . .	loves the believers and willingly shares his life and the gospel with them
2:9. . . .	works hard so as not to be a burden to anyone while preaching the Good News
2:10 . . .	is pure, honest, and faultless toward the believers
2:11 . . .	treats the believers as a good father would treat his own children
2:12 . . .	willingly pleads, encourages, and urges the believers to live in a way that God would consider worthy

THE EVENTS OF CHRIST'S RETURN / 1 Thessalonians 4:15-17

While Christians have often disagreed about what events will lead up to the return of Christ, there has been less disagreement about what will happen once he does return.

1. Christ will return visibly, with a loud command.

2. There will be an unmistakable cry from an angel.

3. There will be a trumpet fanfare such as has never been heard.

4. Believers in Christ who are dead will rise from their graves.

5. Believers who are alive will be caught up in the clouds to meet Christ.

PAUL'S PRAYERS / *1 Thessalonians 3:10*

Reference	Paul prayed . . .
Romans 10:1	. . . that the Jews might be saved by believing in Jesus Christ.
2 Corinthians 13:7, 9	. . . that the believers would not do anything wrong, but would pass the test and be made perfect in Christ.
Ephesians 1:17	. . . that the believers would be given the Spirit of wisdom and revelation so that they would know God better.
Ephesians 3:16-19	. . . that the believers would be filled with the Holy Spirit and experience God's love in its fullness.
Philippians 1:4, 9	. . . that the believers' love for one another would abound more and more in knowledge, depth, and insight.
Colossians 1:9	. . . that the believers would have a knowledge of God's will and be made wise with spiritual wisdom.
1 Thessalonians 3:10	. . . that he and his coworkers could return to the believers and teach them further.
2 Thessalonians 1:11	. . . that God would make the believers worthy of the life to which he called them, and that God would fulfill all their good intentions and faithful deeds.
Philemon 1:6	. . . that Philemon would be active in sharing his faith.

Paul also requested that the believers pray for him:

Reference	Paul requested . . .
Romans 15:30-31	. . . that they join in his struggle for the churches, that he would be rescued from the Jews who persecuted him, and that the Christians would accept the financial gift he was delivering from all the churches.
Ephesians 6:19-20	. . . that God would give him the right words to share the Good News and that he would be able to keep on speaking boldly, despite his chains.
Colossians 4:3	. . . that God would give him and his coworkers many opportunities to preach the Good News.
1 Thessalonians 5:25	. . . that believers pray for him: "Brothers and sisters, pray for us."
2 Thessalonians 3:1	. . . that God's message would spread rapidly and be honored.
2 Thessalonians 3:2	. . . that God would save them from wicked and evil people.

PASSAGES ABOUT CHRIST'S SECOND COMING
1 Thessalonians 5:2

Matthew 13:40-43	"I, the Son of Man, will send my angels, and they will remove from my Kingdom everything that causes sin and all who do evil. . . . Then the godly will shine like the sun."
Matthew 24:27	"For as the lightning lights up the entire sky, so it will be when the Son of Man comes."
Matthew 26:64 (see also Mark 14:62)	"In the future you will see me, the Son of Man, sitting at God's right hand in the place of power and coming back on the clouds of heaven."
Mark 13:24-27	"The sun will be darkened, the moon will not give light, the stars will fall from the sky . . . and he will send forth his angels to gather his chosen ones from all over the world."
Luke 21:25-28	"And down here on earth the nations will be in turmoil, perplexed by the roaring seas and strange tides. The courage of many people will falter because of the fearful fate they see coming upon the earth."
John 14:1-3	"I am going to prepare a place for you. . . . When everything is ready, I will come and get you, so that you will always be with me where I am."
Acts 1:9-11	"Jesus has been taken away from you into heaven. And someday, just as you saw him go, he will return!"
Acts 3:19-21	"[God] will send Jesus your Messiah to you again. For he must remain in heaven until the time for the final restoration of all things, as God promised long ago through his prophets."
1 Corinthians 15:51-53	"None of us will die, but we will all be transformed. . . . For when the trumpet sounds, the Christians who have died will be raised with transformed bodies. And then we who are living will be transformed so that we will never die."
Philippians 3:20-21	"We are citizens of heaven . . . and we are eagerly waiting for him to return as our Savior. He will take these weak mortal bodies of ours and change them into glorious bodies like his own."
1 Thessalonians 2:19	"You will bring us much joy as we stand together before our Lord Jesus when he comes back again."
1 Thessalonians 3:13	"Christ will make your hearts strong, blameless, and holy when you stand before God our Father on that day when our Lord Jesus comes with all those who belong to him."
1 Thessalonians 4:13-18	"When Jesus comes, God will bring back with Jesus all the Christians who have died. . . . The Lord himself will come down from heaven. . . . First, all the Christians who have died will rise from their graves. Then, together with them, we who are still alive and remain on the earth will be caught up in the clouds to meet the Lord in the air and remain with him forever."
1 Thessalonians 5:23	"Now may the God of peace make you holy in every way, and may your whole spirit and soul and body be kept blameless until that day when our Lord Jesus Christ comes again."
2 Thessalonians 1:7-8	"He will come with his mighty angels, in flaming fire, bringing judgment on those who don't know God and on those who refuse to obey the Good News of our Lord Jesus."
2 Thessalonians 2:1-17	"That day will not come until there is a great rebellion against God and the man of lawlessness is revealed. . . . He will exalt himself and defy every god there is. . . . The Lord Jesus will consume [him] with the breath of his mouth and destroy [him] by the splendor of his coming."

PASSAGES ABOUT CHRIST'S SECOND COMING
1 Thessalonians 5:2 Continued

1 Timothy 6:14-15	"For at the right time Christ will be revealed from heaven by the blessed and only almighty God, the King of kings and Lord of lords."
2 Timothy 4:1-8	"Christ Jesus . . . will someday judge the living and the dead when he appears to set up his Kingdom. . . . Now the prize awaits me—the crown of righteousness that the Lord, the righteous Judge, will give me on that great day of his return. And the prize is . . . for all who eagerly look forward to his glorious return."
Titus 2:12-13	"We should live in this evil world with self-control, right conduct, and devotion to God, while we look forward to that wonderful event when the glory of our great God and Savior, Jesus Christ, will be revealed."
Hebrews 9:28	"Christ died only once as a sacrifice to take away the sins of many people. He will come again but not to deal with our sins again. This time he will bring salvation to all those who are eagerly waiting for him."
James 5:7-8	"You must be patient as you wait for the Lord's return. . . . Take courage, for the coming of the Lord is near."
1 Peter 1:7, 13	"If your faith remains strong after being tried by fiery trials, it will bring you much praise and glory and honor on the day when Jesus Christ is revealed to the whole world. . . . Look forward to the special blessings that will come to you at the return of Jesus Christ."
1 Peter 4:12-13	"These trials will make you partners with Christ in his suffering, and afterward you will have the wonderful joy of sharing his glory when it is displayed to all the world."
1 Peter 5:4	"And when the head Shepherd comes, your reward will be a never-ending share in his glory and honor."
2 Peter 3:1-14	"A day is like a thousand years to the Lord, and a thousands years is like a day. The Lord isn't really being slow about his promise to return, as some people think. No, he is being patient for your sake. He does not want anyone to perish, so he is giving more time for everyone to repent. But the day of the Lord will come as unexpectedly as a thief. Then the heavens will pass away with a terrible noise and everything in them will disappear in fire."
1 John 2:28–3:2	"Continue to live in fellowship with Christ so that when he returns, you will be full of courage and not shrink back from him in shame. . . . We can't even imagine what we will be like when Christ returns. But we do know that when he comes we will be like him, for we will see him as he really is."
Jude 1:14	"Look, the Lord is coming with thousands of his holy ones."
Revelation 1:7	"Look! He comes with the clouds of heaven. And everyone will see him."
Revelation 3:10	"Because you have obeyed my command to persevere, I will protect you from the great time of testing that will come upon the whole world to test those who belong to this world."
Revelation 19:11–20:6	"Then I saw heaven opened, and a white horse was standing there. And the one sitting on the horse was named Faithful and True."
Revelation 22:7, 12, 20	"Look, I am coming soon! . . . My reward is with me, to repay all according to their deeds" . . . Amen! Come, Lord Jesus!

GOD IS FAITHFUL / *1 Thessalonians 5:24*

When thinking of faithfulness, a friend or spouse may come to mind. People who are faithful to us accept and love us, even when we are unlovable. Faithful people keep their promises, whether promises of support or promises made in marriage vows. God's faithfulness is like human faithfulness, only perfect. His love is absolute, and his promises are irrevocable. He loves us in spite of our constant bent toward sin, and he keeps all the promises he has made to us, even when we break our promises to him. Listed below are a few of the verses that describe God's faithfulness:

Reference	Verse
Exodus 34:6	"I am the LORD, I am the LORD, the merciful and gracious God. I am slow to anger and rich in unfailing love and faithfulness."
Deuteronomy 7:9	"Understand, therefore, that the LORD your God is indeed God. He is the faithful God who keeps his covenant for a thousand generations and constantly loves those who love him and obey his commands."
Deuteronomy 32:4	"He is the Rock; his work is perfect. Everything he does is just and fair. He is a faithful God who does no wrong; how just and upright he is!"
Psalm 33:4	"For the word of the LORD is right and true; he is faithful in all he does" (NIV).
Psalm 36:5	"Your unfailing love, O LORD, is as vast as the heavens; your faithfulness reaches beyond the clouds."
Psalm 89:1-2, 5, 8	"I will sing of the tender mercies of the LORD forever! Young and old will hear of your faithfulness. Your unfailing love will last forever. Your faithfulness is as enduring as the heavens. . . . All heaven will praise your miracles, LORD; myriads of angels will praise you for your faithfulness. . . . O LORD God Almighty! Where is there anyone as mighty as you, LORD? Faithfulness is your very character."
Psalm 91:4	"He will shield you with his wings. He will shelter you with his feathers. His faithful promises are your armor and protection."
Psalm 100:5	"For the LORD is good. His unfailing love continues forever, and his faithfulness to each generation."
Psalm 117:2	"For he loves us with unfailing love; the faithfulness of the LORD endures forever. Praise the LORD!"
Psalm 145:13	"For your kingdom is an everlasting kingdom. You rule generation after generation. The LORD is faithful in all he says; he is gracious in all he does."
Lamentations 3:22-23	"The unfailing love of the LORD never ends! By his mercies we have been kept from complete destruction. Great is his faithfulness; his mercies begin afresh each day."
1 Corinthians 10:13	"But remember that the temptations that come into your life are no different from what others experience. God is faithful. He will keep the temptation from becoming so strong that you can't stand up against it."

Reference	Verse
1 Thessalonians 5:24	"God, who calls you, is faithful; he will do this."
2 Thessalonians 3:3	"But the Lord is faithful; he will make you strong and guard you from the evil one."
Hebrews 10:23	"Without wavering, let us hold tightly to the hope we say we have, for God can be trusted to keep his promise."
1 Peter 4:19	"So then, those who suffer according to God's will should commit themselves to their faithful Creator and continue to do good."
1 John 1:9	"But if we confess our sins to him, he is faithful and just to forgive us and to cleanse us from every wrong."
Revelation 19:11	"Then I saw heaven opened, and a white horse was standing there. And the one sitting on the horse was named Faithful and True."

CHECKLIST FOR ENCOURAGERS / *1 Thessalonians 5:11-23*

The command to "encourage" others is found throughout the Bible. In 5:11-23, Paul gives many specific examples of how we can encourage others.

Reference	Example	Suggested Application
5:11	Build each other up.	Point out to someone a quality you appreciate in him or her.
5:12	Respect leaders.	Look for ways to cooperate.
5:13	Hold leaders in highest regard.	Hold back your next critical comments about those in positions of responsibility. Say "thank you" to your leaders for their efforts.
5:13	Live in peace.	Search for ways to get along with others.
5:14	Warn the lazy.	Challenge someone to join you in a project.
5:14	Encourage the timid.	Encourage those who are timid by reminding them of God's promises.
5:14	Help the weak.	Support those who are weak by loving them and praying for them.
5:14	Be patient.	Think of a situation that tries your patience, and plan ahead of time how you can stay calm.
5:15	Resist revenge.	Instead of planning to get even with those who mistreat you, do good to them.
5:16	Be joyful.	Remember that even in the midst of turmoil, God is in control.
5:17	Pray continually.	God is always with you—talk to him.
5:18	Give thanks.	Make a list of all the gifts God has given you, giving thanks to God for each one.
5:19	Do not stifle the Holy Spirit.	Cooperate with the Spirit the next time he prompts you to participate in a Christian meeting.
5:20	Do not scoff at prophecies.	Receive God's word from those who speak for him.
5:22	Avoid every kind of evil.	Avoid situations where you will be drawn into temptation.
5:23	Count on God's constant help.	Realize that the Christian life is to be lived not in our own strength but through God's power.

2 THESSALONIANS

MEGATHEMES IN 2 THESSALONIANS

Theme	Explanation	Importance
Persecution	Paul encouraged the church to persevere in spite of troubles and trials. God will bring victory to his faithful followers and judge those who persecute them.	God promises to reward our faith by giving us his power and helping us bear persecution. Suffering for our faith will strengthen us to serve Christ. We must be faithful to him.
Christ's Return	Since Paul had said that the Lord could come at any moment, some of the Thessalonian believers had stopped working in order to wait for Christ.	Christ will return and bring total victory to all who trust in him. If we are ready, we need not be concerned about *when* he will return. We should stand firm, keep working, and wait for Christ.
Great Rebellion	Before Christ's return, there will be a great rebellion against God led by the man of lawlessness (the Antichrist). God will remove all the restraints on evil before he brings judgment on the rebels. The Antichrist will attempt to deceive many.	We should not be afraid when we see evil increase. God is in control, no matter how evil the world becomes. God guards us during Satan's attacks. We can have victory over evil by remaining faithful to God.
Persistence	Because church members had quit working and become disorderly and disobedient, Paul chastised them for their idleness. He called on them to show courage and true Christian conduct.	We must never get so tired of doing right that we quit. We can be persistent by making the most of our time and talents. Our endurance will be rewarded.

THEOLOGY OF TRIALS IN THE NEW TESTAMENT
2 Thessalonians 1:4

As we live for Christ, we will experience troubles because we are trying to be God's people in a perverse world. Some people say that troubles are the result of sin or lack of faith, but the Bible teaches that they may be a part of God's plan for believers. Our problems can help us look upward and forward, instead of inward; they can build strong character; and they can provide us with opportunities to comfort others who are also struggling. Your troubles may be an indication that you are taking a stand for Christ.

Trial	Verse
Suffering is not always the result of sin.	John 9:2-3 . . . "Teacher," his disciples asked him, "why was this man born blind? Was it a result of his own sins or those of his parents?" "It was not because of his sins or his parents' sins," Jesus answered. "He was born blind so the power of God could be seen in him."
God provides hope and love in suffering.	Romans 5:3-5 . . . We can rejoice, too, when we run into problems and trials, for we know that they are good for us—they help us learn to endure. And endurance develops strength of character in us, and character strengthens our confident expectation of salvation. And this expectation will not disappoint us. For we know how dearly God loves us, because he has given us the Holy Spirit to fill our hearts with his love.
Problems help us trust in God's sovereign purpose for our lives.	Romans 8:28-29 . . . And we know that God causes everything to work together for the good of those who love God and are called according to his purpose for them. For God knew his people in advance, and he chose them to become like his Son, so that his Son would be the firstborn, with many brothers and sisters.
Suffering enables us to comfort others.	1 Corinthians 1:3-5 . . . May God our Father and the Lord Jesus Christ give you his grace and peace. I can never stop thanking God for all the generous gifts he has given you, now that you belong to Christ Jesus. He has enriched your church with the gifts of eloquence and every kind of knowledge.
Our eternal reward outweighs our suffering.	2 Corinthians 4:17-18 . . . For our present troubles are quite small and won't last very long. Yet they produce for us an immeasurably great glory that will last forever! So we don't look at the troubles we can see right now; rather, we look forward to what we have not yet seen. For the troubles we see will soon be over, but the joys to come will last forever.
Problems open up opportunities for service.	Philippians 1:12 . . . And I want you to know, dear brothers and sisters, that everything that has happened to me here has helped to spread the Good News.
Problems may be a confirmation that we are living for Christ.	2 Thessalonians 1:5 . . . But God will use this persecution to show his justice. For he will make you worthy of his Kingdom, for which you are suffering.

THEOLOGY OF TRIALS IN THE NEW TESTAMENT
2 Thessalonians 1:4 Continued

Trial	Verse
God uses suffering in his plan for our lives.	2 Thessalonians 1:1-3 . . . This letter is from Paul, Silas, and Timothy. It is written to the church in Thessalonica, you who belong to God our Father and the Lord Jesus Christ. May God our Father and the Lord Jesus Christ give you grace and peace. Dear brothers and sisters, we always thank God for you, as is right, for we are thankful that your faith is flourishing and you are all growing in love for each other.
Through his suffering, Jesus fully identified with us.	Hebrews 2:18 . . . Since he himself has gone through suffering and temptation, he is able to help us when we are being tempted.
Jesus was willing to obey God even when it meant suffering.	Hebrews 5:8 . . . So even though Jesus was God's Son, he learned obedience from the things he suffered.
Trials help train us to be more fruitful.	Hebrews 12:11 . . . No discipline is enjoyable while it is happening—it is painful! But afterward there will be a quiet harvest of right living for those who are trained in this way.
Problems help us mature.	James 1:2-4 . . . Dear brothers and sisters, whenever trouble comes your way, let it be an opportunity for joy. For when your faith is tested, your endurance has a chance to grow. So let it grow, for when your endurance is fully developed, you will be strong in character and ready for anything.
Trials help refine our character.	1 Peter 1:6-9 . . . So be truly glad! There is wonderful joy ahead, even though it is necessary for you to endure many trials for a while. These trials are only to test your faith, to show that it is strong and pure. It is being tested as fire tests and purifies gold—and your faith is far more precious to God than mere gold. So if your faith remains strong after being tried by fiery trials, it will bring you much praise and glory and honor on the day when Jesus Christ is revealed to the whole world. You love him even though you have never seen him. Though you do not see him, you trust him; and even now you are happy with a glorious, inexpressible joy. Your reward for trusting him will be the salvation of your souls.
When we suffer, we share in the suffering of Christ.	1 Peter 4:12-14 . . . Dear friends, don't be surprised at the fiery trials you are going through, as if something strange were happening to you. Instead, be very glad—because these trials will make you partners with Christ in his suffering, and afterward you will have the wonderful joy of sharing his glory when it is displayed to all the world. Be happy if you are insulted for being a Christian, for then the glorious Spirit of God will come upon you.

TROUBLE IN THE CHURCH / *2 Thessalonians 2:1-2*

The second letter to the Thessalonians mentions three groups of people who were troubling the church in Thessalonica.

Persecutors	2 Thessalonians 1:4-10 (see also 1 Thessalonians 1:6; 2:14; 3:3)
False teachers	2 Thessalonians 2:2-3
Lazy people (loafers)	2 Thessalonians 3:6-15 (see also 1 Thessalonians 5:14)

GREAT REBELLION / *2 Thessalonians 2:3*

The New Testament warns about this time of great rebellion:

Matthew 24:10-13	Many will turn away from me. . . . Many false prophets will appear. . . . Sin will be rampant everywhere, and the love of many will grow cold.
John 15:21-22	The people of the world will hate you because you belong to me, for they don't know God who sent me. . . . They have no excuse for their sin.
1 Timothy 4:1-3	In the last times some will turn away . . . they will follow lying spirits and teachings that come from demons.
2 Timothy 3:1-9	In the last days there will be very difficult times. For people will love only themselves and their money. They will be boastful and proud, scoffing at God. . . . They will consider nothing sacred. . . . They will act as if they are religious, but they will reject the power that could make them godly.
2 Peter 3:3-5	In the last days there will be scoffers who will laugh at the truth and do every evil thing they desire. This will be their argument: "Jesus promised to come back, did he? Where is he?"
Jude 1:17-19	In the last times there would be scoffers whose purpose in life is to enjoy themselves in every way imaginable. . . . They live by natural instinct because they do not have God's Spirit living in them.
Revelation 3:10	Because you have obeyed my command to persevere, I will protect you from the great time of testing that will come upon the whole world to test those who belong to this world.

1 TIMOTHY

MEGATHEMES IN 1 TIMOTHY

Theme	Explanation	Importance
Sound Doctrine	Paul instructed Timothy to preserve the Christian faith by teaching sound doctrine and modeling right living. Timothy had to oppose false teachers, who were leading church members away from belief in salvation by faith in Jesus Christ alone.	We must know the truth in order to defend it. We must cling to the belief that Christ came to save us. We should stay away from those who twist the words of the Bible for their own purposes.
Public Worship	Prayer in public worship must be done with a proper attitude toward God and fellow believers.	Christian character must be evident in every aspect of worship. We must rid ourselves of any anger, resentment, or offensive behavior that might disrupt worship or damage church unity.
Church Leadership	Paul gives specific instructions concerning the qualifications for church leaders so that the church might honor God and operate smoothly.	Church leaders must be wholly committed to Christ. If you are a new or young Christian, don't be anxious to become a leader in the church. Seek to develop your Christian character first. Be sure to seek God, not your own ambition.
Personal Discipline	It takes discipline to be a leader in the church. Timothy, like all pastors, had to guard his motives, minister faithfully, and live above reproach. Any pastor must keep morally and spiritually fit.	To stay in good spiritual shape, you must discipline yourself to study God's Word and to obey it. Put your spiritual abilities to work!
Caring Church	The church has a responsibility to care for the needs of all its members, especially the sick, the poor, and the widowed. Caring must go beyond good intentions.	Caring for the family of believers demonstrates our Christlike attitude and exhibits genuine love to nonbelievers.

CHRIST OUR MEDIATOR / *1 Timothy 2:5-6*

God chose the Lord Jesus to be the mediator between God and people. The Son of God, the second person of the Trinity, is the eternal God—equal with the Father. But he willingly took on himself the nature of a man; yet he was without sin. These two complete, perfect, and distinct natures—Godhead and manhood—were inseparably joined in the person of Jesus without being altered or jumbled. Jesus is truly God and truly man.

The following verses show that Jesus was both God and man:

Matthew 16:27	For I, the Son of Man, will come in the glory of my Father.
Matthew 22:42-45	"What do you think about the Messiah? Whose son is he?" They replied, "He is the son of David. . . ." "Since David called him Lord, how can he be his son at the same time?"
Matthew 25:31-40	But when the Son of Man comes in his glory, and all the angels with him, then he will sit upon his glorious throne.
Mark 14: 61-62	"Are you the Messiah, the Son of the blessed God?" Jesus said, "I am."
Luke 9:42-44	But Jesus rebuked the evil spirit and healed the boy. Then he gave him back to his father. . . . Awe gripped the people as they saw this display of God's power.
John 3:35	The Father loves his Son, and he has given him authority over everything.
Romans 5:15	And what a difference between our sin and God's generous gift of forgiveness. For this one man, Adam, brought death to many through his sin. But this other man, Jesus Christ, brought forgiveness to many through God's bountiful gift.
Romans 5:21	So just as sin ruled over all people and brought them to death, now God's wonderful kindness rules instead, giving us right standing with God and resulting in eternal life through Jesus Christ our Lord.
1 Corinthians 15:49	Just as we are now like Adam, the man of the earth, so we will someday be like Christ, the man from heaven.

WOMEN AS TEACHERS / 1 Timothy 2:14

Three views held by Christians on the role of women hinge on how one interprets 1 Timothy 2:9-15.

Nonauthoritative	These people see Paul as expressing his own opinion, not God's, or believe that this passage of Scripture was added later by someone other than Paul. They do not see these words as the Word of God— or as relevant to modern practice.
Authoritative, but culturally limited	This view holds that Paul targeted the Ephesian culture and limited the role of women for this situation and others like it. The general principle to apply today is that we must not hinder the gospel.
Authoritative and absolute	This view holds that women should not be in authority over men in roles such as pastor, elder, or deacon. There is some variety of application as to limits of women's privileges in teaching, such as in Christian schools or in missionary roles.

HISTORY OF CHURCH LEADERSHIP FROM THE NEW TESTAMENT
1 Timothy 3:7

Acts 6:1-6	Seven men were appointed to help the church by "waiting on tables," thereby relieving the disciples of this duty so they could concentrate on preaching the gospel. Many believe this was the beginning of the office of deacon.
Acts 14:23	As Paul and Barnabas prepared to return home to Antioch at the close of their first missionary journey, they appointed elders in each church to care for and continue to teach the newly formed congregations.
Acts 20:17	At the end of Paul's third missionary journey, as he headed toward Jerusalem, he sent for the elders of the church at Ephesus. Clearly this was a recognized group, and to this group Paul gave special instruction (Acts 20:18-35).
Acts 20:28	Paul instructed the overseers to remember their commission by the Holy Spirit and their primary duties—to keep watch over themselves and over their congregations.
1 Thessalonians 5:12-13	Paul gave instructions to the believers in Thessalonica to respect those who labored among them and who had God-given responsibility for them.
Philippians 1:1	Paul greeted the leaders in the church—overseers and deacons.
1 Timothy 5:17	Paul instructed the congregations to recognize the honor due to their leaders.

BEWARE OF FALSE TEACHERS! / *1 Timothy 4:1*

Speaker/Writer	Quote	Section of Warning
Jesus	"For false messiahs and false prophets will rise up and perform miraculous signs and wonders so as to deceive, if possible, even God's chosen ones." (Mark 13:22)	Mark 13:21-23
Paul	"I know full well that false teachers, like vicious wolves, will come in among you after I leave, not sparing the flock. Even some of you will distort the truth in order to draw a following." (Acts 20:29-30)	Acts 20:29-30
Paul	"Please don't be so easily shaken and troubled. . . . Don't be fooled by what they say." (2 Thessalonians 2:1-3)	2 Thessalonians 2:1-12
Peter	"First, I want to remind you that in the last days there will be scoffers who will laugh at the truth and do every evil thing they desire. . . . I am warning you ahead of time, dear friends, so that you can watch out and not be carried away by the errors of these wicked people. I don't want you to lose your own secure footing." (2 Peter 3:3, 17)	2 Peter 3:1-18
Jude	". . . That in the last times there would be scoffers. . . . they are the ones who are creating divisions among you." (Jude 1:18-19)	Jude 1:17-19

WORTHY WIDOWS / *1 Timothy 5:14*

Widows in Ministry (vv.3-10)	Widows in Misery (vv. 11-13)
Good works.	Idle
Hospitality	Going house to house
Active prayer life	Active gossips, busybodies
Helping the afflicted	Saying hurtful things
Hope set on God	Hope set on own desires

MONEY AND CONTENTMENT / 1 Timothy 6:8

Everything comes from God	1 Chronicles 29:11-14; Colossians 1:15-17; 1 Timothy 4:4
Money cannot buy salvation	Proverbs 11:4; Ezekiel 7:19; Matthew 16:26; Luke 16:19-31;18:18-25
Riches do not last	Jeremiah 17:11; 1 Timothy 6:17; James 1:10-11; Revelation 18:11-19
Money never satisfies	Ecclesiastes 5:10-11; Luke 12:15
Don't show favoritism to the rich	James 2:1-9
Money carries responsibility	1 Timothy 6:17-19
Obey God rather than chasing after money	Psalms 17:15; 119:36; Proverbs 19:1; 1 Timothy 6:17
Be content	Philippians 4:11-13; 1 Timothy 6:8; Hebrews 13:5

A PORTRAIT OF GOD / 1 Timothy 6:15

As before in this letter (1:17), Paul needed no excuse at all to launch into an exuberant doxology. In this case, he chose eight wide verbal brushstrokes to picture the awesome nature of God:

Name	What It Means	Other References
Blessed and only Sovereign (Most High)	Control and power are God's alone.	Acts 4:24; Revelation 6:10
King of kings	No king has more power or authority (first used of Babylonian and Persian emperors).	Daniel 4:34; Revelation 17:14; 19:16
Lord of lords	God possesses absolute superiority over all powers, human and divine.	Deuteronomy 10:17; Psalm 136:2-3; Revelation 17:14; 19:16
Immortal	God alone has inherent immortality; ours comes from him.	1 Corinthians 15:53-57
Unapproachable light	God's glory is blinding.	Exodus 24:15-17; Psalm 104:2
Unseen (Invisible)	God is so holy that no one can see him and live.	Exodus 33:17-23; 1 Samuel 6:1-5; John 1:18
Worthy of honor	God is to be honored for who he is and what he has done.	Psalm 96:6; John 5:23; Romans 2:7-10
Eternal dominion (power)	God's power continues from eternity to eternity; it has no end.	1 Peter 4:11; Revelation 1:6

GOD'S ETERNAL AUDIT / *1 Timothy 6:16*

Earthly Treasures: Dangers of money

Forgetting God	Deuteronomy 6:10-13; 8:11-20; Proverbs 18:11; Luke 18:24; 1 Timothy 6:9-10
Acting dishonestly, taking advantage of others	2 Kings 5:20-27; Proverbs 10:2; 22:16; 22-23; Isaiah 5:8-9; Amos 3:10; 5:11; 8:4-7; Micah 6:10-12; James 5:1-6
Being greedy	Exodus 20:17; Luke 12:15-21; Ephesians 5:5
Allowing it to take God's place	Proverbs 11:28; 18:11; Jeremiah 9:23-24; Matthew 6:24; Luke 6:24

Heavenly treasures: Good use of money

Give generously and cheerfully to help the poor	Proverbs 11:24-25; 19:17; 21:13; 22:9; 28:27; Luke 12:33-34; 2 Corinthians 9:7
Giving generously to those who do God's work	Deuteronomy 25:4; Nehemiah 13:10-11; 1 Timothy 5:17
Tithe	Malachi 3:8-10; 1 Corinthians 16:2
Pay your taxes	Romans 13:6-7
Always be honest	Deuteronomy 25:14-16; Proverbs 20:10, 23; Luke 16:10-12
Provide for your family	1 Timothy 5:8
Plan wisely for the future	Proverbs 21:20; 22:3; 24:3-4, 27; 27:23-27

A CHOICE OF TRUST / *1 Timothy 6:18*

Since we cannot trust both God and wealth, we must choose one or the other. We can expect the following results:

Trust in God leads to:	Trust in riches leads to:
Peace	Anxiety
Service of others	Self-centeredness
Satisfaction	Dissatisfaction
Humility	Arrogance
Certainty	Uncertainty
Contentment	Restless greed

2 TIMOTHY

MEGATHEMES IN 2 TIMOTHY

Theme	Explanation	Importance
Boldness	In the face of opposition and persecution, Timothy was to carry out his ministry without fear or shame. Paul urged him to utilize boldly the gifts of preaching and teaching that the Holy Spirit had given him.	The Holy Spirit helps us to be wise and strong. God honors our confident testimony even when we suffer. To get over our fear of what people might say or do, we must take our eyes off of people and look only to God.
Faithfulness	Christ was faithful to all of us in dying for our sin. Paul was a faithful minister even when he was in prison. Paul urged Timothy to maintain not only sound doctrine but also loyalty, diligence, and endurance.	We can count on opposition, suffering, and hardship as we serve Christ. But this shows that our faithfulness is having an effect on others. As we trust Christ, he counts us worthy to suffer, and he will give us the strength we need to be steadfast.
Preaching and Teaching	Paul and Timothy were active in preaching and teaching the Good News about Jesus Christ. Paul encouraged Timothy not only to carry the torch of truth but also to train others, passing on to them sound doctrine and enthusiasm for Christ's mission.	We must prepare people to transmit God's Word to others so that they in turn might pass it on. Does your church carefully train others to teach?
Error	In the final days before Christ returns, there will be false teachers, spiritual dropouts, and heretics. The remedy for error is to have a solid program for teaching Christians.	Because of deception and false teaching, we must be disciplined and ready to reject error. Know the Word of God as your sure defense against error and confusion.

PAUL'S TWO IMPRISONMENTS / *2 Timothy 1:1*

	First Imprisonment A.D. 60–62	Second Imprisonment A.D. 66–67
Reason	Accused by Jews and appealed to Rome	Persecuted by the Roman government
Conditions	Relatively comfortable; in a rented house (Acts 28:30-31)	Cold, dark, lonely dungeon
Relationships	Visited by many friends	Almost totally alone
Freedom	Had many opportunities to witness for Christ—eventually was freed	Was totally confined to prison but was able to read and write
Outlook	Expected freedom (Philippians 1:24-26)	Expected to be executed (4:6), but looked forward to heaven (1:12; 2:8; 4:18)

BE STRONG! / *2 Timothy 2:2*

Scripture gives us many ways to understand the strength God offers his people. We must daily draw on his resources.

Reference	Meaning
Romans 4:20	We have examples to follow (such as Abraham) who were leaders of faith.
2 Corinthians 12:9	We receive strength at our point of weakness. When we acknowledge our limitations, God can use us.
Ephesians 6:10-11	God strengthens us by giving us armor to combat Satan—faith, knowledge, and truth.
Philippians 4:13	God's strength equips us for his service.
1 Timothy 1:12	Our thankfulness to God for the strength he gives enables us to be more receptive.

HEAVENLY REWARDS / *2 Timothy 2:12*

Reference	What It Says about Heaven
Matthew 16:24-27	To follow Christ, take up the cross. To save life, lose it. For Christ will come in glory with his angels and reward each person according to what he or she has done.
Matthew 19:28-30	If we give up material rewards on this earth for the sake of Christ and his kingdom, we are promised a hundred times as much, as well as eternal life with Christ.
Romans 6:8	If we died with Christ, we will also live with him.
Romans 8:17	If we are children of God, then we are his heirs (and coheirs with Christ) of all the riches of glory. We share in suffering; we also share in glory.
1 Corinthians 15:42-58	We will be changed—at the sounding of the last trumpet we will receive imperishable bodies. Christ has the victory!
Colossians 3:3-4	Our lives are hidden with Christ in God. When Christ appears, we will appear with him in glory.
1 Thessalonians 4:13-18	The Lord will come down from heaven with a loud command, with the voice of the archangel, and with a trumpet call. The dead in Christ will rise first. Those who are still alive at his return will be caught up to meet him in the clouds. Then we will be with the Lord together forever.
Revelation 3:21	To the one who overcomes, Christ will give him the right to sit with him on his throne in heaven.
Revelation 21:1-22:21	There will be a new heaven and a new earth. There will be no more death or mourning or crying or pain. The Holy City will be beautiful beyond imagination, and only those whose names are written in the Lamb's Book of Life will allowed to enter. There will be no sun or light, for the Lord himself will be the light. And God's kingdom will remain forever and ever.

LIVING IN THE LAST DAYS / *2 Timothy 3:1*

If society is doomed to degeneration what should believers do as they live in the "last days"? Paul offered advice in several of his letters:

Reference	Application
Romans 13:11-14	Keep close to the Lord.
2 Corinthians 11:13-15 . . .	Avoid masquerading as servants of God.
Ephesians 5:11	Have nothing to do with evildoers and their wicked deeds; instead, expose them. Believers need not allow evil to continue unchecked, but should actively work against it.
Ephesians 5:18	Redeem time.
Colossians 4:2, 5	Believers are to pray, be watchful, be thankful, and be wise in the way they act toward unbelievers, making the most of every opportunity to share the gospel.
2 Thessalonians 3:6-15 . . .	Church members who are lazy and idle must be warned. Christians should not be sitting around waiting for the Lord to return, but should continue working in the ministry.

PREDICTED AND EXPECTED / *2 Timothy 3:11*

Persecution did not take Paul by surprise, for Jesus had predicted it many times. Believers today can take encouragement and courage from Jesus' words and Paul's experiences.

Jesus predicted persecution	Matthew 5:11-12
	Matthew 10:17-23
	Matthew 24:9-11
	Mark 8:34
	Mark 13:9-13
	John 15:18-19, 21
	John 16:33
	John 17:14-15
Paul expected persecution	Romans 8:17
	2 Corinthians 12:9-10
	Philippians 1:29
	1 Thessalonians 3:4

TITUS

MEGATHEMES IN TITUS

Theme	Explanation	Importance
A Good Life	The Good News of salvation is that we can't be saved by living a good life; we are saved only by faith in Jesus Christ. But the gospel transforms people's lives, so that they eventually perform good deeds. Our service won't save us, but we are saved to serve.	A good life is a witness to the gospel's power. As Christians, we must have commitment and discipline to serve. Are you putting your faith into action by serving others?
Character	Titus's responsibility in Crete was to appoint elders to maintain proper organization and discipline, so Paul listed the qualities needed for the eldership. Their conduct in their homes revealed their fitness for service in the church.	It's not enough to be educated or to have a loyal following to be Christ's kind of leader. You must have self-control, spiritual and moral fitness, and Christian character. Who you are is just as important as what you can do.
Church Relationships	Church teaching must relate to various groups. Older Christians were to teach and to be examples to younger men and women. People of every age and group have a lesson to learn and a role to play.	Right living and right relationships go along with right doctrine. Treat relationships with other believers as an outgrowth of your faith.
Citizenship	Christians must be good citizens in society, not just in church. Believers must obey the government and work honestly.	How you fulfill your civic duties is a witness to the watching world. Your community life should reflect Christ's love as much as your church life does.

TITUS GOES TO CRETE / *Titus 1:1-5*

Tradition says that after Paul was released from prison in Rome (before his second and final Roman imprisonment), he and Titus traveled together for a while. They stopped in Crete, and when it was time for Paul to go, he left Titus behind to help the churches there.

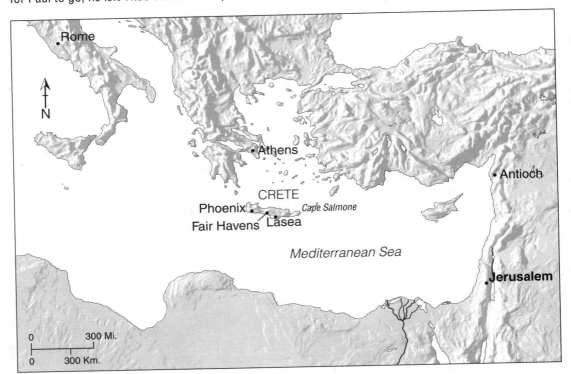

Copyright © 2001 by Tyndale House Publishers

BONDS OF FREEDOM / *Titus 2:6*

Christian freedom does not grant us free and unrestrained use or abuse of the following verses:

Anger	Don't sin by letting anger gain control over you.	Proverbs 29:11
	Don't let the sun go down while you are still angry.	Ephesians 4:26
Tongue	My dear brothers and sisters, be quick to listen, slow to speak, and slow to get angry.	James 1:19
	No one can tame the tongue. It is an uncontrollable evil, full of deadly poison.	James 3:8
Desires	But let the Lord Jesus Christ take control of you, and don't think of ways to indulge your evil desires.	Romans 13:14
	For when we place our faith in Christ Jesus, it makes no difference to God whether we are circumcised or not circumcised. What is important is faith expressing itself in love.	Galatians 5:6
	Run from anything that stimulates youthful lust. Follow anything that makes you want to do right. Pursue faith and love and peace, and enjoy the companionship of those who call on the Lord with pure hearts.	2 Timothy 2:22
	Dear brothers and sisters, you are foreigners and aliens here. So I warn you to keep away from evil desires because they fight against your very souls.	1 Peter 2:16
Money	For the love of money is at the root of all kinds of evil. And some people, craving money, have wandered from the faith and pierced themselves with many sorrows.	1 Timothy 6:10
	Stay away from the love of money; be satisfied with what you have.	Hebrews 13:5
Will	For you have been called to live in freedom—not freedom to satisfy your sinful nature, but freedom to serve one another in love.	Galatians 5:13
	You are not slaves; you are free. But your freedom is not an excuse to do evil. You are free to live as God's slaves.	1 Peter 2:16

THE INDISPENSABLE HOLY SPIRIT / *Titus 3:6*

The following passages show us what an important role the Holy Spirit has in our daily lives.

Passage	Role of the Holy Spirit
John 14:15-31	When Jesus was about to leave the disciples, he told them he would remain with them. How could this be? The Counselor, Helper, Advocate, Spirit of Truth—the Spirit of God himself—would come to care for and guide the disciples after Jesus was gone. The Holy Spirit is a powerful person on our side, working for and with us.
John 20:22; Acts 2	The regenerating power of the Spirit came on the disciples just before Jesus' ascension, and the Spirit was poured out on all the believers at Pentecost, shortly after Jesus ascended to heaven. The Holy Spirit is the very presence of God within us. By faith we can appropriate the Spirit's power each day.
John 14:16	The Holy Spirit will be with us forever.
John 14:17	The Holy Spirit cannot be accepted by the world at large.
John 14:17; Romans 8:9-14	The Holy Spirit lives with us and within us. Although Jesus ascended to heaven, he sent the Holy Spirit to live in believers. To have the Holy Spirit is to have Jesus himself.
John 14:26	The Holy Spirit teaches us. As we study the Bible, we can trust the Holy Spirit to plant the truth in our mind, convince us of God's will, and remind us when we stray from it.
John 14:26	The Holy Spirit reminds us of Jesus' words.
John 15:26	The Holy spirit gives strength to endure the unreasonable hostility many have toward Christ. This is especially comforting for those facing persecution.
John 16:8	The Holy Spirit convicts us of sin, shows us God's righteousness, and announces God's judgment on evil.
John 16:13	The Holy Spirit guides into truth and gives insight into future events. The truth is the truth about Christ.
John 16:14	The Holy Spirit brings glory to Christ.
Romans 8:1-2	The Holy Spirit sets us free.
Romans 8:16; Galatians 4:6-7	The Holy Spirit assures us that we are God's children.
Romans 8:26-27	The Holy Spirit intercedes for us in our weakness and in our prayers.
Ephesians 1:13-14	The Holy Spirit seals us for eternity.

PHILEMON

MEGATHEMES IN PHILEMON

Theme	Explanation	Importance
Forgiveness	Philemon was Paul's friend and the legal owner of the slave Onesimus. Paul asked him not to punish Onesimus but to forgive and restore him as a new Christian brother.	Christian relationships must be full of forgiveness and acceptance. Can you forgive those who have wronged you?
Barriers	Slavery was widespread in the Roman Empire, but no one is lost to God or beyond his love. Slavery was a barrier between people, but Christian love and fellowship are to overcome such barriers.	In Christ we are one family. No walls of racial, economic or political differences should separate us. Let Christ work through you to remove barriers between Christian brothers and sisters.
Respect	Paul was a friend of both Philemon and Onesimus. He had the authority as an apostle to tell Philemon what to do. Yet Paul chose to appeal to his friend in Christian love rather than to order him what to do.	Tactful persuasion accomplishes a great deal more than commands when dealing with people. Remember to exhibit courtesy and respect in your relationships.

THE WORK OF RECONCILIATION / *Philemon 18*

What Paul did for Onesimus parallels what Christ did for us.

Paul and Onesimus

Onesimus had wronged Philemon and thus was separated from him.

Paul had not been involved with Onesimus's guilt.

Paul wrote this letter to reconcile Onesimus and Philemon.

The debt Onesimus had with Philemon had to be paid.

Paul took on a debt that was not his own by promising to repay to Philemon.

Christ and Us

Sinners have wronged God and are thus separated from him (Romans 3:23).

Jesus was sinless, separated from sinners (Hebrews 4:15).

Jesus' work on the cross reconciled sinners and the holy God (2 Corinthians 5:17-21).

The penalty for sin had to be paid (Romans 6:23).

Jesus took on the debt of sin that was not his own (the sins of the whole world) and paid it by his death (John 1:29; Romans 5:8-9; Hebrews 7:27; 9:26, 28).

HEBREWS

MEGATHEMES IN HEBREWS

Theme	Explanation	Importance
Christ Is Superior	Hebrews reveals Jesus' true identity as God. Jesus is the ultimate authority. He is greater than any religion or any angel. He is superior to any Jewish leader (such as Abraham, Moses, or Joshua) and superior to any priest. He is the complete revelation of God.	Jesus alone can forgive our sin. He has secured our forgiveness and salvation by his death on the cross. We can find peace with God and real meaning for life by believing in Christ. We should not accept any alternative to or substitute for him.
High Priest	In the Old Testament, the high priest represented the Jews before God. Jesus Christ links us with God. There is no other way to reach God. Because Jesus Christ lived a sinless life, he is the perfect substitute to die for our sin. He is our perfect representative with God.	Jesus guarantees our access to God the Father. He intercedes for us so we can boldly come to the Father with our needs. When we are weak, we can come confidently to God for forgiveness and ask for his help.
Sacrifice	Christ's sacrifice was the ultimate fulfillment of all that the Old Testament sacrifices represented—God's forgiveness for sin. Because Christ is the perfect sacrifice for our sin, our sins are completely forgiven—past, present, and future.	Christ removed sin, which barred us from God's presence and fellowship. But we must accept his sacrifice for us. By believing in him, we are no longer guilty but cleansed and made whole. His sacrifice clears the way for us to have eternal life.
Maturity	Though we are saved from sin when we believe in Christ, we are given the task of going on and growing in our faith. Through our relationship with Christ, we can live blameless lives, be set aside for his special use, and develop maturity.	The process of maturing in our faith takes time. Daily commitment and service produce maturity. When we are mature in our faith, we are not easily swayed or shaken by temptations or worldly concerns.
Faith	Faith is confident trust in God's promises. God's greatest promise is that we can be saved through Jesus.	If we trust in Jesus Christ for our complete salvation, he will transform us completely. A life of obedience and complete trust is pleasing to God.
Endurance	Faith enables Christians to face trials. Genuine faith includes the commitment to stay true to God when we are under fire. Endurance builds character and leads to victory.	We can have victory in our trials if we don't give up or turn our back on Christ. Stay true to Christ and pray for endurance.

WHAT DID JESUS DO TO OUR SINS? / *Hebrews 1:4*

When we confess a sin to God, he forgives and forgets it because of Jesus' sacrifice. We never need to remember or confess that sin again. When God forgives a sin, it remains forgiven forever.

He took them away 2:17

He forgot them 8:12; 10:17

He freed us from sin's penalty 9:15

He removed sin's power from us 9:26

He offered himself as a sacrifice 10:12

He offered himself as an offering. 10:18

He forgives our sins 10:19

CHRIST AND THE ANGELS / *Hebrews 1:4-14*

The writer of Hebrews quotes from the Old Testament repeatedly in demonstrating Christ's greatness in comparison to the angels. This audience of first-century Jewish Christians had developed an imbalanced belief in angels and their role. Christ's lordship is affirmed without disrespect to God's valued angelic messengers.

Hebrews passage	Old Testament passage	How Christ is superior to angels
1:5-6	Psalm 2:7	Christ is called "Son" of God, a title never given to an angel.
1:7, 14	Psalm 104:4	Angels are important but are still only servants under God.
1:8-9	Psalm 45:6	Christ's Kingdom is forever.
1:10	Psalm 102:25	Christ is the Creator of the world.
1:13	Psalm 110:1	Christ is given unique honor by God.

LESSONS FROM CHRIST'S HUMANITY / *Hebrews 2:14*

God, in Christ, became a living, breathing human being. Hebrews points out many reasons why this is so important.

Christ is the perfect	human leader	and he wants to lead you
	model	and he is worth imitating
	sacrifice	and he died for you
	conqueror	and he conquered death to give you eternal life
	High Priest	and he is merciful, loving, and understanding

JESUS, OUR HIGH PRIEST / Hebrews 2:17

The book of Hebrews is the only place in the New Testament where Jesus is referred to as a High Priest. The role was understood by the Hebrews reading this book because of their religious background.

Jesus is our merciful and faithful High Priest in the service of God.	2:17
We are to focus our thoughts on Jesus, the High Priest whom we confess.	3:1
Jesus is our great High Priest who has gone through the heavens.	4:14
Jesus, our High Priest, is able to sympathize with our weaknesses because he has been tempted as we are but is without sin.	4:15
Jesus did not glorify himself, but he became our High Priest by God's will.	5:5
Jesus is the author of eternal salvation, called by God as High Priest.	5:9-10
Our hope in eternity is sure, for Jesus went before us, having become a High Priest forever.	6:18-20
Jesus is the High Priest who meets our needs; he is holy, blameless, pure, set apart from sinners, and exalted above the heavens.	7:26
Jesus, as our High Priest, sits at the right hand of God's throne in heaven.	8:1
Jesus came as High Priest of the good things to come.	9:11

HOW DOES MOSES COMPARE TO JESUS? / Hebrews 3:3

Moses:	Jesus:
served as a prophet	served as the greatest of prophets
honored God as a servant	remains honored as God's Son
led God's people out of bondage from Egypt	leads people out of bondage to sin
administered the law	fulfills the law
received the law from angels	receives worship from angels
sinned	never sinned
died and was buried	died, but rose from the dead
had a ministry that could only condemn, not save	has a ministry that brings righteousness and eternal salvation
had a fading glory	has glory that is eternal

HOW DOES SIN DECEIVE US? / *Hebrews 3:13*

Because deceitfulness is Satan's weapon, we must arm ourselves against it. We must encourage one another, assemble for worship, clearly warn against those dangers, and constantly show the benefit of faithfully following Christ.

Satan's goal is to deceive us

Genesis 3:1-2	Satan is crafty—he sought to trick Eve
Genesis 3:13	Eve knew that the serpent had deceived her
John 8:44	Satan is a liar; the father of lies
2 Corinthians 2:11	Satan schemes in order to outwit us
2 Corinthians 4:4	Satan blinds the eyes of unbelievers to keep them from the truth
2 Corinthians 11:13	Satan masquerades as an angel of light
2 Thessalonians 2:9	Satan will deceive many in the end times through counterfeit miracles, signs, and wonders
Revelation 12:9	Satan is the deceiver of the whole world

Wealth can deceive us

Deuteronomy 8:11-14	Wealth can cause us to become proud and forget the Lord
Proverbs 11:28	Whoever trusts in riches will be disappointed
Matthew 13:22	The deceitfulness of wealth can choke out the gospel message
1 Timothy 6:9-10	Wealth is a trap that can lead to destruction; the love of money is a root of all kinds of evil

Our desires can deceive us

Ephesians 4:22	Our old nature is corrupted by its deceitful desires
Titus 3:3	Before believing, we were enslaved to and deceived by passions and pleasures
James 1:15-16	Evil desires can deceive us into sinning, which leads to death

THE WORD OF GOD / Hebrews 4:12

The word of God, the Bible, describes itself and its work in many ways:

Isaiah 55:11	God's word will not return to him empty, but will do what God desires and achieve the purpose for which he sent it.
Jeremiah 23:29	God's word is like fire, and like a hammer that can break a rock into pieces.
John 6:63	God's word is spirit and life.
Acts 7:38	God's word is living.
Ephesians 6:17	God's word is part of the believer's armor: the sword of the Spirit—the word of God.
Hebrews 4:12	God's word is living, powerful, sharper than a two-edged sword, judging people's thoughts and intentions.
1 Peter 1:23	God's word is living and enduring; through it people are born again.
Revelation 1:16; 2:12	God's word is a double-edged sword, coming from his mouth.

THE CHOICES OF MATURITY / Hebrews 5:14

One way to evaluate spiritual maturity is by looking at the choices we make. The writer of Hebrews notes many of the ways these choices change with personal growth.

Mature Choices	Versus	Immature Choices
Teaching others	rather than	just being taught
Developing depth of understanding	rather than	struggling with the basics
Self-evaluation	rather than	self-criticism
Seeking unity	rather than	promoting disunity
Desiring spiritual challenges	rather than	desiring entertainment
Careful study and observation	rather than	opinions and halfhearted efforts
Active faith	rather than	cautious apathy and doubt
Confidence	rather than	fear
Feelings and experiences evaluated in the light of God's Word	rather than	according to feelings experiences evaluated

CHRISTIAN MATURITY / *Hebrews 5:14*

Christian maturity is greatly discussed throughout the New Testament. Here are some of the descriptions:

Description	References
Complete	1 Corinthians 2:6; 3:1; Ephesians 4:13; Colossians 1:28; Hebrews 5:14; 6:1
Blameless	Luke 1:6; Philippians 2:15; 3:6; 1 Thessalonians 3:13; 5:23
Whole	Matthew 4:21; 2 Corinthians 13:9-11; Galatians 6:1; 1 Thessalonians 3:10; Hebrews 13:21; 1 Peter 5:10
Disciplined	Hebrews 2:10; 5:9; 12:10
Hope for Resurrection	Luke 13:32; Philippians 3:12; Hebrews 12:23
Love for God and others	1 Corinthians 13:1-13; 14:20; 1 Peter 4:8; 1 John 4:12, 17-21
Christlike	Matthew 5:48; Luke 6:36; Romans 12:2; Colossians 3:10

ABRAHAM IN THE NEW TESTAMENT / Hebrews 6:13-15

Abraham was an ancestor of Jesus.	Matthew 1:1-2, 17 Luke 3:23, 34	Jesus Christ was human; he was born into the line of Abraham, whom God had chosen to be the father of a great nation through which the whole world would be blessed. We are blessed because of what Jesus Christ, Abraham's descendant, did for us.
Abraham was the father of the Jewish nation.	Matthew 3:9 Luke 3:8 Acts 13:26 Romans 4:1; 11:1 2 Corinthians 11:22; Hebrews 6:13-14	God wanted to set apart a nation for himself, a nation that would tell the world about him. He began with a man of faith who, though old and childless, believed God's promise of innumerable descendants. We can trust God to do the impossible when we have faith.
Abraham, because of the faith, now sits in the Kingdom with Christ.	Matthew 8:11 Luke 13:28; 16:23-31	Abraham followed God, and now he is enjoying his reward—eternity with God. We will one day meet Abraham because we have been promised eternity as well.
God is Abraham's God; thus, Abraham is alive with God.	Matthew 22:32 Mark 12:26 Luke 20:37 Acts 7:32	As Abraham lives forever, we will live forever, because we, like Abraham, have chosen the life of faith.
Abraham received great promises from God.	Luke 1:55, 72-73 Acts 3:25; 7:17-18; Galatians 3:6, 14-16; Hebrews 6:13-15	Many of the promises God made to Abraham seemed impossible to be realized, but Abraham trusted God. The promises to believers in God's Word also seem too incredible to believe, but we can trust God to keep all his promises.
Abraham followed God.	Acts 7:2-8 Hebrews 11:8, 17-19	Abraham followed God's leading from his homeland to an unknown territory, which became the Jews' Promised Land. When we follow God, even before he makes all his plans clear to us, we will never be disappointed.
God blessed Abraham because of his faith.	Romans 4 Galatians 3:6-9, 14-19; Hebrews 11:8, 17-19; James 2:21-24	Abraham showed faith in times of disappointment, trial, and testing. Because of Abraham's faith, God counted him righteous and called him his "friend." God accepts us because of our faith.
Abraham is the father of all those who come to God by faith.	Romans 9:6-8 Galatians 3:6-9, 14-29	The Jews are Abraham's children, and Christ was his descendant. We are Christ's brothers and sisters; thus, all believers are Abraham's children and God's children. Abraham was righteous because of his faith; we are made righteous through faith in Christ. The promises made to Abraham apply to us because of Christ.

GIVING A TENTH / *Hebrews 7:4*

Many ancient people observed the practice of tithing—that is, giving a tenth of their earnings (or produce, harvest, etc.) back to a leader or a god. God commanded the Israelites to tithe, and the first instance appears in Abraham's encounter with Melchizedek.

The Israelites were required to tithe of their crops, fruit, and herds.	Leviticus 27:30-32
The tithe was received by the Levites to support them.	Numbers 18:21, 24
The Levites, in turn, gave a "tithe of the tithe" to support the priests.	Numbers 18:26-29 Nehemiah 10:39
The Israelites were to bring their tithes to Jerusalem, and offering them came in the form of a ritual meal in which Levites were invited to share. If Jerusalem was too far for a person to transport the tithe, he could take the tithe there in the form of money. Every third year the tithe could be offered in one's local area, but the person was still to go to Jerusalem to worship.	Deuteronomy 12:5-7, 11-19; 14:22-29; 26:12-15
God promises blessings for those who faithfully tithe, and says that refusing to tithe is like robbing him.	Malachi 3:8-12
Tithing, without love for or obedience to God, amounts to nothing more than a meaningless ritual.	Matthew 23:23; Luke 11:42

HOW CHRIST IS BETTER / *Hebrews 8:6*

The way that Christ opened was far superior than the way provided in the Old Testament. Not only is the way better, but Hebrews says the old way is now no longer an option. There remains one way to God, and that way is discovered by following Christ.

Christ provides better . . .

focus to life	6:9
hope	7:19
covenant	7:22
promises	8:6
sacrifice	9:23
spiritual possessions	10:34
future country	11:16, 35, 40

THE OLD AND NEW COVENANTS / *Hebrews 8:13*

Like pointing out the similarities and differences between the photograph of a person and the actual person, the writer of Hebrews shows the connection between the old Mosaic covenant and the new Messianic covenant. He proves that the old covenant was a shadow of the real Christ.

The Old Covenant under Moses	The New Covenant in Christ	Application
Gifts and sacrifices by those guilty of sin	Self-sacrifice by the guiltless Christ	Christ died for you
Focused on a physical building where one goes to worship	Focuses on the reign of Christ in the hearts of believers	God is directly involved in your life
A shadow	A reality	Not temporal, but eternal
Limited promises	Limitless promises	We can trust God's promises to us
Failed agreement by people	Faithful agreement by Christ	Christ has kept the agreement where people couldn't
External standards and rules	Internal standards—a new heart	God sees both actions and motives—we are accountable to God, not rules
Limited access to God	Unlimited access to God	God is personally available
Based on fear	Based on love and forgiveness	Forgiveness keeps our failures from destroying the agreement
Legal cleansing	Personal cleansing	God's cleansing is complete
Continual sacrifice	Conclusive sacrifice	Christ's sacrifice was perfect and final
Obey the rules	Serve the living God	We have a relationship, not regulations
Forgiveness earned	Forgiveness freely given	We have true and complete forgiveness
Repeated yearly	Completed by Christ's death	Christ's death can be applied to your sin
Human effort	God's grace	Initiated by God's love for you
Available to some	Available to all	Available to you

KEY TABERNACLE PIECES / *Hebrews 9:2-4; Exodus 35*

What can we learn today from the details involved in the building of God's tabernacle? First, the high quality of the precious materials making up the tabernacle shows God's greatness and transcendence. Second, the curtain surrounding the Most Holy Place shows God's moral perfection as symbolized by his separation from the common and unclean. Third, the portable nature of the tabernacle shows God's desire to be with his people as they traveled. For a description of these items, see Exodus 25–31.

Name	Function and Significance
Ark of the Covenant	A golden rectangular box that contained the Ten Commandments
	Symbolized God's covenant with Israel's people
	Located in the Most Holy Place
Atonement Cover	The lid to the ark of the covenant
	Symbolized the presence of God among his people
Curtain	The curtain that divided the two sacred rooms of the tabernacle—the Holy Place and the Most Holy Place
	Symbolized how the people were separated from God because of sin
Table	A wooden table located in the Holy Place of the tabernacle. The holy bread and various utensils were kept on this table
Holy Bread (Bread of the Presence)	Twelve loaves of baked bread, one for each tribe of Israel
	Symbolized the spiritual nourishment God offers his people
Lampstands and Lamps	A golden lampstand located in the Holy Place, which held seven burning oil lamps
	The lampstand lighted the Holy Place for the priests
Altar of Incense	An altar in the Holy Place in front of the curtain
	Used for burning God's special incense and symbolic of acceptable prayer
Anointing Oil	A special oil used to anoint the priests and all the pieces in the tabernacle
	A sign of being set apart for God
Altar of Burnt Offering	The bronze altar outside the tabernacle used for the sacrifices
	Symbolized how sacrifice restored one's relationship with God
Basin	A large wash basin outside the tabernacle used by the priests to cleanse themselves before performing their duties
	Symbolized the need for spiritual cleansing

BIBLE "WAITERS" / Hebrews 9:28

In the Bible we find many people who had to "wait on the Lord," just as believers today must patiently wait for Christ's return. We can learn a lesson in patience from these Bible waiters.

Noah waited for God's timing before leaving the ark	Genesis 8:10, 12
Moses waited on God in the mountain	Exodus 24:12
Job waited for God's answers	Job 14:14
Isaiah waited for God to work in Israel	Isaiah 8:17; 25:9; 26:8; 30:18; 33:2; 40:31; 49:23; 59:9, 11; 64:4
Jeremiah understood the need to wait quietly for God's salvation	Lamentations 3:25
Hosea warned the people to return to God and wait for him to work	Hosea 12:6
Micah waited for the God of his salvation	Micah 7:7
Habakkuk warned the people to hold on to their hope and to wait because it would surely come	Habakkuk 2:3
Zephaniah explained that the Lord wanted his people to wait for him	Zephaniah 3:8
Joseph of Arimathea was waiting for God's kingdom	Luke 23:51
The disciples were ordered by Jesus to wait in Jerusalem for the coming of the Holy Spirit	Acts 1:4
Believers are called to wait for heaven, for the promise is sure	Romans 8:23, 25; Galatians 5:5; 1 Thessalonians 1:10; Titus 2:13; 2 Peter 3:12-14

OBEDIENCE VERSUS SACRIFICES / Hebrews 10:5-6

Often in Scripture, God states that he doesn't want our gifts and sacrifices when we give them out of ritual or hypocrisy. God wants us first to love and obey him.

1 Samuel 15:22-23	Obedience is far better than sacrifice.
Psalm 40:6-8	Instead of burnt offerings, God wants our lifelong service.
Psalm 51:16-19	Instead of penance, God wants a broken and contrite heart.
Jeremiah 7:21-23	Instead of sacrifices, God wants our obedience, and he promises that he will be our God and we will be his people.
Hosea 6:6	Instead of sacrifices, God wants our loving loyalty. Instead of offerings, he wants us to acknowledge him.
Amos 5:21-24	God hates pretense and hypocrisy; he wants to see justice roll on like a river.
Micah 6:6-8	God is not satisfied with offerings; he wants us to be fair and just and merciful, and to walk humbly with him.
Matthew 9:13	Instead of sacrifices, God wants us to give mercy.

ENCOURAGE ONE ANOTHER / Hebrews 10:24-25

Christians are to encourage one another. A word of encouragement offered at the right moment can be the difference between staying strong in the faith or collapsing along the way. Believers ought to be sensitive to one another's needs for encouragement, ready to offer supportive words or actions. The Bible gives several examples of encouragement and commands for believers to encourage each other:

Deuteronomy 3:28	"But commission Joshua and encourage him, for he will lead the people across the Jordan. He will give them the land you now see before you."
Acts 4:36	"For instance, there was Joseph, the one the apostles nick-named Barnabas (which means "Son of Encouragement"). He was from the tribe of Levi and came from the island of Cyprus."
Acts 15:32	"Then Judas and Silas, both being prophets, spoke extensively to the Christians, encouraging and strengthening their faith."
Romans 12:6, 8	"God has given each of us the ability to do certain things well. . . . If your gift is to encourage others, do it."
Romans 15:4-5	"Such things were written in the Scriptures long ago to teach us. They give us hope and encouragement as we wait patiently for God's promises. May God, who gives this patience and encour-agement, help you live in complete harmony with each other— each with the attitude of Christ Jesus toward the other."
Ephesians 6:22	"I am sending him [Tychicus] to you for just this purpose. He will let you know how we are, and he will encourage you."
1 Thessalonians 3:2	"We sent Timothy to visit you. He is our coworker for God and our brother in proclaiming the Good News of Christ. We sent him to strengthen you, to encourage you in your faith."
1 Thessalonians 4:18; 5:11, 14	"So comfort and encourage each other with these words. So encourage each other and build each other up, just as you are already doing. Encourage those who are timid. Take tender care of those who are weak. Be patient with everyone."
2 Timothy 4:2	"Preach the word of God. Be persistent, whether the time is favorable or not. Patiently correct, rebuke, and encourage your people with good teaching."
1 Peter 5:12	"I have written this short letter to you with the help of Silas, whom I consider a faithful brother. My purpose in writing is to encourage you and assure you that the grace of God is with you no matter what happens."

WHAT DOES GOD HAVE IN MIND FOR US? / *Hebrews 11:16*

We need only go to the end of the story, recorded in Revelation 20–22, to find out what God has in mind for his faithful people from across the ages.

Satan is defeated 20:10

Death is defeated 20:14

Sin is banished 21:27

We live with God forever 21:3; 22:5

There will be no more sin, tears, or sorrow 21:4

The heavenly city is revealed 21:2, 10-14

The earth is made new 21:5

Paradise is gained. 22:1-3

TWELVE TESTS OF ABRAHAM / *Hebrews 11:17-18*

Abraham's faith was tested at least twelve specific times. Some of them were not what we might call big tests, but together they establish a picture of Abraham as a person whose faith was genuine. After the last of these, God said, "Now I know that you truly fear God, you have not withheld even your beloved son" (Genesis 22:12).

Each of Abraham's tests can have applications for us:

Reference	Test	Application
Genesis 12:1-7	Abraham left Ur and Haran for an unknown destination at God's direction.	Do I trust God with my future? Is his will part of my decision making?
Genesis 13:8-13	Abraham directed a peaceful separation from Lot and settled at the oaks of Mamre.	Do I trust God with my interests even when I seem to be receiving an unfair settlement?
Genesis 14:13-16	Abraham rescued Lot from the five kings.	Does my faithfulness to others bear witness to my trust in God's faithfulness?
Genesis 14:17-24	Abraham gave a tithe of loot to the godly king of Salem, Melchizedek, and refused the gift of the king of Sodom.	Am I watchful in my dealings with people that I give proper honor to God and refuse to receive honor that belongs to him?
Genesis 15:1-6	Abraham trusted God's promise that he would have a son.	How often do I consciously reaffirm my trust in God's promises?
Genesis 15:7-11	Abraham received the promised land by faith, though the fulfillment would not come for many generations.	How have I demonstrated my continued trust in God during those times when I have been required to wait?
Genesis 17:9-27	At God's command, Abraham circumcised every male in his family.	In what occasions in my life have I acted simply in obedience to God, and not because I understood the significance of what I was doing?
Genesis 18:1-8	Abraham welcomed strangers, who turned out to be angels.	When was the last time I practiced hospitality?
Genesis 18:22-33	Abraham prayed for Sodom.	Am I eager to see people punished, or do I care for people in spite of their sinfulness?
Genesis 20:1-17	Abraham admitted to wrongdoing and took the actions needed to set things right.	When I sin, is my tendency to cover up, or confess? Do I practice the truth that an apology must sometimes be accompanied by restitution?
Genesis 21:22-34	Abraham negotiated a treaty with Abimelech concerning a well.	Can people depend on my words and promises?
Genesis 22:1-12	Abraham prepared to sacrifice his son Isaac.	In what ways has my life demonstrated that I will not allow anything to come before God?

PEACE WITH ALL PEOPLE? / *Hebrews 12:14*

We cannot get around it: Believers—as the salt and light of the world—must pursue peaceful relationships. The verbs, such as "pursue" and "seek," show us that it may not necessarily be easy to do, but God calls us to do it.

Psalm 34:14	Turn away from evil and do good. Work hard at living in peace with others.
Matthew 5:9	God blesses those who work for peace, for they will be called the children of God.
Mark 9:50	Salt is good for seasoning. But if it loses its flavor, how do you make it salty again? You must have the qualities of salt among yourselves and live in peace with each other.
Romans 12:18	Do your part to live in peace with everyone, as much as possible.
Romans 14:19	So then, let us aim for harmony in the church and try to build each other up.
2 Corinthians 13:11	Dear brothers and sisters, I close my letter with these last words: Rejoice. Change your ways. Encourage each other. Live in harmony and peace. Then the God of love and peace will be with you.
1 Thessalonians 5:13	Think highly of them and give them your wholehearted love because of their work. And remember to live peaceably with each other.
2 Timothy 2:22	Run from anything that stimulates youthful lust. Follow anything that makes you want to do right. Pursue faith and love and peace, and enjoy the companionship of those who call on the Lord with pure hearts.
Hebrews 12:14	Try to live in peace with everyone, and seek to live a clean and holy life, for those who are not holy will not see the Lord.
1 Peter 3:11	Turn away from evil and do good. Work hard at living in peace with others.

A BETTER WORD / *Hebrews 12:24*

In contrast to Abel's blood, Christ's blood made a "good word" for us and our salvation.

Good words are clear.	Abel's death left the idea of justice quite ambiguous.	Jesus' death showed clearly the mercy of God to you.
Good words are complete.	Abel's death was unresolved.	Jesus' death was followed by resurrection.
Good words make powerful messages.	Abel's death was tragic. Yet no one says, "I'm a follower of Abel."	Jesus' death was also tragic, yet it saved us. Millions follow him.
Good words explain confusion and point to hope.	Abel's death left humanity with no hope.	Jesus has the most wonderful words of hope for you today. Listen, believe, and obey.

THEOLOGY OF TRIALS IN THE NEW TESTAMENT
Hebrews 12:11

As we live for Christ, we will experience troubles because we are trying to be God's people in a perverse world. Some people say that troubles are the result of sin or lack of faith, but the Bible teaches that they may be a part of God's plan for believers. Our problems can help us look upward and forward, instead of inward, they can build strong character, and they can provide us with opportunities to comfort others who are also struggling. Your troubles may be an indication that you are taking a stand for Christ.

Principle	Key Text
Suffering is not always the result of sin.	"Teacher," his disciples asked him, "why was this man born blind? Was it a result of his own sins or those of his parents?" "It was not because of his sins or his parents' sins," Jesus answered. "He was born blind so the power of God could be seen in him." (John 9:2-3)
God provides hope and love in suffering.	"We can rejoice, too, when we run into problems and trials, for we know that they are good for us—they help us learn to endure. And endurance develops strength of character in us, and character strengthens our confident expectation of salvation. And this expectation will not disappoint us. For we know how dearly God loves us, because he has given us the Holy Spirit to fill our hearts with his love." (Romans 5:3-5)
Problems help us trust in God's sovereign purpose for our lives.	"And we know that God causes everything to work together for the good of those who love God and are called according to his purpose for them. For God knew his people in advance, and he chose them to become like his Son, so that his Son would be the firstborn, with many brothers and sisters." (Romans 8:28-29)
Suffering enables us to comfort others.	"All praise to the God and Father of our Lord Jesus Christ. He is the source of every mercy and the God who comforts us. He comforts us in all our troubles so that we can comfort others. When others are troubled, we will be able to give them the same comfort God has given us. You can be sure that the more we suffer for Christ, the more God will shower us with his comfort through Christ." (2 Corinthians 1:3-5)
Our eternal reward outweighs our suffering.	"For our present troubles are quite small and won't last very long. Yet they produce for us an immeasurably great glory that will last forever! So we don't look at the troubles we can see right now; rather, we look forward to what we have not yet seen. For the troubles we see will soon be over, but the joys to come will last forever." (2 Corinthians 4:17-18)
Problems open up opportunities for service.	"And I want you to know, dear brothers and sisters, that everything that has happened to me here has helped to spread the Good News." (Philippians 1:12)
Problems may be a confirmation that we are living for Christ.	"But God will use this persecution to show his justice. For he will make you worthy of his Kingdom, for which you are suffering." (2 Thessalonians 1:5)
God uses suffering in his plan for our lives.	"Finally, dear brothers and sisters, I ask you to pray for us. Pray first that the Lord's message will spread rapidly and be honored wherever it goes, just as when it came to you. Pray, too, that we will be saved from wicked and evil people, for not everyone believes in the Lord. But the Lord is faithful; he will make you strong and guard you from the evil one." (2 Thessalonians 3:1-3)

THEOLOGY OF TRIALS IN THE NEW TESTAMENT
Hebrews 12:11 *Continued*

Principle	Key Text
Through his suffering, Jesus fully identified with us.	"We all know that Jesus came to help the descendants of Abraham, not to help the angels." (Hebrews 2:16)
Jesus was willing to obey God even when it meant suffering.	"So even though Jesus was God's Son, he learned obedience from the things he suffered."(Hebrews 5:8)
Trials help train us to be more fruitful.	"No discipline is enjoyable while it is happening—it is painful! But afterward there will be a quiet harvest of right living for those who are trained in this way." (Hebrews 12:11)
Problems help us mature.	"Dear brothers and sisters, whenever trouble comes your way, let it be an opportunity for joy. For when your faith is tested, your endurance has a chance to grow. So let it grow, for when your endurance is fully developed, you will be strong in character and ready for anything." (James 1:2-4)
Trials help refine our character.	"So be truly glad! There is wonderful joy ahead, even though it is necessary for you to endure many trials for a while. These trials are only to test your faith, to show that it is strong and pure. It is being tested as fire tests and purifies gold—and your faith is far more precious to God than mere gold. So if your faith remains strong after being tried by fiery trials, it will bring you much praise and glory and honor on the day when Jesus Christ is revealed to the whole world. You love him even though you have never seen him. Though you do not see him, you trust him; and even now you are happy with a glorious, inexpressible joy. Your reward for trusting him will be the salvation of your souls." (1 Peter 1:6-9)
When we suffer, we share in the suffering of Christ.	"Dear friends, don't be surprised at the fiery trials you are going through, as if something strange were happening to you. Instead, be very glad—because these trials will make you partners with Christ in his suffering, and afterward you will have the wonderful joy of sharing his glory when it is displayed to all the world. Be happy if you are insulted for being a Christian, for then the glorious Spirit of God will come upon you." (1 Peter 4:12-14)

FIVE WAYS WE CAN BE THANKFUL / *Hebrews 12:28*

We can be thankful that God answers our prayers.

Psalm 3:4; Isaiah 65:24; John 11:41; 2 Corinthians 1:11

We can be thankful for God's provision for our needs.

Matthew 14:19; 26:26-27; Acts 27:35; Romans 14:6; 1 Corinthians 10:30; 1 Thessalonians 5:18; 1 Timothy 4:4-5

We can be thankful for God's blessings.

1 Chronicles 16:34; Daniel 6:10; Philippians 4:6; Colossians 1:10

We can be thankful for God's character and wondrous works.

Psalm 7:17; 75:1; 2 Corinthians 9:15; Colossians 1:12; Revelation 11:17

We can be thankful for our brothers and sisters in Christ.

1 Corinthians 1:4; Ephesians 1:16; Philippians 1:3-5; Colossians 1:3-4; 1 Thessalonians 1:2; 2 Timothy 1:3; Philemon 4-5

TWENTY-FIVE REASONS FOR PRAISING GOD / *Hebrews 13:15*

We praise God for . . .

his splendor and majesty	Psalm 104:1
giving us salvation	Psalm 96:2; Luke 1:68; 1 Peter 1:3-6
bearing our burdens	Psalm 68:19
hearing our prayers	Psalm 66:20
giving us his strength	Psalm 59:17; 68:35
his marvelous deeds	Psalm 9:1; 26:7; 52:9; 72:18
his guidance	Psalm 16:7
his compassion	Psalm 28:6; 2 Corinthians 1:3
his righteousness	Psalm 48:10
his enduring love	Psalm 106:1
his enduring faithfulness	Psalm 117:1-2; Isaiah 25:1
his comfort	Isaiah 12:1; 2 Corinthians 1:3
his wisdom	Daniel 2:20
his spiritual blessings	Ephesians 1:3-6
forgiving our sins	Hosea 14:2; Ephesians 1:7
We praise God because he made us	Psalm 139:14
he is worthy of praise	2 Samuel 22:4; 1 Chronicles 16:25; Psalm 48:1
he keeps his promises	1 Kings 8:15, 56
he is in control	Ezra 7:27
he is eternal	Nehemiah 9:5
he is powerful and mighty	Psalm 21:13
he is sovereign	Psalm 47:7; 66:4
he is trustworthy	Psalm 56:4
he is holy	Psalm 99:3
he is preparing a glorious future for us	Isaiah 61:11; 62:7-9; Revelation 21–22

DON'T FORGET TO DO GOOD / *Hebrews 13:16*

We are saved by faith in Jesus Christ, but faith ought to result in a changed life and a willingness to do good to others.

What Jesus said . . .	Matthew 5:14-16 Matthew 6:1 John 3:21
What Paul said . . .	2 Corinthians 9:8 Ephesians 2:10 2 Thessalonians 2:16-17 1 Timothy 6:17-19 2 Timothy 3:16-17 Titus 3:14
What James said . . .	James 1:22 James 2:14-26 James 3:13
What Peter said . . .	1 Peter 1:14 1 Peter 2:12
What John said . . .	1 John 2:6 Revelation 14:13

JAMES

MEGATHEMES IN JAMES

Theme	Explanation	Importance
Living Faith	James wants believers not only to hear the truth but also to put it into action. He contrasts empty faith (claims without conduct) with faith that works. Commitment to love and to serve others is evidence of true faith.	Living faith makes a difference. Make sure your faith is more than just a statement; it should also result in action. Seek ways of putting your faith to work.
Trials	In the Christian life there are trials and temptations. Successfully overcoming these adversities produces maturity and strong character.	Don't resent troubles when they come. Pray for wisdom; God will supply all you need to face persecution or adversity. He will give you patience and keep you strong in times of trial.
Law of Love	We are saved by God's gracious mercy, not by keeping the law. But Christ gave us a special command: "Love your neighbor as yourself" (Matthew 19:19). We are to love and serve those around us.	Keeping the law of love shows that our faith is vital and real. When we show love to others, we are overcoming our own selfishness.
Wise Speech	Wisdom shows itself in wise speech. God holds us responsible for the results of our destructive words. The wisdom of God that helps control the tongue can help control all our actions.	Accepting God's wisdom will affect your speech. Your words will convey true humility and lead to peace. Think before you speak and allow God to give you self-control.
Wealth	James taught Christians not to compromise with worldly attitudes about wealth. Because the glory of wealth fades, Christians should store up God's treasures through sincere service. Christians must not show partiality to the wealthy or be prejudiced against the poor.	All of us are accountable for how we use what we have. We should not hoard wealth but be generous toward others. In addition, we should not be impressed by the wealthy nor look down on those who are poor.

CHAPTER SUMMARY / *James 1*

TESTED FAITH IS STRONG FAITH / *James 1:5*

Tested faith brings about a depth of character . . . . Romans 5:3-5

Tested faith enables us to comfort and encourage others . . . . . . 2 Corinthians 1:3-5

Tested faith increases dependence on God for wisdom . . . . James 1:5; 3:17-18

Tested faith encourages us to lead a productive and effective life . . 2 Peter 1:5-9

Tested faith helps us to identify with Christ. . . . . Matthew 4:1-11
Hebrews 5:7-10

Tested faith allows us to focus on our future hope in Christ . . . . . Romans 8:18-24

THE TWO WAYS / *James 1:15*

There is a path before each person that seems right, but it ends in death. Proverbs 14:12

Desire
▼
Temptation
▼
Lust/Sin
▼
Habitual Sin
▼
Death

Jesus told him, "I am the way, the truth, and the life. No one can come to the Father except through me." John 14:6

Trial
▼
Faith
▼
Obedience
▼
Perseverance
▼
Crown of Life

SHOWING FAVORITISM / *James 2*

Why it is wrong to show favoritism to the wealthy:

1. It is inconsistent with Christ's teachings.
2. It results from evil thoughts.
3. It insults people made in God's image.
4. It is a by-product of selfish motives.
5. It goes against the biblical definition of love.
6. It shows a lack of mercy to those less fortunate.
7. It is hypocritical.
8. It is a sin.

JAMES AND PAUL ON FAITH AND WORKS / *James 2:14*

James and Paul each meant something different in using the words *faith* and *works*. Each of them was responding to a different need.

	James	**Paul**
Faith	Concerned with the danger of "dead faith"—he knew that shallow beliefs would never stand up to the trials believers would face in life. People will claim faith, but an unsubstantiated claim will be only empty words (see James 2:14).	Concerned with the exercise of "true faith" or saving faith—this faith not only opens the door for grace, but leads to obedient action (see Ephesians 2:8-10).
Works	Claiming works are the natural product of faith that is alive, he emphasized the post-salvation results of the life of faith. This is very similar to Ephesians 2:8-10.	Called "works" those legalistic efforts to secure one's own salvation—any attempt at self-justification. For Paul, the beginning of salvation was always faith. After that, works followed (see Galatians 3:2).

FAITH THAT WORKS / *James 2:14*

James offers a larger number of similarities to the Sermon on the Mount than any other book in the New Testament. James relied heavily on Jesus' teachings.

Lesson	Reference
Whenever trouble comes your way, be joyful.	James 1:2 Matthew 5:10-12
When your endurance is fully developed, you will be strong in character and ready for anything.	James 1:4 Matthew 5:48
Ask God, and he will answer.	James 1:5; 5:15 Matthew 7:7-12
Those who are poor (who don't amount to much by the world's standards) should be glad, for God has honored them.	James 1:9 Matthew 5:3
Watch out for your anger. . . . It can be dangerous.	James 1:20 Matthew 5:22
Be merciful to others, as God is merciful to you.	James 2:13 Matthew 5:7; 6:14
Your faith must express itself in your actions.	James 2:14-16 Matthew 7:21-23
Blessed are the peacemakers; they plant in peace and reap a harvest of goodness.	James 3:17-18 Matthew 5:9
Friendship with the world makes you an enemy of God.	James 4:4 Matthew 6:24
When you humble yourself and realize your dependence on God, he will lift you up.	James 4:10 Matthew 5:3-4
Don't speak evil against each other. If you do, you are criticizing God's law.	James 4:11 Matthew 7:1-2
Treasures on earth will only rot away and be eaten by moths. Store up eternal treasures in heaven.	James 5:2-3 Matthew 6:19
Be patient in suffering, as God's prophets were patient.	James 5:10 Matthew 5:12
Be honest in your speech; just say a simple yes or no so that you will not sin.	James 5:12 Matthew 5:33-37

SPEECH / *James 3*

When our speech is motivated by	It is full of
Satan	Bitter jealousy
	Selfish ambition
	Earthly concerns and desires
	Unspiritual thoughts and ideas
	Disorder
	Evil
God and his wisdom	Purity
	Peace
	Consideration for others
	Submission
	Mercy
	Sincerity, impartiality
	Goodness

WORD PICTURES ON THE IMPORTANCE OF OUR SPEECH
James 3:2-12

In James 3, several word pictures are used to show the importance of mature speech.

Bit	A small bit controls a large animal.	Can we control our use of the tongue?
Rudder	A small piece of wood steers a huge ship in heavy wind.	The tongue, though small, can create grave consequences.
Fire	A small spark unleashes a destructive force.	Do we recognize the destructive force our words can have?
Animals	People can tame animals.	Can we tame our speech and our impulsive thoughts?
Poison	The venom of a snake kills its prey.	Can we keep our words from poisoning us and others?
Spring	A spring can produce only one kind of water.	Is our speech a spring that is good or foul?
Fig Tree	A tree bears just one kind of fruit.	Is our speech bearing good fruit, or is it mixed with bad?
Tongue	The tongue can be used for good or evil.	Does our speech reflect our Christian maturity?

TWO TYPES OF WISDOM / *James 3:14-18*

Wisdom from Below
Characterized by:

Bitter envy (v.14)

Selfish ambition (v.14)

Boasting (v.14)

Denying the truth (v.14)

Being earthly minded (v.15)

Being unspiritual (v.15)

From the devil (v.15)

Wisdom from Heaven
Characterized by:

Purity (v. 17)—personal transparency or Holiness

Peaceable (v.17)—willing to sacrifice for peace

Considerate (v.17)—gentle, not seeking its own way

Willing to yield (v.17)—agreeable, willing to reevaluate, open

Merciful (v.17)—compassionate

Impartial (v.17)—single-minded toward God and people

Sincere (v. 17)—without hypocrisy

Resulting in:

Disorder (v.16)

Evil Practice/actions (v.16)

Resulting in:

Good fruit (v.17)

Righteousness/good actions (v.18)

THE DOWNWARD SPIRAL OF OUR DESIRES / *James 4:1*

Without submission to God, our desires lead us down a well-worn path that will harm us and those around us (see James 1:14-15; 4:1-3).

Unchecked desires ————————————————— lead to

Not asking God ————————————————— leads to

Coveting, evil desires, wrong motives ————— lead to

Fights and quarrels ————————————————— lead to

Church life marked by death (slander, judging others, name calling, boasting, backbiting)

CHURCH WARS / *James 4:2*

Weapons and strategies are used in church fights and quarrels. James tells us the exact location of the manufacturing plants for all these weapons. The trouble begins in ourselves.

Missiles	Attacking church members from long range.
Guerrilla tactics	Ambushing the unsuspecting.
Snipers	Well-aimed criticisms.
Terrorism	No one is immune from being hurt.
Mines	Ensuring that others will fail in their efforts to serve God.
Espionage	Using friendships to get potentially damaging information about others.
Propaganda	Using gossip to spread damaging information about others.
Cold War	Freezing out an opponent by withdrawing or refusing to talk to him or her.
Nuclear Attack	Being willing to sacrifice the church if the goals of my group are not met.

NO MIDDLE GROUND / *James 4:4*

Why is it impossible to be a friend of the world and a friend of God at the same time? The paths lead in opposite directions and to very different conclusions:

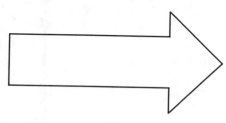

Faith, Hope, Love (1 Corinthians 13:13)

Love, Joy, Peace . . . (Galatians 5:22)

Abundant Living (John 10:10)

Eternal Life (John 3:16)

Love of Neighbor (Matthew 7:12)

Strife/Quarrels (James 4:1-3)

Materialism (1 John 2:15-17)

Hopelessness (Ephesians 2:12)

Egocentric Living (James 4:3)

Death (Proverbs 14:12)

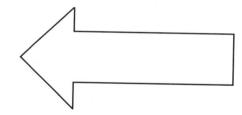

TACTICS AND WEAPONS FOR RESISTING THE DEVIL / *James 4:7*

We are commanded to "resist" the devil, to take a stand against him, now! Those intent on submitting to God ask, "how?"

Tactics	God has not left us without battle plans. Here are some of his instructions:

Refuse to accept Satan's suggestion that we can be separated from Christ.	Romans 8:38-39
Ignore the temptation to doubt God's grace.	1 John 3:19-24
Reject the lie that we are beyond forgiveness.	1 John 1:9
Pray before, during, and after attacks by the devil.	Philippians 4:4-7 1 Thessalonians 5:16-24 James 1:2-8
Allow Christ to replace our way of thinking with his way of thinking.	Philippians 2:5-8; 4:8-9 Romans 12:1-2

Weapons	While the devil employs weapons of terror and illusion, God equips us with weapons of real power. They are only ineffective when we leave them unused. Among them are:

The belt of truth—whenever the truth is spoken and lived, the devil is unwelcome.	Ephesians 6:14 John 8:32; 14:6; 17:17
The breastplate of righteousness—living rightly is the result of advanced training in the faith. When we are living under God's guidance we are on guard against the devil's attacks.	Ephesians 6:14 Hebrews 5:12-14 1 Peter 2:12
The footwear of the gospel of peace—communicating the gospel is taking back territory controlled by the devil.	Ephesians 6:15 Matthew 24:14 Romans 1:16
The shield of faith—our faith in Christ makes him our shield and protector.	Ephesians 6:16 Hebrews 11:1 1 Peter 1:3-5
The helmet of salvation—the salvation that God offers is our eternal protection.	Ephesians 6:17 1 Thessalonians 5:8-9 Romans 1:16
The sword of the Spirit, God's Word—the Bible is a weapon when its truth is put to use, exposing the devil's work and helping those who are losing the battle.	Ephesians 6:17 2 Timothy 3:16 Hebrews 4:12
Prayer—in prayer we rely on God's help.	Ephesians 6:18-20 Hebrews 4:16 James 5:13-16

PERSECUTED PROPHETS / *James 5:10* See also *Mark 12:1-8*

Prophet	Persecution	Passage
Moses	The Israelites complained and rebelled against Moses because they were in the desert and had no water.	Exodus 17:1-7
David	King Saul persecuted David because David was becoming a powerful leader, threatening Saul's position.	1 Samuel 20–27 Psalms 31:13; 59:1-4
Various Prophets	Jezebel killed many of God's prophets because she didn't like having her evil ways pointed out.	1 Kings 18:3-4
Elijah	Elijah had to flee for his life when he confronted King Ahab and Queen Jezebel with their sins.	1 Kings 18:10–19:2
Micaiah	King Ahab thought Micaiah was stirring up trouble rather than prophesying from God, so he threw Micaiah into prison.	2 Chronicles 18:12-27
Elisha	A king of Israel threatened persecution for Elisha because he thought Elisha caused a famine.	2 Kings 6:31
Zechariah	Zechariah was executed by King Joash because he confronted the people of Judah for disregarding God's word.	2 Chronicles 23:20-22
Jeremiah	King Zedekiah thought Jeremiah was a traitor for prophesying Jerusalem's fall, so he had Jeremiah thrown into prison, then into a muddy cistern.	Jeremiah 37:1–38:13
Daniel	Daniel was caught praying and was thrown into the lions' den.	Daniel 6

MONEY: WHAT DOES GOD SAY? / *James 5:1*

Dangers of Money	Forgetting God	Deuteronomy 6:10-13; 8:11-20 Proverbs 18:11 Luke 18:24 1 Timothy 6:9-10
	Acting dishonestly, taking advantage of others	2 Kings 5:20-27 Proverbs 10:2; 22:16, 22-23 Isaiah 5:8-9 Amos 3:10; 5:11; 8:4-7 James 5:1-6
	Being greedy	Exodus 20:17 Luke 12:15-21 Ephesians 5:5
	Allowing it to take God's place	Proverbs 11:28; 18:11 Matthew 6:24 Luke 6:24
Advice about Money	Give generously and cheerfully to help the poor	Proverbs 11:24-25; 19:17; 21:13; 22:9; 28:27 Luke 12:33-34 2 Corinthians 9:7
	Give generously to those doing God's work	Deuteronomy 25:4 Nehemiah 13:10-11 1 Timothy 5:17
	Get out and stay out of debt	Psalm 37:21 Proverbs 3:27-28; 22:7 Romans 13:8
	Tithe	Malachi 3:8-10 1 Corinthians 16:2
	Don't co-sign for another's debt	Proverbs 11:15; 17:18; 22:26-27
	Don't accept bribes	Exodus 23:8 Psalm 15:5 Proverbs 17:23
	Pay your taxes	Romans 13:6-7
	Always be honest	Deuteronomy 25:24-16 Proverbs 20:10, 23 Luke 16:10-12
	Always provide for your family	1 Timothy 5:8
	Plan wisely for the future	Proverbs 21:20; 22:3; 24:3-4, 27; 27:23-27

Correct Perspective on Money	Everything comes from God	1 Chronicles 29:11-14 Colossians 1:15-17
	Money cannot buy salvation	Proverbs 11:4 Ezekiel 7:19 Matthew 16:26 Luke 16:19-31; 18:18-25
	Riches do not last	James 1:1-1 Revelation 18:11-19
	Money never satisfies	Ecclesiastes 5:10-11 Luke 12:15
	Don't show favoritism to the rich	James 2:1-9
	Money carries responsibility	1 Timothy 6:17-19
	Obey God rather than chase after money	Psalms 17:15; 119:36 Proverbs 19:1
	Be content	Philippians 4:11-13 1 Timothy 6:8 Hebrews 13:5
A Word to Employers	Pay wages in full and right away	Leviticus 19:13 Deuteronomy 24:14-15 Jeremiah 22:13 Malachi 3:5
	Severe judgment awaits employers who unfairly withhold wages	Amos 5:11; 8:4-7 James 5:1-6
	Be fair	Proverbs 11:26 Ephesians 6:9 Colossians 4:1

1 PETER

MEGATHEMES IN 1 PETER

Theme	Explanation	Importance
Salvation	Our salvation is a gracious gift from God. God chose us out of his love for us, Jesus died to pay the penalty for our sin, and the Holy Spirit cleansed us from sin when we believed. Eternal life is a wonderful gift for those who trust in Christ.	Our safety and security are in God. If we experience joy in relationship with Christ now, how much greater will our joy be when he returns and we see him face to face. Such a hope should motivate us to serve Christ with greater commitment.
Persecution	Peter offers faithful believers comfort and hope. We should expect ridicule, rejection, and suffering because we are Christians. Persecution makes us stronger because it refines our faith. We can face persecution victoriously, as Christ did, if we rely on him.	Christians still suffer for what they believe. We should expect persecution, but we don't have to be terrified by it. The fact that we will live eternally with Christ should give us the confidence, patience, and hope to stand firm even when we are persecuted.
God's Family	We are privileged to belong to God's family, a community with Christ as the founder and foundation. Everyone in this community is related— we are all brothers and sisters, loved equally by God.	Because Christ is the foundation of our family, we must be devoted, loyal, and faithful to him. By obeying him, we show that we are his children. We must accept the challenge to live differently from the society around us.
Family Life	Peter encouraged the wives of unbelievers to submit to their husbands' authority as a means of winning them to Christ. He urged all family members to treat others with sympathy, love, compassion, and humility.	We must treat our families lovingly. Though it's never easy, willing service is the best way to influence loved ones. To gain the strength we need for self-discipline and submission, we need to pray for God's help.
Judgment	God will judge everyone with perfect justice. We all will face God. He will punish evildoers and those who persecute God's people. Those who love him will be rewarded with life forever in his presence.	Because all are accountable to God, we can leave judgment of others to him. We must not hate or resent those who persecute us. We should realize that we will be held responsible for how we live each day.

THE CHURCHES OF PETER'S LETTER / *1 Peter 1:1*

Peter addressed his letter to the churches located throughout Bithynia, Pontus, Asia, Galatia, and Cappadocia. Paul had evangelized many of these areas; other areas had churches that were begun by the Jews who were in Jerusalem on the day of Pentecost and heard Peter's powerful sermon (see Acts 2:9-11).

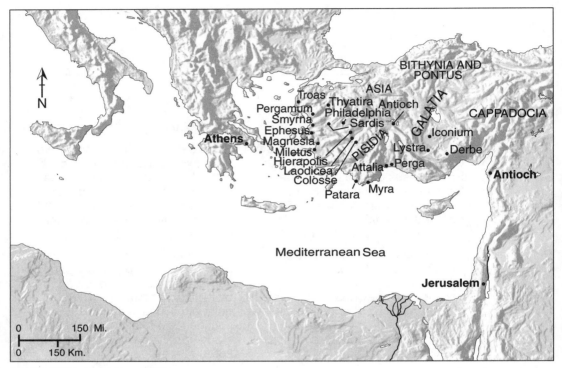

Copyright © 2001 by Tyndale House Publishers

THE INHERITANCE / 1 Peter 1:4

Our promised inheritance comes from our loving Father. We cannot earn an inheritance; it is a gift. The word "inheritance" is described in various ways in Scripture.

The Promised Land	Numbers 32:19
	Deuteronomy 12:9; 15:4; 19:10
	Joshua 11:23
	Psalm 105:11
God Himself	Psalm 16:5
Eternal Life	Daniel 12:13
	Matthew 19:29
	Mark 10:17
	Titus 3:7
The Earth	Matthew 5:5
The Kingdom of God	Matthew 25:34
	1 Corinthians 15:50
	Ephesians 5:5
Glory with Christ	Romans 8:17
Sealed by the Holy Spirit	Ephesians 1:14
A Reward	Colossians 3:24
Salvation	Hebrews 1:14
Eternal	Hebrews 9:15
A Blessing	1 Peter 3:9
Heavenly City, New Jerusalem	Revelation 21:2-7

REASONS TO REJOICE IN TRIALS / *1 Peter 1:7*

Reason	Verses	Application
Trials strengthen our faith.	"We can rejoice, too, when we run into problems and trials, for we know that they are good for us—they help us learn to endure." (Romans 5:3) (See also 1 Peter 4:19)	Trials and suffering burn away self-reliance and promote reliance on God.
Trials help us look forward to the glory we will experience when Christ comes to restore us.	"In his kindness God called you to his eternal glory by means of Jesus Christ. After you have suffered a little while, he will restore, support, and strengthen you, and he will place you on a firm foundation." (1 Peter 5:10)	Trials and suffering teach us not to be so comfortable or dependent upon this life.
Trials expose a deep vein of patience in us.	"But when the Holy Spirit controls our lives, he will produce this kind of fruit in us: love, joy, peace, patience, kindness, goodness, faithfulness." (Galatians 5:22)	Trials and suffering are the only way for us to develop patience.
Trials help us resist worldly desires.	"So then, since Christ suffered physical pain, you must arm yourselves with the same attitude he had, and be ready to suffer, too. For if you are willing to suffer for Christ, you have decided to stop sinning." (1 Peter 4:1)	Trials and suffering help us see the futility of worldly desires so we can devote ourselves to God.
Trials can bring rewards from Jesus.	"God blesses the people who patiently endure testing. Afterward they will receive the crown of life that God has promised to those who love him." (James 1:12) (See also Romans 8:18; 2 Corinthians 4:17; 1 Peter 5:4)	Trials and suffering are slight compared to the eternity of joy that we have been promised.

SUBMISSION / *1 Peter 3*

Submission is voluntarily cooperating with someone, first out of love and respect for God and then out of love and respect for that person. Submitting to nonbelievers is difficult, but it is a vital part of leading them to Jesus Christ. We are not called to submit to nonbelievers to the point that we compromise our relationship with God, but we must look for every opportunity to humbly serve in the power of God's Spirit.

Submission is:

Functional	a distinguishing of our roles and the work we are called to do
Relational	a loving acknowledgment of another's value as a person
Reciprocal	a mutual, humble cooperation with one another
Universal	an acknowledgment by the church of the all-encompassing lordship of Jesus Christ

ALL RISE FOR THE JUDGE / *1 Peter 4:5*

Matthew 12:36

And I tell you this, that you must give an account on judgment day of every idle word you speak.

Acts 10:42

And he ordered us to preach everywhere and to testify that Jesus is ordained of God to be the judge of all—the living and the dead.

Romans 14:9

Christ died and rose again for this very purpose, so that he might be Lord of those who are alive and of those who have died.

2 Timothy 4:1

And so I solemnly urge you before God and before Christ Jesus—who will someday judge the living and the dead when he appears to set up his Kingdom.

Revelation 20:11-15

And I saw a great white throne, and I saw the one who was sitting on it. The earth and sky fled from his presence, but they found no place to hide.

I saw the dead, both great and small, standing before God's throne. And the books were opened, including the Book of Life. And the dead were judged according to the things written in the books, according to what they had done.

The sea gave up the dead in it, and death and the grave gave up the dead in them. They were all judged according to their deeds.

And death and the grave were thrown into the lake of fire. This is the second death—the lake of fire.

And anyone whose name was not found recorded in the Book of Life was thrown into the lake of fire.

2 PETER

MEGATHEMES IN 2 PETER

Theme	Explanation	Importance
Diligence	If our faith is real, it will be evident in our godly behavior. If people are diligent in Christian growth, they won't backslide or be deceived by false teachers.	Growth is essential. It begins with faith and culminates in love for others. To keep growing we need to know God, keep on following him, and remember what he taught us. We must remain diligent in faithful obedience and Christian growth.
False Teachers	Peter warns the church to beware of false teachers. These teachers were proud of their position, promoted sexual sin, and advised against keeping the Ten Commandments. Peter countered them by pointing to the Spirit-inspired Scriptures as our authority.	Christians need discernment to be able to resist false teachers. God can rescue us from their lies if we stay true to his Word, the Bible, and reject those who distort the truth.
Christ's Return	One day Christ will create a new heaven and earth, where we will live forever. As Christians, our hope is in this promise. But with Christ's return comes his judgment on all who refuse to believe.	The cure for complacency, lawlessness, and heresy is found in the confident assurance that Christ will return. God is still giving unbelievers time to repent. To be ready, Christians must keep on trusting and resist the pressure to give up waiting for Christ's return.

GOD'S PATIENCE / 2 Peter 3:9

Exodus 34:6	He passed in front of Moses and said, "I am the LORD, I am the LORD, the merciful and gracious God. I am slow to anger and rich in unfailing love and faithfulness."
Numbers 14:18	The LORD is slow to anger and rich in unfailing love, forgiving every kind of sin and rebellion. Even so he does not leave sin unpunished, but he punishes the children for the sins of their parents to the third and fourth generations.
Psalm 86:15	But you, O Lord, are a merciful and gracious God, slow to get angry, full of unfailing love and truth.
Jeremiah 15:15	Then I said, "LORD, you know I am suffering for your sake. Punish my persecutors! Don't let them kill me! Be merciful to me and give them what they deserve!"
Ezekiel 18:23	Do you think, asks the Sovereign LORD, that I like to see wicked people die? Of course not! I only want them to turn from their wicked ways and live.
Jonah 4:2	So he complained to the LORD about it: "Didn't I say before I left home that you would do this, LORD? That is why I ran away to Tarshish! I knew that you were a gracious and compassionate God, slow to get angry and filled with unfailing love. I knew how easily you could cancel your plans for destroying these people."
Romans 2:4	Don't you realize how kind, tolerant, and patient God is with you? Or don't you care? Can't you see how kind he has been in giving you time to turn from your sin?
Romans 9:22	God has every right to exercise his judgment and his power, but he also has the right to be very patient with those who are the objects of his judgment and are fit only for destruction.
Romans 11:32	God has imprisoned all people in their own disobedience so he could have mercy on everyone.
1 Timothy 2:4	He wants everyone to be saved and to understand the truth.

1 JOHN

MEGATHEMES IN 1 JOHN

Theme	Explanation	Importance
Sin	Even Christians sin. Sin requires God's forgiveness, and Christ's death provides it for us. Determining to live according to God's standards in the Bible shows that our life is being transformed.	We cannot deny our sinful nature, maintain that we are "above" sinning, or minimize the consequences of sin in our relationship with God. We must resist the attraction of sin, yet we must confess when we do sin.
Love	Christ commands us to love others as he loved us. This love is evidence that we are truly saved. God is the Creator of love; he cares that his children love each other.	Love means putting others first and being unselfish. Love is action—showing others we care—not just saying it. To show love we must give sacrificially of our time and money to meet the needs of others.
Family of God	We become God's children by believing in Christ. God's life in us enables us to love our fellow family members.	How we treat others shows who our Father is. Live as a faithful, loving family member.
Truth and Error	Teaching that the physical body does not matter, false teachers encouraged believers to throw off moral restraints. They also taught that Christ wasn't really a man and that we must be saved by having some special mystical knowledge. The result was that people became indifferent to sin.	God is truth and light, so the more we get to know him, the better we can keep focused on the truth. Don't be led astray by any teaching that denies Christ's deity or humanity. Check the message; test the claims.
Assurance	God is in control of heaven and earth. Because his word is true, we can have assurance of eternal life and victory over sin. By faith we can be certain of our eternal destiny with him.	Assurance of our relationship with God is a promise, but it is also a way of life. We build our confidence by trusting in God's Word and in Christ's provision for our sin.

LIGHT VERSUS DARKNESS / 1 John 1:5

In many places in Scripture, the realm of God and the realm of evil are contrasted by the differences between light and darkness:

Darkness	Light	Reference
Despairing condition	Hopeful condition	Isaiah 9:2
Inability to recognize the light	Ability to enlighten the world	John 1:4-5, 9
The power of Satan	The power of God	Acts 26:18
Evil deeds	Good deeds	Romans 13:12-14
Natural heart condition	Gift from God	2 Corinthians 4:6
Fruitless works	Source of all that is good, right, true	Ephesians 5:8-11
Spiritual forces of evil	Armor of God	Ephesians 6:12-13
Powerful captivity	Kingdom of the Son, redemption, forgiveness	Colossians 1:12-14
Inability to exist in God's presence	God's presence, fellowship with God, cleansing of sin	1 John 1:5, 7
Transient nature	Permanent nature	1 John 2:8-11

JOHN COUNTERS FALSE TEACHINGS / 1 John 1:6

John counters two major threads in the false teachings of the heretics in this letter:

1:6, 8, 10	They denied the reality of sin. John says that if we continue in sin, we can't claim to belong to God. If we say we have no sin, we are only fooling ourselves and refusing to accept the truth.
2:22; 4:1-3	They denied that Jesus was the Messiah—God in the flesh. John said that if we believe that Jesus was God incarnate and trust him for our salvation, we are children of God.

A BOOK OF CONTRASTS / 1 John 2:7, 21

One of the distinct features of John's writing style was his habit of noting both sides of a conflict. He wrote to show the difference between real Christianity and anything else. Here are some of his favorite contrasts.

Contrast between	Passage
Light and darkness	1:5
The new commandment and the old commandment	2:7-8
Loving the Father and loving the world	2:15-16
Christ and Antichrist	2:18
Truth and lies	2:20-21
Children of God and children of the Devil	3:1-10
Eternal life and eternal death	3:14
Love and hatred	3:15-16
True prophecy and false prophecy	4:1-3
Love and fear	4:18-19
Having life and not having life	5:11-12

LOVE ONE ANOTHER / 1 John 2:9

The New Testament stresses the centrality of believers showing love to their Christian "brothers and sisters." Such love reaches out beyond its borders and draws unbelievers into the fellowship. Such love builds unity in the church.

John 13:34	So now I am giving you a new commandment: Love each other. Just as I have loved you, you should love each other.
John 15:17	I command you to love each other.
Romans 13:8	Pay all your debts, except the debt of love for others. You can never finish paying that! If you love your neighbor, you will fulfill all the requirements of God's law.
1 Peter 1:22	Now you can have sincere love for each other as brothers and sisters because you were cleansed from your sins when you accepted the truth of the Good News. So see to it that you really do love each other intensely with all your hearts.
1 John 3:11	This is the message we have heard from the beginning: We should love one another.
1 John 3:23	And this is his commandment: We must believe in the name of his Son, Jesus Christ, and love one another, just as he commanded us.
1 John 4:7	Dear friends, let us continue to love one another, for love comes from God. Anyone who loves is born of God and knows God.
1 John 4:11	Dear friends, since God loved us that much, we surely ought to love each other.
2 John 5	And now I want to urge you, dear lady, that we should love one another. This is not a new commandment, but one we had from the beginning.

YOU HAVE CONQUERED THE EVIL ONE / 1 John 2:13

When Jesus came to earth in a human body, his express purpose was to conquer the evil one—Satan. All of humanity is bound in sin and under Satan's rule. Through Jesus' death and resurrection, he bound Satan and shattered his power. Yet Satan is still active until the day when Christ returns to set up his glorious kingdom. Then Satan will be sent to the place of torment reserved for him and his demons.

Believers have been set free from Satan's authority and have been given power over him. Yet the battle rages as spiritual warfare continues between Satan's forces and God's forces. Satan battles against anyone who loves the Lord. But believers are promised power in times of intense spiritual battle. The following steps will help you if you sense that you are fighting a spiritual battle:

1. Realize that the battle is not against "flesh and blood" but against the spirit world and evil forces.

   Ephesians 6:12

2. Trust that Satan's power can be broken in any specific area of his domain, and utilize the powerful spiritual weapons given to you by God for the destruction of Satan's power.

   Acts 26:18
   2 Corinthians 10:4-5
   Ephesians 6:16
   1 Thessalonians 5:8

3. Challenge Satan and his power by believing in Jesus' name, using God's Word, praying in the Spirit, and fasting.

   Matthew 6:16
   Acts 6:4; 16:16-18
   Ephesians 6:17-18

4. Stay fervently committed to God's truth and righteousness.

   Romans 12:1-2
   Ephesians 6:14

5. Proclaim the gospel of the kingdom in the fullness of the Spirit.

   Matthew 4:23
   Acts 1:8
   Romans 1:16
   Ephesians 6:15

6. Pray especially for the Holy Spirit to convict the lost.

   John 16:7-11

7. Keep morally fit by loving God, not the temptations of this world.

   1 Corinthians 10:13
   1 John 2:15-17

GOD VS. THE EVIL WORLD / *1 John 2:15*

John warned believers not to love this world and its selfish pleasures. Christians stand in a war zone. The battle takes place here on earth as the spiritual forces of God battle against those of Satan. While God allows Satan to rule over the earth through the minds of those in rebellion against God, Satan's kingdom will one day be destroyed. Christians live in this world, but are not of it. Satan hates Christians' detachment and will attempt to make life as difficult as possible for Christ's followers. To give in to the senseless lust for possessions and power, to spend money on selfish desires and foolish upgrades in cars, clothes, homes, and equipment while ignoring the needs of others is to lose the cosmic war to Satan. So, Christian, know that Satan wars against you, and remember that you represent the winning side.

Reference	Verse
Matthew 6:24	No one can serve two masters. For you will hate one and love the other, or be devoted to one and despise the other. You cannot serve both God and money.
John 12:31	The time of judgment for the world has come, when the prince of this world will be cast out.
John 14:30	I don't have much more time to talk to you, because the prince of this world approaches. He has no power over me.
John 15:18	When the world hates you, remember it hated me before it hated you.
Ephesians 6:11-12	Put on all of God's armor so that you will be able to stand firm against all strategies and tricks of the Devil. For we are not fighting against people made of flesh and blood, but against the evil rulers and authorities of the unseen world, against those mighty powers of darkness who rule this world, and against wicked spirits in the heavenly realms.
James 4:4	You adulterers! Don't you realize that friendship with this world makes you an enemy of God? I say it again, that if your aim is to enjoy this world, you can't be a friend of God.
1 John 2:16	For the world offers only the lust for physical pleasure, the lust for everything we see, and pride in our possessions. These are not from the Father. They are from this evil world.
1 John 3:1	See how very much our heavenly Father loves us, for he allows us to be called his children, and we really are! But the people who belong to this world don't know God, so they don't understand that we are his children.
1 John 4:4	But you belong to God, my dear children. You have already won your fight with these false prophets, because the Spirit who lives in you is greater than the spirit who lives in the world.
1 John 5:19	We know that we are children of God and that the world around us is under the power and control of the evil one.

TEMPTATIONS / *1 John 2:17*

	Temptation of Eve (Genesis 3:4-6)	Temptation of Christ (Matthew 4:1-11; Luke 4:1-13)	Temptation of the Church Today
Lust of the flesh The desire to fulfill pleasures, physical desires	The fruit looked delicious and would be good to eat.	Turn the stones into bread.	Take what is easier or more pleasurable rather than God's best.
Lust of the eyes The constant craving for more	The fruit was a pleasure to look at.	Gain all the kingdoms of the world, as far as the eye can see.	Respond impulsively, without restraint or self-control.
The pride of life The desire for power or possessions	The fruit was desirable for gaining wisdom; Eve wanted to "be like God."	Throw yourself down and the angels will come and rescue you for God will not allow you to be hurt.	Build a power base rather than seek to serve others.

IN TRUTH AND ACTION / *1 John 3:17-18*

What does the New Testament say about good works? Read the following selection of verses:

Jesus said:

Matthew 5:16 ". . . let your good deeds shine out for all to see, so that everyone will praise your heavenly Father."

Matthew 6:3-4 "But when you give to someone, don't tell your left hand what your right hand is doing. Give your gifts in secret, and your Father, who knows all secrets, will reward you."

Matthew 6:19-21 "Don't store up treasures here on earth. . . . Store your treasures in heaven. . . . Wherever your treasure is, there your heart and thoughts will also be."

Paul said:

2 Corinthians 9:8 "And God will generously provide all you need. Then you will always have everything you need and plenty left over to share with others."

Ephesians 2:10 "For we are God's masterpiece. He has created us anew in Christ Jesus, so that we can do the good things he planned for us long ago."

1 Timothy 2:10 "For women who claim to be devoted to God should make themselves attractive by the good things they do."

1 Timothy 6:17-18 "Tell those who are rich . . . to use their money to do good. They should be rich in good works."

2 Timothy 3:16-17 "All Scripture . . . is God's way of preparing us in every way, fully equipped for every good thing God wants us to do."

Titus 3:8 "These things I have told you are all true. I want you to insist on them so that everyone who trusts in God will be careful to do good deeds all the time. These things are good and beneficial for everyone."

The writer of Hebrews said:

Hebrews 10:24 "Think of ways to encourage one another to outbursts of love and good deeds."

James said:

James 2:15-17 "Suppose you see a brother or sister who needs food or clothing . . . but then you don't give that person any food or clothing. What good does that do? So you see, it isn't enough just to have faith. Faith that doesn't show itself by good deeds is no faith at all—it is dead and useless."

James 3:13 "If you are wise and understand God's ways, live a life of steady goodness so that only good deeds will pour forth. And if you don't brag about the good you do, then you will be truly wise!"

Peter said:

1 Peter 2:12, 15 "Be careful how you live among your unbelieving neighbors. Even if they accuse you of doing wrong, they will see your honorable behavior. . . . It is God's will that your good lives should silence those who make foolish accusations against you."

John said:

1 John 3:18 "Dear children, let us stop just saying we love each other; let us really show it by our actions."

HERESIES / 1 John 4

Most of the eyewitnesses to Jesus' ministry had died by the time John composed this letter. Some of the second- or third-generation Christians began to have doubts about what they had been taught about Jesus. Some Christians with a Greek background had a hard time believing that Jesus was human as well as divine, because in **Platonic thought** the spirit was all-important. The body was only a prison from which one desired to escape. Heresies developed from a uniting of this kind of Platonic thought and Christianity.

A particularly widespread false teaching, later called **Docetism** (from a Greek word meaning "to seem"), held that Jesus was actually a spirit who only appeared to have a body. In reality he cast no shadow and left no footprints; he was God but not man. Another heretical teaching, related to **Gnosticism** (from a Greek word meaning "knowledge"), held that all physical matter was evil, the spirit was good, and only the intellectually enlightened could enjoy the benefits of religion. Both groups found it hard to believe in a Savior who was fully human.

John answers these false teachers as an eyewitness to Jesus' life on earth. He saw Jesus, talked with him, touched him—he knew that Jesus was more than a mere spirit. In the very first sentence of his letter, John establishes that Jesus had been alive before the world began and also that he lived as a man among men and women. In other words, he was both divine and human.

Through the centuries, many heretics have denied that Jesus was both God and man. In John's day people had trouble believing he was human; today more people have problems seeing him as God. But Jesus' divine-human nature is the pivotal issue of Christianity. Before you accept what religious teachers say about any topic, listen carefully to what they believe about Jesus. To deny either his divinity or his humanity is to consider him less than Christ, the Savior.

SIGNS OF THE CULTS / *1 John 4:1*

Following are some common characteristics of the teachings of cults that attack Christianity. Knowing about them will help Christians stand firm.

1. A central authority makes the decisions.

Cults find their authority not in the Bible but in a powerful and dictatorial leader.

2. Special prophets or special revelation show that the cult has "new truth."

Because of so-called "problems" in the Bible or in Christian doctrine, cults appeal to new authorities or new spiritual revelation to counter Christianity.

3. Attacks on the Christian church.

Cults take great pains to show that Christian denominations show the disunity of the Christian church. The cult may point out immorality, racism, and hypocrisy in the Christian church in order to "prove" that it is not the true church.

4. Attacks on Christian doctrine.

To establish their authority, cults try to prove the "unreasonableness" of Christian doctrine. They especially attack the doctrine of the Trinity and of the deity of Christ.

5. Undermine Scripture.

Cults will twist the Scripture's grammatical or textual background, or string together unrelated verses, in order to "prove" some way-out viewpoint.

6. Promote salvation by works.

Cults stress actions—meetings, training, doing the work of the group—as essential to acceptance by God.

7. Undermine the assurance of eternal life in God's grace.

Cults teach that salvation exists in adherence to *their* teaching and practice, not in the merciful love of God through Jesus Christ.

OLD TESTAMENT TESTS FOR FALSE PROPHETS / *1 John 4:2*

In the Old Testament, various signs or works pointed to a true or false prophet. Many of these can be applied today.

1. Does the prophet use fortune-telling?

Divination was expressly forbidden by God (Deuteronomy 18:9-14). No true teacher or prophet would use fortune-telling, tarot cards, or have any dealing with dead spirits (Jeremiah 14:14; Ezekiel 12:24; Micah 3:7).

2. Have the prophet's short-term prophecies been fulfilled?

Deuteronomy 18:22 used this as a test. Do predictions come to pass?

3. Is the prophet marked by a desire to say only what pleases people?

Many false prophets told people what they wanted to hear. A true prophet serves God, not people (Jeremiah 8:11; 14:13; 23:17; Ezekiel 13:10; Micah 3:5).

4. Does the prophet draw people away from God?

Many teachers draw people to themselves or to the system or organization they have built (Deuteronomy 13:1-3).

5. Does the prophet's prophecy confirm the Bible's main teaching?

If a prophecy is inconsistent with or contradictory to Scripture, it is not to be believed.

6. What is the prophet's moral character?

False prophets were charged with lying (Jeremiah 8:10; 14:14), drunkenness (Isaiah 28:7), and immorality (Jeremiah 23:14).

7. Do other Spirit-led people discern authenticity in this prophet?

Discernment by others who are led of the Spirit is a key test (1 Kings 22:7). The New Testament used this a great deal (John 10:4-15; 1 Corinthians 2:14; 14:29, 32; 1 John 4:1).

THREE TESTS FOR BELIEVERS / *1 John 5:1*

Throughout this letter, John has been describing how to determine true believers. The false teachers had done a good job of confusing the believers, so John took them back to the basics and described three basic tests for discerning true believers. Like a three-braided cord, these three "tests" are interwoven, each dependent upon the other, none existing alone in the life of a true believer.

True believers . . .

1. Obey God's commands in his Word.	2:3-6; 2:28–3:10; 5:2-3
2. Love God and other believers; have lifestyles characterized by love.	2:7-11; 3:11-18; 4:7-12; 5:1-3
3. Believe in the truth of the gospel message that Jesus Christ is the Savior.	2:18-27; 4:1-6; 5:1, 4-5

IN JESUS ALONE / 1 John 5:11

John's Gospel contains many of Jesus' words that testify to this fact recorded in 1 John 5:11—eternal life is found only by believing in Jesus Christ.

John 3:15-16	"Everyone who believes in me will have eternal life. For God so loved the world that he gave his only Son, so that everyone who believes in him will not perish but have eternal life."
John 3:36	"All who believe in God's Son have eternal life. Those who don't obey the Son will never experience eternal life, but the wrath of God remains upon them."
John 4:14	"The water I give them takes away thirst altogether. It becomes a perpetual spring within them, giving them eternal life."
John 5:21	"He will even raise from the dead anyone he wants to, just as the Father does."
John 5:24	"I assure you, those who listen to my message and believe in God who sent me have eternal life. They will never be condemned for their sins, but they have already passed from death into life."
John 5:26	"The Father has life in himself, and he has granted his Son to have life in himself."
John 5:39-40	"You search the Scriptures because you believe they give you eternal life. But the Scriptures point to me! Yet you refuse to come to me so that I can give you this eternal life."
John 6:27	"But you shouldn't be so concerned about perishable things like food. Spend your energy seeking the eternal life that I, the Son of Man, can give you. For God the Father has sent me for that very purpose."
John 6:40	"For it is my Father's will that all who see his Son and believe in him should have eternal life—that I should raise them at the last day."
John 6:47	"I assure you, anyone who believes in me already has eternal life."
John 6:53-54	So Jesus said again, "I assure you, unless you eat the flesh of the Son of Man and drink his blood, you cannot have eternal life within you. But those who eat my flesh and drink my blood have eternal life, and I will raise them at the last day."
John 6:68	Simon Peter replied, "Lord, to whom would we go? You alone have the words that give eternal life."
John 10:28	"I give them eternal life, and they will never perish. No one will snatch them away from me."
John 11:25	Jesus told her, "I am the resurrection and the life. Those who believe in me, even though they die like everyone else, will live again."
John 14:6	Jesus told him, "I am the way, the truth, and the life. No one can come to the Father except through me."
John 17:2-3	For you have given him authority over everyone in all the earth. He gives eternal life to each one you have given him. And this is the way to have eternal life—to know you, the only true God, and Jesus Christ, the one you sent to earth.
John 20:31	But these are written so that you may believe that Jesus is the Messiah, the Son of God, and that by believing in him you will have life.

2 JOHN

MEGATHEMES IN 2 JOHN

Theme	Explanation	Importance
Truth	Following God's Word, the Bible, is essential to Christian living because God is truth. Christ's true followers consistently obey his truth.	To be loyal to Christ's teaching, we must seek to know the Bible, but we may never twist its message to our own needs or purposes or encourage others who misuse it.
Love	Christ's command is for Christians to love one another. This is the basic ingredient of true Christianity.	To obey Christ fully, we must believe his command to love others. Helping, giving, and meeting needs put love into practice.
False Leaders	We must be wary of religious leaders who are not true to Christ's teaching. We should not give them a platform to spread false teaching.	Don't encourage those who are opposed to Christ. Politely remove yourself from association with false leaders. Be aware of what is being taught in your church.

3 JOHN

MEGATHEMES IN 3 JOHN

Theme	Explanation	Importance
Hospitality	John wrote to encourage those who were kind to others. Genuine hospitality for traveling Christian workers was needed then and is still important today.	Faithful Christian teachers and missionaries need our support. Whenever you can extend hospitality to others, it will make you a partner in their ministry.
Pride	Diotrephes not only refused to offer hospitality but also set himself up as a church boss. Pride disqualified him from being a real leader.	Christian leaders must shun pride and its effects on them. Be careful not to misuse your position of leadership.
Faithfulness	Gaius and Demetrius were commended for their faithful work in the church. They were held up as examples of faithful, selfless servants.	Don't take for granted Christian workers who serve faithfully. Be sure to encourage them so they won't grow weary of serving.

JUDE

MEGATHEMES IN JUDE

Theme	Explanation	Importance
False Teachers	Jude warns against false teachers and leaders who reject the lordship of Christ, undermine the faith of others, and lead them astray. These leaders, and any who follow them, will be punished.	We must staunchly defend Christian truth. Make sure that you avoid leaders and teachers who distort the Bible to suit their own purposes. Genuine servants of God will faithfully portray Christ in their words and conduct.
Apostasy	Jude also warns against apostasy—turning away from Christ. We are to remember that God punishes rebellion against him. We must be careful not to drift away from a faithful commitment to Christ.	Those who do not seek to know the truth in God's Word are susceptible to apostasy. Christians must guard against any false teachings that would distract them from the truth preached by the apostles and written in God's Word.

REVELATION

MEGATHEMES IN REVELATION

Theme	Explanation	Importance
God's Sovereignty	God is sovereign. He is greater than any power in the universe. God is not to be compared with any leader, government, or religion. He controls history for the purpose of uniting true believers in loving fellowship with him.	Though Satan's power may temporarily increase, we are not to be led astray. God is all-powerful. He is in control. He will bring his true family safely into eternal life. Because he cares for us, we can trust him with our very life.
Christ's Return	Christ came to earth as a "Lamb," the symbol of his perfect sacrifice for our sin. He will return as the triumphant "Lion," the rightful ruler and conqueror. He will defeat Satan, settle accounts with all those who reject him, and bring his faithful people into eternity.	Assurance of Christ's return gives suffering Christians the strength to endure. We can look forward to his return as king and judge. Since no one knows the time when he will appear, we must be ready at all times by keeping our faith strong.
God's Faithful People	John wrote to encourage the church to resist the demands to worship the Roman emperor. He warns all God's faithful people to be devoted only to Christ. Revelation identifies who the faithful people are and what they should be doing until Christ returns.	You can take your place in the ranks of God's faithful people by believing in Christ. Victory is sure for those who resist temptation and make loyalty to Christ their top priority.
Judgment	One day God's anger toward sin will be fully and completely unleashed. Satan will be defeated with all of his agents. False religion will be destroyed. God will reward the faithful with eternal life, but all who refuse to believe in him will face eternal punishment.	Evil and injustice will not prevail forever. God's final judgment will put an end to these. We need to be certain of our commitment to Jesus if we want to escape this great final judgment. No one who rejects Christ will escape God's punishment.
Hope	One day God will create a new heaven and a new earth. All believers will live with him forever in perfect peace and security. Those who have already died will be raised to life. These promises for the future bring us hope.	Our great hope is that what Christ promises will come true. When we have confidence in our final destination, we can follow Christ with unwavering dedication no matter what we must face. We can be encouraged by hoping in Christ's return.

THE SEVEN CHURCHES / *Revelation 2:1–3:22*

The seven churches were located on a major Roman road. A letter carrier would leave the island of Patmos (where John was exiled), arriving first at Ephesus. He would travel north to Smyrna and Pergamum, turn southeast to Thyatira, and continue on to Sardis, Philadelphia, and Laodicea—in the exact order in which the letters were dictated.

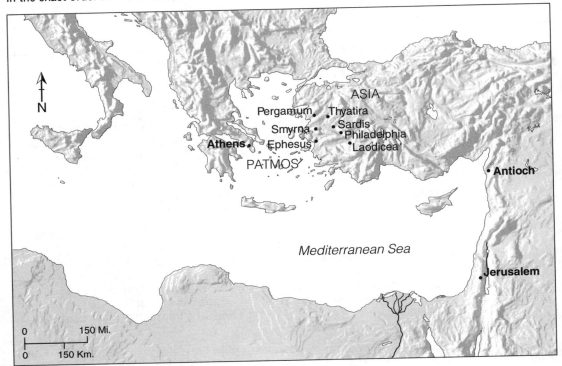

Copyright © 2001 by Tyndale House Publishers

INTERPRETING THE BOOK OF REVELATION / *Revelation 1*

Over the centuries, four main approaches to interpreting the book of Revelation have developed. Each approach has had capable supporters, but none has proved itself the only way to read this book. However, the most basic application question for each approach can be summarized by asking yourself, Will this help me become a better follower of Jesus Christ today?

Approach	Description	Challenge	Caution
Preterist View	John is writing to encourage Christians in his own day who are experiencing persecution from the Roman Empire.	To gain the same kind of encouragement John's first readers gained from the vivid images of God's sovereignty	Do not forget that most biblical prophecy has both an immediate and a future application.
Futurist View	Except for the first three chapters, John is describing events that will occur at the end of history.	To see in contemporary events many of the characteristics John describes and realize that the end could come at any time	Do not assume that we have "figured out" the future, since Jesus said that no one will know the day of his return before it happens.
Historicist View	The book of Revelation is a presentation of history from John's day until the second coming of Christ and beyond.	To note the consistency of human evil throughout history and recognize that names may change but the rebellion against God has not	Be careful before identifying current events or leaders as fulfilling aspects of the book of Revelation.
Idealist View	The book of Revelation is a symbolic representation of the continual struggle of good and evil. It does not refer to any particular historical events. It is applicable at any point in history.	To gain insight into the past, to prepare for the future, and to live obediently and confidently in the present	Do not avoid the book because it is difficult. Try to understand Revelation within its broader literary context.

Revelation is a complex book, and it has baffled interpreters for centuries. We can avoid a great deal of confusion by understanding the literary structure of this book. This approach will allow us to understand the individual scenes within the overall structure of Revelation and keep us from getting unnecessarily bogged down in the details of each vision. John gives hints throughout the book to indicate a change of subject, or a flashback to an earlier scene.

In chapter 1, John relates the circumstances that led to the writing of this book (1:1-20). In chapters 2 and 3, Jesus gives **special messages to the seven churches** of Asia Minor (2:1–3:22).

Suddenly, John is caught up into heaven, where he sees **a vision of God Almighty on his throne**. All of Christ's followers and the heavenly angels are worshiping God (4:1-11). John watches as God gives **a scroll with seven seals** to the worthy Lamb, Jesus Christ (5:1-14). The Lamb begins to open the seals one by one. As each seal is opened, a new vision appears.

As the first four seals are opened, riders appear on **horses of different colors:** war, famine, disease, and death are in their path (6:1-8). As the fifth seal is opened, John sees those in heaven who have been martyred for their faith in Christ (6:9-11).

A set of contrasting images appears at the opening of the sixth seal. On one side, there is a great earthquake, stars fall from the sky, and the sky rolls up like a scroll (6:12-17). On the other side, multitudes are before the throne, worshiping and praising God and the Lamb (7:1-17).

Then, the seventh seal is opened (8:1-5), unveiling a series of God's judgments announced by seven angels with **seven trumpets**. The first four angels bring hail, fire, a mountain of fire, and a falling star—the sun and moon are darkened (8:6-13). The fifth trumpet announces the coming of locusts with the power to sting (9:1-12). The sixth trumpet heralds the coming of an army of warriors on horses (9:13-21). In 10:1-11, John is given a small scroll to eat. Following this, John is commanded to measure the Temple of God (11:1-2). He sees two witnesses, who proclaim God's judgment on the earth for three and a half years (11:3-14).

Finally, the seventh trumpet sounds, calling the rival forces of good and evil to the final battle. On one side is Satan and his forces; on the other side stands Jesus Christ with his forces (11:15–13:18). In the midst of this call to battle, John sees three angels announcing **the final judgment** (14:6-13). Two angels begin to reap this harvest of judgment on the earth (14:14-20). Following on the heels of these two angels are seven more angels, who pour out God's judgment on the earth from **seven bowls** (15:1–16:21). One of these angels from the group of seven reveals to John a vision of a "great prostitute" called **Babylon** (symbolizing the Roman Empire), riding a scarlet beast (17:1-18). After the defeat of Babylon (18:1-24), a great multitude in heaven shouts praise to God for his mighty victory (19:1-10).

The final three chapters of the book of Revelation catalog the events that finalize Christ's victory over the enemy: **Satan's 1,000-year imprisonment** (20:1-10), the final judgment (20:11-15), and the creation of **a new earth and a new Jerusalem** (21:1–22:6). An angel then gives John final instructions concerning the visions John has seen and what to do once he has written them all down (22:7-11).

Revelation concludes with **the promise of Christ's return**, an offer to drink of the water of life that flows through the great street of the new Jerusalem, and a warning to those who read the book (22:12-21). May we pray with John, "Amen! Come, Lord Jesus!" (22:20).

The Bible ends with a message of warning and hope for men and women of every generation. Christ is victorious, and all evil has been done away with. As you read the book of Revelation, marvel at God's grace in the salvation of the saints and his power over the evil forces of Satan, and remember the hope of this victory to come.

THEORIES REGARDING THE TRIBULATION / *Revelation 3:13*

According to the premillenial view, the Tribulation is a seven-year period right before Christ's return when the Antichrist will rule. The premillenial position believes in a literal 1000-year reign of Christ (for more about the millenial positions, see the chart on page 585). All of these theories hold that Christ will return to judge those who have been the enemies of God and his people. (See also the chart on page 583.)

Pre-Tribulation	Christ will come secretly at the beginning of the seven-year period of tribulation and take the church. Then he will return at the end to defeat his enemies.
Mid-Tribulation	Christians will be removed from the earth ("raptured") halfway through the Tribulation (after three and a half years), when the Antichrist defiles the temple. At this time, Christ will return to take the church back, and then he will return again at the end of three and a half years to defeat his enemies.
Post-Tribulation	Christians must endure the catastrophes of the entire Tribulation period. Then, Christ will return at the end of the Tribulation to take all believers to heaven and immediately fight the forces of evil.

THE NAMES OF JESUS / *Revelation 3:14*

Scattered among the vivid images of the book of Revelation is a large collection of names for Jesus. Each one tells something of his character and highlights a particular aspect of his role within God's plan of redemption.

Reference	Jesus' Name	Reference	Jesus' Name
1:13	The Son of Man	12:10	Christ
1:17	The First and the Last	19:11	Faithful and True
1:18	The living one who died	19:13	The Word of God
2:18	The Son of God	19:16	King of kings
3:14	The faithful and true witness	19:16	Lord of lords
5:5	The Lion of the tribe of Judah	22:13	The Alpha and the Omega
5:5	The heir to David's throne	22:13	The Beginning and the End
5:6	Lamb	22:16	The bright morning star
7:17	Shepherd		

THE LETTERS TO THE SEVEN CHURCHES / *Revelation 3:22*

This summary of the letters to the seven churches shows us the qualities our churches should seek and those we should avoid.

Church	Reference	Commendation	Rebuke	Action
Ephesus	2:1-7	Hard work, perseverance	Forsaken first love	Remember and repent
Smyrna	2:8-11	Suffered persecution, poverty	None	Don't fear; be faithful
Pergamum	2:12-17	True to faith	Compromise	Repent
Thyatira	2:18-29	Love, faith, service	Immorality	Repent
Sardis	3:1-6	Effective	Superficial	Wake up; repent
Philadelphia	3:7-13	Faithful	None	Hold on
Laodicea	3:14-22	None	Lukewarm	Be earnest and repent

EVENTS IN REVELATION DESCRIBED ELSEWHERE IN THE BIBLE
Revelation 5:6

Other Reference	Revelation Reference	Event
Ezekiel 1:22-28	4:2-3; 10:1-3	Glowing rainbow around God's throne
Isaiah 53:7	5:6-8	Christ is pictured as a Lamb
Psalm 96	5:9-14	New song
Zechariah 1:7-11; 6:1-8	6:1-8	Horses and riders
Isaiah 2:19-22	6:12; 8:5; 11:13	Earthquake
Joel 2:28-32 Acts 2:14-21	6:12	Moon turns blood red
Mark 13:21-25	6:13	Stars falling from the sky
Isaiah 34:1-4	6:14	Sky rolled up like a scroll
Zephaniah 1:14-18 1 Thessalonians 5:1-3	6:15-17	God's inescapable wrath
Jeremiah 49:35-39	7:1	Four winds of judgment
Luke 8:26-34	9:1-2; 17:3-8	Bottomless pit
Joel 1:2–2:11	9:3-11	Plague of locusts
Luke 21:20-24	11:1-2	Trampling of the holy city of Jerusalem
Zechariah 4	11:3-6	Two olive trees as witnesses
Daniel 7	13:1-10	A beast coming out of the sea
2 Thessalonians 2:7-14	13:11-15	Wondrous signs and miracles done by the evil beast
Jeremiah 25:15-29	14:9-12	Drinking the cup of God's wrath
Isaiah 21:1-10	18:2-3	"Babylon" falls
Matthew 22:1-14	19:5-8	Wedding feast of the Lamb
Ezekiel 38–39	20:7-10	Conflict with Gog and Magog
John 5:19-30	20:11-15	Judging of all people
Ezekiel 37:21-28	21:3	God lives among his people
Isaiah 25:1-8	21:4	Our tears will be wiped away forever
Genesis 2:8-14	22:1-2	Tree of life
1 Corinthians 13:11-12	22:3-5	We will see God face-to-face
Daniel 7:18-28	22:5	Believers will reign with God forever

THE SEVEN SEALS / *Revelation 6:1*

Seal	Reference	Description	Possible meanings
1. Rider on the white horse	6:1-2	A rider on a white horse has a bow and a crown and rides out as a conqueror bent on conquest.	Some believe that this rider symbolizes the spread of the Good News or that the rider is Christ himself. Others suggest that this symbolizes mankind's lust for conquest.
2. Rider on the red horse	6:3-4	A rider on a red horse has agreat sword and is permitted to take peace from the earth so that people will kill one another.	This rider symbolizes coming warfare, even civil warfare, with great bloodshed.
3. Rider on the black horse	6:5-6	A rider on a black horse has a pair of scales and brings famine and pestilence on the earth.	This rider symbolizes famine and pestilence.
4. Rider on the pale horse	6:7-8	A rider on a pale horse is called Death and has the Grave with him.	This rider is called Death, and Hades (the grave) is his inseparable companion. Together they are given power to kill a fourth of the earth's population.
5. Souls of the martyrs under the altar	6:9-11	The souls of the martyrs who were killed for being faithful in their witness are under the altar crying out for vengeance for their blood.	The breaking of this seal announces God's plan to judge those who persecuted believers.
6. Great earthquake	6:12-17	People on the earth face calamities: a huge earthquake and strange occurrences in the sky.	The wrath and power of the Lamb are seen in the cataclysmic earthquake and the supernatural events in the sky.
7. Silence in heaven	8:1	When the last seal is opened, there is complete silence in heaven.	The seventh seal either begins the next cycle of judgments, or it signals the end and Christ's return.

COSMIC DISTURBANCES AT THE DAY OF THE LORD
Revelation 6:12-14

The images in Revelation are not that unusual when compared to the prophets' description of the coming day of the Lord. The Old Testament has many of the same images that John saw.

Isaiah 2:10-22	". . . When the Lord rises to shake the earth, his enemies will crawl with fear into holes in the ground."
Isaiah 13:10	"The heavens will be black above them. No light will shine from stars or sun or moon."
Isaiah 34:4	"The heavens above will melt away and disappear like a rolled-up scroll. The stars will fall from the sky, just as withered leaves and fruit fall from a tree."
Jeremiah 4:24-29	"I looked at the earth, and it was empty and formless. I looked at the heavens, and there was no light."
Ezekiel 32:7-8	"When I blot you out, I will veil the heavens and darken the stars. I will cover the sun with a cloud, and the moon will not give you its light. Yes, I will bring darkness everywhere across your land."
Hosea 10:8	". . . They will beg the mountains to bury them and the hills to fall on them."
Joel 2:11, 31	". . . The day of the Lord is an awesome, terrible thing. Who can endure it? . . . The sun will be turned into darkness, and the moon will turn blood red."
Joel 3:15	"The sun and moon will grow dark, and the stars will no longer shine."
Amos 8:8	"The earth will tremble for your deeds, and everyone will mourn. The land will rise up like the Nile River at floodtime, toss about, and sink again."
Nahum 1:5-6	"In his presence the mountains quake, and the hills melt away; the earth trembles, and its people are destroyed. Who can stand before his fierce anger? Who can survive his burning fury? His rage blazes forth like fire, and the mountains crumble to dust in his presence."
Zephaniah 1:14-18	"The terrible day of the Lord is near. . . . It is a day when the Lord's anger will be poured out. It is a day of terrible distress and anguish, a day of ruin and desolation, a day of darkness and gloom, of clouds, blackness, trumpet calls, and battle cries. . . . He will make a terrifying end of all the people on earth."
Malachi 3:2	"But who will be able to endure it when he comes? Who will be able to stand and face him when he appears? For he will be like a blazing fire that refines metal or like a strong soap that whitens clothes."

THE GREAT TRIBULATION / *Revelation 7:2-3*

Most Christians acknowledge the reality of a time of tribulation, but there is considerable debate concerning when this time will occur and who will be affected by it. (See also the chart located on page 583.)

Dispensational Premillennialism

Dispensational premillennialists believe that Jesus' prophecy of a future Tribulation will affect Israel but not the church. Prior to the Tribulation, the church will be raptured out of the world when Christ suddenly descends from the clouds. The prophecy in Daniel about the Antichrist only deals with God's plans for Israel (Daniel 9:27; Matthew 24:15-22). The rise of the Antichrist begins a seven-year period of tribulation designed to bring Israel back to God. Many Jews recognize Christ as the Messiah. After these seven years of horror, Christ returns to defeat his enemies at Armageddon and begin his thousand-year reign of peace (Matthew 24:29-31).

Historic Premillennialism

Historic premillennialists view the Tribulation as the final manifestation of evil at the end of history. The Antichrist will proclaim himself to be god and launch a worldwide campaign of persecution of Christians (Matthew 24:15-22; 2 Thessalonians 2:3-12). Thus, according to historic premillennialists, Christians will experience this Tribulation and suffer for the cause of Christ. But Christ will sustain his people and protect them from God's dreadful judgments on the Antichrist and his followers. At the height of this period of persecution, Christ will return to defeat his enemies at Armageddon and establish his thousand-year reign.

Amillennialism

Amillennialists believe that the battle between good and evil will climax in a period of intense persecution of Christians at the end of this age, just prior to Christ's second coming. They believe that the Tribulation is not a specific time in the future but instead may refer to this present age as well. The Tribulation occurs anywhere the Good News is being opposed and Christians are being persecuted. Amillennialists point out that Scripture doesn't state that the Tribulation is confined to Israel (Revelation 7:13-14). They believe that all of God's people will be persecuted. When Christ returns, bringing judgment on evil, he will gather believers (Matthew 24:31).

Postmillennialism

Postmillennialists believe that the church itself will usher in the Millennium and that Christ will return after one thousand years of peace on earth. The Tribulation occurs anywhere the Good News is being opposed and Christians are being persecuted. They believe that Jesus' prophecy of the abomination being placed in the temple has already been fulfilled in Titus's destruction of Jerusalem and its Temple in A.D. 70 (Matthew 24:15-22). They don't believe Jesus' prophecy speaks of a future Antichrist.

THE SEVEN TRUMPETS / *Revelation 8:6*

Trumpet	Reference	Description	Results
First	8:7	Hail and fire, mixed with blood, are hurled to the earth.	A third of the earth, a third of the trees, and all green grass are burned up.
Second	8:8-9	A great mountain of fire is thrown into the sea.	A third of the sea becomes blood, killing one-third of its living creatures. One-third of all ships on the sea are destroyed.
Third	8:10-11	A flaming star falls out of the sky.	A third of the earth's water is turned bitter, or polluted, killing many people.
Fourth	8:12-13	One-third of the sun, moon, and stars are darkened.	There is less light from the sky, and people spend more time in darkness.
Fifth	9:1-11	A star falls from the sky and opens the abyss.	Poisonous locusts are let loose to attack people on the earth for five months.
Sixth	9:13-21	A war with huge numbers of mounted troops begins.	A third of all the people on the earth are killed.
Seventh	11:14–14:20	The final struggle between God and Satan—good and evil—takes place first in heaven, then on earth.	Satan acts against God's plan, causing more destruction before he is finally defeated.

THE ANTICHRIST / *Revelation 13:1*

There are many theories regarding the person of the Antichrist, and each has its advocates who have Scripture to back up their views. The actual truth will probably not be clear until the events actually occur. Until then, believers are to remain watchful (Matthew 24:4-5), looking expectantly to Christ's return.

Early Christian Interpreters

Early Christian writings identify the Antichrist as the one who will exalt himself as God. These writers noted that the tribe of Dan is not on the list of the 144,000 "sealed" Jews (see Revelation 7:4-8) and that Dan is the perpetrator in Jeremiah's prophecy of "terror" (Jeremiah 8:15-16). They concluded, therefore, that the Antichrist would be a descendant of the tribe of Dan. This interpretation is not widely held today.

Postmillennialists and Amillennialists

Some believe that the Antichrist will not be a person but, rather, an evil system. Scripture speaks of "many antichrists" (1 John 2:18), and anti-Christian forces have persecuted the church throughout history.

Some believe that the prophecies regarding the Antichrist have already been fulfilled. Some think the Antichrist was Nero, who committed suicide and, then, was expected to come back to life and reclaim his throne. In this theory, the seven-headed beast symbolizes the Roman Empire because the city of Rome was built on seven hills (see Revelation 17:9). There are parallels between the beast and Roman emperors, who took on blasphemous names, such as "lord" or "god" (see Revelation 13:1).

Dispensationalists

Dispensationalists believe that the Antichrist will emerge as the leader of the restored Roman Empire. He will make commitments to Israel (Daniel 7:8, 21-27; 9:24-27; Revelation 17:9-14), then will be assassinated and restored to life. According to this view, the Antichrist will exalt himself in the rebuilt Temple at Jerusalem and begin to persecute the Jews. This will cause Israel to turn to the Messiah. The time of great tribulation will end with military forces converging on Israel to defeat the Antichrist.

Historic Premillenialists and Amillenialists

Historic premillenialists and some amillenialists believe that the Antichrist will be a powerful individual, but they do not believe that the Temple in Jerusalem will be restored.

SATAN'S WORK IN THE WORLD / Revelation 13:2

Satan's . . .	Reference in Revelation
Hatred for Christ	12:13
Hatred for God's people	12:17
Power and authority	13:2
Popularity among unbelievers	13:4
Blasphemy against God	13:6
War against believers	13:7
Ability to deceive	13:14

CITIZENS OF HELL / Revelation 14:9-11

Who will be in hell? Sadly, hell will be populated by people who have willingly rebelled against God and stubbornly refused any offer of repentance.

Reference	Verse
Matthew 25:41-46	Away with you, you cursed ones, into the eternal fire prepared for the Devil and his demons! For I was hungry, and you didn't feed me.
Romans 6:23	For the wages of sin is death.
1 Corinthians 6:9-11	Those who do wrong will have no share in the Kingdom of God. . . . Those who indulge in sexual sin, who are idol worshipers, adulterers, male prostitutes, homosexuals, thieves, greedy people, drunkards, abusers, and swindlers—none of these will have a share in the Kingdom of God.
2 Peter 2:4	For God did not spare even the angels when they sinned; he threw them into hell.
Revelation 20:10	Then the Devil, who betrayed them, was thrown into the lake of fire that burns with sulfur, joining the beast and the false prophet. There they will be tormented day and night forever and ever.
Revelation 20:15	Anyone whose name was not found recorded in the Book of Life was thrown into the lake of fire.
Revelation 21:8	But cowards who turn away from me, and unbelievers, and the corrupt, and murderers, and the immoral, and those who practice witchcraft, and idol worshipers, and all liars—their doom is in the lake that burns with fire and sulfur. This is the second death.
Revelation 21:27	Nothing evil will be allowed to enter [heaven]—no one who practices shameful idolatry and dishonesty—but only those whose names are written in the Lamb's Book of Life.

PERSEVERE TO THE END / *Revelation 14:12*

Scripture Verse

Luke 21:19—By standing firm, you will win your souls.

Lesson

Perseverance grows out of commitment to Jesus Christ. Standing firm is not the way to be saved but the evidence that a person is really committed to Jesus. Endurance is not a means to earn salvation; it is the by-product of a truly devoted life.

2 Timothy 4:5—But you should keep a clear mind in every situation. Don't be afraid of suffering for the Lord. Work at bringing others to Christ. Complete the ministry God has given you.

God will make believers' perseverance worthwhile. He will help his people complete whatever work he has called them to do; he will help them draw others into the kingdom.

Hebrews 3:6—But Christ, the faithful Son, was in charge of the entire household. And we are God's household, if we keep up our courage and remain confident in our hope in Christ.

Perseverance keeps believers courageous and hopeful because they can trust Christ. Because Christ lives in Christians and because he is completely trustworthy to fulfill all his promises, believers can remain courageous and hopeful.

Revelation 14:12—Let this encourage God's holy people to endure persecution patiently and remain firm to the end, obeying his commands and trusting in Jesus.

Believers' ability to persevere is related to the quality of our relationship with God. The secret to perseverance is trust and obedience. Trust God to give you the patience to endure even the small trials you face daily. The fact of God's ultimate triumph can encourage believers to remain steadfast in their faith through every trial and persecution.

BEATITUDES IN REVELATION / *Revelation 14:13*

Seven times in Revelation, God promises blessings upon the believers.

Reference	Verse
1:3	"God blesses the one who reads this prophecy to the church, and he blesses all who listen to it and obey what it says."
14:13	"Blessed are those who die in the Lord from now on. Yes, says the Spirit, they are blessed indeed, for they will rest from all their toils and trials; for their good deeds follow them!"
16:15	"Blessed are all who are watching for me, who keep their robes ready so they will not need to walk naked and ashamed."
19:9	"Blessed are those who are invited to the wedding feast of the Lamb."
20:6	"Blessed and holy are those who share in the first resurrection. For them the second death holds no power, but they will be priests of God and of Christ and will reign with him a thousand years."
22:7	"Blessed are those who obey the prophecy written in this scroll."
22:14	"Blessed are those who wash their robes so they can enter through the gates of the city and eat the fruit from the tree of life."

THE SEVEN BOWLS / Revelation 16:1

Bowl Judgment	Reference	Description	Results
First	16:2	Horrible malignant sores break out on everyone who has the mark of the beast.	Physical pain comes to those who have not repented.
Second	16:3	The sea becomes blood and everything in it dies.	With the death of the sea, all ecosystems are affected.
Third	16:4	The rivers and springs become blood.	With the death of the inland waters, there is no water to drink.
Fourth	16:8	The sun scorches people.	People burned by the heat curse God for it.
Fifth	16:10	Darkness covers the earth.	People are in anguish because of the darkness, but they curse God and refuse to repent. They still have the sores from the first plague and the burns from the fourth plague.
Sixth	16:12	The great Euphrates River dries up.	The drying up of the river provides a way for the armies of the east to march westward without hindrance and gather at the battlefield of Armageddon.
Seventh	16:17-21	An earthquake greater than any that has ever occurred changes the face of the earth. Then comes a terrible hailstorm.	The great city of Babylon is destroyed, islands are engulfed, mountains are flattened. People continue to curse God.

ROMAN EMPERORS / *Revelation 17:10*

Name	Dates of Rule
Augustus	27 B.C.–A.D. 14
Tiberius	A.D. 14–37
Caligula	A.D. 37–41
Claudius	A.D. 41–54
Nero	A.D. 54–68
Galba	A.D. 69
Otho	A.D. 69
Vitellius	A.D. 69
Vespasian	A.D. 69–79
Titus	A.D. 79–81
Domitian	A.D. 81–96

HOW CAN A PERSON KEEP AWAY FROM THE EVIL SYSTEM?
Revelation 18:4

Here are some suggestions:

1. People must always be more important than products.

2. Keep away from pride in your own programs, plans, and successes.

3. Remember that God's will and Word must never be compromised.

4. People must always be considered above the making of money.

5. Do what is right, no matter what the cost.

6. Be involved in businesses that provide worthwhile products or services—not just things that feed the world's desires.

THE RAPTURE / *Revelation 19:11-12*

When Christ returns as the rider on the white horse, is this the point where he "raptures" the church, or has that already happened? There is much discussion regarding the Rapture of the church (never specifically mentioned in Revelation) and the second coming of Christ. What is called the "Rapture" is described in other places in Scripture.

- "No one knows the day or the hour when these things will happen, not even the angels in heaven or the Son himself. Only the Father knows. When the Son of Man returns, it will be like it was in Noah's day. . . . People didn't realize what was going to happen until the Flood came and swept them all away. That is the way it will be when the Son of Man comes. Two men will be working together in the field; one will be taken, the other left. Two women will be grinding flour at the mill; one will be taken, the other left. So be prepared, because you don't know what day your Lord is coming" (Matthew 24:36-37, 40-42).

- "But let me tell you a wonderful secret God has revealed to us. Not all of us will die, but we will all be transformed. It will happen in a moment, in the blinking of an eye, when the last trumpet is blown. For when the trumpet sounds, the Christians who have died will be raised with transformed bodies. And then we who are living will be transformed so that we will never die" (1 Corinthians 15:51-52).

- "For the Lord himself will come down from heaven with a commanding shout, with the call of the archangel, and with the trumpet call of God. First, all the Christians who have died will rise from their graves. Then, together with them, we who are still alive and remain on the earth will be caught up in the clouds to meet the Lord in the air and remain with him forever" (2 Thessalonians 4:16-17).

At the Rapture, Christ will bring his people to be with him. Some Christians think that the Rapture will be a separate event from the Second Coming; others believe they are two names for the same event.

Pretribulationists (dispensational premillennialists) think that the Rapture and the Second Coming are two separate and distinct events. They believe that the church will be raptured before the Tribulation begins. Then, at the end of the Tribulation (seven years later), Christ will return, and this will be the Second Coming.

Midtribulationists also believe that the Rapture and the Second Coming are two separate and distinct events. They believe that the Rapture of all believers will occur halfway through the Tribulation (after three and a half years) so that believers will not be a part of the bowl judgments. Believers will then return with Christ at his second coming, at the end of the Tribulation period.

Posttribulationists (historic premillennialists and amillennialists) think that the Rapture and Second Coming are the same event. Believers will go through the Tribulation. At the end of that time, they will meet the Lord in the air, then they will immediately accompany Christ on his descent to earth as the rider on the white horse.

Postmillennialists also view the Rapture and the Second Coming as the same event; however, they place these events at the end of the Millennium, the thousand-year reign of Christ. After Satan is released from the bottomless pit to deceive the nations and wage war on God's people (20:7-10), Christ will call his people to him; then Christ's people will accompany him as he descends to earth, defeats his enemies, and establishes a new heaven and new earth.

Whenever the Rapture of the church occurs, it is already certain that the rider on the white horse will come in victory and that believers will be with him in heaven. While the various views on these topics can be difficult to understand, it is far more important that every believer knows on which side of the battle he or she is. Those who remain faithful to Christ, no matter what, will receive all that God has promised.

HOW SATAN IS ACTIVE IN THE PRESENT AGE / *Revelation 20:2-3*

New Testament example	Application for today
"Then Satan entered Judas Iscariot." (Luke 22:3)	Satan can cause willing people to do his bidding.
"Peter said, 'Ananias, why has Satan filled your heart?' " (Acts 5:3)	Satan leads people to deceive others.
"Satan, the god of this evil world, has blinded the minds of those who don't believe." (2 Corinthians 4:4)	Satan prevents people from accepting the gospel.
"Satan can disguise himself as an angel of light." (2 Corinthians 11:14)	Satan counterfeits goodness and truth to trap people.
"Satan, the mighty prince of the power of the air . . . is at work in the hearts of those who refuse to obey God." (Ephesians 2:2)	Satan inflames the evil desires of those who reject God.
"We wanted very much to come . . . but Satan prevented us." (1 Thessalonians 2:18)	Satan attempts to block evangelistic efforts.
"Then they will come to their senses and escape from the Devil's trap. For they have been held captive by him to do whatever he wants." (2 Timothy 2:26)	Satan uses church controversies and quarrels to lead people astray.
"Be careful! Watch out for attacks from the Devil, your great enemy. He prowls around like a roaring lion, looking for some victim to devour." (1 Peter 5:8)	Satan attacks the weak, suffering, or lonely Christian, who then withdraws from the church.

VIEWS ON THE MILLENNIUM / *Revelation 20:2-3*

The 1,000 years are often referred to as the Millennium (Latin for 1,000). There are three major views about the Millennium, commonly called premillennialism, amillennialism, and postmillennialism.

Premillennialism

Premillennialism says that the 1,000 years is a literal time period. Christ's second coming will begin the Millennium before the final removal of Satan. (The pre-, mid-, and post-Tribulation views are all "premillennial" in that they all agree that Christ will return at some point around the Tribulation, but before this 1,000-year reign.)

Under this view are two types of understandings:

(1) *Dispensational premillennialists* say that at the end of the Tribulation will come the battle of Armageddon, the imprisonment of Satan, and Jesus' reign over Israel (19:19–20:6). During that 1,000-year reign, the Old Testament promises for Israel will be fulfilled (such as Isaiah 2:4; 9:6-7; 11:6-9; 35:5-6; 42:1). Dispensationalists believe the Millennium will end with Satan leading a brief rebellion against Christ and then being thrown into the lake of fire. Then God will recreate the heavens and earth.

(2) *Historic premillennialists* believe that Christ's second coming will occur after the Tribulation to bring believers into his millennial kingdom. He will defeat the Antichrist's forces at Armageddon and kill the Antichrist, ending a first stage in Christ's defeat of evil. The believers will accompany Christ as he establishes his millennial kingdom on earth. Satan will be chained during that time. Premillennialists believe that the establishment of Christ's millennial reign on earth will cause the nation of Israel to turn to Jesus, thus fulfilling many of the Old Testament prophecies for Israel. Historic premillennialists contend that only believers will be raised from the dead to reign with Christ in the Millennium. The remaining unbelieving dead will be raised to life when the Millennium ends—they will be raised for judgment. At that point, God will bring into existence the new heaven and new earth.

Amillennialism

Amillennialism understands the 1,000-year period to be symbolic of the time between Christ's ascension and his second coming; thus, the Millennium is the reign of Christ in the hearts of believers and in his church and is another way of referring to the church age. This period will end with the second coming of Christ. Amillennialists do not believe in a literal period of Tribulation because they view the Tribulation as including various events during the history of the church. To them, the events of the Millennium described in Revelation 20:1-6 are actually occurring now! Amillennialists believe that as the last days approach, the forces of evil will climax with the Antichrist and the great tribulation he will bring (2 Thessalonians 2:1-3). They believe that the wicked will continue to gather strength, persecuting believers more and more. Only when Christ returns will wickedness be stopped once and for all. After judging both the living and dead, Christ will establish his everlasting reign of peace.

Postmillennialism

Postmillennialism looks for a period of peace on earth ushered in by the church. At the end of this time, Satan will be released, but Christ will return to defeat Satan and reign forever. Postmillennialists believe that Jesus will return to a world that has been "Christianized" by the work of the church. Thus, the Millennium will be established by the church, and Christ will only return to the earth after the Millennium. They believe that the church is now gradually transforming society (Matthew 13:31-33). Postmillennialists believe that the Tribulation symbolizes the constant conflict between good and evil which has existed throughout history.

Postmillennialists believe that the Millennium will end when Satan is released from the bottomless pit. Then Christ will return to judge all people and establish a new heaven and new earth. Postmillennialists believe the church bears the responsibility for spreading the Good News to all the world.

THE CERTAINTY OF THE RESURRECTION / *Revelation 20:11*

The Resurrection is a certainty based on God's Word.

Author	Quote
Job	"I know that my Redeemer lives. . . . And after my body has decayed, yet in my body I will see God." (Job 19:25-26)
David	"When I awake, I will be fully satisfied, for I will see you face to face." (Psalm 17:15)
Descendants of Korah	"But as for me, God will redeem my life. He will snatch me from the power of death." (Psalm 49:15)
Isaiah	"Yet we have this assurance: Those who belong to God will live; their bodies will rise again! Those who sleep in the earth will rise up and sing for joy. For God's light of life will fall like dew on his people in the place of the dead!" (Isaiah 26:19)
Daniel	"Many of those whose bodies lie dead and buried will rise up, some to everlasting life and some to shame and everlasting contempt. . . . You will rise again to receive the inheritance set aside for you." (Daniel 12:2, 13)
Jesus	"He will even raise from the dead anyone he wants to, just as the Father does." (John 5:21)
Jesus	"And this is the will of God, that I should not lose even one of all those he has given me, but that I should raise them to eternal life at the last day." (John 6:39)
Jesus	"I am the resurrection and the life. Those who believe in me, even though they die like everyone else, will live again." (John 11:25)
Paul	"I have hope in God . . . that he will raise both the righteous and the ungodly." (Acts 24:15)
Paul	"The Spirit of God, who raised Jesus from the dead, lives in you. And just as he raised Christ from the dead, he will give life to your mortal body by this same Spirit living within you." (Romans 8:11)
Paul	"And God will raise our bodies from the dead by his marvelous power, just as he raised our Lord from the dead." (1 Corinthians 6:14)
Paul	"Christ was raised first; then when Christ comes back, all his people will be raised." (1 Corinthians 15:23).
Paul	"When we die and leave these bodies—we will have a home in heaven, an eternal body made for us by God himself." (2 Corinthians 5:1)

THE COMING JUDGMENT / *Revelation 20:14-15*

Other places in Scripture describe this judgment.

"The Ancient One sat down to judge . . . the court began its session, and the books were opened." (Daniel 7:9-10)

"For I, the Son of Man, will come in the glory of my Father with his angels and will judge all people according to their deeds." (Matthew 16:27)

"For there is going to come a day of judgment when God, the just judge of all the world, will judge all people according to what they have done." (Romans 2:5-6)

"The day will surely come when God, by Jesus Christ, will judge everyone's secret life." (Romans 2:16)

"Each of us will stand personally before the judgment seat of God. . . . Each of us will have to give a personal account to God." (Romans 14:10, 12)

"For we must all stand before Christ to be judged. We will each receive whatever we deserve for the good or evil we have done in our bodies." (2 Corinthians 5:10)

"Christ Jesus . . . will someday judge the living and the dead when he appears to set up his Kingdom." (2 Timothy 4:1)

"It is destined that each person dies only once and after that comes judgment." (Hebrews 9:27)

"But just remember that you will have to face God, who will judge everyone, both the living and the dead." (1 Peter 4:5)

"The Lord knows how to rescue godly people from their trials, even while punishing the wicked right up until the day of judgment." (2 Peter 2:9)

"And God has also commanded that the heavens and the earth will be consumed by fire on the day of judgment, when ungodly people will perish." (2 Peter 3:7)

"And as we live in God, our love grows more perfect. So we will not be afraid on the day of judgment, but we can face him with confidence." (1 John 4:17)

"Look, the Lord is coming with thousands of his holy ones. He will bring the people of the world to judgment. He will convict the ungodly of all the evil things they have done in rebellion." (Jude 14-15)

THE BEGINNING AND THE END / *Revelation 21:1*

The Bible records for us the beginning of the world and the end of the world. The story of mankind, from beginning to end—from the fall into sin to redemption and God's ultimate victory over evil—is found in the pages of the Bible.

Genesis	Revelation
The sun is created.	The sun is not needed.
Satan is victorious.	Satan is defeated.
Sin enters the human race.	Sin is banished.
People run and hide from God.	People are invited to live with God forever.
People are cursed.	The curse is removed.
Tears are shed, with sorrow for sin.	No more sin, no more tears or sorrow.
The garden and earth are cursed.	God's city is glorified; the earth is made new.
Paradise is lost.	Paradise is regained.
People are doomed to death.	Death is defeated; believers live forever with God.

HEAVENLY REWARDS / *Revelation 21:26-27*

Reference	What It Says about Heaven
Matthew 16:24-27	To follow Christ, take up the cross. To save life, lose it. For Christ will come in glory with his angels and reward each person according to what he or she has done.
Matthew 19:28-30	If we give up material rewards on this earth for the sake of Christ and his kingdom, we are promised a hundred times as much, as well as eternal life with Christ.
Romans 6:8	If we died with Christ, we will also live with him.
Romans 8:17	If we are children of God, then we are his heirs (and coheirs with Christ) of all the riches of his glory. We share in suffering; we also share in glory.
1 Corinthians 15:42-58	We will be changed—at the sounding of the last trumpet we will receive imperishable bodies. Christ has the victory!
Colossians 3:3-4	Our lives are hidden with Christ in God. When Christ appears, we will appear with him in glory.
1 Thessalonians 4:13-18	The Lord will come down from heaven with a loud command, with the voice of the archangel, and with a trumpet call. The dead in Christ will rise first. Those who are still alive at his return will be caught up to meet him in the clouds. Then we will all be with the Lord together forever.
Revelation 3:21	To the one who overcomes, Christ will give him the right to sit with him on his throne in heaven.
Revelation 21:1–22:21	There will be a new heaven and a new earth. There will be no more death or mourning or crying or pain. The Holy City will be beautiful beyond imagination, and only those whose names are written in the Lamb's Book of Life will be allowed to enter. There will be no sun or light, for the Lord himself will be the light. And God's kingdom will remain forever.

WHAT WE KNOW ABOUT ETERNITY / *Revelation 22:1-2*

See also *1 Corinthians 15:54-55*

The Bible devotes much less space to describing eternity than it does to convincing people that eternal life is available as a free gift from God. Most of the brief descriptions of eternity would be more accurately called hints, since they use terms and ideas from present experience to describe what we cannot fully grasp until we are there ourselves. These references hint at aspects of what our future will be like if we have accepted Christ's gift of eternal life.

Description	Reference
We will have a place prepared for us.	John 14:2-3
We will be unlimited by physical properties (1 Corinthians 15:35-49).	John 20:19, 26
We will be like Jesus.	1 John 3:2
We will have new bodies.	1 Corinthians 15
It will be a wonderful experience.	1 Corinthians 2:9
It will be a new environment.	Revelation 21:1
It will be a new experience of God's presence (1 Corinthians 13:12).	Revelation 21:3
We will have new emotions.	Revelation 21:4
There will be no more death.	Revelation 21:4

INDEX

Aaron, 13, 17, 18, 29, 35, 38, 42, 92, 130, 156, 165, 389
Aaron, family of, 34
Abdon, 64
Abednego, 24, 143, 213, 422
Abel, 523
Abel-beth-maacah, 88, 97
Abel-meholah, 65
Abiathar, 102
Abigail, 179
Abihu, 139
Abijah, 112, 144
Abimelech, 67, 389
Abiram, 35
Abishai, 77, 90
Abner, 90
Abraham (Abram), 2, 6, 7, 8, 24, 52, 92, 130, 165, 297, 298, 299, 411, 417, 448, 450, 459, 515, 516, 522
Absalom, 79, 89, 94, 95, 96, 130, 169, 261, 389
Acacia, 50, 53
acceptance, 409
Achaia, 360, 361, 385, 393, 395
Achan, 45
Achish, 85
action, 147, 157
Acts, 359, 365
Adam, 46, 96, 130, 139, 165, 494
Adam, children of, 412
Adonijah, 94, 96, 102, 103, 130
Adullam, cave of, 83
adultery, 216
advice, 163, 181
Aeneas, 362
Aenon, 267
affluence, 46
Agabus, 362

Agrippa. *See* Herod Agrippa II
Ahab, 45, 101, 109, 110, 111, 112, 119, 140, 142, 281
Ahaz, 114, 144, 196, 224
Ahaziah, 96, 113, 122, 144
Ahijah, 112, 124
Ahimaaz, 42
Ahinoam, 94
Ahitub, 42
Ai, 50, 53
Aijalon, valley of, 50, 52, 81
Alexandria, 360
alliances, 196
aloneness, 419
Amalek, 131
Amariah, 42
Amaziah, 113, 144
Ammon, 32, 60, 67, 80, 93, 106, 107, 131, 209
Amnon, 94, 130
Amon, 115, 144
Amos, 114, 124, 216, 222, 226
Amphipolis, 360, 385, 388, 393, 395
Ananias: of Damascus, 399; of Jerusalem, 584; and Sapphira, 366
Andrew, 270, 363, 376
angels, Christ's superiority to, 510
animosity, tribal, 105
Annas, the high priest, 315, 345
announcements, 297
answering to God, 221
Antichrist, the, 578
Antioch of Pisidia, 360, 377, 379, 381, 393, 394, 444, 542
Antioch of Syria, 360, 374, 377, 378, 379, 381, 385, 386, 393, 394
Antipatris, 398

Aphek, 78, 85, 111
Apollonia, 360, 385, 388, 393
Apollos, 362, 368, 392, 459
apostasy, 59, 565
Apostles, fate of the, 376
apostleship, Paul's, 446
appearances: by God (theophanies), 24; of Jesus after the resurrection, 264
Aquila, 368, 392
Arabia, 369
Arad, 32, 38
Aram, 93, 101, 107, 111, 119, 122, 131, 137, 140, 144
Ararat, Mountains of, 2, 5
Aratus, 389
Arimathea, 296, 322
Ark of the Covenant, 25, 51, 74, 78, 89, 104, 129
armor, the Christian's, 462
Arnon River, 38, 39
Artaxerxes, 149, 150
Arumah, 67
Asa, 112, 140, 144, 281, 340
Asahel, 90
Ashdod, 78
Asher, 10, 13, 34
Ashkelon, 62, 69
Ashtoreth, 198
Asia, 360, 386, 393, 394, 444, 456, 472, 542
Assos, 360, 393, 395
assurance, 549
Assyria, 118, 123, 126, 144, 145, 197, 216, 226
Athaliah, 96, 113, 144, 220
Athens, 360, 385, 388, 391, 393, 395, 426, 438
attacking God's work, 389
attacks by Satan (*see also* Satan), 161

coming of the, 237; Jesus as the, 332; names for the, 196; prophecies about, 310, 357
methods, God's, 298
Micah, 61, 70, 114, 125, 196, 216, 228, 419, 519; the prophet, 228
Micaiah, 68, 124, 142, 224, 281
Michal, 91, 94
Micmash, 81
middle ground, 535
Midian, 16, 18, 60, 65
Miletus, 360, 393, 395, 396, 542
Millennium, views of the, 585
mindset, 415
ministers, characteristics of, 482
ministry, Paul's, 479
miracles, 120, 265, 309, 326; Jesus', 356
Miriam, 91, 133, 165, 389
missionaries, New Testament, 368
Mitylene, 360, 393, 395
Mizpah, 60, 74, 78
Moab, 32, 38, 40, 44, 60, 63, 72, 88, 93, 106, 107, 118, 121, 131, 209
Molech, 198
money, 497, 538; advice about, 181
Mordecai, 159, 160
Moreh, Hill of, 60
Moriah, Mount, 8
Moses, 13, 17, 18, 22, 24, 33, 34, 35, 37, 44, 47, 66, 82, 91, 96, 139, 141, 142, 156, 165, 179, 292, 298, 299, 370, 389, 511, 519
Mountains of Ararat, 2, 5
music, 133
Myra, 360, 397, 402, 542
Mysia, 385, 386, 393

Naaman, 119, 120
Naboth, 79
Nadab, 96, 112, 130, 139
Nahum: 125, 229; the prophet, 229
Nain, 296, 304; widow of, 303
names: God's, 4; the Messiah's, 196; Jesus', 336, 372, 571
Naphtali, 10, 13; tribe of, 34
Nathan, 102
Nathaniel. See Bartholomew
nation, the. See Israel, the nation of
nations in the Bible, 6
Nazareth, 244, 246, 253, 266, 267, 296, 299, 301, 322, 324, 330

Neapolis, 360, 385, 386, 393, 395
Nebo, Mount, 47, 198
Nebuchadnezzar: 96, 125, 143, 145, 203, 204, 213, 400; the dream of, 213
Negev, 7, 36, 55, 62
Nehemiah: 141, 149, 150, 154, 155, 156, 389; prayers by, 154
neighbors, love for, 306
new hearts, 201
New Testament books, dates of the, 388
Nicodemus, 293, 349
Nineveh, 197, 226
Nippur, 151, 152
Noah, 2, 5, 46, 92, 130, 165, 519
Nob, 83
Northern Kingdom. See Israel, Kingdom of

Obadiah: 115, 124, 224; the prophet, 224
obedience, 1, 46, 73, 139, 209, 217, 519
objectors, conscientious, 422
Oboth, 38
offerings, 27, 29, 517
Og, King, 33, 39
old self, death of the, 452
Old Testament, Jesus' quotations of the, 318, 347
Olives, Mount of, 244, 257, 260, 266, 279, 289, 296, 307, 311, 322, 361
Olivet discourse, the, 285
Omri, 112
oneness, believers', 460
Onesimus, 508
Ophir, 106
Ophrah, 65, 67
opposition, 147, 359
oppression: 59, 227; of the poor, 221
other gods, 99
others: encouraging, 520; helping, 454; love for, 551; praying for, 474
Othniel, 64

Paddan-aram, 9
Pamphylia, 360, 377, 379, 381, 385, 393, 397, 402
Paphos, 360, 377, 378, 379
parables, Jesus', 355
Paran, Wilderness of, 32, 34
parents, treatment of, 461
passion week, the, 288
Patara, 360, 393, 396, 542

patience, God's, 117, 548
Patmos, 568
Paul: 13, 22, 68, 91, 120, 133, 143, 179, 299, 361, 362, 365, 367, 368, 369, 370, 374, 376, 377, 378, 379, 380, 381, 383, 385, 386, 388, 389, 390, 391, 392, 393, 394, 395, 396, 397, 398, 399, 402, 403, 404, 416, 427, 446, 475, 586; apostle-ship of, 446; conflict with the Judaizers of, 383, 447; credentials of, 441; fund-raising by, 440; God's encouragement of, 398; imprisonments of, 500; journey to Rome, 403; ministry of, 392, 479; prayers of, 466, 483; quotes from the prophets by, 408
peace: 135; the king of, 227
peaceful resistance, 422
Pekah, 114
Pekahiah, 114
people: God's, 127; Jesus' interest in, 295; wise, 179
Peor, Mount, 40
Perea, 244, 257, 296, 309, 322, 338, 341
Perez, 130
perfection, 469
Perga, 360, 377, 379, 381, 542
Pergamum, 393, 542, 568
persecution: 142, 479, 489, 541; expecting, 502; prophets who experienced, 281
persecutors, 389
persevering, 211, 313, 431, 580
Persia, kings of, 150
persistence, 489
personal discipline, 493
personal greatness, 87
perverting faith, 227
Peter, 66, 120, 143, 244, 254, 264, 266, 270, 288, 299, 334, 349, 361, 362, 363, 364, 367, 368, 370, 371, 373, 376, 382, 392, 399, 446, 475, 542, 584
Pharaoh, 19, 420
Pharisees, 247, 268
Philadelphia, 542, 568
Philemon, 508
Philip, 270, 362, 363, 365, 367, 368, 376, 399
Philippi, 360, 385, 386, 388, 393, 395, 438, 464
Philistia, 61, 69, 75, 78, 83, 88, 103, 106, 144, 209
Philistines, 77, 261
Phinehas, 42, 45

LOOK FOR OTHER BOOKS IN:

The Tyndale Reference Library
Bible Resources for Everyone's Library

Tyndale Bible Dictionary
Tyndale Handbook of Bible Charts and Maps
Tyndale Concise Bible Commentary